· CHOICES IN RELATIONSHIPS ·

·CHOICES IN RELATIONSHIPS·

An Introduction to
Marriage and the Family

David Knox
East Carolina University

WEST PUBLISHING COMPANY
St. Paul   New York   Los Angeles   San Francisco

Production credits: Copyediting Elaine Linden
Design Jane Barnard
Composition Carlisle Graphics
Illustrations Barbara Hack Barnett
Cover Design Taly Design Group

Cover art: A detail from Georges Seurat, *Sunday Afternoon on the Island of La Grande Jatte;* 1884–86, oil on canvas, 81 × 120⅜", Helen Birch Bartlett Memorial. © The Art Institute of Chicago. All Rights Reserved.

Library of Congress Cataloging in Publication Data

Knox, David, 1943–
  Choices in relationships.

  Bibliography: p.
  Includes index.
  1. Family life education. I. Title.
HQ10.K59 1985   306.8   84-19495
ISBN 0-314-85257-3
1st Reprint—1985

Photo Credits

1 (left) Historical Picture Service, Chicago; (right) Rose Skytta, Jeroboam. **3** Rich Smolan, Stock, Boston. **7** Owen Franken, Stock, Boston. **10** Kit Hedman, Jeroboam. **18** W. D. Zehr, FPG. **35** Tom Ballard, EKM-Nepenthe. **36** Robert Eckert, EKM-Nepenthe. **40** Cary Wolinsky, Stock, Boston. **41** Barbara Klutinis, Jeroboam. **49** Robert Eckert, EKM-Nepenthe. **50** Peter Grindley, FPG. **59** Tom Ballard, EKM-Nepenthe. **60** Laimute Druskis, Jeroboam. **65** George Gibbons, FPG. **68** Kit Hedman, Jeroboam. **74** Rose Skytta, Jeroboam. **78** (left) Robert Eckert, EKM-Nepenthe; (right) Rose Skytta, Jeroboam. **89** Peter Simon, Stock, Boston. **95** Jerry Howard, Stock, Boston. **97** Jill Cannefax, EKM-Nepenthe. **104** (top) Bradley Green; (bottom left) Willie L. Hill, Jr., FPG; (bottom right) Susan Ylvisaker, Jeroboam. **115** Jerry Berndt, Stock, Boston. **129** (left) Historical Picture Service, Chicago; (right) Tom Ballard, EKM-Nepenthe. **131** Barbara Alper, Stock, Boston. **133** Charles Gatewood, Stock, Boston. **134** John Maher, EKM-Nepenthe. **138** Robert Eckert, EKM-Nepenthe. **142** Bruce Kliewe, Jeroboam. **146** Jeff Albertson, Stock, Boston. **157** James R. Holland, Stock, Boston. **159** Owen Franken, Stock, Boston. **161** Laimute Druskis, Jeroboam. **166** Augusts Upitis, FPG. **172** Jean-Claude Lejeune, Stock, Boston. **185** Lyn Gardiner, Stock, Boston. **188** John Maher, EKM-Nepenthe. **191** Jean-Claude Lejeune, EKM-Nepenthe. **196** John Running, Stock, Boston. **207** James R. Holland, Stock, Boston. **209** John Maher, EKM-Nepenthe. **220** Frank Siteman, EKM-Nepenthe. **222** Frank Siteman, Stock, Boston. **225** Jean-Claude Lejeune, Stock, Boston. **239** (left) The Bettmann Archive; (right) Michael Hayman, Stock, Boston. **241** John Pearsonv, FPG. **242** Bohdan Hrynewych, Stock, Boston. **248** Frank Siteman, Stock, Boston. **254** Karen Rosenthal, Stock, Boston. **262** W. D. Zehr, FPG. **271** Cathy Cheney, EKM-Nepenthe. **273** Lisa Law, Jeroboam. **275** Bohdan Hrynewych, Stock, Boston. **280** Cathy Cheney, EKM-Nepenthe. **281** Arthur Grace, Stock, Boston. **291** James C. Hershey, FPG. **299** Fredrik D. Bodin, Stock, Boston. **306** George Kruse, Jeroboam. **315** Robert W. Young, FPG. **324** Hap Stewart, Jeroboam. **337** Mimi Forsyth, Monkmeyer. **341** Jim Anderson, Woodfin Camp & Associates. **345** James R. Holland, Stock, Boston. **348** Michal Heron, Woodfin Camp & Associates. **361** Jeff Albertson, Stock, Boston. **365** Ellis

(continued following index)

To Frances—my choice.
And to Lisa and Dave
who are beginning
to make choices in relationships
for themselves.

·CONTENTS·

Preface   xvii

· PART ONE ·
Perspectives   1

Chapter 1   Introduction   3

Why Study Marriage and the Family?   4
Self-Assessment: The Relationship Events Scale   6
Benefits of Studying Marriage and the Family   8
What Is Marriage?   10
What Is Family?   13
Ways of Viewing Marriage and the Family   15
Some Cautions about Research   21
Trends   24
Summary   24
Choices
Marriage and Family: An Academic or Personal Search?   26
Choosing Carefully or Choosing by Default   26
Tolerance or Condemnation for the Choices of Others?   27

Chapter 2   Gender Roles   29

Terminology   30
Biological Beginnings   30
Socialization Influences   34
Nature versus Nurture: The Controversy   40
Consequences of Becoming a Woman   43
Self-Assessment: The Sexist Attitudes Scale   45
Consequences of Becoming a Man   49
The Ideal Man   52
The Ideal Woman   53

vii

Trends 53
Summary 54
Choices
Dating: Women Asking Men? 56
Marriage: Role Sharing 57
Employment: Occupational Choices 57

Chapter 3   Love Relationships 59

Origins of Love 60
Definitions and Dilemmas of Love 62
Importance of Love 63
Conditions of Love 64
The Lover Role 68
Romantic and Realistic Love 69
Self-Assessment: The Love Attitudes Scale 70
Styles of Loving 75
Homosexual Love Relationships 78
Love and Sex 81
Jealousy 83
Trends 85
Summary 85
Choices
Heart or Head: Which Should You Listen To? 87
Sex with and without Love: Which Is Better? 88

Chapter 4   Sexual Values and Behaviors 89

Types of Value Systems 90
Personal Sexual Values 93
Society's Sexual Values 94
Masturbation 99
Self-Assessment: Sexual Attitude Scale 100
Petting 104
Sexual Intercourse 107
Trends 121
Summary 122
Choices
Deciding about Intercourse 124
Extramarital Sex? No 125
Extramarital Sex? Yes 126

• PART TWO •

Decisions   129

Chapter 5

Life-Styles   131

Marriage   131
Singlehood   135
Contract Cohabitation   143
Communes   145
Trends   150
Self-Assessment: Life-Style Preference Inventory   151
Summary   152
Choices
Is Marriage for You?   153
Is Singlehood for You?   154
Is Contract Cohabitation for You?   155

Chapter 6

Dating   157

Dating in Historical Perspective   158
Contemporary Functions of Dating   160
Dating Realities   162
Dating Problems   167
Mate Selection   170
Self-Assessment: Needs Assessment Inventory   177
Self-Assessment: Assets and Liabilities Inventory   178
Trends   180
Summary   181
Choices
How Interested Should I Appear to Be?   183
How Available Should I Be?   184
Should I Date One or Several People?   184

Chapter 7

Living Together   185

Definition and Types   186
Why Living Together Is Increasing   186
Characteristics of Live-In Partners   189
The Nuts and Bolts of Living Together   190
Living Together as Preparation for Marriage?   194
Benefits of Living Together   195
Disadvantages of Living Together   196
Living Together as a Permanent Alternative   198

Self-Assessment: Living-Together Consequences
Scale   199
Trends   202
Summary   202
Choices
Should I Live with My Partner?   204
Should We Have One Residence or Two?   204
Should I Tell My Parents I Am Living with My Partner?   205
How Long Should I Live with My Partner?   205

Chapter 8

The Final Choice   207

Selecting a Partner   207
Rejecting a Partner   213
Self-Assessment: The Relationship Assessment
Inventory   214
Timing Your Marital Commitment   221
Becoming Engaged   223
Writing a Prenuptial or Marriage Contract   229
Predicting Your Marital Happiness   230
Trends   235
Summary   235
Choices
Prenuptial Agreement: Yes   237
Prenuptial Agreement: No   237
Prenuptial Agreement: It Depends   238

• PART THREE •

Fulfillments   239

Chapter 9

Marriage Relationships   241

Marriage as a Commitment   242
Rites of Passage   243
Changes after Marriage   249
Sexually Open Marriages   252
College Marriages   253
Mixed Marriages   257
Black Marriages   261
Very Happy Marriages   263
Trends   265
Summary   265
Self-Assessment: Marriage Happiness Scale   266

Choices
Type of Marriage Relationship Desired   268
Partner's Night Out?   268
Separate or Joint Vacations?   269
Parents as Live-ins?   269
Who Will Manage the Money?   269

Chapter 10   **Dual-Income Marriages**   271

The Meanings of Money   271
Dual-Income Marriages   275
Employed Wives: Past and Present   276
Job versus Career   278
Dual-Career Marriages   282
Consequences of Two Incomes in One Marriage   285
Self-Assessment: Does It Pay for a Mother with Small
    Children to Work away from Home?   288
Trends   292
Summary   293
Choices
As a Wife, Do I Want a Dual-Career Marriage?   294
As a Husband, Do I Want a Dual-Career Marriage?   294
How Much Money Should Be Saved and Spent?   295

Chapter 11   **Communication and Conflict**   297

Myths about Marriage   298
Marital Happiness and Adjustment   300
Communication: Some Facts   301
Self-Assessment: The Dyadic Adjustment Scale   302
Conflicts in Marriage   308
Productive and Nonproductive Communication   312
Marital Therapy   318
Marriage Enrichment   323
Trends   326
Summary   327
Choices
How Much Should You Tell?   329
Should You Consult a Marriage Therapist?   329

Chapter 12   **Problems of Violence and Abuse**   331

Violence in Dating Relationships   332
Violence in Living-Together Relationships   336
Violence in Marriage Relationships   337

Self-Assessment: Partner Abuse Scale   339
Child Abuse   344
Incest   350
Parent Abuse   354
Trends   355
Summary   356
Choices
Terminate an Abusive Dating Relationship?   *358*
Terminate Abusive Marriage Relationship?   *359*

Chapter 13   **Sexual Fulfillment   361**

Meanings of Sexual Fulfillment   362
Sexual Fulfillment: Some Prerequisites   364
Sexual Fulfillment: Some Facts   368
Sexual Fulfillment: Some Myths   372
Female Sexual Dysfunctions   377
Self-Assessment: Personal Sex History Inventory   379
Male Sexual Dysfunctions   385
Sexual Fulfillment in Middle Age   388
Sexual Fulfillment in the Later Years   391
Trends   394
Summary   396
Choices
Alone or with Partner?   *397*
Privately or in a Group Setting?   *397*
One or Two Therapists?   *398*

• PART FOUR •

Families   399

Chapter 14   **Planning Children   401**

Do You Want to Have Children?   402
The Child-Free Alternative   409
Self-Assessment: The Attitudes toward Children
   Scale   410
How Many Children Do You Want?   412
Timing Your Children   416
Timing Subsequent Births   420
Trends   421
Summary   421
Choices
Having a Child without a Spouse?   *423*

Chapter 15   **Fertilization and Birth Control   425**

Fertilization   425
Contraception   431
Self-Assessment: The Contraceptive Use Scale   433
Avoiding STDs and Pregnancy   442
Sterilization   444
Abortion   446
Trends   450
Summary   451
Choices
Contraception: Which Method?   453
Sterilization: Yes or No?   454
Abortion: Prochoice or Prolife?   455

Chapter 16   **Having Children   457**

Pregnancy   457
Labor   462
Childbirth Methods   465
When a Woman Becomes a Mother   468
When a Man Becomes a Father   475
When a Couple Becomes a Family   479
Self-Assessment: Impact of Parenthood on Marriage
    Scale   483
Trends   484
Summary   484
Choices
Home or Hospital Birth?   486
For Fathers: Career or Family?   487

Chapter 17   **Rearing Children   489**

Childrearing in Perspective   489
Folklore about Childrearing   494
Approaches to Childrearing   496
Childrearing Problems   506
Self-Assessment: Child Discipline Scale   507
Other Issues Concerning Parents   510
Trends   512
Summary   513
Choices
Which Type of Punishment Is Best?   514
To Reward or Not Reward Positive Behavior?   514
How Much Freedom How Soon?   515
Parent as Friend or Authority?   515

• PART FIVE •

Transitions   517

Chapter 18   Divorce, Widowhood, and Remarriage   519

Divorce   520
Self-Assessment: The Divorce Proneness Scale   532
Widowhood   539
Preparation for Widowhood   542
Remarriage   544
Trends   547
Summary   548
Choices
Who Gets the Children? Custody Criteria of Parents   550
Custody to One Parent?   550
Joint Custody?   550

Chapter 19   Stepfamilies   553

Definition and Types of Stepfamilies   553
Unique Aspects of Stepfamilies   554
Strengths of Stepfamilies   559
Weaknesses of Stepfamilies   560
Women in Stepfamilies   561
Men in Stepfamilies   563
Children in Stepfamilies   565
Developmental Tasks for Stepfamilies   567
Self-Assessment: Stepfamily Success Scale   568
Trends   573
Summary   573
Choices
*Should a Never-Married Man Marry a Divorced Woman with
    Children?   575*
*Should a Never-Married Woman Marry a Divorced Man with
    Children?   576*
*Should a Divorced Woman with Children and a Divorced Man
    with Children Marry?   577*

Epilog   579

Making Choices: Some Facts   579
Five Basic Choices   581
A Last Word   582

· PART SIX ·
Special Topics   583

Special Topic 1   Planning and Investing   585

Developing a Budget   585
Saving and Investing   587
Life Insurance   590

Special Topic 2   Credit   593

Types of Credit Accounts   593
Three C's of Credit   594
Credit Snags to Avoid   595

Special Topic 3   Sexual Anatomy and Physiology   597

Female External Anatomy and Physiology   597
Female Internal Anatomy and Physiology   599
Male External Anatomy and Physiology   602
Male Internal Anatomy and Physiology   603

Special Topic 4   Sexually Transmitted Diseases   607

Gonorrhea   608
Syphilis   609
Genital Herpes   610
Acquired Immune Deficiency Syndrome (AIDS)   612
Getting Help   612
Prevention   613

Special Topic 5   Resources and Organizations   615

References   619
Index   645

· PREFACE ·

The theme of this book is taking charge of your life by making deliberate choices in your personal relationships, especially marriage and family. In no other area of life are choices as important. From these choices come your greatest joys and your greatest sorrows.

We begin with an overview of the basic concepts of relationships, then follow with a developmental framework examining relationships from first meetings through marriage, having and rearing a family, divorce, and remarriage. Along the way we look at gender roles, love relationships, sexual fulfillments, communications, dual-income marriages, and step-families. Choices relevant to each topic are highlighted by special features throughout each chapter:

EXHIBITS

These are boxed inserts that offer practical illustrations of particular topics, such as "How to Meet Anyone on Your Campus" and "Two Views of One Dual-Career Marriage."

DATA

Since the study of marriage and the family (also referred to as "famology") is a social science, we present data on who does what as reported in various professional journals. These data help us to gather as much information as possible with which to make decisions. For example, the fact that those who marry in their teens have two to three times the chance for divorce as those who marry in their mid-twenties has implications for deciding at what age to get married.

CONSIDERATIONS

Sprinkled throughout the text are short paragraphs that also could be labeled "What this may mean for you" or "The point is . . ." or "If you haven't thought of this . . ." These considerations encourage you to think about what you have been reading as it relates to your life and your interpersonal relationships.

SELF-ASSESSMENT INVENTORIES

Consistent with the theme of making decisions, every chapter includes an inventory or scale to enhance your decision making. Examples include the Love Attitudes Scale, the Sexual Attitude Scale, and the Relationship Assessment Inventory. Both you and your partner might want to complete these self-assessment inventories.

Each chapter closes with a special section on choices relevant to the content of that chapter. Examples of the issues discussed include: *Is Marriage for You?*, *Date One or Several People?*, *Should You Live with Your Partner?*, and *Who Will Manage the Money?* Fifty-five choices are examined in the 19 chapters.

These features are presented with one goal in mind—to provide you with a basis for making the best possible personal or interpersonal choices.

Acknowledgments

This book is a result of the work of many people. Gary Woodruff provided direction and support from the inception of the project; Phyllis Cahoon secured reviews and kept the project on schedule; Marilyn Huber proofread selected chapters; Jane Bacon handled permissions; Elaine Linden turned my writing into smooth reading; Mark Jacobsen and Lenore Franzen gave thoughtful consideration to the visual appeal of each page and diligently managed the details of transforming the manuscript into a book. Many professors, expert in the field and experienced teachers of the course for which this book is intended, read the manuscript and offered valuable insights and suggestions: Maggie Hayes, Nina Nahemow, R. Eugene Rice, Jacqueline Whitmore-Hettel, Laura Nathan, Peter Chroman, James Schillinger, David E. Holindrake, Fred T. Adams, William Powers, Kathleen Campbell, Joseph J. Leon, and Fred Stultz. Finally, Christa Reiser and Ken Wilson developed a superb instructor's manual and study guide to accompany the text. Their fine products will facilitate both teaching and learning. Although these individuals have helped immeasurably, responsibility for the book's content remains mine.

David Knox

• CHOICES IN RELATIONSHIPS •

· Part One ·

PERSPECTIVES

There is an old joke among professors who teach marriage and family courses that they can use the same tests year after year because, while the questions remain the

same, the answers keep changing. The percentage of women and men who choose to remain single, who enter marriage as virgins, and who have a dual-career marriage changes continually. Hercalitus said, "Nothing endures but change." This is certainly true of marriage and the family.

Women no longer look to marriage and the family for total fulfillment. Although these continue to be a major source of enjoyment, they are supplemented by success in the work world and by interactions with coworkers and friends. Likewise, although the job remains a primary source of satisfaction for

most men, it is being supplemented by increased interest in the family unit. Some men are particularly becoming more involved in their role as father.

· Chapter 1 ·

INTRODUCTION

CONTENTS

Why Study Marriage and the Family?

Self-Assessment: **The Relationship Events Scale**

Benefits of Studying Marriage and the Family

What Is Marriage?

What Is Family?

Ways of Viewing Marriage and the Family

Some Cautions About Research

Choices

Love is the only thing I know that hurts so good.

DENNIS ROGERS

A sophomore was looking over her university catalog to select courses for the next term. A course on marriage and the family caught her eye. Her immediate reaction was "everybody knows about marriage and the family" and "taking a course on the subject would be a waste of time." But she and her boyfriend had been having trouble lately, her parents were divorced, and her sister was unhappy in her marriage. Perhaps there were some issues worth examining.

In this chapter we review reasons for taking a practical course in marriage and the family and the potential benefits of doing so. We also examine the definitions of marriage and the family and several ways of viewing these institutions. Finally, we suggest some cautions to keep in mind about research in marriage and the family and some basic choices to consider as you begin studying this subject.

In this book we are concerned with the practical aspects of marriage and the family and with your making choices to maximize your happiness in these areas. There are at least eight objectives of this book.

Consider Remaining Single Versus Getting Married

We live in a society in which the overwhelming majority of us marry.

DATA • *About 95 percent of the U.S. population aged 45 and older in 1980 had married. Of those currently aged 25 to 29, about 90 percent of the men and 89 percent of the women will eventually marry.* (Glick, 1984)

But in spite of the fact that our society socializes all of us to seek the role of spouse, we are all no more suited for this role than we are for the role of computer programmer, pharmacist, farmer, or lawyer. One objective of studying marriage and the family is to discover who we are as individuals and to examine the degree to which our personalities, needs, and goals are compatible with the role of spouse. Although most of us will decide to marry, some of us may decide that being single has more positive consequences than being married. The decision to remain single is as valid a choice as the decision to marry.

CONSIDERATION • Some evidence suggests that people are increasingly opting for singlehood. In 1970, 45 percent of the men and 64 percent of the women in their early twenties had already married. But a decade later only 31 percent of the men and 50 percent of the women in this age group had married. "This change may mean only that more young adults are postponing marriage. On the other hand, it could mean that a growing proportion of adults are committing themselves to staying single or living together" (Glick, 1984, p. 22).

Identify a Compatible Marriage Partner

It does not much signify whom one marries, as one is sure to find the next morning it is someone else.

SAMUEL ROGERS

Should you decide to marry, it is important to be able to identify the person with whom you will have the highest chance of achieving a happy marriage. You are no more suited to marry everyone you meet than they are suited to marry you. A goal of studying marriage and the family is to learn how to systematically examine yourself, a potential partner, and your relationship so that you make the best possible choice of a marriage partner. One man said:

> I've been married twice. I was in love both times but the women were very different. In the first marriage, we couldn't agree on anything and we fought all the time. I had thought that it was best to marry someone who was different from me so I wouldn't be bored and would always have something new going on in the relationship. I was wrong. The fighting made the love wear off and we got divorced. I'm now married to someone who likes the same things I like and we enjoy doing things together. It's a lot different than with my first wife.

Learn Conflict Negotiation Skills

Even though you select a compatible marriage partner, you will inevitably disagree about some things—how to spend money, how much time to allocate to spouse or job, how many children to have, and so on. Some couples resolve conflict by getting divorced. But they soon remarry and experience conflict with their new partner. Learning how to reduce conflict and negative feelings by negotiating an acceptable compromise to both you and your partner is an essential skill for success in marriage.

Assess Yourself

Since a prerequisite for wise mate selection and a happy marriage is to "know thyself," one of the goals of this book is to help you assess your feelings and perspectives on an array of marriage and family issues. To achieve this goal, every chapter includes an inventory or scale for self-assessment, for example, a Love Attitudes Scale, Sexual Attitude Survey, and Attitudes Toward Children Scale. As you begin this book, you might take the Relationship Events Scale, which is designed to help you determine your current stage on the continuum of a developing relationship.

Explore Human Sexuality

Sexuality is a part of human relationships. In Chapter 13 we examine the prerequisites, facts, and myths of sexual fulfillment and suggest ways of resolving an array of sexual problems, including lack of orgasm, premature ejaculation, and impotence. We also look at sexuality in the middle and later years.

> Platonic love is love from the neck up.
>
> THYRA SAMTER WINSLOW

Develop Realistic Expectations

Most individuals enter marriage with intense feelings of love for their partner, a commitment to make their marriage work, and positive feelings about the future. Divorce is something that happens to other people, and the thought of divorce in the minds of the partners about to be married is abhorrent. "If people knew how we feel about each other, they would know that our marriage will last," said one bride. But in spite of this common feeling, one-half of marriages do not last. To develop a realistic view of what is necessary to create and maintain a good marriage is another goal of this book.

Prepare for Transitions

We are always in a state of transition from one stage of life or event to the next. The transitions from singlehood to marriage to separation to divorce to remarriage to widowhood are examples. How we might anticipate these changes and successfully adapt to them are emphasized throughout.

THE RELATIONSHIP EVENTS SCALE*

Below is a list of six levels of a developing relationship. After each level is a set of parentheses indicating the number of items in the level that must be true of your relationship before you will have successfully completed it. Being at a particular level is neither good nor bad. The objective of the scale is to give you feedback on how far on a relationship continuum you have progressed.

Level 1 (at least 2)
- My partner has called me an affectionate name (sweetheart, darling, etc.).
- I have called my partner an affectionate name (sweetheart, darling, etc.).
- We have spent a whole day with just each other.
- We have arranged to spend time together without planning any activity.
- We have felt comfortable enough with each other so that we could be together without talking or doing an activity together.

Level 2 (at least 1)
- We have received an invitation for the two of us as a couple.
- My partner has referred to me as his/her girlfriend/boyfriend.
- I have referred to my partner as my girlfriend/boyfriend.

Level 3 (at least 2)
- My partner has said "I love you" to me.
- I have said "I love you" to my partner.

- My partner does not date anyone other than myself.
- I do not date anyone other than my partner.

Level 4 (at least 1)
- We have discussed the possibility of getting married.
- We have discussed living together.

Level 5 (at least 2)
- I have lent my partner more than $20 for more than a week.
- My partner has lent me more than $20 for more than a week.
- We have spent a vacation together that lasted longer than three days.

Level 6 (at least 1)
- We are or have been engaged to be married.
- We have lived together or we live together now.

*Developed by A. Christensen & C. E. King, Published in *Journal of Marriage and the Family,* The relationship events scale: A Guttman scaling of progress in courtship, 1983, *44,* 671–677. © by the National Council on Family Relations, 1910 W. County Road B, Suite 147, St. Paul, Mn. 55113. Reprinted by permission. In their original research the authors presented the items in random order and the respondent did not know the level of relationship selecting the item would indicate.

Prepare for Parenting

One of the major transitions most spouses experience is the movement from a dyad to a triad. Although fewer married couples are choosing to have children than previously, a majority of couples do. In Chapter 14 we examine the relevant issues about whether to have children and the process of adjusting to them.

DATA • *More than 90 percent of young women express a desire to have children.* (Rossi, 1984)

We also examine some ways to rear children effectively and look at needed parenting skills throughout the family life cycle. Children do not remain babies in bassinets and playpens. They become teenagers who want rooms, phones, and cars of their own. Balancing their needs for dependence and independence are important parenting skills. In addition, parents need to continue to nurture their marriage relationship during the childrearing years.

> Most of us become parents long before we have stopped being children.
> MIGNON
> MCLAUGHLIN

CONSIDERATION • Variability is a theme which permeates all of these reasons for studying marriage and the family. Although we tend to think of all marriage relationships as similar to those of our parents or friends, there are more than 50. million married couples in the United States who represent different social classes, generations, races, religions, ethnic backgrounds, and work patterns (one- or two-earner families). To be aware of the various life-styles and patterns of marriage is to increase our range of choices.

Although life is a series of choices, deciding what to do is not always easy.

College courses on marriage and the family are usually one of two types. One type is a practical or functional course, which is designed to help students make personal decisions about marriage and the family. Whether to marry, when to marry, whom to marry, and whether and when to have children are some of the practical issues that are dealt with. The course is usually taken by freshmen and sophomores and is the type of course for which this book is written.

The second type is more theoretical and may view marriage and the family from several perspectives: the structure-functional, family life cycle, social psychological, social class, crisis, cross-cultural, institutional, and historical. Although we briefly review some of these perspectives, we are more concerned with personal issues and decisions.

Since you are enrolled in a practical course on marriage and the family, you will be investing an academic term in the systematic study of this subject. What are some of the potential benefits of such study?

Happier Marriage

By systematically examining yourself, your partner, and your relationship and making informed choices, you might improve your chances of having a happy marriage. One spouse who had taken the course said:

> I learned that you can't depend on love feelings alone to select a compatible marriage partner. And that when you are having a troubled time in your marriage it doesn't mean that you have to get a divorce. All spouses go through bad times and you are going to have to learn how to reduce conflict no matter who you're married to, so you might as well learn to resolve it with the one you're married to.

Couples who participate in a preparation for marriage program emphasizing communication patterns and conflict resolution are less likely to engage in destructive conflict and are less rigid in their roles (Bader et al., 1980; Ridley et al., 1982).

Marriage Insight

Marriage halves our griefs, doubles our joys, and quadruples our expenses.
ANONYMOUS

One of the best-kept secrets in the United States is what happens behind closed doors between spouses. Because marriage is such an intimate relationship, even our parents and married friends disclose very little to us about the nuances of their marriages. We are left to guess what marriage is really like or assume that movies and television portray marriage accurately.

A course in marriage and the family helps us to gain greater insight into marriage by exposing us to the various studies on intimate relationships, including those of spouses and parents. In addition, some instructors ask guest speakers whose life situation parallels the various topics of the course (dual-income marriage, living together, divorce) to share their experiences with the class. Such exposure helps to provide a more realistic perspective of what marriage and family life are all about.

Benefit to Children

One of the greatest gifts you can give your children is to have a good marriage yourself. By displaying positive ways of interacting with your partner, you offer children a positive model. They, in turn, are likely to take many of the patterns you present into their own relationships.

Of course, if you model negative behaviors, they may learn those too. One woman said of her parent's marriage:

> My mother has been divorced three times. I've seen the men come and go in her life so that I know men will be around for only a short time. But what frightens me is that I have developed the same pattern with men. I can't seem to keep one. I end up having a fight with them and they are gone before I know what has happened. I know I need to change what I'm doing but I'm not sure what it is.

Some research suggests that general rather than specific interpersonal competence has a greater impact on children (Filsinger & Lamke, 1983). This means that partners who have good social skills in all relationships, not just marital relationships, may provide the best model for their children.

Relationship Changes

It is not unheard of for students who take a course in marriage and the family to break up with their dating partners before the term is over. One former student said:

> I knew that my partner and I should break up before I took the course. We had different values and goals and a roller coaster, on-and-off-again relationship. The course helped me to see that we had drifted into a pattern of avoiding our problems. I certainly didn't want to be married and have the same problems but somehow I thought if we were married that we would feel differently (more in love or committed or something). So I tried to make things better by asking her to work on the relationship with me. But she said "love isn't something you have to work at," so we didn't work on it and it did die. I'm sad it's over between us but better now than later.

Other students report that the course helps them to talk about specific issues with their partner that they have put off. "I know we wouldn't have talked about how we would manage two careers, children, and his invalid father unless we had had this course," commented one sophomore.

Love, honor, and negotiate.

ALAN McGINNIS

Marriage Therapy and Marriage Enrichment?

A final potential benefit of taking a marriage and family course is to increase the probability of contacting a marriage and family therapist before a relationship drifts into serious trouble. " 'See a therapist before you see a lawyer' is what I got out of our discussion on divorce and marriage therapy," said one student. "I plan to." And for couples who want to strengthen an already good relationship, marriage enrichment is available.

There are several components of the definition of marriage, and at least two major types—monogamy and polygamy. We discuss both the definition and types of marriage in this section.

Definition of Marriage

When a girl marries, she exchanges the attentions of many men for the inattention of one.

HELEN ROWLAND

Marriage in the United States is an arrangement in which two adults of the opposite gender have an emotional relationship and a legal commitment to each other according to the laws of the state in which they reside. Most marriages involve a public announcement and a public ceremony. All require a marriage license, which provides for the transfer of property and legitimizes offspring.

EMOTIONAL RELATIONSHIP

Most people say they want to get married because they are "in love." This motivation reflects that marriage is a relationship sought by two people who care a great deal for each other, who enjoy being together, and who want to share their lives permanently. They want a lover, a friend, a buddy, a person they can trust and talk to in an otherwise competitive and often impersonal world. A 27-year-old single person said, "Marriage is one way of expressing your ultimate love for a person by wanting to spend the rest of your life with that person."

Emotional bonding is one need satisfied by marriage which no other institution can provide.

SEXUAL MONOGAMY

The emotional commitment to each other implies that each partner will be sexually faithful to the other. Although half of all husbands and between 20 and 40 percent of all wives eventually have intercourse with someone other than their partner during the marriage, they usually hide their extramarital encounters from the spouse. With the exception of couples who agree that extramarital partners are acceptable, sexual fidelity is expected.

LEGAL COMMITMENT

Marriage is also a legal commitment that only those of opposite gender (one female, one male), age (usually 18 for the male, 16 for the female), and marital status (neither partner may be married to someone else) may contract. The marriage license certifies that the individuals were married by a legally empowered representative of the state with two witnesses present.

DATA • *Between 2,400,000 and 2,500,000 marriage licenses are issued annually in the United States.*   (National Center for Health Statistics, 1984)

The license entitles each partner to share in the estate of the other. In most states whatever the deceased spouse owns is legally transferred to the remaining spouse at the time of death.

CONSIDERATION • The marriage license also verifies the legal relationship between the woman and the man. Insurance companies that provide life and health protection pay claims for deceased and hospitalized spouses. They do not recognize girlfriends, boyfriends, and live-ins as beneficiaries. If your partner says, "The real marriage is in the heart and the license doesn't make our marriage a real marriage," remember that the law generally does not see it this way. The exception is common law marriage (possible in some states), which means that if a couple present themselves as married they will be regarded as legally married.

LEGITIMACY OF CHILDREN

The marriage license also deems any child born to the marrying couple as legitimate and makes the parents legally responsible for the care of their offspring. Although individuals marry for love, fun, and companionship, the *real* reason (from the viewpoint of the state) for marriage is the legal obligation of a woman and man to nurture and support any children they may have. In our society childrearing is the primary responsibility of the family, not of the state.

Marriage is a relatively stable unit that helps ensure that children will have adequate care and protection, will be socialized for productive roles in society, and will not become the burden of those who did not conceive them. Thus there is tremendous social pressure for individuals to be married at the time they have children. Even at divorce, the legal obligation of the father and mother to the child is theoretically maintained through child-support payments.

PUBLIC CEREMONY

The legal bonding of a couple is often preceded by an announcement in the local newspaper and a public ceremony in a church or synagogue. Of the an-

It is as absurd to say that a man can't love one woman all the time as it is to say that a violinist needs several violins to play the same piece of music.

HONORÉ DE BALZAC

nouncement one groom-to-be said, "The fact that Barbara and I were actually getting married was not real to me until I saw her picture in the paper and read the sentence that we were to be married on June third." The newspaper is not the only means of publicly announcing the private commitment. Telling parents, siblings, and friends about wedding plans helps verify the commitment of the partners and also helps marshal the social and economic support to launch the couple into marital orbit.

Types of Marriage

There are two major types of marriage—monogamy and polygamy. In monogamy one wife and one husband have an exclusive sexual relationship. Monogamy is the only legal type of marriage in the United States. Although people in group and homosexual relationships may regard themselves as married, legally they are not. But as one man from Nigeria said, "Some men in my country have three wives at once; in your country you have three wives but not all at the same time." With 50 percent of U.S. marriages ending in divorce and 80 percent of these resulting in remarriage, we have a system of serial monogamy (individuals having several successive monogamous relationships).

I'd rather have three husbands than one. I should have married *more*.

INGRID BERGMAN

Polygamy is a general term that refers to having several spouses. One form of polygamy is polygyny, in which one husband has several wives. Although illegal, polygyny is practiced in Utah by those of the fundamentalist Mormon faith. Eighty-year-old Albert Barlow lives in Utah with his three wives, 34 children, 270 grandchildren, and 70 great-great grandchildren. In an interview on ABC television, he said, "We don't do it [have several wives] for physical purposes, we do it for spiritual purposes" (ABC's "20/20," 1984). Fundamentalist Mormons believe you must create a large earthly family so that you will have a large heavenly family.

DATA • *It is estimated that between 20 and 40 thousand people (husbands, wives, and children) are living in polygynous families in Utah.* (ABC's "20/20," 1984)

From a worldwide perspective, all societies south of the Sahara Desert in Africa practice polygyny. Specific examples are the Yoruba of Nigeria and the Pokomo of Kenya.

CONSIDERATION • Although most non-Mormon American males view polygyny solely in terms of sexual pleasure with a variety of women, the reality in other societies is quite different. Additional wives are sought to produce heirs and to help with housework and are often encouraged by first wives who view several wives as a symbol of their husband's success. Much as a wife might encourage her husband to buy a new car or house to elevate her own status among her peers, so the wife in certain polygynous societies would want her husband to acquire additional wives. Such wives may also relieve first wives of sexual duty, and the husband of many wives is expected, indeed obligated, to have sex with each of them on a regular basis.

Even though polygyny is permitted in a number of societies, most marriages in these societies are monogamous. Although additional wives produce heirs, they may also cost money and only wealthy men can afford to support several wives and children. If a Pokomo man in Kenya has more than one wife, he must supply each with a house and help each cultivate a separate field.

Another form of polygamy is polyandry in which one wife has several husbands, as do the Buddhist Tibetans. In some cases, these husbands may be brothers. Polyandry is functional economically as several men can pool their resources and support one wife. This not only distributes the economic burden but also benefits the wife who may want several children. Polyandry also helps keep the birthrate low, as each woman can produce only one child every nine months regardless of the number of husbands she has. In contrast, if all the husbands were married to different women, more babies would be born.

• WHAT IS FAMILY? •

As with marriage, family may be similarly defined and typed.

Definition of Family

One definition of family is a social group characterized by common residence (the spouses live together), economic cooperation (the spouses share their money and chores), and sexual reproduction (spouses have or adopt children). This definition does not cover all families, as some dual-career couples live apart, some spouses keep their money separate, and some spouses are child-free. Indeed, not all definitions of the family require the presence of children or spouses. The U.S. Census Bureau defines family as a group of two or more persons who are related by blood, marriage, or adoption. According to this definition, two siblings or two spouses may constitute a family.

Types of Family

Families may be typed according to an individual's function within the family and according to member inclusiveness.

FAMILY OF ORIENTATION
This is the family into which you were born. This represents you, your parents, and your siblings. When you go to your parents' home for the holidays, you return to your family of orientation.

DATA • *Seventy-seven percent of children live in a home with two parents.* (Glick, 1984)

FAMILY OF PROCREATION
This represents the family you will begin if you marry and have children. As noted earlier, more than 90 percent of us choose to marry and to establish our

Call it a clan, call it a network, call it a tribe, call it a family. Whatever you call it, whoever you are, you need one.

JANE HOWARD

own family of procreation. We travel through time from the family of orientation to the family of procreation (see Figure 1.1).

NUCLEAR FAMILY

The family is one of nature's masterpieces.

GEORGE
SANTAYANA

Nuclear family may refer to either your family of orientation or procreation. Your nuclear family consists of you, your parents (or parent) and siblings or of you, your spouse, and your children (or just you and your children). During the transition from your family of orientation to your family of procreation, you are in two nuclear families.

EXTENDED FAMILY

Your extended family includes not only your nuclear family but other relatives as well. In practical terms, if you lived with your extended family, your spouse, children, parents, and siblings would all be there. Whereas many societies emphasize the importance of extended families, ours emphasizes the importance of the nuclear family.

> CONSIDERATION • There are numerous variations of these and other types of families that we discuss later in the book. Single-parent families headed by either a woman or man, child-free families, communal families, and stepfamilies are examples. Awareness of these alternatives expands the range of your choices.

Figure 1.1   **Movement from Family of Orientation to Family of Procreation**

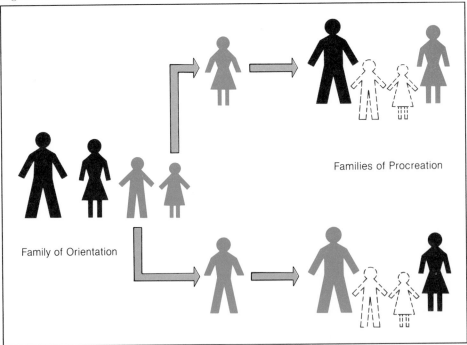

Families of Procreation

Family of Orientation

(The specific number of children a family has will vary from zero to many depending upon the parents' choices.)

Table 1.1 Some Differences Between Marriage and the Family

MARRIAGE	FAMILY
Usually initiated by a public ceremony	Public ceremony not essential
Usually involves two people	Can be as few as two
Ages of the individuals tend to be similar	The individuals represent several generations
Individuals usually choose each other	Members are born or adopted into the family
Ends when spouse dies or is divorced	Continues beyond the life of the individual
Sex between spouses is expected and approved	Sex between near kin is neither expected nor approved
Requires a license	No license needed to become a parent
Procreation expected	Consequence of procreation

Source: Axelson, 1984.

The definitions and types of marriage and the family just described do not emphasize the important differences between these concepts. These are listed in Table 1.1.

• WAYS OF VIEWING MARRIAGE AND THE FAMILY •

There are various conceptual frameworks, perspectives, or ways of viewing marriage and the family. Some of these include the following.

Series of Choices

As noted earlier, viewing marriage and the family as a series of choices is a predominant theme of this book. Although it is common for people to drift into relationships or life-styles by default, the goal of this book is to encourage you to take charge of your life by being aware of your choices, to examine the positive and negative consequences of each choice, and to make a considered decision.

What is not possible is not to choose, but I ought to know that if I do not choose, I am still choosing.

JEAN-PAUL SARTRE

This perspective suggests that you are continually confronted with a range of choices about marriage and the family. To remain single or to get married, separated, divorced or remarried are among them. Each choice leads to an endless array of new choices. There are at least 14 different life-styles from which to choose (Stayton, 1984). See Exhibit 1.1 for examples.

If you choose to be single, you can live alone or with another partner in a heterosexual or homosexual relationship. You can live in a one-room apartment or on a communal farm with 1,600 others (as on the Farm in Tennessee, discussed in Chapter 5). If you choose to marry, there are a variety of marital styles (traditional, open, dual career, child-free) from which to select. If you decide to separate and eventually divorce (as most of us visualize "somebody else" doing), you will be making additional choices to remain single or to remarry. Such a remarriage will involve still other choices of whether to marry a person with children or to be child-free in a subsequent marriage—and so forth and so on.

· Exhibit 1.1 ·

MENU OF LIFE-STYLES

A life-style is the pattern of relationships around which individuals organize their lives. The menu of life-styles available in our society include the following:

- *Traditional Monogamy*: Each spouse is sexually faithful to the other until the death of one partner. Approximately 30–40 percent of Americans continue in one monogamous relationship for life, with no secret affairs or one-night stands.
- *Serial Monogamy*: Individuals have a series of monogamous relationships, marrying, divorcing, and remarrying several times.
- *Sexually Open Marriage*: Spouses regard each other as their primary emotional and sexual partner but may have other transient emotional and sexual relationships outside the marriage.
- *Synergamous Marriage*: Similar to a sexually open marriage except each spouse may develop a committed secondary relationship and may spend significant amounts of time with the other partner. In some cases,

another residence may be set up. Each spouse knows about and approves of the other committed relationship of the mate.

- *Swinging or Group Sex*: Spouses go together to a party or house with the intent of pairing off for sexual experiences with the spouse of another couple. Some swingers seek recreational sex only, whereas others want close emotional ties. Swinging is different from a sexually open marriage, as swingers market themselves as a couple to recruit other sexual partners.
- *Group Marriage*: Although heterosexual monogamy is the only legally recognized form of marriage in the United States, some threesomes, foursomes, and more live together as though they are married. For example, a man and two women or two men and one woman or any of several combinations may live in a common residence, cooperate economically, and sexually reproduce among themselves. They are committed to each other and view their relationship as a marriage.
- *Communes*: Individuals, couples, or families agree to live together, share

expenses, and perhaps rear children. The numbers have ranged from three to 1,600. They may permit sexual relations only with each other or with outsiders or both. They may focus on a common value (such as religion), philosophy (behavioral psychology), or craft (building houses). Commune members are often less committed to each other than those in group marriages.

- *Family Network System*: Such a group is similar to a commune except a small number of families (usually two or three) link their lives together on a regular basis by coming together for meals, sharing tools, and sometimes housing. Only family units are involved.
- *Cohabitation*: Two people who are not blood related who share an emotional and sexual relationship at a common residence for more than just weekends. The partners may be assessing their relationship during the living-together period or committed to marry in the future.
- *Singlehood*: Singlehood is the state of not being married.

Finally, each choice will have both positive and negative consequences. As one spouse said:

Everything is a trade-off. If you get married, you are less free; if you don't get married, you are more lonely. If you have kids, they cost money, make noise, and tear up the house; if you don't have kids, you miss them. If you have an affair, you feel guilty and may lose your marriage; if you don't have sex with others, you wonder what it would be like all the time. So what's the answer?

Although we focus on marriage and the family as a series of choices, there are other perspectives. These include the structure-function, family life cycle, social-psychological, social class, and crisis views.

Structure and Function

The structure-function perspective of marriage and the family emphasizes the functions these institutions serve for the rest of our society. Just as the religious institution helps to explain the unknown, the economic institution ensures the production and distribution of goods and services, and the legal institution provides social control, so the institutions of marriage and the family have three major functions. First, marriage and family serve to replenish society with socialized members. Our society cannot continue to exist without new members, so we must have some way of ensuring a continuing supply. But just having new members is not enough; we need socialized members—those who can speak our language and know the norms and roles of our society. The legal bond of marriage and the obligation to nurture and socialize offspring helps to assure this.

> The family is the nucleus of civilization.
>
> WILL AND ARIEL DURANT

A second function of marriage and family for society is that it promotes emotional stability of the adult partners and gives children a place to belong. Society cannot afford enough counselors to help settle us down when we have problems. Marriage provides an in-residence counselor who is, theoretically, a loving and caring partner. To have someone who loves and cares about us helps keep us stable so that we can adequately perform our work roles in society. Children also need people to love them and to have a place to belong. The affective function of marriage and the family is one of its major strengths. No other institutions focus so completely on fulfilling our emotional needs as do marriage and the family. Finally, by producing and socializing offspring, marriage and the family contribute to other institutions. In fact, all other institutions depend on the family for its members.

Family Life Cycles

That we are all on a conveyer belt of time is illustrated by the family life cycle view of marriage and the family. Examples of these cycles (see Table 1.2) reveal

Our society depends on parents to socialize new members for society.

what is happening to us at various ages. Cycle (a) is for people who marry only once and have two children. Cycle (b) is for people who get divorced and who remarry. Racial origin, family income, and education affect the timing of marital events as people proceed through the life course (Norton, 1983). For example, being black, having lower income, and having completed less than 12 years of education increases a person's chance of divorce. Other factors associated with divorce are discussed in Chapter 18.

Social-Psychological

The social-psychological view emphasizes the importance of social variables as they act upon the individual in marriage and the family. Examples of these variables are self-concept and the self-fulfilling prophecy. The self-concept is affected by family members who are social mirrors into which we look for information about who we are and how others feel about us. If we see approval in our parents and spouses, we develop and maintain a positive feeling about ourselves. One wife displayed her very positive self-concept in the birthday card she gave her husband. It read: "I don't know what to get you for your birthday . . . you've got everything . . . you've got me!"

To love oneself is the beginning of a life-long romance.

OSCAR WILDE

Table 1.2 Alternative Family Life Cycles

(A) FAMILY LIFE CYCLE OF THOSE WHO MARRY ONLY ONCE*	
Life Stage	*Age (Average)*
Marriage	Males: 24
	Females: 22
First child born	Males: 27
	Females: 25
Last child born	Males: 33
	Females: 31
Last child leaves	Males: 51
	Females: 49
Grandparent	Males: 52
	Females: 50
Widowhood	Females: 70
Death	Males: 70
	Females: 78

(B) FAMILY LIFE CYCLE OF THOSE WHO MARRY AND DIVORCE*	
Life Stage	*Age (Average)*
Marriage	Males: 24
	Females: 22
Divorce	Males: 31
	Females: 29
Remarriage	Males: 34
	Females: 33
Widowhood	Females: 70
Death	Males: 70
	Females: 78

*Ages are for white males and females and are taken from 1984 U.S. Vital Statistics data.

The self-fulfilling prophecy implies that we behave according to the expectations of others. If our spouses expect us to be on time, faithful, and productive, we are likely to behave to make those expectations come true. On the other hand, if they expect us to be late, unfaithful, and lazy, we are likely not to disappoint them.

CONSIDERATION • What expectations do you have of your partner and what expectations does your partner have of you in regard to punctuality, faithfulness, and productivity? If these are positive, the behavior is also likely to be positive. In a sense, you find what you look for in your partner and he or she in you.

Social Class

Stratification, a term that has been borrowed from geology, refers to differential ranking of people into higher or lower horizontal layers or strata. When individuals who occupy similar social positions on the scale of prestige are stratified, we say they are in the same social class. Students on your campus have been stratified into the academic classes of freshmen, sophomores, juniors, and seniors.

Marriages and families are also stratified into different social classes. Whether they are regarded as belonging to the upper, middle, or lower class will depend on the criteria used to define social class. Although the most frequently used criteria are income, occupation, and education, others may include dwelling (neighborhood and type of house), family background, values, and goals.

> CONSIDERATION • One way to assess social class is to define it in terms of acceptance, for example, who asks whom to dinner. If you want to know who your social class equals are, look across the table at your next meal.

Crisis

A crisis may be defined as an event for which old patterns of adaptation are no longer helpful. Most individuals, spouses, and parents experience one or more crisis events in their lifetimes. Examples of crisis events include divorce, widowhood, alcoholism, extramarital intercourse, incest, infertility, the birth of a child who has an abnormality, unemployment, military separation, and interpersonal violence. A crisis event may stem from an external source (for example, a recession may cause unemployment) or an internal source (discovery of a spouse's affair may encourage alcoholism).

Although it is assumed that everyone knows about marriage and the family, professional journals are available which report the findings of various researchers.

· SOME CAUTIONS ABOUT RESEARCH ·

This book is based on a comprehensive review of studies in the area of marriage and the family that have been reported in professional journals. These include the following:

Journal of Marriage and the Family
Family Relations
Journal of Family Issues
Family Perspective
Alternative Lifestyles
Journal of Marital and Family Therapy.

Although not specific to marriage and the family, the following journals frequently include studies on interpersonal relationships, divorce, and sexuality:

Journal of Home Economics
Child Development
Parenting Studies
Studies in Family Planning
Journal of Social Issues
Journal of Orthopsychiatry
Family Process
Journal of Divorce
Journal of Sex and Marital Therapy
Sex Roles: A Journal of Research
SIECUS Report

My latest survey shows that people don't believe in surveys.

LAURENCE PETER

Two weekly newsletters report the latest information in marriage and the family:

Marriage and Divorce Today
Sexuality Today

Although the findings of the various studies presented in these publications furnish a basis for making choices in marriage and the family, it is wise to be cautious about research. Some research limitations to be aware of are discussed in the following pages.

Sampling

Most information about marriage and the family is based on sampling—studying a relatively small number of individuals and assuming that those studied are similar to a larger group. For example, suppose you want to know what percentage of unmarried seniors (US) on your campus are living together. Although the most accurate way to get this information is to secure an anonymous yes or no response from every US, doing so is not practical. To save yourself time, you could ask a few USs to complete your questionnaire and assume that the rest of the USs would say yes or no in the same proportion as those who did. To decide who those few USs would be, you could put the names of every US on campus on separate note cards, stir these cards in your bathtub, put on a blindfold, and draw 100 cards. Since each US would have an equal chance of having his or her card drawn from the tub, you would have what is known as a random sample. After administering the questionnaire to this sample and adding the yeses and nos, you would have a fairly accurate idea of the percentage of USs on your campus who are living together.

Because of the trouble and expense of obtaining random samples, most researchers study those to whom they have convenient access (Rubenstein, 1982). This often means students in the researchers' classes. The result is an overabundance of research on "convenience" samples consisting of white, Protestant, middle-class college students.

> CONSIDERATION • Since today's college students comprise only about 5 percent of all American adults, their attitudes, feelings, and behaviors cannot be assumed to be similar to those of their noncollege peers or older adults.

Although the data presented in this book include those obtained from young unmarried college students, they also refer to people of different ages, marital statuses, life-styles, religions, social classes, and societies.

Control Groups

Just as most samples are not representative, most of the marriage and family research is not experimental, as it does not use control groups. The value of a control group is that for particular questions, it allows you to be more certain in your conclusions than if you do not have a control group. In our earlier example, we could not conclude that taking a marriage and family course influenced reported desire to live together (which might be true in the experimental group), if those in the control group also reported an increased desire for living together even though they did not take a marriage and family class. Hence it is essential to include a control group in marriage and family research if we want to know the effect one factor has on another.

Terminology

In addition to being alert to potential shortcomings in sampling and control groups, you should consider how the phonomenon being researched is defined. For example, in the preceding illustration, how would you define *living together*? How many people, of what gender, spending what amount of time, in what place, engaging in what behaviors will constitute your definition?

DATA • *Researchers of living together have used more than 20 definitions.*

What about other terms? What is meant by marital satisfaction, commitment, interpersonal violence, and sexual fulfillment? Before accepting that most people report a high degree of marital satisfaction or sexual fulfillment, be alert to the definition used by the researcher. Exactly what is the researcher trying to measure?

Researcher Bias

Even when the sample is random and the terms are carefully defined, two researchers can examine the same data and arrive at different conclusions. In your study of living together, suppose you find that a quarter of the students on your campus are living together. In discussing your findings, would you emphasize that fact or the fact that the majority of the students (75 percent) were not living together? You can focus on either aspect of the data to make the point you want to make. Many researchers tend to focus on selected aspects of the data they are reporting.

Also, the answer a researcher gets is related to the question she or he asks. In one *New York Times*/CBS poll, 30 percent of the respondents answered yes when asked, "Do you think there should be an amendment to the Constitution prohibiting abortions, or shouldn't there be such an amendment?" But when the same people were asked, "Do you believe there should be an amendment to the Constitution protecting the life of the unborn child?" one-half answered yes.

Time Lag

There is typically a two-year lag between the time a research study is completed and its appearance in a professional journal. Since textbooks are based on these journals and take from three to five years from writing to publication, by the time you read the results of a study, other studies may have been conducted that reveal different findings. Be aware that the research you read in this or any book may not reflect current reality.

Deception

Studies in all fields may have problems of sampling, terminology, lack of a control group, researcher bias, and time lag, but there is another problem specific to social science research, particularly marriage research. That is deception. Marriage is a very private relationship that happens behind closed doors, and we have been socialized not to reveal to strangers the intimate details of our marriages. Therefore we are prone to distort, omit, or exaggerate information—perhaps unconsciously—to cover up what we may feel is no one else's business. This means the researcher sometimes gets inaccurate information. One researcher contends that when 23-year-old Margaret Mead interviewed Samoans about their sexual behavior, reported in *Coming of Age in Samoa* (1928), her respondents told her lies to tease her (Freeman, 1983). Marriage and family researchers only know what people say they do, not what they actually do.

An unintended and probably more frequent form of deception is inaccurate recall. Sometimes researchers ask respondents to recall details of their relationships

> You can fool some of the people all of the time, and all of the people some of the time, but you cannot fool all of the people all of the time.
>
> LINCOLN

that occurred years ago. Since time tends to blur some memories, respondents may not relate what actually happened but only what they think happened.

In addition to deception on the part of the person being surveyed, outright deception on the part of the investigator is not unknown. In response to pressures to publish or from a desire for prestige and recognition, some researchers have doctored their data. For example, the late British psychologist Cyril Burt was renowned for his research designed to test the relative importance of heredity and environment on a person's development. He studied identical twins who had been reared in separate environments since birth and presented data that seemed to indicate clearly that heredity was more important. Five years after Burt's death, evidence came to light that he had altered his data, that his coauthors never existed, and that the investigations were never conducted. Although such research fraud is rare, it "reduces public respect for the findings of scientific research" (Bobys, 1983, p. 47).

> CONSIDERATION • In view of the research problems outlined here, you might ask, "Why bother to report the findings?" The research picture is not as bleak as it may seem at first. A number of studies have been conducted that have none of the research drawbacks mentioned. The articles in *Journal of Marriage and the Family*, for example, illustrate the high level of methodologically sound articles that are being published. Even less sophisticated journals provide us with useful information about what is currently happening. The alternative to gathering data is relying on personal experience alone, and this is unacceptable to social scientists who study marriage and the family.

• TRENDS •

In general, marriage and family will continue to be the most important aspect in the lives of most people, not least because of the multiple functions they perform.

> Woody Allen in the movie *Annie Hall* tells his psychiatrist about his uncle who thinks he is a chicken. The psychiatrist asks, "How long has he been thinking he is a chicken?" "Several years," Allen says. "But why haven't you reported this before now?" asks the psychiatrist. Allen replies, "It's because we need the eggs."

The farther backward you can look, the farther forward you are likely to see.

WINSTON CHURCHILL

For all the problems interpersonal relationships may cause, we continue to seek them. Marriage and family relationships feed the emotional part of ourselves. Families are primary groups of intimate individuals. We tire of impersonal secondary group relationships—like those with whom we interact during the business day—and look forward to more personal interaction at day's end. More than 200,000 respondents identified "love" and "companionship" as the two most important needs that marriage fulfills (*Better Homes and Gardens*, 1983).

• SUMMARY •

Reasons for studying marriage and the family include assessing your suitability for singlehood versus marriage, identifying a compatible marriage partner, learning conflict negotiation skills, and preparing for transitions. Some benefits of taking a practical marriage and family course might include a happier marriage, greater insight into marriage relationships, a positive model for subsequent children, and a greater willingness to contact a marriage therapist if necessary. The course might also effect the relationships of unmarried people. In some cases, individuals become more confident that their relationship has the characteristics of permanence. In other cases, individuals discover they are on the *Titanic* with their partners and terminate the relationship before sinking.

Marriage in the United States is both an emotional relationship and a legal commitment. It usually includes a public announcement, a public ceremony, and sexual monogamy. It always provides for the transfer of property and the legitimizing of children. Marriage in other societies may be monogamous or polygamous. Polygamy may be polygynous when one man has several wives or polyandrous when one wife has several husbands. The latter is rare.

Family in the United States refers to a group of people who live together, cooperate economically, and reproduce. A wife, husband, and children represent the usual American family, although several variations (two spouses or two siblings or one parent–one child) also qualify as a family. The family of orientation is the one into which we are born; the family of procreation is the one we begin with our own spouse.

A primary way of viewing marriage and the family is as a series of choices. We are continually making choices—whether to marry, whom to marry, whether to stay married, whether to have children, how many children to have, and so on. Examining these various choices is a central theme in this book.

Other views of marriage and the family include the structure-function, family life cycles, social-psychological, social class, and crisis views. The structure-function perspective emphasizes the benefits to society of the institutions of marriage and family. Marriage bonds a female and male together in a legal relationship that obligates them to nurture and socialize any offspring they may have. Since society and its institutions depend on marriage and the family for new members, marriage will continue to be a valuable institution in our society.

The research reported in this book should be viewed cautiously. Most research has one or more methodological problems such as use of a small, nonrandom sample, lack of a control group, vague terminology, researcher bias, and outright deception. These cautions do not imply that all research is problematic. Indeed, the journals reporting studies in marriage and family are becoming more sophisticated in their methodology and reflect some excellent research.

Although the form of marriage and family will continue to change (for example, more dual income marriages and single parent households), the importance of marriage and the family as a set of relationships that meets our emotional needs for love and support will continue.

Questions for Reflection

1. How would you feel about having a polygynous or polyandrous marriage?
2. If you knew that studying marriage and the family as a personal search would contribute to the break up of the relationship with your partner, would you still choose to study the subject from this perspective? (Questions two and three will become meaningful after reading the choices section which follows.)
3. Describe several decisions you have made by deciding not to decide.

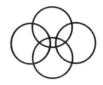

· CHOICES ·

Studying marriage and the family as an academic exercise or a personal search, consciously choosing between two alternatives or choosing by default, and choosing to be tolerant or condemnatory about the decisions of others are basic choices to be made in a marriage and family course.

MARRIAGE AND FAMILY: AN ACADEMIC OR PERSONAL SEARCH?

Until your final grade for this course is posted, you will be involved in the systematic study of marriage and the family. One way to regard this course and the content of this book is as an academic exercise in which you come to class, take notes, skim the book, take tests, and go to the next course without ever becoming involved with the content. This is a legitimate choice. People take marriage and family courses for a variety of reasons and may do so to complete a social science requirement, to fill a transcript, or out of intellectual curiosity.

An alternative reason for studying marriage and the family is to explore the intimate relationship between you and your lover, spouse, or parents with the goal of making better decisions in your own life about marriage and family issues. One student said:

A lot of people I know, including my parents and brother, are divorced or running around on their partners. I want to know all I can about why people do these things so I can help avoid similar things happening to me. My partner and I are taking this course together in hopes that we can beat the odds.

You may choose to regard the study of marriage and the family as an academic or personal search or as both. Some people have mixed feelings.

Somehow I feel that some things should remain a mystery and maybe marriage, love, and sex are things you shouldn't "study"—it might take the spontaneity out of them if you do. On the other hand, I think of marriage the same way I do a garden. Some things make it flourish and some things make it wither. Knowing what those things are could make the differences in being happily married and being divorced three times.

CHOOSING CAREFULLY OR CHOOSING BY DEFAULT

Some of us believe we can avoid making decisions about marriage and the family. We cannot, because not to decide is to decide by default. Some examples follow:

- If we don't make a decision to pursue a relationship with

a particular person, we have made a decision (by default) to let that person drift out of our lives.

- If we don't decide to do those things necessary to keep or improve the relationships we have, we have made a decision to let them slowly disintegrate.
- If we don't make a decision to be faithful to our dating partner or spouse, we have made a decision to be open to situations and relationships in which we are likely to be unfaithful.
- If we don't make a decision to avoid having intercourse with a new partner early in the relationship, we have made a decision to let intercourse occur.
- If we are sexually active and don't make a decision to use some form of birth control, we have made a decision to become a parent.
- If we don't make a decision to break up with our dating partner or spouse, we have made a decision to continue the relationship with him or her.

Throughout the book we consider various choices with which we are confronted in marriage and the family. It will be helpful for us to keep in mind that we cannot avoid making choices—that not to make a choice is to make one.

TOLERANCE OR CONDEMNATION FOR THE CHOICES OF OTHERS?

Regardless of the choices we make about our own behavior and life-styles, we must also make a choice about the rights of others to make choices that are different from ours. Most people are relatively tolerant of the choices others make. "One of my closest friends has started living with her partner," said one woman. "While I wouldn't want to do this myself, I feel it is okay for her to do what she wants."

Some people find it more difficult to be tolerant about homosexuality. "I couldn't believe she was gay when she told me," remarked this same woman of another friend. "I can't handle her being gay and told her so. My tolerance stops when my friends want to be or do something that is unnatural. I guess I'd feel the same way if my boyfriend said he wanted to tie me up to have sex."

· Chapter 2 ·

GENDER ROLES

CONTENTS

Terminology
Biological Beginnings
Socialization Influences
Nature versus Nurture:
 The Controversy
Consequences of
 Becoming a Woman
Self-Assessment:
 The Sexist Attitudes Scale
Consequences of
 Becoming a Man
The Ideal Man
The Ideal Woman
Choices

The woman who most needs liberating is the woman in every man, and the man who most needs liberating is the man in every woman.

WILLIAM COFFIN, JR.

American men are self-reliant and strong; they rarely, if ever, cry; they have full-time careers and support their families; and they are not especially interested in changing diapers, planning a meal, or buying clothes for their children. In contrast, American women need husbands to protect and support them; they are emotional and they cry when they are unhappy; they have a special talent that men lack for nurturing babies, preparing gourmet meals, and finding good buys on food, clothes, and household items.

Do these descriptions sound familiar? If they do, it is not necessarily because the people we know fit the descriptions. Instead, we recognize the stereotypes (simplified beliefs, often inaccurate, about members of a particular group) because we have all learned to varying degrees what the traditional roles of men and women are supposed to be in our society. In this chapter we explore the biological and social origins of gender roles, the consequences for the individuals who assume these roles, the trends regarding such roles, and the decisions we can make in reference to them. We all occupy various social roles; and since the roles of spouse and parent are roles eventually assumed by most of us, it is important for us to be aware of their implications. We begin by defining some basic terms.

· TERMINOLOGY ·

Sociologists, home economists, social workers, and other family life educators often have different definitions and connotations for the terms *gender*, *gender identity*, and *gender role*. We use these terms in the following way:

Gender refers to the biological distinction of being female or male. The primary sex characteristics that differentiate women and men include external genitalia (vulva and penis), gonads (ovaries and testes), sex chromosomes (XX and XY), and hormones (estrogen, progesterone, and testosterone). Secondary sex characteristics like the female's larger breasts and the male's beard are additional distinctions.

In contrast to the biological gender distinction, gender identity is the psychological state of viewing one's self as a girl or boy and later as a woman or man. Such identity is learned and is a reflection of the society's conceptions of masculinity and femininity. A person's gender identity is usually formed at about age 3.

Gender role, also known as sex role, refers to the socially accepted characteristics and behaviors typically associated with a person's gender identity. In our society the traditional concept of being female includes being emotional, dependent, and family-oriented, whereas the traditional concept of being male includes being nonemotional, independent, and career oriented. These gender-role stereotypes are changing. Today more parents are encouraging a wider range of behaviors in their children. Increasingly, women are being encouraged to be assertive and men to be nurturant.

Whether gender roles are primarily a function of biological or social influences is a continuing controversy (examined later in this chapter). Most researchers acknowledge that biological and social factors interact to produce an individual's personality. Although children are born female and male, they learn culturally defined feminine or masculine characteristics. In the following sections we review the biological beginnings of women and men and examine the ways in which they are socialized.

· BIOLOGICAL BEGINNINGS ·

Although all human life begins with a zygote—a fertilized egg (Figure 2.1)—all zygotes are not alike. They carry different chromosomes and hormones, which result in women and men being housed in different bodies.

Chromosomes

Women and men have different genetic makeups. Every normal human ovum (egg) contains 22 "regular" chromosomes (Figure 2.2) and one X chromosome.

Egg

Sperm

Figure 2.1
Fertilization
Fertilization occurs when a sperm penetrates an egg in a Fallopian tube.

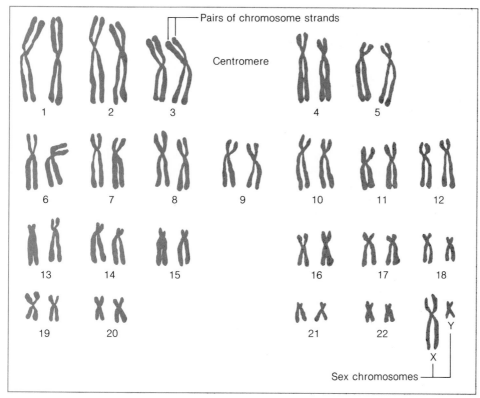

Figure 2.2 **Chromosome Pairs** Twenty-three chromosome pairs are within each cell of a person's body.

Every normal human sperm contains 22 "regular" chromosomes and one X *or* Y chromosome. Whereas the regular chromosomes contain various genes that determine the individual's eye color, hair color, body type, and predispositions to baldness, color blindness, and free bleeding (hemophilia), the extra chromosome determines the biological gender of the individual. Since the sex chromosome in the ovum is *always* X (the female chromosome), the sex chromosome in the male sperm determines the gender of the child. If the sperm contains an X chromosome, the match with the female chromosome will be XX, and a female will result. If the sperm contains a Y chromosome, the male chromosome, the match with the female chromosome will be XY, and a male will result. Hence the normal female has 44 regular chromosomes (22 from each parent) plus an X chromosome from her mother and an X chromosome from her father. The normal male also has 44 regular chromosomes and an X chromosome from his mother but a Y chromosome from his father.

Hormones

Although each gender has hormones of the other (testosterone, estrogen, progesterone), the release of these and others into the bloodstream in varying amounts causes the development of a female or male embryo (the human organism from conception until the end of the eighth week).

Male and female embryos are indistinguishable from one another during the first several weeks of intrauterine life. In both, two primitive gonads and two paired duct systems form about the fifth or sixth week of development (Figures 2.3 and 2.4). The reproductive system of the male develops from the Wolffian ducts and the female reproductive system from the Müllerian ducts, but both are present in the developing embryo at this stage. If the embryo is genetically a male (XY), a chemical substance controlled by the Y chromosome stimulates the primitive gonads to develop into testes. The testes, in turn, begin secreting the male hormone testosterone, which stimulates the development of the male reproductive and external sexual organs. The testes also secrete a second substance, called Müllerian duct-inhibiting substance, which causes the potential female ducts to degenerate or become blind tubules. Thus development of male anatomical structures depends on the presence of male hormones at a critical stage of development.

The development of a female requires that no (or very little) male hormone be present. Without the controlling substance from the Y chromosome, the primitive gonads will develop into ovaries and the Müllerian duct system into Fallopian tubes, uterus, and vagina; and without testosterone the Wolffian duct system (epididymis, vas deferens, ejaculatory duct) will degenerate or become blind tubules.

The impact of hormones becomes even more evident at puberty. The testes and ovaries release hormones necessary for the development of secondary sex characteristics. Higher levels of testosterone account for the growth of facial hair in males and pubic and underarm hair in both males and females. Breast development, on the other hand, results from increasing levels of estrogen.

Figure 2.3 Embryo before Six Weeks with Undifferentiated Sexual Structures

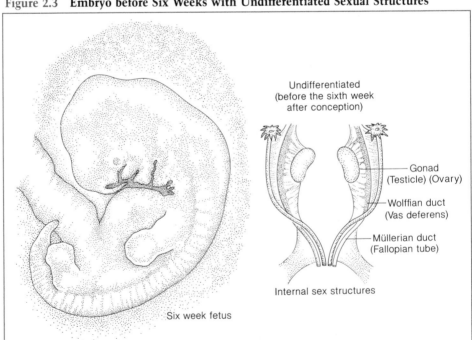

Undifferentiated
(before the sixth week
after conception)

Gonad
(Testicle) (Ovary)

Wolffian duct
(Vas deferens)

Müllerian duct
(Fallopian tube)

Internal sex structures

Six week fetus

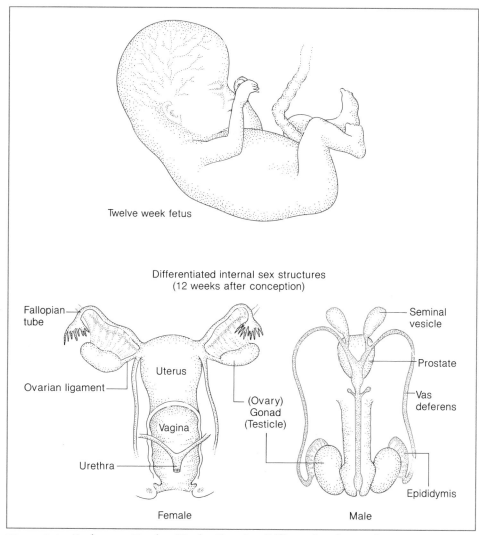

Twelve week fetus

Differentiated internal sex structures
(12 weeks after conception)

Fallopian tube

Ovarian ligament

Uterus

Vagina

Urethra

(Ovary) Gonad (Testicle)

Seminal vesicle

Prostate

Vas deferens

Epididymis

Female

Male

Figure 2.4 Embryo at Twelve Weeks Showing Differentiated Sexual Structures

Anatomy and Physiology

In addition to chromosomal and hormonal differences, a number of physical characteristics differentiate women and men. These differences begin before birth, since the male fetus (the human organism from the eighth week of pregnancy until birth) is more likely to be stillborn than the female fetus during the early months of pregnancy. Male babies, children, and adults are also more likely to die each year than female babies, children, and adults.

DATA • *Females live an average of 8 years longer than males (78 versus 70).* (World Almanac & Book of Facts, 1984)

Although men have higher mortality rates than women, they are taller, heavier, and stronger than women. The average height for the adult man is 5 feet, 8

If I told you you had a beautiful body, you wouldn't hold it against me would you?

DAVID FISHER

inches. For women, it is 5 feet, 3 inches. But regardless of height or frame, men weigh about 10 pounds more than women.

• SOCIALIZATION INFLUENCES •

We learn to engage in behavior that is socially defined as appropriate for our gender role. After reviewing the importance of environmental influences, we look at how parents, teachers, peers, and the media influence us toward gender-specific behavior.

Significance of the Environment

Parents who have raised their child differently are finding that culture has an enormous influence. For example, there is the case of a woman physician whose child says that women can't be doctors.

CAROL JACKLIN

The great majority of characteristics designated as feminine or masculine in any given culture are learned from the material and interpersonal environment in which we grow up. Gender-role prescriptions in our culture not only signal the color of the blanket in which an infant is to be wrapped but they also dictate appropriate toys (doll or football), clothes (panties or briefs), and work roles (baby sitter or paper boy) for children. Gender roles also tell us whether to be aggressive or passive in interpersonal and sexual interaction.

That women's sexual aggressiveness or passivity is learned behavior is illustrated by a study of females attending male strip shows. In such a situation where women receive peer support for sexual aggressiveness, their passivity seems to disappear. After attending a male strip show weekly for eight months, Peterson and Dressel (1982) summarized their observations:

> A primary feature of the club is that it provides the opportunity for women to be assertive in sexual transactions with males. This takes several forms. Members of the audience initiate expressions of sexual interest, and they emulate male-typed courting behaviors by bringing gifts to, or doing favors for, their favorite dancers, as well as by propositioning strippers of their choice. This display of assertiveness by members of the audience is described by strippers as frequently being excessive, with women often becoming verbally and physically aggressive and sometimes engaging in behavior that dancers describe as lewd. (pp. 203–204)

Theories of Gender-Role Learning

Although most theorists agree that the environment has a profound effect on our gender-role development, they do not agree on the specific processes. There are four main explanations of how female and male gender roles are acquired.

SOCIAL LEARNING THEORY

Derived from the school of behavioral psychology, the social learning perspective emphasizes that when gender-appropriate behaviors are rewarded and gender-inappropriate behaviors are punished, a child learns the behaviors appropriate to her or his gender. For example, two young brothers enjoyed playing "lady." Each of them would put on a dress, wear high-heeled shoes, and carry a pocketbook. Their father came home early one day and angrily demanded that they "take those clothes off and never put them on again. Those things are for women," he said. The boys were punished for playing "lady" but rewarded with their father's approval for playing "cowboys," with plastic guns and "Bang! You're dead!" dialogue.

Reward and punishment alone are not sufficient to account for the way children learn gender roles. Direct instruction ("girls wear dresses," "men walk on the outside when walking with a woman") is another way children learn through social interaction with others. But there are too many gender rules to learn. These require the use of other mechanisms like modeling.

The concept of modeling is important in understanding gender-role acquisition from a social learning perspective. In modeling, the child observes another's behavior and imitates that behavior. On Monday afternoon eight-year-old Bill helped his younger sister repair her tricycle. The Saturday before this event, Bill had observed his father putting spark plugs in their Dodge. His father was the "fix-it-man" in their home, and Bill, modeling after him, was the fix-it-man in his father's absence.

The eye's a better pupil and more willing than the ear; Fine counsel is confusing, but example's always clear.

EDGAR A. GUEST

Much of our behavior is learned through modeling.

The impact of modeling on the development of gender-role behavior is controversial. For example, although a modeling perspective implies that children will tend to imitate the parent of the same gender, children are usually reared mainly by the woman in all cultures. Yet this persistent female model does not seem to interfere with the male's developing the appropriate behavior for his gender. One explanation suggests he learns early that males have more status and privileges in our society and he therefore devalues the feminine and emphasizes the masculine aspects of himself. Some research has found that grade school boys are more likely to reject opposite gender behavior than are girls (Bussey & Perry, 1982).

Women also do not strictly model their mothers' behavior. While women who work outside the home usually have mothers who did likewise (Stevens & Boyd, 1980), their mothers may also be traditional homemakers (Haber, 1980).

COGNITIVE-DEVELOPMENTAL THEORY

The cognitive-developmental theory of gender-role acquisition suggests that the mental maturity of the child is a prerequisite to such acquisition (Kohlberg,

Children tend to identify with the same gender parent.

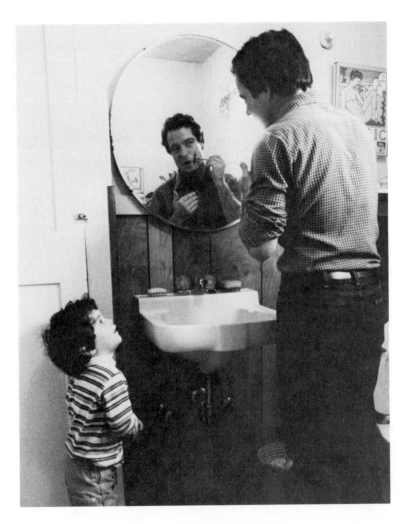

1969). Although 2-year-olds can label themselves and each other as "girl" or "boy," they have superficial criteria for doing so. People who wear long hair are girls and those who never wear dresses are boys. Two-year-olds believe they can change their gender by altering their hair or changing clothes.

Not until age 6 or 7 does the child view gender as permanent (Kohlberg 1966, 1969). In Kohlberg's view this cognitive understanding is not a result of rewards for appropriate gender-role behaviors and punishments for inappropriate behaviors. Rather, it involves the development of a specific mental ability to grasp the idea that certain basic characteristics of people do not change even though their hair style might. Once children learn that gender is permanent, they seek to become competent and proper members of their gender group. For example, a child standing on the edge of a school playground may observe one group of children jumping rope while another group is playing football. Her or his self-concept ("I am a girl" or "I am a boy") connects with the observed gender-appropriate behavior and she or he joins one of the two groups. Once in the group, the child seeks to develop the behaviors appropriate to her or his gender.

> Male and female personalities are socially produced.
>
> MARGARET MEAD

SOCIAL INTERACTION THEORY

The social interactionist perspective of gender-role learning is based on the belief that the meaning of others and events emerges as a result of social interaction. One researcher (Cahill, 1983) has described how children learn gender roles when they are playing.

> In an interaction situation of interrelated roles, such as house playing, the child must fit his or her behavior to that of others. The child not only rehearses his or her own gender but also learns to anticipate the behavior of the other gender. He or she learns to expect certain behaviors of different-sex others. In such play situations, children are extemporaneously scripting cross-sex interactions in much the same way they will be required to do in later life. (pp. 10–11)

IDENTIFICATION THEORY

Identification results when the child takes on the demeanor, mannerisms, and attitudes of the same-gender parent. A child who identifies with her or his parent acts like that parent.

Sigmund Freud, the father of psychoanalysis, said that children identify with the same-gender parent out of fear (1925, 1933). He felt this fear may be one of two kinds: fear of loss of love or fear of retaliation. The first type, which results in both girls and boys identifying with their mother, is caused by their deep dependence on her for love and nurturance. Fearful that she may withdraw her love, young children try to become like her to please her and to ensure the continuance of her love.

According to Freud, about age 4 the child's identification with the mother begins to change, but in different ways for boys and girls. Boys experience what Freud calls the Oedipal complex. Based on the legend of the Greek youth Oedipus who unknowingly killed his father and married his mother, the Oedipal complex involves the young boy's awakening sexual feelings for his mother as he becomes aware he has a penis and his mother does not. He unconsciously feels that if his father knew of the intense love feelings he has for his mother, the father would castrate him (which may be what happened to his mother and sister since they have no penis). The boy resolves the Oedipal struggle—feeling love for father but wanting to kill him because he is a competitor for mother's love—by becoming like his father, by identifying with him. In this way the boy can keep his penis and take pride in being like his father. According to Freud, the successful resolution of this Oedipal situation marks the beginning of a boy's appropriate gender-role acquisition.

While her brother is experiencing the Oedipal complex, the girl goes through her own identification process known as the Electra complex. Around age 4 she recognizes that she has no penis, wishes she did (penis envy), and feels her mother is responsible for its absence. To retaliate, she takes her love away from her mother and begins to focus on her father as a love object. But her desire for a penis is gradually transformed into the need for a baby, and to get a baby from her father she recognizes that she must be more like her mother. So she identifies again with her mother. Her goal now is to be a woman like her mother and to be a mother herself. According to Freud, such gender-role identification is characteristic of a mature female.

Although Freud's identification theories make interesting reading, there is little scientific support for their validity as explanations for gender-role acquisition. Most 3- and 4-year-olds do not know the difference between males and females on the basis of their genitals. Also, it is possible that some girls have status envy rather than penis envy. They may view the male role as offering more rewards, not because men have a penis, but because in many cases they tend to occupy the social positions that are accorded status in our society (heads of corporations, senators, representatives).

Nevertheless, although verification for Freud's identification theories is weak, his belief in the biological basis of gender-role differences has had a significant impact. His dictim "biology is destiny" is still influential in research on gender differences.

> And here's the happy bounding flea—
> You cannot tell the he from she.
> The sexes look alike you see;
> But she can tell, and so can he.
>
> ROLAND YOUNG

CONSIDERATION • In reviewing the social learning, cognitive-developmental, social interactionist, and identification perspectives of how individuals become women and men, it is clear that no one explanation is adequate. Depending on the social situation, the age of the child, the frequency and nature of play interactions, and the attitudes of the child's parents, each process is influential at different times, in different ways, and to different degrees. Young children will at times be rewarded or punished for gender-appropriate or inappropriate behaviors, cognitively choose to engage in gender-appropriate behaviors, learn gender roles through interaction with their peers, and choose to identify with their parents.

Sources of Socialization

The preceding discussion has implied that gender roles are learned through interaction with the environment. Since parents, teachers, peers, and the mass media make up the social environment, what are the effects of each? Researchers have suggested the following answers.

PARENTS
Parents are usually the most important influence in a child's life—the first influence and the longest lasting. Parents affect gender-role learning by reacting

in different ways to their boy and girl children. These differences "may be quite subtle, and adults may be unaware of their own predispositions toward sex stereotyping" (Culp et al., 1983, p. 487).

Parents tend to give their daughters dolls and their sons baseballs or footballs. They are also more protective of their daughters out of fear that they will be sexually molested, although such protectiveness often encourages girls to be less active in exploring their environment. Daughters are more socialized to be family oriented, to be aware of who is having what birthday, and to want the family to be together for various holidays. Finally, daughters are often expected to provide more care for ailing family members and relatives than their brothers.

Parents from different social classes also tend to encourage different gender-role views. Middle-class children tend to be more flexible in their gender-role definitions compared with working-class children. For example, a middle-class child might feel that both men and women could be gentle, whereas the working-class child would more likely view gentleness as characteristic of women only (Romer & Cherry, 1980).

TEACHERS

Although parents have the earliest and most pervasive influence on their children, teachers are a major influence outside the home. Teachers may differentially influence the level of interest girls and boys display in school subjects by the way they present material. When teachers imply that what they are discussing is primarily "for boys," the girls in the class demonstrate less interest by asking fewer questions and remembering less of what is discussed. Similarly, when the material is labeled "for girls," boys are less likely to pay attention. However, when the material is labeled as important for both genders, both girls and boys are more attentive than if it is labeled as relevant for one gender (Bradbard & Endsley, 1983).

PEERS

Peers become an important influence in the life of a child beginning with grade school and continuing through adolescence. The individual looks to his or her peers to discover "the" appropriate language, dress, and interests. Recall your own high school days when you spoke the same language, wore the same clothes, and pursued the same activities as those your age and gender. Parents often recognize the significance of peer group influence and encourage their children to have the "right" friends.

MEDIA

Television plays a significant role in gender socialization. It has been estimated that the typical child and teenager spends more time in front of the television screen than in school. What the child views often presents a male bias and emphasizes stereotyped roles. In a three-year study of television commercials during the Christmas holiday season, researchers found that boys were significantly more likely to be in such commercials than girls (Feldstein & Feldstein, 1982). In another study of children who watch television (McGhee & Frueh, 1980), boys and girls in grades 1, 3, 5, and 7 were classified as heavy TV viewers (25 or more hours per week) or light TV viewers (10 or fewer hours per week) be-

I find television very educating. Every time somebody turns on the set I go into the other room and read a book.

GROUCHO MARX

Television can become a subtle source of gender role stereotypes for children.

fore they took the Sex Stereotype Measure Instrument. Results showed that those who were heavy TV viewers had more stereotyped gender-role perceptions than light viewers; for example, that men were competitive, persistent, not easily hurt, and "rough," whereas women were noncompetitive, lacking drive, sensitive, and "gentle."

Television also affects the degree to which adults believe in gender-role stereotypes. Adults who watch a lot of television tend to have more gender-role stereotypes than those who watch television infrequently (Ross et al., 1982); and feminists, defined as women who agree with the ideals of the women's movement, watch less television than nonfeminists (Lull et al., 1983).

Children and adults are also confronted with the same stereotypes in the art museum. In a study of gender-role imagery in modern Western art, O'Kelly (1980) found that men frequently are depicted doing something, whereas women are more often at rest; "they are merely like plates or fruits painted for shape, texture, and color" (p. 105). Women also are more often seen nude in seductive poses.

CONSIDERATION • Although parents, teachers, peers, and the media represent different sources of gender-role socialization, their impact is the same—to emphasize different gender-role behaviors for women and for men.

• NATURE VERSUS NURTURE: THE CONTROVERSY •

The relative importance of our biological heritage (nature) and our socialization experiences (nurture) in determining who we are continues to be one of the most controversial issues related to gender roles. We now examine both sides of this issue.

Are Gender Role Behaviors Innate?

Those on the "nature" side of the nature-nurture controversy contend that our biological inheritance programs us to be who we are. As we have seen in this chapter, women and men have different chromosomes and hormones, which determine not only gender but also body types and mortality expectations. They also influence an individual's psychological makeup and sexual preference.

Studies of identical twins who were reared apart emphasize the impact of heredity. Also known as monozygotic twins, identical twins develop from a single fertilized egg that divides to produce two embryos. These embryos develop into infants who, from a genetic viewpoint, are identical. If these individuals are exposed to different environments in their infancy and childhood, yet show striking similarities as adults, heredity is the suggested cause.

A team of researchers at the University of Minnesota (Bouchard et al., 1980) have studied more than 15 such pairs of twins, asking each twin about 15,000 questions. The researchers observed a striking tendency for the twins to show very similar physical and psychological characteristics. If one stuttered, had a phobia, had headaches, was shy, anxious, or depressed, or had a particular interest, the other tended to have the same characteristic. Identical twins who were reared apart also tend to be similar in intelligence. Such similarity is related to their genetic inheritance (Bouchard, 1983). In his presidential address to the Society for Psychophysiological Research, David Lykken (1982) said, "I think first, that much more of the variance in human behavior is genetically based than we have previously supposed" (p. 372).

Additional evidence for biological determinism has been suggested by an early study in the Dominican Republic (Imperato-McGinley et al., 1974).

Similarities in identical twins suggest that much of who we are is the result of genetic inheritance.

Owing to a genetic-endocrine problem, a large number of males were born who at birth appeared to be females, having a vaginal pouch instead of a scrotum and a clitoris instead of a penis. The parents, unaware that anything was unusual, reared the biological males as females. But at puberty, a spontaneous hormonal change caused the development of a penis in these individuals and a change in their psychological orientation. These males who had been reared as females began to view themselves as males and to develop a sexual interest in females.

Other researchers feel strongly that sexual identity is innate. Milton Diamond (1982), a specialist in sexual and gender identity, says that each individual has a male or female nervous system, which biases the development of that person's sexual identity and partner choice. Furthermore, one researcher observed that men and women have different brain structures, different biological-neurophysiological makeups, and different hormonal makeups, which possibly explain males being more aggressive and females being more nurturant (Daniel, 1984).

Are Gender Role Behaviors Learned?

With good heredity, nature deals you a fine hand at cards; and with a good environment, you learn to play the hand well.

WALTER C.
ALVAREZ

In contrast to the belief that we are biologically programmed to become who we are, other researchers state just as emphatically that we learn to be who we are. Although the fact that women and men have different biological makeups that result in different body sizes and reproductive outcomes is acknowledged, this group completely rejects the idea that various personality traits and social behaviors are also innate.

We have examined some of the evidence that we are products of our experiences through social learning, modeling, social interaction, and identification. Further evidence for the impact of learning experiences on the development of gender-role characteristics comes from a study at the University of Arizona (Ridley et al., 1982). Twenty-six couples were assigned to a problem-solving skills-training program after taking the Bem Sex Role Inventory (BSRI), designed to assess the degree to which each person viewed herself or himself as masculine or feminine.

The training consisted of meeting in small groups for three hours weekly for eight weeks with an instructor who outlined various problem-solving skills, modeled the skills, and gave feedback to the couples who practiced them. An important aspect of the training sessions was teaching the participants how to disclose themselves to each other and to express their feelings (traditionally associated with a feminine gender role). After completing the training, the participants took the BSRI again. Results showed that both men and women scored higher on the femininity aspects following the training. Similar changes were not observed in the control group of this experiment.

This study emphasizes that self-disclosure, a trait typically associated with women, can be learned. It is not an innate trait but is acquired through social and cultural exposure to various learning situations. The fact that males are typically less self-disclosing than females is a consequence of their socialization, not their heredity. Another study showed that assertiveness is a skill women can learn (McVicar & Herman, 1983). Finally, one study demonstrated that females display autocratic leadership skills similar to that of males when the situational context calls for such behavior (Stitt et al., 1983). Emphasizing that behavior is not innate, one woman said, "Our biological legacy is the ability to choose how we would like to live" (Weisstein, 1982, p. 85).

CONSIDERATION • The fact that the nature-nurture, heredity-environment controversy continues underscores the fact that innate and learning influences interact to produce who we are, what we think, and how we behave. Alice Rossi (1984), in her presidential address to the American Sociological Association, observed:

It makes no sense to view biology and social experience as separate domains contesting for election as "primary causes." Biological processes unfold in a cultural context, and are themselves malleable, not stable and inevitable. So, too, cultural processes take place within and through the biological organism: they do not take place in a biological vacuum. (p. 10)

• CONSEQUENCES OF BECOMING A WOMAN •

A combination of biological factors and feminine gender-role socialization experiences produces a woman. Although most women take pride in being a woman, there are various consequences associated with living in this gender role.

Self-Concept

In some cases, women may have less confidence in themselves than men. In one study (McMahan, 1982), 49 men and 62 women about to take a battery of tests were asked beforehand how they would expect their performance to compare with that of others taking the same tests. The women were much more likely to predict they would perform more poorly than men. In another study (Erkut, 1983) of 116 women and 176 men who were asked before the midterm in a social science class how they thought they would perform, the researcher concluded that "fewer women than men display confidence that they will succeed or believe that they have the ability to succeed" (p. 224).

Women may also have lower self-esteem than men. When 925 females and 928 males took the Rosenberg and Simmons' Self-Esteem Scale (items included "How happy are you with the kind of person you are?" and "Are more of the things about you good, bad, or are they about the same?"), women scored significantly lower than men (Hoelter, 1983). Although the results suggest that women have lower self-esteem than men, it is possible that they are more modest or honest than men in their answers.

Women may also be prejudiced against themselves. When 180 females were asked to evaluate four academic articles, their opinions were less favorable if they thought the articles were written by a woman (Joan T.) than a man (John T.) (Paludi & Bauer, 1983).

Disenchantment with being a woman may be related to sexism, which may be defined as the systematic persecution and degradation of women based on

I am a woman. I am tired of being called a person.

ANONYMOUS

the supposed inferiority of women and the supposed superiority of men. The Sexist Attitudes Scale is a way to assess the degree to which you have prejudicial attitudes toward women.

Marriage: A Personal Disappointment?

Because the role of the wife is closely related to adult feminine identity in our society, many women feel enormous pressure to get married. Some conservative religious denominations such as Adventists, Mormons, and Baptists emphasize that a married woman's activities should "be confined to the home and family" (Rhodes, 1983, p. 104). But the consequences of socializing women for marriage to the exclusion of other options is often negative.

There is evidence that husbands and wives derive different levels of satisfaction from marriage, men being more satisfied (Rettig & Bubolz, 1983). About their marriage, more wives than husbands report frustration, dissatisfaction, problems, unhappiness, and a desire to divorce. About their mental health, more married women than married men feel they are about to have a nervous breakdown, experience more psychological and physical anxiety, and more often blame themselves for their own lack of adjustment (Mugford & Lally, 1981; Rubenstein, 1982).

Marriage is a good deal like taking a bath— not so hot once you get accustomed to it.

LAURENCE PETER

The changed relationship with her partner upon marriage and her role as a housewife are key aspects contributing to the poorer mental health reported by wives. Before marriage the woman is catered to by the man. He tells her how nice she looks, takes her to dinner, movies, and other entertainments, and gives her his undivided attention. She is led to believe that his world revolves around her. After marriage she discovers that his world revolves around his work.

Being a housewife is generally regarded as a low-status occupation. "Lip service is given to the indispensability of the homemaker, but no one equates that to the indispensability of the work of the physician or the accountant" (Chafetz & Dworkin, 1984. p. 50). The homemaker may say, "I am only a housewife," but the accountant would never say, "I am only an accountant."

But increasingly, wives are leaving the home and entering the work force (more than 60 percent now work outside the home), and doing so seems to have positive results. When employed wives are compared with nonemployed wives, the former report greater marital satisfaction (Freudiger, 1983).

Motherhood: A Short Venture?

Whether a married woman is employed outside the home or not, she is likely to want children (95 percent) (Knaub et al., 1983). Her role as mother tends to take priority over other roles. Her children come first in making decisions about the rest of her life. Most feel that their priorities are paying off. In a study of more than 140,000 mothers, 92 percent said they were satisfied with the way their children were turning out (Keating, 1983).

But in perspective, the role of being an active mother is relatively brief. A woman who marries in her early twenties will have children who leave home when she is about 50. Since she can expect to live to about 80, she will have more than a quarter of a century in which her mother role is not primary. The

THE SEXIST ATTITUDES SCALE

Directions: Read each sentence carefully and circle the number which you feel best represents your opinion.

1 Strongly agree (definitely yes)
2 Mildly agree (I believe so)
3 Undecided (not sure)
4 Mildly disagree (probably not)
5 Strongly disagree (definitely not)

	SA	MA	U	MD	SD
1. Women are ruled more by their hormones than men.	1	2	3	4	5
2. Women tend to be less rational than men.	1	2	3	4	5
3. A man would make a better mechanic than a woman.	1	2	3	4	5
4. Women gossip more than men.	1	2	3	4	5
5. A man would make a better employer than a woman.	1	2	3	4	5
6. Women are better at taking care of a family than at any other role.	1	2	3	4	5
7. Women should take their husbands' name when they marry.	1	2	3	4	5
8. Women have become too independent and career-oriented.	1	2	3	4	5
9. Women should think more and talk less.	1	2	3	4	5
10. A woman will get more satisfaction from her family than from her career.	1	2	3	4	5

Scoring: Add the numbers you circled. Since 1 (strongly agree) is the most sexist response and 5 (strongly disagree) is the most egalitarian response, the lower your total score (10 is the lowest possible score), the more sexist you are, and the higher your score (50 is the highest possible score), the more egalitarian you are about gender roles. A score of 30 places you at the midpoint on the sexism–egalitarian continuum.

relatively short-term nature of the mother role emphasizes the need for developing other roles, and employment is a primary alternative.

Marriage and Motherhood: Achievement Barriers?

Being a wife and mother may limit a woman's achievements in areas such as education and employment.

EDUCATION

Women now constitute more than half of all entering college students. Although they earn more than half of all bachelor's degrees and master's degrees, they earn only a third of the Ph.D. and fewer M.D. degrees. Whether the explanation is that women choose motherhood over long-term career preparation, or woman lack educated female models, or they believe there are not enough professional opportunities open to them, the result is the same—women tend to have other priorities than earning academic degrees.

One woman mused about education and her life:

> It seems to me that women in general don't look ahead and ask, "What will I be doing in ten years?" For example, even though I had talent in graduate school and worked for my master's, it never occurred to me to go ahead to a Ph.D. Once I married, I looked forward to having a family. In some ways, I'm glad that I didn't have the pressure of a career while my family was young. I loved that period and made the most of it. (Frankel & Rathvon, 1980, p. 91)

This picture may be changing. As external barriers to professional schools (law, medicine, business) are removed and dual-career marriages increase, more academic degrees will be awarded to women.

EMPLOYMENT

Marriage and motherhood may also interfere with a woman's economic potential. Although most men (88 percent) and women (95 percent) prefer that the wife be employed if there are no children, employment preferences change with their advent. In a national study of high school seniors, almost half felt that the most preferred situation for the family with young children was for the husband to work full time and for the wife to work half time (Herzog et al., 1983).

A graduate student expressed how her interests were becoming reoriented since she had become involved in a relationship.

> It's not a choice between marriage and someone/anyone else. It's between singlehood and relationship. Mike is perfect for me and I don't ever expect to meet anyone who can top him. But this relationship is affecting my career. As a graduate student, I am spending less time on schoolwork, doing poorer quality work, and enjoying it less because I'd rather be with Mike. Also because I'm in the relationship now, I am committed (and want to) spend time on it.

The fact that many women drop out of the labor force during their children's preschool years (compared with almost zero percent for men) has implications for the jobs women have and the money they earn. Two researchers (Kenkel &

Gage, 1983) observed that women tend to select jobs on the basis of how enjoyable they might be rather than for their income-producing value. This may be accounted for by women's lack of job skills and work experience as well as their expectation that work will be interrupted by childrearing.

Women are also discriminated against in employment. They are given lower positions than men with equivalent qualifications and experience resistance when they seek jobs traditionally held by men (Riemer & Bridwell, 1982). Two researchers (Gerdes & Garber, 1983) asked 64 managers to review the job applications of men and women with equal experience, academic qualifications, and intellectual competence. (Women were generally evaluated as being less suitable for the job.) The researchers concluded, "When the job description's stated requirements were not addressed by the application materials, evaluators assumed that the male candidate possessed the required skills, and the female candidate lacked these stereotypically masculine skills" (p. 314). The facts that women earn fewer academic degrees, work in lower-status jobs, and experience barriers to jobs traditionally held by men translate into a lower lifetime income than men achieve.

> Not only am I angry, but I'm also angry at all the years I wasn't angry.
> CAROL KLEINMAN

DATA • *On the average, a man who completes four years of college and works full time will earn $1,190,000 from age 18 to age 64. A college-educated woman who works full time will earn $846,000 (or about 70 percent) between the same ages.* (U.S. Census Bureau, 1983)

CONSIDERATION • With the 50 percent chance of divorce, the likelihood of being a widow for seven or more years, and the almost certain loss of her parenting role midway through her life, a woman without education and employment skills is often left high and dry. One mother said, "The only thing I want my daughter to remember is to become economically independent doing something she enjoys as a first priority. That way if her husband divorces her or dies and her kids are gone, she will still have something left."

Marriage, Motherhood, Job: Who Has the Best of Everything?

Some women view divorce as happening to someone else and the death of their husband as "too far off to worry about." For these women and others, the traditional gender roles of wife and mother offer more rewards than drawbacks. In contrast to many working mothers, full-time homemakers can more freely control and plan their own work and be their own bosses. They are more likely than employed women to see their children's first steps and hear their first words than women who must depend on reports about their child's achievements from a baby-sitter or child-care worker. Women who enjoy the homemaker role find greater fulfillment in caring for those they most love than in working in a more impersonal setting toward more impersonal goals. They do not see the traditional role as an achievement barrier, because they define achievement as providing a good home life for their families and rearing their children successfully.

Although many women might prefer to stay at home with their children, especially when they are young, the 50 percent divorce rate has created a number of female-headed households in which the woman is the sole wage earner. In addition, in couple households inflation and high interest rates may require that the wife work outside the home to achieve the standard of living desired by the couple or simply to make ends meet. Many wives are found to work in jobs they do not enjoy.

Most wives who are employed outside the home are personally happy (Freudiger, 1983). Among the benefits wives derive from such employment include increased interaction with a variety of individuals, a broader base for recognition, improved economic conditions for self and family, and greater equality between self and spouse. But sometimes the assertiveness needed to compete successfully in the employment arena is not viewed as positively when expressed by a woman as by a man. On the job as elsewhere, different standards of behavior may be applied to men and to women.

> A business man is aggressive:
>   a business woman is pushy.
> A business man is good on details;
>   she's picky.
> He loses his temper because he's so involved with his job;
>   she's bitchy.
> He follows through;
>   she doesn't know when to quit.
> He stands firm,
>   she's hard.
> His judgements are
>   her prejudices.
> He is a man of the world;
>   she's been around.
> He drinks because of the excess job pressure;
>   she's a lush.
> He isn't afraid to say what he thinks;
>   she's mouthy.
> He exercises authority diligently;
>   she's power-mad.
> He's close-mouthed;
>   she's secretive.
> He climbed the ladder of success;
>   she slept her way to the top.
> He's a stern task master;
>   she's hard to work for. *

In spite of the prejudice some women experience in the employment arena, most women today expect to successfully combine career, marriage, and children. The simultaneous accomplishment of all three goals may be very difficult, but the advertising industry supports the woman who wants it all. An advertisement for Enjoli perfume states:

> Enjoli—the new 8 hour perfume for the 24 hour woman. You can feed the kids and the gerbils. Pass out the kisses. And get to work by 5 of 9! You can work all

---

* Anonymous poem reprinted in M. Eichler, *The Double Standard* (New York: St. Martin's Press, 1980), pp. 15–16.

Over sixty percent of married women aged 25 to 34 are in the labor force.

day in the old rat race. Even put a smile on sourpuss' face! You can bring home the bacon. Fry it up in a pan. And never let him forget he's a man! Because you're a, ENJOLI woman!*

• CONSEQUENCES OF BECOMING A MAN •

The role of men in our society has its own disadvantages and rewards. We now look at some of these.

The Job Requirement

A recent career advertisement in a national magazine showed a young wife looking at her husband while leaning on his shoulder. The man-to-man caption read, "One day, it suddenly strikes home that we're going to be working for a living the rest of our lives." Just as the woman is more often channeled into the roles of wife and mother, the man is tracked into the world of gainful employment to provide primary support for his wife and children. He has little choice. He must work—his wife, children, parents, in-laws, and peers expect it.

* Used by permission of Charles of the Ritz Group Ltd. © 1978 Charles of the Ritz Group Ltd.

A college senior responded to this observation by saying, "Baloney! I'm not getting caught in the work trap. I'm going to paint houses now and then—just enough to keep me going—and enjoy life." Three years after graduation he reported, "I'm married now and we need money for our child. It's easy to say you don't need money when you're single but when you've got a sick kid who's running up medical bills, you know it's time to get cooking."

A man's responsibility to earn an income and society's tendency to equate income with success have implications for his self-esteem. The assumption is that the man who makes $50,000 annually is more of a man than the one who makes $5,000. Ultimately a man must turn himself into a machine that produces money.

> CONSIDERATION • The pressure to make money may also interfere with a man's development of other roles and skills. Some men have never learned how to cook, wash clothes, or take care of a home. As a result, they feel dependent on a woman for these domestic needs. Some men stay married and others remarry because they feel unequipped to care for themselves. One divorced man said, "I can't cook or wash clothes. I need a woman to look after me."

The Identity-Equals-Job Syndrome

Ask a man who he is and he will tell you what he does. His identity lies in his work. It is the principal means by which he confirms his masculinity. In studies of unemployment during the Great Depression, job loss was regarded as a greater shock to men than to women, although the loss of income affected both.

Men tend to define who they are by what they do.

The identification of self with job becomes a problem when it forces human concerns into a low priority. One father told his 5-year-old daughter who had asked him to play with her, "Don't bother Daddy. I'm busy. Please leave the study." Later that afternoon when he came into the child's room to play with her, she said, "Don't bother me. I'm busy. Please leave my room."

For most men fatherhood is a secondary role, and as we know, role socialization begins early. When 20 middle-class male children were asked what they wanted to be when they grew up, athlete, fire fighter, and police officer headed the list. "Father" was not on anyone's list (Zuckerman & Sayre, 1982).

> To say a man holds a job is to misstate the fact. The job holds the man.
> JAMES G. COZZENS

Emotional Stereotypes

Some men feel caught between society's expectations that they be competitive, aggressive, independent, and unemotional and their own desire to be more open, caring, and emotional. Not only are men less likely to cry than women (Lombardo et al., 1983), but they are also less able to express love, happiness, and sadness (Balswick, 1980). The words "I love you," "I'm happy," or "I'm depressed" do not come easy for some men.

When men do display their emotions, they often do so in a more "forceful," "dominating," "boastful," and "authoritarian" way than women, who are more likely to be gentle in their speech (Kramarae, 1981). "Men have traditionally struggled under the oppression of a role expectation which is self-limiting, destructive of a complete and fulfilling existence, and dangerous to their health and well being" (Isherwood, 1983, p. 229).

CONSIDERATION • One researcher (Pleck, 1981) suggested that parents put too much emphasis on trying to ensure that their sons fit the cultural stereotypes of masculinity. Addressing parental concerns about situations in which the father is away because of divorce or career, he argues that "boys can grow up perfectly well without a strong 'masculine identity' and may be better off without it" (p. 69).

Adapting to Changing Relationships

There is an emerging new equality in relationships between women and men. Modern women, in contrast to traditional women, are more likely to disagree with their partners, challenge their reasons, and suggest alternative explanations and preferences. Acquiescence, submission, and apology are words that less often describe women in today's heterosexual relationships.

CONSIDERATION • There may be a lag between the relationships women want and relationships men are socialized to accept. In one study (Wilson & Knox, 1981), the women viewed themselves as equal and sought egalitarian relationships, whereas the men viewed themselves as traditional and less interested in egalitarian relationships.

The egalitarian issue also expresses itself in couples' attitudes toward higher education. The man no longer asks, "Where will you work to put me through school?" but "How will we finance our educations?" or "Do you want to finish your education before I finish mine?"

Because of women's increasing desire for education, career involvement, and economic independence, men today can expect women to be less interested in early marriage than formerly.

DATA • *In 1970, 64 percent of the women in their early twenties were married in contrast to 50 percent in this age group in 1980.* (Glick, 1984)

Also, when women do marry, they are likely to expect more from their partners in sharing child-care and housekeeping responsibilities than changing a diaper and setting the table. Some feel that liberation for men is not only their freedom to cry but also their willingness to share domestic work.

Finally, women have begun to assert their own sexual needs. Before Masters and Johnson's widespread influence, men could be concerned solely with their own sexual pleasure. Today a man, after ejaculation, may look into the eyes of his frustrated partner who says, "I didn't have an orgasm." He can no longer be the great lover by satisfying only himself.

Although there have been women's support groups for years, some men's groups recently have been formed to assist men in various areas of adjustment. Increasingly, counselors are being trained to conduct such groups. The Male Awareness Leadership Education (MALE) program in Minneapolis, Minnesota, an eight-week course for professionals, covers such topics as "machismo," "male fears," and "violence." These groups offer a forum for men to discuss an array of issues, which few other experiences provide.

• THE IDEAL MAN •

A Man-of-the-Hour is the one whose wife told him to wait a minute.

LAURENCE PETER

Women students in the author's marriage and family class (120 students) were asked to identify the qualities they most desired in a man. The characteristics most frequently mentioned were "loving," "loyal," "affectionate," "responsible," "intelligent," and "hard working." Here are some examples:

My ideal man is a very loving and caring person who is not afraid to "feel" things or to show affection. He is very secure within himself and is not adversely affected or threatened by any of *my* achievements. He is very considerate of my feelings at all times and willing to solve problems by talking. He is a hard worker and very responsible and dependable in his "duties" as an employee, mate, and father. He can be trusted—I don't have to worry about whether or not he is loyal. He cares about his appearance and has a good self-concept.

•

My ideal man is one who respects the new eighties woman, yet at the same time can open the car door for her. He is the man who surprises you by cooking dinner on the night you have to work late. He is the man who gives wonderful back-rubs and foot massages (even when your feet stink). He also actually likes his in-laws. He can apologize when he's hurt your feelings and admit when he's wrong and you're right.

•

My ideal partner must be affectionate because I need positive attention in an intimate relationship. He must also be intelligent and open minded. Of course, physical attractiveness is important—my man can't be ugly! About 5'11" or 6', he would be dark-complected, with a mustache, hairy chest, and nice physique (but not too muscular). He must also be honest with me and teach me that I can trust him when I'm not around.

• THE IDEAL WOMAN •

Male students in the same class were asked to identify the characteristics of their ideal woman. "Physically attractive," "flexible," "trustworthy," "hard working," "intelligent," and "dependable" were the qualities most frequently mentioned by these males.

I want not only a woman with a good head on her shoulders but also with a great body to support her head. In addition, she must be honest and sincere so that I can trust her. A positive outlook toward religion and on life in general are also important to me. I basically want a good person who respects and is good to me and expects the same from me.

•

My ideal woman would first of all have to be attractive if I am to marry her. I also must be able to trust her. I would like her to be nice and have a good personality. Most important, we must be able to get along and have a good time together. When I'm with my friends, I want her to understand that there are other parts to my life than being a spouse.

•

I feel the ideal woman should be loyal and trusting so there will be no misunderstandings about the time we spend apart from each other. I feel that she must be hard working and show incentive to make contributions to the relationship. She should be flexible and have a sense of humor that will alleviate tension. Dependability is important because it shows a genuine concern and will to please.

CONSIDERATION • The respective ideal woman and man are very similar. Both are characterized by loyalty, dependability, and flexibility. While men tend to focus more on physical appearance, woman also want a nice-looking man.

• TRENDS •

Although we continue to recognize that a person's biological heritage has a significant impact on her or his development, our society is becoming less rigid in its gender-role socialization. As a result, there will be fewer roles closed to women and more androgynous people (those with both feminine and masculine characteristics), including more assertive females and expressive males. In the past 10 years, a number of social barriers to women's participation in formerly all-male activities have been removed. No longer are women barred from being vice-presidential candidates, Supreme Court justices, West Point cadets, or astronauts, and girls now play baseball on Little League teams. Today's wom-

I am glad there is no longer a sign, "White Males Only Need Apply." It's our time folks.

GERALDINE FERRARO

an is not only a married housewife with two children living in surburbia. She also may be a never-married woman, a divorced woman, a married woman who works outside the home, or a child-free married woman. Stereotypes of who women are and what they do are fading.

As each gender begins to fill a wider range of roles, the trend toward androgyny will increase. For example, men will feel more free to be gentle and to express their emotions, whereas women will more often be assertive and competitive. Although cross-gender changes are sometimes more difficult for women (Alperson & Friedman, 1983), movement toward these changes will be accelerated by women's greater participation in work outside the home and men's greater involvement in child care. Developing more of the qualities of the opposite gender is often viewed as having the best of both worlds, feminine and masculine, and may also be associated with increased personal satisfaction, good mental health, and ability to cope with stress (Burchardt & Serbin, 1982; Patterson & McCubbin, 1984; Rotheram & Weiner, 1983).

• SUMMARY •

The term *gender* refers to the biological distinction of being male or female. In contrast, a person's gender identity is her or his self-concept as a girl and later a woman or a boy and later a man. Gender roles are the socially accepted characteristics and behaviors associated with a person's gender identity. In our society the traditional role of women is to be emotional, dependent, and home oriented, whereas the male role is to be unemotional, independent, and career oriented. Today these stereotypes are breaking down under the impact of changes in family structure and job participation.

Gender-role behaviors of women and men are a result of the combined effects of biological inheritance and social environment. Biological inheritance includes chromosomes and hormones resulting in sexual differentiation. Only women menstruate, get pregnant, give birth, and nurse their infants. Only males get penile erections and ejaculate semen.

But biological inheritance is overlaid with environmental influences. There are several explanations of how children learn appropriate gender-role behaviors: social learning, cognitive developmental, social interaction, and identification. The social learning perspective states that children learn their roles by being rewarded for gender-appropriate behaviors and punished for inappropriate (opposite-gender) behaviors. In the cognitive developmental view of gender-role learning, children first reach the stage where they understand that their gender is permanent and then actively seek to acquire masculine or feminine characteristics. Social interaction theory suggests that roles are learned in social interaction with playmates. Identification theory suggests that children, either out of fear or love, take on the role of the same-gender parent. Whereas biology through chromosomes and hormones predisposes people to behave in certain ways, society (represented by parents, teachers, peers, and mass media) guides the person's behavior into culturally approved channels, for example, girls playing with dolls and boys playing with cars and trucks.

A long-standing controversy in gender-role development is the relative influence of heredity versus environment, but an interaction effect seems to account for most personal and social behaviors.

Being socialized as a woman or man has varied consequences for the person. Women sometimes have less confidence in themselves than men because of pervasive sexism. Marriage is sometimes a disappointment, since wives discover that husbands are often more interested in work than in family. Women also pursue less education and earn less income than men. Those who do not develop an interest other than their husbands and children may feel a void when those roles terminate.

Men, on the other hand, feel an imperative to earn money and are looked down on by society if they do not. They are also less emotionally expressive and sometimes place human relationships below their work in importance. Adapting to more assertive women and more egalitarian relationships is an increasing demand upon men.

The future of gender roles will include fewer barriers to women in pursuing various life options and a general movement toward androgyny. Some evidence suggests that androgyny is associated with good mental health.

Questions for Reflection

1. Why is there little agreement about the precise way in which gender roles are learned?
2. To what degree do you feel free to exhibit behaviors typically associated with the opposite gender?
3. To what degree do you feel comfortable about your partner engaging in behavior typically associated with the opposite gender?

The result of our society becoming less rigid in its gender-role expectations for women and men is a new array of choices of gender-role behavior. Such choices are becoming increasingly available in dating, marriage, parenting, and employment.

·CHOICES·

DATING:
WOMEN ASKING MEN?

Traditionally, the only socially appropriate way for a woman and man to begin dating was for the man to call the woman up several days in advance and ask her if she would like to have dinner, see a movie, attend a concert, or whatever later in the week. Her role was passive. If she were asked, she could accept or reject. If she asked him out for a first date, it implied that she was inappropriately aggressive—it was the man's role, not the woman's, to do the asking.

This pattern is still dominant. Most women are uncomfortable asking a new person for a date. Three women explain:

I just wouldn't feel right about it. I wouldn't want the guy to think I was too fast or pushy.

•

I couldn't take the rejection. Besides, nine out of 10 guys I would want are already involved with someone else. Even the guys I just find attractive and talk to have steady girlfriends, so I don't want to humiliate myself by asking them out and being turned down.

•

We always had a phone rule in my house: *Never call a guy unless he has called and is expecting you to call him back.* I have three older sisters and my parents have always made sure that my sisters never called their boyfriends (unless it was a serious relationship). Their reason was "if he wants to go out, he'll call you."

But more and more women are asking the man out, and such a choice is becoming more acceptable.

I say "go for it" simply because there are more advantages than disadvantages. The only disadvantage I can think of is the possibility of coming over as pushy. But on the advantage side: (1) Maybe he doesn't know if you're interested. If you wait around for him to ask you and he doesn't, you may never get together. (2) Maybe he's shy. (3) Guys hate to say no to girls so he'll probably go out with you and he may find that he likes you.

The boyfriend I have now I asked out over a year ago (he's shy). Things have been going great ever since. He told me about a month ago that if I had never asked him out, he would never have asked me out first because he thought I wasn't interested. I'm glad I let him know I was.

•

I wouldn't have much of a problem asking a guy out. Of course, I'd wait a little hoping that he would ask first. But some guys need a little push in the "right direction"—my direction.

Women are sometimes interested in what men think about women who call them up. Most men feel positive about being asked for a date and do not regard the woman as too forward. The following are examples of what men in the author's class said when they were asked, "How would you feel about a woman asking you out for a date if you have never dated her before?"

I'd love it. It makes me feel wanted and I like for the female to be aggressive.

•

I prefer that the woman ask me out. I get tired of having to be the aggressor all the time.

•

I'm the traditional type. I'll do the asking.

•

Three girls have called me up for dates in the last year. I went out with two of them and had a terrific time. I made up some excuse for the one who looked like "Godzilla's sister."

Should a woman decide to call a man for a date, what might she say? Does she call him up to borrow his class notebook or a record album and hope he will get the hint that she is interested in him? Or does she mention that there is a new movie in town that has had excellent reviews and wait for him to ask her? Both women who have asked men for dates and men who have accepted say that the direct approach is best. A woman might say "Hi! This is Jill. I'm in your English literature class and am calling to ask if you would like to go out Saturday evening to see the campus movie."

A woman who chooses to call a man for a date may experience what men experience who call a woman for a date—rejection. "She won't get turned down much," said one woman. "But it will happen and she shouldn't feel bad about it when it does. I asked this one guy out who looked like Richard Gere and he told me he was involved with someone and couldn't go—I wasn't surprised."

MARRIAGE: ROLE SHARING

The choices available to spouses regarding their role behavior in marriage are also increasing. More egalitarian relationships mean that either spouse may now be employed, cook supper, clean the house, and call out spelling words for the children. Such role flexibility increases the potential for experientially sharing the work required in marriage and provides the basis for each partner to better understand the feelings of the other. In essence, role sharing allows a greater range of sharing in all aspects of the relationship.

When only the husband worked outside the home and the wife stayed home to take care of the house and children, each spouse had a set of experiences that was unknown to the partner. He would be tired at the end of the day from working at the office; she would be tired from cleaning the house, preparing food, and listening to the bickering of two young children. They were sure they were more tired than their partner and regarded their own role as the most difficult and the partner's role as "easy and nothing to complain about." One outcome of both spouses choosing to engage in a greater range of roles is the increased understanding of what the partner is experiencing. "Since I have been employed and my husband has taken over the meals and child care, we both know what it is like to be tired for different reasons," said one wife.

EMPLOYMENT: OCCUPATIONAL CHOICES

The general trend toward gender-role flexibility is also having its impact on occupational role choices. Jobs traditionally occupied by one gender are now open to the other. Men may now become nurses and librarians and women may become construction workers and lawyers. A match between personality needs and occupational choice is not overridden by arbitrary social restrictions of who can and can't have a particular job or career.

· Chapter 3 ·

LOVE RELATIONSHIPS

CONTENTS

Origins of Love

Definitions and Dilemmas
   of Love

Importance of Love

Conditions of Love

The Lover Role

Romantic and Realistic Love

Self-Assessment:
   The Love Attitudes Scale

Styles of Loving

Homosexual Love
   Relationships

Love and Sex

Jealousy

Choices

Love doesn't make the world go 'round. Love is what makes the ride worthwhile.

FRANKLIN P. JONES

"Because we're in love" is the reason most Americans give for wanting to get married. "Loss of love" is also the reason many couples give for wanting to get a divorce. Because of the importance of love in our decision to marry and divorce, it is imperative that we try to understand the dynamics of love—how it develops, how it dies, and how to keep it alive and flourishing.

   Although parent-child, sibling-sibling, and friend-friend relationships (same or opposite gender) often involve love, heterosexual and homosexual love feelings are the focus of this chapter. In this chapter we explore the origins of love, various definitions of love, the importance of love, and the various types of love. We conclude by an examination of the similarities and differences between love and sex.

The mark of a true crush is that you fall in love first and grope for reasons afterward.

SHANA
ALEXANDER

Psychiatrists, sociologists, psychologists, philosophers, and theologians have tried to explain the origin of love (Hendrick & Hendrick, 1983). Several of these explanations follow.

Sexual Origin

Sigmund Freud (1960) stated that love was a mental feeling of tenderness and affection, which resulted from blocked biological sexual desires and needs. He referred to love as aim-inhibited sex, noting, "Love with an inhibited aim was originally full sensual love and, in man's unconscious mind, is still so" (p. 96). Freud equated love with sexual desire, which when not expressed through intercourse or other sexual behavior became an emotion, a feeling called love. Freud would say that if you just met someone and are physically attracted to him or her, yet have not had orgasm with that person, you are likely to experience love feelings.

Social Origin

Taking the opposite view, Dr. Ian Suttie wrote in *The Origins of Love and Hate* (1952) that love was a positive instinctive feeling based on the need for compan-

Suttie believed that love is based on the innate need for companionship with others.

ionship with others. Love, therefore, was social rather than sexual and derived from a person's self-preservative instincts. He wrote, "The specific origin of love, in time, was at the moment the infant recognized the existence of others" (p. 20). Suttie would say that you have an inherited instinct to love others because of your recognition that your survival (emotional and practical) depends on relationships with others.

Psychic Origin

Theodore Reik (1949), who once studied with Freud, thought that love was neither sexual nor social but psychic. He believed that "the origin of love belongs to the ego-drives" (p.65). By this he meant that love sprang from a state of dissatisfaction with one's self and was a vain urge to reach one's "ego-ideal." Love, therefore, is the projection of your ideal image of yourself onto another person and loving your own image in that person. For example, if you feel that you are not good looking, you are likely to fall in love with someone who is because of your desire to be good looking. Or if you feel as though you lack confidence in yourself, you are likely, according to Reik, to fall in love with someone who displays a great deal of self-assurance. In both of these examples, what you lack you find in someone else and love these qualities in them.

Conditioning Origin

Sociologist Joseph Folsom (1948) focused on the conditioning or learning aspect of love, stating that whatever object was frequently perceived while needs were being satisfied became an object of desire. For example, Folsom would say that if you ate most of your meals with a particular person, you would tend to develop a positive feeling for that person because she or he would become associated with the reduction of a basic need—hunger. In addition, he noted, "We tend to repeat that which was satisfying or that which immediately accompanied a satisfying experience" (p. 165). So Folsom believed that if you and your partner spend enough enjoyable time together, love feelings will result.

The voyage of love is all the sweeter for an outside stateroom and a seat at the captain's table.

HENRY S. HASKINS

Philosophical Origin

A philosophical explanation of love has been suggested by theologian Paul Tillich (1960), who conceived of love as a drive toward the unity of the separated. He wrote, "Reunion presupposes separation of that which belongs essentially together" (p. 25). His belief in the spiritual and physical union that makes up love refers to the ancient myth that women and men were once two halves of the same body. Although split, each half has continued to look for the other half. According to Tillich, half of the world (female) is looking for the other half (male) and vice versa. He would say that when you become involved in a love relationship with a person, you are in a sense being reunited with someone with whom you share a strong spiritual and physical affinity.

Behavioral Origin

A behavioral view of love suggests that you develop love feelings for people based on the way they behave toward you. If someone shows you a lot of attention, tells you that you are good looking, a terrific person, and that he or she loves being with you, and shows you physical affection the way you like it, you are likely to fall in love with that person. Of course, the person must meet various criteria in terms of age, height, weight, and appearance, but after these criteria are met, the person's positive behavior toward you creates love feelings toward him or her.

Your positive behavior toward another is also important in creating love. By investing yourself in another, by doing things for and with the person, and by acting in caring and loving ways, you increase the chance that you will develop love feelings for him or her. Behaviorists say that you can act yourself into a new way of feeling and this is especially true of love. If you engage in behaviors that reflect love, you are likely to fall in love with that person.

CONSIDERATION • If your goal is to fall in love with someone, you might do things for and with the person. If she or he reciprocates your positive behavior, the probability that love feelings will develop is increased. However, love is sometimes elusive and just doing things for a person or having the person do things for you will not always produce love. Physical appearance, values, social class background, friends, career goals, and life-style preferences will also affect your love feelings for each other.

• DEFINITIONS AND DILEMMAS OF LOVE •

La Rochefoucauld said, "True love is like ghosts which everyone has talked about but few have seen." His definition suggests that love feelings are mysterious and the individual alone has access to what she or he experiences. Because the experience is personal, the definitions of love are varied. Some definitions of love include the following:

Love is defined as an expression of positive regard, warmth or comfort that is expressed most easily in paralinguistic communication such as touch, eye contact, posture, proximity, and facial expressions. (Rettig & Bubolz, 1983, p. 498)

•

Love is a set of positive feelings targeted toward another person. It is a statement that says I am willing to spend my time and energy to please you and I want to receive pleasure from you. And I am willing to operate at a minimum profit advantage. (Ridley, 1983, p. 166)

•

Love is an emotion that follows from our decision to cooperate with our partner. We don't cooperate with our partners because we love them. Rather, we love them because we have decided to cooperate. (Croake, 1983, p. 166)

When students in the author's classes were asked to "define the meaning of love," some listed various qualities like "caring," "compassion," "respect," "sharing," and "commitment." One student said that "love is sacrificing because you want to," while another said that "love is being in a crowded room full of beautiful people of the opposite gender and wishing you were alone with your partner."

> CONSIDERATION • The one element all these definitions have in common is that they are different. Since love is a private emotional experience, no single definition can cover all its variety.

Love may not only be defined differently, but it also may express itself in complicated ways that create dilemmas for us. One dilemma includes being in love with two people at the same time. "I know I love my husband," said one woman, "but I also love the man I work with." Such a dilemma is not unusual. The feelings are a consequence of being in two relationships at the same time that have engendered these feelings. It is possible to be involved in several relationships at the same time and to have love feelings for each of the people. But although it is possible to love two or more people at the same time, it is not possible to love them to the same degree at any particular moment because a choice must be made in terms of how one spends his or her time. If you choose to spend time with person X, at least for that moment in time, you value that person more than the others.

The worst of having a romance of any kind is that it leaves one so unromantic.

OSCAR WILDE

> CONSIDERATION • Some people do not like the feeling of being in love with two people at once and try to reduce their feelings for one of them. This is often accomplished by deciding to see only one of the persons and by thinking negative things about the other. For example, Jan who was in love with her husband and colleague, decided to stop seeing her colleague socially; and when she did think of him, she made herself think only of the negative aspects of being involved with him—he was married, he drank heavily, he was 12 years older than she, and he had three children.

Another dilemma of love is being in love with a totally inappropriate person. Someone who is radically different in age, who has severe problems (alcoholism, drug addiction), who values nothing you value, who criticizes you continually, and who lies to you may not be a good partner for you. Nevertheless, you might love that person and feel that everything will turn out all right. Most marriage therapists would empathize with your love feelings and suggest that you look at the payoffs for your loving this person. Does it upset your parents? Do you feel this is what you deserve because you are "no good"? Do you feel pity for the person and want to be her or his therapist? These questions imply that the love relationship is based on some motivations that should be carefully examined.

• IMPORTANCE OF LOVE •

Although people disagree about the definition of love, there is little disagreement about its importance. In a study of 224 husband-wife couples, "love and affection" were more important for marital satisfaction than sex or open communication (Rettig & Bubolz, 1983). In another study of more than 200,000 respondents, "love" was the primary reason for staying married (*Better Homes and Gardens*, 1983).

Health Significance

One's health may be adversely affected by unfulfilled love needs. A specialist in psychosomatic disease (Lynch, 1977) reported that being lonely and unloved often leads to heart disease and premature death for the single, widowed, and divorced. Also, in a study on love and health (Kemper & Bologh, 1981), the respondents who had recently ended a love relationship had the most negative health status. The authors concluded, "A relationship of long duration that is going well appears to have a positive effect on one's health status" (p. 86).

Emotional Significance

The world is a
comedy to those
that think, a
tragedy to those
who feel.

HORACE WALPOLE

In a nationwide study on happiness, the researchers concluded that the presence of a love relationship was essential for many people if they were to be happy (Freedman, 1978). Diana Ross remarked on the Johnny Carson show, "I want to be in love again," partly echoing Tennyson's

> O that 'twere possible
> After long grief and pain
> To find the arms of my true love
> Round me once again!

For some people, love is addictive (Peele & Brodsky, 1976). It produces a feeling of euphoria that a person learns to enjoy and depend on. Once we get accustomed to the euphoria of love, we need to be with our partner to feel the heightened sense of contentment and happiness. Withdrawal symptoms—depression, unhappiness, even somatic complaints—may begin when the love relationship breaks. According to these writers, the person suffering from a broken love relationship goes through withdrawal in much the same way as an alcoholic who has given up alcohol.

CONSIDERATION • Although love may be important for our emotional well-being, we all differ in the degree to which we need love relationships. For some of us, our support system of friends satisfies our need for connectedness. An intense one-on-one love relationship may not be necessary or desirable. "I don't like the obligations that creep into a love relationship," said one woman. "I have a lot of friends and enjoy being with them, but I don't need to be 'deeply in love' with a particular person to be happy or productive in my work." Other people may only feel content when in a love relationship and inordinately depressed if not.

• CONDITIONS OF LOVE •

Love develops under predictable social, psychological, physiological, and cognitive conditions.

Love is a significant aspect of our lives.

Social Conditions

Our society provides a basic context for love feelings to develop by emphasizing the importance of love. Through popular music, movies, television, and novels, the message is clear: Love is an experience to enjoy and to pursue. You are missing something if you are not in love.

Peer influence is also important in creating the conditions for love to develop, as many of our peers establish love relationships and pair off. Their doing so makes love relationships normative and encourages us to seek the same experience. "All but one of my closest friends are involved in a steady love relationship," said one math major. "I'm wondering when I'm going to fall in love and be involved with someone?"

Our society also links love and marriage. Couples who are about to get married are expected to be in love. If they are not, they would be ashamed to admit it. The fact that more than 90 percent of Americans marry suggests that there are few who escape the love feelings that are suppose to accompany courtship and marriage.

Psychological Conditions

There are two psychological conditions sometimes associated with falling in love: a positive self-concept and the ability to self-disclose.

POSITIVE SELF-CONCEPT

The way you feel about yourself is your self-concept. If you have a positive self-concept, you like yourself and enjoy being who you are.

I am larger, better than I thought. I did not know I held so much goodness.

WALT WHITMAN

A positive self-concept is important to the development of love since once you accept yourself, you can believe that others are capable of doing so too. In contrast, a negative self-concept has devastating consequences for the individual and those people with whom he or she becomes involved. Individuals who cannot accept themselves tend to reject others. "My daddy always told me I was no good and would never amount to anything," said one man. "I guess I have always believed him, have never liked myself, and can't think of why someone else would either." Woody Allen has become famous for exploiting a negative self-concept: "I would never want to belong to an organization that would have me as a member."

The way we feel about ourselves and our ability to relate intimately to others have been learned. Our first potential love relationships were with our parents or the person who cared for us in infancy. As babies we were helpless. When we were hungry, cold, or wet, we cried until someone came to take care of us. Our parents became associated with reducing our discomfort. When we saw them, we knew that everything would be okay.

If we were well cared for as infants, we were helped to establish a good self-concept by being taught two things: (1) We were somebody that someone else cared about. (2) Other people were good because they did things that made us feel good. When people learn as young children to love and trust those around them, they can generalize this experience to others and eventually establish loving adult relationships.

SELF-DISCLOSURE

In addition to feeling good about yourself, it is helpful to disclose your feelings to others if you want to love and be loved. Disclosing yourself is a way of investing yourself in another. Once the other person knows some of the intimate details of your life, you will tend to feel more positively about that person because part of you is now a part of them.

In a study (Rubin et al., 1980) of 231 couples who defined themselves as "going together," the researchers observed that the more the partners disclosed themselves to each other, the greater their love feelings for each other and the closer they regarded their relationship. As for what they disclosed, 70 percent of the women and men reported they had disclosed "fully" their feelings about their sexual relationship, and six in 10 had given full information about their previous sexual experiences. "Even in an area in which one would expect the greatest degree of reserve, 38 percent of the women and 35 percent of the men reported that they had revealed fully to their partners the things about themselves they were most ashamed of" (p. 313).

It is not easy for some people to let others know who they are, what they feel, or what they think. They may fear that if others really knew them, they might be rejected as a friend or lover. To guard against this possibility, they may protect themselves and their relationships by allowing only limited access to their thoughts and feelings.

Trust is the condition under which people are willing to disclose themselves. To feel comfortable about letting someone else inside their head, they must feel that whatever feelings or information they share will not be judged and will be kept safe with that person. If trust is betrayed, a person may become bitterly resentful and vow never to disclose her- or himself again. One woman said, "After I told my partner that I had had an abortion, he told me that I was a murderer and he never wanted to see me again. I was hurt and felt I had made a mistake telling him about my intimate life. You can bet I'll be careful before I disclose myself to someone else."

Partners who are successful in disclosing to each other tend to feel better about their relationship, not only in courtship, but also in marriage. In a study of 120 couples (Jorgensen & Gaudy, 1980), those reporting the highest levels of satisfaction also reported the highest levels of self-disclosure. "Being open about fears, problems, self-doubts, feelings of anger or depression, and aspects of marriage perceived to be bothersome to one or both partners, as well as openly sharing positive feelings about the self and other" (p. 286) contributed to the happiness of the respective spouses.

But disclosure must be equal to benefit the relationship. In one study (Davidson et al., 1983), the researchers found that those partners who were similar in affective disclosure had better adjustment than those who were dissimilar.

> "We both love each other at the same level," said one woman. "I tell him that I love him about as often as he tells me. I was once in a relationship where the guy loved me more than I loved him. He would always be telling me that he loved me. I got tired of hearing him say that and it made me feel guilty when he did."

CONSIDERATION • Although it helps to have a positive self-concept at the beginning of a love relationship, sometimes this develops after becoming involved in a love relationship. "I've always felt like an ugly duckling," said one woman. "But once I fell in love with him and he with me, I felt very different. I felt very good about myself then because I knew that I was somebody that someone else could love."

Other partners keep their disclosure at a very low level until after they define themselves as being in love. "I can't tell anybody anything that matters until after I feel that I can trust them," said one man. "When I start to love them, I usually tell them more than they want to know."

Physiological and Cognitive Conditions

After the social and psychological conditions of love are operative, the physiological and cognitive components of love become important. The individual must be physiologically aroused and interpret this stirred-up state in emotional terms (Schacter, 1964; Walster & Walster, 1978). For example, Carol was beginning her first year at a midwestern university. Being three states away from home in an unfamiliar environment, she felt lonely and bored. During registration she met a good-looking junior. They exchanged pleasant glances and small talk and planned to go out together that night around 8:00. Carol became anxious when Brad had not shown up by 8:45. When he finally arrived at 9:00 (car trouble delayed him), they went to a concert, drank some beer, and played video games at a local pub. Carol had a terrific time.

There are many people who would never have been in love if they had never heard love spoken of.

LA ROCHEFOUCAULD

Two days went by before Carol heard from Brad again. He called to ask if she wanted to go home with him for the weekend. By the end of that weekend, Carol felt she was in love. Her loneliness, the fun they had when they were together, frustration (she never knew when Brad would call or come by), and sexual arousal (they had petted but had not yet had intercourse) were enough to induce an agitated, stirred-up state. Since both her roommates were "in love," Carol identified herself as being in the same condition.

CONSIDERATION • Not only are the preceding four conditions important for the development of love feelings, but also the timing must be right. There are only certain times in your life when you are in the "market" for a love relationship. When those times occur, you are likely to fall in love with the person who is there and also "in the market." Hence many love pairings exist because each of the individuals is available to the other and not because they are particularly suited for each other.

• THE LOVER ROLE •

When all of the foregoing conditions are met, the person assumes the role of lover; and like all roles, the role of lover suggests that the person will engage in certain behavior. First, the lover can be expected to idealize the partner. The lover will see qualities that are not there (perhaps the person is "never" selfish) and avoid seeing qualities that are there (such as the beginning of a drinking

Lovers sometimes idealize each other.

problem). Such idealization is functional as it enhances the lover's self-esteem ("I must be a terrific person if I am in a love relationship with such a terrific person").

Another element of the lover role is that of suffering. The lover expects to endure a certain amount of pain, from either longing, unrequited love or outright rejection.

> The suffering element of the lover role has an additional consequence: the lover is allowed to continue suffering because he is in love. If one regularly absorbs abuse from his neighbor and takes no action, his behavior is considered foolish; it is expected that one take immediate action to avoid further pain. However, if one is suffering rejection from his lover, it is expected that he endure the pain while attempting to establish mutual love. (Buehler & Wells, 1981, p. 454)

A final element of the lover role is fantasy. The lover is allowed to spend a great deal of time envisioning a future that may be unrealistic. "The two of us together in a cottage by the sea" is a visual image of how some lovers think of marriage. The demands of working until 10:30 P.M. on one's job or getting up three times a night with an infant who has colic is rarely a part of the fantasy.

• ROMANTIC AND REALISTIC LOVE •

Love for some people is romantic; for others it is realistic. Romantic love (sometimes referred to as infatuation) is characterized by such beliefs as love at first sight, there is only one true love, and love conquers all. The ultimate, almost obsessional form of romantic love has been called limerence (Tennov, 1979). Symptoms include drastic mood swings, palpitations of the heart, and intrusive thinking about the partner.

Emotion has taught mankind to reason.

MARQUIS DE VAUVENARGUES

In contrast to romantic love is realistic love, or conjugal love, which tends to be characteristic of people who have been in love with each other for several years. Partners who know all about each other yet still love each other are said to have a realistic view of love.

The following self-assessment—the Love Attitudes Scale—is a way for you to measure the degree to which you are romantic or realistic. You might want to take the inventory and sum up your numbered responses in a total score. Since 1 (strongly agree) is the most romantic response and 5 (strongly disagree) is the most realistic response, the lower your total score (30 is the lowest possible score), the more romantic you are, and the higher your score (150 is the highest possible score), the more realistic you are about love. A score of 90 places you at the midpoint on the scale of romantic-realistic love.

CONSIDERATION • In taking the Love Attitudes Scale, be aware that you are merely assessing the degree to which you are a romantic or a realist. Your tendency to be one or the other is not good or bad. Both romantics and realists may be happy, mature people.

Some of the beliefs and comments of people who have completed the Love Attitudes Scale follow.

THE LOVE ATTITUDES SCALE*

Directions: Read each sentence carefully and circle the number that you believe best represents your opinion. Be sure to respond to all statements.

1 Strongly agree (definitely yes)
2 Mildly agree (I believe so)
3 Undecided (not sure)
4 Mildly disagree (probably not)
5 Strongly disagree (definitely not)

	SA	MA	U	MD	SD
1. Love doesn't make sense. It just is.	1	2	3	4	5
2. When you fall head-over-heels-in-love, it's sure to be the real thing.	1	2	3	4	5
3. To be in love with someone you would like to marry but can't is a tragedy.	1	2	3	4	5
4. When love hits, you know it.	1	2	3	4	5
5. Common interests are really unimportant; as long as each of you is truly in love, you will adjust.	1	2	3	4	5
6. It doesn't matter if you marry after you have known your partner for only a short time as long as you know you are in love.	1	2	3	4	5
7. If you are going to love a person, you will "know" after a short time.	1	2	3	4	5
8. As long as two people love each other, the educational differences they have really do not matter.	1	2	3	4	5
9. You can love someone even though you do not like any of that person's friends.	1	2	3	4	5
10. When you are in love, you are usually in a daze.	1	2	3	4	5
11. Love at first sight is often the deepest and most enduring type of love.	1	2	3	4	5
12. When you are in love, it really does not matter what your partner does since you will love him or her anyway.	1	2	3	4	5

*From D. Knox, *The love attitudes inventory,* rev. ed. (Saluda, N.C.: Family Life Publications, 1983). Reprinted by permission.

	SA	MA	U	MD	SD
13. As long as you really love a person, you will be able to solve the problems you have with that person.	1	2	3	4	5
14. Usually there are only one or two people in the world whom you could really love and be happy with.	1	2	3	4	5
15. Regardless of other factors, if you truly love another person, that is enough to marry that person.	1	2	3	4	5
16. It is necessary to be in love with the one you marry to be happy.	1	2	3	4	5
17. Love is more of a feeling than a relationship.	1	2	3	4	5
18. People should not get married unless they are in love.	1	2	3	4	5
19. Most people truly love only once during their lives.	1	2	3	4	5
20. Somewhere there is an ideal mate for most people.	1	2	3	4	5
21. In most cases, you will "know it" when you meet the right one.	1	2	3	4	5
22. Jealously usually varies directly with love; that is, the more you are in love, the greater your tendency to become jealous.	1	2	3	4	5
23. When you are in love, you do things because of what you feel rather than what you think.	1	2	3	4	5
24. Love is best described as an exciting rather than a calm thing.	1	2	3	4	5
25. Most divorces probably result from falling out of love rather than failing to adjust.	1	2	3	4	5
26. When you are in love, your judgment is usually not too clear.	1	2	3	4	5
27. Love often comes but once in a lifetime.	1	2	3	4	5
28. Love is often a violent and uncontrollable emotion.	1	2	3	4	5
29. Differences in social class and religion are of small importance as compared with love in selecting a marriage partner.	1	2	3	4	5
30. No matter what anyone says, love cannot be understood.	1	2	3	4	5

Love At First Sight? (Belief 11)

"To love someone 'at first sight,' " said one woman "means that you are only physically attracted to that person. This is usually infatuation, not love." She disagrees that love happens quickly and feels that the longer it takes for love to develop, the longer it will last.

Cher of Sonny and Cher said when she first saw Sonny, "I swear to God, as I saw him walk through the door, everyone else faded away. I just saw *him*—this thin guy with long black hair, Beatle boots and a gold chain around his hand. Everything else was a blur" (Hirschberg, 1984, p. 25).

Another spouse said that love at first sight had happened to him and his wife. "I spotted her in the auditorium in high school when she was reading a part for a school play. I was in love with her before she finished her lines. I asked a friend to introduce us and we started dating. That was 23 years ago; today we have three children. For me, just like the song says, 'Just one look, that's all it took.' "

Love Conquers All? (Belief 13)

Realists disagree that you can work out all your problems if you have enough love. "Loving a person does not come with a guarantee of a problem-free life," said one dual-career wife in Denver. "The spouses can have different personalities and priorities, and love won't be able to resolve everything."

But sometimes love does conquer all. Karen is engaged to a graduate student who lives in another state. She says of their relationship, "Had it not been for the deep love we have for each other, our relationship would never have survived the separations and abortion we had to go through. Love was the glue that kept our relationship together."

One True Love? (Belief 14)

The romantic believes there is only one person that you will love completely. "While you may love more than one person in your lifetime," said one wife of 18 years, "you will have only *one true love.* This is the person who has a special place in your heart and mind even though you can't be with that particular individual."

Sometimes a person believes there is only one true love until that true love is replaced. This happened to one husband who said, "I fell in love with a girl in high school and dated her through two years of college. I was deeply in love with her. But she moved away when her dad was transfered to another state. I thought the end of the world had come until I met the woman who became my wife."

> The magic of first love is our ignorance that it can never end.
>
> DISRAELI

Ideal Mate? (Belief 20)

One husband said he believed in ideal mates because the way his wife talked about her first husband, he must have been one. Romantics feel there is one special person for everybody. Realists disagree and say there are numerous people that any one person can meet, fall in love with, and be happy with. "I'd better tell you," said one husband, "that my wife is the only person I could be happy with because if I didn't, she'd whop me on my bald head with a skillet."

Love Comes Once, Twice, Three Times? (Belief 27)

"He's the only one I've ever really loved" reflects the feelings of the romantic. Such was the experience of Lauren Bacall. She spoke of Humphrey Bogart as her one great love, and while emphasizing that life goes on and that she had adjusted, she remarked that the specialness they shared would never come again. Dionne Warwick sings in one of her songs, "I'll never love this way again."

Realists don't buy that view. They believe there are numerous people with whom you can enjoy a great love relationship. "I've loved many men," said one woman, "and while I've loved each one in a different way, it doesn't mean that I've loved any one of them less than the others." "For All The Girls I've Loved Before" is a song which reflects the theme of various loves.

Who Is Romantic? Who Is Realistic?

Using the Love Attitudes Scale, several studies have been conducted to find out the degree to which various categories of people are romantic or realistic. When 100 unmarried men and 100 unmarried women college students completed the inventory, the results revealed that men were more romantic than women and that freshmen were more romantic than seniors (Knox & Sporakowski, 1968). Similar results were found in a similar study (Knox, 1982), in which 94 was the average score of 97 students, men and freshmen having more romantic scores and women and seniors having more realistic scores. However, after analyzing the results of a romance survey of slightly less than 12,000 *Psychology Today* readers, the researcher concluded that "more women than men say that romance is important and men rate their partners as being more romantic" (Rubenstein 1983, p. 49).

> I don't want realism, I want magic.
>
> TENNESSEE WILLIAMS

Another study (Knox, 1970) compared the love attitudes of 50 men and 50 women high school seniors with 50 husbands and 50 wives who had been married more than 20 years. Both the unmarried and married groups revealed a romantic attitude toward love. These findings had been expected for the high school seniors but not for the older marrieds. It may be that those who have been married for 20 years adopt attitudes consistent with such a long-term investment of their time and energy; that is, the belief that there is only one person with whom an individual can really fall in love and marry justifies those who have done so. Also, some older marrieds grow to love each other. One wife said:

> I knew when I married him I didn't love him. I was pregnant and since you didn't get an abortion back then, I went through with the wedding. Our first years were rough, but we hung on to each other and have had a good marriage. My love for him is now stronger than I would have ever imagined. Love is something you grow into—not something that just happens.

When the high school seniors and older marrieds were compared with 100 couples who had been married less than five years, the latter proved very realistic in their attitudes. For them, moonlight and roses had become daylight and

The business of life often overshadows romantic love.

dishes. This is not to suggest that recently married spouses do not love each other but that their feelings about each other may change as a result of their movement from the role of lover to spouse. Lovers spend all of their time together and orient their day around each other. Spouses spend most of their time earning money and orient their day around their work. One husband said:

> My wife and I have been married for almost 10 months. The first six months were extremely gratifying, sexually and in all other aspects. Since then we have begun working up to 10 or 12 hours per day, six days a week, trying to accumulate enough money to buy a new mobile home. This has put a lot of strain on us. Our sexual activities have been cut drastically to approximately once a week. We are more irritable toward each other and we are overlooking some of each others' needs. I realize that we are losing our "romantic love," and I hope things will improve after I graduate and start working on a less demanding and more stable schedule.

CONSIDERATION • Is romantic love a sound basis for marriage? If the love you have for your partner is based primarily on physical attraction, little time together, and few shared experiences, marrying on this basis may be taking an unnecessary risk. To marry someone without spending a great deal of time with him or her (the minimum is one year) in a variety of situations (your home, your partner's home, four- or five-day camping trips, and so on) may be like buying a Christmas present without knowing what is inside.

Lovers develop different styles of loving. Lee (1974) identified six such styles of loving; Hatkoff and Lasswell (1979) studied more than 500 men and women using Lee's categories. The six types, described here, are ideal constructs and rarely is any one a "pure" type. People tend to have varying degrees of each quality.

Erotic (Romantic) Love

The erotic style of loving is similar to romantic love. Erotic individuals seek a lover who is the perfection of physical beauty. They hold an ideal image in their thoughts and try to match it with a real person. The image is made up of the details of the lover's skin, eyes, hair, body parts, and fragrance. When the person is found, there is the feeling of having known her or him for a long time. Individuals who fall in love often or who have been in love several times are likely to view love through a romantic set of lenses.

> There is no greater or keener pleasure than that of bodily love—and none which is more irrational.
>
> PLATO

Erotic lovers usually experience a chemical or gut reaction on first meeting each other and go to bed soon afterward. "This is the first test of whether the affair will continue, since erotic love demands that the partner live up to the lover's concept of bodily perfection" (Lee, 1974, p. 44). However, the erotic relationship also involves psychological intimacy. Each wants to know everything about the beloved, to become part of him or her. "Erotic lovers like to wear matching T-shirts, identical bracelets, matching colors, order the same foods when dining out, etc." (Hatkoff & Lasswell, 1979, p. 223).

Erotic love is the most transient of the various styles of loving. Because the real must match the ideal in terms of physical beauty and psychological fit, the erotic lover is often disappointed. Although erotic lovers may eventually settle for less, they never forget the compromise and rarely lose hope of realizing the dream.

The erotic style of loving is more characteristic of men than women. As noted earlier, men are more romantic in their conception of love than women. Since male socialization includes an emphasis on female beauty and transient relationships, this finding is not surprising.

Ludic (Self-Centered) Love

In contrast to the erotic lover, the ludic lover views love as a game, refuses to become dependent on any one person, and does not encourage another's intimacy. Like a cat teasing a mouse, the ludic lover keeps the partner at a distance. While the ludic lover is criticized by the erotic lover because of his or her lack of commitment, moralists condemn the ludic's implicit promiscuity or hedonism (Lee, 1974).

Two skills of every ludic are to juggle several people at the same time and to manage each relationship so that none predominate. These strategies help to ensure that a relationship does not deepen into an all-consuming love. The ludic lover may keep two, three, or even four lovers "on the string" at one time.

Sex is self-centered and exploitive rather than symbolic of a relationship (Hatkoff & Lasswell, 1979).

The ludic lover also tends to be a man. Don Juan represents the classic ludic lover. To him the pleasure of the game was in the chase, not in the prize. "Once I am sure that a girl has fallen in love with me, I gradually begin to lose interest in her," is a statement that characterizes Don Juan's modern counterpart.

CONSIDERATION • If you find yourself dating a ludic lover and you decide that you do not want to be one of several lovers or to have your relationship treated as a game, withdrawal may be your only option. The hope that your ludic lover may really fall in love with you and stop dating others may be an illusion. Some ludic lovers remain so throughout their lives.

Storgic (Friendship) Love

The Greeks used the word *storge* to characterize love based on friendship, companionship, and affection. "Storgic lovers are essentially good friends who have grown in intimacy through close association, with an unquestioned assumption that their relationship will be permanent" (Hatkoff & Lasswell, 1979, p. 222). Although neither partner experiences feelings of ecstasy, storgic lovers care deeply for each other. Storgic lovers may not remember a specific point when they felt love for each other, yet they have developed a deep feeling of intimacy that binds each to the other.

The storgic lover is practical and predictable. The emotional component of love is low key. Storgic lovers plan their relationship—for example, what they will do together each night. Spontaneity is lacking. To the ludic or erotic lover, storgic love is a bore (Lee, 1974). But storgic love has its advantages.

> Storgic lovers build up a reservoir of stability that will see them through difficulties that would kill a ludic relationship and greatly strain an erotic one. The physical absence of the beloved, for instance, is much less distressing to them than to erotic lovers; they can survive long separations . . . Also, in the ludic relationship, something is happening all the time (a game is being played) . . . and inactivity leads to boredom . . . In storge, there are fewer campaigns to fight and fewer wounds to heal. (p. 48)

Women are more likely to be storgic lovers than men (Hatkoff & Lasswell, 1979), perhaps because female socialization emphasizes caring, companionship, and affection. Previous research has also revealed that women tend to be more rational about love (Knox, 1982; Knox & Sporakowski, 1968).

CONSIDERATION • Because storge relationships do not involve sex, they are unique when experienced by lovers. Once a couple decide that sex will become a part of their relationship, the nature of that relationship changes forever. Rarely can they return to a nonsexual relationship once sex has occurred. Some couples decide to stabilize their relationship with storge love before introducing the sexual element.

I wish to believe in immortality—I wish to love with you forever.

JOHN KEATS

Agapic (Thou-Centered) Love

The agapic lover has only the best interests of her or his partner at heart. Such a lover "would be more likely to help her or his love object to get medical attention for genital herpes contracted from someone else than to be angry or punitive toward the love object for having a sexual relationship with another" (Hatkoff & Lasswell, 1979, p. 222). "Whatever I can do to make your life happy" is the motif of the agapic lover, even if this means giving up the beloved to someone else.

Neither women nor men are more likely to have an agapic style of love than the other gender. At least this is true of mainland Americans. But among Hawaiians, women are more likely to demonstrate agapic qualities than men. (Hatkoff & Lasswell, 1979). In observing this phenomenon, the researchers remarked:

> The Hawaiian sample which showed women scoring significantly higher than men on the agapic scale, contained a substantial proportion of Orientals. If one looks at the traditions and norms surrounding sex differences in Oriental cultures, this is not at all surprising. Traditionally, women in Oriental cultures were taught to put their husbands before themselves, an agapic quality. (p. 226)

My love is deep;
the more
I give to thee
The more I
have, for both
are infinite.
SHAKESPEARE

Manic (Intense Dependency) Love

The manic lover has difficulty functioning without his or her partner. He or she is obsessed with the beloved. Jealousy and inability to sleep, eat, or think logically characterize the manic lover. The manic lover has peaks of excitement but also experiences the depths of depression.

Women are more likely to be manic lovers than men (Hatkoff & Lasswell, 1979). Traditionally, women were taught to be dependent. "Even in this country women in the very recent past needed a husband's signature and consent to travel abroad, to own property, to borrow money, or even to work" (Safilios-Rothschild, 1977).

Pragmatic (Logical-Sensible) Love

H. L. Mencken once said that love can make a man mistake an ordinary young woman for a goddess or a woman mistake an ordinary young man for a Greek god. Although love may create illusions, there is also some evidence that love sees very clearly.

> Pragmatic lovers are inclined to look realistically at their own assets, decide on their "market value" and set off to get the best possible "deal" in their partners. The pragmatic lover remains loyal and faithful and defines her or his status as "in love" as long as the loved one is perceived as a "good bargain" (Hatkoff & Lasswell 1979, p. 223).

Women are more likely to be pragmatic in their love relationships than men. They are more realistic about love and tend to be more sensitive to issues in a

Friendships,
like marriages,
are dependent
on avoiding the
unforgivable.
JOHN D.
MACDONALD

relationship that predict a bad future. In a study of terminated relationships, women were more likely to initiate the breakup (Rubin et al., 1981).

• HOMOSEXUAL LOVE RELATIONSHIPS •

Although the styles of loving described in the preceding pages were initially defined in terms of heterosexual relationships, lovers may also be homosexual. The love feelings of two homosexual men or homosexual women are the same as the love feelings experienced by two heterosexuals, but the expression of these feelings—behavior—is different. We now examine the definition and incidence of homosexuality and explore gay male relationships and gay female relationships.

Definition and Incidence

Homosexuality refers to both emotional attachment and sexual attraction to those of one's own gender. Homosexual people, who are also called "gay" people, may be either men or women. When most people use the term *homosexual*, they mean a man who has an emotional and sexual preference for other men. The term *lesbian* is used to refer to a woman who has an emotional and sexual preference for other women.

DATA • *Fifty-five percent of 1,000 women aged 18 to 65 felt that homosexuality was not an acceptable alternative life-style.*   (Women's Views Study, 1984)

Love bonds exist between same gender individuals just as they do between those of the opposite gender.

    Rarely is anyone entirely homosexual or heterosexual in both attitudes and behavior. Rather, our sexual orientation can be placed on a continuum devised by Kinsey et al. (1953) and illustrated in Figure 3.1. Gay people cannot be stereotyped or pigeonholed. They are young and old, white and black, single and married, and from all social classes, occupations, and religions. The idea that a homosexual person is instantly recognizable is false. Although some effeminate men are homosexual, others are not.

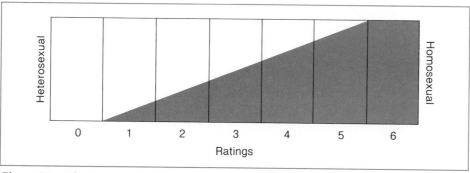

Figure 3.1   The Heterosexual–Homosexual Rating Scale
Source: Kinsey, et al., 1953.

Thirty-five percent of 65,000 adult males and 20 percent of 15,000 adult females have reported a homosexual experience during adolescence (Petersen et al., 1983a). Most of these experiences occurred only once or twice with one or two partners. This kind of experience, which may be a part of adolescent exploration, does not mean that an individual is homosexual.

DATA • *Adult men who are predominantely homosexual—that is, who prefer sex with their own gender but may have had incidental heterosexual sexual experiences—represent 5 to 10 percent of all men in western societies. Adult women who are predominantely homosexual represent 3 to 5 percent of all women.* (Marmor, 1980)   *The percentage of people who are exclusively homosexual—who have had no heterosexual experiences—is lower, about 2 percent of men and 1 percent of women. A task force of the American Sociological Association estimated that there are 20 million Americans with a homosexual orientation.* (Huber et al., 1982)

Gay Male Relationships

To put gay male sexuality in perspective, we begin by looking at heterosexual male sexuality. In traditional heterosexual relationships men are more sexually aggressive than women. When a man and a woman are out for an evening, it is typical that the man will initiate the sexual activity and the woman will act as gatekeeper controlling the pace of his advances. If this is their first date and she feels no emotional attachment to the man, she is less likely to reward his sexual advances.

When two gay men are out for an evening, who will be the gatekeeper? Who will put the brakes on sexual behavior if they have just met? Generally, neither partner. Of 4,000 gay men who were asked, "How often do you go home to have sex with someone you have just met?" only 7 percent replied "never." Fifty percent said they did so frequently (Jay & Young, 1979).

DATA • *In a study of 50 AIDS victims, the Center for Disease Control in Atlanta found that the median number of lifetime sexual partners for these men was 1,100, with a few of the men reporting as many as 20,000. The median number of different partners for a homosexual control group without the disease was 550.* (Meredith, 1984)

Cruising is the term in the gay subculture for going to a bar, bathhouse, or party to pick up a sexual partner. Since people have become aware that contracting AIDS (acquired immune deficiency syndrome) occurs primarily through sexual contact with gay men, the extent of cruising has diminished (Meredith, 1984).

The sexual activities of gay male partners, even when they are intensely enjoyable, are usually not enough to keep the couple together. Many of their relationships are short lived. This is not to say that some gay men do not establish lasting emotional and sexual relationships. One man said the relationship with his partner had lasted longer and was considerably happier than either of his sisters' marriages. However, although stable relationships based on sexual fidelity and emotional intimacy are desired by most gay men (Harry & Lovely, 1979), such relationships are the exception, not the rule.

Several reasons may account for the transitory nature of gay male relationships. Since men have been socialized to be sexually focused in their relationships, gay men as well as heterosexual ones may prefer the variety that transitory relationships provide. But most heterosexual men marry and make a commitment to their wives that they will be monogamous. Women help channel the male's sexual expression into marriage. Homosexual males do not have a partner's expectation of fidelity and their own expectation of punishment if they stray. One gay man said, "If I wanted monogamy I'd get me a wife and stay at home. But being gay means that I can have men, as many as I want, as often as I want with no 'wife' telling me who I can and can't sleep with."

Gay relationships also have few social and economic supports. When a heterosexual couple are in love, they can be public about their feelings and expect that others will approve of their relationship. Many gay couples feel they must hide their love, their "marriage" is illegal, and their living together is suspect. They cannot file joint tax returns, collect Social Security widowhood benefits (even though they may have lived as a married couple for 50 years), or get favorable insurance rates given to married people.

The lack of social support is illustrated in the 1983 family protection bill, which was submitted to the House of Representatives for consideration. The bill states:

> No Federal funds may be made available under any provision of Federal law to any public or private individual, group, foundation, commission, corporation, association, or other entity for the purpose of advocating, promoting, or suggesting homosexuality, male or female, as a life style. (p. 9)

In short, our society does not approve of homosexual relationships and gives the couple no help in establishing or maintaining such a relationship.

Gay relationships are also very intense. Often excluded by the larger society, gay men try to satisfy all needs for each other. In the midst of a hostile social environment, this goal may be unrealistic.

CONSIDERATION • Although many gay male relationships are short lived, they may be very satisfying. In a study of 128 gay men (Peplau, 1981), 80 percent said they were currently in love with their partner and rated their relationships as "best friendships" with the added component of romance and erotic attraction. Some gay male relationships are committed. One researcher studied 50 males who had lived with their respective partners an average of 3.7 years (Lewis et al., 1981).

Gay Female Relationships

Some gay women have transitory sexual encounters but this is unusual. When 1,000 gay women were asked how often they had sexual relations with someone they just met, almost 60 percent said they never did and another 35 percent said they rarely did (Jay & Young, 1979). More often, gay women have relationships that last from three to five years; these are based on emotional as well as sexual attraction. About 60 percent of the women in the Jay and Young study noted that they always had sexual relations with someone with whom they were emotionally involved, and another 35 percent said this was the case very frequently. Most women, including most gay women, have learned that sexual expression "should" occur in the context of emotional or romantic involvement. Ninety-three percent of 94 gay women in one study said their first homosexual experience was emotional; physical expression came later (Corbett & Morgan, 1983). "Lesbians inflate the traditional female role by becoming even more *romantic* than the norm for women" (Cook et al., 1983, p. 212).

CONSIDERATION • So for gay women the formula is love first and sex second; for gay men it is sex first and the emotional relationship second. This pattern is also characteristic of heterosexual women and men.

Although gay female relationships normally last longer than gay male relationships, long-term relationships (20 years or more) are rare. Serial monogamy—one relationship at a time—seems to be the dominant life pattern (Raphael & Robinson, 1980). Loss of romantic love or the inability to sustain the feelings across time seem to be a major reason for the breakup of gay female relationships. Just as strong love feelings brought them together, their absence makes each person in a relationship question why they stay together. "I don't know what happened," said one woman. "I just wasn't in love with her anymore. And I couldn't fake my feelings any longer so I left her."

Gay women also are typically denied the experience of rearing children, which can have a stabilizing effect on relationships. Prejudice against their being parents springs from the belief that their children will also become homosexual. But 36 of 37 children reared by lesbian or transsexual parents had heterosexual gender-role preferences (Green, 1978).

• LOVE AND SEX •

Whether lovers are homosexual or heterosexual, there are similarities and differences between love and sex. We compare these concepts now.

Diane Keaton: "Sex without love is an empty experience." Woody Allen: "Yes, but as empty experiences go, it's one of the best."

Similarities Between Love and Sex

In general, love and sex are more similar than they are different. These similarities include the following:

Both love and sex represent intense feelings. To be involved in a love relationship is one of the most exciting experiences an individual ever has. To know that another person loves us engenders feelings of happiness and joy. "No one ever really loved me until now," remarked one man, "and because of this love I have a very good feeling inside."

Sex has the same capability to generate intense excitement and happiness. Although sex is more than orgasm, the latter is the epitome of intense pleasure.

Both love and sex involve physiological changes. When a person is in an intense love relationship, his or her brain produces phenylethylamine, a chemical correlate of amphetamine, which may result in a giddy feeling similar to an amphetamine high (Liebowitz, 1983). When the love affair breaks up, the person seems to crash and go through withdrawal since there is less phenylethylamine in his or her system. Some heartbroken lovers reach for chocolate, which is loaded with phenylethylamine.

Further support for the idea that love has a physiological component has been suggested by Money (1980), who studied patients who had undergone brain surgery or suffered from a pituitary deficiency. Although they were able to experience various emotions, passionate love was not one of them.

The physiological changes the body experiences during sexual excitement have been well documented by Masters and Johnson (1966) in their observations of more than 10,000 orgasms. Such changes include increased heart rate, blood pressure, and breathing.

Both love and sex have a cognitive component. To experience the maximum pleasure from each, the person must label or interpret what is happening in positive terms. For love to develop, each person in the relationship must define their meetings, glances, talks, and the like as enjoyable. The significance of labeling is illustrated by the experience of two women who dated the same man. Although they spent similar evenings, the first woman said, "I love him—he's great," but the other woman said, "He is a jerk."

Positive labeling is also important in sex. Since each person's touch, kiss, caress, and body type is different, sexual pleasure depends on labeling sexual interaction with that person as enjoyable. "I can't stand the way he French kisses" and "I love the way he French kisses" are two interpretations of kissing the same person. But only one interpretation will make the event pleasurable.

Both love and sex may be expressed in various ways. The expression of love may include words ("I love you"), gifts (flowers or candy), behaviors (being on time, a surprise phone call or visit), and touch (holding hands, tickling). Similarly, sex as well as love may be expressed through a glance, embracing, kissing, fondling, and intercourse.

The need for love and sex increases with deprivation. The more we get, the less we feel we need; and the less we get, the more we feel we need. The all-consuming passion of Romeo and Juliet, perhaps the most celebrated love story of all time, undoubtedly was fed by their enforced separation. The following reflects a similar love-from-afar experience:

> I feel the thing that has affected me the most about love is that we broke up over a year and a half ago and I still think of him every day. I feel that if he walked in the door tomorrow we would start up where we left off—but that will never happen. A month after we became involved he got a girl pregnant in his hometown and married her. This destroyed me completely and for a long time I wouldn't go out with anyone. The thing that bothered me most was when I saw him recently at a bar he told me that he still loved me but that he had to marry her because his parents found out she was pregnant.

Deprivation has the same effect on the need for sex. Statements of people who have been separated from their lover for several weeks may be similar to "I'm horny as a mountain goat," "We're going to spend the weekend in bed," and "The second thing we're going to do when we get together is take a drive out in the country."

Differences Between Love and Sex

There are several differences between love and sex. These include the following:

Love is crucial for human happiness; sex is important but not crucial. After analyzing the data from a study of more than 100,000 people about what makes them happy, one researcher concluded: "Many people are unhappy with their sex lives and many think this is an important lack, but almost no one seems to think that sex alone will bring happiness. Romance and love were often listed as crucial missing ingredients, but not sex; it was simply not mentioned" (Freedman, 1978, p. 56).

Barbara Lockhart (1983), a competitive speed skater on the U.S. Olympic team, commented on sex and love:

> To me, channeling my energies in training was positive, exciting, and rewarding, and so is the channeling of sexual energy. I do not feel sorry for myself, nor do I feel deprived or depraved, not having any "outlet" for sexual feelings. I really enjoy not having sex in my life. It would be wonderful to be able to enjoy sexual intimacy, but as long as I am single, I am experiencing a far greater joy in my life by not having sex be a part of it. (p. 38)

Love is pervasive whereas sex tends to be localized. Love is felt all over, but sexual feeling is most often associated with various body parts—lips, breasts, or genitals. People do not say of love as they do of sex, "It feels good here."

Love tends to be more selective than sex. The standards people have for a love partner are generally higher than those they have for a sex partner. Expressions like "I'll take anything that wears pants," "Just show me a room full of skirts," and "I wouldn't kick him out of bed" reflect the desire to have sex with someone—anyone. Love wants *the* person rather than *a* person.

The standards for a love partner may also be different from those for a sexual partner. For example, some people form relationships with others to meet emotional intimacy needs not met by their sexual partners. A sexual component need not be a part of the love relationship they have with these people.

• JEALOUSY •

Feelings of jealousy are not uncommon in love relationships. Jealousy is a set of emotional feelings which result from the perception that the love relationship they have with a person is being threatened. The specific feelings are those of fear of loss or abandonment, anxiety, pain, anger, vulnerability and hopelessness.

> The jealous are troublesome to others but a torment to themselves.
>
> WILLIAM PENN

DATA • *Seventy-five percent of 103 women and men of varying ages and involvements in relationships reported feeling jealous. One-half of the respondents described themselves as "a jealous person."* (Pines & Aronson, 1983)

Individuals more likely to be jealous are women (who have more reason to be jealous because of the higher infidelity rate among men), those who are not in a monogamous relationship, those who are dissatisfied with the sexual relationship with their partner, and those who are dissatisfied with their relationship in general (Hanson, 1983; Pines & Aronson, 1983).

Causes

Jealousy feeds on suspicion, and it turns into fury or it ends as soon as we pass from suspicion to certainty.

LA ROCHEFOUCAULD

Jealousy may be caused by external or internal factors. An external factor is the behavior of the partner that elicits jealousy. In the Pines and Aronson (1983) study of 103 respondents, most said they became jealous when they were at a party with their partner and their partner spent a great deal of time talking, dancing, and flirting with someone of the opposite gender. "I get to feeling very uncomfortable when I see him enjoying himself and putting his hands all over another woman," remarked one woman. Other behaviors of the partner that create jealousy include the partner expressing appreciation of and interest in someone else, having a close friend of the opposite gender, and involvement in a love or sexual relationship with someone else.

DATA • *Eighty-two percent of the women and 76 percent of the men whose spouses had had an affair reported feeling jealous.* (Buunk, 1982)

Jealousy may also be triggered by thoughts of the individual who has learned to be distrustful in previous situations. "I know my husband is faithful to me," said one wife, "but my ex-husband wasn't and it's hard for me to trust men again."

Jealous feelings may also result from low self-esteem. People who feel inadequate in looks or personality may doubt their ability to get another person to love them and be faithful to them, so they are continually jealous of others whom they fear may take their partner away.

CONSIDERATION • It is not unusual that the interaction of two people in a relationship encourages the development of jealous feelings. Suppose John accuses Mary of being interested in someone else and Mary denies the accusation and responds by saying "I love you" and being very affectionate. If this pattern continues, Mary will teach John the rewards of jealousy. John learns that when he acts jealous, good things happen to him—Mary showers him with love and physical affection. Inadvertently, Mary is reinforcing John for exhibiting jealous behavior. To break the cycle, Mary should tell John of her love for him and be affectionate when he is not exhibiting jealous behavior. When he does act jealous, she should say that she feels badly when he accuses her of something she isn't doing and to please stop. If he does not stop, she should terminate the interaction until John can be around her and not act jealous.

Consequences

Low levels of jealousy are functional for a couple's relationship. Not only does it keep the partner aware that he or she is cared for (the implied message is "I love you and don't want to lose you to someone else"), but also the partner learns that the development of romantic and sexual relationships on the side are unacceptable. "When I started spending extra time with this guy at the office," said one wife, "my husband got jealous and told me he thought I was getting in over my head and asked me to cut back on the relationship because it was 'tearing him up' and he couldn't stay married to me with these feelings. I felt really loved when he told me this and drifted out the relationship I was developing with the guy at the office."

Jealousy may improve a relationship in yet another way. When the partners begin to take each other for granted, involvement of one or both partners outside the relationship can incite the other partner to reevaluate how important the relationship is and can help recharge it.

In its extreme form, jealousy may have devastating consequences, including murder, suicide, spouse beating, and severe depression. "I turned into an alcoholic overnight," said one male. "I just didn't want to be sober because I would think about her and this other fellow. I almost drank myself into oblivion."

· TRENDS ·

The most predictable trend in love relationships is that there will be little change. The excitement of love will still characterize each new love relationship. Although a person may have been disappointed in previous relationships, love feelings help to create the illusion that the current love relationship will be different. That love is something more than illusion, deception, and idealization is something one person cannot convince another of. Such a perception is grounded in experience. Even those with extensive interpersonal experience are not immune to "falling in love" and riding the love wave.

Prejudice against homosexual men and women will also continue. Like a robin among snakes, gay people live in a hostile environment. They are called pejorative names ("queer," "dyke," "faggot"), labeled as having negative characteristics ("sick," "dangerous"), and legally prohibited from marrying each other. Although being a homosexual is not a psychiatric disorder, being homophobic (having an unrealistic fear of homosexuals) is. Because heterosexuals (to their knowledge) have limited interaction with homosexuals, they do not have an opportunity to form more positive feelings about homosexuals. Without more positive experiences, negative stereotypes will continue to guide the perceptions and feelings of heterosexuals.

Social acceptance of homosexual love relationships will be slow. Just as resistance to full participation by blacks in society was first muted by legislative changes, followed by much slower attitudinal change, so will the breakdown of negative feelings against gay people follow legal change. Such changes have included the right of homosexuals to legally adopt their lovers, which gives legal recognition to their relationship and provides for inheritance.

· SUMMARY ·

Love is a crucial element in human happiness. It is also the feeling most people have when they say they want to get married. But whereas most people agree on its importance, they do not agree on the definition of love. Love is a feeling that people experience individually and privately.

The origins of love may be sexual (aim-inhibited sex), social (innate desire for companionship), psychic (search for ego ideal), psychological (a learned experience), or philosophical (a drive toward the unity of the separated). That love is a learned feeling has had the most scientific support.

Love occurs under certain conditions. Social conditions include a society that promotes the pursuit of love, peers who enjoy it, and a set of norms that link love and marriage. Psychological conditions involve a positive self-concept and a willingness to disclose one's self to others. Physiological and cognitive conditions imply that the individual experiences a stirred-up state and labels it as love. All of these conditions are important but not essential. What is essential is a high frequency of positive verbal and nonverbal behavior from the partner to furnish the basis on which love feelings may develop. It is easy for us to fall in love with someone who compliments us, is affectionate, and shares our value system. We rarely develop love feelings for those who criticize us, don't enjoy touching us, and who do not respect our values.

A person who enters the role of lover engages in predictable behaviors. Not only will the person idealize the partner, but she or he will also endure suffering and fantasize about the future with the beloved.

Love may be viewed on a continuum from romanticism to realism. Men, college freshmen, and never-marrieds tend to be more romantic than women, college seniors, and young marrieds.

Styles of loving include erotic (romantic), ludic (self-centered), storgic (friendship), agapic (thou-centered), manic (dependency), and pragmatic (logical) love. While agapic love may be characteristic of either gender, storgic, manic, and pragmatic love are more frequent among women and erotic and ludic love are more frequent among men.

Intense love feelings also occur between members of the same gender. All homosexual relationships tend to be less stable than heterosexual relationships, but gay male relationships are less stable than gay female relationships.

Love and sex are similar and different. Both love and sex represent intense feelings, involve physiological changes, have a cognitive component, are expressed in various ways, and increase with deprivation. The differences suggest that love but not sex is crucial for happiness; love is pervasive whereas sex is localized; and love tends to be more selective than sex.

Jealousy is a common feeling and results from the fear of losing a valued love partner. It may be external or internal. Jealousy may have been learned in previous situations and also may result from low self-esteem.

Trends in love relationships include little change in the romance component in new love relationships, continued prejudice against homosexual people, and slow social acceptance of gay love relationships.

Questions for Reflection

1. To what degree are you comfortable disclosing yourself to others? How did you develop this level of comfort or discomfort?
2. Which of the six styles of loving best characterizes you?
3. To what degree are your decisions dominated by rational versus emotional concerns? (This question will have meaning after reading the choices section which follows.)

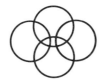

·CHOICES·

Choosing to listen to one's heart or head in making decisions and choosing to have sex with or without love are two important decisions about love relationships. We examine the consequences of each choice here.

HEART OR HEAD: WHICH SHOULD YOU LISTEN TO?

Lovers are frequently confronted with the need to make decisions about their relationships. But they are divided on whether to let their heart or head rule in such decisions. One hundred and twenty students in a marriage and family class were asked whether they used their heart or head in making such decisions. Some of their answers follow.

Heart
Those who relied on their heart for making decisions felt that emotions were more important than logic and that listening to your heart will make you happier. One woman said:

In deciding on a mate, my heart should rule because my heart has reasons to cry and my head doesn't. My heart knows what I want, what would make me most happy. My head tells me what is best for me. But I would rather have something that makes me happy than something that is good for me.

Regarding the guy I'm dating now, my head tells me that he just isn't right for me because he lives his life in the fast lane and he's not worth my trouble. On the other hand, my heart says go for it. He's good looking and I love him and even if he doesn't love me now, I think I can get him to love me.

Other women agreed that love should come first. "I think you should rely on your heart when deciding if you and someone else are right for each other. If you do not have true feelings from the heart, you have nothing," said one person.

Some men also agreed that your heart should rule. One said:

I went with my heart in a situation and I'm glad I did. I had been dating a girl for two years when I decided she was not the one I wanted and that my present girlfriend was. My heart was saying to go for the one I loved, but my head was telling me not to because if I broke up with the first girl it would hurt her, her parents, and my parents. But I decided I had to make myself happy and went with the feelings in my heart and started dating the girl who is now my fiancee.

Relying on one's emotions does not always have a positive outcome, as the following experience illustrates:

Last semester I was dating a guy I felt more for than he did for me. Despite that, I wanted to spend any opportunity I could with him when he asked me to go somewhere with him. One day he had no classes and he asked me to go to the park by the river for a picnic. I had four classes that day and exams in two of them. I let my heart rule and went with him. Nothing

ever came of the relationship and I didn't do well in those classes.

Head
Most of the respondents felt that it was better to be rational than emotional.

In deciding on a mate, I feel my head should rule because you have to choose someone that you can get along with after the new wears off. If you follow your heart solely you may not look deep enough into a person to see what it is that you really like. Is it just a pretty face or a nice body? Or is it deeper than that such as common interests and attitudes? After the new wears off, it's the person inside the body that you're going to have to live with. The "heart" sometimes can fog up this picture of the true person and distort reality into a fairy tale.

•

Love is blind and can play tricks on you. Two years ago, I fell in love with a man whom I later found out was married. Although my heart had learned to love this man, my mind knew the consequences and told me to stop seeing him. My heart said, "Maybe he'll leave her for me," but my mind said, "If he cheated on her, he'll cheat on you." I got out and am glad that I listened to my head.

•

I think it is best to use your head. I am very happy and in love with a girl I have been dating for seven great months. But at the time I met her, I was dating a sexual dynamo. But we were two different people. I gave up the incredible sex for a more compatible partner.

Some feel that both the head and heart should rule when making relationship decisions.

(continued)

When you really love someone, your heart rules in most of the situations. But if you don't keep your head in some matters, then you risk losing the love that you feel in your heart. I think that we should find a way to let our heads and hearts rule together.

SEX WITH AND WITHOUT LOVE: WHICH IS BETTER?

Some individuals feel that sex is best in the context of a love relationship. Of 12,000 respondents in the *Psychology Today* survey on romance, 30 percent of the men and more than 40 percent of the women said that sex without love was either unenjoyable or unacceptable. Half of those under the age of 22 felt this way (Rubenstein, 1983).

Here are examples of what some men and women have said about the importance of an emotional relationship as a context for sexual expression:

As a divorced person I have been involved in a number of sexual encounters. I can only say that none have been as fulfilling or pleasurable as the ones in which there was mutual love, understanding, and consideration involved along with it.

•

Sex is good and beautiful when both parties want it but when one person wants sex only, that's bad. I love sex, but I like to feel that the man cares about me. I can't handle the type of sexual relationship where one night I spend the night with him and the next night he spends the night with someone else. I feel like I am being used.

There are still a few women around like me who *need* the commitment before sex means what it should.

Other people feel that love is not necessary for sexual expression. Indeed, the theme of the book *Sex Without Love* (Vannoy, 1980) is that sex should be enjoyed for its own sake. One person said:

You choose a lover according to how you wish to be loved, and you choose a sex partner according to how you wish to be laid. There is no guarantee whatever that the person you love and the person whom you find most sexually desirable are one and the same. There are just certain things a lover may not be able to give you, and it may be good sex. (p. 24).

The idea that sex with love is wholesome and sex without love is exploitive is a fallacious dualism. Two strangers can meet, share each other sexually, have a deep mutual admiration for each other's sensuous qualities, and go their separate ways in the morning. "Their parting is not evidence that their sexual encounter was exploitation. Rather, it is a sign of their preference for independence and singlehood rather than permanent emotional involvement and marriage" (Vannoy, 1980, p. 26). One woman said:

I have never had sex with a man I was emotionally involved with or committed to. In fact, I *seek* sex without love or emotional ties. For me, the costs of love (devotion of time and energy, loss of personal space and privacy) far outweigh its benefits. Sex without emotional involvement and commitment is erotic and fulfilling.

Each person in a sexual encounter will undoubtedly experience different degrees of love feelings; and the experience of each may differ across time. One woman reported that the first time she had intercourse with her future husband was shortly after they had met in a bar. She described their first sexual encounter as "raw naked sex" with no emotional feelings. But they continued to see each other over a period of months, an emotional relationship developed, and "sex took on a love meaning for us."

Sex with love can also drift into sex without love. One man said he had been deeply in love with his wife but that he had come to despise her because she was seeing other men. "I used to think of her as a princess but now I think of her as a whore," he said. "When we have sex now, there is no love."

Both love and sex can be viewed on a continuum. Love feelings may range from non-existent to intense, and relationships can range from limited sexual interaction to intense interaction. Hence rarely are sexual encounters with or without love. Rather, they will have varying degrees of emotional involvement. Also, rarely are romantic love relationships with or without sex. Rather, they have varying degrees of sexual expression. Where on the continuum one chooses to be, with what degree of emotional and sexual involvement, will vary from person to person and from time to time.

· Chapter 4 ·

SEXUAL VALUES AND BEHAVIORS

CONTENTS

Types of Value Systems
Personal Sexual Values
Society's Sexual Values
Masturbation
Self-Assessment:
  Sexual Attitude Scale
Petting
Sexual Intercourse
Choices

There may be some things better than sex, and some things worse, but there is nothing exactly like it.

W. C. FIELDS

Our sexual values guide our sexual behavior. Think about the following situations.

> Two people are slow dancing to romantic music. Although they met only two hours ago, they feel a strong attraction to each other. Each is wondering how much sexual involvement is appropriate when they go back to one of their apartments later that evening. How much sexual involvement is appropriate in a new relationship?
>
> •
>
> A couple have decided to live together but they know their respective parents would disapprove. If they tell their parents, the parents are likely to withdraw their financial support and each will be forced to drop out of school. Should they tell?
>
> •
>
> While Mary was away for a weekend visiting her parents, the man with whom she is living had intercourse with an old girlfriend. He says he is sorry and promises never to be unfaithful again. Should she take him back?
>
> •

A woman is married to a man whose career requires that he be away from home for extended periods of time. While she loves her husband, she is lonely, bored, and sexually frustrated in his absence. She has been asked out by a colleague at work whose wife also travels. He too is in love with his wife but is lonely for emotional and sexual companionship. They are ambivalent about whether to see each other when their spouses are away. Should they see each other?

The individuals in these situations will make a decision based on their personal value system. Although we may not have experienced these particular encounters, we have confronted others that require examining our own values. In this chapter we look at our sexual values and their behavioral expression in masturbation, petting, and sexual intercourse.

• TYPES OF VALUE SYSTEMS •

Lord give me chastity—but not yet.

SAINT AUGUSTINE

Our sexual values become visible when we choose one course of action over another. This choice may be based on our feeling of what is right and wrong, moral and immoral, or a perception that one course of action will have more positive consequences than another. Sometimes a combination of factors affects our choice. A single woman who felt she was drifting into a love relationship with a married coworker stated:

> Although I felt strongly about him, I thought it was wrong and immoral for me to get involved with him. He also had three kids and the hurt it would cause them and his wife wouldn't be worth it, so I stopped flirting with him and was very careful about what I said to him.

There are several value systems that may offer guidelines for people making decisions about their sexual behavior. These include legalism, situationism, hedonism, asceticism, and rationalism.

Legalism

A legalistic view of sexual ethics involves making decisions on the basis of a set of laws or codes of moral conduct. In the example of the single woman and her married coworker, part of her reasoning was legalistic—it is "wrong" to become involved with a married person.

The official creeds of the Christian and Jewish religions reflect a legalistic view of sexual ethics. Intercourse between a man and a woman is a gift from God to be expressed in marriage only, and violations (masturbation, homosexuality, and extramarital sex) are sins against God, self, and community. The person who adopts a legal set of sexual ethics is generally clear about what is appropriate, right, or moral. "I never wonder when I'm out with my fiancée if we're going to have intercourse or not—we won't," said a devoutly religious man.

Situation Ethics

One of the most prevalent forms of contemporary sexual ethics is situation ethics. This perspective suggests that sexual decisions should be made in the context of the particular situation. Genuine love and goodwill should be the core motives for each decision, and the prediction of positive consequences a basic guideline. The situationist believes that to make all decisions on the basis of rules is to miss the point of human love and to do more harm than good. Whereas the legalist would say it is right for married people to have intercourse and wrong for the unmarried to do so, the situationist would say "it depends" and would ask: "Suppose the married people do not love each other and intercourse is an abusive, exploitative act? Also suppose that the unmarried people love each other and their intercourse experience is an expression of mutual concern and respect. Which couple is being more loving or ethical?"

> . . . no action which is not justified by its results can be right.
>
> GEORGE EDWARD MOORE

CONSIDERATION • It is sometimes difficult to make sexual decisions on a case-by-case basis. "I don't know what's right anymore" reflects the uncertainty of a situation ethics view. Once a person decides that mutual love is the context justifying intercourse, how often and how soon should the person fall in love? Can love develop after two hours of conversation? How does one know that her or his own love feelings and those of a partner are genuine? The freedom that situation ethics brings to sexual decision making requires responsibility, maturity, and judgment. In some cases, individuals may deceive themselves by believing they are in love so they will not feel guilty having intercourse.

Hedonism

A third value perspective suggests that one need not be concerned with moral or contextual issues but with pleasure. "If it feels good, do it" emphasizes the hedonistic ethic that sexual desire is an appropriate appetite and its expression is legitimate. Like hunger and thirst, the sexual urge need not be subject to moral constraints. Too much has been made, says the hedonist, of the sexual act. It should be regarded as one of many pleasures we are capable of experiencing.

Asceticism

The ascetic believes that giving into what he or she considers carnal lusts is unnecessary and calls us to rise above the pursuit of sensual pleasure into a life of self-discipline and self-denial. The spiritual life is the highest good and self-denial helps us achieve it. Monks, nuns, and other celibates have adopted the sexual value of asceticism.

Rationalism

Rationalism refers to the use of reason in determining a course of action. Rationalism is concerned with the intellect rather than with emotions. The rationalist would make a decision on the basis of the facts.

Combining rationalism and situation ethics, which has the component of emotion, one process of making value choices is to consider the positive and negative consequences for a yes and no decision. Exhibit 4.1 illustrates this process.

MAKING DECISIONS ON THE BASIS OF CONSEQUENCES

The following diagrams illustrate the prediction and evaluation of positive and negative consequences for a yes and no decision as the basis for deciding what to do when confronted with a dilemma. For example, Julie is engaged to be married to Louis in three months but has some serious reservations about her impending marriage.

I. Predict Outcomes

In making her decision, she would first predict the consequences of a yes and no decision.

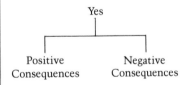

Yes

Positive Consequences   Negative Consequences

Yes—Marry Him

The positive consequence of getting married would be to continue the love relationship she enjoys with Louis. They have been dating since high school and have developed a very close emotional bond. She also views him as good looking, kind, and a person with whom she can really communicate. "We can talk about anything," she says.

The negative consequence of marrying him is that he is not very ambitious. He wants to drop out of school next term and get a job at McDonald's. Although he can make good money as a manager at McDonald's, he doesn't have goals beyond cooking hamburgers. He also doesn't want any children and feels that they are an unnecessary expense. Julie wants children and a solid economic base upon which to rear them.

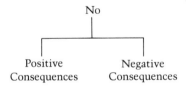

No

Positive Consequences   Negative Consequences

No—Break Up

The positive consequence of deciding to break the engagement is to avoid living with a man whom she feels is not ambitious and who does not want children in their relationship. Breaking up also frees her to become involved in other love relationships oriented toward marriage with men who are ambitious and who love children.

The negative consequence of breaking the engagement is to experience the pain of ending a long-term love relationship. "My whole life has been with Louis," said Julie. The thought of not seeing him again and starting anew with someone else frightens her.

II. Evaluate Outcomes

In evaluating outcomes it is important not only to look at how the positive and negative consequences look on paper but also at how they "feel." Julie's head may tell her it is best to terminate the relationship with Louis but her heart may tell her to stay with him. Some people will act on their emotions, whereas others will act on their rational view of the situation. It is difficult to know which is the best basis for a decision. King Edward VIII of England gave up his throne to marry Wallis Simpson, a divorcée. He did so in the name of love and, at least publicly, said he never regretted his decision.

• PERSONAL SEXUAL VALUES •

There are several ways you can clarify some of your own sexual values. One is a self-administered questionnaire, of which the following is an example. Select one ending for each of the following statements and consider why you chose that answer. You may wish to think of additional statements about sexual behavior that similarly include a range of choices.

For me, it is most important that a sexual experience:

1. Be morally correct.
2. Be fun and pleasurable.
3. Increase the love feelings with my partner.
4. Improve my self-concept.
5. Result in orgasm.

The worst thing I could find out about my sexual partner is that she or he:

1. Has genital herpes.
2. Is homosexual.
3. Is unfaithful or has deceived me.
4. Is sterile.
5. Has been a prostitute.

In a sexual relationship, I would prefer that:

1. My partner is in love with me.
2. I am in love with my partner.
3. Sex means the same thing to both of us.
4. We are married to each other.
5. My partner is uninhibited.

If I am feeling the need for sexual release, I would rather:

1. Have intercourse.
2. Have my partner perform oral sex.
3. Engage in vigorous physical activity.
4. Masturbate.
5. Have a sexual dream resulting in orgasm.

Intercourse is appropriate under the following conditions:

1. The partners are married.
2. The partners are engaged.
3. The partners are in love.
4. The partners feel affection but not love for each other.
5. The partners feel no particular affection for each other.

Women and men differ in their relationship conditions for sexual behavior, women requiring more love and commitment than men. For example, 1 percent of the women in one study (Knox & Wilson, 1981) said that intercourse without affection would be okay in contrast to 10 percent of the men. Differences in sexual values are also evident. In the same study more than 85 percent of both genders said they did not always agree with their dates on how long people should wait before engaging in kissing, petting, and intercourse.

Another way of clarifying sexual values is to think of the degree to which you regard sexual behaviors as acceptable. What category on the following continuum best reflects your sexual values about sex with love, sex without love, abortion, oral-genital sex, intercourse, masturbation, homosexuality, extramarital sex, and virginity at marriage?

Acceptable	Does Not Matter	Unacceptable

Still another exercise in values clarification is to develop an answer to a value dilemma. For example, Kathy and Bob are in love and they plan to be married in June. Kathy is sterile and has been told by her physician that she can never have children. Bob has mentioned children and Kathy knows he wants them. If she tells Bob of her sterility, she is certain that he will end the relationship with her. But she feels that after they are married he will not divorce her and that he will be willing to adopt. Should she tell him she cannot have children?

The goal in examining this and other value dilemmas is to explore our own sexual values. These values are influenced by the society in which we live, in which both liberal and conservative elements coexist. In the following section, we examine the ways in which our society is both sexually permissive and conservative.

• SOCIETY'S SEXUAL VALUES •

We live in a pluralistic society with both liberal and conservative elements. What are these views and what are the social outcomes that result from each? We sometimes make decisions about what works for us out of a synthesis of the societal perspectives to which we are exposed.

A Liberal View

We live in a sensate society, which seeks to excite the senses to their maximum potential. An experience like watching strobe lights flicker on an array of rock concert artists and listening to their amplified voices and blaring guitars feeds our visual and auditory senses to their limit. MTV (music television) specializes in stimulating our senses.

Orgasm, and the erotic feelings leading to it, is another sensation our society seeks to market. The first law of advertising is "sex sells." Our attention is grabbed by sexual appeals in advertising (such as McDonald's slogan in the early 1980s, "We do it all for you"); seminudity is a visual stimulus in countless ads in magazines, billboards, movies, and television.

We continually promote new media stars to personify our ideas of feminine and masculine sexuality. Female sex symbols like Linda Evans, Audry Landers, and Bo Derek are not to be outdone by male sex symbols such as Tom Selleck, Richard Gere, and John Travolta.

In a sensate society, every member is affected by the pervasiveness of sex. From sex grafitti on rest room walls to the grinding hips on "Solid Gold" to the sensuous perfume commercials on television, we are reminded daily that we live in a sexually permissive society. Some of the effects of this sexual permissiveness are described in the following pages.

SEXUAL OPENNESS

Society's increased willingness to tolerate and even encourage openness about sex has positive and negative aspects. Colleges and universities provide a responsible forum for open discussions of sexuality. The course in which you are enrolled is a forum for learning about interpersonal relationships and some aspects of your sexuality. Some universities sponsor conferences on sexuality, contraception, and sexually transmitted diseases. The result is a more systematic examination of human sexuality and a more informed public.

But such university-sponsored discussions on sexuality occur in the context of a media sex blitz. We are bombarded with stimuli from books (the bestseller list regularly features books on sex), magazines (even *Sports Illustrated* has an annual swimsuit issue), television (steamy soap operas and late night cable TV), and music (with sexually explicit lyrics).

SEX AS RECREATION

Sex for the purpose of having children has been replaced largely by sex as recreation. But sex for recreation (nonprocreative sex) is still preferred in the context of a love relationship. "I love sex," said one woman, "but I love it with someone I love and who loves me."

LESS VIRGINITY

Although some people remain virgins until marriage, most do not.

DATA • *Sixty-two percent of the men and sixty-nine percent of the women responding to a questionnaire at a large, mid-Atlantic university reported that they had experienced intercourse.* (Sack et al., 1984)

Despite the trend toward more individuals having intercourse before marriage, there are some individuals for whom virginity is important. One person said, "I have been taught that sex before marriage is wrong and I feel that it is. Besides, I think that waiting till you're married to have intercourse makes it special for you and your partner and gives the two of you a special beginning."

CONSIDERATION • Women today have more freedom to have intercourse with less stigma than women of 20 years ago. But the price of their sexual freedom has been the loss of security. Men today feel less obligated to women they have sex with than previously. In the past men tended to feel more committed to such women. "I thought I should marry her since we had been having intercourse," said a traditional man.

THE SLOW DEATH OF THE SEXUAL DOUBLE STANDARD

The double standard suggests there are different standards for sexual behavior for men and women. Typically, there are fewer negative connotations associated with men having sex with a variety of women than women having sex with a variety of men. The term *promiscuous* is used for women, not men. But attitudes toward which gender should have sex, when, and with how many partners are changing. Loss of virginity no longer necessarily marks a woman as promiscuous if sex is in the context of a loving mutual relationship. Also, the woman is allowed more than one sexual partner if each subsequent partner is one with whom she is emotionally involved.

LIBERAL OBSCENITY LAWS

Although some people in our society enjoy looking at pictures of nude bodies and sexually explicit scenes, others regard them as offensive and obscene. The availability of "adult" magazines and movies suggests that we have a relatively liberal view of what is obscene.

For a group of citizens to close down an adult bookstore or movie theater, they must prove that the materials sold are obscene. There are three criteria for obscenity. First, the dominant theme of the material must appear to a *prurient* (literally, "to itch") interest in sex. Such interest implies that the material is sexually arousing in a lewd way. Second, the material must be patently *offensive* to the community. In general, a community can dictate what its standards are regarding the sale, display, and distribution of sexually explicit materials. The third criterion for obscenity is that the material must have no *redeeming social value*. If the material can be viewed as entertaining or educational, a case can be made for its social value, and a small degree of social value can outweigh prurience and offensiveness. For example, in one community some citizens wanted to close the movie theater that featured X-rated films on the grounds that the films were both prurient and offensive. But a local sex therapist testified as an expert witness that some couples could profit from viewing such films as an aid to overcoming certain sexual dysfunctions. The judge ruled that because such films had therapeutic value, they had more than sufficient social value to justify their continuing availability to the public, and he allowed the theater to remain open.

A Conservative View

Although sex is pervasive and the limit of what is acceptable seems to be expanding, there is a strong conservative religious element in our society working to reverse this trend. Not all conservative or religious people support the Moral Majority, but those who do have mounted a vigorous opposition to permissive sexual values. The percentage of Americans who support the so-called Moral Majority, their background characteristics, and how the Moral Majority affects our society follows.

MORAL MAJORITY OR MINORITY?

The Moral Majority, which takes its name from the loosely organized group founded by Reverend Jerry Falwell in 1979, does not represent the majority of Americans, in spite of the group's claim to the contrary.

DATA • *In a 1981 Gallup Poll, 8 percent of a national sample said they support-ed the Moral Majority. This represents between 12 and 13 million Americans.* (Gallup Report, 1981)

A study conducted by the Connecticut Mutual Life Insurance Company (1981) throws some light on the characteristics of those people making up the Moral Majority.

> There is sin and evil in the world, and we are enjoined by Scripture and the Lord Jesus to oppose it with all our might.
>
> PRESIDENT
> RONALD REAGAN

Some fundamentalist religious groups publicly advocate conservative sexual values.

In this study religious ultraconservatism was measured by agreement that the following 10 activities were morally wrong: adultery, use of hard drugs, homosexuality, intercourse before the age of 16, lesbianism, pornographic movies, abortion, smoking marijuana, living with someone of the opposite gender without being married, and intercourse between two single people. Of 1,610 randomly selected individuals, those most likely to feel that the activities were wrong had similar background characteristics. These characteristics included the following:

1. *Age.* The older the person, the more likely that person was to take a conservative stand on all 10 moral issues.
2. *Region.* Southerners were three times as likely as those in the West to describe all activities as morally wrong. Those in the Northeast and Midwest were between the extremes.
3. *Race.* Whites were more likely than blacks to describe all 10 actions as morally wrong.
4. *Gender.* Women were more conservative than men on these issues.
5. *Income.* Those with lower incomes ($12,000–$25,000) were twice as likely to feel the actions were morally wrong as those with incomes above $25,000.
6. *Education.* Those with less than high school educations were twice as likely as those with college educations to condemn all 10 actions.
7. *Residence.* Those living in small cities or rural areas were twice as likely to object to the actions as those living in large cities or urban areas. *

IMPACT OF THE MORAL MAJORITY

Although the Moral Majority represents only a minority of Americans, it has become an influential force in our society, a "powerful lobbying group of Christian fundamentalists dedicated to electing their own political candidates" (Negri, 1981, p. 4). The movement has identified a number of trends contributing to the country's moral decay: escalating divorce, the prohibition of school prayer, abortion on demand, pornography, homosexuality, drug use, and sex education in the public schools. Falwell (1984) said in a nationally televised address "Moral and Spiritual State of the Union" that "For so long we have neglected to take stock in our moral standards as a nation that we have allowed the very foundation of our country to erode. Our forefathers were proud to bequeath us a government based on biblical principles" (p. s–1).

> Censors are people who know more than they think you ought to.
>
> LAURENCE PETER

With the cooperation of a conservative administration, the Moral Majority has been instrumental in introducing several pieces of legislation into Congress for the following purposes.

1. *Eliminate abortion.* The "human life" bill defines life as beginning at conception, making all abortions a criminal offense.
2. *Encourage chastity.* The adolescent family life bill is a proposed $30 million program to teach teenagers "self-discipline and chastity" and to discourage the use of birth control. The bill's definition of promiscuity is "a person under 21 having intercourse out of wedlock."

---

* *The Connecticut Mutual Life Report on American Values in the '80s: The Impact of Belief.* © 1981 Connecticut Mutual Life Insurance Company, Hartford, Connecticut.

3. *Restrict sex education.* Schools getting federal funds would be required to obtain parental approval of content and course material before providing sex education courses.
4. *Penalize homosexuality.* Any agency or firm that advocates homosexuality as a viable life-style should be denied federal funds. "We believe that homosexuality is moral perversion" (*Moral Majority Report*, 1984, p. 21).

Although at the time of this writing the fate of these proposals is not yet known, they testify to the current strength of the ultraconservative movement.

CONSIDERATION • The future of the conservative view is uncertain. One researcher observed, "Parents are increasingly uncomfortable with the sweeping permissiveness their own pursuit of new options has created" (Yankelovich, 1981, p. 6). As a result, they may desire a more conservative society. The Reagan victory in 1984 suggests that conservative public policy may increase.

To assess the degree to which you are conservative or liberal, take the Sexual Attitude Scale (Hudson, Murphy, & Nurius, 1983). A liberal according to the Sexual Attitude Scale is one who feels that the expression of human sexuality should be open, free, and unrestrained. A conservative is one who feels that sexual expression should be considerably constrained and closely regulated. When 689 students (primarily seniors and graduate students) took the Sexual Attitude Scale, both genders tended to score from borderline low to high-grade liberal (Nurius & Hudson, 1982).

• MASTURBATION •

Masturbation is defined as stimulating one's own body with the goal of experiencing sexual sensations. In this section we review attitudes toward masturbation, who does it, and benefits of masturbation.

DATA • *Ninety-eight heterosexual men in a sexually active stable relationship reported masturbating an average of five times during the past four-week period.* (Reading & Wiest, 1984)

Attitudes Toward Masturbation

Masturbation has traditionally had a "bad press." It is almost as though religion, medicine, and pyschotherapy have conspired to give masturbation a bad name.

RELIGION

Whereas the Jewish and Catholic religions have been most severe in their stand against masturbation, Protestants have not been very positive. Ancient Jews considered masturbation a sin so grave that it deserved the death penalty. Catholics once regarded masturbation as a mortal sin which, if not given up, would

Joyful masturbation and self-love naturally flow over into sexual exchange with another person. We can give and receive love best when we feel good about ourselves.

BETTY DOBSON

SEXUAL ATTITUDE SCALE

This questionnaire is designed to measure the way you feel about sexual behavior. It is not a test, so there are no right or wrong answers. Answer each item as carefully and accurately as you can by placing a number beside each one as follows:

1 Strongly disagree
2 Disagree
3 Neither agree nor disagree
4 Agree
5 Strongly agree

	SD	D	U	A	SA
1. I think there is too much freedom given to adults these days.	1	2	3	4	5
2. I think that the increased sexual freedom seen in the past several years has done much to undermine the American family.	1	2	3	4	5
3. I think that young people have been given too much information about sex.	1	2	3	4	5
4. Sex education should be restricted to the home.	1	2	3	4	5
5. Older people do not need to have sex.	1	2	3	4	5
6. Sex education should be given only when people are ready for marriage.	1	2	3	4	5
7. Premarital sex may be a sign of a decaying social order.	1	2	3	4	5
8. Extramarital sex is never excusable.	1	2	3	4	5
9. I think there is too much sexual freedom given to teenagers these days.	1	2	3	4	5
10. I think there is not enough sexual restraint among young people.	1	2	3	4	5
11. I think people engage in sex too much.	1	2	3	4	5

	SD	D	U	A	SA
12. I think the only proper way to have sex is through intercourse.	1	2	3	4	5
13. I think sex should be reserved for marriage.	1	2	3	4	5
14. Sex should be only for the young.	1	2	3	4	5
15. Too much social approval has been given to homosexuals.	1	2	3	4	5
16. Sex should be devoted to the business of procreation.	1	2	3	4	5
17. People should not masturbate.	1	2	3	4	5
18. Heavy sexual petting should be discouraged.	1	2	3	4	5
19. People should not discuss their sexual affairs or business with others.	1	2	3	4	5
20. Severely handicapped (physically and mentally) people should not have sex.	1	2	3	4	5
21. There should be no laws prohibiting sexual acts between consenting adults.	1	2	3	4	5
22. What two consenting adults do together sexually is their own business.	1	2	3	4	5
23. There is too much sex on television.	1	2	3	4	5
24. Movies today are too sexually explicit.	1	2	3	4	5
25. Pornography should be totally banned from our bookstores.	1	2	3	4	5

Scoring: Reverse the scores for statements 21 and 22 in the following way: 1 = 5, 2 = 4, 4 = 2, 5 = 1. For example, if you wrote 1 for statement 21 ("There should be no laws prohibiting sexual acts between consenting adults"), change that number to 5 for scoring purposes. Reverse score statement 22 similarly.

Add the numbers you assigned to each of the 25 statements. Your score may range from a low of 25 (strongly disagreed with all items: $1 \times 25 = 25$) to a high of 125 (strongly agreed with all items: $5 \times 25 = 125$). If you scored between 25 and 50, you might be regarded as a high-grade liberal, between 50 and 75, a low-grade liberal. If you scored between 100 and 125, you might be regarded as a high-grade conservative; between 75 and 100, a low-grade conservative.

Source: Hudson, W. W., Murphy, G. J., & Nurius, P. S. A short-form scale to measure liberal vs. conservative orientations toward sexual expression. *Journal of Sex Research,* 1983, 19, 258–272. A publication of the Society for the Scientific Study of Sex. Reprinted by permission.

result in eternal damnation. Although Protestants felt that neither death nor eternal hellfire were appropriate consequences for masturbation, hell on earth (as a consequence of intense guilt) was.

> CONSIDERATION • The basis for the negative view of religion toward masturbation is that masturbation is nonprocreative sex, and any sexual act that cannot produce children is a sin and an unnatural act. "Against nature" is a term that suggests an action is contrary to its essential purpose—or nature. For example, the essential purpose of eating is to sustain life and the essential purpose of sexual activity, according to Catholic thought, is to procreate. To perform an act so that its essential purpose—its nature—cannot be met is to perform an unnatural act (Gregersen, 1983).

MEDICINE

The medical community reinforced religion's prohibition of masturbation by bringing "scientific validity" to bear on their description of its hazards. In 1758 Samuel Tissot, a French physician, published a book in which he implied that the loss of too much semen, whether by intercourse or masturbation, was injurious to the body and would cause pimples, tumors, insanity, and early death (Tissot, 1766).

Adding to the medical bias against masturbation was Sylvester Graham, an American. In 1834 he wrote that the loss of an ounce of semen was equal to the loss of several ounces of blood. Graham believed that every time a man ejaculated, he ran the risk of contracting a disease of the nervous system. His solution was Graham crackers, which would help the individual control the release of sexual energy (Graham, 1848). By the mid-nineteenth century, Tissot's theories had made their way into medical textbooks and journals. In spite of a lack of data, physicians added to the list of disorders resulting from masturbation— loss of hair, weak eyes, and suicidal tendencies.

Masturbation—
it's sex with
someone I love.
WOODY ALLEN

PSYCHOTHERAPY

In the early twentieth century, psychotherapy joined religion and medicine to convince people of the negative effects of masturbation. Psychotherapists, led by Freud, suggested that masturbation was an infantile form of sexual gratification. People who masturbated "to excess" could fixate on themselves as a sexual object and would not be able to relate to others in a sexually mature way. The message was clear: If you want to be a good sexual partner in marriage, don't masturbate; and if you do masturbate, don't do it too often.

> CONSIDERATION • The result of religion, medicine, and psychotherapy taking aim at masturbation was devastating. Those who masturbated felt the shame and guilt they were intended to feel. The burden of these feelings was particularly heavy since there was no one with whom to share the guilt. In the case of a premarital pregnancy, responsibility could be shared. But with masturbation, the "crime" was committed alone.

Benefits of Masturbation

Shame, guilt, and anxiety continue to be common feelings associated with masturbation in our society, but new attitudes are emerging. Although the attitudes of some religious leaders are still negative, most physicians and therapists are clearly positive about the experience. Masturbation is not only approved but recommended. Specific benefits of masturbation include the following:

1. *Self-knowledge.* Masturbation gives you immediate feedback about what you enjoy during sexual stimulation. You can tell another what turns you on sexually by exploring your own feelings, rhythms, and responses in private.
2. *More likely orgasm.* Ninety-two percent of a sample of more than 1,000 women said they achieved orgasm most of the time when they masturbated, but only 30 percent achieved orgasm regularly when they had intercourse (Hite, 1977). In another study of almost 15,000 women, masturbation was preferred among women who had difficulty climaxing during intercourse (Cook et al., 1983).
3. *Pressure off partner.* When one partner in a relationship does not want to have intercourse or other sexual involvement, masturbation is a way of experiencing sexual pleasure without obligating the partner.
4. *No partner necessary.* Masturbation provides a way to enjoy sexual feelings if no partner is available.
5. *Unique experience.* When combined with one's own fantasies, masturbation is a unique sexual experience. It is different from petting, intercourse, mutual stimulation of the genitals, and oral sex.
6. *Avoidance of sexual involvement.* Extramarital or extrapartner entanglements can be avoided by masturbation. Sexual tensions can be released by one's self without risking sexual involvement with a partner external to the primary relationship.

CONSIDERATION • In spite of the benefits of masturbation, it remains a private experience and the decision whether to engage in the behavior is personal. Neither persons choosing not to masturbate nor those choosing to masturbate should feel guilty about their decision.

Correlates of Masturbation

Frequency of masturbation tends to be associated with several factors: gender, religion, and marital status.

GENDER

Men have higher masturbation rates than women. Not only do a higher percentage of males masturbate, they do so more often.

DATA • *The median number of masturbation experiences per year for the more than 65,000 men in one survey was 140; for the slightly less than 15,000 females in the same survey, the number was 44.* (Petersen et al., 1983b)

The explanations for higher masturbatory rates among men include greater genital availability (a male's penis is easy to touch and rub—a woman's genitals are more hidden), the greater need for release of periodic seminal buildup, and the greater socialization of males to view sexuality as release rather than relationship.

RELIGION

Masturbation rates are lower among those who attend church or synagogue and who regard themselves as devout. This is not surprising in view of the traditional negative attitude of religion toward masturbation.

MARITAL STATUS

Unmarried, separated, divorced, and widowed individuals are more likely to masturbate than those who are married or who are living with someone. Those who are married or have a regular sexual partner often have a private masturbatory life, but their frequency of masturbation is lower.

DATA • *Forty-three percent of the husbands and 22 percent of the wives in one study reported masturbating more than once a week in contrast to 61 percent of the single males and 37 percent of the single females.* (Petersen et al., 1983b)

• PETTING •

Whoever called it necking was a poor judge of anatomy.
GROUCHO MARX

Petting is the term that traditionally has been used to describe interpersonal physical stimulation that does not include intercourse. (Although the term may seem out of date, no new one has replaced it.) For some couples, petting acts as a substitute for intercourse. For example, a highly religious couple may engage in petting to orgasm and still see themselves as virgins. The following sections describe some of these petting behaviors from least to most involved.

DATA • *Although there are great differences, the actual time partners in one study spent in foreplay before intercourse was slightly less than five minutes.* (Levitt, 1983)

Kissing

A kiss isn't just a kiss. There are different types of kissing. In one style of kissing, the partners gently touch their lips together for a short time with their mouths closed. In another, there is considerable pressure and movement for a prolonged time when the closed mouths meet. In still another, the partners kiss with their mouths open, using gentle or light pressure and variations in movement and time. Kinsey referred to the latter as deep kissing (also known as soul kissing, tongue kissing, or French kissing).

One woman described a good kiss:

> Variably soft and hard, but never rough. Tender touching of the lips, gentle parting—not too wide—playful archery and tactile explorations with the

tongues. Letting emotions control the intensity of the contact—sucking, licking, and kissing.

Kissing may or may not have emotional or erotic connotations. A goodnight kiss may be perfunctory or may symbolize in the mind of each partner the ultimate sense of caring and belonging. It may also mean different things to each partner.

People who throw kisses are hopelessly lazy.

BOB HOPE

DATA • *Seventy percent of the women and 83 percent of the men in one study reported they felt kissing was appropriate by the end of the first date.* (Knox & Wilson, 1981)

Breast Stimulation

As the relationship becomes more involved, the man will usually stimulate the woman's breasts. "More involved" usually means by or after the sixth date for 60 percent of college women and by the fourth date for 60 percent of college men (Knox & Wilson, 1981). In our society the female breasts are charged with erotic potential. A billion-dollar pornographic industry encourages the male to view the female's breasts in erotic terms. An array of adult magazines feature women with unusually large breasts in seductive poses.

CONSIDERATION • Not all women share men's erotic feelings about breasts. They rarely manually stimulate their own breasts and seem to neglect the breasts of their male partners. The latter may be unfortunate as male breasts have the same potential for erotic stimulation as female breasts. For some males breast stimulation by their partners is particularly important.

Manual Genital Stimulation

Manual genital stimulation may be done by either partner. When the woman stimulates the man's genitals, it is often the man who takes his partner's hand and moves it to his genitals. Other men use body language. Once manual caressing begins it may result in ejaculation or be a prelude to oral stimulation, intercourse, or both. Sometimes the woman becomes aroused by observing her partner's erection and ejaculation as a result of her manual stimulation.

The man who stimulates the woman's genitals may be trying to ready her for intercourse or doing so as an end in itself. Regardless of the motive, the style of stimulation may vary. Some partners rub the mons veneris area (see Sexual Anatomy and Physiology in Part Six), putting indirect pressure on the clitoris. Others may apply direct clitoral pressure. Still others may insert one or several fingers into the vagina, with gentle or rapid thrusting, at the same time they stimulate the clitoris.

Not all women enjoy the insertion of the man's finger or fingers in their vagina during petting. Some women permit it because their partners want to do it, and often the man wants to do it because he assumes that the woman wants something in her vagina. But the key to sexual pleasure for many women is pressure on and around the clitoris, not necessarily insertion.

Cunnilingus

Cunnilingus is the stimulation of the clitoris, labia, and vaginal opening of the woman by her partner's tongue and lips.

DATA • *Sixty-eight percent of 250 sophomore women reported that their partners had performed cunnilingus on them.* (Herold & Way, 1983).

Women most likely to have experienced cunnilingus have high self-esteem, masturbate, have intercourse, are emotionally involved, and are religious (Herold & Way, 1983). Regarding self-esteem, women who feel good about themselves are better able to assert themselves in their sexual lovemaking and are less concerned about being rejected or having their actions viewed negatively. Masturbation and intercourse are linked with cunnilingus, as those who are highly active in one sexual area are likely to be active in other areas. Greater emotional involvement and cunnilingus are associated because cunnilingus is regarded as a very intimate sexual behavior. "I can't let a guy do that to me if I don't care about him," reported one woman. Having a high frequency of church attendance is positively related to cunnilingus "perhaps because vaginal virginity is the prime concern among the highly religious, they might feel less guilty about oral sex than about coitus" (p. 335).

Fellatio

In contrast to cunnilingus, fellatio is oral stimulation of the male's genitals by his partner. While fellatio most often refers to the woman's putting her partner's penis in her mouth and sucking it, fellatio may also include licking the shaft and glans, frenulum, and scrotum.

DATA • *Sixty-one percent of 250 sophomore women reported they had engaged in fellatio.* (Herold & Way, 1983)

In spite of the reported high frequency of fellatio, it remains a relatively taboo subject. In many states legal statutes prohibit fellatio as a "crime against nature." "Nature" in this case refers to reproduction and the "crime" is sex that does not produce babies.

People engage in fellatio for a number of reasons. Beyond the issues of pleasure and the desire to remain a technical virgin are motives of acceptance, dominance, and variety. One man said that his partner fellating him meant she really loved him and enjoyed his body. "It means total acceptance to me," he said. In one study (Blumstein & Schwartz, 1983), husbands who reported that their wives performed fellatio tended to be more happily married than husbands whose wives did not.

Dominance may be another reason for the enjoyment of fellatio. A common theme in pornographic movies is forcing the woman to perform fellatio. In this context the act implies sexual submission, which may give the male an ego boost. Aware of this motive, some women refuse to fellate their partners. One woman said her partner viewed her as a prostitute when she fellated him, she did not like such a perception, and therefore she had stopped doing so.

Variety is another motive for fellatio. Some lovers complain that penis-in-vagina intercourse is sometimes boring. Fellatio adds another dimension to a couple's sexual relationship. The greater the range of sexual behaviors a couple has to share, the less likely they are to define their relationship as routine and uninteresting.

• SEXUAL INTERCOURSE •

Sexual intercourse, or coitus, refers to the sexual union of a man's penis in a woman's vagina. It is the event most people think of when the phrase "they had sex" is used. But sexual intercourse is also a means of communication that occurs for various reasons and in different contexts—before marriage, during marriage, outside marriage, and after marriage, as well as independently of marriage.

Intercourse is more than two bodies in motion. Each partner brings to the intercourse experience a motive (to express emotional intimacy, to have fun,); a psychological state (contentment, excitement, hostility, boredom); and a physical state (aroused, relaxed, tense, exhausted).

DATA • *Although there are great variations, the actual time couples in one study spent engaging in intercourse was between two and three minutes.* (Levitt, 1983)

CONSIDERATION • The combination of these motives and states may change from one sexual encounter to the next. Tonight one partner may feel aroused and seek intercourse mainly for physical pleasure. But the other partner may feel tired and only have intercourse out of a sense of duty. Tomorrow night both may feel relaxed and loving and have intercourse as a means of expressing their feelings for each other.

The verbal and nonverbal communication preceding intercourse may also give the partners information about how each feels about the other. "I can tell how we're doing," said one woman, "by whether or not we have intercourse and how he approaches me when we do. Sometimes he just rolls over when the lights are out and starts to rub my back. Other times he plays with my face and kisses me while we talk and waits till I reach for him. Still other times we each stay on our side of the bed so that our legs don't even touch."

Motivations for Intercourse

People initiate intercourse for a number of reasons. These may be positive or negative, ranging from the desire for intimacy to the desire for revenge.

EXPRESS EMOTIONAL INTIMACY

In our relatively impersonal society, sexual intercourse may help a person feel emotionally connected to another. The physical closeness of intercourse may signify a more general closeness between the people sharing the relationship.

Mike and I have known each other for three and a half years, can talk about anything, and love each other with our souls as well as our bodies. When we make love, we feel the full expression of our love for each other. The closeness and tender touching result in intense pleasure which we share only with each other. Intercourse is our way of expressing in a physical way the love we have for each other in an emotional way.

DATA • *When 234 undergraduates were asked to describe the motive for their most recent intercourse experience, "emotional intimacy" followed by "love" were the most frequently mentioned motives by both women and men.* (Ratcliff & Knox, 1982)

HAVE FUN

"Having fun" was the third most frequently mentioned motive for having intercourse by the respondents in the preceding study.

> Don't get me wrong—I'm not the "wham-bam, thank-you-ma'am" type of guy. I admire females and respect what they represent. I would much rather have intercourse with someone who I am emotionally involved with and care for a great deal. But as unromantic as this may sound, sex can merely be fun—that's just the way I feel.

ENHANCE EGO

Although a couple may engage in intercourse primarily for fun, one (or both) of the partners may be attempting to boost his or her own ego, even at the expense of the partner. This is relatively rare for both women and men, but men are more likely to have intercourse so they may tell their friends about it than women are.

A classic example is a man who told his roommate that he had had intercourse with the university homecoming queen. Since the roommate expressed disbelief, a plan was devised so he could verify the event. The scheme called for the roommate to hide in the closet of the bedroom while his friend made love to the campus beauty. The reader can imagine this proof of manhood being executed. Notice that the man's actions were in reference to his roommate, not the woman.

Such sexual behavior to secure the approval of one's friends is not unique to men. One college woman said she was dating a man who had a particularly long penis. Since her girlfriends were disbelieving, she arranged for them to hide in her closet (three of them) while she had intercourse with the man in her apartment.

RELIEVE PEER PRESSURE

Peer pressure can influence an individual to have intercourse. One woman said of such pressure:

> Unfortunately, I am one of those girls who has never had intercourse. I'm probably the only one in the room. You know the new definition of a virgin: an awfully ugly third grader.

Men are not immune to peer pressure either. One said:

> Peer pressure is enormous, pushing you toward and down the path of sexual expression and intimacy. Not commiting yourself to this path of sexual intimacy brings on social scorn which causes low self-esteem and self-worthlessness. Males pressure other males into sex before they are ready or prepared for this intimacy.

RELIEVE PARTNER PRESSURE

Pressure toward intercourse may also come from the partner, since only one partner may be interested in moving the relationship toward intercourse. "I put pressure on him by telling him how frustrated I was. We joked about it a lot, but I believe it did influence him to have intercourse with me. He felt sorry for me."

IMPROVE RELATIONSHIP

Some couples have intercourse in the hope that it will improve their relationship. It is impossible to predict the specific effect intercourse will have on a relationship. One partner reported, "Intercourse for us was the best thing that ever happened. Since we began having sex over a year ago we have felt more emotionally involved with each other. It's really magic." But another said, "It was a mistake for us to have intercourse. I thought it would draw us closer together but it hasn't. My partner has been avoiding me lately and things are not the same. I regret that it happened."

DATA • *Thirty percent of 234 college students said the effect of their last intercourse experience was to improve their relationship, 8 percent said things got worse, and 62 percent said their relationship remained the same.* (Ratcliff & Knox, 1982)

These motives for intercourse are not exhaustive. Others include conceiving a baby, expressing passion, relieving sexual tension or boredom, duty, reconciliation, revenge, and rebellion against parents. Also, motives are often mixed. Rarely is an intercourse experience just for intimacy, fun, or passion: it includes a combination of motives.

Premarital Intercourse

In this section we review first intercourse experiences, characteristics of those who have intercourse before marriage and how many partners they have.

FIRST INTERCOURSE EXPERIENCES

Because people attach a great deal of emotional and social significance to intercourse, the first experience is likely to be memorable. Some confusion, anxiety, and frustration about the when, who, why, and how of first intercourse are typical. The following statements reflect such feelings: "I'd like to get it over with"; "My closest friend has intercourse regularly; I wonder when I'll be doing it?"; "I feel that I should already have had intercourse by now, but I haven't." Compounding these concerns are those about the partner (Will my partner respect me?), pregnancy (How lucky will I be?), and genital herpes (Will I get it?). (See Exhibit 4.2 for reactions to first intercourse experiences).

Weiss (1983) collected data from 130 university women about their first intercourse experience. He found that women who perceived their first coital partners as gentle, loving, and considerate were also likely to experience pleasure and less likely to experience guilt or anxiety. These partner behaviors were more important in women reporting a positive first intercourse experience than whether they had just met their partner, were going steady, or were engaged. "Conversely, men who were seen as unloving, inconsiderate, and rough were associated with more negative affect even if the couple were engaged at the time of the woman's first intercourse" (p. 228).

• Exhibit 4.2 •

FIRST INTERCOURSE EXPERIENCES

Students in the author's marriage and family class were asked to describe their first intercourse experience. Although there was no typical description, elements of pain, fear, anxiety, and awkwardness were not unusual. Some of the various experiences included the following:

• My first intercourse was actually very nice—both physically and emotionally. I dated the same guy for four years in high school and it wasn't until my senior year when we actually made love. I was nervous and we did not use any contraception, which doubled my nervousness. Also, for years my mother preached, "Nice girls don't." My philosophy is that nice girls do because they are the ones with the steady boyfriends.

• I had been dating this guy for almost a year when we first made love. The first time was not the best. It was quite painful physically and I couldn't understand how people could find such enjoyment from sex.

• My first time I really felt nothing. I didn't know what to expect. I didn't feel guilty or sad or happy. I wasn't sorry it happened. I was not forced into the situation and the guy was not in it just for sex because we are still dating.

• My first intercourse experience was a disaster. Both the girl and I were virgins and had no idea what we were doing. Actually, we really didn't have intercourse the first time; she was so tight that I couldn't get inside of her. We gave up after 15 minutes.

• I was 15 and my partner was 16. I had two fears. The first was my fear of getting her pregnant the first time. The second was of "parking" in dark and desolate areas. Therefore, once we decided to have intercourse, we spent a boring evening waiting for my parents to go to sleep so we could move to the station wagon in the driveway.

After near hyperventilation in an attempt to fog the windows (to prevent others from seeing in), we commenced to prepare for the long-awaited event. In recognition of my first fear, I wore four prophylactics. She, out of fear, was not lubricating well, and needless to say, I couldn't feel anything through the four layers of latex.

We were able to climax, which I attribute solely to sheer emotional excitement, yet both of us were later able to admit that the experience was disappointing. We knew it could only get better.

• My first intercourse experience was simply terrible. There was no romance involved. He just came like a bull. He was the worst lover, ever. I was very hurt when he left me but now I'm glad he did.

WHO HAS PREMARITAL INTERCOURSE?

Some people are more likely to have intercourse than others. Among college students, the factors most likely to influence intercourse before marriage include the following.

Gender   In most studies, men are more likely to report having had premarital intercourse than women. For example, in a random sample of never married, white, undergraduate students at Michigan State University, 65 percent of the men and 57 percent of the women reported having had intercourse (Kallen et al., 1983). However, some studies report females having a higher incidence of premarital intercourse. For example, 69 percent of the women and 62 percent of the men at a large, mid-Atlantic university reported having had premarital intercourse. (Sack, et al., 1984).

Egalitarian gender role orientation   The more egalitarian a woman is in her view of gender roles, the more likely she is to approve of premarital intercourse, to be assertive in sexual activities, and to instruct her partner in ways to enhance her own sexual pleasure (Koblinsky & Palmeter, 1984).

Education   More education is associated with an increased approval of intercourse before marriage. In one study of 1,000 women (Women's Views Survey 1984), 60 percent of those who had attended college compared with 40 percent of those who attended high school only approved of intercourse. In another study (Earle & Perricone, 1982), 46 percent of the freshmen women reported they had had intercourse in contrast to 82 percent of senior women.

Emotional relationship   Those who are involved in a reciprocal love relationship are more likely to feel that intercourse is appropriate (Knox & Wilson, 1983).

Religious affiliation   Protestant college women have a higher incidence of intercourse than either Catholic or Jewish women (Bell & Coughey, 1980).

Church attendance   The less often a college student attends church or synagogue, the more likely that person is to have had intercourse (Diederen & Rorer, 1982). This is particularly true of women (Notzer et al., 1984).

Race   Black men and women are more likely to have premarital intercourse than white men and women (Zelnik & Kantner, 1977).

Peers having intercourse   Individuals, particularly men, who have close peers of the same gender who have had premarital intercourse are more likely to have premarital intercourse than those individuals whose close friends have not had premarital intercourse (Sack et. al., 1984).

Divorced parents   Individuals whose parents are divorced are more likely to have had premarital intercourse than individuals whose parents are still married to each other (Booth et al., 1984). This relationship may be a function of the norm-breaking model the parents provide by divorcing.

CONSIDERATION • These characteristics do not imply causation. Females, freshmen, Catholics, frequent church attenders, whites, those whose parents are married to each other, or a person with all of these characteristics may also have intercourse before marriage.

DATA • *In a nationwide sample, the average age at first intercourse for women was 16.2; for men, 15.2. The sexual partners of the women were about three years older; the sexual partners of the men were about six months older.*   (Zelnik & Shah, 1983)

NUMBER OF PREMARITAL PARTNERS

In a study of readers of *Playboy* magazine, both unmarried women and men reported having had an average of 19 sexual partners (Petersen et al., 1983a). In another study of students at a conservative southern university, more than 90 percent of the women and 80 percent of the men had from one to five premarital partners (Earle & Perricone, 1982). Some individuals have more than one lover with whom they have an ongoing sexual relationship. One fourth of 42 never-married professional women reported they were currently engaging in sexual intercourse with more than one sex partner (Davidson & Darling, 1983). "It's not as hard to keep the men separate in my mind as I thought it would be," reported one woman.

Although some individuals don't have concurrent sexual relationships, they try to have intercourse with as many people as possible. "I'm up to 99," said one man. "And I'm looking for someone special to break the magic 100."

Marital Intercourse

Intercourse after marriage is different from intercourse before marriage. Marriage is the traditional social context for most intercourse experiences.

UNIQUE ASPECTS OF MARITAL INTERCOURSE

Marital intercourse is unique in terms of its social legitimacy, declining frequency over the course of the marriage, and varying importance to the partners.

Social legitimacy   In our society marital intercourse is the most legitimate form of sexual behavior. Homosexual, premarital, and extramarital intercourse do not enjoy society's approval, although attitudes and laws are changing. It is not only okay to have intercourse when married, it is expected. People assume that married couples make love, and if they do not, something is "wrong."

Declining frequency   Marital intercourse is also characterized by declining frequency.

> I wonder what Adam and Eve think of it [marriage] by this time.
>
> MARIANNE MOORE

DATA • *In one study spouses who had been married for one year had intercourse an average of 15 times per month. But those who had been married six years reported they had intercourse six times per month.* (Greenblat, 1983)

For some couples it does not take long for the frequency of intercourse to diminish. A traditional wedding prank is for someone to give the bride and groom a half-gallon jar on their wedding day with the following instructions taped on it: "Every time you have intercourse during your first year of marriage, put a penny in this jar. Then beginning with your second year, take a penny out every time you have intercourse. It will take you five years to empty this jar, which you will fill in one."

Reasons for declining frequency are careers or jobs, children, and satiation. Regarding the impact of employment, one spouse said:

> Exhaustion is a very big problem. I never thought it could happen. When I'm working and running my business, it is totally absorbing and it takes me a long time to decompress at night, by which time Jerry is usually sound asleep! And I guess Jerry, unlike when we first got married, has a lot of responsibility in his position—so it's work that's taking its toll on our sex life! (Greenblat, 1983, p. 296)

Children also decrease the frequency of intercourse by their presence and by the toll they take on the caretaker's energy. "After taking care of a 3-year-old and a 9-month-old all day, I'm in no mood for sex. I'll tell you that straight out," said one mother. Also, the mere fact that children are in the house and can walk into the bedroom at any time translates into the couple having intercourse late at night when the children are asleep or early in the morning before they awaken. "It shoots spontaneity in the neck," said one husband.

Satiation in psychology means that repeated exposure to a stimulus results in the loss of its ability to reinforce. For example, the first time you listen to a new record album you derive considerable enjoyment and satisfaction. You play it over and over the first few days. But after a week or so, listening to the album is no longer new and does not give you the same level of enjoyment that it did at first. So it is with intercourse. Having intercourse with the same person the first few times is not as new and exciting the thousandth time. "Everything gets old if you do it often enough," said one spouse.

Commenting on the loss of sexual focus from courtship to marriage, one researcher (Schmidt, 1982) said:

> There is the illusion that a couple's relationship can be continuously and permanently compatible with the intensive sexuality experienced in the early days of falling in love. This is impossible because the closeness that comes from living together, sleeping, eating, and spending leisure time together, and bringing up children together cannot additionally cope with sexual symbiosis [having intercourse continually]. (p. 95)

Varying importance   How important is intercourse to married couples? The range is very wide. Whether for physiological or psychological reasons, some married couples stop having intercourse. For them, sex is not a meaningful event. Yet they may love each other deeply and delight in the companionship they share.

Other couples regard sex as the only positive aspect of their relationship. One husband said that he and his wife had decided to separate, "and since we both knew that I would be moving out on Friday we had intercourse twice a day that week." A year after the separation, he said, "Sex with us was the best there is. I don't miss the fights we had, but I do miss the sex."

Between the extremes of "sex is nothing" and "sex is everything" is "sex is good but not everything." "It's the icing on the cake," said one man. "If you've got a good out-of-bed relationship, sex only makes things better. But sex can't make a bad marriage good."

Extramarital Intercourse

The terms *playing around* and *cheating* refer to the same phenomenon—having intercourse with someone other than one's own spouse.

DATA • *Although it is difficult to know how many spouses have extramarital intercourse (there is a tendency to be dishonest about this very private aspect of one's life), various studies suggest that about 50 percent of husbands and between 20 and 40 percent of wives have at least one such encounter.* (Frank & Enos, 1983; Hassett, 1981; Petersen et al., 1983b)

All such encounters are not alike. The nature of the event, the participants, their motives, and the consequences for themselves and their marriages vary tremendously.

Most affairs involve a reciprocal emotional relationship.

TYPES OF EXTRAMARITAL ENCOUNTERS

Intercourse outside of marriage may be a brief encounter, a full-blown affair, or an event shared with the spouse.

The brief encounter   The lyrics to the song "Strangers in the Night" describe two people exchanging glances who end up having intercourse "before the night is through." Although the partners may see each other again, more often their sexual encounter is a "one-night stand."

DATA • *In one study 28 percent of the men and 5 percent of the women said their last extramarital encounter was a one-night stand.*   (Spanier & Margolis, 1983)

The affair   An affair implies a relationship with the partner beyond the sexual involvement. The various combinations of pairs include married man-single woman, married man-married woman, and married woman-single man. Most relationships develop as a result of the partners meeting and interacting at work. This is the case for most people since time away from the partner is usually time at work.

It's hard for an old rake to turn over a new leaf.

LAURENCE PETER

Intense reciprocal emotional feelings characterize most affairs. Such feelings are more a function of the conditions under which the relationship exists than any magical matching of the partners involved. For one thing, the time together is very limited. Like teenagers in love who are restricted by parents, adult lovers are restricted by their spouses and other family responsibilities. Such limited access makes the time they spend together very special. In addition, the lover is not associated with the struggles of marriage—bills, children, house cleaning—and so is viewed through a more romantic set of lenses.

Swinging   In the traditional affair, one or both of the spouses has intercourse with someone outside the marriage without the partner's knowledge. Swinging, also referred to as comarital sex, is another form of extramarital intercourse in which the spouses of one marriage or pair-bonded relationship have sexual relations with the spouses or partners of another relationship. Swinging is different from an affair as the former implies no deception (both partners are aware of the extramarital encounter) and both partners (rather than one) are usually involved. When 35 swinging couples were compared with 35 married couples who did not engage in swinging, the former reported greater satisfaction with their marital sexual relationship. The researchers (Wheeler & Kilmann, 1983) commented:

> Thus, for comarital couples, engaging in recreational sexual activities with outside partners apparently does not interfere with each member's perception of a positive marital sexual relationship; for these couples, it may be that their marital sexual relationship is enhanced by agreed-upon sexual contact with outside partners. This may not be the case for couple members who engage in covert extramarital sexual relationships, often as an "escape" from a dysfunctional marital relationship. (p. 304)

WHO HAS EXTRAMARITAL INTERCOURSE?

The factors most likely to influence a partner to have extramarital intercourse include the following:

Gender   The incidence of husbands who have extramarital intercourse is at least 10 percent higher than wives. Reasons why women are less likely to have an affair include more limited opportunities and social constraints—businessmen have affairs with secretaries, pilots with flight attendants, physicians with nurses, and teachers with colleagues and students. Although married women are joining the work force in increasing numbers, about 40 percent still spend most of their time at home. Since an affair is dependent on knowing someone to have an affair with, the wife's contacts and opportunities are more limited.

Sexual experience   Having had intercourse before marriage is also characteristic of those who have intercourse outside of marriage (Thompson, 1983). Not only do most premaritally sexually experienced people have more than one sexual partner, but they also learn how to break norms. Both behaviors are involved in extramarital affairs.

Marriage quality   Spouses who report low marital satisfaction, infrequent intercourse, and poor quality intercourse are more susceptible to extramarital involvements (Thompson, 1983).

Peer influence   Having a close married friend who has been sexually involved in an extramarital relationship is also related to an individual's becoming involved in an affair (Atwater, 1982).

Length of marriage   How long a person has been married is also related to having an affair. Although some spouses report having had extramarital intercourse during their honeymoon, most report that several years of married life (seven or more) go by before their first experience (Petersen et al., 1983b).

Divorce   Spouses who have been married previously are more prone to having an extramarital relationship, possibly because they are less concerned about breaking social constraints.

MOTIVES FOR EXTRAMARITAL INVOLVEMENTS

There are a number of reasons why spouses have intercourse with someone other than their mate. Some of these reasons are discussed here.

Variety   One of the characteristics of marital sex is the tendency for it to become boring and routine. Before marriage the partners cannot seem to get enough of each other. But with constant availability, the attractiveness and excitement of intercourse seems to wane.

The Coolidge Effect helps to explain the need for sexual variety.

> One day the President and Mrs. Coolidge were visiting a government farm. Soon after their arrival they were taken off on separate tours. When Mrs. Coolidge passed the chicken pens she paused to ask the man in charge if the rooster copulates more than once each day. "Dozens of times" was the reply. "Please tell that to the President," Mrs. Coolidge requested. When the President passed the pens and was told about the rooster, he asked "Same hen every time?" "Oh no, Mr. President, a different one each time." The President nodded slowly, then said, "Tell that to Mrs. Coolidge." (Bermant, 1976)

Men seem more motivated by the need for variety than women.

DATA • *Fifty percent of wives who have an affair do so with only one partner.* (Tavris & Sadd, 1977) *But husbands have an average of seven partners.* (Yablonsky, 1979) *And twice as many men have extramarital intercourse for sex only (without an emotional component) than women.* (Thompson, 1984)

Although men typically have more opportunity and fewer social constraints, the desire for variety is difficult to overlook.

CONSIDERATION • One anthropologist (Symons, 1979) suggests an evolutionary reason for men having more desire for sexual variety than women. The male who achieved the greatest reproductive success—who had the most surviving progeny—would be the one who impregnated the greatest number of females. On the other hand, reproductive success for the female depended on mating with the most fit male to ensure that her offspring would have the greatest possible chance of survival. She did not need a variety of partners.

Friendship   Some people view intercourse outside their marriage as a natural consequence of a developing relationship. "It's not that I'm crazy about sex; it's just that I enjoy relationships with other women and sex is only a part of that," is an expression that typifies this feeling. Such relationships usually develop when people work together. They share the same world eight to ten hours a day and over a period of time may develop good feelings for each other that eventually lead to a sexual relationship.

Apathetic or uncooperative spouse   Some spouses have affairs because their partner is not interested in sex. "He doesn't like sex and never has," remarked one wife. "And it frustrates me beyond description to have intercourse with him when I know it's just a duty to him. So I've found someone who likes sex and likes it with me."

Although a spouse's lack of interest in intercourse is often a reason for an affair, some go outside the marriage because their spouse will not engage in other sexual behaviors they want and enjoy. The unwillingness of the spouse to engage in oral sex, anal intercourse, or sexual positions like rear entry sometimes encourages the partner to look elsewhere for satisfaction.

Unhappy marriage   It is commonly believed that people who have affairs are not happy in their marriage. But this is more likely to be true of wives than husbands. Although husbands are more likely to have an affair than wives, they usually are not "dissatisfied with the quality of their marriage or their sex life with their wife" (Yablonsky, 1979, p. 15). Rather, men seem to seek extramarital relationships as an additional life experience. This is generally not true of wives. In one study only 6 percent of wives who had been involved in an affair said they were happy in their marriage (Tavris & Sadd, 1977). Most wives "appear to seek extramarital sex when they experience some deficit—sexual, emotional, or, perhaps, economic—in their marriage, or perceive another man as being superior to (not merely different from) their husbands" (Symons, 1979, p,. 238). Although trapped in a bad marriage, they may not want a divorce. "So they turn to an affair or a series of them as a means of treading water, keeping the marriage afloat for the time being until their children grow up or they [the wives] earn a degree, etc." (Schaefer, 1981).

Aging   A frequent motive for intercourse outside of marriage is the desire to reexperience the world of youth. Our society promotes the idea that it is good to be young and bad to be old. Sexual attractiveness is equated with youth, and having an affair may confirm to an older partner that he or she is still sexually desirable. Also, people may try to recapture the love, excitement, adventure, and romance associated with youth by having an affair. For some, it is viewed as the last opportunity to be young again.

One 47-year-old woman said she felt that life was passing her by and that "before long, it will all be over. To be in love is the most magical feeling I have ever experienced and I want to have that feeling once more before I end up in a nursing home somewhere."

Absence from spouse   Circumstances have more to do with some extramarital relationships than specific motives. One factor that predisposes a person to an extramarital encounter is prolonged separation from the spouse, which may make the partner particularly vulnerable to other involvements. Some wives whose husbands are away for military service report that the loneliness can become unbearable. Some husbands who are away say that it is difficult to be faithful. "You've almost got to be a saint to get through two years of not having intercourse if you're going to be faithful to your spouse," one air force captain said. "Most of the guys I'm stationed with don't even try."

> You are only young once, but if you do it right—once is enough.
>
> LAURENCE PETER

CONSIDERATION • An extramarital sexual involvement will not occur because of these reasons alone. Other factors must be operative before an affair will actually take place. One factor is a value system that permits extramarital involvement under certain conditions. Some people have decided that extramarital sex is wrong and they will not permit such involvement under any conditions. Others feel that extramarital sex is justified under certain conditions. "I didn't get married to be unhappy," said one spouse. "So if I can't find a responsive partner at home, I'll look somewhere else."

Other conditions under which extramarital sex is likely to occur include the availability of a willing partner and an opportunity to engage in the behavior so that the spouse will not find out. "When I was overseas, I had plenty of women," said one partner. "And there's no way my wife was going to find out." The reason some people do not have extramarital encounters is the lack of favorable conditions.

Postmarital Intercourse

Postmarital intercourse by the divorced and widowed is the last type of intercourse situation that we consider in this chapter. First, we look at the situation of the formerly married.

INTERCOURSE AMONG THE DIVORCED

About two and a half million people get divorced every year. Most will have intercourse within one year of being separated from their spouse. The meanings of intercourse for the separated or divorced vary. For many, intercourse is a way to reestablish, indeed repair, their crippled self-esteem. Divorce is often a shattering emotional experience. The loss of a lover, the disruption of daily routine, and the awareness of a new and negative label ("divorced person") all converge on the individual. Questions like "What did I do wrong?" "Am I a failure?" and "Is there anybody out there to love me again?" loom in the mind of the divorced. One way to feel loved, at least temporarily, is through sex. Being held by another and being told that one feels good gives a person some evidence that he or she is desirable. Since divorced people may be particularly vulnerable, intercourse is a lifeboat they may reach for. "I felt that as long as someone was having sex with me, I wasn't dead and I did matter," said one recently divorced person.

Whereas some use intercourse to mend their self-esteem, others use it to test their sexual adequacy. The divorced person may have been told by the former spouse that he or she was an inept lover. One man said his wife used to make fun of him because he was occasionally impotent. Intercourse with a new partner who did not belittle him reassured him of his sexual adequacy and impotence ceased to be a problem. A woman described how her husband would sneer at her body and say no man would ever want her because she was so fat. But she found men who thought her attractive and for whom her weight was not a problem. Other divorced men and women say that what their spouses did not like, their new partners view as turn-ons. The result is a renewed sense of sexual desirability.

Beyond these motives for intercourse, many divorced people simply enjoy the sexual freedom their divorced state offers. Freed from the guilt that spouses experience when having extramarital intercourse, the divorced are free to have intercourse with whomever they choose. Most choose to do so with a variety of partners.

DATA • *In one study, divorced men and women reported having an average of 30 and 22 sexual partners, respectively. These averages were higher than those among singles, marrieds, remarrieds, and live-ins.* (Petersen et al., 1983b)

Before getting remarried, most divorced people seem to go through predictable stages of sexual expression. The initial impact of the separation is followed by a variable period of emotional pain. It is during this time that the divorced look to intercourse for intimacy to soothe some of the pain, although this is rarely achieved.

This looking-for-intimacy-through-intercourse stage overlaps with the feeling-of-freedom stage and the divorced person's desire to explore a wider range of sexual partners and behaviors than marriage provided. "I was a virgin at marriage and was married for 12 years. I've never had sex with anyone but my spouse so I'm curious to know what other people are like sexually," one divorced person said.

But the divorced person soon tires of casual sex. One man said he had been through 22 partners since his divorce a year ago. He likened his situation to that of a person in a revolving door who is in motion but isn't going anywhere. "I want to get in a relationship with someone who cares about me and vice versa." The pattern is typical. Most divorced people initially use sex to restore their ailing self-esteem and to explore sexual parameters. But they soon drift toward sex within the context of an affectionate love relationship. "You get tired of screwing people or being screwed," said one person. "You get to where you want to love the person you're holding."

INTERCOURSE AMONG THE WIDOWED

The 12 million widowed in the United States are different from the divorced in their sexual behavior. In general, widowed men and women have intercourse less frequently than those who are divorced. A major reason is the lack of an available partner. But others have intercourse less frequently because they feel they are "cheating" on the deceased. "It's a guilty feeling I get," expressed one widower, "that I shouldn't want to get involved with someone else and that I shouldn't enjoy it."

Social expectations also do not support sexual expression among the widowed. Most are considered "too old" for sex. The lack of an available sexual partner, feelings of guilt at the idea of cheating on the deceased, and an unsupportive social context seem to conspire against the widowed. When a group of widows (ages 67 to 78) were asked how they coped with their sexual feelings when they had no partner, they responded:

Only by keeping busy. Keep occupied with various activities and friends.

•

Do physical exercise. Have many interests, hobbies.

•

We just have to accept it and interest ourselves in other things.

•

By turning to music or other arts, painting, dancing is excellent . . . using nurturant qualities, loving pets, the elderly, shut-ins. Reading, hiking . . . lots more. My mind controls my sex desires. (Starr & Weiner, 1982, pp. 165–167)

Other widows, particularly young widows, enjoy active sex lives with a new partner. "Just because your spouse is gone doesn't mean you're dead," said one 43-year-old widow. "I figure I've got half my life left and I'm not about to give up sex yet."

Widowers have more access to sexual partners because there is an abundance of widows competing for a small number of men at later ages. Also, since our society supports male aggressiveness, widowers are more likely to initiate contacts than widows.

> In the long run we are all dead.
>
> JOHN MAYNARD KEYNES

• TRENDS •

The trend toward using a rational-situation ethics perspective in contrast to a rigid legalistic one in making decisions about sexual behavior will continue. Individuals will rely more on their own judgment than on the rules of official religion.

Masturbation, the last great taboo, will become a more accepted behavior and topic of discussion in the media, particularly television. For example, on a segment of "The Tonight Show," Johnny Carson discussed masturbation with a sex therapist. But because most people have been socialized to feel embarrassment and shame about masturbation, this trend will be slow.

Trends toward sexual involvement with more partners before marriage will continue. As the age at marriage continues to rise, more people will be sexually available for a longer period of time. Also, since single relationships are less stable than marriage relationships, there is a greater turnover of partners.

Extramarital sexual encounters will also increase, particularly among wives. As more wives join the labor force (now about 62 percent) they will have increasingly frequent contact with men. Also, since women are having fewer babies, they will be less homebound. The result will be more freedom and opportunity to become involved in extramarital encounters.

· SUMMARY ·

Sexual values are moral guidelines for appropriate behavior. Legalism, situationism, hedonism, and asceticism are basic value frameworks within which an individual makes decisions.

There are both liberal and conservative elements in our society's attitude toward sexuality. On the one hand is the increased openness about sexual matters, especially in the media, changing standards of sexual behavior for women, and relatively liberal obscenity laws. On the other hand is the reaction of the Moral Majority to increased liberalization, especially of abortion, gay rights, and sex education.

Masturbation is sexual self-stimulation. Traditionally, religion, medicine, and psychotherapy have considered masturbation immoral and harmful. However, attitudes toward masturbation are changing. Although religious leaders may still express disapproval, most physicians and therapists are clearly positive.

Petting is a frequent sexual behavior involving any sexual contact that does not include intercourse. Examples include kissing, breast stimulation, cunnilingus, and fellatio. There are different types of kissing, and kissing may or may not have emotional or erotic connotations. Cunnilingus means oral contact with the female genitals; fellatio means oral contact with the male genitals.

Sexual intercourse is a method of communication. People initiate intercourse for a number of reasons, including the desire to feel emotionally close, to express love, and to have sensual fun with one's partner. Intercourse also occurs in different interpersonal contexts: before, during, outside, and after marriage. Premarital intercourse is significant because it represents first intercourse for most people and does not have the legitimacy of marital intercourse. Most people who have premarital intercourse do so with relatively few partners and in the context of an affectionate love relationship. The effect of premarital intercourse on the subsequent relationship is minimal.

Marriage is the traditional social context for most intercourse experiences and marital intercourse is the most socially approved form of sex. Its frequency declines the longer the couple is married.

Various studies suggest that about 50 percent of husbands and between 20 and 40 percent of wives have extramarital sex. Motivations include variety, absence of spouse, unhappy marriage, and aging.

Intercourse among the divorced and widowed are two types of postmarital intercourse. The divorced typically have very active sex lives that include a number of sexual partners. But after an initial period of casual sex, the divorced usually drift into monogamous relationships.

The widowed are usually more socially isolated and have more difficulty finding sexual partners than the divorced. Widows more than widowers often resign themselves to diverting their sexual interest with hobbies and other interests.

Questions for Reflection

1. How have your sexual values and behaviors changed in the last five years? To what degree are these changes related to your education, peers, and love relationships?
2. What impact do you think having a number of sexual partners has on the individual involved? Is it positive or negative? Why?
3. What motives have you had for your various sexual experiences?

· CHOICES ·

Deciding whether to have intercourse in a new relationship and whether to have extramarital sex are choices with which most people are confronted.

DECIDING ABOUT INTERCOURSE

In each new relationship a decision about whether to have intercourse must be made. Since the first meeting, each partner muses about this. You might consider the following issues in making this decision.

Personal Consequences
How do you predict you will feel about yourself after you have intercourse? An increasing number of individuals feel that if they are in love and have considered their decision carefully, the outcome will be positive.

I believe intercourse before marriage is okay under certain circumstances. I believe that when a person falls in love with another, it is then appropriate. This should be thought about very carefully for a long time, so as not to regret engaging in intercourse. I do not think intercourse should be a one-night thing, a one-week thing, or a one-month thing. You should grow to love and care for the person very much before giving that "ultra" special part of you to your partner. These feelings should be felt by both partners; if this is not the case, then you are not in love and you are not "making love."

Those who are not in love and have sex in a casual con-text sometimes feel badly about the expereince.

I viewed sex as a new toy—something to try as frequently as possible. I did my share of sleeping around and all it did for me was to give me a total loss of self-respect and a bad reputation. Besides, guys talk. I have heard rumors that I sleep with guys I have never slept with.

•

The first couple of guys I had sex with pressured me and I regret it. I don't believe in casual sex; it brings more heartache than pleasure. It means so much more when you truly love the partner and you know your love is returned.

But not all people who have intercourse in the context of a love relationship feel good about it.

The first time I had intercourse, I was in love and I thought he loved me. But he didn't. He used me and I have always hated him for it.

Some prefer to wait until marriage to have intercourse.

The person I marry will respect my wishes and wait until marriage. I don't want to sneak around and feel bad when I'm giving up an important part of myself. I want to be married, to be in our bed, and feel good that we have waited. I know that people have different values and to each his own. But I feel that my decision to wait until I'm ready is as good as anybody elses.

The effect intercourse will have on you personally will be influenced by your religious values, your personal values, and the emotional involvement with your partner. Strong religious and personal values against intercourse plus a lack of emotional involvement usually mean guilt and regret following an intercourse experience. In contrast, values that regard intercourse as appropriate in the context of a love relationship are likely to result in feelings of satisfaction and contentment after intercourse.

Two researchers (Darling and Davidson, 1984) compared the psychological and sexual satisfaction of 123 females who had had intercourse with 79 females who had not had intercourse. Among the sexually experienced females, 75 percent were psychologically satisfied and 77 percent were physiologically satisfied with their sex lives whereas among those who had not experienced coitus, only 46 percent reported psychological satisfaction and 47 percent reported physiological satisfaction with their sex lives.

Partner Consequences
Since a basic moral principle is to do no harm to others, it may be important to consider the effect of intercourse on your partner. Whereas intercourse may be a pleasurable experience with positive consequences for you, your part-

ner may react differently. What are your partner's feelings about intercourse and her or his ability to handle the experience? If you suspect your partner will not feel good about it or be able to handle it psychologically, then you might reconsider whether intercourse would be appropriate with this person.

One man reported that after having intercourse with a woman he had just met, he awakened to the sound of her uncontrollable sobbing as she sat in the lotus position on the end of the bed. She was guilty, depressed, and regretted the experience. He said of the event, "If I had known how she was going to respond, we wouldn't have had intercourse."

Relationship Consequences

Does intercourse affect the stability of a couple's relationship? Apparently not. Hill et al. (1976) studied the sexual behavior of 5,000 college sophomores and juniors who had ongoing sexual relationships. In a two-year follow-up, the researchers found that those who had had intercourse were no more likely to have broken up than those who had not. In another study (Ratcliff & Knox, 1982), less than 2 percent of 234 respondents said their relationship terminated as a result of their last intercourse. "Remained the same" was the most frequently chosen description of the effect intercourse had on the relationship.

Contraception

Another potential consequence of intercourse is pregnancy. Once a couple decide to have intercourse, a separate decision must be made as to whether intercourse should result in pregnancy. If the couple wants to avoid pregnancy, they must choose and effectively use a contraceptive method. But many do not. Thirty percent of white women aged 15–19 and almost 50 percent of black women in the same age group who had premarital intercourse reported they became pregnant (Zelnik & Kanter, 1980). In general, the interval between first intercourse and the use of a prescription method of birth control is about one year (Zelnik et al., 1984). Religiously devout individuals who have intercourse before marriage are particularly prone not to use contraceptives (Notzer et al., 1984). In most cases the pregnancy was a surprise. One woman recalled:

It was the first time I had had intercourse so I didn't really think I would get pregnant my first time. But I did. And when I told him I was pregnant, he told me he didn't have any money and couldn't help me pay for the abortion. He really wanted nothing to do with me after that.

Sexually Transmitted Diseases

Avoiding sexually transmitted diseases (STDs) is an important consideration in deciding whether to have intercourse. The result of increasing numbers of people having more frequent intercourse with more partners has been the rapid spread of the bacteria and viruses re-

sponsible for numerous varieties of STDs. For some, the fear of contracting genital herpes is a deterrent to having intercourse with someone they do not know. Twenty-two percent of 1,505 single people (aged 18 to 37) agreed with the statement, "I have changed my behavior to avoid the risk of contracting herpes" (Boston Globe Newspaper Co., 1983). One man said, "A close friend got herpes on a one-night deal and has been plagued by it ever since. Intercourse isn't worth getting herpes so I've decided to be very careful about who I sleep with." Some people are taking no chances. One woman told her new partner that she wouldn't sleep with him until he showed her a statement from a physician that he did not have a STD.

Although no method is completely safe, a sexually active person can reduce the chances of getting an STD by not having sex with someone who has multiple partners; by using a condom or contraceptive such as foam, cream, or jelly; by looking for sores or discharge and washing exposed areas after contact; and by urinating after contact.

EXTRAMARITAL SEX? NO

As noted earlier, about 50 percent of husbands and between 20 and 40 percent of wives report they have had intercourse with someone other

(continued)

than their spouse (Frank & Enos, 1983; Petersen et al., 1983b). Conversely, about 50 percent of husbands and between 60 and 80 percent of wives decide not to have an affair. Eighty-five percent of the wives in a recent study said they disapproved of extramarital sex (Women's Views Survey, 1984).

Some of those not having an affair feel that it causes more trouble to themselves and their partners than it is worth. "I can't say I don't think about having sex with other women, because I do—a lot," said one husband. "But I would feel guilty as hell and if my wife found out, she would kill me."

Although his wife probably wouldn't "kill him," she likely would express her pain and disillusionment by asking, "How could you do this to me?" Extramarital intercourse is still regarded as adultery in an emotional sense. Like conspiring with a thief to rob their home, the adulterer is seen as conspiring with another to invade the privacy of the marriage. As a result, the partner may develop a deep sense of distrust, which often lingers in the marriage long after the affair is over. "I can forgive you," said one husband, "but I'll never forget what you've done." A wife said that whenever her husband was away on a business trip she has visions of him being in bed with another woman. "I just don't trust him anymore."

In addition to guilt and distrust as outcomes of an affair, another danger is the development of a pattern of having affairs. "Once you've had an affair, it's easier the second time," said one spouse. "And the third time you don't give it a thought." Increasingly, the spouse looks outside the marriage for sex and companionship.

Spouses who establish a pattern of affairs also invest increasing amounts of time and energy with someone other than the spouse. Although this commitment of self to the new person helps build the relationship with that person, it does nothing to improve the relationship with the spouse.

Thirty percent of 108 marriages in which one of the spouses had an affair ended in divorce (Humphrey & Strong, 1978). "When you have an affair, you are playing with a ticking time bomb," said one spouse. "I was able to hide mine for three years before she found out, but when she did, she threw me out of the house. When I think about what I actually did, I traded something good for something new. It was a terrible mistake."

EXTRAMARITAL SEX? YES

A small percentage of spouses who have an affair feel that it has positive consequences for them, their marriage, and their partner. One wife said, "I felt wanted, loved, desired, and sexually attractive. And every time I was with him I felt I was someone special." In contrast to the spouse who has become familiar and inattentive, the lover is new and exciting—and makes the partner feel this way too.

Benefits to the marriage may also occur. Some partners become sensitive to the fact that they have a problem in their marriage. "For us," one spouse said, "the affair helped us to look at our marriage, to know that we were in trouble, and to seek help." The thesis of the book *Beyond Affairs* (Vaughn & Vaughn, 1980) is that couples need not view the discovery of an affair as the end of their marriage but as a new beginning.

A final positive effect of a partner discovering an affair is that the partner may become more sensitive to the needs of the spouse and more motivated to satisfy them. The partner may realize that if spouses are not satisfied at home, they will go elsewhere. One husband said his wife had an affair because he was too busy with his work and did not spend time with her. Her affair taught him that she had alternatives—other men who would love her emotionally and sexually—and to ensure that he did not lose her, be became intent on satisfying her.

Although an affair is dangerous for most marriages, one researcher (Britton, 1984) interviewed 276 spouses who had had an affair and identified the conditions under which an extramarital encounter is least likely to have negative consequences.

1. The spouses have a solid marriage relationship. The one who has the affair has a strong emotional commitment to the mate. The lover is viewed as short term only, not as a potential replacement for the mate.
2. The spouses compartmentalize easily. The one who has the affair can keep the lover and the mate separated in time, place, and thought. Memories of the experiences with the lover are not allowed to blend into the relationship with the spouse so that behavior is adversely affected.
3. The spouses avoid disclosure. Disclosure is like a rattlesnake in the relationship, which strikes the spouse and introduces a deadly venom. Few spouses can tolerate the information that their partner had or is having a sexual relationship with someone else.
4. The spouses limit contacts. Frequent contacts with one or more lovers take the energy away from the marriage and increase the chance of getting caught.
5. The spouses seek recreation only. Sexual experiences that are for spontaneous recreation do the least damage. Those that are carefully orchestrated for emotional impact take time and energy away from the mate.

Part Two

DECISIONS

More than a century ago, young men and women faced great obstacles to spending time with each other. Not only were coeducational opportunities rare, but also the boy was expected to be introduced to the girl's parents before the partners could see each other socially. If her parents decided the boy was not suitable, no relationship would develop. If the partners did get together with their parents' approval, they were usually not alone. If they went out, the girl was often accompanied by a chaperone who would arrange the time, place, and events of the meetings between the partners. If they stayed inside, the boy would visit in the girl's house. They were expected to stay in the same room (usually the kitchen) with her parents. Private conversations were further limited because there were no telephones and no cars to escape adult monitors.

Today dating and mate selection decisions are made by the individual. While sitting in your marriage and family class, you might glance across the room and spot someone who is particularly attractive to you. You may envision a developing relationship with this person, including a number of dating events—dining

together, going to parties, seeing movies, and attending concerts. The only obstacle to initiating the relationship is your instructor's lecture, which will be over in another 20 minutes. You may plan to approach this person after class and ask if you can borrow yesterday's class notes. If that person is not involved in another relationship and views you as a potential partner, your dating relationship will have begun.

· Chapter 5 ·

LIFE-STYLES

CONTENTS

Marriage
Singlehood
Contract Cohabitation
Communes
Self-Assessment: **Life-Style Preference Inventory**
Choices

I would be married, but I'd have no wife, I would be married to a single life.

RICHARD CRASHAW

One way to view your life is as a series of activities experienced alone or with other people. Eating, working, sleeping, seeing movies, attending concerts, and clipping coupons are all activities that occur in the context of a life-style choice. Although most people opt for marriage, it is only one of an array of life-style choices. Others examined in this chapter include singlehood, contract cohabitation, and communal living. As we noted, the process of making life-style choices and reevaluating your decisions is continual. Some people have chosen and experienced all of the life-styles discussed here, and some more than once.

· MARRIAGE ·

DATA · *Of all life-styles, marriage is the option chosen by more than 90 percent of all Americans. Every year about 5 million people choose to tie the marital knot.* (National Center for Health Statistics, 1984)

Social forces and individual motivations account for most people opting for marriage. Let's examine these reasons.

Society and Marriage

As we noted earlier, marriage and the family have traditionally served three main functions in our society: to replace old members with new socialized members, to regulate sexual behavior, and to stabilize adult personalities by providing companionship.

> CONSIDERATION • The companionship function of marriage has become more important as the form of marriage has changed. Unlike the traditional marriage, which was formal and authoritarian, emphasizing ritual and discipline, the modern marriage pattern is delineated in terms of interpersonal relationships, mutual affection, sympathetic understanding, and comradeship. The need for intimacy and companionship has become so strong that many couples consider divorce when they no longer feel "in love" or "able to communicate" with their partners. Other differences between the traditional and modern marriage are presented in Table 5.1.

Recently, the traditional justifications for marriage have been questioned. There is little concern now that our society would "disappear" if people stopped marrying. Children would continue to be born; and the increase in single-parent families suggests that the husband and wife team is not the only pattern for rearing children.

The argument that marriage tends to regulate sexual behavior is true, as most spouses have intercourse with each other most of the time. But again, the issue is children, and the development of contraceptive technology has made it possible for individuals to make love without making babies. It is the use of contraceptives, not marriage, that now prevents unwanted children.

Table 5.1 **Traditional and Modern Marriage Compared**

TRADITIONAL MARRIAGE	MODERN MARRIAGE
Emphasis on ritual and roles	Emphasis on companionship
Couples do not live together before marriage	Couples may live together before marriage
Wife takes husband's last name	Wife may keep her maiden name
Man dominant—woman submissive	Neither spouse dominant
Rigid roles for husband and wife	Flexible roles for spouses
One income (the husband's)	Two incomes
Husband initiates sex—wife complies	Sex initiated by either spouse
Wife takes care of children	Parents share childrearing
Education important for husband, not for wife	Education equally important for both
Husband's career decides family residence	Family residence decided by career of either spouse

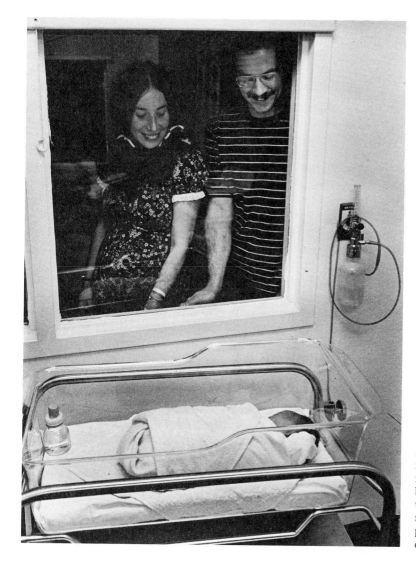

A major social function of marriage is to bind two adults together to nuture and protect their offspring.

The emotional support each spouse derives from the marital relationship remains one of the basic functions of marriage. In our social world, which consists mainly of impersonal secondary relationships, a sense of belonging may be particularly important. But proponents of singlehood are quick to point out that soaring divorce rates suggest that marriage does not offer much emotional support for some people and that an array of intimate friendships may be superior to the one-to-one marital relationship. Still, most of us have been socialized to believe that it is better to have one relationship for 50 years rather than 25 relationships of two-year durations.

The Individual and Marriage

Although the social justifications for marriage are being questioned, marriage continues to be the life-style of choice.

DATA • *When 1,600 respondents were asked which of three life-styles they preferred (marriage, singlehood, living with someone), 92 percent said marriage. (Connecticut Mutual Life Insurance Report, 1981)*

Reasons for most of us being drawn to marriage include personal fulfillment, companionship, security, and parenthood.

Personal fulfillment   We are socialized as children to believe that getting married is what adult men and women do. Even if our parents are divorced, we learned that being married is what they wanted, but it didn't work out. Marriage often becomes a goal to achieve, and achieving that goal is assumed to give us a sense of personal fulfillment.

Companionship   Many people marry primarily for companionship—for a primary group relationship. Primary groups are characterized by intimate, affectionate associations in which there is mutual love and caring. The family in which you grew up is a primary group. Your parents loved and cared for you more than anyone else.

Although marriage does not ensure it, companionship is the greatest expected benefit of marriage. Companionship is talking and doing things with someone you love; it is creating a history with someone. "Only my husband and I know the things we've shared," said one wife. "The shrimp dinner at Ocean City, the walk down Bourbon Street, and the chipmunk in our backyard are part of our joint memory bank."

To have and to hold from this day forward
For better, for worse, for richer, for poorer
In sickness and in health, to love and to cherish
Till death do us part.

BOOK OF
COMMON PRAYER

Companionship is a primary reason people get married.

DATA • *There are 52,543,000 married men and 53,625,000 married women in our society. As a group, married people represent 67.2 percent of our population.* (*Statistical Abstract of the United States*, 1984)

Security   People also marry for the emotional and legal security marriage can provide. A 32-year-old single person remarked, "I've been through three relationships in the past year, and it's getting old. I want security. I want to get in a relationship where my partner and I will let ourselves completely go and commit ourselves to each other for the full trip."

Parenthood   Some people marry to have children. Although some are willing to live with someone, it is rare that they express a desire for children outside of marriage. There is a strong presumption in our society that only spouses should have children. Role entry to parenthood is through marriage. One couple (both Ph.D.'s) who had lived together for seven years said they decided to marry "so we could begin our family."

Other benefits   There are also some side benefits from being married. From an economic viewpoint, two can definitely live together more cheaply than they can live apart. In addition, while single people aren't unhappy, married people by comparison tend to be happier, healthier, more satisfied with their relationships, and have higher incomes (Ward, 1979). If a person divorces, the desire to get remarried is high. Five of six men and three of four women remarry. Regardless of the reason, marriage seems to offer what most people want and miss once they have experienced it.

• SINGLEHOOD •

The life-style choice being considered by an increasing number of Americans is singlehood. Law separates people into "marrieds" and "singles." No matter how married a couple feel they are, if they are not legally married by ceremony or common law, they are two single individuals. Also, regardless of how single a married person may view himself or herself, unless the marriage has been dissolved by law or death of the spouse, the person is still married.

> We are witnessing a population explosion of "solos"—people who live alone, outside a family altogether.
>
> ALVIN TOFFLER

Categories of Singles

There are about 60 million single adults over the age of 18. But they are not all alike. The different categories of singles include the never married, the separated or divorced, and the widowed.

NEVER-MARRIED SINGLES
The largest proportion of singles in the United States are those who have never married. Since 1970 there has been a dramatic increase in the percentage of men and women between the ages of 20 and 24 who are single. In 1970, 55 percent of the males and 36 percent of the females in these age ranges were single; by 1980 these percentages had jumped to 69 percent and 50 percent respectively (Glick, 1984).

DATA • *The never married represent 19,125,000 men and 15,262,000 women over the age of 18. As a group they represent 24.5 percent of our population. (Statistical Abstract of the United States, 1984)*

There are several reasons for a larger percentage of single people at these ages now than in previous years. These include a greater number of women in college, increased employment opportunities for women, more social support for singlehood (the women's movement, peers), availability of effective contraception, and the "marriage squeeze." The latter refers to an excess of young women at the currently most "marriageable" age. Women tend to marry at age 22 and men at age 24. There are more women turning 22 than men turning 24 in any given year, so these women must compete for the smaller number of men. As a result, more are left without partners.

Beyond numbers, there is a new wave of youth who feel that their commitment is to themselves in early adulthood and only later to marriage. This translates into staying in school, establishing one's self in a career, and becoming economically and emotionally independent. The old pattern was to leap from school to marriage. The new pattern is look (wait and prepare) before leaping.

"I could get married tomorrow," said one college senior. "But my mom married before she finished school and has regretted it ever since. Besides, I want to go to law school and I don't want to try and juggle law books and a husband at the same time."

> It is true that I never should have married, but I didn't want to live without a man. Brought up to respect the conventions, love had to end in marriage. I'm afraid it did.
>
> BETTE DAVIS

SEPARATED AND DIVORCED SINGLES

There is a tendency to think of single people as only those who have never married. But statistics show otherwise.

DATA • *There are 4,605,000 divorced men and 6,895,000 divorced women in our society who are "single again." As a group, the divorced represent 5.9 percent of our population. (Statistical Abstract of the United States, 1984)*

For many of these people, the return to singlehood is not an easy transition. In a study of more than 2,000 respondents in the Chicago area, depression was much more characteristic of the recently separated and divorced than of the never married or the married (Pearlin & Johnson, 1977). Emotional and physical well being also seem more precarious for this group (Sommers, 1979).

After the initial impact of separation and divorce, most remarry or adjust to and enjoy singlehood. One divorced man said, "I can stand being alone. Perhaps I even have a gift for it. What I can't stand is taking what's available 'until something better comes along.'"

WIDOWED SINGLES

Whereas some separated and divorced people have chosen to be single rather than remain in an unhappy marriage, the widowed are forced into singlehood. When widowhood occurs in later life it may be particularly stressful. Those who are widowed exhibit higher rates of mortality and suicide and evaluate their health more negatively. Lacking money and feeling lonely may also be problems (Ward, 1984). But widowhood may also have its positive aspects. One widow said, "I miss my husband but I'm not going to grieve about something I can't change. I've got friends and time to travel. I feel like I've been given a second life and I'm going to make the most of it."

DATA • *There are 1,860,000 widowed men and 10,795,000 widowed women in America. As a group the widowed represent 2.4 percent of our population. (Statistical Abstract of the United States, 1984)*

Attitudes Toward Singles

Married people tend to have a negative view of single women. At least that is the finding of one Australian study (Stolk & Brotherton, 1981) in which 48 spouses were asked how they felt most people would respond when asked to complete the sentence "I think of single women over 30 as . . ."

Seven in 10 husbands and four in 10 wives said that "spinster," "failure," and "hasn't met the right person" would be how most people would respond. But these negative feelings seemed to be a result of other than personal contact with singles—20 percent of the spouses didn't know a single woman and half had never had a single woman in their home.

Americans have their own prejudices against singles. In one study, undergraduate students rated never-married persons as less secure and less reliable than marrieds (Etaugh & Malstrom, 1981).

This prejudice against singles exists for at least two reasons: First is the attitude that singlehood is deviant. Although being unmarried is normative in your teens and early twenties, it becomes deviant when you are 30. Since most people marry, those who don't become somewhat suspect. Then too, since most singles express a desire to be married and to have children, marrieds assume that since they don't have what they want, they must be frustrated and unhappy.

> The whole idea of marriage and swearing before a judge or God—promising to love in sickness and in health till death do you part—almost promises to program hypocrisy into society.
>
> SHIRLEY MACLAINE

Stereotypes of Singles

Singles are also victims of stereotypes (simplified beliefs about members of a particular group). The "swinger" and "lonely loser" are two stereotypes that are often used to describe adult unmarrieds.

SWINGERS

The stereotype of the swinger has been described as follows:

Singles are swingers—the beautiful people who are constantly going to parties, who have uncommitted lives—and a lot of uncommitted sex . . . They frolic on clean, sun-drenched beaches and ski the French Alps. They drink Pepsi-Cola. They shop at Lord and Taylor or Neiman Marcus. They vacation in the Hamptons or Rehobeth Beach or with the Club Mediterranée. During the winter, they go to the Caribbean or to Mexico. They have clear complexions and blonde hair, and they look like self-assured winners. They are never ill, never poor, and never overweight. (Stein, 1976, pp. 2–3)

To test this stereotype, one researcher (Cargan, 1981) interviewed 151 never-married and divorced singles about their number of sexual partners, frequency

Singlehood is increasingly being viewed as a viable life-style alternative.

of intercourse, and satisfaction with their sexual relationships. Their answers were compared with 249 married people. Results showed that the singles, particularly the divorced, had more sexual partners than the marrieds. About one-third of the divorced had 11 or more sexual partners, compared with 15 percent of the never-marrieds and 6 percent of the marrieds. The charge that "singles are swingers" seems true for only a minority of singles and most of those are divorced.

LONELY LOSER

The second stereotype about singles is that they are lonely losers. They are unhappy, depressed, and in therapy. They wish, so the saying goes, that they were married.

> They live by themselves and consume great quantities of frozen TV dinners and diet sodas. The women in the group are in constant communication with their mothers, who periodically send them clippings from the local paper announcing yet another engagement of a former high-school classmate. The men in this group visit their mothers every other Sunday. They live by themselves and drink a lot. (Stein, 1976, p. 3)

Cargan (1981) also asked his respondents about the degree to which they felt depressed when alone or felt as though there was no one with whom to share or discuss things. More singles than marrieds felt depressed and lonely. About one in three of the singles said they often had no one to share their life with in contrast to one in 10 of the marrieds.

CONSIDERATION • It should be emphasized that most of the singles in this study were neither depressed nor lonely. Being lonely is a result of perception, not a result of the single life-style. "I am often alone but never lonely," said a single woman.

Singlehood as a Life-Style Choice

To the never married, separated, divorced, and widowed, singlehood has different meanings. But there are two basic ways of viewing it—as a life-style or as a stage leading to marriage or remarriage. In spite of the less than positive attitudes and stereotypes about singles, an increasing number of people are choosing singlehood as a life-style. The reasons for this involve a desire to enjoy the benefits of singlehood and avoid the entanglements of marriage. These reasons are detailed in Table 5.2.

THE BENEFITS OF SINGLEHOOD

Benefits of deciding to remain single include freedom, autonomy, and spontaneity. Regarding freedom, being single permits the individual to pursue a range of activities with which marriage and children might interfere. Individuals who wish to establish themselves in a career without the interference of a spouse and babies might find singlehood particularly rewarding. Singlehood also permits a larger sense of freedom. "Being single allows me to do what I want to do, when I want to do it, and with the person or persons I choose," said a 27-year-old computer programmer. "There are no fences around what I want to do, and a spouse is the thickest, tallest fence I know of."

I want to be alone.

GRETA GARBO

Freedom for the single person may also mean freedom to select different values, have sex with different people, travel more, and have no responsibility for others. The single person enjoys the freedom to change philosophies or lifestyles without considering the effect on another. "In the past two years since I've joined the health club, I've made many new friends," a graduate student said. "Just as I have changed friends, I think I would have needed to change spouses if my partner had not had the same experience." B. F. Skinner, the famous behavioral psychologist, said that one of the reasons he could not join the Twin Oaks commune (which used his book *Walden Two* as a model) is because he would have to get a divorce. "Communes are not my wife's cup of tea," he remarked.

The single person may also change sexual partners at will. The freedom to have a variety of sexual relationships is regarded as a major advantage of being single. "When you're married," remarked a divorced college teacher, "you have to act like you aren't sexually attracted to others and you dare not put your

Table 5.2 Reasons to Remain Single

BENEFITS OF SINGLEHOOD	DISADVANTAGES OF MARRIAGE
Freedom to have multiple sex partners	Restriction to one sex partner
Freedom to have a variety of interpersonal relationships	Restriction to one basic relationship
Freedom to move from city to city	Restriction of career mobility
Freedom to travel	Travel restricted by spouse and children
Responsibility for one	Responsibility for spouse and children
Not required to interact with others on intimate basis	Required to interact with others in household
Spontaneity	Life sometimes too routine

thoughts into action. Although the sex life of the single person isn't what married people fantasize it is, it has its advantages."

Freedom from responsibility and freedom to travel are other advantages of the single life-style. Mates are responsible to each other and for any children they may have; the single person is responsible only to those he or she chooses. A recent graduate who is single said, "I don't have to use my paycheck to buy anything except what I want, nor do I need to spend my time cooking or running other people's errands."

People who choose singlehood may be attracted by the spontaneity that the life-style offers. The married person is probably better able to predict when he or she will be doing what than the single person. Some single people abhor regimentation. A friend may call, a new person may be met at work, or someone may drop by, and this will affect the activities for that evening or weekend. "I live not knowing what's going to happen next," observed a 32-year-old accountant, "and I like it that way."

Exhibit 5.1 reflects the insights of an attractive 32-year-old woman in her first year in law school. She comments on both the positive and negative aspects of singlehood.

Most people remain single for a combination of the reasons we have discussed, but some do so because of responsibility for an ill or aging parent, physical disability, homosexuality, or no available partner. Some people also have a fear of marriage. One senior art student said:

> My mom has been divorced three times. Marriage to me means nothing but arguments, misery, and grief. Why would anyone want to get married? I can't think of a reason.

Whatever the reason, marriage does not attract everyone. Among those who have remained single throughout their lives are Plato, Isaac Newton, Leonardo da Vinci, Jonathan Swift, Henry David Thoreau, Emily Dickinson, and Florence Nightingale. Contemporary people who have never married (at the time of this writing) include Gloria Steinem, Ralph Nader, Barbara Jordan, Jerry Brown, Bernadette Peters, Steve Martin, and Jacqueline Bisset. These individuals have chosen singlehood as a life-style and view it as a positive experience.

THE DISADVANTAGES OF MARRIAGE

As Table 5.2 indicates, those who opt for singlehood may view marriage as restricting their potential for personal growth, trapping them in an undesirable role (spouse), or restricting their mobility. A single journalist wrote:

> I'm not the kind to be locked up in one room with one person for 50 years. I'd much rather take my chances with the singles who don't have stable relationships. I feel smothered by a one-to-one relationship and really don't like it. I need the space. And I would go nuts having to ask permission or consider someone else's needs every time I made a decision about something.

Related to the feeling that a person rarely maximizes his or her potential inside the marital relationship is the conviction that the specific roles of wife and husband are undesirable. Some women feel the role of the wife is to be a nurse and waitress to her husband. Some men feel their role as husband is a greater trap than the wife's. One middle-aged man remarked, "As a husband, I am expected to be economically responsible for everything, eat breakfast and dinner

· Exhibit 5.1 ·

A SINGLE WOMAN'S VIEW

At this point in my life I enjoy being single. Of course, there are disadvantages to singlehood, but I like the privacy and independence that it affords me.

Singlehood gives me a tremendous amount of freedom and time. Since I am responsible only for myself, I can decide to relocate and/or continue my education. This freedom allows me to change, grow, and develop as a person. Part of my growth is dependent on maintaining diverse relationships, including male friendships. Being single, I can consciously choose to become romantically involved with males who would not be threatened by my male friends. Singlehood permits all sorts of small but important freedoms. For example, I can sleep late, read in bed, travel, visit with friends after work, and eat odd meals at unusual times. I also have the option not to prepare meals, clean the house, or answer the phone.

Being single has made me more aware of the importance of developing a positive self-image and learning to "pat myself" on the back. It has been essential for my mental health to develop a good support system and to confide in close friends. I have also discovered the need to be competent in traditionally male areas of expertise such as car and house repairs. Learning simple tasks like replacing a windowpane, repairing the lawn mower, and tuning the car engine increases my self-confidence and sense of independence.

I feel comfortable with my single status after listening to some of my married female friends discuss what is expected of them in terms of their role as a wife and mother. This is not a feeling of superiority because being comfortable with my choice does not prevent an occasional sense of ostracism for not being married. Also, feeling good about myself does not eliminate all the anxiety I have about singlehood. For example, I wonder if I am possibly missing something wonderful by not having children.

One of the most difficult aspects of singlehood to cope with is the attitude and behavior of a few of my peers. The belief that being single indicates a personality defect makes me defensive about my life-style. Occasionally I feel that I am viewed as a threat to married females, particularly if I have a professional relationship with their husbands. Also, my family is not completely supportive of my single status. Although my father was pleased and proud of my independence, his death removed much of my family support, and I believe that my mother and sisters would be relieved if I married.

The fact that I am single does not mean that I do not want a serious long-term relationship. However, being single is a challenge because, to be independent and to be comfortable enough to live alone, I have to like myself. So even though there are times I am lonely, overall I enjoy being single.

Although others may assume that single people are lonely, many singles prefer and enjoy their choice of life-style.

with my wife, stay in the house from six at night until morning, have sex only with my wife, and enjoy weekends with a two-year-old."

The spouse role can also isolate a person from other people. In a traditional marriage, the partners must carefully control the level of each new relationship for the sake of their marriage. Such control may result in feelings of isolation and loneliness. One woman remarked that she had been more lonely since she had married than when she was single. "My single friends don't call me anymore because they assume I have a built-in companion. I live in the same house with Rex, but *companion* isn't the word I would use to describe him. I'm terribly lonely."

Even those who have good marital relationships often feel it is unrealistic to expect their partner to satisfy all their emotional, social, physical, and sexual needs. "To be all things to one person is impossible," one married man concluded. "My wife and I love and care for each other, but we feel that we've got to find some way to take the heavy responsibility off each of us to be everything to the other. We haven't found the answer."

The land of marriage has this peculiarity, that strangers are desirous of inhabiting it, whilst its natural inhabitants would willingly be banished from thence.

MONTIGUE

Some people also feel that marriage is no longer necessary. Society has encouraged marriage for the care and protection of children, but individuals may marry for different reasons. Men have traditionally married for sex and women for economic security. In today's society the idea that sex is justified in the context of a love relationship decreases the importance of marriage for sex and the increasing economic independence of women removes that particular reason for marriage. A divorced woman who recently received her Ph.D. remarked, "For the past 11 years, I needed my husband for food and shelter. Now I am economically self-sufficient. For the first time, getting married can be a choice for me. And although I may change, I doubt I'll choose to remarry." Indeed, two researchers observed that occupational achievement among women is associated with remaining single (Mueller & Campbell, 1977).

Singlehood as a Stage

Instead of being a permanent choice, singlehood for some people is a stage between various life-style choices that are made throughout their lives. A not unusual pattern is for a person to experience singlehood, marriage, divorce (return to singlehood), living together, and remarriage. The decision to opt for any of these at any given time may be complex. Contributing to the selection of one alternative is the perception of the positive and negative consequences of doing so when compared with the other alternatives. The single person may be free but lonely and perceive marriage as worth the cost of lost freedom to gain companionship. The married person may be secure but bored and view singlehood with its variety as worth the cost of security. The person who lives with another may enjoy the spontaneity of "a relationship based on love, not law" but not like the lack of permanence of the relationship. Legitimizing the relationship with marriage may be worth the risk of losing some spontaneity.

CONSIDERATION • Decisions to end or maintain a specific relationship can be explained in terms of exchange theory. People enter and remain in relationships (or life-styles) only as long as the relationships and life-styles are evaluated by the individuals to be profitable (profit in exchange terms is rewards minus costs). "I know it sounds crazy," said one 40-year-old bachelor, "but I feel it's time for me to be married because the advantages of this freedom don't mean anything anymore."

• CONTRACT COHABITATION •

Some people want to remain single and to live with someone of the opposite gender. Although some want to live together in an emotional and marriage oriented relationship, others do not. In Chapter 7 we discuss living together in the usual sense. In this chapter we discuss contract cohabitation. Under this arrangement the individual simply hires someone as a companion. Edmund Van Deusen (1974), a California writer, did so, recalling, "My principal need was for someone to talk to . . . Second, I needed a warm body to go to bed with." He placed the following advertisement in the *Los Angeles Free Press*, interviewed several applicants, and selected the woman who best fit his job description:

> Free-lance writer looking for woman who would be interested in room, board, and $500 a month. Send name, phone number, and photo to Tom Smith, Box 1251, Laguna Beach, California 92652, (p. 25).

Contract Details

Contract cohabitation includes the following elements: (1) It is an eating, sleeping, and living arrangement between employer and employee, based on a written or unwritten employment contract. (2) All contract items, including salary, are defined by the employer and accepted in advance by the employee. (3) Free hours, annual vacations, and social or work activities outside the relationship are guaranteed by the terms of the contract. (4) Sex is expected but cannot be demanded or denied. (5) The employment contract can be canceled at any time by either party without reason or explanation.

An example of a job description for a contract cohabitation relationship follows:

> Specific Tasks—Light housekeeping, meal preparation, household shopping, estimated time per day: two hours. Companionship—Weekdays: 6:00 to 8:00 P.M.; Saturday: 3:00 P.M. on; Sunday: All day; Bedtime: Normally 11:00 P.M.; Night off: Wednesday; Vacation: One week with pay per year; Client entertaining: optional; Social entertaining: Required (Van Deusen, 1974, p. 111)

The philosophy behind contract cohabitation is that the best way to get what you want from an interpersonal relationship is to specify the expectations in advance and pay for it. But beyond the specific exchange of money and services is the capacity for a caring relationship that is not encumbered by the roles of husband and wife. Van Deusen writes:

> This leaves me free to cherish Elaine, [the first woman who became involved in Van Deusen's contract cohabitation], whom I have no need or desire to change. Why should I? In thirty days I may never see her again. I can enjoy her for who she is, and she can enjoy me in return. Neither of us is trying to force the other into a preconceived fantasy image. Neither of us feels possessive or possessed. Neither of us is depending on the other for self-image or identity. (p. 99)

An Evaluation

But what happened to Elaine? And how does Van Deusen evaluate contract cohabitation 10 years later? In a phone interview from his Laguna Beach home in 1984, Van Deusen shared the details:

> She was here for six years, which was a time of learning and growth for both of us. We both felt that the time had come for us to split. She was entering a young-grandmother role and wanted to devote more time to her family. I've got grandkids of my own (I'm 58) and didn't want to go through that again.
>
> In addition, my money had run out at the time. I am a writer and my income fluctuates tremendously. I paid her throughout the six years as we agreed but I had to cut back on expenses for a few months. We are still the best of friends.

During the six-year-period, for a year and a half, Van Deusen experimented with bringing another woman into the relationship. He paid her the same salary as Elaine and said they split the work. He commented:

> Two actually works better than one for me. Two people under contract cohabitation guarantees separateness. If there is just me and a woman, we're not too different from another monogamous unit in terms of what other people see and relate to. But if there are two women, that's different and people don't treat us like a traditional couple. In addition, by having two on the job, I'm not asking one person to be everything I need and want.
>
> It is also easier for two to share the work. I need coverage seven days a week. With two, one of them can always be "on duty," which gives the other a break. And since there is always employee turnover, having two provides a smoother transition. As one phases out, another phases in. It's my preferred arrangement . . . as long as I can afford it.

It is also a mistake to try to establish two parallel, identical relationships. Each person's needs, expectations, and contributions are too different. Triads have the "glue" of love to hold the threesome together. In my case, however, it seems to work better to treat each relationship as a separate entity.

Van Deusen offered some additional insights about contract cohabitation. First, he felt, six years is on the edge of being too long, while less than 12 months is too short. Between one and two years is best. As for salary, he said, "The amount of money doesn't seem to make the difference of a person getting into the groove as an employee in a contact cohabitation relationship. I have also had people stay here for free, but that doesn't work. You need at least a nominal salary to establish self-respect."

Most contractors are men. "I know of only one woman who has entered into a contract cohabitation relationship as an employer. The ads are placed predominately by men. But this should change as women move up the executive ladder."

What kind of women apply for contract cohabitation? "Our sexually liberated, me-generation, short-term commitment society has spawned a generation of women who are willing to become involved in contract cohabitation relationships. In fact, the women are more concerned about whether or not they will be turned on by me as a sexual companion rather than whether or not they will please me." According to Van Duesen, the woman most suited for contract cohabitation is goal oriented and has something she wants to do that is more important than any relationship. Contract cohabitation is basically an impersonal, businesslike arrangement—it is not relationship or commitment oriented.

CONSIDERATION • Van Deusen concludes that contract cohabitation, like all other life-style alternatives that involve another person, is something you have to work at. "But contract cohabitation has been good to me and the women who have become involved. You get to know someone very well and you avoid the entrapment of a love affair or marriage."

• COMMUNES •

Single individuals and married couples (with or without children) may choose a life-style that includes an array of interpersonal relationships and join a commune. Also referred to as an intentional community, a collective, or cooperative, a commune is a group consisting of three or more adults who live together by free choice rather than because of legal or blood ties. Whereas many groups have about six members, the Farm in Summertown, Tennessee, has more than 1,600 members.

Historical analysis has shown communal movements are not randomly distributed across time and space but flourish only at points of relatively sharp social and cultural discontinuity.

ANGELA AIDALA

CONSIDERATION • Specific information on more than 750 communes in the United States, Canada, and other countries is detailed in the 1983 Directory of Communities available from Communities, Box 426, Louisa, Va. 23093. The most extensive library on communes has been collected by the Center for Communal Studies on the Indiana State University, Evansville campus (8600 University Blvd., Evansville, Ind. 47712). These sources will be helpful in locating a commune with the values and life-style consistent with your interests.

The primary motivations for joining a commune are interpersonal and economic.

DATA • *It is estimated that there are a total of 2,500 communal groups in North America.* (Levine, 1984)

Types of Communes

Communes may be categorized as either rural or urban, with urban communes often clustering around universities. Membership in urban communes tends to be more fluid than in rural communes, which call for greater commitment. A commune member in Boston can move into a solo apartment at any time, whereas moving out is harder for the communard of rural Twin Oaks, in Louisa, Virginia.

In addition to the urban-rural dichotomy, there are a variety of other types of communes. Spiritual communes include such groups as the Amish, Abode of the Message, and Agahpay Fellowship. People join religious communes to share a spiritual experience with others. The Farm in Exhibit 5.2 is an example of a spiritual commune.

Ideological communes (Twin Oaks, Cold Mountain Farm) are committed to secular themes, such as behavioral psychology or Marxism. Those who join an ideological commune wish to participate in planning and implementing a miniature society consistent with specific ideological principles. Youth communes that do not fall into the hip or ideological categories are usually composed of young people who simply want to share the economic or interpersonal advantages of group living. Group marriage communes (the Family, Harrad West) have the primary goal of working out new styles of interpersonal and family relationships. Finally, communes for the elderly include the Share-A-Home Association in Winter Park, Florida. This group has a manager who oversees the day-to-day operation of the home. Under this arrangement, they can enjoy the companionship of each other without being bothered by the details of running a home, planning meals, etc.

Motivations for Joining a Commune

Interpersonal and economic motivations are primary in joining a commune. "I wanted to feel a connectedness to a variety of people, not just one," said one communard. "In marriage or in a living-together relationship, you're stuck with one other person. In a commune, you're not." Group living is also cheaper. Most communes have central dining facilities and large houses or dorms for inexpensive sleeping quarters.

Women often have another incentive for communal living—equality. Child-rearing is often considered a community task and is assignable to men as well as women. Household chores are also equally divided.

> I chose to live with a group of people I see being support for the personal changes I have been and expect to continue going through.
>
> A COMMUNE MEMBER

Problems of Communal Living

In spite of the potential benefits of communal living, there are also problems. These include lack of organization or structure, uncontrolled membership, determining division of labor, defining ownership, economic maintenance, and interpersonal conflicts.

ORGANIZATION OR STRUCTURE

There is a real difference among communes over the degree of organization they want. Communes that fail to organize their work and their decision-making tend to find that work stays undone. While earlier communes (like Oneida and the Shakers) were autocratically governed by church elders, many contemporary communes are less structured. Government and laws are rejected, as are leaders and rules (Kephart, 1982).

MEMBERSHIP

Regardless of the organizational framework a commune develops for itself, it must deal with the issue of who can be a member. Although some communes

THE FARM: A SPIRITUAL COMMUNE[*]

Located in Summertown, Tennessee (one hour south of Nashville), 1,600 people live in one of the most successful and enduring communes in America. Begun in 1971 under the leadership of Stephen Gaskin, the Farm is a spiritual community which emphasizes attunement to the "astral" (higher cosmic) level of human relationships and nature. The Buddhist regard for the sacredness of life and the unity of all spirits is an ideological theme of the commune.

Members
Of the 1,600 people on the Farm, about half are children and a third of those are adopted. As an outgrowth of the commune's belief in the sacredness of life, the Farm offers pregnant women the opportunity to have their babies there. If the mother does not want the child, the community offers to adopt it with the understanding that the mother can return to adopt it at any time.

The adults range in age from teenagers to middle age. Most come from privileged middle- and upper-class backgrounds. While many are educated, others are not, and some

come from poor southern rural communities. New members are welcome but must live in the commune and "soak" for a period of five months before making their pledge to the farm.

Finances
Joining implies giving all worldly goods and money to the commune. No outside bank accounts, property, or income are allowed. Food, clothing, and shelter are all provided through the Farm.

The commune's economy is based on work both outside the community on construction or agricultural crews or inside the community on such services as the bicycle shop, bakery, pottery shop, printshop, and birthing clinic. Of the 1,750 acres, 150 are used for growing crops to feed the communal members.

Sexuality
Permissiveness in the community is discouraged. Most of the adults in the commune are married and fidelity is a strongly held value. Male-female relationships are egalitarian although women tend to be more involved in childrearing than men.

Organization
While Stephen Gaskin is recognized as the

charismatic leader of the commune, he is not viewed as a dictator. Discussions regarding work assignments and various concerns of the commune are held at Sunday meditation. This is a communitywide meeting. The results are forwarded to the Council, a group of appointed people who help guide or organize the community.

Community Service
The Farm serves society though their "Plenty Network," which provides a variety of free services such as ambulances, health care, midwives, and agricultural advice to local people and third-world countries.

Joining
Further information about the Farm can be obtained from The Farm, Route 1, Box 197A, Summertown, Tenn. 38483.

[*]Excerpted from A. Rubissow, The Farm, *Communities: Journal of Cooperative Living*, April/May 1982, p. 9 et passim. Used by permission of Ariel Rubissow.

have an open door policy, most have membership requirements. A member of a commune in Chicago observed, "At first, anybody could join, and we soon found that anybody (including drunks, addicts, and criminal fugitives) did join. Our rules now include no hard drugs, no couples, no minors, and no children. Membership is still dependent on a unanimous vote of every member, which we take after the person has been here six months."

DIVISION OF LABOR
"Doing your own thing" rarely works in a commune because, for most people, peeling potatoes, washing dishes, and taking out the garbage isn't "their thing." Twin Oaks commune has a labor credit system whereby each member is expected to work 40 hours during a seven-day week, with labor credits assigned to each chore. The more undesirable the work, the greater the point value. Those who choose not to do their share of the work are allowed to goof off a few days in hopes they will be able "to get it together again." One communal member wanted to play his drums all day and avoid basic chores. After a "warning," he continued to play his drums and was asked to leave.

OWNERSHIP
Commune property is usually held in common. Land, houses, and in some cases, clothes belong to everyone. Problems occur when individual members try to claim as their own what belongs to the commune. In one group a couple became upset with other members of the commune and took a bench they had made with them when they left the commune.

ECONOMIC MAINTENANCE
A commune must have economic resources to survive, and these are often somewhat unreliable. Some typical resources include a large garden, welfare checks, windfalls (inheritance, birthday checks, gifts), animals (chickens for eggs, goats for milk), barter (exchange of vegetables and goat milk for grain, hardware, or clothes), gathering (blackberries, plums, blueberries, strawberries), and scavenging (looking for discarded food in alleys behind grocery stores). Whereas these sustenance sources are more characteristic of rural communes, urban communes survive through members who have "straight" jobs, deal dope, play in bands, or offer a service like building construction or auto repair. In some cases, one or two members will support the entire group. A university teacher who gave his check to the commune each month was asked, "How do you feel about being the entire economic base of your commune?" He replied, "I don't mind giving all my money to the commune. My only regret is that I can't be here with them during the day to help them build our house." But two months after this individual left the commune, it folded.

INTERPERSONAL CONFLICTS
The problem in communal living for many communards is interpersonal. Whereas the marriage relationship requires a person to accommodate his or her needs to one other individual, a commune necessitates an adjustment to several people. Conflicts over what food to eat, what time to serve it, what music to play at what volume, and what temperature to keep the main house are examples.

Stability of Communes

The combination of problems common to communes makes their survival difficult.

DATA • *In one study of 52 communes, only 20 lasted two and a half years.* (Jansen, 1980) *In another study, the researcher observed that of more than 400 individuals who had left home abruptly to join a commune, over 90 percent returned home within two years.* (Levine, 1984)

> CONSIDERATION • Commenting on the reasons most communes have relatively short lives, one researcher (Gardner, 1978) said, "Community requires giving up a certain measure of individual freedom and letting people penetrate our lives. But the children of prosperity were trained to think they were special, and their parents' values of achievement, individualism, and privacy were more deeply planted than they knew. In many ways, they had trained incapacities for the communal experience. The deep incapacity of all, perhaps, was the inability to put group success above individual destiny" (p. 251).

Most communes die, but some seem eternal. The Farm (Summertown, Tennessee) and Twin Oaks (Louisa, Virginia) are now in their second decades. One explanation for the survival of Twin Oaks is planning. Every year Twin Oaks sculpts an economic framework for the next 11 months. A member of the commune (Stewart, 1984) wrote:

> Many people view long-range planning as an attempt to achieve control over an organic and complex reality by reducing it to numbers and labels. The truth is that long-range planning, in some form of implicit or explicit thinking about the future, is an effective means by which we can take part in shaping our way of life. (p. 41)

We have reviewed some of the basic life-style choices available to us. In assessing the degree to which you want to experience each of these life-styles, you might take the Life-Style Preference Inventory.

• TRENDS •

Marriage will continue to be the dominant life-style choice for most Americans. Its lure of companionship, commitment, and economic security seems to offer more than the alternatives. Although some people may delay getting married for educational or career reasons, there is no evidence of a major trend away from marriage.

Contract cohabitation has not attracted a large following and will probably continue to be a rare form of singlehood. Unlike contract cohabitation, communal living has historical precedents (Shakers, Oneida, Amish) and is the life-style of about a quarter of a million people. However, for an individual to be happy in a commune, she or he must reconcile personal and community goals. The existence of more than 750 communes worldwide suggests that a number of people are not only capable of but enjoy this merging of individual and group goals.

No matter how many communes anybody invents, the family always comes back.

MARGARET MEAD

LIFE-STYLE PREFERENCE INVENTORY

Below is a list of life-style choices. To indicate your preference, assign a number from 0 to 10 for each life-style. Zero indicates no desire to experience this life-style, whereas 10 indicates a strong desire.

Life-Style	Preference	Life-Style	Preference
Sexual		*Children*	
Heterosexual	_____	None	_____
Homosexual	_____	One	_____
Bisexual	_____	Two	_____
		Three	_____
Singlehood		Four or more	_____
Single until meet "right" person	_____		
Single until become career established	_____	*Live Together*	
		To further assess relationship	_____
Single forever	_____	As a prelude to marriage	_____
		As a permanent alternative to marriage	_____
Marriage		For economic convenience	_____
Traditional roles	_____		
Shared roles	_____	*Housing*	
One income or career	_____	Live alone	_____
Two incomes or careers	_____	Live with someone of same gender	_____
Sexually monogamous	_____		
Sexually open	_____	Live with someone of opposite gender	_____
Group marriage	_____	Live in commune	_____
		Live in contract cohabitation arrangement	_____

Based on the preferences you selected, write a brief description of the life-style you prefer. If you are involved in a relationship, you might ask your partner to indicate her or his preferences for each of the life-styles.

• SUMMARY •

Traditionally, marriage has existed to replenish society with socialized members, to regulate sexual behavior, and to stabilize adult personalities. But the problem of overpopulation and the availability of convenient, effective contraception have undermined the first two functions. Emotional support remains the primary function of marriage.

The decision to marry involves assessing the advantages and disadvantages. Marriage offers a potentially intense primary relationship over time and avoids the potential loneliness associated with singlehood. But singlehood offers freedom to do as one wishes and avoids the obstacles to personal fulfillment associated with marriage. For many Americans, the decision to marry or be single is not permanent. While many singles contemplate marriage, many marrieds ponder whether they should stay married.

Older individuals (primarily men) who have the economic resources sometimes choose contract cohabitation. This arrangement involves an employer–employee relationship in which behavioral expectations are specified, agreed to, and paid for.

Communal living is another life-style option. There are hundreds of communes to select from, including those that emphasize religion, ideology, or group marriage. The advantages of communal arrangements include living with several people in an intimate environment and sharing expenses.

Marriage will continue to be the dominant choice for most Americans.

Questions for Reflection

1. Which life-style do you feel offers the most benefits? Why?
2. How would you defend your involvement in each of the life-style choices to your grandparents?
3. What do you think will be the dominant life-style in the year 2000?

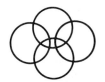

·CHOICES·

Because our society is becoming more tolerant of alternative life-styles, a number of choices are realistic options for you. The basic options and issues to consider follow.

IS MARRIAGE FOR YOU?

The decision to marry or not might be based on the perceived consequences (positive and negative) of the respective life-styles. The primary benefits of marriage include increased companionship, security, parenthood, and the development of a shared history. Although cohabitants may have made an emotional commitment to each other, spouses additionally have made a social and legal commitment. The blend of these commitments result in married people feeling more secure with each other and their relationship. "When your partner wants to marry you," said one male, "you know she is serious about you. Otherwise, she could disappear the next day and you might never see her again."

Marriage also furnishes the socially appropriate context for children. Although some individuals opt for single parenthood, most want to be married when they become parents. Persons who are not married and who choose parenthood will have a more difficult time than those who are married.

The experience of parenthood is one of numerous events spouses share over the course of their life together. Partners who don't get divorced have 50 or so years of memories. One 40-year-old husband said, "My wife and I have been seeing a movie a week since we began dating more than 20 years ago. We have already seen close to 1,000 movies together and some of them have become a part of us. We still enjoy *Casablanca*." Neil Simon in his play *Chapter Two* likened a relationship to the alphabet. People who have just met are in the As and Bs, whereas those who have known each other for years are in the Rs and Ss. One of the frustrating aspects of divorce is that we lose the shared history with a person and must begin at the As and Bs with a new person.

The disadvantages of marriage include loss of freedom, an increased risk of becoming a divorcee or widow, and financial responsibility for others. The person who travels fastest, travels alone. If you have a career goal or want career success, the involvement of another person in your life can hinder your achievement of that goal. Not only may your career mobility be restricted, your freedom to become involved sexually with others will be eliminated. "If you want to be married, you have to give up other women," said one spouse. "You can't have it both ways."

Since at least half of all brides and grooms in the United States become divorced, by avoiding marriage they avoid the traumatic experience of divorce. In addition, since most women outlive their husbands by eight or so years, most wives have inadvertently signed up for several years in the widow role.

(continued)

Financial responsibility for children, for homes, and for all the things married people buy is part of the marital package. Some people don't like to get in debt or to be obligated to pay for things someone else (the spouse) wants. If you marry, you will incur the financial obligations of your partner and vice versa.

The decision to marry may not be a one-time decision. Many of us will make the basic decision of marriage versus singlehood many times throughout our lives. The single decide whether to marry, and the married decide whether to stay married. For the divorced, the question is whether to remain single or to remarry.

IS SINGLEHOOD FOR YOU?

Singlehood is not a unidimensional concept. There are many styles of singlehood from which to choose. As a single person you may devote your time and energy to career, travel, privacy, heterosexual or homosexual relationships, living together, communal living, or a combination of these experiences over time. The essential difference between traditional marriage and singlehood is the personal and legal freedom to do as you wish.

But although singlehood offers freedom, the issues of loneliness, money, education, and identity need to be dealt with.

Loneliness

For some singles, being alone is a desired and enjoyable experience. "The major advantage of being single," expressed one 29-year-old man, "is that I don't have to deal with another person all the time. I like my privacy." Henry David Thoreau, who never married, spent two years alone on 14 acres bordering Walden Pond. He said of the experience, "I love to be alone. I never found the companion that was so companionable as solitude."

Others view solitude as an opportunity to become deeply involved in their work. A single-by-choice woman artist remarked, "Marriage would interfere with what I most enjoy, my work. I am most creative when I am alone. Fixing supper for someone else, changing a baby's diapers, or having to talk to someone else every night would be dreadful chores to me." Steve Martin said in one of his talk-show interviews, "I like to be alone and to be private."

Still others live with someone to minimize feelings of loneliness. But the choice of who one lives with may be important. In a study of 22,000 people who were living alone, those who had lived with their parents said they were more lonely than those who were living alone (Shaver & Rubenstein, 1980).

The strategy most singles use to avoid feelings of loneliness is to develop a "network of human relationships that meet their needs for intimacy, sharing, and continuity" (Stein, 1981, p. 16). "Marriage is a sustained friendship with one other person," said a single person. "But marriage is also confining. So I enjoy two very close friendships but don't have the 'marriage' problems with either of them."

Economic Self-Sufficiency

Having social relationships or developing an enjoyment for being alone are not the only prerequisites to successful single living. It takes money. Money is less likely to be a problem for a man who has been socialized to expect to work all of his life and who usually earns about a third more than a woman. A woman who decides not to marry is giving up the potentially larger income her husband might earn. Also, both men and women who decide not to marry give up the possibility of a two-income family.

Education

Since good incomes are often associated with higher education, the person considering singlehood as a life-style might stay in school. Women completing four years of high school can expect to earn an average of $381,000 in their lifetime, about 27 percent less than the estimate of $523,000 for women completing four years of college. For men, the figures are $861,000 and $1,190,000 (U.S. Department of Commerce, 1983). "It earns to learn" is a phrase that educators have used to promote the importance of education.

Personal Identity

Single people must establish an identity—a role—that helps to define who they are and what they do. Spouses eat together, sleep together, party together, and cooperate economically. They mesh their lives into a cooperative relationship that gives them the respective identity of being on their own marital team. On the basis of their spousal roles, we can predict what they will be doing most of the time. For example, on Sunday at noon they are most likely to be having lunch together. Not only can we predict what they will be doing, their roles as spouses tell them what they will be doing—interacting with each other.

The single person must find other roles. A meaningful career is the avenue most singles pursue. A career provides structure, relationships with others, and a strong sense of identity ("I am an interior decorator"). To the degree that singles find meaning in their work, they are successful in establishing autonomous identities independent of the marital role.

In evaluating the single lifestyle, to what degree, if any, do you feel that loneliness would be a problem for you? What are your educational and career plans to ensure a launch into your chosen field and the standard of living you desire?

The old idea that you can't be happy unless you are married is no longer credible. Whereas marriage will be the first option for some, it will be the last option for others. One 76-year-old single-by-choice woman said, "A husband would have to be very special to be better than no husband at all."

IS CONTRACT COHABITATION FOR YOU?

Being an employer in a contract cohabitation relationship requires that you live in a relatively large city (to avoid ostracism) and that you have the money to pay for the services (domestic, emotional, sexual) of a person or persons. Van Deusen's experience makes it clear that such relationships require social skills, insight into relationship dynamics, and tolerance for change. Unless these characteristics are true of you, the outcome of a successful cohabitation relationship may be less positive than anticipated.

· Chapter 6 ·

DATING

CONTENTS

Dating in Historical Perspective

Contemporary Functions of Dating

Dating Realities

Dating Problems

Mate Selection

Self-Assessment: **Needs Assessment Inventory**

Self-Assessment: **Assets and Liabilities Inventory**

Choices

An ideal wife is any woman who has an ideal husband.

BOOTH
TARKINGTON

You will recall that a central goal of marriage from the viewpoint of society is to bond two people together who will produce, protect, nurture, and socialize children to be productive members of society. To ensure that this goal is accomplished, society must make some institutional provision for sexually mature females and males to meet, interact, and pair off in permanent unions for eventual parenthood. The dating institution serves this function and guides woman-man interaction through an orderly process toward mate selection.

There are different patterns of dating—in groups and in nonexclusive and exclusive relationships. Some opposite-gender members date by "hanging around" and "getting together" in various size groups; others prefer one-to-one relationships. The latter may be "open"—each partner may date others—or "closed"—the partners date each other exclusively. Such exclusive dating may or may not be oriented toward marriage.

Even pairings that lead to marriage are not permanent. Rather, individuals are likely to pair with a number of others over the course of their lifetime. Also, the criteria for choosing a partner at one stage in life may be different from the criteria at another time. One divorced man said:

> The first time around I wanted someone who was a visual knockout. I married a real beauty and because we argued all the time, she began to look like Cyclops to me. The next time I will choose in reference to similar values and goals because I've found that looks become much less important after you get the person home.

After reviewing how the Industrial Revolution changed the dating relationships of women and men, we explore the various problems women and men experience in dating. Since dating is the primary mechanism of mate selection, we examine the various cultural, sociological, psychological, and sociobiological reasons you may be attracted to a particular person.

• DATING IN HISTORICAL PERSPECTIVE •

In colonial America a man who wanted to marry a woman had to ask the father's permission to do so. The following is a letter from (William Byrd around 1705) to Daniel Parke asking his permission to marry his daughter (Woodfin & Tinling, 1942):

> Since my arrival in this country I have had the honour to be acquainted with your daughters, and was infinitely surpriz'd to find young ladys with their accomplishments in Virginia. This surprize was soon improv'd into a passion for the youngest for whom I have all the respect and tenderness in the world. However I think it my duty to intreat your approbation before I proceed to give her the last testimony of my affection. And the young lady her self whatever she may determine by your consent will agree to nothing without it. If you can entertain a favourable opinion of my person, I dont question but my fortune may be sufficient to make her happy, especially after it has been assisted by your bounty. If you shall vouchsafe to approve of this undertaking I shall indeavour to recommend myself by all the dutiful regards to your Excellency and all the marks of kindness to your daughter. Nobody knows better than your self how impatient lovers are, and for that reason I hope youll be as speedy as possible in your determination which I passionately beg may be in favour of your & c.

The Industrial Revolution

The transition from a courtship system controlled by parents to the relative freedom experienced today occurred in response to a number of social changes. The most basic change was the Industrial Revolution, which began in England in the middle of the eighteenth century. No longer were women needed exclusively in the home to spin yarn, make clothes, and process food from garden to table. Commercial industries had developed to provide these services, and women transferred their activities in these areas from the home to the factory. The result was to place them in frequent contact with male workers.

Female involvement in factory work decreased parental control, since parents were unable to dictate the extent to which their offspring could interact with those they met at work. Hence values in mate selection shifted from the parents to the children. In the past, parents had approved or disapproved of a potential mate on the basis of their own values: Was the person from "good stock"? Did the man have property or a respectable trade? Did the woman have basic domestic skills? In contrast to these parental concerns, the partners focused more on love feelings.

Parental Influence Today

As a result of the Industrial Revolution and the gradual loss of parental control, young women not only became acquainted with young men outside the family circle but also felt free to look at them as possible mates. Then with the development of the automobile in the twentieth century came a radical change in the conditions of social interaction of unmarried men and women. Couples could now escape from their respective parents to do as they wished. Movies provided an additional place to share an evening away from friends. Within one generation, courtship had changed from parental to couple control. But parents still try to influence the person their offspring dates and marries. This is especially true of daughters.

DATA • *In a random sample of 334 university students, 60 percent of the women compared with 40 percent of the men said their parents had tried to influence the people they dated.* (Knox & Wilson, 1981)

Both the kind and amount of parental influence were approved of by the offspring. More than 80 percent (women more than men) said it was important to

Today there are few barriers to meeting a person of the opposite gender.

them to date the kinds of people their parents approved of. "I may not like it sometimes," said one math major. "But my parents are usually right when it comes to knowing who's good for me."

> CONSIDERATION • Parental interference sometimes drives dating partners to be together more often—even to marry. If your parents don't want you to date someone, try to separate the issue of why they disapprove of the person from the issue of whether you can see your partner. You can date and marry whomever you like. In a power struggle with your parents, you will win. The more important concern is why do they object? Your parents know you fairly well, love you, and probably have your best interests in mind. You may still decide to go against their wishes (it is your life), but do so because you genuinely disagree with their perceptions and concerns, not because you want to show them you can marry whom you want whether they like it or not.

For the older unmarried adult or the divorced person, parental influence is less intense. "I'm really on my own when it comes to getting involved with someone," remarked a recently separated person. "It's not that my parents don't care about me; it's just that they feel so removed from what I'm doing."

Aside from direct interference, parents may have a more subtle influence on the dating behavior of their offspring. In a study (Booth et al., 1984) that compared the dating behavior of individuals whose parents were divorced with those whose parents were still married to each other, the former were dating more frequently than the latter. The researchers suggested that the offspring may be modeling on the dating behavior of their parents.

• CONTEMPORARY FUNCTIONS OF DATING •

Since most people regard dating or "getting together" as a natural part of getting to know someone else, the functions of dating are sometimes overlooked. There are at least five—confirmation of a social self, recreation, companionship, socialization, and mate selection.

Confirmation of a Social Self

It's what you learn after you know it all that counts.

JOHN WOODEN

One of the ways we come to be who we are is through interaction with others who hold up social mirrors in which we see ourselves and get feedback on how we are doing. When you are on a first date with a person, you are continually trying to assess how that person sees you (Does he or she like me? Will he or she want to be with me again?). When the person gives you positive feedback through speech and gesture, you feel good about yourself and tend to view yourself in positive terms. Dating provides a context for confirmation of a strong self-concept in terms of how you perceive your effect on other people.

Recreation

Dating, hanging around, or getting together is fun. These are things we do with our peers, away from our parents, and we select the specific activities because

Many couples combine work and play in their dating.

we enjoy them. "I get tired of studying and being a student all day," a straight-A major in journalism said. "Going out at night with my friends to meet guys really clears my head. It's an exciting contrast to the drudgery of writing term papers."

Companionship

A major motivation for dating is companionship. The impersonal environment of a large university makes a secure dating relationship very appealing. "My last two years have been the happiest ever," remarked a senior in interior design. "But it's because of the involvement with my fiancé. During my freshman and sophomore years I felt alone. Now I feel loved, needed, and secure with my partner."

Some students prefer an exclusive relationship to casual dating. One physics major remarked, "I've had it with trying to get all the dates I can. They turn out to be like a revolving door; I have to tell the same stories, act the same superficial way, and read the same script for the first several dates. With one person, I can relate in a more open, relaxed way."

Socialization

Before puberty boys and girls interact primarily with their own gender. An individual may be laughed at if he or she shows an interest in someone of the opposite gender. Even when boy-girl interaction becomes the norm at puberty, neither gender may know what is expected of them. Dating offers the experience of learning how to initiate conversation and the opportunity to develop an array of skills in human relationships such as listening and expressing empathy. It also permits an individual to try out different role patterns like dominance or submission and to assess the "feel" and comfort level of each.

Sexual socialization is also a part of dating. Learning how to become physically close to another and to experience intimate encounters with different people is a typical pattern. "People make love differently—they hold you differently and have different preferences," said a drama major.

Mate Selection

Finally, dating may serve to pair off two people for marriage. For those who want to get married, dating is a process of finding a person who has a similar agenda and the desired characteristics.

> CONSIDERATION • Which dating function is most important will vary from person to person and for a particular person over time. "I've gone full circle," said one banking employee. "Dating used to be for fun which led to companionship and marriage. But I'm recently divorced and am not interested in marriage. I'm dating just for the fun again with no goal whatsoever of getting involved with anyone."
>
> But another person said, "The big time-have a party-get drunk-fun aspect of dating is getting old to me. I'm bored being in crowded smokey rooms listening to loud music. I want a relationship, a companion. I'm ready for marriage."

• DATING REALITIES •

Dating begins with finding a partner—and not just any partner but the one that you want. After discussing various mechanisms for meeting someone, we examine what people look for in the people they date and what they do on dates.

Finding a Partner

Just as people have a variety of motives for seeking a dating partner, there are a number of mechanisms for doing so—through friends, independently, through magazines or newspapers, computers, and video cassettes.

FRIENDS
Table 6.1 shows how students in one study met the person they were currently dating. Their responses emphasize the importance of same-gender friendships in meeting new dating partners. The message seems to be, "When you don't have a date (and want one) go with a friend." Both you and your friend are connections to dating partners for each other.

Table 6.1 How 334 University Students Met Their Dating Partner*

WAYS OF MEETING	FEMALE	MALE
Through a friend	33%	32%
Party	22	13
At work	12	5
Class	6	9
Other	27	41

*Female: N = 227; male: N = 107.
Source: Knox & Wilson, 1981.

INDEPENDENTLY

Since it is traditionally assumed that the man will initiate dating relationships, 200 women in a courtship and marriage class were asked, "How would you go about getting a man to ask you out?" Most said they would either ask a friend to introduce him or engage him in conversation. Others mentioned that "being friendly," "smiling at him," and "being where he'll be" were effective ways of encouraging a man to ask for a date. Some said they would ask a man outright for a date. "I would just call him up, tell him I'm in his history class and ask him out," said a sports medicine major. Exhibit 6.1 suggests a way you can meet anyone on your campus.

MAGAZINES AND NEWSPAPERS

Because two people suited for each other may never meet by chance, formal mate selection networks have developed to make such people aware of each other. The following advertisements are typical of those designed to seek a particular type of partner or to offer one's self for someone who may be looking. They might appear in national magazines such as *Intro* and the *Mother Earth News* or in local newspapers.

> MALE, 32, attractive, professional looking for single, white, female, for fun and frolic. Must be herpless but not hopeless, helpless, or hapless. Mike, P.O. Box 24, Arcola, In. 46704
>
> •
>
> LADY, 28, seeks gentle Paul Bunyan for loving, working, the rest of my life. Nancy, Route 2, Box 54B Republic, Wash. 99166
>
> •
>
> SINGLE mother, 34, 135, two biracial adopted children, former model now technical writer, humorous, handy, desires corespondence with same type person. Mary Mitchener, 228 Culpepper Ave., Dothan, Ala. 35226

Whereas these ads give the information necessary for the parties to contact one another, other magazines function as go-betweens in which parties can contact each other only through the publisher of the magazine. "An interested reader makes contact by writing letters in response to one or more advertisements. Each letter is sealed and identified by a number. These are then mailed to the publisher who, for a fee, addresses and forwards each letter" (Jedlicka, 1980). Suzanne Douglas, publisher of *Intro* magazine says one advertisement results in an average of 14 replies. As to the truthfulness of the advertisements,

HOW TO MEET ANYONE ON YOUR CAMPUS

The following suggestion is a way for you to meet anyone on your campus.

Turn to page 70 on which you will see the Love Attitudes Scale. Hand the book to someone you are intereted in meeting and say, "I'm enrolled in a marriage course on campus and have been requested to ask a person of the opposite sex to take this love test. Would you take a couple of minutes and complete it for me?"

Persons who are interested in some level of interaction with you will agree to complete the form. They may ask you questions about it ("What does the third statement mean?"), establish eye contact, and indicate (through smiles and gestures) a willingness to interact with you.

Not all persons will be receptive. The goal is to meet someone, not for him or her to fall in love with you at first sight. If you ask 20 people to complete the inventory, expect only one to show an interest in you beyond the inventory. But you only need one. The dating world can be a very rejecting place—expect to meet some frogs before you find the prince or princess.

she said that men tend to lie about their age and women tend to lie about their weight.

DATING SERVICE ORGANIZATIONS

A number of organizations exist for the purpose of finding mates for their members. Although many of these are for the general public, some are specialized. Examples include Jewish Dating Service (to match Jewish singles), Preferred Singles (to match singles who are overweight), Chocolate Singles (to match black singles) and Execumatch. The latter, for a fee of $100,000, finds a marriage partner for the wealthy.

COMPUTERS

Computers can figure out all kinds of problems, except the things in the world that just don't add up.

JAMES MAGARY

The computer revolution has introduced another way to meet a dating partner. Campus bulletin boards and newspapers often feature advertisements for computer-matched dates. Titles such as "Pick A Date," "Computer Match," and "Why Be Lonely?" are followed by the promise to find the "right" date for the person who completes the questionnaire. The information requested is designed to help the computer match respondents on the basis of social background, personal attitudes, and complementary needs. The individual's profile is matched with similar profiles in the computer and he or she is given a list of several names, usually three.

The suitability of the partners for each other will depend on how accurately they completed the questionnaire. For example, individuals may indicate they are more physically attractive than they actually are for fear that otherwise they may be paired with the son or daughter of Frankenstein's monster.

Computers may also serve as an initial contact between two people. Compuserve Information Services of Columbus, Ohio, offers the CB Simulator, which allows individuals with home computers to use any of its 36 channels to "talk" with another subscriber. In effect, individuals sit at their respective computer terminals and send written communications to each other. (If more than two users at a time want to talk privately, they can scramble their messages by a mutually agreed-upon code.) "I first met my spouse by conversing with her through written messages on the computer," said a computer hacker. "Soon we set up a lunch date and were married about a year later. Some of my friends also talk with a girlfriend or boyfriend through their computer."

VIDEO CASSETTES

The newest method of partner finding is having yourself interviewed on videotape and letting others watch your cassette in exchange for your watching those already on file. If you like what you see, you can contact the person directly for a date (and vice versa).

Great Resources (New York), Great Expectations (Los Angeles), and Couple Company (Boston) offer to make a videotape of you and permit you to view the tapes of others. The price at Resources is $350 for a six-month membership. One woman reported that for her money she received 40 invitations and sent out nine in the six months she was a member (Kellogg, 1982).

CONSIDERATION • Although some people view finding dating partners through magazines, computers, or video services embarrassing, others regard it as an adventure. Some even feel it is easier than random dating, as it is possible to prescreen a large number of individuals who have the desired qualities rather than spend money on dinner to find out that the person smokes or loves cats and you don't. These relatively new forms of finding a partner should be considered as viable alternatives.

Characteristics of Desired Partner

Regardless of the mechanism for recruiting a dating partner, men and women seem to emphasize different qualities. Physical beauty heads the list for most men. Somehow most men assume if their partner is beautiful whatever problems that may occur in the relationship can be worked out (or would be worth working out).

Women are also concerned about the physical appearance of their partners but less so than men. Honesty, consideration, respect, and a good personality are priority characteristics for most women. One nurse said, "I've had a lot of good-looking guys lie to me to get to me sexually so I'm not as intersted in their looking like Tom Selleck as I used to be. He's got to be attractive to me, but good communication and honesty with him are more important."

Unmarried college students typically look for good looks in a dating partner. Older persons who are divorced and dating again are less likely to emphasize physical appearance. "Once you live with a person for years at a time, your per-

Beauty is a quality, not a form; a content, not an arrangement.

IRVING HOWE

Most males list physical attractiveness as a very important characteristic in a desired partner.

ception of them is colored by how you feel about them," said a separated post office employee. "If you're upset with your partner all the time, the person will look like ET to you no matter how beautiful you thought he or she was in courtship."

Dating Activities

There is considerable variation in the places college students go on dates, the topics they discuss, and the degree to which their activities include sex and drugs. In one study more than 300 students in a random sample revealed their dating experiences (Knox & Wilson, 1981).

Going out to eat, to a football game (the data were collected during football season), to a party and back to his or her room was the typical agenda for an evening of dating. For those who didn't do all of these, eating out and going back to his or her place seemed to be the most important. Going to concerts and movies were also important.

Regardless of where they were, "our relationship" was the most frequent topic of conversation. About a third of the respondents reported that this topic dominated their talk. Though less frequent, school and friends were other topics of conversation. Sex was discussed less than 5 percent of the time.

More than half of the students said they drank alcohol on their last date; fewer reported using marijuana. One-quarter of the men and 20 percent of the women said they smoked marijuana on their last date. Cocaine, although less frequently used than alcohol and marijuana, is also a part of campus life. Alcohol remains the predominant drug on campus.

This society seems to have swallowed the notion that there is a chemical solution for all problems, including the problem of how to spend one's spare time.

JOEL FORT

He could have given us a lot more laughs, but nooooooooooo.

ANONYMOUS
SIGN LEFT ON
GRAVE OF JOHN
BELUSHI

• DATING PROBLEMS •

Dating can sometimes involve problems. One study sought to identify dating problems from the viewpoint of 227 college women and 107 men in a random sample (Knox & Wilson, 1983).

The Woman's View

Table 6.2 lists the most common problems these college women experienced on their dates.

UNWANTED SEXUAL PRESSURE

Unwanted pressure to engage in sexual behavior was the most frequent problem reported by women students. Almost one-fourth felt that men wanted to move the relationship toward sex too quickly. "How quickly he can get his hand in my blouse and up my skirt is what every guy I date seems to have in the front of his brain," said one student. "Too quickly" is usually defined as before an emotional relationship has developed. "I can't get physical with a guy unless I care about him and I know he cares about me," recalled another female. "It just doesn't feel right to do sex with a guy I'm not involved with."

The dilemma expressed by many of the women was not wanting to have too much sex too soon in the relationship but showing enough interest in the man so he would ask her out again. A related concern was getting him to slow down on his sexual advances without hurting his feelings.

Women differed in how they reacted to a sexually aggressive man on dates. Most told their date to "stop it," put their hands on his and moved him away. "You have to be serious when you tell a guy to stop or he'll keep right on," said one education major.

Table 6.2   **Dating Problems Experienced by 227 University Women**

PROBLEMS	PERCENTAGE
Unwanted pressure to engage in sexual behavior	23
Places to go	22
Communication with date	20
Sexual misunderstandings	13
Money	9

Source: Knox & Wilson, 1983.

Other students went along with what their dates wanted to do sexually even though it was not what they preferred. "It seemed important to him, and I knew it wouldn't kill me, so we left the party early and went back to his place. I wanted to stay at the party, but it wasn't worth fighting over."

Still other students kept their distance and ignored sexual advances. "I acted like I didn't know he was hustling me and I kept away from him," recalled a parks and recreation major.

PLACES TO GO

Almost as frequent as the problem of sexual aggressiveness was that of where to go on dates. Eating out was the typical beginning of a date, but what to do afterward seemed to be a problem for about 20 percent of the women. "There isn't much to do in this town—seeing a movie and going back to his place are nice but that gets old after awhile," one student said. "And sometimes the man doesn't dance, drink, or have a car so it limits the options of things you can do."

The intensity of the problem of where to go and what to do seemed to depend on the couple's relationship. For those involved in a mutual, escalating love relationship, "places to go" didn't seem to be as much of a problem. "When we're together, it doesn't matter where we are," said an engaged woman.

COMMUNICATION

Regardless of where the couple spent their time, talking with their partner was a problem for about a fifth of the women. A major concern was trust. As already mentioned, honesty is the most important quality college women look for in their dating partners.

Knowing what to say and how to say it were other communication concerns. Part of the uneasiness grew out of the different levels of interest in the relationship of the respective partners. "I didn't want to get too involved with him so I didn't tell him anything about myself. It was very awkward to keep the conversation on safe subjects like classes and his fraternity."

Jealousy was also a problem. "When I know he's out with someone else the nights he's not with me, I boil with anger," said one woman. "And when I see him having a beer with her at a local bar, I want to strangle him (and her)."

OTHER PROBLEMS

"Sexual misunderstandings" was a dating problem for 10 percent of the women students. Accidently leading a man on when you really don't want to have intercourse is an example. One woman explained that she had been very affectionate with her date throughout the evening: "we danced closely and I was thoroughly enjoying being with him. But he interpreted my affection as a desire to have intercourse. I didn't and the evening ended in a terrible argument."

Money was also viewed as a problem on dates by 10 percent of the women students. "Sometimes it gets so bad," said one sophomore, "we eat out of cans heated on the hot plate in my dorm room. We go to the free campus movies and drink a lot of beer at happy hour prices. Sometimes we would just like a few bucks so we could do something different."

Another aspect of the money problem on dates was who pays. The typical pattern was for the man to pay for everything the first few dates. After that, and from time to time, the woman would pick up the tab for both of them. "I know

The older I grow, the more I listen to people who don't say much.

GERMAIN G.
GLIDDEN

he has a lot of money at the first of the month when he gets paid. But by the second or third week, that's gone so I start paying for things."

Some women said they would always pay for their own expenses on dates. "A guy buys you a beer and he thinks he owns you. If he takes you out to eat, he expects sex later, so I just pay as I go and avoid feeling obligated."

The Man's View

The most common problems experienced by 107 college males on their dates are outlined in Table 6.3.

COMMUNICATION

"Communication with date" was the major problem for a third of the men. "I never know what to say," said one man. "If I ask her a lot of questions, she tells me I am interrogating her. If I don't ask her questions, she says I'm not interested. If I talk a lot and tell stories, she thinks I don't care what she has to say. If I don't talk much, she says I'm boring—so what am I supposed to do?" (Communication is discussed in detail in Chapter 11).

Others complained that they felt anxious and nervous when they knew the conversation was dragging. "After awhile you run out of small talk about the weather and your classes. When the dialogue dies, its awful," expressed one senior.

Some communication concerns decreased after the first few dates with the same person. "After I get to know a girl, I feel comfortable being with her and less self-conscious about what I say. The communication seems to flow more smoothly with someone you know," recalled an engaged male.

SHYNESS

A related problem is shyness, mentioned by 20 percent of the men. Some felt uncomfortable with what they perceived as responsibility for everything. One man said, "I'm supposed to call her up, think of intelligent or cute things to say, know how to read her mind, and ensure that she has a good time—give me a break!"

Other men said they did not meet people well and felt particularly shy the first part of the first date. "I really get nervous and feel awkward," commented a basketball player.

Table 6.3 Dating Problems Experienced by 107 University Men

PROBLEMS	PERCENTAGE
Communication with date	35
Places to go	23
Shyness	20
Money	17
Honesty/openness	8

Source: Knox & Wilson, 1983.

Like women, men also said places to go and money were problems. The men said they got tired of going to the same places. Also, although lack of money was a problem for almost one in 10 men, no man said that who pays was a problem. It is true that role relationships in our society are becoming more flexible and women are more often paying for expenses on dates, yet it seems that men still accept paying for expenses as part of their role.

Honesty and openness were also problems for about one in 10 of the male respondents. How much to tell how soon were concerns. One man said he didn't want to get hurt so he kept a close guard on what he said. There was also the feeling that neither partner knew what the other was thinking and that attempts to get the other to open up were frustrating. "She just sat there all night and didn't say a word unless I would ask a question," mused an anthropology major.

The reports of these college students suggest that women and men are experiencing the same dating event differently. Almost a quarter of the females were frustrated by the necessity of warding off sexually aggressive males, but only 2 percent of the men were troubled by women being sexually aggressive.

While women are coping with unwanted sexual advances on dates, men are struggling to get and keep communication going on dates. Also, they feel much more shy than the women they date. Twenty percent of the men said that shyness was a problem on dates in contrast to only 5 percent of the women. This situation is a curious contrast in perceptions. University women view university men as sexually aggressive, but university men view themselves as shy.

CONSIDERATION • What is needed is more openness about what the respective partners are feeling. The woman might let the man know she is turned off by sexual aggressiveness and turned on by behaviors that are more personally focused. The man might stop taking complete responsibility for "everything working out fine" and relax, which may reduce his expectation that communication flow in a certain way. Lowered anxiety and expectations would increase the probability of more relaxed communication.

• MATE SELECTION •

The mutual selection of Prince Charles and Lady Diana, Johnny Cash and June Cash, Phil Donahue and Marlo Thomas, and Jane Fonda and Tom Hayden did not occur by chance. Various cultural, sociological, psychological, and, some sociobiologists say, biological factors combined to influence their meeting and marriage.

Cultural Aspects of Mate Selection

Cultural norms for mate selection vary. The degree of freedom an individual has in choosing a marriage partner depends on the culture in which he or she lives. In some cultures arranged marriages predominate; in others, including our own, "free" choice is the rule. But some arranging takes place in all cultures. No culture permits absolute free choice. In this section we explore arranged marriages and the cultural pressures that operate within a system of free choice.

ARRANGED MARRIAGES

If your marriage were arranged, several people might participate in the selection of your mate. Depending on whether you lived in Ghana (West Africa), Tepostlan (Mexico), or Japan, your father, both your parents, or your parents with the help of a matchmaker would select your life's companion for you (Stephens, 1982).

Their criteria for selecting a mate for you would include bride price, social status, and family custom. If you are a female, your father would arrange your marriage with the boy whose family would pay him the most. The bride price would be your father's compensation for taking care of you until marriage. When you married, you would no longer be available to your birth family to cook, tend children, or help with the crops. Your marriage would mean the loss of valuable services, and your father would expect to be well paid. If you are a male, your new wife would be your father's expense.

Social status is another consideration in arranging a marriage. Since marriage is the joining of social equals, the respective families are concerned that their offspring marry someone of equal (or perhaps higher) social standing.

Your marriage also might be arranged according to the sororate or levirate custom. In the sororate system, a sister replaces a deceased wife. For example, assume that you, a woman, had a sister whose marriage had included an expensive bride price. After your sister moved in with her new husband, her health deteriorated and she died. Since your father received so much money for your sister, he feels he cheated the young husband by giving him a sick woman. You would replace your sister to fulfill your father's promise of a good wife for a good price.

The levirate system implies the inheritance of a dead man's wife by his brother or other male kin. For example, if you are a man, your brother's wife would become yours when he died. This obligation of the man's family assures continued married status for the woman and, more important, that children of the union will remain within the deceased man's family.

Arranged marriages usually occur in societies with extended rather than nuclear family systems (Lee & Stone, 1980). Ours is a nuclear family system with one husband, one wife, and their children. Extended families include not only the nuclear family but also the parents of the husband and wife and perhaps other relatives such as aunts and uncles all living together.

Arranged marriages are considered an alliance between two families rather than a union of two individuals (Kurian, 1979). Hence family ties are more important than such considerations as physical appearance or love. However, for those individuals who have strong personal preferences, it is not unusual for a society that promotes arranged marriages to provide an alternative—elopement. Individuals can disobey their elders, choose their own mates, run away with them, and then wait and hope that the marriage will finally be approved.

Although arranged marriages are usually thought of as characteristic of preliterate and Eastern societies, they have also been part of Western society. The novel and movie *The Godfather* depicted an arranged marriage in the 1940s between a young Sicilian woman and the son of a powerful New York Mafia fig-

The sacramental nature of marriages is still dominant in India where arranged marriages continue to exist. Most youths believe that parents and close relatives will strive their best to find the most suitable match.

V. V. PRAKASA AND NANDINI RAO

ure. A great many American marriages have been arranged up to modern times, both in poor rural areas and in high society (for example, the marriage of Consuelo Vanderbilt to the Duke of Marlborough in 1895). The Reverend Sun Myung Moon of the Unification Church personally matched and married 2,075 couples in a mass Madison Square Garden ceremony in New York in the early eighties.

ENDOGAMOUS-EXOGAMOUS PRESSURES

Whereas some societies exert specific pressure on individuals to marry predetermined mates, other societies are more subtle. The United States has a system of free choice that is not exactly free. Social approval and disapproval restrict your choices so that you don't marry just *anybody*. Endogamous pressures encourage you to marry those within your own social group (racial, religious, ethnic, educational, economic), and exogamous pressures encourage you to marry outside your family group (to avoid marriage to a sibling or other close relative).

The pressure toward an endogamous mate choice is especially strong where race is concerned. One white woman said, "Some of my closest friends are black. But my parents would disown me if I were to openly date a black guy." In contrast, a black man said, "I would really like to date a girl in my introductory psychology class who's white. But my black brothers wouldn't like it and while my parents wouldn't throw me out of the house, they would wonder why I wasn't dating a black girl."

These individuals resisted endogamous pressures to marry someone of their own racial heritage.

These endogamous pressures aren't operative on all people at the same level or may not work at all. Those over 30, those who have been married before, and those from large urban centers are more likely to be color-blind in their dating and marrying. In Hawaii interracial dating and marriage are normative.

In contrast to endogamous marriage pressures, exogamous pressures are mainly designed to ensure that individuals who are perceived to have a close biological relationship do not marry each other. Incest taboos are universal. In no society are children permitted to marry their parent of the opposite gender. In the United States, siblings and first cousins (in some states) are also prohibited from marrying each other.

> CONSIDERATION • Mate selection in the United States is free only to the extent that the individual is willing to marry as the laws of his or her state permit and is capable of withstanding the social pressures for a choice that is not culturally approved. The wife of an interracial couple remarked, "I married Reid because I loved him. I still do. But the cost has been high. My father wouldn't speak to me. My mother is heartbroken. Most of my friends approve of my marriage, but there is more grief than I thought."
> The effect of the cultural influences just described is to narrow your choice of a mate from anybody to those outside your immediate family and to those of the same race, religion, and social class.

Sociological Aspects of Mate Selection

There are several sociological factors at work in the attraction of two people to each other. These concepts include homogamy, role compatibility, and propinquity.

HOMOGAMY
The homogamy concept of mate selection states that you are attracted to and become involved with those who are similar to you in age, physical appearance, education, social class, marital status, and religion.

Age When a friend gets you a date, you assume the person will be of an age similar to yours. Your peers are not likely to approve of your becoming involved with someone twice your age. A student who was dating one of her former teachers said, "He always comes over to my place and I prepare dinner for us. I don't want to be seen in public with him. Although I love him, it doesn't feel right being with someone old enough to be my father." Such a concern for age homogamy is particularly characteristic of never-married individuals. Those who have been married before are much more likely to become involved with someone who is less close to their age (Bytheway, 1981).

How old would you be if you didn't know how old you was?

SATCHEL PAIGE

DATA • *The median age at which American men first marry is 24; for females, it is 22.* (National Center for Health Statistics, 1984)

The tendency for men to marry down and women to marry up in age, social class, and education is referred to as the mating gradient. Such pairing results in some high-status women and low-status men remaining single. As a function of the mating gradient, the upper-class girl will receive approval from her parents and peers only if she marries someone of equal status. On the other hand, approval is usually forthcoming for the man who marries below himself in age and status.

> CONSIDERATION • The mating gradient results in an oversupply of unmarried older, bright, attractive, educated, professional women. Men might consider the personal, social, and economic benefits of including such women in their pool of potential partners, and women might reconsider the idea that their mate must be older, educated, and professionally established. Solid happy relationships can result from a number of different pairings. The mating gradient may be an artificial restriction.

Beauty is altogether in the eye of the beholder.

GENERAL LEW WALLACE

Physical appearance   Love may be blind but it knows what the person looks like. In general, people tend to become involved with those who are similar in physical attractiveness. When you look in the mirror you evaluate the degree to which you are physically attractive and assess the level of physical attractiveness of the person or persons whom you feel would be interested in you. A look at the various pairings on campus may show this concept in operation. Are the "good-looking people" paired off with each other? Or are they mismatched? If they are mismatched, is the girl better looking than the boy? Some data suggest this would be the case (Janda et al., 1981).

Education   In addition to age and appearance, the level of education you attain will influence your selection of a mate. A sophomore who worked in a large urban department store during the Christmas holidays remarked, "The two weeks Todd and I spent selling record albums and tapes were great. But our relationship never gathered momentum. I was looking forward to my last two years of school, but Todd said college was a waste of time. I don't want to get tied to someone who thinks that way."

This student's experience suggests that you are likely to marry someone who has also attended college. Not only does college provide an opportunity to meet, date, and marry another college student, but it also increases the chance that only a college-educated person will be acceptable. Education affects not only what you know but also what you are aware of. The very pursuit of education becomes a value to be shared.

Social class   You have been reared in a particular social class, a term that reflects your parent's occupation, income, and education as well as your residence, language, and values. If you were brought up in the home of a physician, you probably lived in a large house in a nice residential section of town. You were in a higher social class than if your parents were uneducated and worked as clerks at K-Mart.

The social class in which you were reared will influence how comfortable you feel with a partner. "I never knew what a finger bowl was," recalled one man, "until I ate dinner with my girlfriend in her parents' Manhattan apartment. I knew then that while her life-style was exciting, I was more comfortable with paper napkins and potato chips. We stopped dating."

Previous marital status There is a tendency for the divorced to marry the divorced, the widowed to marry the widowed, and the never married to marry the never married. A divorced mother of twin boys remarked, "The only person who really understands me is a divorced father. He knows what a lonely experience divorce is and how important children are."

Religion Some religious denominations socialize their members to seek mates of a similar religious orientation. Mormons (Marie Osmond married another Mormon), Jews, Catholics, and to some extent, fundamentalist Protestants encourage homogamous religious mate selection. "Don't date anyone you wouldn't marry, and don't marry anyone who is not of your faith," said one religious leader to his congregation.

PROPINQUITY

An American man married a woman who was born in Vienna, Austria, but she had spent her senior year of high school in his parents' home as a foreign exchange student. Their marriage illustrates the concept of "residential propinquity," which states that the probability that A and B will marry each other decreases as the distance between their residences increases.

It is obvious that we can only marry those with whom we interact, but the propinquity aspect of mate selection also includes convenience. Being in the same class or working at the same job or living close to each other permits convenient interaction. Referring to his former fiancée, a library science major said, "When I first transferred to State, I would drive the 300 miles each way to see her on weekends. I did that three times. Then I noticed a girl in one of my classes and we began studying together. I soon stopped the ten hours of driving each weekend to see the other girl. It was only five minutes from my apartment to the new girl's place."

Psychological Aspects of Mate Selection

Beyond the cultural and sociological factors that restrain and guide your choice of a partner, various psychological variables are involved. These include complementary needs, exchange, and parental image. All are concerned with the way the individual, independent of his or her society, views the mate selection process.

COMPLEMENTARY NEEDS

"In spite of the women's movement and a lot of assertive friends, I am a shy and dependent person," remarked a transfer student. "My need for dependency is met by Warren, who is the dominant, protective type." The tendency for a submissive person to become involved with a dominant person (one who likes to control the behavior of others) is an example of attraction based on complementary needs. Partners can also be drawn to each other on the basis of nurturance and receptivity. These complementary needs suggest that one person likes to give and take care of another while the other likes to be the benefactor of such care.

That partners select each other on the basis of complementary needs was suggested by Winch (1955), who noted that needs could be complementary if they were different, as dominant and submissive, or if the partners had the same need but at different levels of intensity. As an example of the latter, two individuals may have a complementary relationship when both want to do advanced graduate study. But both need not get Ph.D.s. The partners will complement each other if one is comfortable with his or her level of aspiration, represented by a master's degree, but still approves of the other's commitment to earn a Ph.D.

Winch's theory of complementary needs, commonly referred to as "opposites attract," was based on the observation of 25 undergraduate married couples at Northwestern University. The findings have been criticized by other researchers who have not been able to replicate Winch's study. Two researchers said, "It would now appear that Winch's findings may have been an artifact of either his methodology or his sample of married people" (Meyer & Pepper, 1977).

Two questions have been raised about the theory of complementary needs: (1) Couldn't personality needs be met just as easily outside the couple relationship rather than through mate selection? For example, a person who has the need to be dominant could get such fulfillment in a job that involved an authoritative role, such as head of a corporation or an academic department and (2) What is a complementary need as opposed to a similar value? For example, is the desire to achieve at different levels a complementary need or a shared value?

Whether complementary or not, you expect your partner to meet certain of your needs. The Needs Assessment Inventory is designed to help you identify the needs you expect your partner to fulfill and the degree to which she or he does so.

> Wel-married, a man is winged: il-matched, he is shackled.
>
> HENRY WARD
> BEECHER

EXCHANGE THEORY

Since your parents will not be haggling with your partner's parents over bride price or other matters, you are your own broker. Your selection will involve various exchanges.

Exchange theorists suggest that you will marry the person who offers you the greatest rewards at the lowest cost of all the people who are available to you (Nye, 1980). Four concepts help to explain the exchange process in mate selection: (1) Rewards are behaviors (your partner looking at you with the "eyes of love"), words (saying "I love you"), resources (being beautiful or handsome, having money), and services (driving you home, typing for you) your partner provides for you that you enjoy and that influence you to continue the relationship, (2) Costs are unpleasant consequences of a relationship. One man said, "I have to drive across town to pick her up, listen to her nagging mother before we can leave, and be back at her house by midnight;" (3) Profit is the excess reward when the costs are subtracted from the rewards, (4) Loss occurs when the costs exceed the rewards. The Assets and Liabilities Inventory (p. 178) is a way for you to assess the profit you are experiencing in the relationship with your partner.

Exchange concepts operate at three levels of the dating relationship—who can date whom, the conditions of the dating relationship, and the decision to marry. As for whom you date, you are attracted to those who have something to exchange. If you are an attractive, self-confident senior with the social skills of Lady Diana, you will expect a lot in exchange from the partner you date. An un-

• Self-Assessment •

NEEDS ASSESSMENT INVENTORY*

Identify the needs you expect your partner to meet in column A by ranking them in importance from 1 to 16. Next, write in column B the degree to which you feel your partner can or does satisfy each of the needs you ranked (0 = low, 10 = high). You might also ask your partner to complete this exercise.

(A)	(B)		(A)	(B)	
_____	_____	Companionship	_____	_____	Intellectual exchange
_____	_____	Recreation	_____	_____	Make me feel secure
_____	_____	Affection	_____	_____	Provide direction
_____	_____	Good sex partner	_____	_____	Have children with
_____	_____	Good traveling partner	_____	_____	Love me
_____	_____	Support my career	_____	_____	Have money
_____	_____	Share my values	_____	_____	Accept my values
_____	_____	Take care of me	_____	_____	Good communication

*This inventory was developed on the basis of an idea suggested by Lynda Harriman (1982).

ASSETS AND LIABILITIES INVENTORY*

According to exchange theory, your partner brings both assets and liabilities to your relationship. List these assets and liabilities.

Assets	Liabilities
1. _____	1. _____
2. _____	2. _____
3. _____	3. _____
4. _____	4. _____
5. _____	5. _____

An example of assets and liabilities listed by one person included the following: *Assets:* good looking, polite, honest, educated, and ambitious. *Liabilities:* divorced, one child, low self-esteem, in debt, and smokes. After identifying the assets and liabilities, assign each a number from 1 (not too significant) to 5 (very significant). Add the numbers for assets and subtract the total from the sum of the liabilities. The resulting score will be your profit in the relationship. For example, the sum of the assets of the person's partner mentioned above was 22 (good looking = 4, polite = 4, honest = 5, educated = 4, and ambitious = 5), and the sum of the liabilities of the partner was 15 (divorced = 3, one child = 3, low self-esteem = 2, in debt = 4, and smokes = 3). The profit in dating this person was found by subtracting the liabilities (15) from the assets (22) = +7. The higher the number the greater the profit. The maximum profit in this case would be 25.

*This inventory was developed on the basis of an idea suggested by Lynda Harriman (1982).

attractive, inept high-school student has little hope of becoming involved in a dating relationship with you, having little to exchange for your looks, status, and skills.

Once you identify a person who can offer the equivalent of what you have to exchange, other bargains are made about the conditions of your continued relationship. Waller and Hill (1951) observed more than 30 years ago that the person who has the least interest in continuing the relationship can control the relationship. This "principle of least interest" is illustrated by the woman who said, "He wants to date me more than I want to date him so we end up going where I want to go and doing what I want to do." In this case, the woman trades her company for the man's acquiescence to her choices.

Additional exchanges take place as the couple move toward marriage. They make a marital commitment when each person feels that he or she is getting the partner who offers the most rewards of all those currently available. A graduating senior and groom-to-be remarked, "It's easy. I've decided to marry Maria because sharing life with her is more fun than being with anyone else. And marriage is one way to help ensure that we will be together to share our lives across the years."

CONSIDERATION • Partners are more likely to continue their involvement in a relationship as long as they derive more profit from that relationship than from any other available to them (Lloyd et al., 1984). They discontinue relationships where the costs exceed the rewards unless they have no alternative relationship. In this case, they may choose to suffer in an unhappy relationship rather than be alone or go through what they regard as the trauma of divorce.

PARENTAL IMAGE

Whereas the complementary and exchange theories of mate selection are relatively recent, Freud earlier suggested that the choice of a love object in adulthood represents a shift in libidinal energy from the first love objects, the parents. This means that a man looks for a wife like his mother and woman looks for a husband like her father. In a study of almost 7,000 spouses, Jedlicka (1984) observed that selecting a partner similar to the opposite-gender parent occurs more often than can be expected by chance.

Sociobiological Aspects of Mate Selection

Sociobiology suggests there is a biological basis for all social behavior—including mate selection. Based on Darwin's theory of natural selection, which states that the strongest of the species survive, sociobiologists contend that men and women select each other as mates on the basis of their concern for producing offspring most capable of surviving.

According to sociobiologists, men look for an attractive, bright, sexually conservative woman who will care for their offspring. Men also look for young women. One researcher (Daniel, 1984) observed, "It is advantageous for males to have good form vision for females between the ages of 15 and 40. It serves no advantage for men to deposit their cheap sperm in matronly women, at least as far as procreation is concerned. Doing so increases the possibility of congenital aberrations (retardation, cleft palate, etc.)."

Women, in contrast, look for a strong, faithful, working man who will provide for her children. If a person ignores these variables, the sociobiologists say, his or her genes are likely to die off and not be perpetuated (Warner, 1982).

G. Gordon Liddy, the convicted Watergate conspirator, said that he selected his wife, in part because of her genes. She was taller than him (he didn't want small kids) and bright (she did calculus problems for recreation the way he did crossword puzzles). As a result, all of their kids are strong, healthy, and bright (Liddy, 1980). Of course, this argument is flawed, as Liddy's children might have inherited his size and presumed lesser intelligence.

The sociobiological explanation for mate selection is extremely controversial. Critics say that biological concerns are rarely conscious if present at all. Men and women think more about their partner than about offspring when selecting a mate.

· TRENDS ·

The future of dating relationships will include more people spending more time in a number of such relationships, a gradual shift away from traditional dating practices, increased interracial, interreligious, and interethnic dating, and increased confusion about roles in dating relationships. As noted in the last chapter, both women and men are marrying later than in previous years. The result of such delay is that each person will have more time to become involved with a variety of people. More time spent dating also has implications for how dating is perceived—initially more for recreation than for mate selection.

Because of this shift in dating focus from mate selection to recreation, the traditional dating pattern, which is geared toward early marriage, will become less functional. "Hanging out" and "getting together," whereby individuals go where they can meet members of the opposite gender in informal ways without an introduction, will increase. The women's movement has been instrumental in making some women feel comfortable about going to singles' bars and initiating relationships.

The future of dating relationships will also include increased interracial, interreligious, and interethnic dating as desegregation continues and as endogamous pressures subside.

Differences in role expectations will also become more apparent. Whereas the women's movement has sensitized women to seek equalitarian relationships with men, socialization of men to perceive women in other than traditional roles has been less extensive. As a result, there may be more confusion during first encounters when the new woman and the traditional man meet. Also, since the women's movement has not influenced all women and since some men are nontraditional, the man seeking a woman who wants an equalitarian relationship may be surprised to find a traditional woman and vice versa.

Other trends in dating will include greater use of mate selection technology. As our society becomes more populated, urban, and industrial, there will be fewer personal networks within which to meet eligible mates. Increasingly, individuals will place more advertisements in newspapers or magazines, and join computer and videotape dating clubs, linking persons who might not otherwise meet through traditional dating patterns.

Finally, as the liberal norms of Western societies continue to spread, parents in other societies will come under increasing pressure from their offspring to let them participate in selecting the person they will spend their life with. The movement away from arranged marriages is already occuring in India, Africa, Israel, and Malaya (Murstein, 1980).

• SUMMARY •

Dating is the primary mechanism by which men and women pair off into exclusive committed relationships. Its functions involve confirmation of a social self, recreation, companionship, socialization, and mate selection.

Although dating may be in groups or in one-to-one relationships, finding a partner isn't always easy. Most meet through a friend or at a party; others establish contacts through newspaper advertisements, computer dating clubs, or video cassettes.

The typical dating event involves going out to eat, seeing a movie or football game, and going back to his or her apartment. Conversation most often focuses on the couple's relationship.

Women view unwanted sexual pressure as the biggest problem on dates. Communication—not knowing what to say or do—is the most frequent problem reported by men.

As dating moves toward mate selection, the partners are influenced by various cultural, sociological, psychological, and perhaps biological factors. Although marriages in some cultures are arranged by parents or other relatives, our culture relies mainly on endogamous and exogamous pressures to guide mate choice.

Sociological aspects of mate selection include homogamy—people prefer someone like themselves—and propinquity—people prefer someone with whom it is convenient to interact.

Psychological aspects of mate selection include complementary needs, exchange, and parental image. Complementary needs theory suggests that people select others who have opposite characteristics to their own. They may also seek each other if they both have the same need but at different levels of intensity.

Exchange theory posits that one individual selects another on the basis of rewards and costs. As long as an individual derives more profit from a relationship with one partner than another partner, the relationship will continue. Exchange concepts influence who dates whom, the conditions of the dating relationship, and the decision to marry.

The parental image theory of mate selection says that a man looks for a wife like his mother and a woman looks for a husband like her father.

The sociobiological view of mate selection suggests that men and women select each other on the basis of their biological capacity to produce and support healthy offspring. Men seek young women with healthy bodies and women seek ambitious men who will provide economic support.

Trends in dating relationships include a longer period of dating, a gradual shift from the traditional dating pattern to a more informal one, increased interracial, religious, ethnic dating, increased confusion over dating roles, greater reliance on technology in finding dates, and increased participation by offspring in other societies in their arranged marriages.

Questions for Reflection

1. How does exchange theory help to explain your involvement in your most recent relationship? What specifically are or were the rewards and costs?
2. To what degree, if any, do you consider sociobiological factors when selecting a marriage partner?
3. What kinds of influence do your parents have on your dating relationships?

·CHOICES·

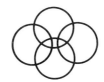

Beginning to date someone involves a number of choices. These include how interested you should appear to be, how available you should be, and whether to date one or several people.

HOW INTERESTED SHOULD I APPEAR TO BE?

"If I let a man know I'm interested in him, I lose him," said one woman. "It happens every time. I'm learning to be very distant and cold with men." But her roommate said, "If you don't show your interest, he'll think you're not interested and he'll go away."

A frequent dilemma in dating is whether to let someone know you are interested in her or him. Like all decisions, looking at the positive and negative consequences of each course of action may suggest an answer.

One benefit of showing interest in someone is to give the person the feeling that he or she is attractive and desirable to you. Having the person reciprocate your feelings may not be your goal. "I just wanted her to know that I thought she was stunningly beautiful," said one guy. "If she never gives me another thought, it doesn't matter."

Another benefit is that by showing your interest, the other person doesn't have to guess whether you are interested. If you never get together, it won't be because the other person was unaware that at least one of you had an interest in the other. "A lot of men are shy," said one woman. "If you don't hit them between the eyes with a two by four, they don't know that it's time to ask you out."

The drawbacks of showing your interest in another are possible rejection, investment without profit, and social withdrawal. Since all people will not like you no matter who you are or what you look like, to extend yourself to another is to risk rejection. Some people handle rejection as a part of the dating game and are relatively unbothered by it. Others are devastated by rejection.

Another drawback is the fact that you may have invested your time and have nothing to show for it—time you could have used doing something else. "I spent a semester flirting with this girl and when I finally called her up for a date, she didn't even know my name," said one man. "What a waste," he said.

A final problem with showing your interest in another is that if you are rejected you may develop a pattern of avoidance and become depressed, withdrawn, and self-pitying. Such avoidance behavior may perpetuate itself. By being depressed and withdrawn you ensure that someone will not be interested in you, which further confirms your feelings of self-doubt.

Perhaps the best answer to whether to show your interest in another is yes, a little at a time. Being friendly by saying "hello" and smiling are sufficient expressions of your interest in another to stimulate a response if the other person is

(continued)

interested. Smiling back and being friendly might be met by further escalation of friendliness on your part. If the person does not reciprocate your overtures, you might conclude that he or she is not interested in you. But rather than decide that something is wrong with you, you might consider that something is wrong with the person because he or she is not attracted by someone as terrific as you and take your affections elsewhere.

HOW AVAILABLE SHOULD I BE?

Assuming that someone is showing an interest in you and wants to date you, how available should you be? If the person asks you out on Thursday for Friday night, should you go? If you agree to go out Friday will the person think you have nothing else to do but sit in your dorm all weekend because no one else wants you? If you don't go, will the person ask someone else and begin a dating relationship with her or him? The best answer might be to say, "I would really like to go out but cannot go tomor-row night. Please ask me another time." If the person is interested in you, your not being available will more likely spur than deter interest. Making your partner wait a week to get a date with you increases your value to that person and makes you both feel good about each other the first date.

One suggestion to the person doing the asking. Rather than say, "Are you doing anything next Friday?", say "Would you like to go out to dinner and see a movie next Friday?" The latter question avoids the possibility that people will feel bad by having to tell you that no one has asked them out and they aren't doing anything but watching paint dry.

SHOULD I DATE
ONE OR SEVERAL PEOPLE?

Is it best to date one or several people? The answer will vary. One advantage of dating one person is to learn what it is like to manage a sustained relationship. The longer you date someone, the greater the chance for conflict and the greater the need for negotiating conflict. Being able to re-solve conflict in an interpersonal relationship is a very valuable skill.

Dating one person will also prevent you from dating others. If you begin to date one person in your freshman year and continue until your senior year, you will miss the experience of knowing a variety of people with different interests and values.

On the other hand, dating one person whom you enjoy may be more desirable than dating 50 others whom you don't enjoy. "Why should I date around, when all I want to do is be with Stan," said one woman.

Partners who date only each other for a sustained period of time are more likely to have intercourse and oral sex than those who date casually. Some see this as an advantage, whereas others see it as a reason for delaying monogamous dating.

A pattern some people adopt is to first date a wide variety of people. Then around age 20 they begin to focus on the one person they might want to marry and date him or her exclusively for a period of several years.

· Chapter 7 ·

LIVING TOGETHER

CONTENTS

Definition and Types

Why Living Together Is Increasing

Characteristics of Live-In Partners

The Nuts and Bolts of Living Together

Living Together as Preparation for Marriage?

Benefits of Living Together

Disadvantages of Living Together

Living Together as a Permanent Alternative

Self-Assessment:Living-Together Consequences Scale

Choices

The practice of nonmarital cohabitation is not restricted to the young . . .

ROY WATSON

One of the major changes in our society has been the gradual acceptance of a couple's living together before marriage. This acceptance (in some cases tolerance) has increased among people of all ages, races, and social classes. Some view living together as a necessary stage in a developing relationship before making a permanent commitment.

In this chapter we examine the characteristics of those who live together, their motivations for doing so, and how they evaluate the experience. In addition, we assess the potential benefits and disadvantages of becoming involved in a living-together relationship. Finally, since the courts are indicating increased concern, we look at the legal implications of living together as a permanent alternative to marriage. The terms used to describe live-ins include *co-habitants* and *POSSLQ* (people of the opposite sex sharing living quarters), the latter used by the U.S. Census Bureau.

• DEFINITION AND TYPES •

We define living together as two unmarried adult lovers who share a common bed or residence over a consistent period of time. "A consistent period of time" may include living together on weekends if the partners do so for several months. A continual emotional and sexual relationship with the sharing of a physical space (apartment or house) is a necessary ingredient in living together.

DATA • *More than 25 percent of all college students in the United States are living together.* (Macklin, 1980) *In the larger population, about 3 percent of all couple households consists of unmarried couples who are living together.* (Glick, 1984) *In one study of Canadian married couples, 64 percent reported they had lived together before marriage.* (Watson, 1983)

The various types of living-together relationships include individuals who are emotionally involved but not ready for marriage, those who are waiting to get married, those who view living together as a permanent alternative to marriage, and those who live together for economic reasons (it is cheaper). Most individuals who live together have a strong affectionate relationship with their partners, but they have not yet made a commitment to marry each other. In traditional terms, they are "going steady" but they have also moved in together. This "involved but not committed to marriage" pattern of living together was expressed by one student who said:

> The only thing I know about is today. And today I'm happy with my partner. Tomorrow? Who knows? While we both intend to get married someday, we're not sure that it will be to each other.

The bond of love and trust which holds two people together is much stronger than the legal bond authorized by church and state.

LIFE

Other couples are committed to marry each other and are living together until the time is right. Although they may not be officially engaged, they plan to be married and are consciously assessing their compatibility. "The idea of agreeing to spend the rest of your life with someone you've never lived with is nonsense," said one live-in partner. "We love each other very much and feel very secure with each other. But we want to see if we can pull it off on a day-to-day basis."

A few people (about 1 percent) live together as a permanent alternative to marriage. Many of these have been married and do not want to marry again, but want a live-in lover relationship.

• WHY LIVING TOGETHER IS INCREASING •

Living together is not a recent phenomenon. In the 1920s Judge B. B. Lindsey suggested the living-together alternative out of his concern for the number of divorcing couples he saw in his court. He reasoned that if couples lived together before marriage, they might be able to better assess the degree to which they were compatible with each other. The idea did not catch on until the early sixties, when half a million couples were living together. By the eighties the number had increased to 1.8 million couples. About 28 percent of these couples have children living with them (Spanier, 1983).

DATA • *According to the latest census count, 1,863,000 couples were living together in the United States.* *(Statistical Abstract of the United States,* 1984)

New patterns in relationships do not develop in a vacuum. A number of social, psychological, and technological changes have influenced more people to live together. These changes include new sex norms, availability of contraceptives, off-campus apartments and coed dorms, peer support, and more tolerant parents.

New Sex Norms

Social criticism and the fear of it have often functioned to control people's actions, and until quite recently, any woman who was living with a man she was not married to was said to be a "slut" who was just "shacking up."

Such an expression reflected the double standard—the idea that nonmarital sexual satisfaction was appropriate for men but not for women. Because of the double standard, many women felt they had to withhold sex until they could get a commitment for marriage. But the double standard is no longer so widely adhered to in American society. This is owing in part to the women's movement, which encouraged women to stop regarding marriage as the ultimate experience and to stop bargaining with sex but rather to enjoy it.

The double standard is being replaced by the acceptance of sex as part of a love relationship. If two partners care for each other emotionally, their sexual relationship is socially justified. "When you're living with someone," said one woman, "everybody knows you're having sex. But you don't live with a guy unless you care about each other—and that's what makes living together okay."

Related to this is the idea that having intercourse before marriage is also acceptable. The stigma that used to be associated with premarital intercourse has been replaced by the stigma associated with being a virgin. "If a person is 20 and hasn't had intercourse, what's wrong with them?" asked one student.

Availability of Contraceptives

Although most live-in partners have an ongoing sexual relationship, they typically do not want children of their own until they are married. The separation of lovemaking and babymaking is made possible by the availability of safe and effective contraceptives. More than 80 percent of college students in one study (Ratcliff, 1983) reported they used contraception the last time they had intercourse. The percentage for those who used contraception who were living together was even higher. The pill continues to be the most frequently used contraceptive.

Off-Campus Apartments and Coed Dorms

Liberal sexual norms and effective contraception have combined with new housing patterns to encourage students to live together. University officials made living together more convenient by rejecting the *in loco parentis* philosophy, the belief that administrators had an obligation to "stand in the place of parents" and to monitor the moral behavior of students. An increasing number of officials have relaxed various restrictions that were designed to keep the sexes in separate beds. Twenty-four-hour visitation rights, dorms with no curfew, coed dormitories, and allowing students to live off campus in private apartments have virtually eliminated the structural barriers to living together. Although most universities do not officially allow live-in relationships, they do not attempt to prevent them. A student in an all-girl dorm said, "Guys stay in this dorm all the time and some of them might as well live here."

More tolerant landlords have also made it more convenient for two people to live together. Many landlords now permit two people to sign a lease without concern for their marital relationship, whereas in the past some landlords would not rent to an unmarried couple.

Peer Support

A number of students have indicated considerable peer support, particularly among college youth, for living together (Macklin, 1980). Such support when

Today's society
more willingly
condones
students living
together.

combined with knowing friends who live together may be influential in encouraging others to live together. "While I had never considered living together before coming to college, a lot of my friends are doing so," observed one freshman. "That makes it easier for me to consider moving in with my partner."

DATA • *Twenty-seven percent of over 5000 students from four universities said that they would live with someone before marriage.* (Martin and Martin, 1984)

But peer support is not specific to youth. Many divorced people are aware of their friends who are living together. "It's not the hush-hush thing it used to be," said a recently separated person. "Plenty of my friends are living together and told me they would never get married again without first living with their partner."

More Tolerant Parents

Although most parents disapprove of their offspring living together, an increasing number are becoming more tolerant. "I don't like my daughter moving in with her boyfriend," said one mother, "but I'd rather she do that than be married to the bum." Another parent said, "My son isn't ready for marriage (he's 18). Maybe living together will settle him down and give him an idea of what a stable relationship is all about."

Even some very religious parents for whom living together is a moral issue indicate an attitude of tolerance. At a weekend conference for Quakers, some of the parents whose children were living together said they "had survived the ordeal without losing love or respect for their sons and daughters" (Mace, 1981).

• CHARACTERISTICS OF LIVE-IN PARTNERS •

The social climate is conducive to living together, but most unmarried (single, divorced, widowed) have not done so. What are the differences between those who live together and those who do not?

Nonchurch Attenders

In a comparison of cohabitants and noncohabitants (Watson, 1983), 75 percent of the former reported never attending religious services in contrast to a quarter of the latter. The cohabitors were also more likely not to be members of a church. Among those who were members, Catholics were the most likely to live together and fundamentalist Protestants the least likely.

Drug Users

Couples who live together may be more likely to use drugs than those who don't. In a comparison of 30 married couples who lived together before they were married with 30 married couples who did not, the former were more frequent users of alcohol, marijuana, LSD, and speed (Markowski & Johnston, 1980).

Androgynous

When androgyny is defined as having both masculine and feminine characteristics, living-together partners are more likely to be androgynous than those who do not live together (Macklin, 1980). Such androgyny suggests that the partners are less rigid in their roles. "We don't see the world as his or her responsibility but ours," said one live-in partner. "If something needs to be done, the one who's there does it."

Formerly Married

People who have been married before are more likely to live together than those who have not been married before (Watson, 1983). "I'm not about to marry a man without living with him first," said one woman. "My first husband was an alcoholic but I didn't find out until after the wedding." Another person said, "I'm just not interested in marriage anymore—I've done that. What I want is a close emotional relationship without the pressure of having to 'get along' that marriage creates."

DATA • *About half of all individuals who live together have been previously married.* (Spanier, 1983)

Black and Urban

Couples who are black and urban are also more likely to be found among those who live together than those who are white and rural.

DATA • *The rate of blacks living together is two times that of whites.* (Spanier, 1983)

That couples who live together tend to be in large urban centers is not surprising. Cities offer anonymity and a context for liberal thinking and behavior that smaller towns do not.

In summary, there are several differences between couples who live together and those who do not. But they are also similar to each other in terms of making good grades, being interested in marriage, wanting children, and being committed to marriage (Booth et al., 1984; Macklin, 1980; Markowski & Johnston, 1980).

• THE NUTS AND BOLTS OF LIVING TOGETHER •

What is living together like on a day-to-day basis? In this section we explore such issues as the decision to live together, commitment, intimacy, and problems.

Deciding to Move in Together

As anyone who lives together knows, there is rarely a time that a couple specifically discuss living together. Rather, the partners become emotionally involved with each other, spend increasingly larger amounts of time together, and gradually drift into a living-together arrangement. The typical pattern is to first spend an occasional night together, then a weekend, then a night before or after the weekend, and so on. This escalation usually takes place over a period of months.

DATA • *In one study the partners knew each other 10½ months before they moved in together.* (Risman et al., 1981)

"We just enjoyed spending time together and the more, the better. We weren't aware that we were gradually moving in together—but that's what was happening," recalled an English major.

Another couple recalled their experience: "We were at his place fooling around when I said how nice it would be to have my stereo to listen to. We decided to go to my dorm and get it. Doing so was symbolic because in the next few days we had moved my other stuff into his apartment. We never talked about living together, only 'getting my stuff.' "

Feelings about Marriage

What do couples who live together feel about marriage in general and about marriage to each other? When 40 college couples who were living together were

When individuals move in together, "mine" and "yours" sometimes becomes "ours."

asked these questions, 93 percent of the women and 85 percent of the men said they would eventually marry (Risman et al., 1981) "Just because we're living together doesn't mean we're anti-marriage," said one live-in partner.

Although most partners in living-together relationships plan to eventually marry, they are less certain about marrying each other. Women are slightly more likely to feel that they will marry the person they are currently living with than vice versa.

DATA • *More than 85 percent of both partners believe they will marry someday, but women think there is about a 60 percent chance they will marry the person they are currently living with, whereas only 50 percent of the men think that way.* (Risman et al., 1981)

Intimacy

When 40 couples who were living together were compared with 191 couples who were "going steady," (Risman et al., 1981) the living-together couples were more intimate—they disclosed more to each other, indicated greater love for each other, had sexual intercourse more often, and viewed their relationship as closer. Hence although the living-together couples weren't sure about their future life together, they had drifted into a very intimate relationship. Also, they were enjoying it. About 80 percent of both genders reported they were satisfied with their relationship. These percentages were slightly above the satisfaction levels of those partners who were "going steady."

Division of Labor

Who does the work in living-together relationships? Who cooks the food, cleans the bathroom, washes the clothes, and puts oil in the car? Although many couples share the work in their relationships, there seems to be a drift toward traditional roles, the woman doing more of the work. This traditional division of labor may be the unconscious replication of the role relationships the respective partners observed in their parents' marriages. One woman who cooks, cleans, and does the laundry said, "I really don't mind. I'd rather be taking care of things around the apartment than just sitting around." One might predict that her mother also takes care of her father in a similar manner and feels guilty "just sitting around."

But others feel frustrated and angry at the traditional drift. One graduate student who had recently moved in with her partner said:

> Moving in together has caused some unanticipated problems. Things prior to that had been quite egalitarian and I liked the way Bob treated me. After we moved in, the boxes had not even been unpacked and I became a *housewife*! I worked all day on *our* house while he went to school. It was horrible and I was miserable. We talked about it and two days later I was the housewife again. I'm hoping that since we're moved in and things are unpacked and cleaned, this problem will be gone.

Problems

Partners who live together report certain problems in their relationships about parents, jealousy, roles, and sex.

PARENTS

Most college students are reluctant to tell their parents they are living together. They fear their parents' disapproval and, in some cases, retribution. "My dad would cut off my money if he knew Mark and I were living together," said one junior.

DATA • *In a study of Canadian cohabitants, 80 percent of the women and 87 percent of the men said their parents knew they were living together.* (Watson, 1983)

Some don't care if their parents know they are living together, but those who hide it feel guilty about the deception. "I don't feel good about being dishonest with my folks but I tell myself it would hurt them more if they knew," one partner said.

Still others are sorry they can't share their feelings about their companion with their parents. "I've never been happier than since I moved into Carl's apartment. But the fact that my folks don't know and would be disappointed if they did bothers me. Carl is a very important part of my life, and I feel sad that I can't share him with my parents," observed a music major.

Older, noncollege, divorced people who live together also have parental concerns. "No matter how old I am," said one 36-year-old woman, "I'm still my mother's child and she thinks living together is wrong." As noted earlier, not all parents disapprove of living together. Some prefer it to their offspring marrying too early or marrying the wrong person.

JEALOUSY

Since about half of the partners who live together aren't committed to marrying each other, it is not surprising that jealousy sometimes occurs. "When she doesn't come in until late and I know she's been with another guy, it hurts me terribly," said one partner. "I know I don't own her but I can't help being jealous."

LOSS OF FREEDOM

Some live-in partners complain that the relationship restricts their freedom. One woman said:

Liberty is the one thing you can't have unless you give it to others.

WILLIAM ALLEN WHITE

> Last week I hit a new low point. I felt very trapped and that all my independence and freedom were gone. I had earlier insisted that we have an open relationship (sex with others allowed), but it didn't occur to me until now that I am part of a *couple* and no one's going to be interested in me. Also, I felt I'd have no alone time except when I'm working (we do not have separate bedrooms and we use one car to go back and forth to school). I've had nightmares

about being married and even awakened one night terrified because I had rolled over and felt someone in bed with me (guess I'd been dreaming I was 'single' again).

OTHER PROBLEMS

Partners who live together experience many of the same problems as married couples. Lack of money, lack of space, and sexual problems are not uncommon. Regarding the latter, differences over frequency of intercourse, lack of orgasm, premature ejaculation, and impotence may sometimes occur. A woman remarked how living together had changed her sex life with her partner. "Before we started living together, we had intercourse less frequently because we weren't as available to each other. But when we were sleeping together every night, intercourse was always a possibility. It became a hassle because I wanted it more often, and he felt that only the male should be the aggressor."

In many ways, couples who live together are very similar to married couples. In a review of six studies comparing the two, Macklin (1980) concluded that the main dissimilarity is "commitment": Married couples view their relationship as more permanent. "If you're married," one spouse said, "you kind of know that you and your partner will be together next year. But if you're living together, you aren't sure where you or your partner will be."

• LIVING TOGETHER AS PREPARATION FOR MARRIAGE? •

Does living together result in happier marriages? Two researchers compared the marriages of 30 couples who lived together before they were married with 30 couples who did not live together. They concluded that ". . . cohabitation with a mate prior to marriage seemed neither to greatly benefit nor greatly harm the marriage relationship during the first year of marriage" (Markowski & Johnston, 1980, p. 125).

In another study (Jacques & Chason, 1979), 54 spouses who had lived together (not necessarily with each other) were compared with 30 spouses who had not experienced a live-in relationship. Each spouse was asked to indicate her or his marital satisfaction in reference to sexual satisfaction, need satisfaction, relationship stability, physical intimacy, sexual attractiveness, openness of communication, closeness to ideal partner, and the degree to which they worked on their relationship. Results revealed that those who had living-together experiences did not describe their marriages as different from those who had not had such experiences.

In still another study of 309 spouses (DeMaris & Leslie, 1984), those who had lived together before they were married reported *lower* marital satisfaction than those who had not lived together. Of this unexpected finding, the researchers concluded:

> Rather than acting as a filter that effectively screens out the less-compatible couples, cohabitation appears to select couples from the outset who are somewhat less likely to report high satisfaction once they are married. This may be due to the fact that those individuals expect more out of marriage from the beginning. Alternatively, these may be individuals who adapt less readily to the role expectations of conventional marriage than do the more traditional respondents. In either case, it is most probably the difference between the kinds

of people who do and do not choose to cohabit before marriage, rather than the experience of cohabitation itself, that accounts for these findings. (p. 83)

CONSIDERATION • These studies suggest that you should not live with a partner before marriage if your sole goal is to help ensure a happy marriage with that partner. There is no data to support such a causal relationship.

• BENEFITS OF LIVING TOGETHER •

Although having a successful marriage is not a predictable result of living with someone before marrying them, there are some aspects of a living-together relationship that may be beneficial. The most pervasive benefit is that most couples who live together report it is an enjoyable, maturing experience. There are other potential benefits as well.

Delayed Marriage

Individuals who marry in their mid- and late twenties are more likely to stay married and to report higher levels of marital satisfaction than those who marry earlier. To the degree that living together functions to delay the age at which a person marries, it might be considered beneficial. "I married when I was 20," remarked one woman, "because you just didn't live together in those days. I wish I had waited to get married and had had the option of living together in the meantime." Lana Turner, the blond Hollywood "sweater girl" of the forties, said one of the reasons she had seven marriages is that it was expected that when two people became involved they didn't live together—they got married. (Turner, 1982)

Ending Unsatisfactory Relationships before Marriage

When you are involved in a relationship before marriage and break up with the person, at worst our society labels it a "broken engagement." After the wedding the label changes to "divorce." Living together may clearly indicate that you and your partner are not suited for each other. "I love him, but know that we are incapable of living in the same house," said one man. Finding this out before tying the legal knot will eliminate some unnecessary grief.

CONSIDERATION • A team of researchers studied the termination of various premarital relationships and concluded. "The best divorce you get is the one you get before you get married" (Hill et al., 1976).

Less Idealization

You have been to a dance and seen suspended from the ceiling a ball made up of small square glass mirrors that cast reflections from a light shining on it as it

A benefit of living together is the opportunity to view the partner in a variety of settings and roles.

turns. Traditional courtship usually gives information about a person in small units much like the light reflected from a couple of the mirrors. In contrast, living together may give you more information—you will see more facets of the person by being around her or him more of the time. You may like what you learn about your partner from increased exposure or you may not.

Markowski & Johnston (1980) found that living together helps to break down idealization of the partner, at least for men. Men who had lived with their partners were much less likely to regard them as always composed, lighthearted, happy, and reasonable. Idealization was not reduced for women in the study.

• DISADVANTAGES OF LIVING TOGETHER •

"Never again" said a man who had formerly had a living-together relationship. "I invested myself completely and felt we would eventually get married. But she never had that in mind and just took me for a ride. The next time I'll be married before moving in with someone." Living together does have negative consequences for some people.

Feeling Used

When levels of commitment are uneven in a relationship, the partner with the most commitment feels used. "I always felt I was giving more than I was getting," said one partner. "It's not a good feeling."

Feeling Tricked

Some partners feel they have been deceived. "I always felt we would be getting married, but it turns out that she was seeing someone else the whole time we were living together and had no intention of marrying me," recalled one partner.

Desiring to be more than true, you are worse than false.

ARMAND
BASCHET

> CONSIDERATION • Since many living-together relationships do not end in marriage, if you agree to live together with the specific goal of marrying that person, you may be disappointed. By not requiring that the relationship end in marriage, you increase the chance that you can successfully emerge from the living-together arrangement regardless of the outcome.

Developing Hostility

The feelings of being tricked and used often combine to create deep hostile feelings, not only against the partner, but also against others in general. Sometimes the person feels incapable of initiating or maintaining another relationship. "What's the use," remarked one partner who had recently terminated a relationship, "I'm burned out on investing myself in people."

Relationships to Avoid

A team of researchers identified the types of living-together relationships that had negative consequences for those involved (Ridley et al., 1978). These included the following.

The "Linus blanket" relationship   In this pattern the individuals had an overwhelming need to be involved with someone, anyone. The fear of breaking up caused the partners to defer to each other on almost every issue. As a result, the partners had no practice in problem solving, and they hid their real needs from each other. "We were always being nice to each other and never really disclosed ourselves to each other . . . I guess that's why we broke up," said a business major.

The emancipation relationship   Often one partner lives with another as a symbol of independence from parents and rebellion against tradition. But there are usually feelings of guilt and the person soon withdraws from the relationship. Unless the person works out his or her ambivalent feelings about living together, the consequences are likely to be negative.

The one-sided convenience relationship   Although some live-in relationships involve mutual convenience, others do not. In the latter pattern, one partner manipulates the other to continue sexual, domestic, or other favors while withholding any semblance of commitment. Since there is little reciprocity, the relationship becomes exploitive.

To assess the degree to which living together may have a positive or negative outcome for you and your partner, you might take the Living-Together Consequences Scale.

• LIVING TOGETHER AS A PERMANENT ALTERNATIVE •

Whereas most people regard living together as a stage to a future marriage (though not necessarily with the person they are currently living with), some view it as a permanent alternative to marriage. They enjoy living together, but they do not plan to marry anyone, ever.

Who Lives Together Permanently?

Those who select living together as a permanent alternative to marriage have usually been married before and don't want the entanglements of another marriage. Others feel that the "real" bond between two people is (or should be) emotional. They contend that many couples stay together because of the legal contract even though they do not love each other any longer. "If you're staying married because of the contract," said one partner, "you're staying for the wrong reason."

Still others live together instead of getting married because of the economic advantages. This is particularly true of older couples. "If we got married," said one 67-year-old man, "they would take her Social Security benefits away from her. We know a lot of couples who are doing what we're doing." Whether old or young, most couples who live together instead of getting married do not have children.

Legal Implications of Living Together

The law is reason free of passion.

ARISTOTLE

In recent years, the courts have become increasingly involved in living-together relationships as a number of legal problems have surfaced.

MISCELLANEOUS PROBLEMS

Unmarried couples who live together are sometimes refused apartments or homes by landlords, refused automobile or home coverage by insurance companies or charged higher rates. They may also be refused employee's family health care or group insurance coverage and denied United States citizenship, food stamps, or Social Security survivors' benefits. A live-in partner cannot be listed as a dependent, which would provide a tax deduction.

LIVING-TOGETHER CONSEQUENCES SCALE

This inventory is designed to measure the degree to which living together will have positive or negative consequences for you and your partner. There are no right or wrong answers. After reading each sentence carefully, circle the number that best represents your feelings.

1 Strongly disagree
2 Mildly disagree
3 Undecided
4 Mildly agree
5 Strongly agree

	SD	D	U	A	SA
1. I have a fairly liberal background and living together is not against my values.	1	2	3	4	5
2. If we break up after living together without getting married, I will not be devastated.	1	2	3	4	5
3. I have thought a lot about the pros and cons of living together and feel that it is right for me and my partner.	1	2	3	4	5
4. I will not feel used if my partner breaks up with me and doesn't marry me.	1	2	3	4	5
5. I am not living with my partner so that I can get back at my parents.	1	2	3	4	5
6. I want to live with my partner because of love, not because of convenience.	1	2	3	4	5
7. My partner and I have known each other for a long time.	1	2	3	4	5
8. I am not counting on living together to help us have a stronger relationship.	1	2	3	4	5
9. My partner and I have discussed our future.	1	2	3	4	5
10. My parents would not disown me if they found out that I was living with my partner.	1	2	3	4	5

Scoring: Add the numbers you circled. Since 1 (strongly disagree) is the most negative response and 5 (strongly agree) is the most positive response, the lower your total score (10 is the lowest possible score), the greater the negative consequences of living together, and the higher your score (50 is the highest possible score), the greater the positive consequences of living together. A score of 25 places you at the midpoint between positive and negative consequences of living together.

COMMUNITY PROPERTY AND INHERITANCE

The couple who lives together for several years will probably accumulate considerable property in the form of a house, furniture, a car, stereo equipment, and so on. But it is no longer clear what belongs to whom if they separate. In the case of Michelle Triola Marvin and actor Lee Marvin who lived together for almost seven years, the California Supreme Court ruled that "The fact that a man and woman live together without marriage, and have a sexual relationship, does not in itself invalidate agreements between them relating to their earnings, property, or expenses" (Myricks, 1980, p. 210). In essence, this case makes it possible for former live-in lovers to sue each other for a division of property.

Regarding inheritance, if an individual fails to make proper provision for the distribution of his or her estate (property) after death, the law of the state in which the death occurs will dictate the disposition of the property. In such cases, a legal spouse is usually automatically entitled to inherit between one-half and one-third of the mate's estate. But a living-together partner may get nothing. Rather, the next of kin to the deceased partner may be the benefactor of the estate.

PALIMONY

A take-off on the word *alimony*, palimony refers to the amount of money one "pal" who lived with another "pal" may have to pay if the pals split up. Actor Lee Marvin was ordered to pay Michelle Marvin $104,000 by the Los Angeles Superior Court for "rehabilitative purposes." The amount was arrived at by taking the highest weekly amount she earned as a singer ($1,000) and computing it for a two-year period. Judge Arthur Marshall reasoned that Ms. Marvin acted as a companion and homemaker to Lee Marvin to the detriment of her career and should be given money to retool her skills.

In the past, partners in living-together relationships had no legal rights in reference to each other because their arrangement was viewed as sexually illicit. Today such arrangements are recognized as licit, and the parties can be held liable to each other and forced to pay money at the court's discretion. Exhibit 7.1 describes a number of court cases on living together.

But the courts may disagree. In 1982 the California Second District Court of Appeals overturned the $104,000 award to Ms. Marvin, saying there was no basis for the rehabilitative award—she had sustained no damages.

CONSIDERATION • If you and your partner decide to live together instead of getting married, depending on the state, the judge, and the court, palimony is possible if there is a lawsuit after separating. Division of property is not just possible, but likely.

CHILD CUSTODY

If an unmarried couple have a child or children, the custody issue may arise should the parents decide to separate. The case of *Stanley* v. *Illinois* illustrates the legal consequences of having children without converting the living-together relationship into a legal marriage. Joan Stanley lived intermittently with Peter Stanley for 18 years. Although they were never married, they had three children. When Joan died, Peter lost custody of his three children. Under Illi-

• Exhibit 7.1 •

COURT CASES ON LIVING TOGETHER

Although the case of *Marvin v. Marvin* has been the most widely publicized, other live-ins have gone to court over palimony, child support, and division of property.

Kozlowski v. Kozlowski
A woman who lived with a man (as his spouse) for 15 years was awarded money by the New Jersey Supreme Court, which stated that the man had assured her he would provide for her for the rest of her life. The court felt he was obligated to make good on his promise.

McCullon v. McCullon
A man who lived with a woman for 28 years was required to pay alimony and child support for her 18-year-old daughter. The New York Supreme Court said they had presented themselves as a married couple, filed joint tax returns, and held property in common.

Carlson v. Olsen
The Minnesota Supreme Court ruled that the property of a couple who had lived together for 21 years should be equally divided. The rationale was that the woman performed wifely and motherly services during the living-together years and was entitled to half of what the couple owned.

In other cases, the courts have viewed agreements between live-ins as illegal and unenforceable.

Warren v. Warren
A woman who sought a division of property with her former live-in lover was awarded nothing by the Nevada Supreme Court. The court did not recognize love letters as evidence of an implied contract to create a partnership.

McCall v. Frampton
Penny McCall sued Peter Frampton for half of his earnings during the five-year period she lived with him. She also asked for one-half interest in a 53-acre estate and a portion of his future income. The New York Supreme Court ruled that McCall committed adultery in living with Frampton and that she was not entitled to anything since her relationship with him was illegal.

Sources: Kozlowski v. Kozlowski, 395 A.2d 913 (1978); McCullon v. McCullon, 410 New York Supp. 226 (1978); Carlson v. Olsen, 256 N.W.2d 249 (1977); Warren v. Warren 579 P.2d 722 (1978); McCall v. Frampton *Family Law Reporter*, 1979,5,3077.

nois law the children of unwed fathers become wards of the state upon the mother's death. There was no hearing to determine the father's fitness as a parent, since the presumption was that all unwed fathers are unfit to raise their children.

> CONSIDERATION • If you have been married and do not plan to remarry (but want a sustained companionship relationship), permanent living together may meet your needs. Even if you have not been married but want to avoid marriage and children, a permanent live-in relationship may be for you. Obviously, the person you live with should also feel that never getting married is acceptable or preferable. It is not unusual for only one partner to view the relationship as a permanent alternative to marriage. "The biggest conflict we have," said one cohabitant, "is that he always wants to get married and I don't."

• TRENDS •

If current patterns continue, an increasing number of couples will live together. Although prevalence rates are not likely to reach the 60 percent rate reported by Watson (1983), living together will likely become a more accepted feature of woman-man relationships. Particularly among the previously engaged and formerly married, living together may be viewed as a stage of getting to know someone before making a marital commitment.

DATA • *By 1990, 5 percent of all couple households will consist of couples who are living together.* (Glick, 1984)

Those who decide to live together will also become more cautious about the legal implications of their relationship. This will be particularly true of those who live together for a considerable period of time. In such relationships implied agreements between the partners may be enforceable. Rod Stewart, Nick Nolte, Alice Cooper, and Rod Steiger have all been sued by their former live-in partners. The caution light is on for living-together relationships.

Parents will also become more accepting of the living-together relationships of their offspring. One parent said their first child was divorced after a year of marriage and "it would have been better if they had lived together rather than becoming legally tied." One young woman said, "My parents were very upset when my sisters lived with their boyfriends. But they've gotten used to it and they think very little of me living with my boyfriend." In one study, 55 percent of the females and 72 percent of the males said their parents would approve of their living with a partner (Watson, 1983).

• SUMMARY •

Living together may be defined as two unmarried adult lovers sharing a residence over an extended period of time. About a fourth of all college students and 3 percent of all couples sharing a household are living together. Although most have a wait-and-see attitude about their relationship, others are committed to eventual marriage. A small number view living together as a permanent alternative to marriage.

Various sociological, psychological, and technological factors have led to increasing numbers of couples living together. These changes include changing sex norms, the availability of effective contraception, off-campus apartments, peer support, and parental tolerance.

In general, couples who live together are similar to those who do not live together. But live-ins also tend to be nonchurch attenders, use drugs more, be androgynous, and to have been previously engaged or formerly married.

Live-ins most often drift into a living-together relationship, few have formally discussed it. They report high levels of satisfaction in their relationships and divide the housework along traditional lines. Many seem troubled that their parents do not know of their relationship and feel they would be disappointed if they did know. Some live-ins complain of jealousy, loss of freedom, and lack of money as problems.

Living together before marriage does not seem to increase or decrease one's chances of having a happy marriage. With one exception (DeMaris & Leslie, 1984), studies report that couples who lived together before they were married say similar things about their marriage in terms of sexual satisfaction, need satisfaction, openness of communication, and negotiation of conflict as couples who did not live together. Potential benefits of living together include delaying marriage, ending unsatisfactory relationships before marriage, and reducing idealization. The disadvantages of living together involve feeling used, tricked, and hostile toward the opposite gender.

Only a small percentage (one percent) of unmarried couple households consist of those who are living together as a permanent alternative to marriage. These relationships may cause problems if they terminate, since the courts are increasingly willing to enforce implied agreements made by live-ins.

Trends in living together include an increase in the number of couples doing so, greater social tolerance for the pattern, and increased parental tolerance for their offspring living together.

Questions for Reflection

1. To what degree are any of the relationships to avoid mentioned in this chapter (see p. 197) part of your background?
2. To what degree do you share the characteristics of those who live together and how do you feel about your suitability for the relationship?
3. How would you handle the issue of disclosure to parents if you lived with your partner?

· CHOICES ·

Choices about living together include whether to live together, whether to maintain two residences, whether to tell parents, and how long to live together. Careful decision making may help to make living together a more positive experience.

SHOULD I LIVE WITH MY PARTNER?

There are three conditions under which you should not live together. First, if your values are such that you believe living together is wrong, the arrangement will have only negative consequences for you. You will lose respect for yourself, your partner, and your relationship. Second, if you expect that marriage will result from living with your partner and you will be devastated if it does not, you should not live together. Living together is not equivalent to engagement and it is not unusual for the partners who live together to have different goals about marriage. Even partners who view themselves as being engaged and who plan to marry may not do so after they have

lived together. "I found out that I couldn't live with him," "I found out I didn't want to live with her," and "I found out I wasn't ready for marriage" are some of the comments made by those who live together but do not end up getting married. Third, it is unwise to live with someone you feel is exploiting you—regardless of the reason.

Aside from these three cautions, living together seems to have limited harmful effects and some beneficial ones. The primary benefit is that it may help partners to discover before they get married that they are unsuited for marriage.

SHOULD WE HAVE ONE RESIDENCE OR TWO?

When a couple drift into living together, they often end up living in the man's residence while the woman maintains her own place. The latter furnishes a cover story for both sets of parents, a place for her to get her mail, and a haven to retreat to when conflict erupts in the relationship. One woman who maintained her own apartment said, "I needed a place I could go back to, to call my own and to see my friends. Having a place of your own is expensive but it gives you flexibility by not putting all your eggs into the living-together basket. I ended up breaking up with my partner and I'm sure the adjustment was a lot easier because I had a place to retreat to when I needed it."

The disadvantage of maintaining a separate place may be the flip side of the advantage. If you have a place to retreat to, the skills of managing conflict with your partner may not be as easily learned. Since you can walk out when you want to, your motivation for working things out may be lower. "I'm sure we would be apart," said one cohabitant "if I had not given up my dorm room. But because I had no place to escape to, we worked out our differences and have a stronger relationship for it."

SHOULD I TELL MY PARENTS I AM LIVING WITH MY PARTNER?

The decision to tell one's parents about the living-together relationship will depend on one's parents, the relationship with them, the values of honesty and kindness, and the ability to hide the living-together experience.

Some parents are very conservative and would be devastated to learn that their son or daughter is in a living-together relationship. One mother said, "When we found out our daughter was living with her boyfriend, we were hurt more than we were shocked. We have a Christian home and always thought we had brought her up right. Her behavior was a slap in the face at everything that we had taught her." Other parents don't approve of their children living together but view their doing so as part of the liberalization of the whole society. "We know that a lot of young folks are living together these days," said one father. "Our son went to one of these liberal colleges and learned all sorts of things we don't ap-

prove of. But we trust his judgment and don't figure that living together will hurt him. Besides, we would rather he live with his girlfriend than get married as young as he is."

Just as some parents are conservative and others more liberal, the relationship offspring have with their parents will vary. "I've always been fairly open with my parents no matter what it was," said one cohabitant. But another said, "I can't tell my parents anything without them criticizing me, so I've learned to live my life and let them know as little as possible." Whether you tell your parents about your living-together relationship will depend not only on who they are but, also on your relationship with them.

The values of honesty and kindness are often in conflict when it comes to making a decision about telling one's parents of a living-together relationship. If you value being honest with your parents, you will tell them you are living with your partner. But doing so may hurt them and give them a problem to live with. As an alternative to being honest, you might choose to be kind and not tell them, sparing them the

burden of living with such information.

Of course, your parents may already know of your living together or will find out without your telling them. Keeping such a secret is difficult under the best of circumstances. The only way to ensure that your parents do not find out is to avoid the behavior. "I don't care whether my parents find out or not," said one person, "It's my life." But another said, "I couldn't do that to my parents."

HOW LONG SHOULD I LIVE WITH MY PARTNER?

Is there a good and bad period of time to live together if your goal is to have a happy marriage? There is no evidence that living together before marriage for any length of time is predictive of a successful marriage relationship. However, it is known that relationships in which the partners have known each other for at least a year have a higher chance of marital success than relationships of shorter duration.

· Chapter 8 ·

THE FINAL CHOICE

CONTENTS

Selecting a Partner

Rejecting a Partner

Self-Assessment:
 The Relationship
 Assessment Inventory

Timing Your Marital
 Commitment

Becoming Engaged

Writing a Prenuptial or
 Marriage Contract

Predicting Your
 Marital Happiness

Choices

Keep your eyes wide open before marriage, half shut afterwards.

BENJAMIN
FRANKLIN

After a period of casual friendships, dating, and perhaps living together, individuals narrow their choice of a marriage partner to one. This chapter is about maximizing the chances for a successful marriage by selecting a compatible companion, rejecting those partners who are not compatible, and looking at the various issues that should be considered before marriage. To the degree that you use the premarital period to examine and evaluate your relationship, you can feel more secure in your final choice of a marriage partner.

· SELECTING A PARTNER ·

One of the most important topics of this text is identifying the person or persons with whom you will have the highest chance of a successful marriage. If you were to date 50 people, some of them would be a more suitable mate for you than others; and you can't always depend on love to tell you the difference. As noted earlier, love feelings can alter your perception and judgment when it comes to choosing a marital partner. "I was so much in love with her, I knew we could work out any differences we might have," said one divorced man. "I was wrong."

A basic consideration in evaluating a potential partner is compatibility—the quality of being able to get along well with another person. Compatibility is important because it reduces conflict. Whatever your interests, they are shared by the people you choose as close friends. Consider the difficulty of being *married* to someone who does not like at least some of the things you like.

Of course, it is not necessary (nor is it possible) that you and your partner feel the same way about everything. It is important that you feel the same way about issues the two of you regard as important. Achieving a compatible relationship means identifying those issues that are important to you and selecting a partner who shares your views. "The phrase to remember in choosing a mate," emphasizes one marriage and family teacher, "is 'know yourself and marry yourself.'" As a means of increasing your self-understanding and identifying a compatible partner, consider each of the following issues and how important it is to you that you and your partner are similar.

Many other bodies exist around mine, of which some are to be avoided, and others sought after.

RÉNÉ DESCARTES

Recreational Compatibility

When asked what he saw in his fiancée, an engaged man replied, "She's incredibly fun to be with." Since one of the reasons for your getting married may be the hope of continuing fun times with your partner, to what degree do you share recreational interests? What are your respective feelings about attending cultural events (opera, ballet, symphony, the theater), watching sports (football, tennis, swimming), participating in sports (jogging, skiing, bowling, dancing, fishing, hunting, tennis, golf, racketball), or more sedentary activities (watching TV, going to movies, reading, listening to music). What is your idea of a good time? While some like to go to parties and drink beer, others feel that a weekend of camping is fun.

CONSIDERATION • It does not matter what recreational interests you enjoy. It only matters that your partner share those interests at a level that you mutually regard as desirable.

Need-for-Partner Compatibility

Partners also vary in the degree to which they need each other. One partner said, "I need a great deal of freedom. I love Jim but I don't want to be around him all the time and I certainly don't want him clinging to me." But Jim said, "I'm different. I need to be with Pam and am depressed when I'm not. I know she loves me but sometimes I interpret her not wanting to be with me as rejection. Our different needs for each other's time has been a problem in our relationship." To what degree do you and your partner have similar needs for being with each other and how much does it matter?

Partners who have similar interests have fewer conflicts about how to spend their free time.

Sexual Compatibility

For some partners, having a compatible sexual companion is essential to a happy relationship. Sexual compatibility most often refers to a mutually satisfactory sexual relationship that includes similar feelings about the frequency of intercourse and agreement on what is enjoyable and permissible. "We both love sex," said one student. "But she loves it more than I do and it's been a problem for her understanding that I just don't want to do it all the time."

Career and Family Goals Compatibility

More important than recreational and sexual compatibility is the extent to which you and your partner agree on having a dual-income marriage and the number of children you want. Failure to discuss the issues of jobs and children

The world is full of willing people; some willing to work, the rest willing to let them.

ROBERT FROST

is to assume that you and your partner have the same goals. "We were like two people in a bus station with tickets to different destinations," said a 26-year-old insurance adjuster. "I wanted her to stay home and for us to have a family. But she wanted a career in fashion merchandising and said that children would interfere with that."

Role Compatibility

I know a couple who got a divorce because they were incompatible—he had no income and she wasn't patable.

GROUCHO MARX

Having compatible roles is as important as having similar goals. As a potential husband or wife, what do you expect to do in each of the following areas and what do you want your spouse to do? Who "should" pay the bills, cook the food, wash the dishes, do the laundry, mop the floor, vacuum the house, and clean the bathroom? If you have children, at what age is it appropriate to put them in a day care center? Who is to care for the child when he or she is an infant? Who stays home from work when a child is sick? Who drives the kids to piano, ballet, and gymnastics lessons? The answers to these questions will help you to evaluate the degree to which you and your partner agree on your respective marital roles.

CONSIDERATION • Your role expectations are less important than you and your partner viewing your roles the same way.

DATA • *The fact that 176 individuals who had been dating their partner for a year were no more likely to have role compatibility than when they first started dating indicates couples may pay little attention to role compatibility in courtship. Hence, role compatibility was not necessary for continuing the relationship.* (Leigh et al., 1984)

Value Compatibility

Although concern for the compatibilities just discussed are critical to selecting the right partner, using a wide-angle lens on yourself and your partner may also be important. Your philosophy of life will influence many of your interests and activities. For example, a person with an intellectual philosophy of life is likely to read extensively, attend lectures, and pursue graduate study. Consider the degree to which each of the following orientations and their behavioral expression characterize you and how much you want them to characterize the person you marry.

RELIGION

How important is religion to you? How important should it be to your partner? If you are a religiously devout person, to what degree is it important that your partner participate in religious activities with you, provide a religious example for your children, and relate to your friends who are also religious?

Many religious doctrines view marriage as a permanent relationship. "Until death do us part" is a phrase from the traditional marriage ceremony. What is your concept of the permanence of marriage (Is divorce justifiable under any conditions?) and what is the concept held by your partner? Some people have a "let's see if the marriage works out" view, whereas others regard it as a lifetime commitment. To what degree do you and your partner see marriage the same way and how much does it matter to you if your views are different?

LIFE-STYLE

What is the sexual and economic life-style you would like for your marriage? The concept of open marriage suggests that although married partners will regard each other as their primary relationship, each may have emotional or sexual relationships outside the marriage. How do you and your partner feel about open marriage and about fidelity?

CONSIDERATION • It is less important what your and your partner's values are than that you know what they are and that you both agree on the values or agree to disagree.

The economic life-style that you expect in your relationship is also important. The social class in which you and your partner were reared will furnish a good index of what you are accustomed to. If your parents held high-status, high-income jobs like physician or lawyer, you have been reared in an economic life-style quite different from someone whose parents were laborers. Such rearing will have an influence on the economic expectations in your own relationship. Also, such expectations can have the reverse impact. One geology major said his parents were physicians and he had been "ignored while they did their careers." As a result, he did not want nor was he comfortable with the "things" his parents surrounded him with. He wanted the "simple life" and is now living in a commune.

POLITICS

The women's movement, abortion legislation, nuclear armaments, gun control, censorship, and the rights of gay people are all political concerns. Whereas some individuals are involved in these issues through thought, discussion, financial support, and organized effort, others are oblivious to their existence as problems. Some feel that politics at any level on any issue is a colossal bore. Also, two people may have the same political concerns but different beliefs about the issues. To what degree do you and your partner share similar political orientations and to what degree does the similarity or dissimilarity matter?

SELF-ACTUALIZATION

A number of people are involved with "getting in touch with their feelings," increasing self-awareness, and actualizing their full potential. For some, this translates into transcendental meditation, yoga, and seeking inner peace. How much importance do you attach to these experiences and how important is it to you that your partner share them with you?

No man can completely know another but by knowing himself, which is the utmost extent of human wisdom.
SAMUEL JOHNSON

DATA • *The fact that 176 individuals who had been dating their partner for a year were no more likely to have similar values than when they first started dating indicates couples may pay little attention to value compatibility in courtship. Hence, value compatibility was not necessary for continuing the relationship.* (Leigh et al., 1984)

Communication

All of the preceding issues are important in selecting a mate, but none takes precedence over the quality of good communication in your relationship. You will bring certain wants, needs, values, and expectations into the relationship with your partner. The probability that your partner's wants and so on will be compatible with yours on every issue all the time is zero.

CONSIDERATION • Good communication not only helps to get the "hidden agendas" up front but also helps to negotiate differences so that each partner continues to benefit from the relationship. Where most couples drift into trouble is when their needs are not expressed, go underground, and later resurface in a negative way. "I hated the way he treated me," said one woman, "but I never said anything. Finally, one day I just told him I was leaving. We never discussed why."

In Chapter 11 we discuss couple communication in detail. For now it is relevant to point out that being able to talk about what you are thinking, feeling, and experiencing with your partner is a highly important issue in selecting a partner.

Flexibility

We rarely find that people have good sense unless they agree with us.

LA
ROCHEFOUCAULD

Since you and your partner do have differences and will change in unpredictable ways throughout your relationship, it is highly desirable that you link yourself with someone who has the capacity to minimize the stress associated with the differences and change. In chapter 11 on communication we will discuss how you can negotiate differences with your partner. But your partner must be willing to negotiate!

Body Clock Compatibility

Some of us are "morning people," some of us are "night people." Characteristics that differentiate the two are listed in Table 8.1. "If one partner rises early every morning ready for a hearty breakfast and the other cannot deal well with either early morning or breakfast, their rhythms do not match and thus they are said to exhibit assynchrony. Synchrony would be achieved, on the other hand, by the marriage of two larks or two owls, both of whom love to . . . bound from the bed at 6 A.M. and go to sleep at sundown or do not truly awaken until mid-afternoon" (Darnley, 1981, p. 33).

To what degree does it matter if partners are matched or mismatched in terms of body clocks? Two researchers (Adams & Cromwell, 1978) who studied 28 married graduate students observed that some out-of-phase couples have

Table 8.1 Morning and Night People

MORNING PERSON	NIGHT PERSON
Awakens at dawn	Awakens late morning or early afternoon
Goes to bed by 10:30	Watches TV past midnight
Wants to leave party early	Enjoys staying at party till over
Rarely active at 2:30 A.M.	Often active at 2:30 A.M.
Feels most creative in morning	Feels most creative at night

less serious conversation, fewer shared activities, less sex, poorer marital adjustment, and more managed conflict.

Related to the body clock issue is that of different energy levels. What is your energy level, and how does it compare with the energy level of your partner? If they are not similar, each of you will need to be able to tolerate the differences or define the differences as unimportant.

Love

"It don't mean a thing if it ain't got that swing," is the lyric to an old song from the big band era. Its message points up the importance of love in a relationship. Even if all the compatibilities discussed were present in your relationship, it would probably be a mistake to marry someone you did not love. In the United States we have been socialized to only marry those people for whom we feel a deep emotional attachment. To marry without love is to begin a relationship with a missing element, which may or may not develop.

In evaluating your total relationship, you might take the Relationship Assessment Inventory.

> We don't want to live with anyone unless there is love—not some silly idea of romantic love, but the sort of love that nourishes the soul and enables people to grow.
>
> EDA LeSHAN

• REJECTING A PARTNER •

Suppose after evaluating your relationship with a particular person, you decide it is best to terminate it. In a study of 220 dating couples, 103 of them broke up within a two-year period (Hill et al., 1976). After examining why they broke up, when they did so, and who initiated the breakup, we explore how you might end a relationship.

Why 103 Relationships Ended

The individuals who broke up told why they did so. Some of their reasons include the following.

MINIMAL INVOLVEMENT

Dating other people, hesitancy to define themselves as being "in love," not feeling close to the partner, and not viewing the partner as a potential spouse were among the reasons for termination of their relationships (Hill et al., 1976).

· Self-Assessment ·

THE RELATIONSHIP ASSESSMENT INVENTORY

Assuming you are involved in a relationship that is oriented toward marriage, the following questions are designed to increase your knowledge of how your partner thinks and feels about a variety of issues. You may want to read the questions to your partner and ask your partner to read them to you.

Careers and Money

1. What kind of job or career will you have? What are your feelings about "working in the evening" versus "being home with the family"? Where will your work require that we live? How often do you feel we will be moving? Where are the places you would refuse to move to? How much will your job require that you travel?

2. How much money will you make the first year we are married?

3. What are your feelings about joint versus separate checking accounts? Which of us do you want to pay the bills? How much money do you think we will have left over each month? How much of this do you think we should save?

4. When we disagree over whether to buy something, how do you suggest we resolve our conflict?

5. What "big ticket item"—house, car, boat, or whatever—do you think we should buy first when we have the money?

6. How often will you want to go on vacation? Where will you want to go? How will we travel? How much money do you feel we should spend on vacations each year?

7. How do you feel about my having a career? Do you expect me to earn an income? How much annually? To what degree do you feel it is your responsibility to cook, clean, and take care of the children? When the children are under age 3, do you want me to stay at home with them or do you think they should be put in a day care center? When they are sick and one of us has to stay home, who will that be?

8. What is your parents' annual income?

9. Do you want me to account to you for the money I spend?

10. How much money do you think we should give to charity each year?

Religion and Children

1. To what degree do you regard yourself as a religious person? What do you think

about religion, a supreme being, prayer, and life after death?

2. Do you go to religious services? Where? How often? Do you pray? How often? What do you pray about? When we are married, how often would you want to go to religious services? In what religion would you want our children to be reared? What responsibility would you take to ensure that our children had the religious training you wanted them to have?

3. How do you feel about abortion? Under what conditions, if any, is abortion justified?

4. What do you think about children? How many do you want? Why? When do you want the first child? At what intervals would you want to have additional children? What do you see as your responsibility for child care—changing diapers, feeding, bathing, playing with children, and taking them to piano lessons? To what degree do you regard these responsibilities as mine?

5. Suppose I did not want to have children or couldn't have them, how would you feel? Would you want to adopt children?

6. To your knowledge, can you have children? Are there any retarded or otherwise abnormal children in your family history?

7. Do you want our children to go to public or private schools?

8. How should children be disciplined? How were you disciplined as a child?

Sex

1. How much sexual intimacy do you feel is appropriate in casual dating, involved dating, and engagement?

2. What do you think about masturbation, oral sex, homosexuality, S & M, and anal sex?

3. What type of contraception do you suggest? Why? If that method does not prove satisfactory, what method would you suggest next?

4. What are your values regarding sex outside of marriage? Suppose I were to have an affair and later told you; what would you do? Why? If I had an affair, would you want me to tell you? Why?

5. What sexual behaviors do you most and least enjoy? How often do you want to have intercourse? How do you want me to turn you down when I don't want to have intercourse? How do you want me to approach you for intercourse? How do you feel about just being physical together— hugging, rubbing, holding, but not having intercourse?

6. If we had a problem we couldn't work out, would you consider seeing a marriage counselor?

7. What does an orgasm feel like to you? By what method of stimulation do you experience an orgasm most easily?

8. Tell me one of your sexual fantasies.

(continued)

Partner Feelings

1. If you could change one thing about me, what would it be?

2. What would you like me to do to make you happier?

3. What would you like me to say or not to say to make you happier?

4. What do you think of yourself? Describe yourself with three adjectives.

5. What do yo think of me? Describe me with three adjectives.

6. What do you like best about me?

7. Do you think I get jealous easily? How will you cope with my jealousy?

8. How do you feel about me emotionally?

Feelings about Parents

1. How do you feel about your mother? Your father?

2. What do you like and dislike about my parents?

3. What is your feeling about living near our parents? How would you feel about my mother living with us? What will we do with our parents if they can't take care of themselves?

4. How do your parents get along? Rate their marriage on a 0–10 scale (0 unhappy; 10 happy). What are your parents' role responsibilities in their marriage?

Other Questions

1. If one of us has to make the final decision on an issue, who should that be?

2. What sports, interests, and hobbies do you enjoy?

3. How often do you like to drink beer, wine, or liquor? How often, if at all, do you like to smoke marijuana, snort coke, or take other drugs? Specify. To what degree do you want me to participate with you?

4. Suppose we couldn't get along: Would you be willing to get a divorce?

5. Would you sign a prenuptial contract if I asked you to?

6. After we are married, how often will you want to be away from home at night with your friends? How do you feel about me being out at night with my friends?

These reasons might suggest that the individuals never felt very strongly about each other, yet more than half reported they were in love at the time of the initial survey two years earlier. So the idea that "love will keep us together" was not true for these couples.

DIFFERENCES

Being dissimilar was also related to breaking up. Specifically, those partners who were different in age, educational plans, intelligence, and physical attractiveness were more likely to break up than those who were alike in these respects. But the differences in other background variables, including social class, religion, and desired family size, didn't seem to matter.

> Can two walk together except they be agreed?
>
> AMOS 3:3

DIFFERENTIAL INVOLVEMENT

There was a greater likelihood that a relationship would break up when one partner was more involved than the other. Fifty-four percent of such relationships were terminated by the end of the two-year period. In contrast, only 23 percent of the relationships had been terminated in which the partners were equally involved (Hill et al., 1976). One partner being more involved than another is not unusual. Of 150 romantically involved couples at UCLA, more than half saw themselves as more involved than their partners (White, 1977).

In a study of 537 university student relationships the researchers (Walster et al., 1978) concluded, "It is in equitable love relationships that men and women feel most content and happy. Inequitable love relationships are volatile relationships—the underbenefited feel resentful and the overbenefited feel guilty" (p. 91).

CONSIDERATION • Level of involvement in a relationship is difficult to control. Inevitably, the partners will enter the relationship at different levels and experience varying degrees of intensity throughout its course. The film *Anne of a Thousand Days* illustrates this phenomenon. At one point Anne Boleyn observes that she and King Henry VIII spent 1,000 days in a love relationship. But for only one of those days were they in love with each other. The rest of the time he was in love with her but not she with him or vice versa.

One partner in an eight-month relationship explained how it feels to be out of phase with one's lover. "I'm losing the love feelings I had for her and I can't really explain why. I don't want to hurt her but I'm beginning to view her as the clinging vine type. I know she knows I'm slipping. I doubt we'll be together by Christmas."

SEPARATION

Although not mentioned in the Hill et al. study, some couples indicate that separation was a major factor contributing to their break up. "When we were separated over the summer," said one partner, "I think both of us got tired of being lonely so we drifted into other relationships."

CONSIDERATION • It is sometimes said that the effect of separation on a relationship is much like water on a fire—a little makes it blaze but too much can put it out.

The Calendar and Breakups

DATA • *Among college students breakups tend to occur with the school calendar. June (school is over), September (summer vacation is over), and January (the first term is over) are the months in which couples are most likely to break up.* (Hill et al., 1976)

As one student said, "I told him that I wanted us to date others (translation: I wanted to date others) while we were separated during the summer. As it turned out, I didn't write after that, became involved with someone else, and didn't see him again."

Who Breaks Off a Relationship?

Relationships are rarely ended by mutual agreement. In the Hill et al. (1976) study, eight in 10 of the women and men said that one person wanted to end the relationship more than the other. That person is most often the woman. Fifty-one percent of the relationships were ended by the woman, 42 percent by the man, and the rest mutually.

CONSIDERATION • One possible explanation of why women are more likely to terminate a relationship is that women may be more sensitive to signs of trouble. For example, in the preceding study women not only cited more problems in the relationships than men but they also pointed to different kinds of problems. Whereas women expressed concern about "differences in interests" and "differences in intelligence," men were more likely to cite "living too far apart" as a reason to break up.

Having more and better alternative relationships is another reason women may be more likely to end a relationship. In a study of 150 romantically involved couples (White, 1977) the women reported having significantly more opposite-gender friends than the men. The researcher also found that the larger the number of opposite-gender friends a partner has, the less involved that person regards his or her present relationship.

Breaking Up with Your Partner

Last night I wrote
I loved you
and your oat-
meal cookies;
tonight I write
I hate you
but I still love
your oatmeal
cookies.

HAL J. DANIEL III

"Break it to me gently" sings Juice Newton in her song of the same name. The lyrics imply that one of the most painful experiences we ever have is ending a relationship. Even though we may not be married to the person, the termination represents cutting off an intimate companion.

It sometimes happens that you are involved in a relationship that, for whatever reason, you feel the need to terminate. Some guidelines you might consider include the following:

1. Decide that terminating the relationship is what you want to do. In some cases, it may be easier to "fix" the relationship rather than drop the partner and get another one. Negotiating differences, compromising, changing expectations, and giving the relationship more time are alternatives to ending it. But in other cases, it may be wiser to terminate a wounded relationship than try to keep it alive. Rhett Butler says to Scarlett O'Hara in *Gone With The Wind*:

I was never one to patiently pick up broken fragments and glue them together and tell myself that the mended whole was as good as new. What's broken is broken—I'd rather remember it as it was at its best than mend it and see the broken pieces as long as I lived (Mitchell, 1977, p. 945).

2. Acknowledge and accept that the other person will probably be hurt when you terminate the relationship and that there may be no way you can stop the hurt. One person said, "I can't live with him any more but I don't want to hurt him either." The two feelings are incompatible. To end a relationship with someone who loves you is usually to hurt him or her.

CONSIDERATION • But to continue a relationship with someone because you don't want to hurt him or her is to hurt yourself (you will continue to be frustrated and ask yourself "Why can't I get the nerve to end it?"), your partner (you are living with him or her out of pity), and your relationship (it only exists out of fear of what will happen if you do end it).

3. Having decided that termination is the goal and that hurting the partner cannot be avoided, tell the partner that you do not want to continue the relationship for a reason that is specific to you ("I need more freedom," "I want to go to graduate school in another state," "I'm not ready to settle down," and the like). Don't blame your partner or give him or her a way to make things better. If you do, the relationship will continue because you may feel obligated to give your partner a second chance. By making the reason specific to yourself and your needs, you take away the option of your partner doing something to keep you.

Although some prefer to tell the partner in person, others feel that a letter is easier. "I know it's chicken," said one history major, "but I just can't tell her to her face. I've tried twice and she's talked me out of it both times." Still others prefer the phone. One person used a cassette tape. "I didn't want the coldness of a letter or to get trapped in a phone conversation and hear him start crying, so I made him a cassette tape and mailed it to him."

4. Cut off the relationship completely. If you are the person ending the relationship, you will be less involved in the relationship than your partner. Your lower level of involvement may make it possible for you to continue to see the other person without feeling too hurt when the evening is over. But the other person will have a more difficult time and will best heal if you stay away completely. To let the person stay in your life is to keep his or her hurt alive. Once you have decided to terminate the relationship, you need to get it over with.

5. Start new relationships. By going out with others you force your ex-partner to acknowledge that you are serious about ending the relationship. You should also encourage your ex-partner to see others. Time usually heals all wounds but meanwhile another partner is an alternative source of reinforcement.

When Your Partner Breaks Up with You

Suppose you are on the other end of the breakup and you are the one being dropped? What might you do to get over the terminated relationship and to ease the transition to a new relationship? Here are some possibilities:

1. Recognize that the pain is temporary. Although the hurt you feel when a

Temporary loneliness is one of the potential consequences of a terminated relationship.

partner withdraws from you will be intense, keep in mind that it will not last forever. You will get over it, and in most cases, completely.

2. Focus on negatives of the partner. When you think about your ex-partner, be careful not to dwell on the positives—how good the sex was, how much he or she once loved you, how you enjoyed the day at the beach or the Willie Nelson concert. These memories will only keep your hurt alive. Instead, focus on the negative aspects of your partner—he or she deceived you, saw someone else while still involved with you, was always late, drank too much, wanted too many or too few kids, or whatever you regard as the disadvantages of the relationship.

3. Discard mementos of the person. If you have been involved with someone for a while, you may have various symbols of your relationship—gifts, pictures, stones you collected at the beach. If you discard these things that remind you of the person, you may minimize your pain—at least in the short run. Later you will be able to see the same items and perceive them differently. If they bother you, put them away. Shakespeare said, "Praising what is lost makes the remembrance dear."

4. Stay away. One of your greatest needs will be to make contact with the person and get your ex-partner to relate to you as he or she once did. Fight the need and stay away. Don't call, drop by, or write. The best way to get over your feelings is cold turkey.

5. Initiate new relationships. The best antidote to a terminated relationship is a new one.

CONSIDERATION • Although you may not feel like initiating contact with others, it will eventually heal the pain to get back into the stream of life by doing so. Don't wait until you feel like seeing others—do it immediately. But watch the level of involvement in a new relationship. Because you have just come from a terminated relationship, you may be particularly vulnerable or susceptible to a new love. For now the goal should be to see others and have fun, not to fall in love or find a new partner.

Women seem to cope with terminations better than men, which isn't surprising in view of the fact that, as we have noted, they most frequently initiate them. In a study of 231 involved couples, among those who ended their relationships, the women were likely to be less depressed, lonely, and unhappy afterward (Rubin et al., 1981).

• TIMING YOUR MARITAL COMMITMENT •

Launching a communications satellite into space requires precise timing. If lift-off occurs at other than the exact moment, the satellite will miss its orbit and be lost in space (RCA once lost a multimillion dollar satellite in space). Getting into a successful marital orbit also requires timing. Issues to consider in timing your commitment to marriage are age, education, and career.

Age

Your age and that of your partner at the time of your marriage are highly predictive of future marital happiness and stability. Individuals who get married in their teens report greater marital unhappiness and have higher divorce rates than those who delay marriage (Carlson & Stinson, 1982). Although age itself does not increase marital happiness and stability, increased age at marriage is associated with greater personal maturity, higher education, better income, and parental approval of the marriage. Those who are older are more likely to have prepared for marriage by clarifying their values and goals, establishing an economic base, and working out good relationships with parents and in-laws.

But how old is "older"? How old do you and your partner need to be to maximize your potential for a good marriage?

DATA • *Women who marry when they are 25 and men who marry when they are 28 report greater marital satisfaction and have lower divorce rates than those who marry earlier.* (Lasswell, 1974)

After hearing these statistics in a marriage and family class, one student responded, "Getting married at my age [18] would be like being operated on by a surgeon with one arm. I'd have half the chance of coming out of the thing alive."

CONSIDERATION • One of the concerns in our society is the escalating divorce rate. We could radically reduce the percentage of couples who get divorced by passing legislation requiring people to be age 25 or older before marriage. Of course, such a law will never be passed because of our value for individual freedom. In addition, studies disagree on the effect of age at marriage on marital satisfaction. One study (Bahr et al., 1983) found no relationship.

Education

The amount of education you get and whether you or your partner has more education may also affect your marital happiness and the stability of your relationship. Men who complete college have a lower rate of divorce than men who complete only high school or who leave college without graduating. The reason for greater marital stability among college-educated men is not the education itself but the economic potential associated with increased education. The adage "The more you learn, the more you earn" is still true.

DATA • *The lifetime income of a male who completes high school is $861,000; who completes college, $1,190,000. The lifetime income of a female who completes high school is $381,000; who completes college, $523,000.* (U.S. Bureau of the Census, 1983)

A college degree is not only associated with increased income but with a greater chance of staying married.

Increased education for women is also predictive of marital stability, but not if she has more education than her husband. This is particularly true if she is a college graduate and her husband isn't (Glick, 1984).

Career Plans

The timing of your marriage will also depend on your career plans. Some individuals feel they want to become established in a career for a couple of years and to be economically independent before they get married. "My sister married a guy in college and threw her career plans to the wind," said one woman. "She's now divorced and is on the job market for the first time at age 31. I'm not going to let that happen to me."

Other people feel they have to make a choice between their career and their partner and fear losing the partner if they choose the career. "I can't put my partner on hold for two years while I find out what it is like in the business world," said another woman. "I'm confident that I'll be a great success in my work but I don't know how much it will mean if I'm not married to Bill. It is a real dilemma."

• BECOMING ENGAGED •

Having selected a partner after rejecting some partners, and perhaps having been rejected yourself, your mutual commitment to marriage with a compatible partner usually means an engagement. What are the implications of this stage and how can you use it to increase future happiness?

Engagement has two meanings—in war, it's a battle; in courtship, it's a surrender.

LAURENCE PETER

Implications of an Engagement

The engagement period is usually regarded as serious, partner-exclusive, public, and as preparation time for the wedding.

SERIOUS

An engagement is a specific commitment to marry. Once the words "let's get married" are spoken and agreed to, the relationship assumes a different status. The other person is no longer viewed as a casual partner but as a future spouse. Although a few regard engagement lightly, most take it seriously.

PARTNER-EXCLUSIVE

Engagements carry the expectation that all outside relationships (romantic and sexual) will terminate. Seeing other people during the engagement period is often regarded as a reason to break the relationship. "After I found out he had been seeing his old girlfriend," said one fiancée, "I figured he would also be unfaithful to me when we were married. I confronted him and he lied about it. We broke up."

PUBLIC

Before the announcement of a future wedding, the love relationship belongs solely to the partners. But whereas love is private, engagement is public. Parents and peers become involved in the event and communicate their evaluations of each partner's marital choice. One business major recalled, "When I was just dating Laura, my best friend said nothing about her one way or the other. But when I told him we were getting married after graduation, he told me she had a 'for rent' sign in her head and that I would be signing up for the nightmare of my life if I married her." Indeed, the opinions of peers and parents are influential in strengthening or breaking an engagement (Surra & Wareham, 1981).

PREPARATIONS

Eighty percent of first weddings take place in a traditional setting—a church or synagogue—with bridesmaids and ushers. Such an event requires tremendous preparation, and for many couples, is a time of intense stress. "We were both under so much pressure preparing for the wedding," recalled one bride, "at one time we considered calling it off. My daddy told us if it was going to be that big of a hassle, to elope and he would give us the $2,500."

Using Your Engagement Period Productively

Marriage is a great institution, but I'm not ready for an institution yet.

MAE WEST

"He's not the man I married," said a spouse one year after her wedding. This is as often said of a wife. People often do not know the person they are marrying very well. "What you see is what you get" is not true of marriage partners. You really don't know what you have got until you relate to the person in the role of spouse over a period of time. But there are some things you can do to help minimize the surprises after marriage. These include systematically examining your relationship, visiting your future in-laws, and considering premarital counseling.

EXAMINE YOUR RELATIONSHIP

In a commercial for an oil filter, a mechanic says he has just completed a "ring job" on a car engine that will cost the owner over $400. He goes on to say that a $5.98 oil filter would have made the job unnecessary and ends his soliloquy with, "Pay me now, or pay me later." The same idea applies to the consequences of using or not using your engagement period to examine your relationship. At some point you will take a very close look at your partner and your relationship; but will you do it now or later? Doing so now may be less costly than doing so after the wedding.

In examining your relationship, consider the compatibility issues discussed earlier in this chapter. To what degree are you and your partner compatible, similar, or dissimilar on the issues that matter to each of you?

RECOGNIZE DANGEROUS PATTERNS

As you examine your relationship, you should be sensitive to issues that suggest you may be on a collision course. Three such issues are breaking the relationship frequently, constant arguing, and inequality resulting from differences in education, social class, and the like. A roller coaster engagement is predic-

During the engagement period, looking at your relationship is more important than selecting a ring.

tive of a marital relationship with the same pattern. But the psychic and social costs of separating during a marriage are higher.

The same is true of frequent arguments in a relationship.

CONSIDERATION • Lover's arguments become the married couple's fights. Use the premarital period to develop a pattern of resolving differences. If this is not possible, consider the consequences of being married to someone with whom you will have a roller coaster relationship punctuated by quarrels.

Relationships in which the partners are regarded as being unequal to each other are precarious. Such was the case of Bill and Susan. He was a divorced physician with two children. She was a nurses aide, and although she held him in awe they had little in common. Although lovers may view each other with awe, spouses rarely do. Eventually, he may feel cheated because he does not have a companion equal to his life and educational experience. She may feel stress at continually trying to be what she is not to appease him. So persons who are radically different in age, education, social class, and values should also be cautious about marrying. Friends select each other because they have something in common and will maintain their relationship for the same reason. Lovers may select each other on the basis of love feelings, but when these feelings dissipate, what they have in common is likely to maintain their interest in each other.

OBSERVE YOUR FUTURE IN-LAWS

Since engagements often mean more frequent getting together with each other's parents, you might seize the opportunity to assess the type of family your partner was reared in and the implications for your marriage. When visiting your in-laws-to-be, observe their standard of living, the way they relate to each other, and the degree to which your partner is like the parent of the same gender. How does their standard of living compare with that of your own family? How does the emotional closeness (or distance) of your partner's family compare with that of yours? Such comparisons are significant because both you and your partner will reflect to some degree your respective home environments. If you want to know what your partner may be like in 20 years, look at his or her parent of the same gender. There is a tendency for a man to become like his father and a woman like her mother.

CONSIDER PREMARITAL COUNSELING

Most clergy offer three premarital sessions before marrying a couple. These may consist of information about marriage, assessment of the couple's relationship, or resolving conflict that has surfaced in the relationship. Those who do not plan to be married in a church or synagogue or choose to see a clergyman for premarital counseling sometimes see a marriage counselor. A third party can be helpful in assisting a couple to assess their relationship. Although the couple might deny the existence of a problem for fear that looking at it will break them up, the counselor can help them examine the problem with the goal of working it out. Most couples who voluntarily become involved in premarital counseling regard the experience in positive terms (Schumm & Denton, 1979). Those premarital programs which use married couples as models seem to be the most effective. One such program is offered by the Office of Social Concerns and Family Life Ministry in New Ulm, Minnesota which involves a happily married couple talking about the realities of marriage, negotiating conflict, and managing money (*Marriage and Divorce Today*, 1984).

DATA • *Almost 80 percent of over 5,000 students from four universities said that they believed that they had the necessary skills to make a good marriage.* (Martin and Martin, 1984)

Prolong Your Engagement If . . .

Even though you and your partner may have examined your relationship, seen a counselor, and feel confident about your impending marriage, there are four conditions under which you might consider prolonging your engagement. In combination, these conditions argue against getting married at this time.

SHORT COURTSHIP

We all know happily married people who married soon after they met, but the probability of marital success is low for such couples. In general, the longer a couple know each other before they marry, the better their chance of staying married and having a happy relationship. An extended period of time before the wedding gives you an opportunity to observe your partner in a variety of settings.

> CONSIDERATION • A year is the minimum length of time a couple should know each other before getting married. During this period the partners should spend time with each other, their respective parents, and friends. Taking the Relationship Assessment Inventory (see page 214) will be helpful in addressing the important issues in one's marriage.

LACK OF MONEY

A divorced woman listened intently as her lover explained the details of his finances: "Since I too am divorced, I pay alimony and child support. The money that's left barely pays for my food and rent. I'm writing a novel now and will be financially okay if it sells. If it doesn't, my money situation will be tight." The woman refused to see this man again and said, "I love him, but I loved my first husband too. We literally ate soup, bologna, and peaches for most of our meals. I'm tired of being poor. People who say that love is all you need to make a marriage work must have money." Two researchers (Rosenblatt & Keller, 1983) observed that couples who experience economic distress also tend to blame each other more often.

PARENTAL DISAPPROVAL

A parent recalled, "I knew when I met the guy it wouldn't work out. I told my daughter and pleaded that she not marry him. She did and they are divorced." Such parental predictions (whether positive or negative) often come true.

Even though parents who reject the commitment choice of their offspring are often regarded as unfair, their opinions should not be taken lightly. The parents' own experience in marriage and their intimate knowledge of their offspring combine to help them assess how their child might get along with a particular mate. Should your parents disapprove of your marital choice, try to evaluate their concerns objectively. Their insights may prove valuable.

PREMARITAL PREGNANCY

Three in 10 white women aged 15–19 and almost five in 10 black women in the same age group who had premarital intercourse reported they became pregnant (Zelnik & Kanter, 1980). The spouses of such marriages have a higher risk of marital unhappiness and divorce than those who do not conceive children before marriage (Kraus, 1977). Combined with a short premarital period, lack of money, and parental or in-law hostility, premarital pregnancy represents an ominous beginning for newlyweds.

NEGATIVE REASONS FOR GETTING MARRIED

In addition to premarital pregnancy, other questionable reasons for getting married include rebound, escape, and pity.

Rebound   A rebound marriage results when you marry someone immediately after another person has terminated a relationship with you. It is a frantic attempt to reestablish your desirability in your own eyes and in the eyes of the partner who just dropped you. One man said:

> After she told me she wouldn't marry me, I became desperate. I called up an old girlfriend to see if I could get the relationship going again. We were married within a month. I know it was foolish but I was very hurt and couldn't stop myself.

CONSIDERATION • To marry on the rebound is questionable because the marriage is made in reference to the previous partner and not to the partner being married. In reality, you are using the person you intend to marry to establish yourself as the winner in the previous relationship. To avoid the negative consequences of marrying on the rebound, you might wait until the negative memories of your past relationship have been replaced by positive aspects of your current relationship. In other words, marry when the satisfactions of being with your current partner outweigh any feelings of revenge.

Escape   A partner may marry to escape an unhappy home situation. The parents are often seen as oppressive and overbearing and their marriage as discordant. Their continued bickering may be highly aversive, causing the partner to flee the home by marrying. A family with an alcoholic parent may create an escape situation. One woman said:

> I couldn't wait to get away from home. Ever since my dad died, my mother has been drinking and watching me like a hawk. "Be home early, don't drink, and watch out for those horrible men," she would always say. I admit it. I married the first guy that would have me. Marriage was my ticket away from that woman.

CONSIDERATION • Marriage for escape is a poor idea. Far better is to continue the relationship with the partner until mutual love and respect, rather than the desire to escape an unhappy situation, becomes the dominant force propelling you toward marriage. In this way you can evaluate the marital relationship in terms of its own potential rather than solely as an alternative to an unhappy situation.

Pity   Some partners marry because they feel guilty about terminating a relationship with someone who has undergone a radical physical change. The boyfriend of one woman got drunk one Halloween evening and began to light fireworks on the roof of his fraternity house. As he was running away from a Roman candle he had just ignited, he tripped and fell off the roof. He landed on his head and was in a coma for three weeks. A year after the accident his speech and muscle coordination were still adversely affected. The woman said she did not love him any more but felt guilty about terminating a relationship now that he had become physically afflicted. She was ambivalent. She felt it was her duty to marry her fiancée, but her feelings were no longer love feelings.

CONSIDERATION • In such a situation where one partner loses a limb, becomes brain damaged, or is otherwise affected so that a normal physical life is impossible, it is important to keep the issue of pity separate from the advisability of contracting the marriage. The decision to marry should be based on factors other than pity or gratitude to the partner. This is a value judgment based on the potential long-term negative consequences of contracting a relationship in which one partner has become afflicted late in the courtship process. Although the short-term consequences of marrying one's afflicted fiancé may be positive as the partner can avoid the guilt of withdrawal and be steadied by the idea that "I did the responsible thing," the long-term consequences may have a debilitating effect on the relationship. Negative consequences may be thoughts such as "I married only half a person" or the difficulties of continuing to cope with living with an afflicted person. It is very important to accurately assess the way you feel about your partner if she or he has experienced a physical impairment.

Delaying marriage until all of the "right" conditions are met may be extremely difficult. Most of us assume that *our* marriage will be different, will not end in divorce, and that love is enough to compensate for factors like a premarital pregnancy or lack of money. But is this a reasonable assumption in the light of factors suggesting that we delay the wedding?

Even though all of the indications for a successful marriage are present, either you or your partner may be reluctant to make a commitment. Reluctance may be related to a negative experience in a previous relationship or the perception that making a commitment may be followed by the other person losing interest or beginning to date others. Such was the case of one student who said, "As long as you don't make a commitment, you've got them. Once they know they've got you, they don't want you."

• WRITING A PRENUPTIAL OR MARRIAGE CONTRACT •

When a couple marry they enter into an unwritten contract with the state. The legal obligations of the contract are that the husband is responsible for the economic support of his family and the wife is responsible for various domestic services and child care. Such obligations may be rejected by husbands who feel that their wives should share in the economic support of the family and by wives who want their husbands to share the domestic work and childrearing. Nevertheless, the law does not allow either party to absolve themselves of their responsibility.

Beyond the essential elements of the unwritten marriage contract, some couples want to specify for themselves the rights and obligations of their own marriage. One-fourth of 283 students said they would be interested in developing a contract with their marital partner, (Vander Mey & Rosher, 1981). Both women and men were equally interested in doing so. Some of the items they were interested in including in their contract related to each partner having an equal voice in where they lived, how they spent their money, and how their children would be reared. That each was to earn an income and help with domestic and childrearing responsibilities were also important items.

Persons who have been married before are often concerned that money and property be kept separate in a second marriage. One established widowed physician wanted his property and assets to go to his children. The woman he was to marry was also a widow and wanted her estate to go to her daughter. They drew up an agreement stating that whatever property and assets they had would not become the spouse's in the event of death or divorce.

Where only one party has assets, a prenuptial contract can have negative consequences for the other party. Sherry, a never-married 22-year-old, signed such an agreement. "Paul was adamant about my signing the contract. He said he loved me, but would never consider marrying anyone unless we signed a prenuptial agreement stating that he would never be responsible for alimony in case of a divorce. I was so much in love it didn't seem to matter. I didn't realize that basically he was and is a selfish person. Now, five years later after a divorce, I go to the court begging for alimony while he lives in a big house overlooking the lake with his new wife."

Although most people marrying for the first time will not opt for a prenuptial agreement, a higher proportion of those in their second marriages will. Some agreements will be designed to keep property separate. Other agreements will be informal and designed to clarify expectations in the relationship. Exhibit 8.1 is the marriage contract of spouses who had been married before.

CONSIDERATION • When the goal of a personal marital contract is to keep property separate, contact an attorney. One attorney warns, "Don't try to write a contract yourself. A little sacrifice of a legal fee at the time of drafting that will hold up in court can save a great deal of grief later on. If you do it yourself, you are destined to experience *Tu Errabais* (liberally translated: 'You will screw it up')" (Wright, 1984).

• PREDICTING YOUR MARITAL HAPPINESS •

Whether or not you develop a marriage contract with your partner, you will make a prediction about the success of your marriage. But how can you be sure you are right? You can't. It is not possible to predict what your level of marital satisfaction will be even three days after your wedding. There are several reasons why.

Illusion of the Perfect Mate

The illusion that you have found the perfect partner—one who will be all things to you and vice versa—will carry you through courtship. But the reality is very different. You have not found the perfect mate—there isn't one. Anyone you marry will come with a minus quality and the one quality that is lacking may become the only one you regard as important (Sammons, 1984). When some people discover that their partner lacks something they think is essential ("the ability to communicate", "being faithful", "loves me"), they consider a divorce. Columnist Ann Landers (1977) asked her readers, "If you had it to do over again, would you marry the same person?" She received 50,000 responses. Fifty-two percent replied "no" and 48 percent said "yes." Marital happiness is hard to predict because the drug of the premarital period—love—alters your view of the partner; but this view is only an illusion.

Deception During the Premarital Period

Your illusion of the perfect mate is helped along by some deception on the part of your partner. At the same time, you are presenting only favorable aspects of

· Exhibit 8.1 ·

MARRIAGE CONTRACT

Pam and Mark are of sound mind and body, have a clear understanding of the terms of this contract and of the binding nature of the agreements contained herein; they freely and in good faith choose to enter into this PRENUPTIAL AGREEMENT and MARRIAGE CONTRACT and fully intend it to be binding upon themselves.

Now, therefore, in consideration of their love and esteem for each other, and in consideration of the mutual promises herein expressed, the sufficiency of which is hereby acknowledged, Pam and Mark agree as follows:

Names
Pam and Mark affirm their individuality and equality in this relationship. The parties believe in and accept the convention of the wife accepting the husband's name, while rejecting any implied ownership.

Therefore, the parties agree that they will be known as husband and wife and will henceforth employ the titles of address: Mr. and Mrs. Mark Stafford, and will use the full names of Pam Hayes Stafford and Mark Robert Stafford.

Relationships with Others
Pam and Mark believe that their commitment to each other is strong enough that no restrictions are necessary with regard to relationships with others.

Therefore, the parties agree to allow each other freedom to choose and define their relationships outside this contract and the parties further agree to maintain sexual fidelity each to the other.

Religion
Pam and Mark reaffirm their belief in God and recognize He is the source of their love. Each of the parties have their own religious beliefs.

Therefore, the parties agree to respect their individual preferences with respect to religion and to make no demands on each other to change such preferences.

Children
Pam and Mark both have children. Although no minor children will be involved, there are two (2) children still at home and in school and in need of financial and emotional support.

Therefore, the parties agree that they will maintain a home for and support these children as long as needed and reasonable. They further agree that all children of both parties will be treated as one family unit and each will be given emotional and financial support to the extent feasible and necessary as determined mutually by both parties.

Careers and Domicile
Pam and Mark value the importance and integrity of their respective careers and acknowledge the demands that their jobs place on them as individuals and on their partnership. Both parties are well established in their respective careers and do not foresee any change or move in the future.

Therefore, the parties agree, however, that if need or desire for a move should arise, the decision to move shall be mutual and based on the following factors:

(a) The overall advantage gained by one of the parties in pursuing a new opportunity shall be weighed against the disadvantages, economic and otherwise, incurred by the other.
(b) The amount of income or other incentive derived from the move shall not be controlling.
(c) Short-term separations as a result of such moves may be necessary.

Mark hereby waives whatever right he may have to solely determine the legal domicile of the parties.

Care and Use of Living Spaces
Pam and Mark recognize the need for autonomy and equality within the home in terms of the use

(continued)

of available space and allocation of household tasks. The parties reject the concept that the responsibility for housework rests with the woman in a marriage relationship while the duties of home maintenance and repair rest with the man.

Therefore, the parties agree, to share equally in the performance of all household tasks, taking into consideration individual schedules, preferences, and abilities of each.

The parties agree that decisions about the use of living space in the home shall be mutually made, regardless of the parties' relative financial interests in the ownership or rental of the home, and the parties further agree to honor all requests for privacy from the other party.

Property; Debts; Living Expenses

Pam and Mark intend that the individual autonomy sought in the partnership shall be reflected in the ownership of existing and future-acquired property, in the characterization and control of income, and in the responsibility for living expenses. Pam and Mark also recognize the right of patrimony of children of their previous marriages.

Therefore, the parties agree that all things of value now held singly and/or acquired singly in the future shall be the property of the party making such acquisition. In the event that one party to this agreement shall predecease the other, property and/or other valuables shall be disposed of in accordance with an existing will or other instrument of disposal that reflects the intent of the deceased party.

Property or valuables acquired jointly shall be the property of the partnership and shall be divided, if necessary, according to the contribution of each party. If one party shall predecease the other, jointly owned property or valuables shall become the property of the surviving spouse.

Pam and Mark feel that each of the parties to this agreement should have access to monies that are not accountable to the partnership.

Therefore, the parties agree that each shall retain a mutually agreeable portion of their total income and the remainder shall be deposited in a mutually agreeable banking institution and shall be used to satisfy all jointly acquired expenses and debts.

The parties agree that beneficiaries of life insurance policies they now own shall remain as named on each policy. Future changes in beneficiaries shall be mutually agreed on after the dependency of the children of each party has been terminated. Any other benefits of any retirement plan or insurance benefits that accrue to a spouse only shall not be affected by the foregoing.

The parties recognize that in the absence of income by one of the parties, resulting from any reason, living expenses may become the sole responsibility of the employed party and in such a situation, the employed party shall assume responsibility for the personal expenses of the other.

Both Pam and Mark intend their marriage to last as long as both shall live.

Therefore the parties agree that should it become necessary, due to the death of either party, the surviving spouse shall assume any last expenses in the event that no insurance exists for that purpose.

Pam hereby waives whatever right she may have to rely on Mark to provide the sole economic support for the family unit.

Evaluation of the Partnership

Pam and Mark recognize the importance of change in their relationship and intend that this CONTRACT shall be a living document and a focus for periodic evaluations of the partnership.

The parties agree that either party can initiate a review of any article of the CONTRACT at any time for amendment to reflect changes in the relationship. The parties agree to honor such requests for review with negotiations and discussions at a mutually convenient time.

The parties agree that, in any event, there shall be an annual reaffirmation of the CONTRACT on or about the anniversary date of the CONTRACT.

The parties agree that, in the case of unresolved conflicts between them over any provisions of the CONTRACT, they will seek mediation, professional or otherwise, by a third party.

Termination of the Contract

Pam and Mark believe in the sanctity of marriage; however, in the unlikely event of a decision to terminate this CONTRACT, the parties agree that neither shall contest the application for a divorce decree or the entry of such decree in the county in which the parties are both residing at the time of such application.

In the event of termination of the CONTRACT and divorce of the parties, the provisions of this and the section on "Property; Debts; Living Expenses" of the CONTRACT as amended shall serve as the final property settlement agreement between the parties. In such event, this CONTRACT is intended to affect a complete settlement of any and all claims that either party may have against the other, and a complete settlement of their respective rights as to property rights, homestead rights, inheritance rights, and all other rights of property otherwise arising out of their partnership. The parties further agree that in the event of termination of this contract and divorce of the parties, neither party shall require the other to pay maintenance costs or alimony.

Decision Making

Pam and Mark share a commitment to a process of negotiations and compromise which will strengthen their equality in the partnership. Decisions will be made with respect for individual needs. The parties hope to maintain such mutual decision making so that the daily decisions affecting their lives will not become a struggle between the parties for power, authority, and dominance. The parties agree that such a process, while sometimes time consuming and fatiguing, is a good investment in the future of their relationship and their continued esteem for each other.

Now, therefore, Pam and Mark make the following declarations:

1. They are responsible adults.
2. They freely adopt the spirit and the material terms of this prenuptial and marriage contract.
3. The marriage contract, entered into in conjunction with a marriage license of the State of Illinois, County of Wayne, on this 12th day of June, 1984, hereby manifests their intent to define the rights and obligations of their marriage relationship as distinct from those rights and obligations defined by the laws of the State of Illinois, and affirms their right to do so.

4. They intend to be bound by this prenuptial and marriage contract and to uphold its provisions before any Court of Law in the Land.

Therefore, comes now, Pam Hayes Carraway who applauds her development which allows her to enter into this partnership of trust and she agrees to go forward with this marriage in the spirit of the foregoing PRENUPTIAL and MARRIAGE CONTRACT.

_____
Pam Hayes Carraway

Therefore, comes now, Mark Robert Stafford who celebrates his growth and independence with the signing of this contract and he agrees to accept the responsibilities of this marriage, as set forth in the foregoing PRENUPTIAL and MARRIAGE CONTRACT.

_____
Mark Robert Stafford

This contract and covenant has been received and reviewed by the Reverend Ralph James, officiating.

_____
Ralph James

Finally, comes Karen James and Bill Dunn who certify that Pam and Mark did freely read and sign this marriage contract in their presence, on the occasion of their entry into a marriage relationship by the signing of a marriage license of the State of Illinois, County of Wayne, at which they acted as official witnesses. Further, they declare that the marriage license of the parties bears the date of the signing of this PRENUPTIAL and MARRIAGE CONTRACT.

_____
Karen James

_____
Bill Dunn

yourself to the other person. The deceptions are often not deliberate but an attempt to withhold undesirable aspects of one's self for fear that the partner may not like them. One male student said he knew he drank too much but that if his date found out, she would be disappointed and maybe drop him. He kept his drinking hidden throughout their courtship. They married and are now divorced. She said of him, "I never knew he drank whiskey until our honeymoon. He never drank like this before we were married."

Confinement of Marriage

Another factor that makes it impossible to predict your continued happiness is the different circumstances of the premarital period and marriage. Although premarital norms permit relative freedom to move in and out of relationships, marriage involves a legal contract. One recently married person described marriage as an iron gate that clangs shut behind you, and "getting it open is almost impossible." One's freedom to leave a relationship is transformed by the wedding ceremony. Thereafter there is tremendous social pressure to work things out and a feeling of obligation to do so that was not previously present. The new sense of confinement often brings out the worst in partners who seemed very cooperative before marriage.

Balancing Work and Relationship Demands

Predicting marital happiness is also difficult because the partners must necessarily shift their focus from each other to the business of life. Careers and children emerge as concerns that often take precedence over spending time with each other, going to parties, and seeing movies. Time and energy spent on jobs and childrearing often leave marriage partners too tired to interact with each other. "I never see my partner" is often heard by marriage counselors. Also, the more abrasive communication encouraged by conditions of stress has negative consequences for the way partners feel about each other. "Whenever we do get together, we fight," said one partner.

Inevitability of Change

Times change and we change with them too.

FROM OWEN'S EPIGRAMMATA

One of the major themes of this text is that you are continually changing. Just as you are not the same person you were 10 years ago, you will be different 10 years from now. The direction and intensity of these changes are predictable neither for you nor for your partner. You, your partner, and your relationship will not be the same two years (or two days) in a row. Reflecting on change in her marriage, one woman recalled, "When we were married we were very active in politics. Now I have my law degree and am enjoying my practice. But Jerry is totally immersed in meditating and taking health food nutrients. He also spends four nights a week playing racketball. I never imagined that we'd have nothing to say to each other after only three years of marriage."

CONSIDERATION • Whether you will be happily married after your wedding cannot be predicted. Although selecting a compatible partner is basic, giving up any illusions of finding a perfect mate, minimizing premarital deception, accepting (and enjoying) the confinement of marriage, balancing work and relationship demands, and adapting to whatever changes that occur are crucial for marriage success.

• TRENDS •

With more than 50 percent of marriages ending in divorce, some couples are becoming more cautious about entering marriage. The growing possibility that "divorce may happen to me too" may reduce the number of hasty, ill-conceived marriages. The fact that age at marriage is inching upward may reflect a greater determination to marry when the conditions are right, not when the emotions are ready. Also, the use of marriage contracts reflects a concern that each partner be aware of the other's expectations to prevent misunderstandings.

In addition to greater caution in entering marriage, alternatives to the traditional formal engagement will become more acceptable. Although the engagement ring and announcement will continue to be the script for most people, a growing number, particularly those who live together, will bypass the formality of an engagement period.

> It appears to me that finding someone one can truly enjoy is, to some extent, a happy accident.
>
> JAMES WALTERS

• SUMMARY •

In selecting a marital partner, you might consider the degree to which you are compatible in the areas of recreation, sex, career and family goals, roles, and values (religion, life-style, politics, self-actualization).

Communication, flexibility, and body clock compatibility are also critical issues to assess in selecting a partner. Being able to talk about your feelings, needs, and expectations and being able to negotiate differences when they occur are probably the most essential characteristics in selecting a partner. Flexibility is important since life will continually involve change. Body clock compatibility, while less significant than the ability to communicate with a flexible partner, will make day-to-day living, working, and playing with your spouse a little easier.

The process of selecting a partner may involve rejecting some partners. This usually cannot be done without hurting the partner, but giving reasons specific to yourself, not blaming the partner, and dating others will help to heal the hurt in a shorter period of time. When you are rejected, as we all are, the adjustment can be enhanced by recognizing that the pain is temporary, focusing on the negative aspects of the terminated relationship, and instigating new relationships immediately. The only caveat of new relationships is to avoid any immediate new commitments.

You can use the engagement period productively by systematically examining your relationship, observing your future in-laws for clues about your partner's background and character, and going for premarital counseling. Conditions under which you might want to prolong your engagement include having known each other for less than a year, having an inadequate or unstable source of income, having parents who disapprove of your marriage, and being pregnant.

Some couples decide to write a marriage contract to specify the understandings of their relationship. If these involve the disposition of property and assets, a lawyer should be asked to draw up the agreement. Otherwise, the document may not be in legal terms recognized by the courts.

Regardless of what you do, you will not be able to guarantee yourself and your partner a happy marriage. The illusion of the perfect mate, deception during the premarital period, the confinement of marriage, the demands of careers and children, and the inevitability of change make prediction of future marital happiness impossible.

Trends in marital commitments include the possibility of greater caution in entering marriage (the fact that people are marrying later is some evidence for this) and the bypassing of some formal aspects of the engagement period.

Questions for Reflection

1. Most people in marriage feel that if the partners love each other enough, a personal marriage contract is unnecessary and is a violation of the spirit of marriage. How do you feel? Would you develop a contract for your marriage or agree to do so if your partner were to ask?
2. Why is it difficult to terminate a relationship that an individual knows is not a good one?
3. What are the conditions under which you would terminate a relationship before making a marital commitment?

· CHOICES ·

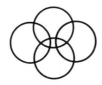

Because of the possibility of divorce, some couples are considering a prenuptial or antenuptial agreement that specifies that the money and assets a person brings into a marriage remain his or hers in the event of a divorce. The agreement may also specify how the person's assets will be distributed to one's children from a previous marriage. When such agreements are not made, the assets of the partner become accessible to the spouse. Although these agreements are currently enforceable in only about half of the states, the number of these states is growing. Seventy students in a marriage and family class were asked if they would sign or ask their partners to sign such an agreement. About 40 percent said "yes," 40 percent said "no," and 20 percent said "it depends."

PRENUPTIAL AGREEMENT: YES

Those opting for a prenuptial agreement gave a variety of reasons:

I didn't have one in my previous relationship and it caused a lot of problems because I didn't. I have a large inheritance and my partner wanted to get his hooks into it.

•

Such a contract will make a divorce settlement less complicated.

•

It is always a good idea to discuss the money and have things clear between the two of you. A prenuptial agreement is a fair, just, and reasonable idea.

•

If I brought something into the marriage such as a savings account, I wouldn't want my partner to have one cent of it if we got divorced.

•

You know what happened to Johnny Carson. If he had had such an agreement, he would have gotten off easier in the settlement.

•

Although we may marry for love, we divorce in a state of hate. A contract about who gets what would come in handy at that time.

•

Love has a great tendency to blind couples who are planning to get married. By discussing the financial terms of your relationship in a rational way, your marriage would be stronger because of your open communication with each other. If your partner won't sign such an agreement, it suggests that he or she is after your money and you will know it is time to dump them.

•

Although you marry when you are in love, feelings change and it's hard to predict the future. I am a very independent person and I would like my husband to be independent also. Although our relationship will be based on emotional dependence on each other, I want each of us to be financially independent.

•

I am an only child and I would hate for the money that my parents and grandparents worked so hard for to go to somebody outside the family.

PRENUPTIAL AGREEMENT: NO

An equal number (40 percent) said they would not sign a prenuptial agreement or ask their partner to do so. Their reasons follow:

Asking your future spouse to sign such an agreement would mean that you don't trust them. I wouldn't

(continued)

marry someone unless I was absolutely positive that he or she was the one for me and that we would be together for the rest of our lives.

•

In my case, there wouldn't be any need to sign a contract. I don't have any money and neither does he.

•

In the wedding vows it states, "All that I am, and all that I have, I give to you." To me, those vows are sacred and everything that I have, material possessions and spiritual, I will give to my partner.

•

Signing a prenuptial agreement implies that your marriage won't last. It's a bad way to start a marriage.

•

It [prenuptial agreement] would weaken the marriage from the start by making it easier to get out if something goes wrong. It also doesn't show complete trust which is a core issue in any successful marriage relationship.

•

I wouldn't have the nerve to bring up a prenuptial agreement. It would be like slapping my partner's face.

•

I'm not going to worry about "who gets the goods" if there were to be a divorce and I would not want to marry someone who would worry that he would get shafted by me.

•

A prenuptial agreement in my opinion is like saying that I want as much as I can get and I just don't like the feel of such an agreement. In a marriage relationship there should be a special trust and if you don't have that, you're in trouble.

•

Marriage is an emotional commitment of each partner to the other that results from the love each feels for the other. If either partner asks the other to sign such an agreement, this takes all the emotion out of the relationship and you're headed toward a divorce.

PRENUPTIAL AGREEMENT: IT DEPENDS

About 20 percent of the respondents in the marriage and family class said they would sign or ask their partner to sign such an agreement under certain conditions.

I would definitely consider a prenuptial agreement if I were a widow or a divorcée with children and had a considerable estate or money. While a prenuptial agreement would take a lot of the "glitter" and "romance" out of a second marriage, my first priority would be to protect my money for my children.

•

If I were making myself financially secure and found the girl of my dreams, I wouldn't ask her to sign such an agreement. But if I had already made my fortune and then found someone I loved, I would consider asking her to sign such an agreement.

•

No matter how much in love a couple is, whenever one owns anything of monetary value and the other one does not, that person should think with his head about keeping what is rightfully his. Some people do marry for money and you need to watch out for them.

One student emphasized the importance of open communication.

I believe that both people must want a prenuptial agreement to alleviate some of the anxieties that might arise such as distrust and misunderstanding. Moreover, I believe both people should communicate openly their fears, conceptions, and feelings about a prenuptial agreement. Further, I believe that if both have decided after lengthy dialogue that a prenuptial agreement is in order, both parties should sign on the dotted line. I want to emphasize that this must be a *mutual decision* with shared responsibility.

· Part Three ·

FULFILLMENTS

When the United States was primarily rural, family members looked to each other to fulfill a variety of their needs—religious, recreational, educational, economic, and protective. Although people went to church, family members would gather around the open fire in the evening while father read from the Bible. Instruction in honesty, faithfulness, and obedience was part of the

family's religious ritual. Education was also home generated; and although there was much work to do on the farm (milking cows, repairing fences, and tending crops), the family was also the recreational unit. Finally, the rifle over the mantle was both a symbol of family protection and sometimes a practical necessity.

Today all of these needs can be met outside the family. Churches and synagogues compete for membership. The state has taken over the education function. Recreation is no longer home oriented and family members look to events outside the family for fun and people outside the family to have fun with. Family members also earn their living outside the family by working for private industry or business. The family

spirit generated from working together as a family is gone. Finally, public police protection has replaced the need for a rifle over the mantle.

Although most of the needs of family members can be met outside the family, the need to feel emotionally connected to others, to be a part of others' lives, continues to be a major fulfillment that only marriage and the family offer.

· Chapter 9 ·

MARRIAGE RELATIONSHIPS

CONTENTS

Marriage as a Commitment
Rites of Passage
Changes after Marriage
Sexually Open Marriages
College Marriages
Mixed Marriages
Black Marriages
Very Happy Marriages
Self-Assessment:
  Marriage Happiness Scale
Choices

We were such a good and loving invention. An aeroplane made from a man and wife. Wings and everything. We hovered a little above the earth. We even flew a little.

YEHUDA AMICHAI

Having made the final choice of a marriage partner, the lovers make a marital commitment, get married, and move into their new roles as spouses. Such a transition involves various rites of passage and personal, social, and legal consequences. In this chapter we examine these changes as well as an array of marriages of different groups and types—sexually open, college, mixed (interfaith, interracial, age-discrepant), black, and "very happy" marriages. The prevailing theme of this chapter is that there is no one marriage relationship—there are only marriage relationships. They differ by social class, ethnicity, religion, physical ability (or disability), presence or absence of children, degree of freedom or intimacy, and education of spouses, among other variables. These differences imply that your marriage will be unique—special to you and your partner.

• MARRIAGE AS A COMMITMENT •

Maxim Gorky said, "When a woman gets married, it's like jumping into a hole in the ice in the middle of winter; you do it once and you remember it for the rest of your days." One of the reasons our getting married leaves such an indelible memory is the significance of the commitment. Marriage represents a multilevel commitment—person to person, family to family, and couple to state.

DATA • *Ninety-two percent of over 5000 students in four universities view marriage as a lifelong commitment.* (Martin and Martin, 1984)

Person to Person

Commitment may be defined as an intent to maintain a relationship. Saying "I do" in a marriage ceremony implies that you and your partner are making a personal commitment to love, support, and negotiate differences with each other. You are establishing a primary relationship with your partner—all other relationships become secondary. Commitment may also mean a promise or pledge, dedication or devotion, and attachment or bond (Quinn, 1982). Persons who are committed to each other are pledged to each other, devoted to each other, and attached to each other.

Family to Family

Marriage also involves commitments by each of the marriage partners to the family members of the spouse. Recently married couples are often expected to divide their holiday visits between both sets of parents. In addition, each

Parents continue to care about their children after they are married and may visit them often.

spouse becomes committed to help his or her in-laws when appropriate and to regard family ties as part of marital ties. For some older couples, this means caring for disabled parents who may live in their home. "We always said that no parent was ever going to live with us," said one spouse. "But my wife's father died and her mother had no place to go. Her living here was an initial strain but we've learned to cope with the situation quite well."

Not all couples accept the family to family commitment. Some spouses have limited contact with their respective parents. "I haven't seen my folks in years and don't want to," said one woman in her second marriage.

Couple to State

Finally, the spouses become legally committed to each other according to the laws of the state in which they reside. This means they cannot arbitrarily decide to terminate their own marital agreement. Just as the state says who can marry (not close relatives, the insane, or mentally deficient) and when (usually at age 18 or above), legal procedures must be instigated if the couple want to divorce. The state's interest is that a couple stay married, have children, and take care of them.

DATA • *Around two and a half million marriage licenses are issued to couples every year. These represent a legal bond, not only between the individuals, but also between the couple and the state.* (National Center for Health Statistics, 1984)

• RITES OF PASSAGE •

The transition from one social status to another that is marked by some specific event is referred to as a rite of passage. The first day in school, getting a driver's license, and graduating from college are all events that mark major role transitions (to those of student, driver, and graduate). For lovers the marriage ceremony is a rite of passage to the role of spouse.

Weddings

In preparation for the wedding, some states require a blood test of each partner certifying that neither has a sexually transmitted disease (or that it is not in the communicable stage). This document is then taken to the county courthouse where the couple make application for a marriage license. Two-thirds of the states require a waiting period between the issuance of the license and the wedding (Table 9.1 details state laws on marriage.) Eighty percent of the couples take their license to a clergyman to be married; 20 percent seek a justice of the peace (most of these marriages are remarriages).

Although some couples may agree to a religious ceremony and perfunctorily participate because of their parents' wishes, others accept the emphasis in traditional religious weddings that marriage is a sacred relationship ordained by God. The religious official, the setting, the music, and the words of the ceremony ("holy matrimony") take marriage from the secular into the spiritual realm.

The "band of gold" has not always been gold . . . Only in the 17th century did social pressure dictate that the ring should be gold, pure and nontarnishing.

BARBARA CHESSER

Table 9.1 State Laws on Marriage*

STATE	WITH CONSENT		WITHOUT CONSENT		BLOOD TEST**		WAIT FOR LICENSE	WAIT AFTER LICENSE
	Men	Women	Men	Women	Required	Other State Accepted		
Alabama(b)	14	14	18	18	Yes	Yes	none	none
Alaska.	16	16	18	18	Yes	No	3 days	none
Arizona	16(g)	16	18	18	Yes	Yes	none	none
Arkansas.	17	16(h)	18	18	Yes	No	3 days	none
California	18(g)	18	18	18	Yes	Yes	none	none
Colorado.	16	16	18	18	Yes	. . .	none	none
Connecticut	16	16(j)	18	18	Yes	Yes	4 days	none
Delaware.	18	16(k)	18	18	Yes	Yes	none	24 hrs. (c)
District of Columbia	16	16	18	18	Yes	Yes	3 days	none
Florida.	16	16	18	18	Yes	Yes	3 days	none
Georgia	16(g)	16(g)	18	18	Yes	Yes	none (k)	none
Hawaii.	16	16	18	18	Yes	Yes	none	none
Idaho	16	16	18	18	Yes	Yes	none	none
Illinois (a)	16	16	18	18	Yes	Yes	none	1 day
Indiana	17(k)	17(k)	18	18	Yes	No	72 hours	none
Iowa.	—(k)	—(k)	18	18	Yes	Yes	3 days	none
Kansas.	14	12	18	18	Yes	Yes	3 days	none
Kentucky	—(k)	—(k)	18	18	Yes	No	3 days	none
Louisiana (a)	18(k)	16(h)	18	16	Yes	No	none	72 hours
Maine	16(h)	16(h)	18	18	No	No	5 days	none
Maryland.	16	16	18	18	none	none	48 hours	none
Massachusetts	—(k)	—(k)	18	18	Yes	Yes	3 days	none
Michigan (a)	16	16	18	18	Yes	No	3 days	none
Minnesota.	16(e)	16(e)	18	18	none	. . .	5 days	none
Mississippi (b).	17(l)	15(l)	21	21	Yes	. . .	3 days	none
Missouri	15	15	18	18	none	Yes	3 days	none
Montana	15	15	18	18	Yes	Yes	none	3 days
Nebraska.	17	17	18	18	Yes	Yes	2 days	none
Nevada	16	16	18	18	none	none	none	none
New Hampshire (a).	14(e)	13(e)	18	18	Yes	Yes	5 days	none
New Jersey (a)	—(g)	12	18	18	Yes	Yes	72 hours	none
New Mexico	16	16	18	18	Yes	Yes	none	none

Indeed, the ending of the traditional ceremony emphasizes God's presence and approval: "Therefore, whom God hath joined together, let no man put asunder." The solemnity of the ceremony is designed to impress upon the couple the seriousness of the responsibilities they are undertaking to each other, to their future children, and to their respective families.

It is no longer unusual for couples to have weddings that are neither religious nor traditional. Only friends of the couple and members of the immediate families may gather in the backyard of the bride. Rather than the traditional white gown, the bride may wear her favorite dress. The groom may wear a suit (he just as well may not), and everyone else wears whatever they think is appropriate.

Table 9.1 *Continued*

STATE	WITH CONSENT		WITHOUT CONSENT		BLOOD TEST**		WAIT FOR LICENSE	WAIT AFTER LICENSE
	Men	Women	Men	Women	Required	Other State Accepted		
New York	16	14(e)	18	18	Yes	No	none	24 hrs.(f)
North Carolina (a)	16	16	18	18	Yes	No	none	none
North Dakota (a).	16	16	18	18	Yes	. . .	none	none
Ohio (a)	18	16	18	18	Yes	Yes	5 days	none
Oklahoma.	16	16	18	18	Yes	No	none	none
Oregon	17	17	18	18	Yes	No	3 days	none
Pennsylvania	16	16	18	18	Yes	No	3 days	none
Rhode Island (a) (b)	14	12	18	18	Yes	Yes	none	none
South Carolina	14	12	18	18	none	none	24 hrs.	none
South Dakota	16	16	18	18	Yes	Yes	none	none
Tennessee (b)	16	16	18	18	Yes	Yes	3 days	none
Texas.	14(k)	14(k)	18	18	Yes	Yes	none	none
Utah (a)	14	14	18	18	none	Yes	none	none
Vermont (a)	16	16	18	18	Yes	. . .	none	5 days
Virginia (a).	16	16	18	18	Yes	Yes	none	none
Washington.	17	17	18	18	(d)	. . .	3 days	none
West Virginia	16	16	18	18	Yes	No	3 days	none
Wisconsin.	16	16	18	18	Yes	Yes	5 days	none
Wyoming.	16	16	19	19	Yes	Yes	none	none
Puerto Rico.	18	16	21	21	Yes	none	none	none
Virgin Islands	16	14	18	18	none	none	8 days	none

*Marriageable age, by states, for both males and females with and without consent of parents or guardians. In most states, the court has authority to marry young couples below the ordinary age of consent, where due regard for their morals and welfare so requires. In many states, under special circumstances, blood test and waiting period may be waived.

Many states have additional requirements; contact individual state. (a) Special laws applicable to nonresidents. (b) Special laws applicable to those under 21 years; Ala., bond required if male is under 18, female under 18. (c) 24 hours if one or both parties resident of state; 96 hours if both parties are non-residents. (d) None, but both must file affidavit. (e) Parental consent plus court's consent required. (f) Marriage may not be solemnized within 10 days from date of blood test. (g) Statute provides for obtaining license with parental or court consent with no state minimum age. (h) Under 16, with parental and court consent. (i) If either under 18, wait 3 full days. (j) If under stated age, court consent required. (k) If under 18, parental and/or court consent required. (l) Both parents' consent required for men age 17, women age 15; one parent's consent required for men 18–20 years, women ages 16–20 years.

Source: *World almanac & book of facts 1984*, p. 93. © Newspaper Enterprise Association, Inc., 200 Park Avenue, New York, NY 10166 Used by permission.

In the exchange of vows, neither partner promises to obey the other, and their relationship is spelled out by themselves rather than by tradition. Vows often include the couple's feelings about equality, individualism, humanism, and openness to change (see Exhibit 9.1).

Part of the preference for less lavish, less traditional weddings is economic.

DATA • *Bridal consultants estimate that the average cost of a wedding which includes a church hall reception is $3000. A hotel reception with champagne can easily cost $2000 more.* (Mills, 1984)

· Exhibit 9.1 ·

AN EXCHANGE OF VOWS

I love you and want to be with you. I do not belong to you nor do I want you to belong to me, but rather I want us to have a relationship in which we will want to be with each other and in which we will nurture each's growth while maintaining our own separateness and individuality. In that interest, I express the following goals, promises, and commitments.

First of all, I accept responsibility for myself. I will not depend on you for my fulfillment as a person. I will accept my ultimate aloneness in life and the responsibility for my own happiness. But out of my aloneness I desire to share time and space with you. I will be with you while intimately sharing past and present experiences along with hopes, dreams, and plans for the future.

I will be reliable and open to you so that we will maintain a basis of trust between us. I will love and trust myself in order to continually become a more trustworthy person to you and add fidelity, security, and depth to our relationship. I will grow and change, but through honest dialogue I will maintain your trust in me.

I will respect you as an individual person and will cherish your uniqueness. I will strive to help you become more of yourself even though that may differ from what I would like for you to be. I will take pride in you and your differences from me. I will consistently remember those qualities and traits that are beautiful about you and consistently communicate my love by recognizing your inner and outer beauty through words and actions.

In times of need I will care for you and for myself. I understand that there will be times of pain as well as joy in our relationship. In troubled times I will try to be considerate, compassionate, caring, nonjudgmental, and forgiving. I understand that you and I in our humanness have limitations and will make mistakes. I will accept those limitations in myself and in you and will not expect either of us to be perfect. I understand that in your love you have exposed your human vulnerabilities. I will respond with consideration to cherish and invite you to feel protected without undue pain.

I will not take you for granted. I will consistently be aware and emotionally present to you. I will listen to you when you speak and I will encourage you whenever I possibly can.

In giving myself to you I will give from my inner joy and not from duty. I will consistently enjoy sharing those parts of myself that you enjoy. I will enrich and preserve my body, mind, and spirit for you and me. I will continue to change, striving to become a more mature and stimulating person. I will accept changes in you as well as in myself. I will gracefully accept the limitations of aging for both of us. As I grow older I will try to develop wisdom and integrity of character, and I will encourage and appreciate similar growth in you.

I will consistently make time available for being together, for communication, for work, for fun, and for love. No matter how many demands or enticements I experience for success or childrearing, I will set aside and give the highest priority to our time together.

I will share in the

parenting experience of providing care, setting limits, and giving opportunities for Megan Carol and any other children born to us. I will share in helping them to grow as persons and achieve their own wishes, hopes, and dreams. With you I will give them roots and stability, but I will also let them go to develop their own wings.

I will share with you in the development of a community of friends and family. I will share with you in contributing to our larger community around us.

As much as possible, I will try to be aware of a sense of values, of eternal values. I will try to consider those things that are of real consequence as well as respond to the cares of the moment.

Most of all, I will try to be a real person to you. I will try to give you the kind of love that will encourage the realness in you. Let our lives be filled with effort, expectation, and desire and something evermore about to be.

Hal and Sherry

Reprinted by permission of Hal G. Gillespie, M.D. and Cheryl L. Gillespie, R.N., M.S.

CONSIDERATION • The alternative to spending such large sums on a wedding is elopement. Some couples make a deal with their parents that they will either elope or have a small wedding in the back yard. One bride said, "The marriage license costs us $10 and we're using the $4,000 my dad gave us as a down payment on a mobile home." However, other couples want the experience of a big wedding. "I'm only going to get married once," said one bride-to-be. "And I want it to be a big church wedding with a horse-drawn carriage to take us away after the reception."

Honeymoons

Couples who live together before their marriage are less likely to take a honeymoon following their wedding.

DATA • *In one study about 60 percent of couples who lived together took a honeymoon.* (Risman et al., 1981)

After brunch, dinner, or party, they may return to their apartment or house much as they would at the end of a normal day. "The newness is gone once you've lived with someone," remarked a new husband. "And while being married is supposed to be different, it doesn't *feel* that way."

DATA • *In contrast, more than 95 percent of couples who have not lived together take a honeymoon.* (Risman et al., 1981)

For honeymooners, their first week or 10 days as a married couple are often spent in one resort location, traveling each day to a new place, or loafing for several days with no schedule of places to be or things to do. Disneyland, the Bahamas, and camping are favorites for many couples.

The most important thing to know about a honeymoon is to take one.

Regardless of where the couple go, the honeymoon serves various social, and personal functions. The social function of the honeymoon is to make it normative for the couple to isolate themselves from others. Although a few people will play pranks like tampering with the couple's car, hiding their luggage just after the wedding, or handcuffing the new husband to a doorknob, most people are socialized to view honeymooners as deserving of privacy.

The period of undisturbed privacy provides a personal function of the honeymoon—recuperation. Since traditional weddings may include bridal showers, a rehearsal, a rehearsal dinner, and a long reception, the bride and groom often feel exhausted by the time they reach their first night's destination. The bride is usually more fatigued, since she has assumed greater responsibility for the wedding than her partner. "I was sick when we got to the motel room," recalled an exhausted bride. "I hadn't slept soundly in three days and had eaten only peanuts and cookies. I was a wreck." But the honeymoon dictates no responsibilities, plenty of sleep, and good food—the physician's prescription for fatigue.

The honeymoon is over when he phones that he'll be late for supper—and she has already left a note that it's in the refrigerator.

BILL LAWRENCE

CONSIDERATION • In making a decision whether to take a honeymoon, remember that there is only one honeymoon for each marriage and it can only take place right after the wedding. Although a couple may take subsequent trips, their first days following the wedding (particularly if they have not lived together) are unique. You can't have a honeymoon later.

• CHANGES AFTER MARRIAGE •

Whether a couple go on a honeymoon or not, they will become aware of various changes—personal, social, and legal—that occur as a result of getting married.

Personal Changes

An initial enhanced self-concept is a predictable consequence of getting married. Your parents and closest friends will arrange their schedules to participate in your wedding and will give you gifts to express their approval. In contrast, there is no rite of passage if you decide to remain single. There is no ceremony, no fussing and excited parents or friends, no gifts—only the implied question, "Is something wrong with you?" As a married person you are assumed to be normal and to have made the right decision. The strong evidence that your spouse approves of you and is willing to spend a lifetime with you also tells you that you are okay.

The married person also begins adopting new values and behaviors consistent with the married role. Although new spouses often vow that "marriage won't change me," it does. For example, rather than stay out all night at a party, which is not uncommon for singles who may be looking for someone to bed, spouses (who are already paired off) tend to go home early. Their roles of spouse, employee, and later, parent, force them to adopt more regular hours. The role of married person implies a different set of behaviors from that of single person. Although there is an initial resistance to "becoming like old married folks," the resistance soon gives way to the realities of the role.

Another result of getting married is disenchantment. It may not happen in the first few weeks or months of marriage, but it is almost inevitable. Farrah Fawcett once said, "Marriage—that's when the blazing torch of love slowly turns into a pilot light." Whereas courtship is the anticipation of a life together, marriage is the day-to-day reality of life together—and reality does not always fit the dream. Daily marital interaction exposes both partners as they really are—human beings who get tired and irritable. "Burt never snapped at me about anything when we were dating, but I never acted like a mean bitch (his term) before we were married either," expressed a wife of six months.

The disenchantment is also related to the couple's shifting focus of interest away from each other. The husband often makes the most dramatic shift. He "pursues his dream(s) of success, i.e., money, achievement, power, while his wife is left home to deal with the 'realities' of life, i.e., children, house, chores, etc." (L'Abate & L'Abate, 1981). If the woman is not home oriented, she may shift her interest into her career. Either way each partner gives and gets less attention than in courtship.

The speed of the disenchantment process may be related to the number of other changes going on in the partners' lives. Bob and Louise, a newly married couple, moved to another city and bought a house. Louise wrote her dissertation for her Ph.D. while Bob changed careers and enrolled in medical school. They also decided to begin their family—Louise became pregnant.

> Almost all newlyweds like sex in the beginning.
>
> ELLEN FRANK & CAROL ANDERSON

CONSIDERATION • However, disenchantment is balanced by more positive aspects of the new relationship. When compared with singles, married people are happier, healthier, more satisfied with their relationships, have higher incomes, and are less lonely (Cargan, 1981; Ward, 1979). "I've been single, and I've been married," said one spouse. "Marriage is better." Most people agree.

Parents, In-Laws, and Friendship Changes

Marriage affects relationships with parents, in-laws, and friends of both partners. Parents are likely to be more accepting of the partner following the wedding. "I encouraged her not to marry him," said the father of a recent bride, "but once they were married, he was her husband and my son-in-law, so I did my best to get along with him."

Just as acceptance of the mate by one's parents is likely to increase, interaction with one's parents is likely to decrease. This is particularly true when the newly married couple move to a distant town. "I still love my parents a great deal," said a new husband, "but I just don't get to see them very often." Parents whose lives have revolved around their children may feel particularly saddened at the marriage of their last child and may be reluctant to accept the reduced contacts. Frequent phone calls, visits, invitations, and gifts may be their way of trying to ensure a meaningful place in the life of their married son or daughter. Such insistence by the parents and in-laws may be the basis of the first major conflict between the spouses. There is no problem if both spouses agree on which set of in-laws or parents they enjoy visiting and the frequency of such get-togethers. But when one spouse wants his or her parents around more often than does the partner, frustration will be felt by everyone.

CONSIDERATION • Most marriage counselors believe that when the spouses must choose between their partner and parents, there are more long-term positive consequences associated with choosing the partner than vice versa. Ideally, of course, such choices should be avoided. For partners to try to deny their mate access to the mate's parents is risky. When an individual marries, he or she marries into an already existing family, and the parent and in-law relationships come with the marriage.

Marriage also affects relationships with friends of the same and opposite gender.

DATA • *In a study of 419 students at Pennsylvania State University, students who were married reported having the fewest friends of all.* (Johnson & Leslie, 1982)

Less time will be spent with friends of the same gender because of new role demands from the spouse. In addition, friends will assume that the newly married person now has a built-in companion and is not interested in (or would be punished by the spouse for) barhopping, moviegoing, or whatever.

Opposite-gender relationships also change. The single person is free to seek and become involved in new sexual relationships. But unless the married couple have an open marriage and agree that outside sexual partners are appropriate, each spouse is expected to carefully monitor the level of interaction with people of the opposite gender to ensure that an affair does not develop. Although, as we have noted, half of all husbands and about 40 percent of all wives do have intercourse outside their marriage at least once, it is clearly a violation of their agreement not to do so.

> CONSIDERATION • What spouses give up in same- and opposite-gender friendships, they gain in developing a close relationship with each other. "We still enjoy our friends but we end up spending more time with each other than with anyone else. We like it that way," said an elementary school teacher.

Legal Changes

Unless the partners have signed a prenuptial agreement specifying that their earnings and property will remain separate, the wedding ceremony involves an exchange of property. Once the words "I do" are spoken, each spouse is entitled to inherit a portion of the other's estate. Although the amount varies by state, many states permit between one-third and one-half of the estate to be inherited. Also, as noted earlier, the husband becomes legally responsible for the economic support of any children produced in the marriage. Even if the couple divorce, he cannot arbitrarily decide that he no longer wants to support his children. The law says it is his responsibility.

> The people can change Congress but only God can change the Supreme Court.
>
> GEORGE W. NORRIS

Sexual Changes

Sex will also undergo some changes during your first year of marriage. Frequency declines for most married couples but the quality improves. "The urgency to have sex disappears after you're married," said one wife. "After a while you discover that your husband isn't going to vanish back to his apartment at midnight—he's going to be with you all night, every night. You don't have to have sex every minute because you know you've got plenty of time. Also, you've got work and other responsibilities, so sex takes a lower priority than before you were married."

Even though the constant availability of a sexual companion and increased responsibilities may reduce the frequency of sex, such a decline does not imply that sex becomes less meaningful. Rather, sex in marriage takes on a richer and deeper quality. You are now a committed couple, not only in a personal, but also in a legal sense. You have extended yourself to each other to the fullest, and your sexual relationship will express itself in the context of that commitment. "Jim and I enjoyed sex before we were married," recalled one bride of 11 months. "And it was good then. But it feels better or closer now and I'm not talking about the physical part."

Quality improves, not only because you feel more comfortable with each other, but also because you become more aware of each other's preferences. "I thought I knew what she liked before we were married," shared one new husband. "But now she's more comfortable telling and showing me what turns her on. And I'm still learning." A quality sexual relationship results from such feedback and time. Like the Boston Pops orchestra, it sounds good because they've been practicing.

About 20 percent of spouses will not have intercourse before their wedding night. Mostly because of religious values, they will enter marriage as virgins. The fact that they have waited to have intercourse with each other will give them a unique feeling of commitment. But they also will experience a decline in the frequency of intercourse the longer they are married.

• SEXUALLY OPEN MARRIAGES •

> The core of our book [*Open Marriage*] referred to open marriage as a relationship of commitment and equality in which each partner's individual growth contributes synergistically to the marriage bond.
>
> NENA O'NEILL

When married partners have intercourse with someone other than their spouse, their mate is usually unaware of their doing so. As an alternative to a secretive extramarital affair, some spouses (a very small percentage) acknowledge their mutual desire for a sexually open marriage. In 1972 the O'Neills noted that sexually open marriages offer the freedom for spouses to experience emotional and sexual encounters with others while regarding each other as their primary emotional and sexual companion. One psychologist observed that traditional monogamous marriages no longer provide adequately for the intimacy needs of some individuals and that sexually open marriages are an alternative for achieving such needs inside the marital relationship (Peabody, 1982).

Who Selects This Option?

Researchers have studied the characteristics of those spouses who have sexually open marriages. In one study of 23 sexually open marriages (Knapp & Whitehurst, 1978), the couples' ages ranged from 20 to 63. They were upper-middle-class professionals living in urban areas and somewhat dissatisfied with the restraints of conventional marriage. They wanted a secure emotional relationship but the freedom for personal growth and autonomy and perceived that a sexually open marriage offered the best of both worlds.

In another study of 130 spouses in sexually open marriages (Rubin, 1982), 40 was the average age for females; 43 for males. The average family income was $36,000 and more than 50 percent had master's degrees. The social class of these spouses was also upper middle-class.

CONSIDERATION • Although it is sometimes assumed that spouses in sexually open marriages are less happy or neurotic or have personality flaws, there is limited evidence to support this assumption. To the contrary, when the 130 spouses in sexually open marriages in the Rubin study were compared with 130 spouses in sexually exclusive marriages (where the partners agree that neither will have outside sexual relationships), there were no significant differences in the degree of happiness or relationship adjustment reported by the two groups. (Rubin, 1982) In a five year follow-up of the marriages in the respective groups, 68 percent of the sexually open couples in contrast to 82 percent of the sexually exclusive couples were still together. These differences were not statistically significant. (Adams and Rubin, 1984)

Problems

Jealousy was a problem reported by 80 percent of the respondents in one study of sexually open relationships (Buunk, 1981). Such jealousy was the result of one or both spouses being able to decide intellectually that having an open marriage was desirable but emotionally unable to handle the jealous feelings when the spouse had intercourse with someone else. "Although we had agreed that sex with others was okay," said one wife, "the first time I did it, I told Jim and he called me a slut. I was horrified that he changed the rules on me so quickly but he said he couldn't help how he felt."

Several other problems were an outgrowth of the jealousy problem: Loneliness—what was the other partner to do when the mate had a date? Free time—suppose one spouse wanted to spend time with the mate but the mate had already arranged to be with someone else? Physical arrangements—was the spouse to stay away from home till the date left? Still other problems related to maintaining relationships with straight friends who would not approve of an open relationship. "It's just that meeting others becomes such a big part of your life that you like to share it with your friends. And if they can't accept what you're up to, you tend to change friends," said one spouse. In some cases, those in sexually open marriages will seek new friends through magazines such as *Select* where couples advertise for potential partners. The couple might invite another couple over and exchange partners for all or part of an evening.

Benefits

Most spouses in the small number of sexually open marriages that have been studied report they feel better about themselves ("other people like me too") and better about each other ("we have something else to talk about and share") since becoming involved in a sexually open relationship. "It's been good for us," said one spouse.

CONSIDERATION • Since no study has been conducted on those partners who have become disenchanted with a sexually open marriage and returned to a monogamous relationship, one should probably be cautious about becoming involved in a sexually open relationship. Conditions that seem to be associated with positive outcomes include the following: (1) The spouses have a strong primary relationship including a high degree of mutual affection, respect, understanding, and agreement about choice of life-styles. (2) The spouses possess the personality traits and interpersonal skills necessary to deal effectively with complex and potentially stressful relationships. (3) The outside partners with whom the spouses become involved have no need or desire to compete with the spouse for primacy in the relationship.

• COLLEGE MARRIAGES •

DATA • *Twenty percent of college students are married. This percentage represents both the younger student (18–22) who married while in college and the older married person who returns to school.* (U.S. Bureau of the Census, 1981)

This proportion of married college students is radically different from those of earlier years. Before 1940 it was not uncommon for a college or university to deny admission to married students or to require enrolled students to drop out

Research indicates that married students with children tend to have higher grade point averages.

if they married. It was believed that married students would have an undesirable influence on other students. After World War II, the return of married veterans to college established the social legitimacy of the college marriage (and even high school marrieds are acceptable now).

In general, married college students make good grades.

DATA • *In a study of 600 full-time juniors and seniors attending a southwestern university, students who were married and who had children had the highest grade point averages; those who were married and had no children had intermediate averages; those who were unmarried had the lowest averages.* (Ma, 1983)

Young Married College Students

DATA • *About 30 percent of married students attending college are age 24 or below.* (U.S. Bureau of the Census, 1981)

Although most college students prefer to finish their degrees before getting married, others seem compelled by the desire to be married now. A language major asked, "Why not marry? We're tired of waiting, don't believe in living together, and are miserable living in the dorms." Her fiancé said, "It's simple. I'm happiest with her and she feels the same way about me. We talked to our parents during semester break, and while they would prefer that we wait until we graduate, they will support us if we decide to marry now. We've decided."

Marriage while in college seems to have a positive effect on completing college; at least this seems true for men. In a study of more than 200 males (Adler, 1982), those who married while in college were much more likely to complete college (65 percent) than those who did not marry (37 percent).

ROLE CHANGES

In addition to the role of spouse, the young married student may take on the additional roles of employee and parent. Unless their parents continue to support them, one of three patterns develop: Both the husband and the wife get part-time jobs; the husband drops out of school while his wife continues; or the wife drops out while her husband continues. The first pattern especially may be stressful because of the difficulty in managing the respective roles. Some are surprised at the lack of control they have over the employee role. "As a student, you can miss a class or 'study later' if you need to. But when you're working for somebody, they expect you to do exactly what they want, when they want it, or you're fired," reflected a student working at a McDonald's near campus. "And if you've got a test that day, your boss doesn't care. Those hamburgers still have to be served."

Although most couples who marry in college plan to delay having children until after graduation, unwanted pregnancies may occur; and an unplanned pregnancy after marriage is often handled differently from a premarital one. After marriage there is an increased chance the couple will have the baby. "I might have had an abortion had I gotten pregnant when we were living together," recalled a wife who had been married three months. "But now it's different. We're going to have the baby, and I will finish school later."

CONSIDERATION • Although role strain is not unique to the college marriage, one role may be added to another without sufficient time to adjust to the previous role. Stacking the roles of student, spouse, employee, and possibly parent requires a greater degree of adaptation than is required of the single college student with fewer roles to juggle. Aware of the role-stacking effect, most students opt to delay marriage until after graduation.

MONEY PROBLEMS

Some parents disapprove of their offspring getting married while in college and stop financial support after the wedding. Lack of money is not unique to the newly married young college student couple, but it introduces a variable that was not present when they were single and engaged. A sophomore who married in his freshman year wrote:

> We began our marriage without any help from our parents. The result was a tremendous strain on our once happy relationship. Not having enough money put us both under tensions that neither of us had known before. We struggled to make rent, utilities, tuition, and other payments. We squeezed our budget for money to buy food with. Our recreational life-style had changed drastically because we rarely had money to eat out or to see a movie. We bought no new clothes—birthdays were the only times we got new ones. The result was unhappiness which we would not let others know about because of our pride. We were both from middle-class families, but we were poor.

Older Married College Students

DATA • *More than 70 percent of married college students are age 25 or older. Most of these are 30 and older, with more married husband than wife students. About half of these older married students attend school part time.* (U.S. Bureau of the Census, 1981)

A look around any college classroom reveals a number of older students, many of whom are married. In contrast to the young college set, many of these spouses have been or are employed in full-time jobs and have children.

But how does returning to school affect the marriage relationship? In a study of 361 women (age 26 and over who were married and had at least one child), half of those who dropped out before completing their degree and one-third of those who did complete their degree reported that their return to school had resulted in some strain on the marriage (Berkove, 1979). This showed itself in the husbands' jealousy in competing with his wife's new interest and his annoyance over occasional late meals and a cluttered house. One student wife said of her husband,

> He mentions how much money my education is costing (even though I've worked part time off and on) and how much time I spend away from the family (he spends as much time away from the family as I do). He has stopped commenting on the state of the house, since I told him that if it was too dirty to suit him, he was welcome to clean it, because it suited me just fine.

Benefits also resulted from the wife's return to school. Most of the wives reported increased personal and intellectual development, and half reported that their husbands showed greater appreciation of, satisfaction with, and pride in the fact that their wives had returned to school (Berkove, 1979).

In another study (Van Meter & Agronow, 1982), married female students reported the least amount of role strain when they "placed the family role first" and did not allow the role of student to interfere with that of wife and mother. Under these conditions their husbands were very supportive of their wives going back to school. An additional finding was that husbands who had also attended college were much more supportive of their wives going to school.

Student wives who are also mothers report positive benefits for their children. In a study of 40 such women (Kelly, 1982), more than half said the relationships with their children had improved since returning to school. Their children had showed an increased interest in their own schoolwork, and there was a new mutuality of interest—both mother and child would talk about "having to get my homework done."

Making good grades and keeping their husbands and children happy often came at the expense of the student wife's sleep. In essence, the wife and mother "added her study (sometimes a full-time student load) to her existing program and what she cut back on was sleep and leisure time. It is little wonder that one of the main problems cited by mature-age female students is chronic tiredness" (Kelly, 1982, p. 291).

Although the personal, marital, and parent-child relationships tend to improve when the wife returns to school (assuming she continues to put her family role first), what happens when the older married husband returns to school? McRoy and Fisher (1982) studied 20 couples in which the husband only was in

College professor—someone who talks in other people's sleep.

BERGEN EVANS

graduate school and compared them with 20 couples in which the wife only was in graduate school and 20 couples in which both spouses were in school. Results showed that the husband being in school was associated with less money and less marital satisfaction than either of the other two groups. It seems that when the husband does not contribute economically to the marriage and family, everyone suffers. "But that's not true of us," said one student husband who was being supported by his wife. "I put her through school and now it's her turn to earn the money. We both agreed on this plan and it hasn't been a problem for either of us."

CONSIDERATION • For those marriages in which one or both spouses are considering returning to school, it seems important for the wife to give her family priority to keep her husband's support high and conflict with him low. For men it may be important to maintain some level of employment or economic contribution to the relationship.

• MIXED MARRIAGES •

Interreligious, interracial, and age-discrepant marriages are examples of marriages in which the partners differ from each other in a particular way.

Interreligious Marriages

DATA • *Although most people marry those within their own faith, 18 percent of Catholics marry non-Catholics, 7 percent of Protestants marry non-Protestants, and 11 percent of Jews marry non-Jews. When the percentage of those who marry someone with "no religion" or from a religion other than Protestant, Catholic, or Jewish is calculated, 15–20 percent of existing marriages are between spouses with different religious preferences.* (Glenn, 1982)

There has been a consistent trend in the willingness of people to marry someone who does not share their religious background. Even among Catholics who have traditionally been socialized to seek a mate of the same faith, there seems little concern that their partner be Catholic. In a study of 162 Catholic students, only 8 (5 percent) said they were strongly opposed to interfaith marriages (Egelman & Berlage, 1982). This perspective might reflect "a continued secularization of the institution of marriage and a continued diminution of the influence of the church and the extended family on marital choice and on marriage relationships" (Glenn, 1982, p. 556).

Are people in interreligious marriages less satisfied with their marriages than those who marry someone of the same faith? The answer depends on a number of factors. First, people in marriages in which one or both of the spouses profess to "no religion" tend to report lower levels of marital satisfaction than those in which at least one spouse has a religious tie. Second, men in interreligious marriages tend to report less marital satisfaction than men in marriages where the partners have the same religion. This may be owing to the fact that children of interreligious marriages are typically reared in the faith of the mother, so that the father's influence is negligible whether he is or is not religious. Third, wives who marry outside their faith don't seem less happy from wives who marry inside their faith (Glenn, 1982).

CONSIDERATION • The impact of a mixed religious marriage seems to depend on the degree of devoutness of the individual. If religion is a core value for you, to marry someone who does not share your faith may weaken your subsequent marital happiness. This may be particularly true if you are a man.

Interracial Marriages

Although interracial marriages may involve many combinations including American whites, American blacks, Indians, Chinese, Japanese, Korean, Mexican, Malaysian, and Hindu mates, this section will focus on black-white marriages in the United States.

DATA • *Of the 50 million married couples in the United States, 697,000 or .014 percent are interracial marriages.* (*Statistical Abstract of the United States, 1984*)

Most black-white marriages consist of a black man and a white woman. In those cases in which the wife is black, the husband tends to be older, to have been previously married, and to have low educational attainment (Spanier & Glick, 1980).

DATA • *Of the 50 million married couples in the United States, only 155,000, or .0031 percent, are black-white couples. Of these, 108,000, or .0022 percent, consist of a black husband and white wife and 47,000, or .0009 percent, consist of a black wife and white husband.* (*Statistical Abstract of the United States, 1984*)

PROBLEMS

Disapproval of parents and discrimination by employers and landlords is a problem for some black-white couples; and these vary with the degree to which those people have been socialized to perceive interracial unions as appropriate or inappropriate. Rural, conservative, dogmatic individuals are likely to look at such couples with hostile eyes. Liberal people who live in large metropolitan centers are more likely to have a "live and let live" philosophy and to regard such couples neutrally or with admiration.

We've not run into any problems. Some people may disagree, but we don't have to cope with them.

HERSCHEL WALKER OF HIS INTERRACIAL MARRIAGE TO CINDY DEANGELIS

Given the range of reactions, how are black-white couples actually treated by their parents, employers, and landlords? In general, both sets of parents reject the interracial marriage of their son or daughter. One white husband said, "My parents have never accepted my marriage to a black woman. We have not visited or talked in nearly four years."

Such parental rejection springs from their concern about how the marriage will affect the parents' own status and their fear for the couple and the problems they must face. Hostility often disappears when the couple have a baby (the parents want access to their grandchild) or tragedy strikes (one partner becomes seriously ill). Difficulties with employers and landlords are less predictable. Some employers and landlords discriminate against an individual or couple if they know of the interracial marriage. Others, particularly those in larger cities, are indifferent to the marital status or choice of marriage partner of their employee or tenant.

Black-white spouses must also contend with problems concerning their children. Children of mixed marriages "will learn quickly that their lineage is a rarity that shapes friendships and futures, that white boys and white girls seldom date tan girls and tan boys, that color is not forgotten. That life in between is at once injustice and insight" (Harrington, 1982, p. 12).

STABILITY

In view of the problems experienced by some black-white couples, are they more likely to get divorced? Yes. When same-race and interracial marriages are compared, the latter are more likely to get divorced (Price-Bonham & Balswick, 1980). The lack of social support, overt hostility, and lack of similar background may contribute to a higher divorce rate. Lena Horne, the famous black singer, said of the divorce to her white husband, "We had a good life together, and I loved him but he didn't know what it meant to be black." Sammy Davis, Jr., and Mary Cunningham also divorced their respective spouses in earlier interracial marriages. Interracial Family Alliance (P.O. Box 20290, Atlanta, Georgia 30325) is a support group for interracial couples. The group is particularly concerned about the social and psychological development of the children of interracial couples. Their unhappiness can affect the stability of interracial couples.

> The trend in interracial dating apparently is not only on the increase, but the secretiveness previously associated with it is also declining.
>
> ERNEST PORTERFIELD

CONSIDERATION • Although individuals contemplating an interracial marriage might assess the degree to which different racial backgrounds will affect the relationship with their partner, such divergent backgrounds are only one aspect of the decision to marry equation. Different racial backgrounds, in themselves, do not necessarily lead to subsequent divorce. Rather, this variable must be considered in the context of the total relationship.

Age-discrepant Marriages

Although some women marry men much younger than themselves, the most common age-discrepant marriage is between younger women and older men. The man is typically in his fifties or above and is usually divorced or widowed. Senator Strom Thurmond, *Washington Post* editor Ben Bradley, Governor George Wallace, and Dr. Benjamin Spock married women considerably younger than themselves.

> Despite the popular interest in age-discrepant unions, very little is actually known about them. People who enter what is considered to be an unconventional relationship are not anxious to make their personal lives visible. Consequently, there is much speculation and stereotyping about the people involved, what their motives and their life-styles might be, but little in the way of scientific fact. (Berardo et al., 1983, p. 57)

Keeping in mind the absence of hard data, the following observations have been made about May–December marriages.

MOTIVES

Instead of marrying a middle-aged woman with three children, the man in the May–December marriage often marries a young woman with whom he can start life over. From his young wife's perspective, she is marrying a man who has already made his mark in the world. She begins her marriage with instant status and probably an ample bank account. U.S. Supreme Court Justice William O. Douglas was 68 when he married a 23-year-old bride.

INTERESTS

Although partners of very different ages may develop mutual interests, there is a greater potential for their interests to be different. The younger partner might enjoy Van Halen; the older partner may delight in Glenn Miller. The younger partner may feel that her mate is "showing his age" by such a preference.

CHILDREN

The May–December couple may experience several difficulties about children: (1) The wife may want children, but he may feel too old to be a father and may fear his wife's transition from lover to mother. (2) Children from a husband's previous marriage may require child-support payments, limiting the money available for the couple. The wife may resent not being able to take a family vacation because money is being drained off to send to his children in whom she has little emotional investment. (3) Visits by the husband's children may be unwelcome because the wife resents playing the role of mother—preparing extra meals, doing extra laundry, making extra beds, and performing other such tasks. One man who had married a younger women said:

> She married me knowing that I wasn't totally convinced that I wanted to have children . . . I guess as I looked at it, the relationship of two people, their own lives for themselves, can be as selfish as my living my own life for myself . . . we were both working, and weren't sharing with anyone. We talked about it. (They have since had two children). (Darling, 1981, p. 38-39)

SEX

A 60-year-old man may not be able to meet the sexual demands of a much younger wife. As a consequence, she may seek a sexual companion outside the marriage. The husband might be threatened by such competition and the marriage relationship jeopardized.

EARLY WIDOW

Since men in America die approximately seven years earlier than women, the wife in the May–December marriage is likely to be a widow longer than the woman married to someone closer to her age. But reflecting on this concern, one woman said, "I'd rather have 15 years with this man than 50 with anybody else."

CONSIDERATION • None of these concerns is necessarily unique to the May–December marriage. Conflicts over sex, children, and recreation may occur in marriages in which the partners are the same age, and no newlywed is guaranteed that his or her spouse will be healthy and alive tomorrow. As for the success of such unions, two researchers (Bumpass & Sweet, 1972) compared married couples who stayed together with married couples who got divorced. They found that May–December couples were just as likely to stay together and just as likely to divorce as couples in which both partners were of similar age.

LaPatra (1980) summarized his feelings on age-discrepant relationships:

Our lives are enriched by our friends, lovers, and spouses. Requiring that these people have ages similar to ours never made much sense. We don't have to do that anymore . . . More and more Americans are challenging the age barrier, confronting the social stigma, learning to deal with their self-doubts, and enriching their lives with age-different relationships. Widowed older people find young lovers; disenchanted victims of coeval divorce try an age-different relationship the second time; men and women of all ages who feared the dangers of traditional marriage and delayed their unions now join in age-different marriages; and new styles of friendship flourish.

• BLACK MARRIAGES •

For many white people, *The Jeffersons*, a weekly TV sitcom, has been their only exposure to the internal dynamics of a black marriage. George and Louise are portrayed as an upwardly mobile New York couple with a maid, a plush apartment, and interracial friends. Although black marriages like this do exist, the program tells us little about other black families. We now examine some of their distinguishing characteristics.

DATA • *There are 3,535,000 black married couples (7 percent) in the United States compared with 45,007,000 white married couples.* (Statistical Abstract of the United States, 1984)

The Context of Racism

Black marriages occur in the context of continued racism, discrimination, and economic insufficiency. Blacks have higher levels of stress and die earlier than whites. Many feel powerless to defend themselves against racial pressures. One spouse said:

They cut off expectations. I mean no matter how good you are, you will always be a nigger. Hey, that puts strains on people. I mean you can be smart, have a lot of bread, but you know that you will not be able to give your children or yourself an equal chance and this takes its toll. A lot of really good people have a lot on the ball, end up on dope, alcohol, or one thing or another. I mean everyone that I know has one of these problems because of this racist society. Let me tell you, I do not have any hope for the future. (McAdoo, 1982, p. 484)

Much of the discrimination is economic. The median family income for blacks is 57 percent that of whites (Ball, 1982). Living with "not enough money" on a daily basis can create havoc in a marriage. In one study "household expenses" was the issue over which black spouses said they had the greatest disagreement (Gary & Leashore, 1982).

A racially integrated community is a chronological term timed from the entrance of the first black family to the exit of the last white family.

SAUL ALINSKY

For black couples, marriage has the added stress of dealing with racism and discrimination.

Kinship Ties

Black spouses continue to maintain close ties with their parents and kin after they are married. In some cases they may live with their parents. But even if they do not, their parents continue to be important for emotional and economic support. The importance of kinship ties often supersedes that of the marital relationship. Two researchers (Aschenbrenner & Carr, 1980) who studied marriage relationships among blacks concluded, "The black family is not primarily based on a conjugal relationship or a single household, as in the case of the idealized American family. Rather, it consists of a wide reaching group of relatives involved in relationships of exchange and coparenting; and a collective and cooperative spirit prevails . . ." (p. 469).

Marital Roles

The strong emphasis on ties to one's parents and the larger kinship system seem to affect the marriage relationship. In many cases the mother-child relationship seems to take precedence over the wife-husband relationship. Whether this tie is maintained because of her feeling that her economically disadvantaged husband will not be able to support her or he will not stay around to do so (desertion rates among black males are higher than among white males) is uncertain. But not all black wives give allegiance to their kinship ties over their husbands.

Just as role importance will vary from couple to couple, so will the division of power. One researcher (Gray-Little, 1982) who interviewed 75 black urban couples found that 76 spouses described their marriage as "husband-led;" 53 as "egalitarian;" and 21 as "wife-led." The common assumption that black marriages are wife dominated was not true for these couples.

Another aspect of marital roles among black spouses is that they are most likely to be both employed. The black wife's employment is more often an economic necessity than that of the white wife. Sixty percent of black wives compared with 40 percent of white wives in one study listed "financial necessity" as their reason for working (Landry & Jendrek, 1978).

Marital Satisfaction

How happy are black spouses compared with white spouses? Indirect evidence (higher divorce rates and more single-parent households), suggest they are less happy. Moreover, a study comparing black married women with black single-parent women found insignificant differences in reported satisfaction. The researchers (Ball & Robbins, 1983) reasoned that "this lack of clear-cut difference perhaps can be explained by the employment difficulties faced by many black men. Lacking economic and psychic reward from the employment available to them, many men become deficient in their familial roles. Thus women may find little to be gained from marriage in either the instrumental or expressive realms."

Marital satisfaction is even more strained when the wife achieves more than the husband. "The greater a woman's educational level and income, the less desirable she is to many black males. While a male's success adds to his desirability as a mate, it detracts from a woman's. Hence, the women in this group are less likely to marry and remain married, if they do marry. It is a classical case of success in the labor market and failure in the marriage arena" (Staples, 1981, p. 175).

• VERY HAPPY MARRIAGES •

The type of marriage most of us want is the happy marriage—not the "we-get-along" or "things-are-okay" marriage but the type of marriage that continues the love feelings and fun we had in courtship. To find individuals in such marriages, two researchers studied 72 middle-aged, middle-class spouses who answered most of the following items positively (Ammons & Stinnett, 1980):

My spouse and I enjoy doing many things together.

I enjoy most of the activities I participate in more if my spouse is also involved.

I receive more satisfaction from my marriage relationship than most other areas of my life.

My spouse and I have a positive, strong emotional involvement with each other.

Black Americans are still spatially segregated from the majority of the more affluent white citizenry, and certain cultural values distinguish their family life, in form and content, from the middle-class, white Anglo-Saxon model.

ROBERT STAPLES

The companionship of my spouse is more enjoyable to me than most anything else in life.

I would not hesitate to sacrifice an important goal in life if achievement of that goal would cause my marriage relationship to suffer.

My spouse and I take an active interest in each other's work and hobbies. (p. 38)

These spouses also took a personality test (Edwards Personal Preference Test) that revealed their various personality needs and characteristics. The goal was to find out what kind of people live in very happy marriages. The answers follow.

Sex

Almost nine in 10 of the spouses reported having a moderately high to very high need for sexual activity. Sex was seen as a way of expressing a very deep emotional involvement with each other—a meeting of their souls. Also their sexual needs were similar. Both partners enjoyed the sexual aspect of their relationship.

Empathy

The happily married spouses also had a need to be understanding and supportive of their partners. In contrast to a selfish, narcissistic orientation, they felt best when they were nurturing the needs of their partners. "I love to love her and do things for her," said one husband. The result was a relationship in which each spouse felt loved, supported, and cared for by the partner.

Commitment

The starting point in making a marriage work is working on ourselves.

SALLY OLDS

These spouses were also deeply committed and determined to make their marriage work. "My marriage is the most important thing in the world to me and I'm not going to let anything happen to it," said one spouse. "But as anyone who's married knows, the relationship won't spin by itself—you've got to work at it. This means that we work out problems as they come along and don't let things build up."

Another spouse said, "Most folks getting divorced today aren't committed to making their marriage work. You've got to want it to work before it will. Everything follows from your commitment and determination that it will succeed."

Two Strong Egos

Although a major focus of these very happily married spouses was each other, each partner was also an autonomous person, functioning independently of the other in her or his respective careers and roles. Their relationship was like a yardstick that can be best supported horizontally at each end. If the two supports are too close to the middle, the yardstick will topple. So it is with marriage—two individuals standing independently give the best support for their relationship. If they are immersed in each other to the exclusion of developing themselves and their interests, their relationship will be less stable.

Other Characteristics

In a subsequent nationwide study of an additional 438 spouses ranging in age from 20 to 78 who viewed themselves as having a strong family, Stinnett et al. (1982) identified communication, love, religion, and respect as contributing factors. When the respondents were asked what they did as a family that seemed to strengthen their relationship, enjoying the outdoors, taking vacations, going to church, and attending sporting events headed the list.

CONSIDERATION • The studies on very happy marriages suggest that they share four essential elements—commitment, communication, love, and shared activities. A strong commitment to each other to work out the problems in the relationship is basic. But this requires effective communication skills to negotiate differences. Motivation to talk out differences springs from an intense emotional connection between the partners. Their love feelings also propel them into sharing a wide range of activities. To assess your own marital satisfaction, take the Marriage Happiness Scale.

• TRENDS •

Weddings will continue to take place in a variety of settings and represent the desires of the spouses more than their parents. Because more couples are living together, fewer will take the traditional honeymoon. Also, because of changing male-female relationships, traditional marriages, which have been characterized by male dominance, will become less frequent. The trend toward equalitarian relationships will continue. Marriage relationships continue to exhibit a wide range of variation.

• SUMMARY •

All marriage relationships represent a commitment between the partners, the respective families, and the couple and the state.

The wedding is a rite of passage signifying the change in role from lover to spouse. Although couples who have lived together are less likely to have a traditional wedding and honeymoon, most couples getting married for the first time have both.

Marriage results in various personal, social, and legal changes for the spouses. Personally, most spouses experience an enhanced self-concept since they are living with a person who loves and cares for them to the extent of making a "permanent" commitment. Society also approves of a couple's marriage and encourages them to feel good about their decision. But the reality of marriage also involves disenchantment—the gradual process whereby each spouse

MARRIAGE HAPPINESS SCALE

This inventory is designed to measure the way you feel about your spouse. There are no right or wrong answers. After reading each sentence carefully, circle the number that best represents your feelings.

1 Strongly disagree
2 Mildly disagree
3 Undecided
4 Mildly agree
5 Strongly agree

	SD	D	U	A	SA
1. My partner and I enjoy spending our free time together.	1	2	3	4	5
2. My partner and I have never discussed separation.	1	2	3	4	5
3. My partner lets me know that I am loved.	1	2	3	4	5
4. I let my partner know that I love her or him.	1	2	3	4	5
5. My partner and I have a lot in common.	1	2	3	4	5
6. My partner and I rarely argue.	1	2	3	4	5
7. My partner and I have a good sex life.	1	2	3	4	5
8. My partner and I are able to talk about anything.	1	2	3	4	5
9. My partner is supportive of my interests.	1	2	3	4	5
10. My partner and I are committed to make our marriage work.	1	2	3	4	5

Scoring: Add the numbers you circled. Since 1 (strongly disagree) is the most negative feeling you could have and 5 (strongly agree) is the most positive feeling you could have, the lower your total score (10 is the lowest possible score), the less happy you are in your marriage, and the higher your score (50 is the highest possible score), the more happy you are in your marriage. A score of 30 places you at the midpoint between an unhappy and a very happy marriage.

of these wives may have outdistanced their husbands in their career aspira-
tions, it is more often the case that they are married to men who are temporar-
ily having difficulty getting a job paying a higher wage.   (U.S. Bureau of the
Census, 1983a)

Two researchers studied 46 spouses who were involved in marriages in which
the wife's occupation was given priority over the husband's (Atkinson & Boles,
1982). Specific criteria for being included in the study included the husband's
willingness to relocate to further his wife's career, the perception by the
spouses that if they moved it would more likely be because of the wife's career,
and the perception by the spouses that the family was organized around the
wife's career. The spouses were in their forties and had been married an average
of 12½ years. The men had flexible jobs (42 percent were self-employed).

The wives and husbands in these marriages were asked to talk about the
costs and rewards of this type of dual-career marriage. Wives said the costs included being responsible for the economic support of the family, being tired,
feeling guilty over not being a good wife, lacking time to do things, and watching the husband suffer by comparison with the wife—for example, others viewing the husband as lazy, irresponsible, and unmasculine. "If he was any kind of a
man, he wouldn't be moving just because of her job," said a father of his son.

The major costs of this arrangement from the viewpoint of the husbands
were sacrifices in their own careers and the wife being away from home. Also,
occasionally, the husband would have to deal with a cryptic remark like, "Does
she manage you too?" a question addressed to the husband of an office manager.

Both spouses saw more rewards than costs. Wives talked of the opportunity
to pursue their careers, financial gain, independence, freedom from household
chores, enhanced self-esteem, having emotional support from husbands, time
for husbands to spend with children, additional resources for children, and
flexible gender-role models for their children. One mother said:

> I think I show her (my daughter) that a woman can do things. I don't want my
> girl taking a back seat to a man. I know women who stayed home with their
> husbands because they were afraid to leave . . . to go out on their own. Those
> women are trapped—like slaves. I don't want that kind of life for my girl. If
> she's going to live with a man it's going to be because she wants to.

Husbands also saw more rewards than costs of the HER/his career pattern.
They felt relieved of the major responsibility for the economic support of the
family and enjoyed the freedom and resources to pursue their own interests.
One attorney said, "Her job has allowed me to pick and choose cases. I only handle cases in my area of specialization. Most lawyers have to take cases they
don't find interesting or challenging."

As for the happiness of these marriages, more husbands than wives felt "very
happy" or "somewhat happy." Ninety-five percent of the husbands selected one
of these phrases to describe their marriage in contrast to 77 percent of the
wives.

Not all research on marriages in which the wife has a higher-status job and
earns more than the husband reflects as positive a picture as the Atkinson and
Boles research. In a summary of three studies he made on these marriages, Rubenstein (1982) concludes:

> When a wife has a job that outshines her husband's, sex lives may suffer and
> feelings of love diminish. In addition, these couples run a high risk of mutual

psychological and physical abuse, which leads to a significantly higher rate of divorce. Finally, for some underachieving husbands whose wives are over-achievers, premature death from heart disease is 11 times more frequent than normal. (p. 37)

A husband married to a physician may sometimes tire of the attention his wife gives to her career:

> Last night was the first night she was home before 7:30 in I don't know how long. Her schedule this rotation is incredible. The patients are really sick on her service and I know she has to be there a lot. But last night I really wanted to be with her—to talk, to have sex, to enjoy ourselves. Well, she came home and said she just wanted to take a short nap first. Well, you can guess the rest. She didn't want to get up; she didn't want to talk, she didn't want sex. I tried to joke with her. I told her that I'm getting rusty, that I'm afraid I'll forget. So she yells "leave me alone" and gives me "the finger." (Gerber, 1983, pp. 106–107.)

DATA • *About 30 percent of today's medical students are female.* (Mathis, 1984)

Some husbands married to career oriented women become househusbands. One researcher (Beer, 1984) observed that househusbands tend to have had fathers who were a positive role model in terms of doing housework, tend to have an extraordinary sense of fair play regarding domestic work roles, and tend to be professionals who can more easily control their own time.

THEIR Careers

Sometimes spouses view each other as equals and their careers as equally important (Yogev, 1981). "We respect each other's career commitment, try to support each other, and feel that we mutually benefit from keeping two strong careers going," said one spouse. In Exhibit 10.1 (see pages 286–287) a couple share their views of their dual-career marriage.

One researcher (Berardo, 1982) studied 81 marriages in which both spouses were in professional or managerial positions and worked full time (more than 35 hours each week) and compared them with the marriages of 1,500 other families. The study indicated that the dual-career couples were more educated, had higher incomes, were younger, were child-free (60 percent), or had fewer children (three-quarters of those with children had one or two), and tended to live in urban areas.

Housework done by the husbands in the dual-career marriages was no more than that done by other husbands. However, wives in the dual-career marriages did less housework than wives in other marriages. In another study (Bird et al, 1984), the researchers observed that as the status of the wife's work and her income increase, the husband is more likely to help with meal preparation, house cleaning, and childrearing.

One researcher (Mathis, 1984) commented on the phenomenon of physician-physician marriages. He noted that although the advantages include an affluent life-style and a companion who understands the language and work stress of a physician's life, the disadvantages are not being able to find the work environment that may satisfy both partners, little time together, and no one to be the "wife" at home. "I know of no reliable data, but my experience, socially and professionally, indicates that these marriages tend to be considerably above average in stability " (p. 196).

Commuter Marriages

A variation of THEIR careers is the commuter marriage, where each spouse has a strong commitment to her or his career and needs to live close to a particular place of employment that happens to be a different place from where the spouse lives. A study of 43 spouses in such marriages revealed ambivalent feelings about their involvement in the pattern. One spouse asked:

> I think that's how we both saw it. We knew that neither of us was willing to give up the course we were going on so we couldn't ask the other to. Yet implicit in that was the realization that somehow you are making the statement that at least some aspect of your career is more important than being together. I think that's a real issue for today. I get really angry and feel like why do I even have to make these choices, one against the other. It doesn't seem right. There's obviously still a lot of pain. (Gross, 1980, p. 573)

The researcher noted that these marriages experience less strain if the spouses are older, have been married longer, and are free from childrearing responsibilities.

• CONSEQUENCES OF TWO INCOMES IN ONE MARRIAGE •

Regardless of the type of dual-income marriage couples have, there are various consequences for the spouses and their marriage.

Consequences for the Wife

It is clear that most wives who are employed outside the home are personally happy (Gilbert et al., 1981) and feel happy about their marriages (Blumstein & Schwartz, 1983). Among the benefits wives derive from outside employment are increased interaction with a variety of individuals, a broader base for recognition, enhanced self-esteem, and greater equality between self and spouse. Although the family will usually benefit from the increased income, the amount of income must be carefully calculated. If you are a woman, the self-assessment on page 288 may help you decide whether it is worthwhile for you to work when you have small children.

One dual-income wife said, "By having a career you don't put all your eggs in the marriage and family basket. A career gives you another sphere of life to enjoy and in which to feel good about yourself. You can bring more to your husband and children when you're happy doing what you like."

One cost associated with being a dual-income wife is less time for self due to the tendency of the wife to extend herself in both roles (career and wife-mother) as a way of coping with the conflict between the roles. Thus, her major coping strategy is to "do it all." This was the finding of a study of 97 wives in dual career families who had preschool children (Elman and Gilbert, 1984, p. 324)

TWO VIEWS OF ONE DUAL-CAREER MARRIAGE

Chris is a 40-year-old division chief at the New York Public Library in Manhattan. Janie is five years younger and is a full-time professional writer for national magazines. They have been married 14 years and have twins. They agree that the label "dual-career marriage" is an important part of their self-definition. "You know," said Janie, "It's like 'tell me 10 words that describe you' . . . Dual-career couple is well up on the top of the list of phrases that describe us. A dual-career marriage is rigorous. It shapes everything." But their feelings about their dual-career marriage are quite different.

Chris
We maintain this arrangement with my approval but I have strong reservations. There are simply too many pieces in the puzzle. Our children live in a realm where time is beautifully unimportant. Parents with career lives are caught in time. Here we are, seeing ourselves as the radical left, institutionalizing our children in a nursery school from 9 to 3 and then farming them out to a sitter. Somebody else is raising our kids!

I would warn a couple contemplating a dual-career marriage in these terms: Do you think your children are in a state of suspended animation from 8:00 A.M. to 7:00 P.M.? Look at my day outside the job. I wake everybody up, dress one child, and make the lunch boxes if I'm downstairs first. I try to leave Janie upstairs with the twins (age 4) so they can be relaxed together before she leaves. Then I drive the children to their school (50 minutes round trip) before taking the commuter train into Manahattan. I'm home just before 7:00 P.M. Also, we're forced into everything ready made: frozen foods and coloring books instead of a game of cards that involves interacting as a family.

What I see, principally, is that my wife is sharing in the goodies of a man's career world—her lunch friends, her college club in the city, her involvement in work that she finds exciting. I list all the negatives because Janie tends to see her job so rosily.

Janie
Our happiness is work, love, and children. I feel I have everything, more than most people, more than I knew married life could contain. The many roles—wife, mother, worker, friend, editor, family arranger—are invigorating. My perfectionism has diminished. The stages of life have softened. Motherhood doesn't have to replace a professional career.

I feel a very positive model to my 4-year-old daughter. She helps me choose clothes each day . . . her ideas are (honestly) better on sartorial matters than mine. She loves her French-American school, and we share our delight in each other's days. The ache I feel is more with her twin, my son. Beneath his quiet, fun-loving, busy nature, is there a mirror of the loneliness I feel for him during the day? Does he need more alone time than his day allows?

Our intimacy as a married couple certainly does not suffer. Once a week Chris and I meet for lunch—our Thursday tryst—between our places of work. We are happy so it is easy to be affectionate and generous-spirited toward each other.

In her novel *Happy Marriages*, Laurie Colwin says to her old-fashioned, stay-at-home mother, "Stop hectoring me—my children are arranged for, coddled, and loved." That's what I feel. The guilt is only fretting. What childrearing situation is perfect?

Finally, the surprise to this dual working couple—when your income goes up so there is some discretionary income and each week you spend it.

Another cost for the wife in a dual income marriage involves self doubts about one's own feminity. The career wives studied by Atkinson and Boles (1982) said they were sometimes seen as unladylike, domineering, and manipulative. Some wives feel that their career changes the way they see themselves, their spouses, and their marriages. One wife said:

> My career has advanced more rapidly than my husband's, which has been the source of some tension (never verbalized though). As I have established professional identity, become more independent and sure of myself, my expectations of marriage have changed . . . I wish for sharing intimacy which I find is no longer there. Professional training has made me critical of my husband. (Poloma, et. al. 1981, p. 219)

Consequences for the Husband

How do husbands feel about the employment of their wives? The answer seems to be related to the husband's education, whether or not his mother worked outside the home, when his wife began her employment (Ferber, 1982), and his gender-role orientation (Bird et al., 1984). The higher the husband's education, the more likely he is to approve of and support his wife's employment. More educated husbands tend to prefer less rigid roles in their marital relationships, which translates into tolerance for their wife's career involvement.

Husbands who grew up with a mother who worked outside the home are also more supportive of their wives' occupational pursuits. Such an experience suggests that the wife's employment is normative.

Husbands whose wives work outside the home from the beginning of the marriage are more tolerant than husbands whose wives delay such employment. Husbands get accustomed to their wives preparing the meals, cleaning the house, and taking care of the children and miss these services when they stop. Husbands don't help much around the house whether or not their wives work. True house husbands are rare (Beer, 1984). However, the husband of an employed wife does more than the husband of a full-time homemaker. "Since women help bring home the bacon, they expect their husbands to help fry it," says Ann Landers. Also, husbands who have an egalitarian view of gender roles are more likely to take responsibility for meal preparation, cleaning, and child-rearing (Bird, et al., 1984).

Although some husbands may complain about the extra housework they feel pressed into doing, most enjoy the economic benefits of the two-income marriage. "When you've got two people putting money in the kitty, it fills up faster

DOES IT PAY FOR A MOTHER WITH SMALL CHILDREN TO WORK AWAY FROM HOME?

Job satisfaction is certainly a worthwhile reason for a mother to seek employment. But will it pay to work full time while your children are young? Or in the long run, would you be better off acquiring and polishing skills at night school, during hours when your husband can baby-sit, and then stepping into a higher paying job—and probably a more satisfying one—after the children are more independent?

Sadly enough, from a financial standpoint, you will often find that when there are children needing care in your absence, a second family income is mostly illusory. You can sometimes save more money by serving two meatless dinners a week and sewing your own and the children's clothes than you can earn going to work.

Estimate your family's increase in spendable money if you take a job by filling in the following cost sheet. Remember, no matter how attractive your pay may seem, it is only what you get to keep that counts.

Daily transportation	_____ × 250 =	$ _____
Lunches	_____ × 250 =	$ _____
Baby-sitter or day care per week	_____ × 50 =	$ _____
Additional clothes		$ _____
Extra cost of convenience foods to substitute for your cooking	_____ × 250 =	$ _____
Union or professional association dues	_____ × number of payments per year	$ _____
Group life and health insurance (your share)	_____ × number of payments per year	$ _____
Your share of pension plan contributions (this is really long-term savings, but it is not spendable cash for now)		$ _____
	Subtotal of costs	$ _____
Add 10 percent of subtotal costs for office contributions, coffee breaks, and other inevitable and unexpected dollar dribbles		$ _____
	Total costs	$ _____

Now subtract these total costs from your take-home pay, that is, your net after deductions for taxes, Social Security, and disability insurance. What is left is what you are actually going to earn. Is it worth it?

Staying home may turn out to make more economic sense because of the high cost of child care and other expenses. This does not mean you shouldn't work if you want to, however. Consider the kind of work you would really like to do. Then consider spending the time of your children's early years improving your skills with evening classes. Instead of starting as a file clerk, you could be a dental hygienist; instead of starting at assembly-line work, you could be a management supervisor. The early years of childrearing can be an opportunity, not only for your family, but for yourself as well. One-half of mothers with children under 6 do not work outside the home (Thornton and Freedman, 1983).

and you can buy what you want now." Some couples who have adjusted to a standard of living based on two incomes view dropping back to one income as a disaster.

DATA • *The median income of a family with two earners is $30,112 compared with $22,800 where the husband is the sole earner.* (U.S. Bureau of the Census, 1983a)

A wife's career commitment may affect her husband's career. In a study of more than 300 husbands (Sharda & Nangle, 1981), the researchers found that the career mobility of a husband tends to be restricted when he is married to a wife in a high-status occupation. "Both husbands and wives tend to accommodate each other by restricting their own mobility" (p. 148).

A husband may also miss the emotional support of his wife.

> While homebound wives have traditionally depended on their husbands' achievements for much of their sense of worth, husbands have been at least as dependent on their wives—as listeners, consolers, and ego-builders—for their emotional sustenance. When the wife has a career of her own, however, the exchange is altered. The wife is less dependent on her husband for her own self-esteem, and she may also be less attentive to his needs and problems. (Rubin, 1983, p. 72)

Marital Consequences

What are the consequences for their marriage when the wife is employed? Results of studies differ. Two surveys found no effect of the wife's employment or the degree of interest in her work on the marital adjustment of the couple or their companionship feelings for each other (Locksley, 1980; Piotrkowski & Crits-Cristoph, 1981).

In direct contrast, two other studies found that both husbands and wives reported higher marital satisfaction if the wife worked outside the home (Bahr & Day, 1978; Simpson & England, 1981).

These different conclusions suggest that the wife's employment by itself does not determine whether a couple's marriage will be happy. Issues that do influence happiness in the dual-income marriage are more likely to include the husband's support of his wife's employment, flexibility of roles, and commitment by each spouse to allocate time to their relationship. "The bottom line of making a dual-income marriage work," said one spouse, "is to help your partner and be committed to your relationship."

Employment of the wife alters the traditional pattern of the marriage relationship in the direction of equality as the money she earns increases her power in the marriage (Rank, 1982). An interior designer said, "Now that I make a good income, my preferences are given equal weight by my husband. Whether we eat out or not, where we eat, and where we vacation are now joint decisions. Before, my husband would say, 'We can't afford it . . . ' and I would acquiesce." The adage "He who pays the piper calls the tune" summarizes the relationship between money and power. In the dual-income marriage, there are two pipers and two potential tunes.

Time is a particular problem for spouses who work different shifts.

DATA • *Of all nonfarm U.S. households, one-third of couples have at least one spouse who works other than a regular day shift. One in 10 couples work entirely different shifts.* (Presser & Cain, 1983)

CONSIDERATION • To minimize the lack of time dual-income spouses have for each other, one of the partners needs to be responsible for ensuring that the couple spend time together. Much like a gardener, this person looks after the relationship and sees that it is properly nourished. Although wives typically assume this role, about 40 percent of the husbands in one study said they did so (Blumstein & Schwartz, 1983).

Consequences for the Children

Most husbands and wives feel that the wife's employment has more positive than negative personal and marital consequences, but they are more ambivalent about the consequences for their children. Most parents think it is best for their children for the mother to be with the children when they are small. As we noted, only half of mothers with preschool children do not work outside the home. As children get older, the labor force participation of their mothers increases.

Negative effects of a mother's employment on her children's self-concept, school achievement, and vocational development have not been verified. At least one report states that children whose mothers are employed are not significantly different from children whose mothers stay home with them (Rosenthal & Hansen, 1981).

When children are asked how they feel about their mothers' working outside the home, their answers differ depending on gender and age. In a survey of 50 elementary school children (Trimberger & MacLean, 1982), the girls liked it less than the boys. This may have been because they were assigned more domestic tasks than their brothers. The older children also liked it less than the

When both parents work, more responsibility is usually placed on the children.

younger children. They had no older person to play with them (mom was gone) and were assigned more work than their younger siblings.

Domestic work by children also seems to increase as domestic work by their father increases. In a study of 94 married couples with children, the researchers found that fathers who shared a greater amount of tasks involving child care, meal preparation, and cleaning indicated that their children participated to a greater extent in meal preparation, cleaning, and self care (Bird and Ratcliff, 1984).

Mothers who work outside the home often feel guilty about doing so. "I'm very tired when I get home from teaching third grade all day and I don't feel like going to Parents Night at my child's school," said one mother. "But I ask myself, 'What kind of a parent am I if I don't go to my own child's school functions?' and the guilt is usually enough to get me there."

Although most children are not harmed by their mother's employment, "latchkey" children are. The term refers to children who come home from school to an empty house, using their own key to get in. With no one to care for them until after 5:00 P.M. the children have an increased accident risk, may feel rejected ("Since no one's here, I guess no one cares about me"), and may be at greater risk for sexual crimes (Garbarino, 1981).

DATA • *It is estimated that there are 6.5 million children who come home daily to an empty house.* (Long & Long, 1983)

To help allay children's fears, PhoneFriend is available in State College, Pennsylvania, and other areas such as Boston and Houston. By calling a specified number, the children have someone they can talk to in times of stress.

> One recent afternoon brought a panicky call from a 10-year-old girl who needed to use the bathroom, but couldn't because it was occupied by a mouse. Dr. Guerney (director of the program) happened to be at the phone that day, so she and the girl talked it over and came to the conclusion that the mouse was probably more frightened than the girl, and in fact, was probably looking for an excuse to leave. The solution: Make noise and scare it away. This seems to have worked; the girl didn't call back. (*Psychology Today*, 1983, p. 77)

Other Consequences

Couples in two-income marriages note that household chores, childrearing responsibilities, and time priorities are potential problems. Since each spouse's occupational role makes considerable demands, each needs a "backup." In the traditional marriage, this is the nonworking wife who prepares meals and the like. The dual-income marriage has no such backup.

Patterns of response to the "no wife at home" problem vary. As already noted, wives typically extend themselves and do much of the domestic labor and child care in addition to their paid employment. Some husbands help—particularly those who make less money or have jobs of less status than the wife. Other couples hire "wife" substitutes. One such couple hire a woman to come to their home Monday through Friday from 7:30 A.M. to 5:30 P.M., during which time she takes care of the couple's infant, cleans the house, and prepares dinner.

Regardless of how the work gets done, two-income couples complain that they have little time for each other. "We have to schedule Saturday from five till midnight for ourselves. If it weren't for the Saturday nights alone together, we would be divorced. If you don't spend time with each other, you grow away from your partner," remarked a real estate broker.

Because they have limited leisure time and that is usually allocated to the children and each other, the two-income couple sometime feel isolated from others. They have fewer friends. The friendships that do develop tend to be with other dual-income couples, which helps to validate their own life-style.

• TRENDS •

The number of married women employed in the labor force will continue to increase. Most will continue to have jobs, but an increasing number will become involved in careers. For some brides, the understanding that they will pursue a career during their marriage is a nonnegotiable issue. "I want to be married," said one woman, "but I won't let it interfere with my career in business."

The percentage of husbands with supportive attitudes toward a wife's employment will also increase. Economic necessity, male peers with working wives, and being reared by mothers who were employed outside the home will all contribute to this increase. Whether this support translates into an equal sharing of domestic and child-care tasks remains to be seen. Unless men take on more of the workload at home, women will continue to be burdened with the two major roles of worker and homemaker.

More mothers with young children will enter the work force. To encourage more young parents to continue working, more companies will offer flextime, a system that permits a worker to select the eight hours he or she will work between 7:30 A.M. and 6:30 P.M. About one in five American companies and one in four U.S. government agencies offer a form of flextime (Newsweek, 1980). These numbers will increase.

• SUMMARY •

Employed wives are becoming increasingly common, particularly in the middle class. Before 1940 female workers were primarily poor, black, and immigrant, but with World War II, middle-class wives flooded the labor force. At the end of the war, about 20 percent of married women were employed; by 1985 that figure had jumped to over 60 percent.

In general, although wives are motivated by money and the desire for adult interaction, their labor force participation is related to the stage of their families' development. Wives with no children are the most likely to be employed, and those with preschool children are the least likely to work outside the home. Half of the mothers with children under 6 are not employed.

When a career is defined in terms of training, commitment, continuity, and mobility, most wives seem to have jobs rather than a career. The responsibility for children and having no "wife" at home are among the obstacles married women must overcome in pursuing a career.

Dual-career marriages may be described as "his", "hers," or "theirs." When wives are asked to evaluate the effect of their employment on themselves, their marriages, and their children, most report being happier individuals and happier in their marriages. Husbands report mixed feelings about their wives' employment. Although many are delighted that their wives are happier and enjoy the economic benefits of a two-income marriage, they may also miss the personal and domestic attentions of their wives and feel pressed into doing more housework. Trends in two-income marriages include more two-income marriages, more mothers of small children working outside the home, and more companies offering flextime.

Questions for Reflection

1. Does the work role you foresee for yourself approximate a career or a job?
2. How much do you want the person you might marry to be involved in a career? A job?
3. How does having money or not influence your mood, feelings about yourself, and your interaction with others?

· CHOICES ·

Making decisions about a dual-income marriage involves different issues for the wife and the husband. How much to spend and how much to save may also become issues.

AS A WIFE, DO I WANT A DUAL-CAREER MARRIAGE?

Personal needs, your husband's support, and your desire for children are issues you might consider in making a decision to pursue a career during your marriage. It is clear that some women are miserable in the sole roles of wife and mother. A newswoman for a television station said, "My employment offers me the chance to stay alive. When my children leave home or if my husband dies, I will still be a journalist. Otherwise I'd be nothing."

The husband's emotional support for his wife's employment is another important consideration. "I've got the best husband you could imagine," said one university professor. "He has always encouraged my involvement in whatever I wanted to do and he struggled through the grind of

a Ph.D. program with me." Not all husbands are this supportive. Your husband's enthusiastic support is critical if your goal is to pursue a meaningful career.

Finally, think about your desire for children. Unless your husband is willing to share the responsibility of rearing children fully (he takes the children to piano lessons or sees that someone else does; he calls out the spelling words; he helps with the math homework), your career advancement may suffer. As noted earlier, it is common for wives to reduce the conflict between children and job demands by reducing job demands to meet family needs. This strategy will work as long as you are involved in a job, not a career. If career is your goal, you must forego children, your husband must be equally committed to child care, or you must have a

lot of money to pay for child care.

AS A HUSBAND, DO I WANT A DUAL-CAREER MARRIAGE?

As a current or potential husband, you might assess the degree to which you want your wife to pursue a career. In general, husbands point to the companionship aspects, more money, and the knowledge that their wives are happier working than being at home as primary benefits of a wife's employment. One husband said, "When your wife has a career, she understands what the stress of the work world is like. She knows what it is to meet deadlines, to have conferences that are boring, and to be exhausted by traveling. The empathy that each of you have for the other's work stress is a major benefit."

Increased money is also an advantage to the husband. Not only does more money improve the couple's immediate life-style (Home Box Office, new cars, a swimming pool), it may prolong the life of the man. One husband said:

My dad died of a coronary when he was 46. I'm sure that one of the reasons for his early death was the fact that he was totally responsible for earning all the money. Since my mother did not work outside the home, he worked himself crazy with the stress of two jobs. Since my wife earns a terrific income, I don't worry as much about money and certainly don't feel that I am responsible for sending our three kids to college on the money that I earn.

A final benefit to the husband of the wife's career involvement is her happiness. "I'm living with a happy woman," said one husband. "Although she is very busy and exhausted half the time, she loves her work. She's not the kind that can sit home and cut out orange juice coupons all day long."

Husbands also point to several disadvantages of being married to a woman who has a career, especially missing the services of a domestic wife, feeling obligated to help more around the house, and feeling threatened by the wife's own income, increased power, and independence. Missing the services of the domestic wife is more characteristic of husbands whose wives were first homemakers and then career wives. Husbands who began marriage with the career wife don't know what they are missing.

The domestic obligation husbands feel increases as the career demands of the wife escalate. Some husbands respond to this feeling in a cooperative spirit and take over the cooking, cleaning, shopping, and laundry. Other husbands negotiate with their wives to hire a person to come in once or twice a week to take care of the house. Some dual-career spouses have full-time live-in help so that neither is burdened with housework.

The wife's economic independence is a problem for some men. Suddenly they recognize they are no longer needed economically. For the man who has a low sense of self-esteem and needs his wife's constant adulation, her independence may be a problem.

In evaluating these advantages and disadvantages, questions husbands might ask include the following: "Is the loss of domestic services counterbalanced by more income?" "Is my wife's absence from home made up for by her greater fulfillment?" and "Am I willing to share the responsibility of parenting?"

HOW MUCH MONEY SHOULD BE SAVED AND SPENT?

Dual-income spouses usually have a great deal more income than when the husband only has a job. A discussion about what to do with the surplus money is usually a good idea. Some couples prefer to bank one income and live off the other. "We were putting my salary in a money market fund and using hers to pay for our monthly expenses," said one husband.

Other couples prefer to live high and spend all of both incomes each month. "Neither of us had ever had any money, so we decided to go for it," said one wife. "We bought a two-bedroom apartment overlooking the lake, take trips to Aspen to ski, and go to New York to shop and see plays. We figure if we don't spend the money, we will be dead and it won't do us any good in the bank. Besides, we don't have kids so we don't have to save for their college educations or anything like that."

· Chapter 11 ·

COMMUNICATION AND CONFLICT

CONTENTS

Myths about Marriage

Marital Happiness and
  Adjustment

Communication: Some Facts

Self-Assessment: The Dyadic
  Adjustment Scale

Conflicts in Marriage

Productive and Nonproductive
  Communication

Marital Therapy

Marriage Enrichment

Choices

*My wife said I don't listen to
her—at least that's what I
think she said.*

LAURENCE PETER

The role shift from lover to spouse sometimes turns an exhilarating love relationship into one fraught with conflict. Part of the difficulty of this transition may be our unrealistic expectations about marriage. But we need to communicate about our relationship and we need to learn to manage conflict with our partner. In this chapter we look at several myths about marriage and explore a systematic way to manage conflict. We also review basic factors in communication, the differences between productive and nonproductive communication, and characteristics of spouses who communicate well with their partners. For those of us who need help in these areas, we explore marriage therapy and marriage enrichment.

Marriage has a great deal to offer, but it is not a magic kingdom where the usual principles don't apply and where you get something for nothing.

DAVID AND VERA MACE

In their classic book, *The Mirages of Marriage*, Lederer and Jackson (1968) wrote that marriage is "like taking an airplane to Florida for a relaxing vacation in January, and when you get off the plane you find you're in the Swiss Alps. There is cold and snow instead of swimming and sunshine . . . After you buy winter clothes and learn how to talk a new foreign language, you can have just as good a vacation in the Swiss Alps as you can in Florida. But . . . it's one hell of a surprise when you get off that marital airplane . . ." (p. 39).

One of the reasons we are surprised by the actual experience of marriage is that we have a poor idea of what day-to-day living together in marriage is really like. Our assumptions are often distortions of reality. Some of the more unrealistic beliefs our society perpetuates about marriage are discussed here.

"Our Marriage Will Be Different"

All of us know married people who are bored, unhappy, and in conflict. Despite this, we assume our marriage will be different. The feeling before marriage that "it won't happen to us" reflects the deceptive nature of courtship. If we are determined that our marriage will be different, what steps are we taking to ensure that it is? This question is relevant because many of us who enter marriage believing that ours will be different blindly imitate the marriage patterns of others instead of making a conscious effort to manage our own relationship to make it as fulfilling as we expect.

"We Will Make Each Other Happy"

We also tend to believe that we are responsible for each other's happiness. "When my husband tried to commit suicide," one woman recalled, "I couldn't help but think that if I had been the right kind of wife he wouldn't have done such a thing. But I've come to accept that there was more to his depression than just me. He wasn't happy with his work, he drank heavily, and he never got over his twin brother's death."

CONSIDERATION • Although you and your partner will be a tremendous influence on each other's happiness, each of you has roles (employee, student, sibling, friend, son or daughter, parent, and so on) beyond the role of spouse. These role relationships will color the interaction with your mate. If you have lost your job or flunked out of school, your father has cancer, your closest friend moves away, or your mother, who can no longer care for herself, resists going to a nursing home, it will be difficult for your spouse to "make you happy." Similarly, although you may make every effort to ensure your spouse's happiness, circumstances can defeat you.

"Our Disagreements Will Not Be Serious"

Many couples acknowledge that they will have disagreements, but they assume theirs will be minor and "just part of being married." But "insignificant"

Another myth of marriage is that courtship lasts forever. The reality is that marriage focuses on the business of life as in buying houses and rearing children.

conflict that is not resolved can threaten any marriage. "All I wanted was for him to spend more time with me," recalled a divorced woman. "But he said he had to run the business because he couldn't trust anyone else. I got tired of spending my evenings alone and got involved with someone else."

"Children Will Make Our Marriage Even Happier"

Just as we have been socialized to believe that getting married is part of being an adult, we also tend to believe that having children is part of being married. We have been taught that children are a sign of the love between a woman and a man and that children make the couple happier. But some research suggests the opposite is true. Although having children may increase personal happiness (particularly the wife's), children tend to decrease positive marital interactions. In a study comparing couples who intentionally had children with those who intentionally were child-free, the latter reported having more "positive marital interactions" such as fun away from home, working together on a project, and having sexual relations (Feldman, 1981, p. 597). Spouses are happiest before children come and after they leave home. This negative effect of children on marriage is true for both spouses of all races, major religious preferences, educational levels, and employment status (Glenn & McLanahan, 1982).

"My Spouse Is All I Need"

All of us have needs requiring the support of others. These range from wanting to see a movie with someone to needing someone to talk to about personal problems to needing the physical expression of a partner's love. Although it is encouraging to believe that our partner can satisfy all our intellectual, physical, and emotional needs, it is not realistic.

CONSIDERATION • Perhaps a more accurate way to think of these five beliefs about marriage is to recognize that our marriage *may* be different, that we will be *one* important influence on our partner's happiness, that our disagreements *may* not be serious, that children *may* increase our marital happiness, and that we will be able to satisfy *some* of our partner's needs.

• MARITAL HAPPINESS AND ADJUSTMENT •

With or without a belief in various myths, most of us enter marriage expecting to be happy. But what does "being happy" mean? Let us examine the subjective and dynamic nature of marital happiness and various factors that influence it.

What Influences the Perception of Happiness?

Happiness is a subjective term. The nature of happiness depends on one's point of view. One husband remarked that he had an incredible relationship with his wife because each was free to have sex with others. But another spouse said their relationship was "top of the line" because they were faithful to each other.

In addition to being subjective, marital happiness is constantly changing. Marriage is a process, not a state. When one spouse was asked, "How happy are you in your marriage?" he replied, "It depends on when you ask me. If you ask me when the kids are raising hell in the living room and when it's been 10 days since my wife and I had some good dialogue and sex, I'll tell you, 'Not too happy.' But if you ask me when the kids are with a sitter and my wife and I are enjoying a nice dinner by ourselves, I'll tell you, 'Terrific.' " Every marriage has its good and bad periods.

CONSIDERATION • Most couples find that an essential ingredient in a happy relationship is spending time together sharing mutually enjoyable activities like dining or seeing a movie. Couples who don't spend time together gradually drift apart.

Other factors that affect how spouses rate their marriage include their relationships with other people, their fantasies about the happiness of other marriages, and their comparisons of their own marriage now with their marriage in happier times. One 25-year-old career woman explained how an outside friendship affected her feelings about her marriage: "I guess I was happily married until I met Max. Since we worked together we spent a lot of time together. I felt I could talk with him, and I began to compare the time with him with the time I spent with my husband. Within a few months, I defined my marriage as a failure and wanted out."

Even without a rewarding alternative relationship, imagining that other spouses are very happy may decrease one's own marital happiness. "I feel like

I'm caught in a bum marriage," observed one spouse. "My best friend and his wife have the kind of marriage I want. They are both professionals, like the same things, and seem to enjoy being with each other. They've got it made."

Comparing one's own marriage as it now is with the way it once was may be even more devastating. "Before the twins came," recalled a young mother, "Roger and I used to spend all our time together. Now we never go out to eat, see movies, or take vacations. I feel stuck and life is no fun anymore."

Finally, marital satisfaction seems to be related to knowing what your partner wants you to do to please him or her. In a study of 152 couples, those who understood their partner's needs were more likely to be satisfied with their marriage than those who were oblivious to their partner's expectations (Tiggle et al., 1982).

Measuring Marital Adjustment

The concept of marital happiness may be somewhat elusive, but one way of arbitrarily measuring relationship happiness is to complete a form similar to the Dyadic Adjustment Scale (see pages 302–303).

Scores on marital adjustment scales are sometimes deceptive since it cannot be assumed that any one score is "good" or "bad." Disagreement on a variety of fronts does not necessarily imply poor relationship adjustment. "We don't agree on a lot of issues, but we agree on what matters," said one spouse. Conversely, total agreement does not imply a happy relationship. One partner said that she and her husband agreed on "everything" but had "nothing" in common.

Another problem with measuring marital adjustment is that people tend to answer the way they think they should rather than to report the way things actually are (Hansen, 1981). This tendency to give socially desirable answers (conventionalization) keeps the marriage experience hidden and makes it difficult to determine the degree of marital satisfaction spouses actually experience.

Keeping these cautions in mind, some of the characteristics of spouses who tend to score high on marital adjustment and happiness scales include the following:

- More highly educated spouses (Locksley, 1982)
- Understanding spouses (Tiggle et al., 1982)
- More husbands than wives (Rhyne, 1981)
- Spouses whose children have left home (Rhyne, 1981)
- Spouses who have no children (Rhyne, 1981)
- Spouses who view themselves as emotionally mature (Cole, 1980)

• COMMUNICATION: SOME FACTS •

As we have noted in several earlier contexts, communication is one of the most important aspects of marital adjustment, "We can't communicate" is one of the most frequent complaints heard by marriage therapists. Such feelings are also expressed by dating couples. In a study of a random sample of 334 university students, "communication with date" was the top problem reported by males and one in five females (Knox & Wilson, 1983).

I Know You Believe You Understand What You Think I Said, But I Am Not Sure You Realize That What You Heard Is Not What I Meant.

UNKNOWN

THE DYADIC ADJUSTMENT SCALE

This scale measures four aspects of a relationship: consensus (agreement in philosophy of life, decision making, and so on), affection (demonstrations of affection, sex relations), satisfaction (feeling good about the relationship, not regretting the commitment), and cohesion (working on projects together and the like).

To measure your relationship, circle a number indicating the approximate extent of agreement or disagreement between you and your partner for each of the following 32 items and compare your total score with those of 218 married and 94 divorced individuals.* The average score for those married was 114.8; for those divorced, 70.7.**

	Always agree	Almost always agree	Occasionally disagree	Frequently disagree	Almost always disagree	Always disagree
1. Handling family finances	5	4	3	2	1	0
2. Matters of recreation	5	4	3	2	1	0
3. Religious matters	5	4	3	2	1	0
4. Demonstrations of affection	5	4	3	2	1	0
5. Friends	5	4	3	2	1	0
6. Sex relations	5	4	3	2	1	0
7. Conventionality (correct or proper behavior)	5	4	3	2	1	0
8. Philosophy of life	5	4	3	2	1	0
9. Ways of dealing with parents or in-laws	5	4	3	2	1	0
10. Aims, goals, and things believed important	5	4	3	2	1	0
11. Amount of time spent together	5	4	3	2	1	0
12. Making major decisions	5	4	3	2	1	0
13. Household tasks	5	4	3	2	1	0
14. Leisure time interests and activities	5	4	3	2	1	0
15. Career decisions	5	4	3	2	1	0

	All the time	Most of the time	More often than not	Occasionally	Rarely	Never
16. How often do you discuss or have you considered divorce, separation, or terminating your relationship?	0	1	2	3	4	5
17. How often do you or your mate leave the house after a fight?	0	1	2	3	4	5
18. In general, how often do you think that things between you and your partner are going well?	5	4	3	2	1	0
19. Do you confide in your mate?	5	4	3	2	1	0
20. Do you ever regret that you married? (or lived together)	0	1	2	3	4	5
21. How often do you and your partner quarrel?	0	1	2	3	4	5
22. How often do you and your mate "get on each other's nerves"?	0	1	2	3	4	5

	Every day	Almost every day	Occasionally	Rarely	Never
23. Do you kiss your mate?	4	3	2	1	0

	All of them	Most of them	Some of them	Very few of them	None of them
24. Do you and your mate engage in outside interests together?	4	3	2	1	0

How often would you say the following events occur between you and your mate?

	Never	Less than once a month	Once or twice a month	Once or twice a week	Once a day	More often
25. Have a stimulating exchange of ideas	0	1	2	3	4	5
26. Laugh together	0	1	2	3	4	5
27. Calmly discuss something	0	1	2	3	4	5
28. Work together on a project	0	1	2	3	4	5

These are some things about which couples sometimes agree and sometimes disagree. Indicate if either item below caused differences of opinions or were problems in your relationship during the past few weeks. (Check yes or no)

Yes No

29. 0 1 Being too tired for sex
30. 0 1 Not showing love.
31. The dots on the following line represents different degrees of happiness in your relationship. The middle point, "happy," represents the degree of happiness of most relationships. Please circle the dot which best describes the degree of happiness, all things considered, of your relationship.

0	1	2	3	4	5	6
Extremely Unhappy	Fairly Unhappy	A Little Unhappy	Happy	Very Happy	Extremely Happy	Perfect

32. Which of the following statements best describes how you feel about the future of your relationship?

___5___ I want desperately for my relationship to succeed, and *would go to almost any length* to see that it does.

___4___ I want very much for my relationship to succeed, and *will do all I can* to see that it does.

___3___ I want very much for my relationship to succeed, and *will do my fair share* to see that it does.

___2___ It would be nice if my relationship succeeded, but *I can't do much more than I am doing* now to help it succeed.

___1___ It would be nice if it succeeded, but *I refuse to do any more than I am doing* now to keep the relationship going.

___0___ My relationship can never succeed, and *there is no more that I can do* to keep the relationship going.

*The 218 spouses had an average age of 35.1 years and had been married an average of 13.2 years. They had an average of 13 years of education and 2 children. The 94 divorced individuals had an average of 30.4 years and had been married for an average of 8.5 years. They had an average of 14 years of education and 1.6 children.
**The standard deviation for the marrieds was 17.8. This means that scoring 114.8 plus or minus 17.8 is about the same as scoring exactly 114.8. The standard deviation for the divorced individuals was 23.8. This means that scoring 70.7 plus or minus 23.8 points is about the same as scoring exactly 70.7.
Source: Spanier, G. B. Measuring dyadic adjustment: New scales for assessing the quality of marriage and similar dyads. *Journal of Marriage and the Family,* 1976, *38,* 15–28. © National Council on Family Relations, Fairview Community School Center, 1910 West County Road B, Suite 147, St. Paul, Mn. 55113. Reprinted by permission.

DATA • *Seventy-eight percent of over 5000 students in four universities said that they would like to learn better ways to express themselves in a relationship.* (Martin & Martin, 1984)

What is communication and how can we learn to communicate more effectively with our partners? Communication includes a number of basic elements.

Communication Is Symbolic

Communication uses symbols (words) to transmit messages. When you write a letter you are selecting symbols that refer to agreed-upon meanings that the receiver can understand. When you and your partner discuss where you would like to have dinner, you are using symbols that make is possible to convey your respective preferences.

Because we rely on words to express ideas and feelings, it is important that we attach common meanings to symbols in communicating with our partners. The result of not doing so may be merely comical, as in the following situation:

> One Sunday morning early in our marriage, my wife told me that every Sunday morning before the wedding she had coffee and peanuts to start the day off right. So, being a sensitive bridegroom I trotted off to the kitchen and returned with coffee and a handful of peanuts to meet the (rather unusual) request of my bride. After a full minute of hilarious laughter, she calmed down enough to inform me that she expected coffee and the newspaper with the "Peanuts" cartoon strip. I went away feeling like Charlie Brown . . . .(Galvin & Brommel, 1982, p. 6)

Silence gives consent, or a horrible feeling that nobody's listening.

FRANKLIN P. JONES

Communication Is Interactive

Symbols alone do not constitute communication. They must be used by one person who is interacting with another. Each of us lives in a private world of our own thoughts. Direct communication requires being in the presence of another person or talking on the phone (letters are one-way delayed communication). Communication is interaction, expressing our thoughts, finding out those of others, and reacting to the messages.

The interactive nature of communication means that the communication process is dynamic. As the psychological state (happy or energetic, sad or depressed) and physical state (healthy, hungry, tired, sick) of each partner changes, so will his or her communication patterns. "I had the flu but Martin wanted to discuss our relationship," said a telephone employee. "I told him it was a bad time and to wait until I felt better. He thought I was trying to put him off, so we discussed it and broke up. If I had been feeling well, I'm sure we would still be together."

CONSIDERATION • Since psychological and physical states change, it may be important to be sensitive to such things as mood and health before bringing up a difficult issue for discussion with your partner. As the preceding experience illustrates, the outcome of a discussion at time A may be very different from that at time B.

Communication Affects Feelings and Behaviors

"Sticks and stones may break my bones but words can never hurt me" is a familiar children's chant. But words can and do hurt us, just as they can fill us with joy. Recall the time someone complimented you or told you they loved you or the time you said similar things to someone else. Such occasions are usually accompanied by a swell of good feelings.

> CONSIDERATION • During courtship, dating partners take time to be together, to compliment each other, and to share positive experiences. Their time and energy is directed toward each other, not toward work and children. In marriage it is easy to drift into a pattern of not spending time together, of not complimenting, of not sharing positive experiences. But not to cultivate the relationship is to let it die. If your goal is to maintain good feelings about your partner and your partner about you, it is important that you take the time to nurture your relationship as you did in courtship.

Words also affect behaviors. Physical violence in interpersonal relationships often follows name calling or criticizing. "I told her she was a worthless slut and the next thing I knew, she hit me with the lamp," one husband said.

Words also affect future behaviors. The self-fulfilling prophecy says we sometimes act to make the expectations of others come true. If your partner tells you he or she doesn't trust you and knows you will have an affair sooner or later, the chance that you will do so increases.

Communication Occurs in Context

All communication occurs in a previously understood context. When you stand in front of an elevator door that has just opened, the person inside (stranger, lover, friend, professor, spouse) will provide the context for the communication to follow. The interactions with each of these people will be different.

Part of the context is the social mirror each person holds up to you, reflecting her or his perception and feelings about you. If you feel that people have a positive image of you, your manner of interacting with them will be quite different than if you feel they see you negatively. Each person is a stimulus for the response of the other and the cycle repeats itself.

People with an established relationship also tend to know what to expect when they interact. One woman said the sequence of her and her partner's interaction during a conflict was rather predictable: "I get hurt and start complaining, he gets angry and starts yelling. Then we both yell. I always cry and sometimes he does too. Then we part for a while and are silent. Usually, one or the other of us apologizes shortly thereafter and then we hold each other" (Hennon 1981, p. 476).

Communication Occurs at Two Levels

All communication operates at two levels—verbal and nonverbal. The verbal is the literal content of the message, for example, "I'll see you." The nonverbal,

Communication includes nonverbal behavior as well as verbal exchange.

sometimes referred to as metacommunication, is the message about the message. It conveys to the receiver the "real" message through gesture, facial expression, tone, inflection, or body language. For example, "I'll see you" can be said to convey excitement and anticipation of the next meeting, or it can be said to convey lack of interest and the intention to never see the person again.

Other examples of discrepant messages include

- angrily saying "I'm fine"
- avoiding eye contact when saying, "I wouldn't lie to you"
- saying "I'll write soon" and then not doing so for six months
- saying "I really want to be with you" but never making the time to do so
- saying "It was great!" but having a gloomy appearance.

Forty-one couples were studied to assess the degree to which the respective spouses could read the nonverbal cues of their partners (Gottman & Porterfield, 1981). Results showed that marital satisfaction was higher if the spouse could "read" the nonverbal message sent by the mate. This was particularly true for husbands.

CONSIDERATION • It is important that our verbal and nonverbal communication be consistent. Sending confused messages only confuses the receiver about what we mean.

Marital Communication Is Intense

The German philosopher Schopenhauer told the story of two porcupines huddled together on a cold winter's night. As the temperature dropped, they moved closer together. But getting warmer through the closeness also meant getting "stuck" by the quills of the other. As the night wore on they shuffled and changed positions to receive the maximum amount of warmth with the least amount of sticking.

In some ways marriage represents an attempt on the part of two people to achieve the maximum amount of emotional warmth with the least amount of discomfort. Having to deal with conflict is one source of discomfort that accompanies marriage. Alford (1982) identified six styles of handling conflict:

1. Avoidance—avoiding each other or the subject
2. Discussion—discussing the conflict without expressing anger or raising one's voice
3. Argument—a more intense form of discussing without yelling or making insulting remarks
4. Fight 1—raised voices, angry looks, mildly insulting remarks
5. Fight 2—yelling, screaming, and making personal insults
6. Fight 3—yelling, screaming, pushing, shoving, hitting, throwing things, and making extremely insulting personal references (p. 365)

When the same researcher asked 455 respondents to identify which disputing style they used in what relationships, the closer the relationship, the more intense the disputing style. For example, they would avoid conflict with a neighbor but would argue with the spouse. Marriage, the most intimate relationship, generates intense interaction between spouses.

It is a luxury to be understood.

RALPH WALDO
EMERSON

Gender Differences Exist in Communication Patterns

Wives typically display more emotion in communicating with their husbands than vice versa. In one study (Notarius & Johnson, 1982), wives and husbands were videotaped as they discussed a "salient relationship issue." The tapes were then watched and coded for various aspects of positive (warm, tender, affectionate, cheerful) and negative (cold, impatient, sarcastic, blaming) communication. Wives were much more likely to display emotion (positive or negative) than their husbands. This finding is consistent with previous research indicating that men, compared with women, are less expressive of love, happiness, and sadness (Balswick, 1980). Also, when men do display their emotions, they often do so in a more "forceful," "dominating," and "authoritarian" way than women (Kramarae, 1981).

Another study (Sherman & Haas, 1984) of 166 women and 110 men revealed similar gender specific communication patterns. Women wanted empathy and men wanted facts they could use when they were talking with someone. Women were also much more likely to call other women "just to talk" than were men likely to call other men.

DATA • *Sixty-three percent of the women in contrast to forty-three percent of the men in one study reported that they called a person of their own gender "just to talk."* (Sherman & Haas, 1984)

CONSIDERATION • "Consider then the marriage of a man who has had most of his conversations with other men, to a woman who has had most of her conversations with other women, probably the typical situation. He is used to fast-paced conversations that typically stay on the surface with respect to emotions, that often enable him to get practical tips or offer them to others and that are usually pragmatic or fun. She is used to conversations that, while practical and fun too, are also a major source of emotional support, self-understanding, and the understanding of others. Becoming intimate with a man, the woman may finally start expressing her concerns to him as she might a close friend. But she may find, to her dismay, that his responses are all wrong. Instead of making her feel better, he makes her feel worse. The problem is that he tends to be direct and practical, whereas what she wants more than anything else is an empathetic listener." (Sherman and Haas, 1984, p. 73.)

If the respective genders are to enjoy talking with each other, men might provide more empathy and reflective listening while women might get to the point.

• CONFLICTS IN MARRIAGE •

One of the major reasons for marital dissatisfaction is conflict. As one professor in a marriage and family class said, "If you haven't had a disagreement with your partner, you haven't known him or her long enough." In this section we explore the inevitability, desirability, sources, and types of conflict.

> We sleep in separate rooms, we have dinner apart, we take separate vacations—we're doing everything we can to keep our marriage together.
>
> RODNEY DANGERFIELD

Inevitability of Conflict

If you are alone this Saturday evening from six until midnight, you are assured of six conflict-free hours. But if you plan to be with your partner, roommate, or spouse during that time, the potential for conflict exists. Whether you eat out, where you eat, where you go after dinner, and how long you stay must be negotiated. Although it is relatively easy for you and your companion to agree on one evening's agenda, marriage involves the meshing of desires on an array of issues for up to 60 years.

Although most brides and grooms have reached agreement on many issues, new needs and preferences arise throughout the marriage. Changed circumstances sometimes call for adjustment of old habits. "I can honestly say that before we got married, we never disagreed about anything," a wife of three years recalled. "But things were different then. Both my husband and I got money from our parents and never worried about how much we spent on anything. Now I'm pregnant and unemployed, and Neal still acts like we've got someone to pick up the tab. He buys expensive toys like a computer and all the games and software he can carry. He thinks that because he uses VISA we can pay the monthly minimum and still live high. We're getting over our heads in debt, and we're always fighting about it."

CONSIDERATION • You and your spouse may not disagree on who spends how much on what, but the probability that you will agree throughout your marriage on every issue related to sex, in-laws, recreation, religion, and children is zero. Marital conflict is inevitable.

Desirability of Conflict

Not all conflict is bad. One study found that confronting an issue may be healthy for the couple's marriage (Hayes et al., 1981). When 138 divorced people were asked to talk about the communication patterns in their previous marriages, almost half said they seldom quarreled and only two in 10 said they constantly quarreled. The researchers concluded that "conflict was not an important variable because there often was no communication whatsoever occurring between the couple" (p. 23).

In another study of how spouses cope with marital distress (Menaghan, 1982), ignoring and resigning one's self to a problem actually increased the stress level experienced by the spouses. Although negotiating differences may not reduce immediate stress (it is often upsetting and uncomfortable to discuss a conflict in the relationship), such discussions were associated with fewer problems at a later time among the 758 interviewed spouses.

CONSIDERATION • When you or your partner are concerned about an issue in your relationship, discussing it may have more positive consequences than avoiding it. You may not like what your partner has to say about the reason you are upset (and vice versa), but resolving the conflict becomes a possibility. Brooding over an unresolved issue may lead to further conflict.

By expressing your dissatisfactions, you alert each other to the need for changes in your relationship to keep your satisfactions high. One wife with a full-time job said she was "sick and tired of picking up her husband's clothes and wet towels from the bathroom floor." He, on the other hand, was angered by his wife talking on the phone during mealtime. After discussing the issues, he agreed to take care of his clothes in exchange for her agreement to take the phone off the hook before meals. The payoff for their expressing their negative feelings about each other's behavior was the agreement to stop those behaviors. Referring to the need for conflict, one researcher and husband observed, "Because we think of love as a peaceful phenomenon, marriages experiencing conflict are usually considered unloving. This is unfortunate, for conflict can exist precisely because we both care for each other" (Scoresby, 1977, p. 137).

Sources of Conflict

There are numerous sources of conflict. Some of these are easily recognized while others are hidden inside the web of marital interaction.

BEHAVIOR

The preceding example in which one spouse left dirty clothes on the bathroom floor and the other talked on the phone during mealtime illustrates how the behavior of the partner can sometimes create negative feelings and set the stage for conflict. In your own relationship, you probably become upset when your partner does things you do not like (is late or tells lies). On the other hand, when your partner frequently does things that please you (is on time, is truthful), you tend to feel good about him or her and your relationship.

PERCEPTION

Aside from your partner's actual behavior, your *perception* of a behavior can be a source of satisfaction or dissatisfaction. One husband complained about the fact that his wife "was messy and always kept the house in a wreck." This same wife became interested in collecting coupons to get food discounts and began to stack boxes of various "proofs of purchase" all over the house. As a result, the house became even more messy. But because she was now saving more than $100 from their grocery bill each month, her husband saw money when he saw the array of boxes in their living room. The wife's "negative behavior" actually increased. But the husband's perception of that behavior became positive so that a problem no longer existed.

CONSIDERATION • When dissatisfaction with your partner results from your partner engaging in behavior you do not like, consider if it may be easier for you to change your perception of the behavior rather than asking your partner to change the behavior.

VALUE DIFFERENCES

Because you and your partner had years of socialization in different homes before you met, some of your values will be different. One wife, whose parents were both physicians, resented her mother not being home when she grew up. She vowed that when her own children were born she would stay home and take care of them. But she married a man who wanted his wife to actively pursue a career and contribute money to the marriage. This is only one value conflict a couple may have. Other major value differences may be about religion (one feels religion is a central part of life, the other does not), money (one feels uncomfortable being in debt, the other has the buy-now-pay-later philosophy), and in-laws (one feels responsible for parents when they are old, the other does not).

CONSIDERATION • Value differences in a relationship are not themselves bad. "What happens depends less on the degree of difference in what is valued than on the degree of rigidity with which each partner holds his or her values. Dogmatic and rigid thinkers, feeling threatened by value disagreement, try to eliminate varying viewpoints and typically produce more conflict. But partners who recognize the inevitability of difference usually try to accept in each other what they cannot successfully compromise" (Scoresby 1977, p. 142).

INCONSISTENT RULES

All relationships develop a set of rules that helps them to function smoothly. These unwritten but mutually understood rules include what time you are supposed to be home after work, whether you should call if late, how often you can see friends alone, when and how you make love. Conflict results when the partners disagree on the rules or inconsistent rules develop in the relationship. For example, one wife expected her husband to take a second job so they could afford a new car. But she also expected him to go out and party with her at night after he got off work at 10.

LEADERSHIP AMBIGUITY

Unless a couple has an understanding about which partner will make decisions in which area (for example, the husband will decide over which issues to "ground" teenage children; the wife will decide how much money to spend on vacations), each may continually try to "win" a disagreement. All conflict is seen as an "I win-you lose" encounter since each partner is struggling for dominance in the relationship. "In low conflict marriages, leadership roles vary and are flexible, but they are definite. Each partner knows most of the time who will make certain decisions . . ." (Scoresby, 1977, p. 141).

Styles of Conflict

Spouses develop various styles of conflict. If you were watching a videotape of various spouses disagreeing over some issue, you would notice at least three styles of conflict (Bateson, 1972; Lederer & Jackson 1968; Watzlawick et al., 1967). These styles have been explicated in *The Marriage Dialogue* (Scoresby, 1977).

COMPLEMENTARY

In this pattern the wife and husband tend to behave in opposite ways: dominant-submissive, talkative-quiet, active-passive. Specifically, (a) one person lectures the other about what should or should not occur. (b) The other person says little or nothing and becomes increasingly unresponsive. For example, a husband was angry because his wife left the outside lights of their house on all night. He berated her the next morning, saying she was irresponsible. She retreated in silence.

SYMMETRICAL

Both partners react to each other in the same way in the symmetrical style. If she yells, he yells back. If one attacks, so does the other. The partners try to "win" their positions without listening to the other's point of view. In the preceding incident, the wife would blast back at the husband, stating he lived there too and was equally responsible to see that the lights were out before going to bed.

PARALLEL

Both partners deny, ignore, and retreat from addressing a problem issue. "Don't talk about it and it will go away" is the theme of this conflict style. There are several consequences of this style. Gaps begin to develop in the relationship, neither feels free to talk, and both gradually come to believe that they are misunderstood. Both eventually become involved in separate activities, rather than spending time together. In the outside light example, neither partner would say anything about the lights being left on all night but the husband would resent the fact that they were.

Every marriage probably uses all three styles to some degree. Nevertheless, knowing which style is characteristic of your relationship is a beginning for developing more effective communication.

• PRODUCTIVE AND NONPRODUCTIVE COMMUNICATION •

Beyond the information-giving ("I got the milk"), information-getting ("Did you get the wine?"), and sharing ("Look at that.") functions, communication is essential for resolving difficulties as they crop up in a relationship. But there are productive and nonproductive ways of communicating about conflict. Knowing which ways to use and which to avoid is one of the most valuable skills a spouse or couple can possess. In a study of almost 500 couples, Brandt (1982) noted that their marriage success had much more to do with their communication skills than with factors such as age at marriage or lack of money.

Productive Communication

Productive communication increases the emotional closeness of the partners and brings into alignment their respective expectations and behaviors. Suppose one partner expects the other to be punctual and they discuss the issue. Their communication will be productive to the degree that they feel closer as a result of the discussion and either the partner agrees to be more punctual or the other partner decides the issue isn't worth getting upset about and drops the expectation. Here is an example of productive communication:

> Mary and Bob have been living together about six months. When they first moved in together they agreed that because they were both in school and had part-time jobs, they would share the chores—cooking, washing dishes, laundry, and keeping the apartment neat. It seemed to Mary that she was gradually drifting into the role of housewife, which she thought was counter to their agreement. Since she felt Bob wasn't going to start doing his share unless she brought it up, she mentioned the subject one evening as she was preparing dinner.
> MARY: You know, I thought we agreed that we would do the cooking and other stuff together.
> BOB: Well, I guess we did . . . (feeling somewhat guilty for not living up to his part of the deal). What do you want me to do?
> MARY: Since I've got classes Tuesday and Thursday nights, it would be nice for you to take care of the cooking and washing the dishes those nights. I'll handle it MWF and we can worry about the weekend later."
> BOB: Okay. I guess I'm cooking Thursday night, eh? What would you like?

Nonproductive Communication

Nonproductive communication increases the emotional distance between the partners and leaves unchanged the discrepancy between their respective expectations and behaviors. An example follows:

> Alice and Jeff have the same problem as Mary and Bob. Jeff hasn't been helping around the apartment and Alice is upset.

ALICE: Jeff, I'm really fed up with your lying around the apartment while I do all the work. Didn't we agree to do this stuff together?

JEFF: Maybe we did but I've got all I can do with school and work so you'll just have to do it yourself.

ALICE: You aren't being very sensitive to my needs—I go to school and work too.

JEFF: What would you know about sensitivity?

ALICE: You're being hateful and mean.

JEFF: I guess you're being real sweet when you talk like that aren't you? I guess this means no sex again tonight.

ALICE: Right again, Sherlock. And besides, you're the lousiest lover I've ever had.

JEFF: And you've had plenty so I must be real bad. You slut.

ALICE: I'm not listening to this crap.

JEFF: Yeah! What are you going to do about it?

ALICE: Leave—that's what.

JEFF: Go ahead.

What began as a discussion about Jeff helping Alice around the apartment has escalated into a decision to terminate the relationship.

Productive and Nonproductive Communication Compared

Mary and Bob did everything right in handling the housework issue; Alice and Jeff did everything wrong. Table 11.1 compares the two styles.

In a study of 40 married couples, researchers observed what styles of communication were associated with marital happiness (Honeycutt et al., 1982). Spouses who were relaxed, friendly, and empathetic in relating to each other

Table 11.1 **Characteristics of Productive and Nonproductive Communication**

PRODUCTIVE COMMUNICATION (Mary and Bob)	NONPRODUCTIVE COMMUNICATION (Alice and Jeff)
1. Avoidance of behaviors in column 2.	1. Blaming—"your lying around the house while I do the work."
2. Neutral statement rather than accusation—"I thought we agreed . . ."	2. Name calling—"lousy lover," "slut."
3. Acknowledgment of responsibility for partner's discomfort—"Well, I guess we did discuss my sharing the work."	3. Threatening—"I'm going to leave."
4. Expression of willingness to alleviate problem—"What do you want me to do?"	4. Using sarcasm—"What would you know about sensitivity?" "Right again, Sherlock."
5. Positive labeling of suggestion—"It would be nice if . . ."	5. Being judgmental—"You're being hateful and mean."
6. Reciprocity—"I'll handle it MWF."	6. Changing issues—"no sex again tonight."
7. Positive expression at end of conflict— "Okay. I guess I'm on for Thursday night, eh?"	7. No attempt to stop escalation of conflict.
8. Brief—Mary and Bob took two turns each speaking.	8. Lengthy—Alice and Jeff took six turns each speaking.

were happier than those who were rigid, distant, and cold. Mary and Bob's communication patterns reflect these qualities.

Couples concerned about their relationship also establish unwritten rules about the parameters of communication and conflict in their relationship. Some of the rules identified by 33 couples include the following (Hennon, 1981):

1. Never go to bed mad.
2. Never hit each other.
3. Never fight in public.
4. Try not to "pick" arguments.
5. Do not let argument affect sex life.
6. Never walk out when fighting.
7. Do not have sex when partner is angry.
8. Angry or not, do not avoid sleeping together since a good discussion might develop while just lying in bed.

Good communication patterns also imply each partner's participation in stopping negative interaction from escalating, in focusing on issues rather than personalities, and in responding to each other with supportive comments (Krueger & Smith, 1982).

Avoid Use of Defense Mechanisms

Couples who have established good communication patterns avoid using defense mechanisms (any behavior which protects the psyche from anxiety). These temporarily minimize anxiety and avoid emotional hurt, but they also interfere with conflict resolution. Defense mechanisms include the following.

ESCAPISM

I drink to make other people interesting.

GEORGE JEAN NATHAN

When a problem is too difficult or painful to face, a spouse may deny that it exists and try to escape from dealing with it. The usual form of escape is avoidance. The spouse becomes "busy" and "doesn't have time" to think about or deal with the problem, or he or she may escape into recreation, sleep, alcohol, marijuana, or work. The longer an unresolved conflict continues, the less time the spouses spend talking with each other, sharing sex, and going places together.

RATIONALIZATION

Some spouses may try to rationalize a problem away. For example, the wife who is having an affair may justify her involvement with another man on the basis that her husband is unwilling to have intercourse as often as she desires. "I'm tired of begging my husband to make love to me," one wife said. "The man I'm involved with makes it clear that he wants me."

PROJECTION

Projection occurs when one spouse who is guilty of a particular behavior unconsciously accuses the other spouse of the same behavior. For example, the

A spouse who drinks heavily often does so to escape.

wife having the affair may accuse her husband of being unfaithful to her. Such blaming shifts the focus from her affair and puts her husband on the defensive.

Projection may be seen in statements like "You spend too much money" (projection for "I spend too much money") and "You want to break up" (projection for "I want to break up"). Projection interferes with conflict resolution by creating a mood of hostility and defensiveness in both partners, while the issues to be resolved in the relationship remain unchanged and become more difficult to discuss.

DISPLACEMENT

Displacement shifts the frustration one spouse may be experiencing in other role relationships to the other spouse. The wife who is turned down for a promotion and the husband who is driven to exhaustion by his boss may direct their hostilities (displace them) on each other rather than against their respective employers. "I hate to admit it, but our marital happiness is usually a reflection of how happy I am in my work," expressed the manager of a fast-good chain. "At the end of the month when the regional manager drops in to check the books, I get nervous. I am under pressure to increase profits, and I feel on edge by the time I get home. Last night my wife asked me to pass her the TV guide and I blurted, 'Get it yourself.' My real problem is the regional manager, but there is no way I can vent my anger on him."

EMOTIONAL INSULATION

Emotional insulation interferes with conflict resolution by reducing the commitment of the partner to the relationship. One married person said, "I was emotionally devastated by my first marriage because I let myself be vulnerable. I hid nothing and loved as fully as possible. But my partner took advantage of my love and did not reciprocate. I don't want it to happen again so I am very guarded in my current relationship."

The partner has developed a protective posture to avoid being hurt. But the price of such protection may be high. "Getting hurt sometimes happens when you get involved," observed a divorced person. "And if you take your resentments with you into the next relationship, you've had it. You can't make your new partner responsible for something your previous partner did (you can't shoot all the dogs because some of them have fleas). I know, I would not drop my guard, become vulnerable, and let my love feelings go and it cost me my second marriage."

> CONSIDERATION • By knowing about defense mechanisms and their negative impact on resolving conflict, you can be alert to their appearance in your own relationships. The essential characteristics of all defense mechanisms are the same: They are unconscious and they distort reality. Where a conflict continues without resolution, one or more defense mechanisms may be operating.

A Plan to Communicate Successfully about Conflicts

It is helpful to have an overall plan to resolve conflict. Such a plan might include at least six stages.

ADDRESS RECURRING DISTURBING ISSUES

If you or your partner are upset about a recurring issue, talking about it may help. Pam was jealous that Mark seemed to spend more time with other people at parties than with her. "When we go someplace together," she blurted, "he drops me to disappear with someone else for two hours." Her jealousy was also spreading to other areas of their relationship. "When we are walking down the street and he turns his head to look at another woman, I get furious." If Pam and Mark don't discuss her feelings about Mark's behavior, their relationship may deteriorate because of a negative response cycle: He looks at another woman, she gets angry, he gets angry at her getting angry and finds that he is even more attracted to other women (who don't get angry), she gets angrier because he escalates his looking at other women, and so on.

Seldom, or perhaps never, does a marriage develop into an individual relationship smoothly and without crises; there is no coming to consciousness without pain.

CARL JUNG

ASK YOUR PARTNER FOR HELP IN COPING WITH AN ISSUE

To bring the matter up, Pam might say something like "I feel jealous when you spend more time with other women at parties than me . . . I need some help in dealing with these feelings." By expressing her concern in this way, she has identified the problem from her perspective and asked her partner's cooperation in handling it.

FIND OUT YOUR PARTNER'S VIEW

We usually assume that we know what our partner thinks and why our partner does things. Sometimes we are wrong. Rather than assume how our partner feels about a particular issue, we might ask him or her to tell us how he or she sees a situation. Pam's words to Mark might be, "What is it like for you when we go to parties? How do you feel about my jealousy?" Notice that both of these sentences are open-ended: Mark is asked to generate his own thoughts about a situation. Such questions are to be preferred to closed-ended questions—Do you still like me when I'm jealous? Do you want to go alone to parties? These questions require the other person to answer yes or no and make elaboration difficult, if not useless, once a single-word response has been given.

NONJUDGMENTALLY SUMMARIZE YOUR PARTNER'S VIEW

Once your partner has shared his or her thoughts about an issue, it is important for you to summarize your partner's perspective and to do so in a nonjudgmental way. Summarizing serves three functions: It makes sure you understand the situation from your partner's point of view (if you don't summarize correctly, your partner will correct you). It lets your partner know that you know what his or her perspective is. It validates the partner's right to view the situation as she or he does.

After Mark told Pam how he felt about their being at parties together, she summarized his perspective by saying, "You feel that I cling to you more than I should and that you would like me to let you wander around without feeling like you're making me angry." (She may not agree with his view, but she knows exactly what it is and Mark knows that she knows.)

EXAMINE ALTERNATIVE SOLUTIONS

After each partner has told the other how he or she views the situation and has nonjudgmentally summarized the other's perspective, they should make various suggestions about how the problem can be resolved. Such "brainstorming" is crucial since partners often feel upset when they know how their partner sees a situation (Warmbrod, 1982). Brainstorming shifts the focus from criticizing each other's perspective to working together to develop alternative solutions. The partners suggest as many alternatives as possible and no suggestion is "put down." Alternatives suggested by Pam and Mark included the following: (1) Pam should stop being jealous. (2) Mark should stop spending time away from Pam at parties and stop looking at other women, (3) They should break up. (4) They should stop going to parties together, (5) Pam should start spending time away from Mark at parties and begin dancing with other men. (6) Pam should start turning her head to look at other men while walking down the street. (7) They should keep things as they are but not talk about the issue any more. (8) They should stop seeing each other for a week or two.

SELECT A PLAN OF ACTION

After generating a number of solutions, one or a combination of them should be selected. Pam and Mark, for example, selected aspects from several alternatives from which they derived specific actions. They agreed that they would spend 45 minutes of each hour at a party talking and dancing together; Mark would be responsible for initiating and maintaining their time together and Pam would be responsible for initiating their time away from each other. They also agreed that Pam would say nothing about the time they were apart unless Mark brought it up. They further agreed that it was okay for each of them to look at members of the opposite gender when they were with each other but that neither was to say anything about the other partner's looking.

Here are some other examples of agreements reached by partners in conflict:

She wanted a half-carat diamond for her engagement ring; he thought it would be silly to spend $2,000 for a "rock." She put up half the money for the diamond; he put $1,000 on a down payment for a car for her.

•

He wanted to snow ski in Vermont on their honeymoon; she wanted to go to the Bahamas. They went to Disney World.

•

He wanted to buy Carnation Instant Breakfast because he likes its taste; she wanted to buy cereal because it would save them money. They bought both and alternate what they have for breakfast each morning.

•

He wanted her to get a job to put him through school; she wanted him to get a job and put her through school. They decided to work part time and go to school part time.

•

She wanted a baby; he didn't (he had two children from a previous marriage). He agreed to have a baby in exchange for her agreeing to wait two years. (She waited and they had their baby.)

> You cannot do a kindness too soon, for you never know how soon it will be too late.
>
> RALPH WALDO EMERSON

As we noted, some spouses view the resolution of their conflicts in win-lose terms rather than as compromises. In one study (Bell et al., 1982), 60 spouses representing 30 marriages were interviewed about relationship conflicts and their outcomes. The results showed that husbands "win most conflicts regardless of the strategies they or their wives employ." (p. 111) Catholic and Mormon husbands were particularly likely to swing a disagreement their way. However, among couples in which the wife was a member of NOW (National Organization for Women), seven in 10 of the conflicts were "won" by the wife.

• MARITAL THERAPY •

Sometimes it is impossible for spouses to resolve a conflict by themselves. Contacting a marriage therapist is an alternative. Examples of problems spouses bring to marriage therapy are described in Exhibit 11.1 (see page 320).

Questions about Marriage Therapy

If you decide to see a marriage therapist (see Choices at the end of this chapter) whom do you contact, how much will it cost, and what are the chances of a successful outcome? Your therapist should be a specialist with training in marriage therapy. She or he should also be a state-certified marriage and family therapist or a clinical member of the American Association for Marriage and Family Therapy (AAMFT). Since only seven states (Utah, California, Michigan, Nevada, New Jersey, North Carolina, and Florida) license or certify marriage therapists, it is important to verify the training of your therapist. Don't be embarrassed to ask.

DATA • *Although psychologists devote 40 percent of their time to marital therapy, a survey of the American Psychological Association revealed that fewer than 1 percent of the training programs for clinical psychologists approved by the Association offer even one course in the subject. (Psychology Today, 1982) Furthermore, although there are notable exceptions, many "family therapists" in mental health centers possess only general knowledge and minimal skill levels. (Markowski & Cain, 1983)*

The cost of marriage therapy is between $35 and $100 per hour (for private therapy). You can obtain a list of AAMFT members in your area by looking in the Yellow Pages or by writing to AAMFT at 1717 K St., N.W., Suite 407, Washington, D.C. 20006 (Phone: 202-429-1825). Members of AAMFT also conduct therapy in mental health centers where the fee is considerably less.

Most therapy sessions last about 50 minutes, during which the spouses will usually be seen together in what is referred to as conjoint marriage therapy. How long it will take a couple to achieve their goals is difficult to predict. Some exceptional couples need only one session. Others may stay in therapy for years. Most spouses can anticipate therapy lasting a minimum of six sessions.

DATA • *Marriage therapists report that about 35 percent of the couples they see in marital therapy experience an improved relationship, 16 percent experience individual improvement, and 9 percent experience help in achieving a positive separation. When couples seen in marital therapy are asked about the results of their therapy, 42 percent report relationship improvement, 15 percent report individual improvement, and 10 percent report having been helped to achieve a positive separation. (Wolcott, 1984)*

Whether a couple stays together will depend on their motivation to do so, how long they have been in conflict, the severity of the problem, and whether one or both of the partners is involved in an extramarital affair. A moderately motivated couple with numerous conflicts of several years are less likely to work out their problems than a highly motivated couple with minor conflicts of short duration.

Styles of Marriage Therapy

Marriage therapists are not alike. Their main differences are in the ways they identify the causes of marital problems and the ways they attempt to resolve them. The various approaches to marriage therapy include the following.

They saw this girl with a perfect body, perfect husband, perfect children, perfect life. Someone who was in total control. They never knew that, in reality, I was falling apart.

CATHY RIGBY

• Exhibit 11.1 •

PROBLEMS COUPLES BRING TO MARRIAGE THERAPY

Sex

Lack of sexual desire
Infrequent or no orgasm
Pain during intercourse
Vagina too tight for
    penetration
Premature ejaculation
Impotence
No ejaculation
Differences over how sex
    occurs:
  Too little foreplay
  Spouse crude in
    approach
  Oral sex
  Positions
  Too little affection
Disagreement about
    frequency of
    intercourse
Disagreement about when
    sex occurs
Extramarital affair

In-Laws

Talking over the phone to
    in-laws
How often in-laws visit
Borrowing money from in-
    laws
Living with in-laws
How often to visit in-laws
In-laws' dislike of spouse
In-laws' interference in
    children's lives
Loaning/giving money to
    in-laws

Recreation

No sharing of leisure time
Desire of spouse for
    separate vacations
Competition (egos may be
    hurt if one spouse is
    more athletic than
    partner)
Disagreement over
    amount of money to
    allocate for vacation
Spouse doesn't like family
    vacations
Disagreement over what is
    fun
Where to spend vacation
How long to be on
    vacation

Children

Discipline of children
Care of children
Time with children
Number of children
Spacing of children
Infertility
Whether or not to adopt
Rivalry for children's love
Activities children should
    be involved in
Sex education for children
Distress at children's
    behavior
Child abuse by one spouse
Retarded, autistic, or
    otherwise
    handicapped child
Stepchildren

Communication

Don't feel close to spouse
Rarely alone with spouse
Spouse complains/
    criticizes
Don't love spouse
Spouse doesn't love me
Spouse is impatient
Too little time spent
    communicating
Nothing to talk about
Intellectual gaps
Unhappiness with type of
    conversation
Spouse is unhappy and
    depressed
Arguments end in spouse
    abuse/violence

Money

Too little money
Wife's job
Husband's job
Conflict over who buys
    what
Gambling
Borrowing
Excessive debts

Religion

Which church to attend
Wife too devout
Husband too devout
Wife not devout enough
Husband not devout
    enough
Religion for children

Money to church	Different friends	Amount of money spent
Observance of religious holidays and rituals such as circumcision	Confidences to friends	on alcohol/drugs
	Time with friends	Flirting as a consequence of drinking
Breaking of vows	**Alcohol or Drugs**	Influence of drinking/drug habits on children
Friends	Spouse drinks too much	Violence as a consequence of drinking
Too few friends	Spouse smokes too much marijuana	
Too many friends	Spouse takes too many pills	

SYSTEMS THERAPY

Systems therapy suggests that marriage problems can best be viewed and treated by examining the spouses in the larger context of their relationships with their children, in-laws, and friends—how spouses are connected to other people in their interpersonal system. "It is necessary to focus on the whole and to see parts only in the context of the whole, rather than to collect parts and hope someday they will add up to the whole" (Bavelas & Segal, 1982, p. 102).

Problem marital behaviors such as chronic drinking are viewed in terms of how they serve to keep the couple functioning at a stable level. For example, does the wife protect the husband from the consequences of his drinking so that she can play the role of nurse? If he gets well, will he need her? In systems therapy intervention, the therapist explains to the spouses what "rules" they have developed to perpetuate their problems. Spouses can then decide to adopt new rules to achieve new goals. For example, the wife of the alcoholic may decide to stop covering up her husband's alcoholism so that he may eventually seek treatment.

BEHAVIOR THERAPY

The behavioral marriage therapist believes that spouses are unhappy because each is engaging in behavior that upsets the other. The therapist encourages each spouse to engage in behaviors of the kind and at a frequency desired by the partner and develops a behavior contract with each spouse to encourage new behavior. Exhibit 11.2 is an example of a behavior contract drawn up for a husband whose wife complained that he "leaves his clothes all over the house," "never helps me with meal preparation," "never says anything good about me," and "always criticizes me." Notice that the husband agrees to punish himself if he "forgets" to do what he agreed to do. By accepting a negative consequence, he teaches himself not to forget. A contract specifying what the wife would do for the husband (based on his requests) would also be developed. In this way each spouse is changing his or her behavior consistent with the expectations of the partner so that each will have a better behavioral basis for feeling positively about the other. Behavior contracts are one result of therapy, but a great deal of time is also spent on assisting the couple to develop positive communication and negotiation skills.

Find out what a person will work for and what he or she will work to avoid, systematically manipulate these contingencies, and you can change behavior.

JACK TURNER

· Exhibit 11.2 ·

BEHAVIOR CONTRACT

Name _Tom Griffin_   **Date** _October 18_

	Behaviors	M	T	W	T	F	S	S
1.	Put clothes in closet or hamper by 8:30 a.m. every morning.	__	__	__	__	__	__	__
2.	Prepare and serve evening meal Monday and Thursday at 7:00 p.m.	__	__	__	__	__	__	__
3.	Compliment Theresa twice daily.	__	__	__	__	__	__	__
4.	Make no negative statements to Theresa.	__	__	__	__	__	__	__

Terms _If I fail to do any of the above as specified, I forfeit reading the newspaper and watching T.V. news._   __ __ __ __ __ __ __

RATIONAL-EMOTIVE THERAPY

Working from the theories of Albert Ellis, the executive director of the Institute for the Advanced Study of Rational Psychotherapy, the rational-emotive therapist believes that spouses are unhappy because of irrational beliefs they have about themselves and each other. Partners are encouraged to examine their beliefs and to change them if they have a negative impact on the marriage. For example, the belief that "My spouse should care more about me than anything or anyone else" would be examined for its potential negative consequences on the relationship. Other beliefs that interfere with marital happiness include "I should always be happy with my partner," "We should be as happy as we were in courtship," and "My spouse should never do anything that upsets me."

TRANSACTIONAL ANALYSIS

The "TA" therapist believes that spouses are unhappy because one spouse is interacting with the other as though the mate were someone else. For example, a wife may act toward her husband as though he were her father or a husband may relate to his wife as though she were his mother. The TA therapist encourages spouses to examine the ways in which their role relationships with others have been problems and how they may have introduced these unresolved conflicts into their marriage relationship.

ADLERIAN THERAPY

Applying the theories of the Austrian psychiatrist Alfred Adler, the Adlerian marriage therapist views marital discord as a result of power struggles. The individual is seen as trying to compensate for feelings of inferiority that began with the helplessness of infancy. The therapist seeks to improve the marital relationship by helping couples to feel secure and to regard their power struggles as unnecessary.

Systems, behavioral, rational-emotive, transactional, and Adlerian therapy are only a few of the different approaches used in marriage therapy. Gestalt, psychoanalytic, humanistic, reality, and paradoxical therapy are others. Although systems therapy is currently attracting a new wave of therapists, no one therapy can be regarded as superior.

CONSIDERATION • All of the different styles of therapy can be placed in two basic categories—directive and nondirective. In behavioral, rational-emotive, and reality therapy, the therapist is more likely to be directive. He or she suggests specific ways in which the spouses can improve their marriage. Therapists of the systems, transactional, Adlerian, Gestalt, and psychoanalytic persuasions may or may not make specific recommendations. Whereas some clients want specific direction, others want to explore their relationships and develop insight into the dynamics of marital interaction. Should you decide to consult a therapist, you should seek the therapist who will offer the style of therapy you want. Regardless of particular orientation, the trained marriage therapist can be expected to express a genuine concern for your difficulty, to be nonjudgmental, and to regard all information as confidential.

• MARRIAGE ENRICHMENT •

Marriage therapists are often looked upon as the last resort, the final chance before seeking a divorce. They are thought of as an emergency medical team at the bottom of a cliff that ministers to those who have fallen in the hope of reviving them. But why not a guardrail at the top to prevent couples from slipping off the edge? Such preventive intervention is the goal of marriage enrichment programs. There are more than 50 of them including Worldwide Marriage Encounter, International Marriage Encounter, the Minnesota Couple Communication Program, Conjugal Relationship Enhancement (Pennsylvania), and Training in Marriage Enrichment (TIME). Many of the couples who have attended these programs are members of the Association of Couples for Marriage Enrichment (ACME), which has chapters in all states and several foreign countries.

One marriage enrichment exercise is to feel the face of your spouse while your eyes are closed.

Who Attends?

DATA • *More than one million couples have participated in marriage enrichment programs, paying from nothing to $300 for a series of weekly evening or weekend sessions.* (Hof & Miller, 1981).

Couples who attend marriage enrichment programs are more satisfied with their marriages than those who seek marital therapy, but they are less satisfied with their marriages than those who don't attend marriage enrichment programs (Powell & Wampler, 1982). Couples who attended a Worldwide Marriage Encounter weekend tended to be in their thirties, had been married an average of 12 years, had two children, and had attended school an average of 14 years (Becnel & Levy, 1983).

Marriage enrichment is also available for newlyweds. David Mace, (Mace and Mace, 1984) co-founder of ACME, observed:

. . . so often we put newlyweds into a sort of limbo, the impression being now that you're married, you are happy, you are living happily ever after, you don't need any help, and heavens, they do need help! (p. 22)

Growth in Marriage for newlyweds is a marriage enrichment program for the recently married and is offered in Kansas City.

What Is the Program?

The content of a typical program includes enhancing communication, learning problem-solving skills, and discussing the nature of marital interaction. Many of these issues are dealt with through exercises. Exhibit 11.3 details one such exercise designed to clarify each partner's feelings.

· Exhibit 11.3 ·

MY WORLD OF FEELINGS

Please complete the following statements:

1. In our marriage, when we relate together, I am happiest when—
2. In our marriage, when we relate together, I am saddest when—
3. In our marriage, when we relate together, I am angriest when—
4. The best thing about our marriage is—
5. I feel most afraid when—
6. I feel most loved when—
7. I feel appreciated when you—
8. My greatest concern/fear for our marriage is—
9. What I like most about myself is—
10. What I dislike most about myself is—
11. What I like most about you is—
12. My greatest concern/fear for you is—
13. The feelings that I have the most difficulty sharing are—
14. The feelings that I can share most easily with you are—
15. Right now I feel . . . towards you.
16. Right now I feel . . . towards myself.
17. I feel . . . sharing these feelings with you.

Source: Hof & Miller, 1981, p. 99.

One of the most well-known marriage enrichment programs is Marriage Encounter. Like some others, it is sponsored by religious groups. Led by a married couple and a trained religious leader, "the weekend invites and even urges couples to significantly reframe their concepts of marriage, to begin viewing matrimony from a sacramental commitment perspective, and to live out that perspective in an everyday way. In esssence, the weekend calls for a conversion experience" (Stedman, 1982, p. 126).

How Effective Are Marriage Enrichment Programs?

What is the impact of an encounter program on a couple's relationship? After reviewing the data on all marriage enrichment programs, two researchers concluded that "some optimism about the effectiveness of marital enrichment programs is warranted" (Hof & Miller, 1981, p. 63). More self-disclosure, open communication, and empathy are reported by encounter couples.

In another study (Lester & Doherty, 1983), 80 percent of 200 couples who had attended a National Marriage Encounter weekend four years earlier reported they had a totally positive experience. The most positive aspect of the weekend was learning to express their feelings to each other. The most negative aspect was identifying needs during the weekend that were not subsequently fulfilled.

For example, a wife said she wanted more frequent intercourse, which, at follow-up, had still not occurred. During this time the husband had felt inadequate and the wife frustrated.

Complete openness during an encounter weekend may be dysfunctional. One husband felt that, to be honest, he needed to disclose a previous affair to his wife. The encounter weekend was over before the effects of his disclosure were resolved by the couple.

Many of the skills learned in marriage enrichment training sessions do not generalize beyond the sessions. In one study of the enduring effects of specific training in active listening skills (which was part of a larger marriage enrichment program), the researcher concluded, "Despite extensive practice time both in the sessions and as assigned in homework, and despite leaders' observations that participants could, indeed, demonstrate the skills, the couples did not generalize the use of skills beyond the practice sessions" (Garland, 1981, p. 302). A similar study of 17 married couples who participated in a couple communication program revealed that marriage satisfaction increased immediately after the training program but was not maintained at a five-month follow-up (Joanning, 1983). However, any of several marriage enrichment experiences are better than none at all in terms of increasing marriage and family adjustment (Ford et al., 1984).

CONSIDERATION • To minimize the negative effects of exposure to a marriage enrichment program, you should not regard the experience as a place to solve problems or to deal with difficult issues in your relationship. These should be dealt with alone or in marriage therapy. Rather, such a program should be regarded as a place to improve communication skills.

Couples who wish to experience a marriage enrichment program might consider the relative benefits of a weekend versus a series of five weekly evening meetings. When the two formats were compared, participants in the five-week program showed "more positive indications of marital adjustments than participants in the weekend program. "This may be so because a five-week marriage enrichment group allows more time for program materials to be discussed and implemented, and the task assignments to be completed" (Davis et al., 1982, p. 89).

• TRENDS •

The most significant trend about conflict and communication in marriage is the increased willingness of couples to "go public" with their problems. The realization that it is normal for couples to be faced with problems in their relationships is replacing the old ideas that happy couples don't have conflicts. The continuing popularity of marriage enrichment groups, encounter weekends, and marriage seminars reflect this trend.

A second trend concerns raising standards for people who do marriage therapy. More states are enacting laws to create a classification of "certified marriage therapist," denoting that the person has the equivalent in training and background as that required for admission to the American Association for Marriage and Family Therapy. This requires a minimum of a master's degree, including specific training in marriage and family therapy, human sexuality, and ethics. Furthermore, the person must have conducted 1,500 hours of marriage and family therapy with at least 100 of these hours under the supervision of an approved supervisor. The hoped-for result will be a supply of highly trained and experienced marriage therapists sufficient to meet the growing demand for such services.

• SUMMARY •

Our society perpetuates various myths about marriage. These include the notions that love will keep a couple together, that children increase marital happiness, and that each spouse can fulfill all the other's needs. A more realistic view is that love *may* help to keep spouses together, that children *may* improve a marriage and that spouses will fulfill *some* of each other's needs.

Although being happily married is a major goal of most Americans, there is little agreement on what constitutes happiness. Marital happiness is subjective, constantly changing, and is affected by multiple influences. Although marital adjustment may be assessed through the use of various scales, the results are often distorted by the desire of respondents to report a happy marriage whether they have one or not.

Communication is the core of any relationship. It involves the use of words and gestures between two people, which convey a message. Productive use of communication skills in conflict resolution include the use of neutral statements rather than accusations, positive labeling rather than sarcasm, and not allowing a negative mutual-blame cycle to develop.

But marital conflict can erupt at any time. It is both inevitable and, under certain conditions, desirable. The causes of interpersonal conflict include behavior, perception, and value differences. Spouses also develop various styles of conflict—complementary (one dominant, the other submissive), symmetrical (both react the same way to each other), and parallel (both partners avoid confronting the problem).

Having a plan to communicate about conflicts is essential. Such a plan includes deciding to address recurring issues rather than suppressing them, asking the partner for help in resolving the issue, finding out the partner's point of view, summarizing in a nonjudgmental way the partner's perspective, brainstorming for alternative solutions, and selecting a plan of action. To the degree that the plan of action includes suggestions made by each partner, the potential for success in resolving the problem is maximized. When we participate in a solution, we are more committed to seeing it work.

Some couples who can't resolve a conflict by themselves contact a marriage therapist. Since these therapists are not regulated by law in all states, care should be exercised in selecting one. Also, since there are many theoretical approaches, it is important to select a therapist who offers the style of therapy you want. Most spouses report positive outcomes for involvement in marriage therapy.

Marriage enrichment programs are for couples who have good marriages and who want to keep them that way. The marriage enrichment movement, spearheaded by ACME, is gaining increased attention and attracting many spouses who meet to share common problems and solutions.

Trends in conflict and communication include an increasing number of couples becoming involved in marriage enrichment or marriage therapy. Ensuring the adequate training of therapists who provide the latter service has become a priority for some state legislatures.

Questions for Reflection

1. How open have you been with your various partners? Do you feel the consequences have been positive or negative?
2. Which style of conflict (complementary, symmetrical, parallel) tends to be characteristic of you and your partner? How functional or dysfunctional is this style for you?
3. Would you be willing to become involved in marriage enrichment or marriage therapy? Why or why not?

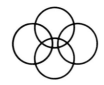

·CHOICES·

A basic choice of individuals in a relationship is deciding how much of themselves they should share with the other person. After examining how much openness is productive for a relationship, we look at the question of whether to consult a marriage therapist when relationship conflict becomes unmanageable.

HOW MUCH SHOULD YOU TELL?

Since good communication often implies open communication, how much is good for a marital relationship? Does a "we tell each other everything" disclosure philosophy have more positive consequences then a "discreet disclosure" philosophy? One therapist suggested that in spite of all the suggestions to "be open" and "let it all hang out," to "jump on the bandwagon for fully uncensored communication is a ride couples should not take" (Stuart, 1980, p. 218).

Adopting a "norm of measured honesty" in a relationship may be advisable for two reasons. First, negative information carries more weight than positive information. When partners disclose negatives, their partners may have difficulty keeping the disclo-

sure in the context of other positives. A minister said that he and his wife had the pattern of being completely open with each other. "One night she told me that she didn't like my beard, which I had become very proud of. After I knew how she felt, I didn't want to kiss her or be near her because of what she had said. I know she loves me but I can't help feeling bad." In his classic study of marital communication, Bienvenu (1970) found that the one item on his inventory that best discriminated well-communicating couples from poorly communicating couples was a negative answer to the question "Does your spouse have a tendency to say things that would be better left unsaid?"

The second reason for measured honesty is that all relationships may need some illusions to survive. Part of this perfectionistic thinking is that our partner loves and is sexually attracted to only us. When our partner tells us, "I am really attracted to this new

person at work," we may appreciate the honesty but feel rejected at the content. The lyrics to an old song, "How may arms have held you but I really don't want to know," aptly describe our ambivalence.

However, certain items that may be painful to the partner should probably be disclosed, particularly if the partners are dating and considering marriage. These issues include previous marriages and children, a sexual orientation different from what the partner expects, alcohol or drug addiction, having a sexually transmitted disease such as genital herpes, and any known physical disabilities such as sterility. Disclosures of this nature include anything that would have a significant impact on the relationship.

SHOULD YOU CONSULT A MARRIAGE THERAPIST?

Most people are reluctant to consult a marriage therapist. In a study of more than 1,000 families, only 7 percent had sought counseling (Olson, 1983). There are several reasons for this reluctance to make an appointment with a therapist.

Most spouses have been taught that seeing a therapist

(continued)

about personal problems means they are mentally ill. "It's the crazy folks that see those counselors," said one woman. Other spouses feel that their marriage is private and nobody else's business. "You don't talk to strangers about those kinds of things," said another spouse. Still other spouses feel that if couples are really in love with each other, they will be able to work out anything. They assume it is only the people who don't love each other who can't work out their problems.

Each of these beliefs is a myth. Seeing a therapist does not mean that you are mentally ill. On the contrary, we are never more mentally and emotionally healthy than when we can acknowledge that we have a problem and seek help for it.

The fact that marriage is a personal and private affair does not mean we cannot discuss our concern with a specialist. Our bodies are also personal and private, but this does not stop us from seeing a physician when we have a physical problem. Our mental health is as important to our feeling good as is our physical health. Both physicians and marriage therapists can be expected to treat the information we share with them with strict confidentiality. This is required by their code of professional ethics.

Finally, as we have seen earlier in this chapter, love is not enough to ensure the resolution of all conflicts. Two people can love each other intensely and not be able to resolve their conflicts or to live together happily. "We loved each other," said one spouse. "but we just couldn't make a go of it together,"

Signs to look for in your own relationship that suggest you might consider seeing a therapist include feeling distant and not wanting or being able to communicate with your partner, avoiding each other, drinking heavily or taking drugs, privately contemplating separation, being involved in an affair, and feeling depressed.

If you are experiencing one or more of these concerns with your partner, it may be wise not to wait until it reaches a stage beyond which repair is impossible. Relationships are like boats. A small leak will not sink it. But if left unattended, the small leak may grow larger or new ones break through. Marriage therapy sometimes serves to mend relationship problems early by helping the partners to sort out values, make decisions, and begin new behaviors that will help them start feeling better about each other.

However, in spite of the potential benefits of marriage therapy, there are some valid reasons you might not want to do it.

Not all spouses who become involved in marriage therapy regard the experience positively. Some feel that their marriage is worse as a result. Saying things the spouse can't forget, feeling hopeless at not being able to resolve a problem "even with a counselor," and feeling resentment over new demands made by the spouse in therapy are reasons for negative outcomes. About the latter, a husband said the result of therapy was that he did more housework because his wife was earning half their income. "Before I came to therapy I wasn't doing anything at home," he said. "Now I still don't do much but resent it when I do."

Therapists also may give clients an unrealistic picture of loving, cooperative, nonsexist, and growing relationships in which partners always treat each other with respect and understanding, share intimacy, and help each other become whomever each wants to be. Such expectations may encourage clients to focus on the shortcomings in their relationship and to feel discouraged about their marriage (Zilbergeld, 1983).

· Chapter 12 ·

PROBLEMS OF VIOLENCE AND ABUSE

CONTENTS

**Violence in Dating
  Relationships**
**Violence in Living-Together
  Relationships**
**Violence in Marriage
  Relationships**
Self-Assessment:
  Partner Abuse Scale
Child Abuse
Incest
Parent Abuse
Choices

The group to which most people look for love and gentleness is also the most violent civilian group in our society.

MURRAY STRAUS

Shakespeare's statement "The course of true love never did run smooth" is a truth most of us reluctantly accept. Things do not always seem to go right with those we love. Developing and maintaining a positive, enduring, committed relationship takes a great deal of energy and skill.

   Although we expect there will be some difficulties in the relationships with those we care about, we are less likely to expect our partners to become violent with us. We may be even more surprised if we become violent toward them. In this chapter we examine violence among couples who are dating, living together, and married. We also look at abuse among family members—parents abusing children, incest, and children abusing parents.

• VIOLENCE IN DATING RELATIONSHIPS •

Violence between dating partners may be categorized as general or sexual.

General Violence

Dating partners sometime become aggressive toward each other to the point of violence. Such courtship violence usually involves pushing, slapping, threatening, and punching; choking or use of a weapon is rare.

DATA • *Thirty percent of 461 college students reported they had either been the victim of premarital violence or been violent toward a premarital partner.* (Bernard & Bernard, 1983)

Here is one student's experience:

We had been engaged two months after a three-year courtship and the subject came up about one of his old girlfriends. I said some bad things about her that we both knew were true when all of a sudden he slapped me. I was really shocked because he had always been so gentle. He was shocked too and started crying and saying he didn't know why he did it because he loved me so much.

Five months later he slapped me again. This time it was in front of six guys because I didn't want to go back to his apartment and drink beer. He apologized greatly and begged me not to leave him. I didn't but I started to examine the wisdom of marrying this guy.

The next four months he slapped me 11 more times, pushed me against a wall four times, and pulled my hair it seemed like 1,000 times. When I suggested that maybe we should break up he said that since our parents had already spent $11,000 on the wedding I couldn't back out now. When I said, "I don't give a damn about the money," he went into a rage and blacked my eye, broke my nose, and fractured my collarbone. That was enough for me so I broke the engagement. He begged me to take him back saying he just couldn't live without me but I didn't. I felt pity for him and I'm glad I got out while the getting was good.

Although males are more likely to be the abuser than females, in almost 70 percent of the cases of courtship violence, both partners have been both the victim and the abuser. "Consequently, premarital violence for a large number of couples was more a case of 'abusive relationships' rather than 'abusive individuals'" (Cate et al., 1982, p. 83).

My partner and I get in an argument sometimes. We slap each other and push each other around. But we apologize and make up and everything is okay.

Courtship partners also tend to express violence toward each other after they have been dating awhile. This implies that the more intimate partners become, the more likely violence is to become a part of their relationship.

DATA • *In a study of 355 college students, 80 percent said the first abusive act had occurred after the relationship had become intimate.* (Cate et al., 1982)

Violence usually occurs after people become angry. The partners have been arguing over an issue and one or both of them erupt with a violent act. Rarely is the abuse deliberate or premeditated. "She got right in my face and told me I was a liar," said one man. "The next thing I knew I shoved her across the room and she hit her head on the refrigerator door." In many cases, alcohol may help precipitate a violent act. A third of the students in one study who reported being abused said they had been drinking at the time. Fifty percent said their partner had been drinking (Makepeace, 1981). Jealousy may also be involved. One student revealed:

> He would always start pouring down the beers when he saw me dance with someone else. Then he would start trouble. First it was verbal, then physical. He would grab me and shove me or push me or yank on me or pull on me or throw me. He only hit me once but the rest was pretty rough treatment.

CONSIDERATION • Since anger (sometimes jealous anger) and alcohol are two precipitating factors in the expression of violent behavior, partners who want to avoid such violence might be sensitive to the combined effects and carefully monitor not only their alcohol intake but also the escalation of their anger (and that of their partner's). By doing so they can withdraw from each other before the violence erupts. One couple who had had problems with violence in their relationship agreed to withdraw from each other (one partner would leave the apartment) when either of them felt their anger had climbed above a level of 3 on a 10-point scale.

Once abuse occurs, it is not unusual for it to recur. Since the abuse happens after the partners have become emotionally as well as sexually involved, the partners are less likely to view it as a reason for terminating the relationship.

DATA • *Forty percent of the students in one study who had experienced violence in their relationships were still involved in the abusive relationship.* (Henton et al., 1983)

Some couples state their relationship became stronger after violence had occurred. This was reported by 40 percent of respondents in the Cate et al. (1982) study referred to earlier. Another 40 percent said their relationship was unchanged, and 20 percent reported a negative effect of the abuse on the relationships. Violence that ended in the partners breaking up tended to be either frequent or severe (hitting or beating).

Why do partners who experience abuse in a relationship stay together? Some stay because they see the violence as only a small part of the relationship. One woman said:

> Even though he slapped me around a lot I never left him because when he wasn't hurting me he was so gentle and sweet. He would tell me that he loved me and that I was the only one in the world that really understood him. Besides, he never *really* hurt me.

Others continue the relationship because there is no perceived alternative. "If I leave him because he's rough with me now and then," said one woman, "I don't know what I would do. He's such a part of my world that I can't imagine life without him." Still others stay because they label the abusive acts as expressions of love. Much like children who were told when they were about to be punished, "I'm doing this because I love you; it hurts me more than you," so

Nothing multiplies more easily than force.

NORMAN COUSINS

the dating partner interprets the violent acts as those only a person who loves him or her would engage in. A lyric from a popular song reflects the mixing of love and violence. "Cruel to be kind means I love you, baby . . . You gotta be cruel to be kind."

DATA • *More than 25 percent of the victims of interpersonal dating violence in one study interpreted the violence as an expression of love.* (Henton et al., 1983)

Still others remain in an abusive relationship because they perceive violence to be a legitimate part of an intimate relationship. In one study (Bernard & Bernard, 1983), those who had been exposed to violence in the home when they were growing up (either through observation or experience) were more likely to be abusers and to use the same form of abuse they were exposed to than those who had not seen or experienced violence. One person in an abusive relationship said:

> I grew up watching my dad get drunk and hit on my mother. I don't think it's right to hit a woman but it happens and it's not the end of the world. Folks who live together are bound to hit each other sometime.

Once violence occurs in a person's own relationship, he or she develops increased tolerance toward it. In the Cate et al. (1982) study of 355 college students, those who had been abused or who were abusers were more likely to approve of violence in dating relationships than those who had not been involved in violence.

Finally, some courtship partners may continue a relationship after they have been abused because they feel they deserve such abuse ("I deserve to be pushed around and beaten; I'm no good") or they caused the abuse ("It was my fault he got angry and beat me . . . I was just asking for it"). But they may also blame themselves for tolerating the violence (Miller & Porter, 1983).

CONSIDERATION • If you have experienced violence in the relationship with your dating partner, be aware that such expressions are likely to become a pattern in your relationship. Couples who do not make a conscious attempt to stop such violence are making an unwritten agreement that such behavior is going to be tolerated in their relationship.

Sexual Violence

Sometimes general violence leads to sexual violence.

> I once dated a guy I was very much in love with. Our pattern was that when we argued about something he would get real mad and slap me around. I would cry and he would beat me harder and my crying would get him sexually aroused and he would want to make love.

Sexual aggression occurs when a person persists in forceful attempts to achieve a sexual goal, even though these actions are disagreeable and offensive to the other person. As noted in Chapter 6, "unwanted pressure to engage in sexual behavior" was the most frequent problem encountered on dates by a group of female university respondents (Knox & Wilson, 1983). But sexual aggression is not confined to one gender.

DATA • *Sixty-two percent of the females and 25 percent of the males in a random sample reported they had been victims of sexual aggression by their dating partners.* (Wilson & Faison, 1983)

Sometimes sexual aggression toward women goes beyond forceful attempts and becomes rape. Such rapes are known as acquaintance rapes or "date rapes" because the rapist is someone the woman knows.

DATA • *Ten percent of the female undergraduates in the same study reported "encountering violence or threat of violence from their male companions who were trying to force sexual intercourse."* (Wilson & Faison, 1983)

One student described the experience of being raped by her boyfriend:

Last spring I met this boy and a relationship started which was great. One year later he raped me. The term was almost over and we would not be able to spend much time together during the summer. So we decided to go out to eat and spend some time together.

After dinner we drove to a park. I did not mind nor suspect anything for we had done this many times. Then he asked me into the back seat. I got into the back seat with him because I trusted him and he said he wanted to be close to me as we talked.

He began talking. He told me he was tired of always pleasing me and not getting a reward. Therefore, he was going to "make love to me" whether I wanted to or not. I thought he was joking so I asked him to stop playing. He told me he was serious and after looking at him closely, I knew he was serious.

I began to plead with him not to have sex with me. He did not listen. He began to tear my clothes off and confine me so that I could not move. All this time I was fighting him. At one time I managed to open the door, but he threw me back into the seat, hit me, then he got on me and raped me. After he was satisfied, he stopped, told me to get dressed and to stop crying. He said he was sorry it had to happen that way.

He brought me back to the dorm and expected me to kiss him good night. He didn't think he had done anything wrong.

Before this happened, I loved him very much, but afterward, I felt great hatred for him. I wished that I had the courage to kill him.

My life has not been the same since that night. I do not trust men as I once did, nor do I feel completely comfortable when I'm alone at night with my present boyfriend. Also my present boyfriend wants to know why I back off when he tries to be intimate with me. I can't tell him because he knows the guy who raped me.

As noted above, one-fourth of the males in one study reported they had "made forceful and offensive attempts for intercourse" against their dates (Wilson et al., 1983). Characteristics of these men included a history as victims of abuse when they were growing up. Such abuse teaches a person to associate violence and intimate relationships.

Acquaintance rapists also tend to believe certain myths about rape, female sexuality, and legitimate victims. For example, believing that rapists are strangers absolves the boyfriend from labeling himself as a rapist. He views his attempts at sexual intercourse as a natural part of the dating situation. Since female sexuality is often defined as passive and unresponsive, male aggressiveness is a necessary part of sexual encounters. Further, legitimate victims for sexual aggression are women who deserve to be raped (so the myth goes) because they advertise their sexual availability by, say, going to a bar to pick up a man and then put limits on the sexual relationship. "These women are really advertising lettuce [sex] but selling cabbage [date me awhile] and deserve what they get," said one man. By viewing the woman and his actions in this way, the man may feel he has done nothing wrong.

Finally, acquaintance rapists, when compared with males who do not use force to gain intercourse, score high on measures of irresponsibility and lack of conscience on personality tests. When sexually coercive males and those who did not use such force were given a battery of psychological tests, results showed that those who used force had personality traits similar to those of rapists in criminal populations (Rapaport & Burkhart, 1983).

• VIOLENCE IN LIVING-TOGETHER RELATIONSHIPS •

Violence may also occur between partners who live together.

DATA • *In a study of 40 cohabitants, more than one-fourth of the relationships included severe violence such as punching, biting, hitting with an object, beating up, and an attack with a knife or gun.* (Yllo & Straus, 1981)

Income and age were related to violence in the cohabiting relationships in this study. The lower the couple's income, the greater the violence. Forty percent of those couples with incomes less than $10,000 reported violence in contrast to those with incomes more than $20,000, in which there was *no* violence. "When there isn't enough money to pay the bills or buy something nice or do something fun once in a while, you feel frustrated and trapped. Fighting with your partner is one way to release the tension," recalled one cohabitant.

Younger cohabitants are also more likely to be involved in violent relationships. More than 40 percent of those under the age of 30 reported violence in contrast to *no* violence being reported by those over 30.

CONSIDERATION • Younger people are more likely to regard violence as an act of love ("He beats me because he cares about me."). The older person is more likely to view violence as an act of hostility. "A person who loves you doesn't hurt you," said one 35-year-old woman. "Getting beat up, hurts."

I used to be cruel to my woman. I beat her and kept her apart from the things that she loved.

JOHN LENNON

Violence rates among cohabitors who had not been married before were also higher than among those who had. Separated or divorced persons were much more likely not to tolerate abuse from their partner. In explaining this difference, the authors state, "Perhaps those people who choose to cohabit rather than marry are quite cautious about their new involvement and are less inclined to tolerate any abuse" (p. 345).

Abusive behavior is sometimes the result of an escalating argument.

• VIOLENCE IN MARRIAGE RELATIONSHIPS •

Persons who experienced violence in the homes in which they grew up and in their dating and cohabiting relationships also tend to experience violence in marriage.

DATA • *Thirty-six percent of the couples in one study had at least one spouse who reported violence in their relationship. The nature of the violence included pushing, grabbing, shoving, hitting the partner with something, throwing something at the partner, slapping, and beating the partner up.* (Szinovacz, 1983).

One wife said:

My husband was usually violent toward me after he'd been out drinking with "the boys." When he got home, a simple "hello" would often trigger it. He'd start out yelling at me, and then slapping, punching, or kicking me, depending on his mood. On two different occasions, I ended up with broken bones.

After the violence he was always very apologetic and swore he'd never do it again . . . but he always did.

The issues over which spouses argue and become violent can be anything. Although conflicts over children was the most frequent issue among violent couples in a national sample (Straus et al., 1980), arguments over sex, money, and housekeeping were not unusual. Often the issue seemed trivial, as illustrated in the following examples:

> He had come home from work and he'd been drinking. He was late and I'd started cooking his meal, but I put it aside, you know, when he didn't come in. Then when he came in I started heating it because the meal wasn't ready. I was standing at the sink, and I was sorting something at the sink, and he just came up and gave me a punch in the stomach. I couldn't get my breath. He'd punched me and the wind was knocked out of me. I just sort of stood there, and I couldn't get my breath, and that was the first time I remember that he ever touched me. It was only because his tea wasn't ready on the table for him. (Dobash & Dobash, 1979, p. 101)

> It didn't matter what I did. When he wanted to hit me, he'd do it for *no* reason or *any* reason at all! If I talked, I was hit; if I didn't talk, I was hit. It could start over anything—you name it. Maybe he didn't like the way I fried his eggs, or the way I made a bed; say the sheets weren't tucked in right. It didn't matter, he'd start yelling at me, and between punches he'd ask me questions. If I tried to answer he'd hit me, and if I didn't understand his question and couldn't think of what he wanted me to say, he'd hit me again. It was a case of damned if you do and damned if you don't; you can't win. I used to think maybe it was something about me that was wrong; maybe I was doing things to make him mad like that. But after 16 years I finally came to the conclusion that it wasn't me—that the problem was him! (Pagelow, 1981, p. 66)

DATA • *In a study of all the homicides in Chicago in one year, 2.6 percent were those in which one spouse killed another.* (Zimring et al., 1983)

Whereas the nature of the violence between spouses it typically pushing, grabbing, shoving, slapping, throwing something at the spouse, or hitting the spouse with something, sometimes the abuser does something that leaves no visible evidence.

> He'd twist my arms behind my back, pulling them up so hard I thought they'd come out of the shoulder socket. He knew better than to make marks on my body—and that doesn't make marks—but it's painful as hell. And there's no way to pull away; you can't do anything. (Pagelow, 1981, p. 85)

The Partner Abuse Scale is designed to help you predict the possibility of abuse becoming a part of your current relationship.

Reasons for Violence

It seems ironic that those individuals who commit their lives to each other in a wedding ceremony are also the most likely to physically hurt each other. Why do people in marriage relationships behave violently toward each other?

PREVIOUS FAMILY LEARNING

As noted earlier, being a participant or an observer of violence in the home in which one was reared is associated with being violent toward one's own partner. "I grew up watching my dad slap my mother around," said one man. "And he beat on me a few times too." In a study of more than 2,000 spouses (Kalmuss,

PARTNER ABUSE SCALE

This scale is designed to predict the potential for violence and abuse in your current relationship. There are no right or wrong answers. After reading each sentence carefully, circle the appropriate number.

1 Never
2 Rarely
3 Occasionally
4 Frequently
5 Very frequently

	N	R	O	F	VF
1. I get irritated easily.	1	2	3	4	5
2. At least one of my parents was abusive to the other.	1	2	3	4	5
3. I was abused as a child.	1	2	3	4	5
4. I have hit my partner before.	1	2	3	4	5
5. Partners who love each other sometimes abuse each other.	1	2	3	4	5
6. I am under a lot of pressure most of the time.	1	2	3	4	5
7. I drink a lot of alcohol.	1	2	3	4	5
8. I lose my temper when I drink.	1	2	3	4	5
9. I have felt the impulse to strike my partner.	1	2	3	4	5
10. It is hard for me to control my temper.	1	2	3	4	5

Scoring: Add the numbers you circled. Since 1 (never) represents the lowest probability for potential abuse and 5 (very frequently) represents the highest probability for potential abuse, the lower your total score (10 is the lowest possible score), the lower the chance of abuse in your relationship, and the higher your score (50 is the highest possible score), the higher the chance of abuse in your relationship. A score of 30 places you at the midpoint between a nonabusive and abusive relationship.

1984), having observed hitting between one's parents was more strongly related to severe marital aggression than being hit as a teenager by one's parents, although both were factors.

HIGH CONFLICT POTENTIAL

Conflict is inherent in any interpersonal relationship, but the potential for conflict is higher among spouses because they must negotiate hundreds of issues over the span of a marital career. Getting one's own way all the time is virtually impossible and some spouses resort to force to ensure compliance with their desires.

DISPLACEMENT OF TENSION

Sometimes being violent may have nothing to do with winning an argument or getting one's way. Rather, the partner may feel frustrated owing to unemployment or limited income, irritated by the bickering of children in a crowded house, or angry at harrassment by his or her boss. These factors can produce a feeling of anxious tension, which is released on the spouse out of displacement (discussed in Chapter 11). The spouse may be blamed for the partner's unhappy frustrated feelings and violence toward the spouse is a way of getting back. "I felt frustrated and alone," said one wife. "I hit him on the head with a skillet and just about killed him. A part of me wishes I had."

> Argument is the worst sort of conversation.
>
> JONATHAN SWIFT

REINFORCEMENT OF VIOLENCE

The law of reinforcement states that any behavior followed by a reward will increase the frequency of that behavior in the future. When spouses get their way as a result of being violent, the odds are increased that they will use violence in the future. "I've found that I can control my wife by beating her up now and then," said one husband. "She's due for another licking soon."

NO REFEREE

Marriage is private; there are no referees to intervene in cases of an escalating conflict. Spouses are judged to be in control of their own relationship without interference from the state. But this freedom has sometimes been taken to extreme so that in some cases the marriage license has been regarded as a hitting license.

VIOLENCE IN SOCIETY

We see social models for violence on television and in movies. Clint Eastwood's Dirty Harry is only one example. Furthermore, our legal system tolerates a great deal of spouse abuse.

> It is not necessary to understand things in order to argue about them.
>
> PIERRE-AUGUSTIN de BEAUMARCHAIS

DATA • *In the cases of 350 wives who were beaten by their spouses, not one of the husbands was arrested, tried, found guilty, and sentenced to jail on a charge of assault and battery. In 60 percent of the cases, the police refused to make an arrest.* (Pagelow, 1981)

Rape in Marriage

Violence in marriage sometimes includes rape.

Some researchers feel that pornography encourages violence against women.

DATA • *Fourteen percent of a random sample of 644 married women in San Francisco reported they had been sexually assaulted by their husbands.* (Russell, 1982)

Sexual assault may have included not only intercourse but also other types of sexual activities the wife did not want to engage in, most often fellatio and anal intercourse.

Two researchers identified several types of marital rape (Finkelhor & Yllo, 1983).

BATTERING RAPE

These rapes occur in the context of a regular pattern of verbal and physical abuse. The husbands yell at their wives, call them names, slap, shove, and beat them. These husbands are angry, belligerent, and frequent alcohol abusers.

> One afternoon she came home from school, changed into a housecoat and started toward the bathroom. He got up from the couch where he had been lying, grabbed her, and pushed her down on the floor. With her face pressed into a pillow and his hand clamped over her mouth, he proceeded to have anal intercourse with her. She screamed and struggled to no avail . . . Her injuries were painful and extensive. She had a torn muscle in her rectum so that for three months she had to go to the bathroom standing up. (p. 123)

NONBATTERING RAPE

These rapes occur in response to a long-standing conflict or disagreement about sex. The violence is not generalized to the rest of the relationship but specific to the sexual conflict.

In the scale of the destinies, brawn will never weigh as much as brain.

JAMES RUSSELL
LOWELL

Their love-making on this occasion started out pleasantly enough, but he tried to get her to have anal intercourse with him. She refused. He persisted. She kicked and pushed him away. Still, he persisted. They ended up having vaginal intercourse. The force he used was mostly that of his weight on top of her. At 220 pounds, he weighs twice as much as she. "It was horrible," she said. She was sick to her stomach afterward. She cried and felt angry and disgusted. He showed little guilt. "He felt like he'd won something." (p. 124)

OBSESSIVE RAPE

These rapes may also be categorized as bizzare. The woman is used as a sex object to satisfy an atypical need of the husband.

"I was really his masturbating machine," one woman recalled. He was very rough sexually and would hold a pillow over her face to stifle her screams. He would also tie her up and insert objects into her vagina and take pictures which he shared with his friends. The interviewee later discovered a file card in her husband's desk which sickened her. On the card, he had written a list of dates, dates that corresponded to the forced sex episodes of the past months. Next to each date was a complicated coding system which seemed to indicate the type of sex act and a ranking of how much he enjoyed it. (pp. 124–125)

Impact of Marital Rape

Being raped by a husband can be more devastating than being attacked by a stranger. The primary effect is to destroy the woman's ability to trust a man in an intimate interpersonal relationship. In addition, the woman raped by her husband lives with her rapist and may be subjected to repeated assaults. Most of the women in the preceding study were raped on multiple occasions.

CONSIDERATION • The law is little help to most women who are raped by their husbands. In 36 of the 50 states and the District of Columbia, the law does not consider a situation where a husband forces his wife to have intercourse as rape. Historically, the penalties for rape were based on property right laws designed to protect a man's property (wife or daughter) from forcible rape by other men. A husband "taking" his own property was not considered rape. Changing such laws has been opposed on the premise that there would be a rash of fabricated complaints. People who favor a law in which a wife could accuse her husband of rape tend to be female, young, single, and educated (Jeffords & Dull, 1982).

Some states do recognize marital rape. James Creitien of Salem, Massachusetts, was convicted and sentenced to three to five years in prison for raping his wife.

Why Wives Stay Married to Husbands Who Rape Them

Many wives who are raped by their husbands do not put up much of a fight. Some feel that it would not do any good no matter how hard they resisted since their husbands are bigger and stronger. In addition, some wives feel that if they resisted, their husbands would hurt them even more.

> I tried once to fight back and he really flipped out and beat me worse than ever. He told me if I ever tried that again he'd kill me. I never tried again. I believe he would.

Still other women feel they are to blame for their husbands anger or frustration. "I've put him off so long, I guess men just go crazy when they don't have sex." Related to these reasons is that the women have no alternative—no place to go, nobody to go to. With no options they take the view of "appeasement rather than massive resistance" (Finkelhor & Yllo, 1983, p. 126).

Man is the hunter, woman is his game.

TENNYSON

Furthermore, women who do not have employment outside the home and who are not economically independent are more constrained to put up with their husbands' abusive behavior. Finally, those who have been married for several years because they feel committed to make the marriage work "no matter what" are likely to continue to stay in the relationship (Strube & Barbour, 1983). One woman who was abused weekly by her partner said, "I have always felt that 'you just don't get divorced.' "

Help for Spouse Abuse

> CONSIDERATION • Wives who are abused by their husbands should consider calling the police and having their husbands arrested. Although there is the risk of making the husband angrier, there is some evidence that husbands may be less likely to be abusive if they know their wives will have them arrested if they are.

A study conducted by the Minneapolis Police Department revealed that of 314 cases in which the police were called because of the husband abusing the wife, arresting the husband was associated with fewer repeated incidences of spouse abuse than counseling both parties on the spot or separation (having the husband leave the residence for at least eight hours).

DATA • *Ten percent of the men arrested for wife beating repeated the offense within six months, compared with 24 percent of those required to leave the residence for eight hours and 19 percent of those who were counseled by the officers.* (Sherman and Berk, 1984)

For those wives who decide to leave their abusing husbands, most go to their parents or relatives, an apartment of their own, a motel or car, or just wander. The fewest number go to a shelter for battered women, which are available in some communities to furnish protection from further violence.

DATA • *Twelve percent of battered women who left their husbands went to a shelter for battered women; 40 percent went to their parents or relatives.* (Pagelow, 1981)

The existence of such shelters is a stimulus for the abusers to seek help. "I knew that when she left me and went to that place for battered women that I needed help," said one abusing husband.

DATA • *There are about 800 shelters throughout the United States which provide temporary housing for abused women and their children.* (*Time*, 1983)

Help usually means marital therapy directed at improved communication and management of conflict in the relationship. The spouses may also become involved in group therapy. But first both spouses must be aware that spouse abuse need not be tolerated. One woman wrote:

> I was one of the battered wives who for years screamed quietly so that the neighbors would not hear. I remember a very alert neighbor told me to scream *loudly* so that they *would* hear—I never forgot that bit of counseling . . . . It (her marriage) was a terrible experience for a naive, trusting, inexperienced woman. I couldn't figure out what was the matter and no one would help me. He was a successful businessman in his own lumber business and I was blamed for everything . . . The conspiracy of silence in the medical, scientific, and publishing circles has been successful . . . Fortunately, because the modern woman is not accepting rape and beating as her just due—we are being forced to study behavior and hopefully expose sick behavior. (Pagelow, 1981, p. 222)

• CHILD ABUSE •

Violence between parents and children and between children and their parents is another abuse pattern. Such violence, although often physical, may also include neglect.

As more is learned about child abuse, it becomes increasingly evident that the plight of children in contemporary society is alarming.

JOHN MEIER

Child abuse may be defined as any interaction or lack of interaction between a child and his or her parents or caregiver that results in nonaccidental harm to the child's physical or developmental well-being. The definition includes what a parent may do (beat, burn, scald) and may fail to do (feed the child, provide a caretaker for a young child, take the child to the doctor) that brings either physical harm to the child or negatively affects the child's development. Parents who refuse to take their ill and suffering child to the doctor are just as guilty of child abuse and neglect as the parents who poison their infant by putting arsenic into the baby bottle.

DATA • *Between 1 and 1.5 percent of all children (from birth to age 18) are abused or neglected each year. This represents about 900,000 children.* (Helfer, 1982)

Parents sometimes become abusive in response to a behavior (lying) or lack of behavior (failure to perform household chores) on the part of the child. In a study of more than 800 abusive events, 69 percent were in response to something the child had done (Kaduskin & Martin, 1981). Some examples follow:

> Child, 3, was held and struck with hands by father because she kicked her mother.

> •

> Child, 9, fighting with her friend while riding in parent's car. Parent became irritated and threatened child. Child did not stop. Mother dragged child by neck into house and slapped child on face.

> •

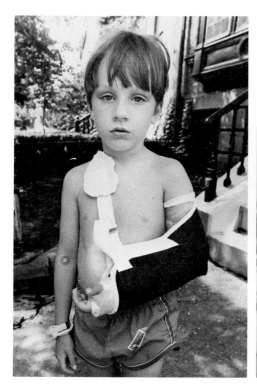

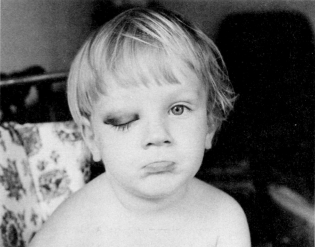

Rosemarie, 13, was taping a song that was on the radio and told her mother to be quiet. When she wasn't. Rosemarie swore at her, which made Mrs. B angry. She threw her tea at Rosemarie, pushed her to the floor, kicked her in the back, and hit her with a belt.

•

Child, 8, wrote on siblings with a magic marker and then lied to father about it. Beaten with belt by father. Bruised and hospitalized for three days with an eye injury.

•

Mother overreacted to her 2-year-old son's unwillingness to eat his dinner. She allegedly threw the child 10 feet across a room and then beat him with her shoe on his head and on one side of his body. The child's cuts required outpatient medical treatment.

•

Irving, 5, was blowing the car horn while father worked on the motor. Irving refused to stop doing this and father, who had been drinking, threw the child from the car to the ground, resulting in a bone fracture.

•

The stepfather warned Gabriel, 13, that if he was suspended from school once more he would kick him all the way back to school. That is exactly what happened (pp. 116–122).

Almost a million children are abused or neglected every day.

There are twice as many cases of neglect as abuse, mothers being somewhat more likely to neglect their children and fathers to abuse them (Downing, 1982). The children are most often normal (for example, not retarded, emotionally disturbed, or physically handicapped) and require some form of treatment for bruises, welts, lacerations, burns, and bone fractures in about 20 percent of the cases. Only in about 5 percent of the cases is hospitalization required. Skull fracture, bleeding within the skull, and severe burns require hospitalization.

DATA • *In one study of abused children under 5 years of age, 51 percent were boys, 49 percent were girls. The average age of the victims was 18.5 months.* (Smith & Hansen, 1983)

Long-term consequences for the child may be devastating. These include brain damage, mental retardation (as a result of improper nutrition), and physical deformities. Twenty-one of 134 battered children died (Smith & Hansen, 1983).

Characteristics of Child Abusers

Some research has suggested that the less income and education parents have, the greater the chance of abuse and neglect. Being black has also been associated with higher incidences of child maltreatment (Downing, 1982). Other researchers have found income, education, and racial background to be unreliable predictors of child abuse (Schumm et al., 1982). For example, when blacks and whites of similar income are compared, the differences in child maltreatment are very small (Garbarino & Ebata, 1983). In addition, middle- and upper-class families are more able to hide abuse from professionals.

However, some factors are predictive of child abuse. These include the following (Oates et al., 1983):

1. The pregnancy is unplanned and the father does not want the child.
2. The birth is complicated and unpleasant.
3. Mother-infant bonding is lacking.
4. Childrearing techniques are strict and harsh and include little positive reinforcement for the child.
5. The child is compared unfavorably with other children and the parents have an unhappy relationship.

Causes of Child Abuse

There is no agreement on the cause or causes of child abuse. The best explanations point to a number of variables that, in combination, offer an explanation for some cases of child abuse.

PARENT PSYCHOPATHOLOGY

Child abuse has been associated with parents who are anger-prone, rigid and domineering, dependent on alcohol or drugs, and who have low self-esteem and difficulty with self-control and handling stress (Burgess & Garbarino, 1983; Engfer & Schneewind, 1982). "Child abusers tend to get violently angry quickly," said one social worker who specializes in child abuse. "And they act on their impulses without thinking what they are doing. All parents, whether they admit it or not, have had the urge to hit or harm their child in some way. What separates the nonabusers from the abusers is the ability to stop their impulses before they hurt the child."

PARENTS MODELING ON ABUSIVE PARENTS

Parents who were themselves abused or the victims of harsh physical punishment tend to duplicate these patterns in their own families (Herrenkohl et al., 1983). One father said:

> My father beat on me as long as I can remember. And for no reason at all. One time it was because I walked over a newspaper in the living room and didn't pick it up. He got up from the couch and shoved me against the wall while yelling obscenities at me. Then he proceeded to sock me with his fists. He did that for years until I was finally old enough to leave home. I never want to go back. But when I had my own kids, I noticed that I had the impulse to do like my dad. I am able to control it most of the time, but at other times, it gets the best of me.

DISPLACEMENT OF AGGRESSION

One cartoon shows several panels consisting of a boss yelling at his employee, the employee yelling at his wife, the wife yelling at their child, and the child kicking the dog who chases the cat up a tree. Some child abuse can be explained by our social norms that the strong dominate the weak. Both genders displace their anger. Of women's aggression, Washburne (1983) observed, "Women's abuse of children stems directly from their own oppression in society and within the family . . . some women displace their frustration and anger on their children, the family members who are less powerful than they" (p. 291).

PARENTAL ISOLATION

Unlike most societies of the world, we rear our children in closed and isolated nuclear units. In extended kinship societies other relatives are always present to help with the task of childrearing. Our isolation means that there is no relief from the parenting role as well as no supervision by others who might interfere in child-abusing situations. One father who stayed with his 2-year-old all day when his wife was in the hospital having another child said, "I've never been so frustrated and will be glad to get back to work. Being with a kid all day is horrendous."

ENVIRONMENTAL STRESSORS

Dissatisfaction with marriage, problem children, lack of home conveniences, feeling lonely, and being exhausted from working all day or being unemployed are examples of stressful situations that further fray the parents' nerves and ability to cope with the role of parenthood (Herrenkohl et al., 1983). "It seems like everything is wrong with everything I touch," said one spouse whose child was dyslexic. "My marriage, job, and child. Nothing seems to work out."

CONSIDERATION • No single factor is likely to result in child abuse, but several in combination increase the likelihood. An unemployed, alcoholic, single parent with four children who was abused when she was a child is much more likely to abuse her child than an employed, chemically free, married woman with one child who was not herself abused as a child.

Agency Response to Child Abuse

Social worker Patricia Capps has furnished the following information on how one state (North Carolina) responds to reported child abuse. Child abuse is normally discovered by a school counselor, neighbor, or physician who calls the local social service department, which is responsible for investigating the abuse. A social worker is required by law to visit the home of the alleged abused child within 24 hours if the abuse is physical and 48 hours if the abuse is neglect. Parental response to these visits ranges from denial ("What are you talking about?") to anger ("Get off my porch!") to apology ("We're sorry it happened"). If the parents are cooperative, the caseworker discusses the nature and context of the abuse and ways to prevent it from recurring. Weekly visits are made by the social worker to ensure that the abuse or neglect has been eliminated. If the parents are not cooperative, the social worker gets a court order to remove the child temporarily from the home. In rare cases, the child is placed in a foster home.

Treatment for the Child Abuser

Since behavior is learned, the most effective way to treat child abuse is to train parents how to behave more appropriately with their children. Several clinicians observed that the best setting for such learning may be small groups of parents that meet for eight twice-weekly sessions, focusing on self-control, alternative actions, and effective childrearing procedures (Barth et al., 1983).

Therapy for the couple is often indicated in cases of child abuse.

SELF-CONTROL

Parents are shown a videotape of parental reactions to a child spilling milk. In one scene the reaction is volatile, in the other, self-controlled. After the first scene, parents identified factors that may have made the parent vulnerable to abuse—fatigue, frustration over work, hunger, and impending illness. The second tape showed the parent talking aloud to herself or himself to identify these factors and "recognize his vulnerability to provocation" (p. 317). After the child's accident, the parent stopped, took a deep breath, and consciously responded appropriately. After the video demonstration, first the group leader and then the members assumed parent and child roles. "Initially guided by the script, then progressively without prompts, group members rehearsed the use of self-talk, impulse delay, and relaxation to the 'spilled milk' situation" (p. 317).

ALTERNATIVE REACTIONS

Group leaders and parents determine alternative behaviors to expressing anger aggressively—telephoning another parent, vacuuming the house, doing aerobic exercises, or looking in the mirror while smiling and saying positive things. Parents learn to yell "stop" subvocally and to engage in one of these behaviors. An additional alternative is for parents to relax by means of deep breathing exercises and tranquil fantasies.

CHILDREARING PROCEDURES

Harsh physical punishment has negative consequences for children and their parents. It teaches children to fear and sometimes hate their parents. Although it may be effective in suppressing behavior temporarily, it does not teach the child appropriate behavior.

CONSIDERATION • Concerned that the use of corporal punishment may have negative consequences for the child, Sweden passed a law in 1979 legally prohibiting such punishment by parents or other persons having care and custody of children. Although enforcement of such a law has been difficult, Swedish attitudes about corporal punishment in subsequent years have become more consistent with the law (Ziegert, 1983).

Positive reinforcement and time out are two alternative techniques parents can use to encourage the behavior they want in their children. "Catch the child doing good" and praise him or her—this reinforces children for positive behavior rather than waiting until they drift into expressing negative behavior that angers the parent. Parents are encouraged to systematically praise and compliment their children every day for the things they do that the parents approve of.

Time out, also known as time out from reinforcement, is an effective way of punishing children for negative behavior that avoids long-term negative consequences for the parent-child relationship. When the child misbehaves, the parent instructs the child to go to an isolated place in the home (for example, the bathroom) for about five minutes. Children usually do not like time out; it mildly punishes the behavior they were engaging in so that the behavior is less likely to recur.

Prevention of Child Abuse

The ultimate solution to child abuse and neglect is the early socialization of parents. Two steps can be taken to execute this solution. First, educate the public through the mass media that child abuse and neglect do occur and that it is unacceptable. Second, provide community adult education programs on marriage and family relationships including interpersonal communication, coping with stress, and parent skills training. More one-on-one training might involve a home health visitor program for *all* new parents for one to two years after the birth of their firstborn (Helfer, 1982). Such a program would be particularly valuable for new parents who were abused by their parents. Unless this high-risk group learns alternative ways of relating with infants and children, the cycle of abuse is likely to continue.

For young parents who discover they are abusive, Parents Anonymous is a national organization with 1,500 local chapters that will provide immediate help and support (22330 Hawthorne Blvd. Torrance, CA 90505; phone: 800-421-0353).

• INCEST •

A variation of child abuse is incest. Incest is defined as sexual relations between close relatives such as father and daughter, mother and son, and brother and sister. Although "sexual relations" may imply intercourse, it may also include fondling of the breasts and genitals, and oral sex. "Relatives" usually implies biologically related individuals but may also include stepparents and stepsiblings.

DATA • *About 15 million individuals in the United States have been victims of incest.* (Stark, 1984)

Incest, particularly parent-child incest, is an abuse of power and authority. It is usually coercive and thus considered a form of family violence (Gordon & O'Keefe, 1984). A child is not in a position to consent to a sex act instigated by an adult. The following describes the experience of a woman who as a child was forced to have sexual relations with her father.

> I was around 6 years old when I was sexually abused by my father. He was not drinking at that time; therefore he had a clear mind as to what he was doing. On looking back, it seemed so well planned. For some reason, my father wanted me to go with him to the woods behind our house to help him saw wood for the night. I went without any question. Once we got there, he looked around

for a place to sit and wanted me to sit down with him. In doing so, he said, "Susan, I want you to do something for daddy." I said, "What's that daddy?" He went on to explain that "I want you to lie down and we are going to play mama and daddy." Being a child, I said "okay" thinking it was going to be fun. I don't know what happened next because I can't remember if there was pain or whatever. I was threatened not to tell, and remembering how he beat my mother, I didn't want the same treatment. It happened approximately two other times. I remember not liking this at all. Since I couldn't tell mama, I came to the conclusion it was wrong and I was not going to let it happen again.

But what could I do? Until age 18, I was constantly on the run, hiding from him when I had to stay home alone with him, staying out of his way so he wouldn't touch me by hiding in the corn fields all day long, under the house, in the barns, and so on until my mother got back home, then getting punished by her for not doing the chores she had assigned to me that day. It was a miserable life growing up in that environment.

DATA • *In a study of more than 6,000 cases of child sexual abuse (children aged 1 to 18), 40 percent of those victimizing the child were the natural parents, 21 percent were stepparents, and 17 percent adoptive or foster parents.* (Finkelhor, 1983)

Father-Daughter Incest

Father-daughter incest has received the most attention in our society. Unlike the experience of the 6-year-old girl just described, incest may begin by affectionate cuddling between father and daughter, which is often enjoyable for both. Over time the cuddling may involve more extended bodily contact, stroking of the genitals, oral sex, and intercourse. Both father and daughter usually give each other mixed signals. Both may enjoy the physical contact but feel it is wrong. One woman expressed the ambivalence she experienced as a child:

My daddy never touched me unless he wanted to have me play with his genitals. I didn't like touching him there but he was affectionate to me and told me how pretty I was. I was really mixed up about the whole thing.

Because of her ambivalence, the daughter may continue to participate in sexual activity with her father. Not only may she derive attention and affection from the relationship but also she may develop a sense of power over her father. She may even demand gifts as the price of her silence. If her parents have an unhappy relationship (this is usually the case), she may enjoy her role as the "little wife."

DATA • *Father-daughter incest usually begins when the daughter is between 6 and 11 and lasts for at least two years.* (Stark, 1984)

Father-daughter incest may begin by force. There are a few cases of fathers having raped their daughters when they were very small—even babies—injuring them badly. Baby incest is difficult for the wife to overlook, but she may sanction the sexual relations of her husband and daughter in her desire to preserve the family unit. One woman said that her "nerves" were about to "snap" because her husband and daughter were having sex. But she did not say anything about it because if she did, her husband, on whom she depended economically, might leave her alone with the children. "At least," she said, "his playing around is kept in the family."

Mother-Son Incest

Incest between mothers and sons occurs less frequently than father-daughter incest. It rarely includes intercourse but is usually confined to various stimulating behaviors. The mother may continue to bathe her son long after he is capable of caring for himself, during which she stimulates him sexually. Later she may stimulate her son to ejaculation.

The mother may also sleep with her son. Although no specific sexual contact may occur, she may sleep in the nude—this behavior is provocative as well as stimulating. In some cases there is sexual contact; one mother had intercourse with her son two to three times a week from the time he was 13 until he left for college (Sarrel & Masters, 1982).

Brother-Sister Incest

One of the most common and least visible forms of incest is that between siblings. Siblings are peers. Their incest may seem natural to them and they may wonder why there is a taboo against it.

Whether brother-sister incest is a problem for siblings depends on a number of factors. If the siblings are young, of the same age, have an isolated sexual episode, engage only in exploratory, nonintercourse behavior, and both consent to the behavior, there may be only limited harm. But a change in any of these factors increases the chance that such incest will have negative consequences for future heterosexual relationships.

If the siblings are young (4 to 8), they will have had less exposure to the idea that sexual behavior among siblings is inappropriate. Although they may have vague feelings that their parents would not approve of their sexual behavior, they will probably not feel the guilt usually associated with such behavior. As they grow older, they may relabel their former behavior as "child's play," minimizing its impact.

Being of the same age will minimize the negative consequences of sibling incest. Although in most cases the siblings are of the same age, it is not uncommon for an older brother to seduce his younger sister into having intercourse with him. It is less common for an older sister to become sexually involved with a younger brother. A difference in age increases the chance that the sexual relationship will be exploitive.

A childhood sexual experience with a sibling that occurs once or twice is also less consequential than a series of such experiences that takes place over a number of years. Most such experiences are limited, but some develop into a pattern and continue for years.

The nature of the sexual behavior is also important. Playing doctor or strip poker or "you show me, I'll show you" probably has minimal impact on siblings. Siblings learn that these are common childhood experiences. But intercourse may increase the potential for negative effects.

DATA • *In one study 18 percent of the brother-sister incest experiences in which the siblings were over the age of 13 involved intercourse. Half of the reactions to the experiences were positive, half were negative.* (Finkelhor, 1980)

Consent is important if the negative consequences are to be minimal. Particularly when one sibling is older than the other, a brother or sister may use blackmail, bribery, or force to get the sibling to comply, as in the case of Jim, age 15, and his sister, Michelle, age 12.

> Michelle had stolen money from her mother to buy some marijuana. Jim threatened to tell their mother if Michelle did not let him fondle her when she was naked. After Michelle consented, Jim threatened her repeatedly over a period of three years. The parents never knew.

Impact of Incest

Father-daughter and mother-son incest have the most undesirable consequences. Daughters of such incest relationships usually develop one of two behavior patterns. One is to become promiscuous, having sexual relations with anyone; the other is to become fearful of sex, avoiding men. One woman said:

> My daddy has been having sex with me since I was a little girl. I can't stand myself for letting him do it and I can't stand to let any man touch me. I hate sex and the thought of it turns me off. I've had three husbands and sex with them was terrible. I'm very sad about the whole thing.

Although a negative attitude toward sex can be unlearned and a more positive attitude learned, it takes time and the direction of a skilled therapist who helps the woman to understand that it was the parent's responsibility, not hers, to see that sexual behavior between them did not occur.

Men may become impotent as a consequence of intimate, quasisexual relationships with their mothers. Having been confronted with a sexually inappropriate stimulus, they had to learn to turn themselves off sexually. Such negative learning can usually be reversed in therapy.

Not all who have incestuous sexual encounters with parents and siblings have difficulties as adults. Indeed, many learn to relabel what happened when they were younger so there is minimal guilt or concern. Subsequent sexual relationships not only provide pleasurable experiences but also help to temper the effects of the earlier sexual encounters. Sometimes, in spite of the incest, a strong love bond can exist between a daughter and her father. In one case, a 16-year-old daughter who had been having sex with her father for two years told the judge that she loved her father and pleaded with him not to send her father to prison.

Treatment for Incest Abusers and Victims

More than 4,000 children and their families have been treated by the Child Sexual Abuse Treatment Program in Santa Clara County, California. In a typical case, a girl will tell a school nurse or counselor that she is being sexually molested by her father. The mother is called, apprised of the situation, and asked to come get the child. The police department is also called and an officer is sent to get an initial statement from the girl. If the investigation suggests there is sufficient evidence to warrant an arrest and referral to the district attorney for prosecution, the father is arrested and placed in jail or released on his own recognizance. But he is not allowed to make contact with the daughter or return to the home; if he does return home, the child is removed to a foster home or care shelter.

Counseling begins immediately. "Incestuous families are badly fragmented as a result of the original dysfunctional family dynamics, which are further exacerbated upon disclosure to civil authorities. The child, mother, and father must be treated separately before family therapy becomes productive" (Giarretto, 1982, p. 263).

The mother and father are also contacted by telephone by a member of Parents United (P.O. Box 952, San Jose, CA 95108-0952; phone: 408-280-5055) who has been through a similar experience and who becomes their "sponsor." In addition to personal contacts, the sponsor invites the clients to Parents United and prepares them for the initial group sessions where other parents discuss the incest that has occurred in their homes.

Meanwhile, depending on the circumstances and recommendation of the social worker, the father might face criminal proceedings. If he is charged with a felony (usually for child molestation or statutory rape), two court-appointed psychiatrists determine if he is a mentally disturbed sex offender. If he is, he is sent to the state psychiatric facility for chronic sex offenders. If not, he may be sent to prison or receive a suspended sentence if he agrees to participate in a treatment program of individual, group, and family counseling. The average length of treatment is about nine months.

> Their body belongs to them and they can decide who touches it.
>
> JUDITH HOOPER

Prevention of Incest

The Committee for Children (P.O. Box 15190, Seattle, WA 98115; phone: 206-524-6020) is an organization to help children acquire knowledge and skills that will help protect them from sexual abuse. Through various presentations in the elementary schools, children are taught how to differentiate between appropriate and inappropriate touching by adults or siblings, to understand that it is okay to feel uncomfortable if they do not like the way someone else is touching them, to say "no" in potentially exploitive situations, and to tell other adults if the offending behavior occurs.

• PARENT ABUSE •

Child abuse and incest focus on how the parent harms or exploits the child. Another form of family abuse is parent abuse—how children harm and exploit their parents, particularly older parents.

There are a number of ways in which children abuse their parents (O'Toole et al., 1983):

1. Physical abuse: hitting parent in the face with a fist or object.

2. Emotional abuse: screaming at parent, ignoring parent, keeping parent locked in room.
3. Nutritional neglect: failing to feed parent for twenty-four hours.
4. Medical neglect: not giving parent medication; not keeping medical appointments.
5. Cleanliness neglect: leaving parent on filthy mattress; leaving parent with infected sores; leaving dirty clothes on parent for days.

DATA • *It is estimated that the number of cases of abused, neglected, or exploited elderly ranges from 600,000 to 1 million, or 4 percent of the elderly population.* (Eastman, 1984)

One 79-year-old woman testified before a joint hearing of the U. S. Senate Special Committee on Aging:

> The past three years have gotten worse. My daughter locked me in the garage and left me there for more than an hour. She always parked her car behind mine in the garage so I could not get my car out except by her permission.
> If she found me using the electric toaster oven, my food was thrown on the floor and the toaster oven was removed and hidden for several days.
> Always hurting me physically and mentally; kicking me, pushing me, grappling with me, telling me to get out, at one time throwing a drawer down the stairs at me, calling me names, telling me I belonged in a nursing home and why didn't I go. (Eastman, 1984, p. 30)

Reasons for parent abuse vary. In some cases the children are frustrated with the burden of having to care for their elderly parents. In other cases they are "getting back at them" for their maltreatment as children. In still other cases parental abuse is one expression of a larger pattern of abuse (which may also include child and spouse abuse).

• TRENDS •

Trends in handling violent and abusive relationships include greater public awareness that such behavior occurs in intimate relationships, an increased number of shelters for battered women, and a less punitive approach to sexually abusive fathers.

Newspapers, magazines, and television often feature stories of violence and abuse in marriage and family relationships. "Sixty Minutes," the CBS news program, devoted a segment to the murder of a father by his son, who could no longer tolerate his father beating him and his sister. Previously they had reported the case of a wife who took out a murder contract on her husband because he had been abusive. Violence is no longer known to only those behind closed doors.

Because of the increasing visibility of violence in intimate relationships, more shelters for battered women will be established. Although most battered women prefer to go to the home of a relative, those who have no place to go to escape the violence will seek refuge in a shelter.

Prosecuting and jailing fathers who abuse their daughters is also abating. The current trend is toward putting the father on probation, thereby keeping the family together, and involving family members in individual and group counseling. Imprisonment only further loosens the family members' emotional ties and, in many cases, economically devastates the family. One social worker commented:

> Once you take the father out of the home, the breadwinner is gone. And although the mother may work, she can't produce the income two of them would produce. Also, it is assumed that every daughter wants her father to be sent to prison because of what he did to her. But that simply isn't so. I was in a courtroom when a judge sentenced a father to 15 years in prison for molesting his 15-year-old daughter. The daughter was in the courtroom at the time of the sentencing and went absolutely berzerk. After regaining her composure, she pleaded with the judge not to "send my daddy to prison."

The Institute for the Community as Extended Family (same address as Parents United, see page 354) will continue to train professionals to develop child sexual abuse treatment programs such as the one described in Santa Clara County, California. The institute has also developed another organization, Adults Molested as Children, to provide help to adults still adversely affected by earlier sexual abuse experiences.

· SUMMARY ·

Violence occurs in about 30 percent of dating relationships, usually after several months of dating. Such violence includes pushing, slapping, threatening, and punching. Either or both partners may be the abuser. It is not unusual for couples to continue their relationship after violence has occurred. For some individuals, violence is viewed as part of a love relationship. Others have no alternative to the primary relationship. Still others feel they deserve the abuse.

Courtship may also involve sexual aggression; about 10 percent of women have reported that their dating partner had tried to or succeeded in raping them. Some men view women as legitimate victims and legitimize the rape in their own mind.

Violence also occurs with couples who live together. Those who are younger, have lower incomes, and who have not been previously married have higher rates of violence in their relationship than older, more affluent, previously married cohabitants.

Violence extends into marriage. Marital violence may be explained by previous family learning, the perceived reinforcement following violence, the lack of controls in our society, and the modeling of violence in the larger society.

Rape occurs in marriage as well as outside of it. These rapes may be part of a larger context of violence in the relationship or a specific conflict over sex. Marital rape is potentially more devastating than rape by a stranger as the woman lives with the rapist. Having the husband arrested for violence and abuse seems to reduce the frequency of such abuse. Therapy that focuses on communication and conflict resolution are the most desirable responses to marital violence.

Child abuse is action resulting in nonaccidental harm to the child's physical or developmental well-being. Child abusers may be found in all races, income, and educational levels. A primary predictive factor is the lack of emotional bonding with the child. Although there is no single cause of child abuse, factors involved are lack of impulse control, parental experience of abuse as children, displacement of aggression, and environmental stressors. Successful treatment of child abuse includes teaching parents to exercise self-control and to use time out and positive reinforcement for good behavior as alternatives to harsh punishment.

Incest may be between father and daughter, mother and son, or brother and sister. Although brother-sister incest is probably the most prevalent, parent-offspring incest is the most destructive. The parent or stepparent uses his authority to coerce the child into a pattern of sexual relations. The child often is not sure what is happening but senses it is wrong since she or he is enjoined to secrecy and may even be threatened.

Treatment for incest should involve the whole family in individual, marital, and family therapy for several months. Teaching young children that it is not okay to let other adults touch them in ways that make them uncomfortable and to tell another adult if someone tries to do so is an incest prevention technique.

Children may also abuse their parents. Examples of such abuse include yelling obscenities at aging parents, hitting them, and not taking food to invalid parents. Congressional hearings to assess the extent of such abuse and to recommend ways to alleviate it may have a positive effect.

Trends in handling violence and abuse are greater visibility of the subject, more shelters for abused wives, and a less punitive approach to parents who abuse their children.

Questions for Reflection

1. Do you feel that rape by a boyfriend or spouse would be more devastating than by a stranger? Why?
2. Have you experienced violence or abuse in your intimate relationships? How has this affected your relationships?
3. What are your feelings about criminal prosecution of a parent who has sex with his or her child versus being put on probation and immersed in individual, marital, and family therapy?

· CHOICES ·

Choices about abusive relationships are basically the decision to terminate or to continue such relationships.

TERMINATE AN ABUSIVE DATING RELATIONSHIP?

People disagree on whether to terminate an abusive courtship relationship. Seventy students in a marriage and family class were asked if they would continue a relationship with someone they were dating who hit and kicked them. Their answers follow.

End Dating Relationship

Most said they would end the dating relationship because such violence is intolerable in an intimate relationship, because they would lose respect for their partner or because they would fear that the abuse would recur.

If my partner hit me out of anger or jealousy it would be the first and last time. I would absolutely terminate the relationship. My reasoning being that if a person hits you once he will more than likely hit you again, and again. There is no acceptable reason whatsoever for a male to hit a female.

•

I would terminate the relationship immediately because I am totally against any type of violence. Striking anyone is an inhumane gesture, especially if it is done out of anger.

•

If a problem arises, I feel we should be able to discuss it in an adult manner. Hitting me would be uncalled for. If my partner hit me, I would hit him back and the relationship would be over.

•

If he feels that he could do it once and get away with it, he may do it again. If we were to marry, he would probably do it even more so I would get out of such a relationship while I could.

•

I would have no desire to nurture a violent relationship and would leave the bum.

•

I would lose all respect for that person and couldn't trust him again. Besides, if he hit me, he might hit our child.

Continue Dating Relationship

A few said they would continue the dating relationship with the partner but that it would depend on the circumstances.

If the infraction was not severe and if the person was "sorry" for her actions and if she thought she had lost control for a split second, I would want us to continue our relationship. But if she hit and kicked me on a regular basis and showed no remorse, I would end the relationship.

•

I would not terminate a dating relationship if my partner hit or kicked me because I would want to find out my partner's rationale for her behavior. Maybe it was something that I did that provoked her anger. . . maybe I deserved it.

•

It would really depend on the situation or the severity of the blows. If it was for my own good and the violence was minimal, I would stick around. But violence is not the kind of thing I would put up with too often.

•

I would probably let it slide the first time, yet I would tell him that he had one and only one more chance. If it ever happened again, I would probably leave him. It also would depend on how long I had been dating him. If it was a second date, I'd leave him in a heartbeat because there are other fish in the sea. If I had been dating him for a long time, I could tell if his outburst was intentional or emotional.

TERMINATE ABUSIVE MARRIAGE RELATIONSHIP?

These students were also asked if they would end their marriage if the spouse hit and kicked them. Although some said they would seek a divorce, most felt that they should try to work it out.

Seek a Divorce
Those opting for divorce basically felt they couldn't live with someone who had or would abuse them.

I abhor violence of any kind and since a marriage should be based on love, kicking is certainly out of the norm. I would lose all respect for my mate and I could never trust him again. It would be over.

Continue
Marriage Relationship
Most felt that marriage was too strong a commitment to end if the abuse could be stopped.

I would not divorce my spouse if she hit or kicked me. I'm sure that there's always room for improvement in my behavior although I don't think it's necessary to assault me. I recognize that under certain circumstances it's the quickest way to draw my attention to the problem at hand. I would try to work

through our difficulties with my spouse.

•

The physical contact would lead to a separation. During that time I would expect him to feel sorry for what he had done and to seek psychiatric help. My anger would be so great it's quite hard to know exactly what I would do. I would feel like killing him.

•

I wouldn't leave him right off. I would try to get him to counseling. If we could not work through the problem, I would leave him. If there was no way we could live together, I guess divorce would be the answer.

•

I would not divorce my husband because I don't believe in breaking the sacred vows of marriage. But I would separate from him and let him suffer!

•

I would tell him I was leaving but that he could keep me if he would agree for us to see a counselor to ensure that the abuse never happened again.

· Chapter 13 ·

SEXUAL FULFILLMENT

CONTENTS

Meanings of Sexual Fulfillment

Sexual Fulfillment:
  Some Prerequisites

Sexual Fulfillment: Some Facts

Sexual Fulfillment:
  Some Myths

Female Sexual Dysfunctions

Self-Assessment: Personal Sex
  History Inventory

Male Sexual Dysfunctions

Sexual Fulfillment in
  Middle Age

Sexual Fulfillment in
  the Later Years

Choices

Too much of a good thing can be wonderful.

MAE WEST

"Sexual fulfillment for me," said a 26-year-old woman "is having sex with someone I love. He accepts my sexuality and is not turned off to my strong responses. In addition he is responsive to my needs and is willing to invest the time it takes to excite me. Good sex takes love, time, patience, caring, and experimentation."

In this chapter we look at the meanings, prerequisites, facts, and myths of sexual fulfillment. We also examine sexual dysfunctions common to women and men. Finally, since growing older is something we all do, we look at sexuality in the middle and later years.

• MEANINGS OF SEXUAL FULFILLMENT •

Sexual fulfillment means different things to different people—and at different times.

Individual Definitions

Sexual fulfillment may mean

- Achieving physical pleasure with someone you are emotionally involved with
- Letting yourself go from social restrictions and really enjoying sex
- A relationship that releases a need for bodily involvement
- Bringing each other to orgasm and sharing the feelings of love and oneness
- A feeling of mental and physical completeness
- Responsiveness of each partner to the emotional and physical needs of the other
- Both partners (not just one) enjoying each other sexually
- Having all the sex you want with the person you want to have it with
- Making love with showers, massages, candlelight, wine, and conversation all night long

According to the *Connecticut Mutual Life Report* (1981), people who regard a sexually fulfilling relationship as important are more often male, young, married, and of higher income and education (Figure 13.1).

Sexual fulfillment depends in part upon having a good sexual partner. In a survey conducted by the author, 100 respondents were asked to specify the characteristics of a good sexual partner. The most frequent characteristic mentioned by both genders was being loved or cared for by their sexual partner. "Having sex with someone is easy," said one person. "It's the person behind the genitals who cares about you that makes it special." But other respondents did not mention the emotional relationship with a partner. Rather, they focused on characteristics such as variety, aggressiveness, patience, and endurance. One woman said, "If he can't stay erect for two hours I wouldn't want him."

Sexual Fulfillment and Intercourse

I have steak and sex the same way—very rare.

RODNEY
DANGERFIELD

The variety of definitions associated with sexual fulfillment make it clear that there is no specific element, including intercourse, in a sexual relationship that must be present for sexual fulfillment.

A couple who never has intercourse may also be sexually fulfilled. One couple reported:

> We've been married for 43 years and haven't had intercourse in 10 years or so. The idea that you need to have intercourse with your spouse to be sexually and emotionally happy is nonsense. We love each other, go everywhere together, and have three beautiful grandchildren. There is more to life than intercourse.

There are a number of reasons why intercourse is not necessary for some couples who define themselves as sexually fulfilled and happy: (1) There is little

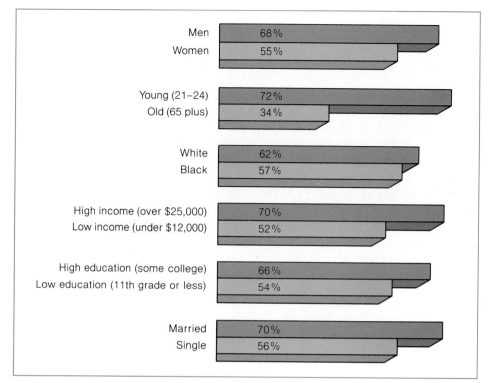

**Figure 13.1   Characteristics of People
Who Say a Sexually Fulfilling Relationship Is Important**

peer pressure for spouses to have intercourse. (2) Sexual experiences may not have been particularly enjoyable—perhaps the man ejaculated prematurely or the woman did not climax. (3) Masturbation may be preferred over intercourse. (4) Other shared interests are more enjoyable than sexual involvement. (5) Physical problems (arthritis, slipped disc, or the like) may make sexual participation painful or unpleasant. (6) Definitions such as "we're too old for that" or "that part of our life is over" may be adopted by the couple who feel that sex should diminish with age. (7) Mutual playful physical affection (hugging, holding, kissing) may have become a substitute rather than a prelude to intercourse. (8) One partner may initially be more disinterested in sex than the mate and discourage sexual advances; over time, the mate learns not to expect sex from the partner.

Sexual Fulfillment Over Time

The degree of sexual fulfillment also varies with time. After conducting interviews with 80 spouses about the frequency of intercourse in their marriages, Greenblatt (1983) concluded that from the first year on "almost everything—children, jobs, commuting, housework, financial worries—that happens to a couple conspires to *reduce* the degree of sexual interaction and almost nothing leads to increasing it." (p. 294)

DATA • *Fifteen was the average number of times per month spouses in one study reported having intercourse during their first year of marriage. Those who had been married six years reported having intercourse an average of six times per month.* (Greenblatt, 1983)

However, couples do not necessarily define fulfillment in terms of frequency. "It's how you do it when you do it, not how often you do it that matters," said one woman. Change in circumstances (and sometimes partners) is inevitable. But the impact of those changes and their definition is less certain.

• SEXUAL FULFILLMENT: SOME PREREQUISITES •

Regardless of variations in the definition of sexual fulfillment, there seem to be several prerequisites for its existence: self-knowledge, a good relationship, open communication, realistic expectations, and a display of sexual interest in the partner.

Self-Knowledge

Being sexually fulfilled implies having knowledge about yourself and your body. To be in touch with yourself and your own body is to know how you can best experience sexual pleasure. "I've read all the books on how to get the most out of sex," said one man, "and I've concluded that the experts know a lot about what some people like sexually, but nothing about what *I* like. Good sex for me is more related to the context than to the technique. And I'm sure that for the next person it's something else."

A Good Relationship

A rule among therapists who work with couples who have sexual problems is "Treat the relationship before focusing on the sexual issue." The sexual relationship is part of the larger relationship between the partners, and what happens outside the bedroom in day-to-day interaction has a tremendous influence on what happens inside the bedroom. The statement "I can't fight with you all day and want to have sex with you at night" illustrates the social context of the sexual experience. One woman described this very clearly.

> *Is not the true romantic feeling—not the desire to escape life, but to prevent life from escaping you?*
>
> THOMAS CLAYTON WOLFE

I don't understand him. He's ready to go any time. It's always been a big problem with us right from the beginning. If we've hardly seen each other for two or three days and hardly talked to each other, I can't just jump into bed. If we have a fight, I can't just turn it off. He has a hard time understanding that. I have to know I'm needed and wanted for more than just jumping into bed. (Rubin, 1976, p. 50)

A good out-of-bed relationship includes spending time together, being affectionate, communicating, and sharing similar values. Also, the nature of a couple's economic relationship can affect their sex life. In a study of dual-career marriages (Johnson, Kaplan, & Tusel, 1979), the researchers reported that the

A good general
relationship is
essential for a
good sexual
relationship.

wives became much more assertive and sexually demanding after they were employed. This was viewed as a function of the wife's increased economic power and self-esteem once she began to bring money into the marriage. "Many wives seemed less likely to accept the blame for unsatisfactory sexual performance . . . Some attempted to get their husbands to read sex manuals or were more vocal about the staleness of their sexual relationship" (p. 7).

The type of relationship also may be important. Hatfield et al. (1982) separately interviewed the spouses of 53 newlywed couples to assess the degree to which having an equitable relationship contributed to their sexual satisfaction. The researchers concluded that equitably treated men and women were more satisfied with their sexual relationships overall than those who felt they were getting more or less out of the relationship than were their partners.

So the effects of a couple's overall and sexual relationship are intertwined. Someone observed that when sex goes well it is 15 percent of a relationship, and when it goes badly it is 85 percent; undoubtedly many partners agree. The sexual relationship positively influences the couple's relationship in several ways: (1) as a shared pleasure, a positively reinforcing event; (2) by facilitating intimacy, since many couples feel closer and share their feelings before or after a sexual experience; and (3) by reducing tension generated by the stresses of everyday living and couple interaction (McCarthy, 1982).

• Intercourse communicates how the partners are feeling and acts as a barometer for the relationship. Each partner brings to intercourse, sometimes unconsciously, a motive (pleasure, reconciliation, procreation, duty); a psychological state (love, hostility, boredom, excitement); and a physical state (tense, exhausted, relaxed, turned on). The combination of these factors will change from one encounter to another. Tonight the wife may feel aroused and loving and seek pleasure. But her husband may feel exhausted and hostile and only have intercourse out of a sense of duty. But tomorrow night both may feel relaxed and have intercourse as a means of expressing their love for each other.

The verbal and nonverbal communication preceding, during, and after intercourse also may act as a barometer for the relationship. "I can tell how we're doing," said one wife, "by whether or not we have intercourse and how he approaches me when we do. Sometimes he just rolls over when the lights are out and starts to rub my back. Other times he plays with my face while we talk and kisses me and waits till I reach for him. And still other times we each stay on our side of the bed so that our legs don't even touch."

Open Sexual Communication

Good communication is as stimulating as black coffee, and just as hard to sleep after.

ANNE MORROW
LINDBERGH

Sexually fulfilled partners are comfortable expressing what they enjoy and do not enjoy in the sexual experience. Unless both partners communicate their needs, preferences, and expectations to each other, neither is ever sure what the other wants. A classic example of the uncertain lover is the man who picks up a copy of *The Erotic Lover* in a bookstore and leafs through the pages until the topic on how to please a woman catches his eye. He reads that women enjoy having their breasts stimulated by their partner's tongue and teeth. Later that night in bed, he rolls over and begins to nibble on his partner's breasts. Meanwhile, she wonders what has possessed him and is unsure what to make of this new (possibly unpleasant) behavior. Sexually fulfilled partners take the guesswork out of their relationship by communicating preferences and giving feedback. This means using what some therapists call the touch-and-ask rule. Each touch and caress may include the question "How does that feel?" It is then the partner's responsibility to give feedback. If the caress does not feel good, she or he can say what does feel good. Guiding and moving the partner's hand or body are also ways of giving feedback.

But open sexual communication is more than expressing sexual preferences and giving feedback. Women wish that men were more aware of a number of sexual issues. Some of their comments follow:

- It does not impress women to hear about other women in the man's past.
- If men knew what it is like to be pregnant, they would not be so apathetic about birth control.
- Most women want more caressing, gentleness, kissing, and talking *before* and *after* intercourse.
- The loss of a woman's virginity may have negative psychological effects.
- Sometimes the woman wants sex even if the man does not. Sometimes she wants to be aggressive without being made to feel that she shouldn't be.
- Intercourse can be enjoyable without a climax.
- Many women do not have an orgasm from penetration only—they need direct stimulation of their clitoris by their partner's tongue or finger. Men should be interested in fulfilling their partner's sexual needs.

- Most women prefer to have sex in a monogamous love relationship.
- When a woman says "no," she means it. Women do not want men to expect sex every time they are alone with their partner.
- Many women enjoy sex in the morning, not just at night.
- Sex is *not* everything.
- Women need to be lubricated before penetration.
- Men should know more about menstruation.
- Many women are no more inhibited about sex than men.
- Women do not like men to roll over, go to sleep, or leave right after orgasm.
- Intercourse is more of a love relationship than a sex act for some women.
- The woman should not always be expected to supply a method of contraception. It is also the man's responsibility.
- Women tend to like a loving, gentle, patient, tender, and understanding partner. Rough sexual play can hurt and be a turn-off.
- Men should know that all women are not alike. Not all women are ready to jump in bed the same night you meet them, nor are they all as cold as a deep freeze. Each one is different.

Men also have a list of things they wish women knew about sex.

- Men do not always want to be the dominant partner—women should be aggressive.
- Men want women to enjoy sex totally and not be inhibited.
- Women should learn how to kiss passionately.
- Women need to return love while in bed. They should know how to give pleasurable fellatio.
- Women need to know a man's erogenous zones.
- Oral sex is good and enjoyable—not bad and unpleasant.
- Many men enjoy a lot of romantic foreplay and slow, aggressive sex. One man says, "I hate a dead screw."
- Men cannot keep up intercourse forever. Most men tire more easily than women.
- Looks are not everything.
- Women should know how to enjoy sex in different ways and different positions.
- Women should not expect a man to get a second erection right away.
- Many men enjoy sex in the morning.
- Pulling the hair on a man's body can hurt.
- Many men enjoy sex in a caring, loving, exclusive relationship.
- It is frustrating to stop sex play once it has started.
- Women should know that all men are not out to have intercourse with them. Some men like to talk and become friends.

Realistic Expectations

To achieve sexual fulfillment, expectations must be realistic. A couple's sexual needs, preferences, and expectations may not coincide. Women and men not only have different biological makeups but they also have been socialized differently. It is unrealistic to assume that your partner will want to have sex with the same frequency and in the same way that you do on all occasions.

A Healthy Attitude Toward Sex

The best way to hold a man is in your arms.

MAE WEST

Sexual fulfillment also depends on having a positive attitude toward sex. Inces-tuous or traumatic sexual experiences may create an intense negative attitude toward sex. Any sexual advance or contact causes the individual to become anxious and engenders the desire to escape or avoid the situation. Such nega-tive reactions to sex are best dealt with through therapy.

Negative attitudes about sex may also be learned from one's parents or peers. As an example of the latter, one wife said to another, "Sex is all men are inter-ested in. I just don't see what is so interesting about sex. I can certainly live without it."

• SEXUAL FULFILLMENT: SOME FACTS •

Sexual fulfillment also requires an awareness of basic facts about human sex-uality. In addition to the information about anatomy and physiology in Part VI (see pages 597–605), other facts important to sexual fulfillment relate to learned attitudes and behaviors, sex as a natural function, the development of sexual communication, "spectatoring" as an interference with sexual function-ing, the sexual response cycles of women and men, and the effects of health on sexual performance.

Sexual Attitudes and Behaviors Are Learned

Whether you believe that "Sex is sinful" or "If it feels good, do it," your sexual attitudes have been learned. Your parents and peers have had a major impact on your sexual attitudes, but there have been other influences as well: school, church or synagogue, and the media. Your attitudes about sex would have been different if the influences you were exposed to had been different.

The same is true of sexual behavior. The words you say, the sequence of events in lovemaking, the specific behaviors you engage in, and the positions you adopt during intercourse are a product of your and your partner's learning history. The fact that learning accounts for most sexual attitudes and behaviors is important since negative patterns can be unlearned and positive ones learned.

Sex Is a Natural Function

Although your sexual attitudes and behaviors are learned, your genital reflexes are innate. "To define sex as natural means that just as an individual cannot be taught to sweat or how to digest food, a man cannot be taught to have an erec-tion, nor can a woman be taught how to lubricate vaginally" (Kolodny et al.,

1979, p. 479). Sex therapy is often aimed at minimizing the impact of negative learning experiences so that the natural processes can take over.

Effective Sexual Communication Takes Time and Effort

Most of us who have been reared in homes in which discussions about sex were infrequent or nonexistent may have developed relatively few skills in talking about sex. Shifting to sex talk with our partner from, say, talking about current events may seem awkward. Overcoming our awkward feelings requires retraining ourselves so that sex becomes as easy for us to talk about as what we had for lunch. Some suggestions that may be helpful in developing effective sexual communication include the following.

SAY SEX WORDS

Develop a list with your partner that contains all of the technical and slang words you can think of about sex. Then alternate with your partner, reading one word after the other from the list. Laughter, embarrassed or otherwise, usually accompanies the first few readings, but repeat the readings until each of you is as comfortable with the words on the sex list as with those on a grocery list. It usually takes several readings over a period of weeks before you will develop a neutral reaction to the sex words. This reaction is important for you to feel comfortable talking about sex with your partner.

READ SEXUALITY BOOKS; SEE MOVIES

To give you and your partner a common focus for discussing sexual issues, you might consider reading a chapter or two from one of several books available in your local bookstore. *For Each Other: Sharing Sexual Intimacy* (Barbach, 1982), *How to Make Love to a Woman* (Morgenstern, 1982), and *How to Make Love to a Man* (Penney, 1981) are examples. Or consider seeing a sexually explicit R- or X-rated film. Although some people are offended by such films, others find them exciting. Whatever your reaction, the value of the book or movie will be in its initiating communication about sex.

ASK OPEN-ENDED QUESTIONS

To learn more about your partner, ask specific questions that cannot be answered with a yes or no. Examples include "What does orgasm feel like to you?" "Tell me about the sexual activities you like best," and "How often do you feel the need for sex?"

GIVE REFLECTIVE FEEDBACK

When your partner shares a very intimate aspect of her- or himself, it is important to respond in a nonjudgmental way. One way to do this is to reflect back what your partner tells you.

Suppose Mary tells Jim that the best sex for her is when he is holding and caressing her, not when they are actually having intercourse. An inappropriate response by Jim to her disclosure would be "Something must be the matter with you." This would undoubtedly stop Mary from further telling her feelings to

We are programmed always to have a purpose, to strive, to succeed, but not to relax and enjoy being alive and feeling good.

LONNIE BARBACH

Jim. But Jim's reflective statement, "Our being close is what you like best in our relationship," confirms for Mary that he understands how she feels and that her feelings are accepted.

"Spectatoring" Interferes with Sexual Functioning

One of the obstacles to sexual functioning is spectatoring. When Masters and Johnson (1970) observed how individuals actually behave during sexual intercourse, they reported a tendency for sexually dysfunctional partners to act as spectators by mentally observing their own and their partners' sexual performance. The man would focus on whether he was having an erection, how complete it was, and whether it would last. He might also watch to see whether his partner was having an orgasm. His partner would ask corresponding questions about herself and him.

CONSIDERATION • Spectatoring as Masters and Johnson conceived it interferes with each partner's sexual enjoyment because it creates anxiety about performance; and anxiety blocks performance. A man who worries about getting an erection reduces his chances of doing so. A woman who is anxious about achieving an orgasm probably will not. The desirable alternative to spectatoring is to relax, focus on and enjoy your own pleasure, and permit your body's natural sexual responsiveness to take over.

Spectatoring is not limited to sexually dysfunctional couples and is not necessarily associated with psychopathology. Spectatoring is a reaction to our concern that we and our partners are performing consistent with our expectations. We all probably have engaged in spectatoring to some degree. It is when spectatoring is continual that performance is impaired.

Women and Men Have Different Sexual Response Cycles

As the spectatoring problem reveals, human sexuality has a psychosocial component. The other major component is the biophysical, which includes the sexual response cycle. Masters and Johnson, who observed the sexual response cycles of more than 10,000 individuals, reported that women and men do not necessarily progress through the cycle the same way (see Figures 13.2 and 13.3).

The four phases of the sexual response cycle are excitement, plateau, orgasm, and resolution. These phases represent what people report they experience when they have sexual intercourse. First, there is the period when sexual activity is about to begin (excitement); then the partners give pleasure to each other for some time but not to the point of orgasm (plateau); then one or both have a climax (orgasm phase); and this is followed by a period of relaxation and a return to the state that preceded sexual excitement (resolution phase).

The female alternative sexual response cycles are illustrated in Figure 13.2. Once sexual excitement begins, there may be three outcomes: progression from excitement to plateau to orgasm to resolution (see line C); or progression from excitement to plateau to orgasm to plateau to orgasm (or to a number of additional orgasms) to resolution (see line A); or progression from excitement to plateau to resolution without experiencing an orgasm (see line B).

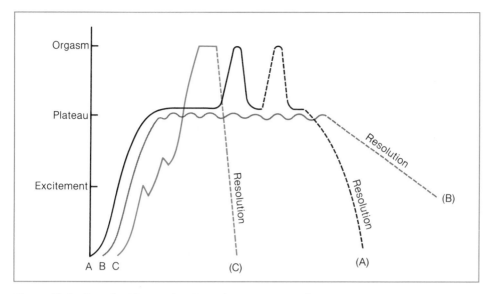

Figure 13.2 **Female Alternative Sexual Response Cycles**
The female may experience one of three patterns in her response to sexual stimulation: Pattern C, the typical response, involves moving from excitement to plateau to orgasm (one) to resolution. Pattern B involves becoming excited, stabilizing at the plateau phase, and moving toward resolution. Pattern A involves having an orgasm, returning to the plateau phase, and then back to another orgasm. This latter pattern may be repeated again and is referred to as multiple orgasm.

Source: Human Sexual Response by William H. Masters and Virginia E. Johnson, Boston: Little, Brown and Company, 1966. Copyright by Masters and Johnson, 1966. p. 5.

The male alternative sexual response cycles are illustrated in Figure 13.3. Once sexual response begins and assuming that both partners are willing for the male to complete the cycle, there is essentially only one outcome—progressing through plateau to orgasm to resolution. Although men may have additional orgasms, there is usually a considerable refractory (or recovery) period before doing so.

CONSIDERATION • Observation of the sexual cycles of the two genders reveals two essential differences: (1) The male usually climaxes once during sexual intercourse, but the female may not climax at all or may climax several times. (2) When the female does experience several climaxes, she is capable of doing so with only a brief time (seconds) between climaxes. In contrast, the male needs a considerable refractory period (minutes to hours) before he is capable of additional orgasms.

Physical and Mental Health Affect Sexual Performance

Effective sexual functioning requires good physical and mental health. Physically, this means regular exercise, good nutrition, lack of disease, and lack of fatigue. Regular exercise, whether through walking, jogging, swimming, or bicycling, is associated with increased sexual activity (Frauman, 1982). Also, as might be expected, lack of disease is related to good sexual functioning. Sexual

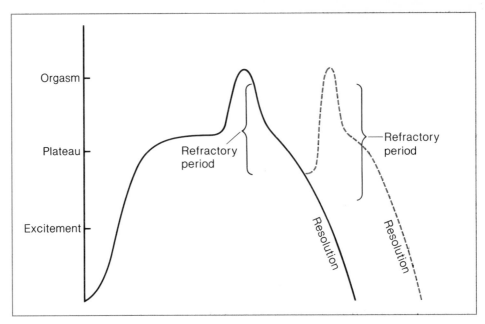

Figure 13.3 Male Alternative Sexual Response Cycles
The male typically experiences the pattern indicated by the solid line in his response to sexual stimulation. He becomes excited and moves through the plateau, orgasm, and resolution phases of the sexual response cycle. The pattern indicated by the dotted line describes the pattern whereby, after a brief refractory period during which the male does not want additional stimulation, he enters the cycle at the plateau phase and has another orgasm, which is followed by another refractory period and resolution.

Source: Human Sexual Response by William H. Masters and Virginia E. Johnson, Boston: Little, Brown and Company, 1966. Copyright by Masters and Johnson, 1966. p. 5.

> I got the bill for my surgery. Now I know what those doctors were wearing masks for.
>
> JAMES BORAN

behavior is dependent on the proper nerve connections between the brain, spinal cord, and genitals. Any disease that affects neural transmission, such as multiple sclerosis, may result in an impairment in sexual performance.

Physical illness may lead to depression, which may affect a person's sexuality. The ill person may feel emotionally devastated and lose all desire for sex (Mathew & Weinman, 1982). "When I found out that I had cancer, I went numb. And sex seems to have disappeared as a meaningful part of my life," said one man. But there may be other causes for depression than physical illness. Failing in school, at work, or in a love relationship can also trigger feelings of depression and temporarily turn off sexual interest. Premenstrual syndrome is an example of how sexuality may be affected by physical and mental factors (Exhibit 13.1) and how sexual fulfillment depends on a healthy body and mind. When these factors are optimum, sexual happiness is likely to soar.

• SEXUAL FULFILLMENT: SOME MYTHS •

Sexual fulfillment also involves recognizing that some of the information that passes for fact in our society is actually myth. Let us examine some of the more prevalent myths.

Good physical health is associated with increased sexual activity.

Myth 1: Simultaneous Orgasm Is the Ultimate Sexual Experience

Having an orgasm at the same time as your partner may be an enjoyable experience, but there are two problems in achieving such a goal. First, it is difficult to fully enjoy your own orgasm while trying to do what is necessary to assist your partner in achieving his or hers. Second, men and women react differently in their bodily movements at the time of orgasm. As McCary (1976) expressed it:

> The man's tendency is to plunge into the vagina as deeply as possible at the moment of his orgasm, to hold this position for a length of time, and to follow, perhaps, with one or two deep deliberate thrusts. The woman's tendency, on the other hand, is to have the same stroking, plunging movements of the earlier stages of intercourse continued during the orgasmic reaction, with perhaps an acceleration of the thrusts and an increase of pressure in the vulva area. These two highly pleasurable patterns of movement are obviously incompatible. Since they cannot both be executed at the same time, whichever pattern

· Exhibit 13.1 ·

PREMENSTRUAL SYNDROME*

Also known as PMS, premenstrual syndrome refers to the physical and psychological problems a woman experiences from the time of ovulation to the beginning of, and sometimes during, menstruation. There are a number of symptoms, which may include the following.

Psychological
Tension
Depression
Irritability
Lethargy

Excessive energy
Altered sex drive

Neurological
Migraine
Epilepsy

Respiratory
Asthma
Rhinitis

Dermatological
Acne
Herpes

Orthopedic
Joint pains
Backaches

But it is the experience of the woman that makes the syndrome real.

Alice A., a 35-year-old housewife and mother, is usually a friendly and productive person, but two weeks out of each month she is overwhelmed by extreme irritability, tension, and depression. "It's as if my mind can't keep up with my body. I cook things to put in the freezer, clean, wash windows, work in the yard—anything to keep busy. My mind is saying slow down, but my body won't quit. When I go to bed at night, I'm exhausted. And everything gets on my nerves—the phone ringing, birds singing—everything! My skin feels prickly, my back hurts, and my face feels so tight that it's painful. I scream at my husband over ridiculous things like asking for a clean pair of socks. I hate myself even when I'm doing it, but I have no control. I can't stand being around people, and the only way I can even be civil at parties is to have several drinks.

This lasts for about a week, and then I wake up one morning feeling as if the bottom has dropped out of my life. It's as if something awful is going to happen, but I don't know what it is, and don't know how to stop it. I don't even have the energy to make the beds. Every movement is an effort. I burst out crying for no reason at crazy times, like when I'm fixing breakfast or grocery shopping. My husband thinks I'm angry with him, and I can't explain what's wrong because I don't know myself. After about four days of fighting off the depression, I just give up, take the phone off the hook, and stay in bed. It's terrifying. I feel panicky—trapped.

Then one morning I wake up and suddenly feel like myself. The sun is shining, and I like life again.*

Between 5 and 10 percent of women experience PMS to the degree that Alice does. Some people have attributed instances of child abuse, alcoholism, divorce, and suicide to PMS. Recently, two British women introduced PMS as part of their legal defense for murder.

Other women experience a milder form of PMS, including different symptoms in varying degrees. But because more than 150 symptoms have

*Premenstrual syndrome: The world's oldest disease? Copyright © by Rebecca R. Davis. Reprinted by permission.

been associated with PMS, there is little agreement about when a person is experiencing the phenomenon. The only agreement on premenstrual syndrome seems to be that the individual's specific symptoms occur together at regular intervals.

There also is no agreement on the causes of PMS and even less agreement on the cure. Hormones, diet, and culture are among the suggested causes. Some physicians treat the woman with PMS as though it is all in her head and will go away in a few days. Others view the problem as an imbalance of hormones and prescribe progesterone (Dalton, 1977). Still others focus on nutrition and exercise. Diet changes include eliminating alcohol, sugar, salt, and caffeine. Eating several small meals every two to four hours is also suggested (Harrison, 1982).

But increasingly, PMS is being recognized as a legitimate set of symptoms requiring treatment. The Premenstrual Syndrome Clinic in Reading, Massachusetts, has treated more than 1,000 women. Their approach to therapy is multidimensional, including diet, exercise, vitamins, and progesterone (if necessary). They also assist women in diagnosing PMS and demonstrating its impact on their lives. Such diagnosis is facilitated by getting women to chart their reactions consistent with their cycle.

The National PMS Society (P.O. Box 11467, Durham, NC 27703; phone 919-489-6577) may be contacted for further information and help.

is carried out during simultaneous orgasm must perforce detract from the full pleasure of one of the partners. (p. 287)

To avoid these incompatibilities and distractions, many couples adopt a "my turn-your turn" pattern in their lovemaking. The man delays his climax until his partner has climaxed (one or more times). In this way the woman can focus on the sexual sensations that are being produced in her body without worrying about whether her partner is climaxing. After she has achieved sexual satisfaction, she can devote her attention to her partner, and he can focus on enjoying his own climax.

Myth 2: Intercourse During Menstruation Is Harmful

Although a woman may prefer not to have intercourse during her period because of an unusually heavy flow or because of cramps, there is no harmful effect on her or on her partner if they do so.

DATA • *Seventy percent of the respondents in one study who were under age 35 reported having intercourse during menstruation.* (Paige, 1978)

Some women report that orgasm helps to relieve menstrual cramps. A couple's doubts about engaging in intercourse during this time may be associated with feelings about menstrual blood, which many people have been taught is "bad."

The taboo against intercourse during menstruation is culturally pervasive and has a long history. Both genders often learn to call menstruation "the curse," "doomsday," or "being sick." The Old Testament warns that a man sleeping with a woman during her period "shall be unclean seven days and every bed whereon he lieth shall be unclean" (Lev. 15:24). For many, breaking this taboo is difficult.

Myth 3: Sex Equals Intercourse and Orgasm

Once a couple begin kissing, embracing, and taking off their clothes, it is assumed that intercourse and orgasm must follow. This may be the preference of both partners, but it is not always the case.

DATA • *Seven of 10 women in a study of 20,000 women said achieving orgasm was not essential for a satisfying sex life.* (Sarrel & Sarrel, 1980)

One woman said, "Intercourse is really for him. I'd just as soon cuddle next to him, have him kiss me, play with my face, and curl my hair with his fingers." For these people sexual interaction is pleasure producing though not necessarily orgasm producing.

It is also assumed that to omit intercourse from lovemaking is to leave things incomplete, to be a failure. Since so many values in our culture are encapsulated by ideas like "finish what you start," the partner who is not particularly interested in intercourse nonetheless may feel compelled to have intercourse.

A pleasurable sexual experience does not necessarily include orgasm.

This feeling, in turn, may create negative feelings toward the partner and the relationship. Such feelings might be avoided if the partners do not insist on intercourse or orgasm each time they want to enjoy each other's sexuality.

Myth 4: Sexual Boredom Is Inevitable

Since the frequency of intercourse tends to decrease the longer the partners know each other, it is assumed that sexual boredom is the cause and that such boredom is inevitable. But many partners avoid boredom by introducing variety into their sex lives. Some sex partners vary the time of their sexual encounters (from weekend nights to weekend afternoons), place (from bed to bath or shower), context (from home to motel or friend's apartment), and behaviors (oral sex and different positions). Others use pornography (an X-rated video cassette), devices (vibrators), lotions, and erotic clothes (like those from Frederick's of Hollywood). Still others play "flip a page" to enhance their sexual relationship. One woman gave her partner a copy of *More Joy of Sex* on their anniversary and said, "You pick a page and let's do it."

CONSIDERATION • Variety only works in dissipating sexual boredom when the partners feel emotionally connected to each other, care about each other, and demonstrate this care through words and behaviors.

Myth 5: Masturbation Ends with Marriage

In a study of more than 1,000 married women, 61 percent reported they enjoyed masturbating (Grosskopf, 1983). Although unavailability of the husband (through absence, illness, or disinclination) is the primary motivation for masturbation among wives, some prefer it as a variation. "I climax best when I masturbate," said one wife, "and while I enjoy my husband's penis inside me, I also enjoy turning myself on."

DATA • *Husbands masturbate more than wives. In one study 43 percent of the husbands in contrast to 22 percent of the wives reported masturbating more than once a week.* (Petersen et al., 1983b)

Just as masturbation before marriage occurs in private, the same pattern continues in marriage. More than 70 percent of the wives in Grosskopf's sample said their husbands did not know of their masturbating. Some spouses are shocked to learn that their partners occasionally masturbate and regard their doing so as rejection of themselves. These people firmly believe that masturbation should end with marriage.

• FEMALE SEXUAL DYSFUNCTIONS •

It is not uncommon for a sexually involved couple to have a sexual problem. Sex therapists refer to such problems as sexual dysfunctions. The existence of a sexual dysfunction implies that the partners want something to happen that is not happening (for example, achieve orgasm) or to stop something from happening that is happening (vaginismus). In this section we examine lack of sexual desire, inability to achieve orgasm, pain during intercourse (dyspareunia), and inability to control constrictions of the vagina (vaginismus) as the major sexual dysfunctions among women.

> CONSIDERATION • Although we discuss treatments for both female and male sexual dysfunctions in this chapter, sex therapy is usually indicated. The name of a certified sex therapist in your area can be located by calling 202-462-1171 or by writing to the American Association of Sex Educators, Counselors, and Therapists (11 Dupont Circle, NW, Suite 220, Washington, D.C. 20036). A sex therapist will usually ask you to complete a form similar to the Personal Sex History Inventory.

Lack of Sexual Desire

The person who lacks sexual desire, a problem also referred to as inhibited sexual desire, never initiates sexual activity and is rarely receptive to another who does. Sex is a bore and a chore. Although women more frequently experience lack of sexual desire, men may also lack such interest. Lack of sexual desire may be primary (the person has never been interested in sex) or secondary (in the past the person demonstrated interest in sex with the same or different partner but does not do so presently).

A problem well stated is a problem half solved.

CHARLES F. KETTERING

DATA • *Two percent of 367 college-educated women characterized their sexual satisfaction as "I don't care one way or the other."* (Coleman et al., 1983)

Several reasons may account for a lack of sexual desire or low libido.

Restrictive child rearing The unresponsive woman usually was told as a child that sexual stimulation and sexual pleasure were sinful and dirty. As a result, she has learned to feel guilty and ashamed of her sexual feelings.

Passive sexual role In addition, the woman with low libido has often been taught to be a passive and dependent sexual partner. The silent message of her socialization has been that it is not feminine to lose herself in sexual ecstasy. Since such abandonment is incompatible with the passive feminine role, she does not permit herself to become sexually excited.

Psychological factors The person who lacks interest in sex may be depressed because of individual or relationship dissatisfaction, may want to avoid sexual involvement because of fear of pregnancy or genital herpes, or may be reacting to previous negative experiences such as incest or rape.

Physical factors Disease, drugs, fatigue, and infection may also erase a person's sexual responsiveness. A nurse said, "After I take care of the kids all day and work the night shift at the hospital, sex is the last thing in the world I'm interested in. And when my partner touches me, I just have to tell him the truth—I'm not interested."

PERSONAL SEX HISTORY INVENTORY

The purpose of this inventory is to obtain information about your sexual self. By answering these questions as completely and as accurately as you can, you will facilitate your therapeutic program. Please complete this history when you are alone and do not discuss your answers with your partner. It is understandable that you might be concerned about what happens to this form. Because much or all of this information is highly personal, your inventory is strictly confidential. No outsider is permitted to see your answers without your written permission.

I. General   Date _____

Name _____

Address _____

Telephone numbers: Office _____

Home_____

Relationship status: Married_____;
Divorced_____; Separated_____;
Single_____; Living together_____;
Widowed_____

Are you currently living with a
partner?_____ How long?_____

How do you feel about the person with
whom you are currently involved or with
whom you have been most recently
involved? _____
_____

Is your sexual orientation
Heterosexual_____? Homosexual_____?
Bisexual_____?

II. Background

1. What did you learn about sex from your parents? Your teachers? Your church? Your peers?
2. What sexual behaviors make you feel guilty?
3. How much emotional involvement have you had with your sexual partners? How have you felt about this level of involvement?
4. What sexual fantasies do you have? How do you feel about your fantasies?
5. What is the content of your sexual dreams? How do you feel about your sexual dreams?
6. How do you feel about your mother? Your father?
7. When you use the word *sex*, what do you mean? List five adjectives for sex.
8. What are your feelings about your body? The body of someone of the opposite gender? The same gender?
9. List the various sexual experiences you have had, your age at the time of first occurrence, how you felt about the

(continued)

experience then, and how you feel about having similar experiences now. Use a form like the following:

Experience

Age_____

Feelings Then_____

Feelings Now_____

10. Describe any sexual experiences you would label "negative."
11. Have you or any sexual partner ever had a sexually transmitted disease? Name or describe these diseases. What was the outcome?
12. What are your feelings about oral sex?
13. What drugs do you take? How often?
14. When did you first masturbate? What is your current frequency? How do you feel about masturbation?
15. Describe any specific sexual problem you are having. How long have you had this problem? What has your partner's response been to this problem?
16. What have you done to try and resolve the problem? What was the result?
17. Have you consulted a therapist before? Who? When?
18. What is the state of your physical health? Are your menstrual periods regular? Do you have menstrual cramps or premenstrual tension? How severe are these problems?
19. Have you experienced what you define to be an orgasm?
20. On a scale from 0 to 10, how would you describe your level of interest in sex?

Sex therapy for low libido in a woman may involve R & R (rest and relaxation), reeducation, improving the relationship with her partner, the use of sensate focus, and masturbation or hormones. Reeducation includes systematically examining the thoughts, feelings, and attitudes the woman was taught as a child and reevaluating them. The goal is to redefine sexual involvement so that it is viewed as a positive, desirable, pleasurable experience. Reeducation also means discarding the belief that one must feel interest in sex before one can enjoy it. Rather, the therapist recommends that the woman become involved in sexual activity first. The premise is that "you can act yourself into a new way of thinking quicker than you can think your way into a new way of acting."

CONSIDERATION • The woman's relationship with her partner is central to her sexual enjoyment with him. Does she love him? Does she trust him? Does she feel emotionally close to him? Unless the relationship with her partner is loving and reciprocal, gains in increasing sexual responsiveness may be minimal.

The woman and her partner are also encouraged to practice sensate focus exercises. Introduced more than 20 years ago by Masters and Johnson, sensate focus (see Figure 13.4) is the mutual exploration and discovery of the partners through touch, massage, fondling, or tracing. Specific guidelines for the exercises include the following: (1) Both partners are nude. (2) The partners are not to have intercourse or touch each other's genitals, and the man is not to touch the woman's breasts. (3) One partner is to give pleasure by touching and gently massaging the other. (4) The other partner is to pay attention to the pleasurable feelings of being touched and gently massaged and to let the other know when he or she does something that is or is not pleasurable. (5) The partners are to switch roles so that each gives and gets sensual pleasure. Sensate focus creates an environment in which the woman is permitted to explore her sexual feelings without having to perform for her partner.

The woman may be encouraged to masturbate—a suggestion also made to women who have difficulty climaxing. Some physicians recommend testosterone to increase a woman's interest in sex. Although unwanted facial hair may occur in 10 to 15 percent of the cases, it may heighten her libido (Greenblatt, 1980).

Inability to Achieve Orgasm

Masters and Johnson characterized women who have never had an orgasm as having primary orgasmic dysfunction (also known as primary anorgasmia or preorgasm). Those who have had an orgasm by any other means at any time in the past but who are unable to do so currently are regarded as having secondary orgasmic dysfunction (also known as secondary anorgasmia).

DATA • *Thirteen percent of 365 college-educated women said they never experienced orgasm.* (Coleman et al., 1983)

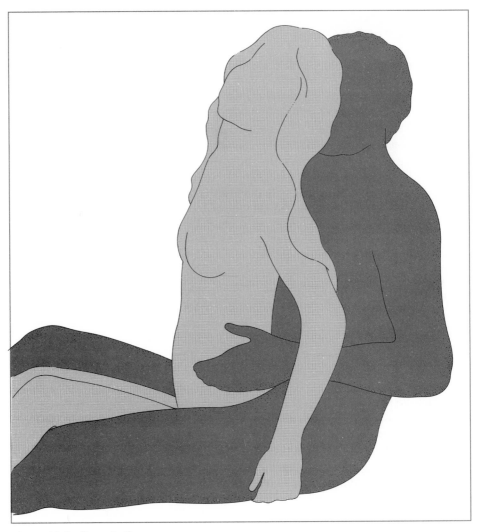

Figure 13.4 Sensate Focus

Source: Human Sexual Inadequacy by William H. Masters and Virginia E. Johnson. Published by Little, Brown, and Company, Boston, Mass.: 1966, p. 300. Reprinted by permission.

Some of the causes of inability to achieve orgasm are similar to those for lack of sexual interest (restrictive childrearing, passive sexual role, and so on. Other causes include the following.

Focusing on partner   Many women have been taught to feel it is their duty to satisfy their partners sexually. But having an orgasm requires that a woman focus on the sexual sensations she is experiencing. If a woman is overly intent on pleasing her partner, she may do so at the expense of her own orgasm.

Negative feelings about mate   If the woman is angry at her partner or feels that he is using her sexually, she may "withhold" having an orgasm. "If I have an orgasm, he'll think I'm having a good time and really enjoying him," said one woman. "I wouldn't give him that kind of pleasure. I'm very mad at my partner now because I just found out he has been seeing other women when I'm not around."

Too little stimulation   The duration of stimulation is associated with whether a woman climaxes. In a study of about 1,000 wives (Brewer, 1981), two-fifths reported climaxing after one to 10 minutes of foreplay. When foreplay lasted 21 minutes or more, three-fifths reported climaxing almost every time. Similarly, the longer her husband's penis stayed erect and inside her, the greater her chance of having an orgasm during intercourse. If penetration was one minute, 25 percent reported orgasm; between one and 11 minutes, 50 percent reported climax; and if penetration lasted more than 15 minutes, two-thirds reported climax. A woman's orgasm is also related to how accurately her partner is aware of what he does that gives her sexual pleasure (Kilmann et al., 1984).

Fear of letting go   Some women feel it would be too embarrassing to lose control in an orgasmic experience, so they deliberately block their sexual arousal.

Too much alcohol   While moderate drinking of alcohol has the effect of inducing relaxation and increasing sexual arousal, heavy drinking has a depressant effect on the woman's orgasmic response.

Too little self-knowledge   Some women have not discovered the kinds of stimulation that produce orgasm either through masturbation or with a partner. Most women report that stimulation on or around the clitoris is necessary for them to achieve an orgasm.

Too high expectations   Some women feel they should have an orgasm during every sexual encounter and that not doing so is evidence that they are not normal. But such expectations produce a great deal of anxiety, which blocks the ability to have an orgasm even though they may try desperately to do so.

DATA • *In a study of 30 students, 22 percent expressed a desire for more frequent orgasms.*   (Sholty et al., 1984)

Since the causes for primary and secondary orgasmic dysfunction are extremely variable, the treatment must be tailored for the particular woman. We have already discussed sensate focus exercises to encourage a woman to explore her sexual feelings and to increase her comfort with her partner. In addition, the therapist may recommend that the woman masturbate to orgasm. Such self-stimulation has the benefit of providing direct feedback to the woman of the type of stimulation she enjoys, eliminates being distracted by a partner, and gives her complete control of the stimulation.

A detailed discussion of using masturbation to encourage orgasm can be found in *Becoming Orgasmic: A Sexual Growth Program for Women* (Heiman et al., 1976). The book deals with all aspects of masturbation, including the feelings of shame and guilt often associated with it.

After the woman has learned how to bring herself to orgasm through masturbation, she is encouraged to teach her partner how to stimulate her manually to orgasm, first while not having intercourse. Finally, if the partners prefer, the woman is taught how to have an orgasm during intercourse by using the "bridge method."

> The couple make love until the woman is aroused. Then the man penetrates, either in the female superior position or one of the variations of the side-to-side position. Then, with the penis contained, the man (or the woman) stimulates the woman's clitoris. When she nears orgasm, clitoral stimulation ceases at her signal, and the couple commence thrusting actively to bring about her orgasm. (Kaplan, 1974, p. 138)

Pain During Intercourse

Pain during intercourse, or dyspareunia, occurs in about 10 percent of gynecological patients and may be caused by vaginal infection, lack of lubrication, a rigid hymen, or an improperly positioned uterus or ovary. Because the causes of dyspareunia are often medical, a physician should be consulted. Sometimes surgery is recommended to remove the hymen.

Dyspareunia also may be psychologically caused. Guilt, anxiety, or unresolved feelings about a previous trauma such as rape or child molestation may be operative. Therapy may be indicated.

Constricted Vagina

A less common sexual dysfunction in which the vaginal opening and outer third of the canal constricts involuntarily, making penetration impossible, is known as vaginismus. Like anorgasmia, vaginismus may be primary or secondary. Primary vaginismus means that the vaginal muscles have always constricted to prevent penetration of any object, including tampons. Secondary vaginismus, the more usual variety, suggests that the vagina has permitted penetration in the past but currently constricts when penetration is imminent.

Vaginismus is most often found in women whose background has included traditional religious teachings suggesting intercourse is dirty and shameful. Other background factors include rape, incest, repeated childhood molestation, or organic difficulties. Examples of the latter are a poorly healed episiotomy (an incision in the perineum to prevent injury to the vagina during childbirth), a poorly stretched hymen, infections or sores near the vaginal opening, or a sexually transmitted disease. The woman who fears pain during penetration will try to avoid it, sometimes unconsciously.

Assuming that vaginismus is not caused by an organic or physical problem (for which a physician should be consulted), the treatment is first to have the woman introduce her index finger into her vagina while she relaxes. Then two fingers are introduced into the vagina and this exercise is repeated until she feels relaxed enough to contain the penis. Once the woman learns that she is capable of vaginal containment of the penis, she is usually able to have intercourse without difficulty. Of course, therapy focusing on the woman's cognitions and perceptions about sex and sexuality with her particular partner precede the finger exercises.

Sexual dysfunctions among women are only one side of the bed. Men may be troubled by sexual apathy, inability to achieve and maintain an erection (erectile dysfunction), inability to delay ejaculation as long as they or their partners would like (premature ejaculation), or inability to ejaculate at all (ejaculatory incompetence).

Sexual Apathy

It is a myth that men are always ready for sex. Some are apathetic or completely uninterested. "I just don't have any desire for sex," said one man. "And if I never have to do it again, I'll feel relieved."

There are many causes for a low sex drive in men: negative feelings about the partner, hormonal insufficiency, career fatigue, fear of parenthood, terror of intimacy, guilt over extrapartner relationships, drugs, and a "too aggressive partner." In addition, the cultural expectation that men are always interested in sex may threaten a man's feelings of masculinity. Treatment for sexual apathy among men often begins with giving them permission not to be interested in sex. The therapist tells the male client not to masturbate or have intercourse until the next session. Then the contributing factors can be explored.

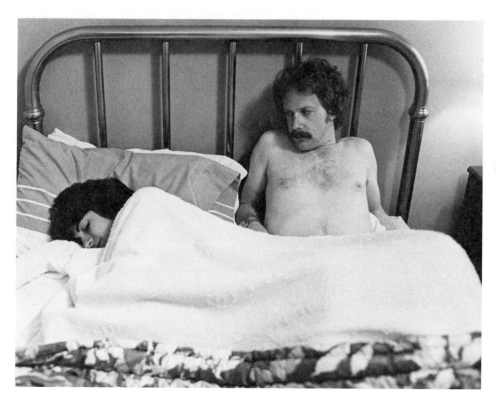

At times either partner may feel sexual apathy.

Erectile Dysfunction

Erectile dysfunction, also known as impotence, is the lack or loss of an erection firm enough for intercourse, which may occur during foreplay, the moment of penetration, or intercourse. Generally, a man who cannot get an erection feels humiliated and embarrassed. Few problems are as devastating to the man as a penis that will not become and remain erect.

Like some female sexual dysfunctions, erectile dysfunction may be primary (the man has never been able to have intercourse) or secondary (he is currently unable to have intercourse). Erectile dysfunction may also be situational—the man can get an erection in one situation (say, through masturbation) but not in another (such as intercourse). Occasional, isolated episodes of inability to get an erection do not warrant the label of erectile dysfunction, nor is treatment necessary.

Primary or secondary impotence may be caused by organic or psychosocial (psychogenic) factors. Organic factors include endocrine malfunctions like diabetes, low testosterone levels, neurologic disorders like multiple sclerosis, and medications such as those for high blood pressure. Treatment of organically caused dysfunction is medical and may include the use of a penile implant, which consists of either semirigid rods of silicone rubber that are surgically inserted into the penis to make it hard, resulting in a permanent semierection, or inflatable cylinders implanted in the penis.

CONSIDERATION • More often, erectile dysfunction is caused by psychosocial factors, and anxiety heads the list. The anxious man cannot get an erection because an erection depends on a state of relaxation. For example, as a male, assume you are in a classroom and a platoon of Russian soldiers walks through the door, putting a gun to the head of each male student. Their leader announces, "You guys have 30 seconds to get an erection or we'll blow your heads off." The demand for such a performance will create intense anxiety, and no man in the class will be capable of getting an erection.

A similar situation may happen in the bedroom. The woman makes it clear to the man that she expects him to have an erection and to have intercourse with her. Whereas such an expectation is a welcome situation for some men, the man who has been impotent in the past begins to fear that he will not be able to get an erection and satisfy her. His anxiety about performing and fear of her disapproval if he fails help to ensure that he will not get an erection. What follows is a devastating cycle of negative experiences locking the man into impotence at each sexual encounter: anxiety, impotence, embarrassment, followed by anxiety, impotence, and so on.

The man also has his own ideas of how he is supposed to perform as a male. Even if the partner is sympathetic and supportive, it may be his own self-imposed performance demands that create the anxiety that interferes with achieving an erection.

Anxiety may also be related to alcohol use. After more than the usual number of drinks, the man may initiate sex but fail to achieve an erection. He becomes anxious and struggles even more to get an erection, ensuring that he will not. Although alcohol may be responsible for his initial failure, his impotence continues because of his anxiety.

Treatment for erectile dysfunction of psychosocial origin begins with the instruction that the couple not have intercourse. If there is no expectation for intercourse, the associated anxiety is minimized. The therapist then discusses with the couple how anxiety (and alcohol, if this is an issue) inhibits erection. The purpose of this information is to help the partners understand the man's erectile dysfunction rather than continue to be mystified by its occurrence.

The partners are also instructed to begin sensate focus exercises and the man is encouraged to give pleasure to his partner through manual or oral stimulation. After several sensate focus sessions, during which there is no pressure to perform and the man learns alternative ways to pleasure his partner, he is more likely to have an erection.

Premature Ejaculation

Premature ejaculation, also known as rapid ejaculation, is the man's inability to control the ejaculatory reflex.

DATA • *Eighty-one percent of more than 65,000 men in one survey reported that there are times they ejaculate too quickly (7 percent said it happened frequently).* (Petersen et al., 1983a)

Whether a man ejaculates too soon is a matter of definition, depending on his and his partner's desires. Some partners define a rapid ejaculation in positive terms. One woman said that she felt pleased that her partner was so excited by her that he "couldn't control himself." Another said, "The sooner we get it over with, the better."

The cause of premature ejaculation lies in early learning experiences. Men report that their early masturbation and intercourse experiences were hurried. They felt pressure to ejaculate as soon as they could. One example is the male who had to masturbate quickly before his parents could discover what he was doing; another is the man whose prostitute partners would try to make him climax quickly so they could get to the next customer.

DATA • *The average duration of intercourse before ejaculation in men is two minutes.* (Hong, 1984)

Use of the squeeze technique developed by Masters and Johnson, is the most effective procedure for treating premature ejaculation. The woman stimulates her partner's penis manually until he signals her that he feels the urge to ejaculate. At his signal she places her thumb on the underside of his penis and squeezes hard for three to four seconds. The man will lose his urge to ejaculate. After 30 seconds she resumes stimulation, applying the squeeze technique again when her partner signals. The important rule to remember is that the woman should apply the squeeze technique whenever the man gives the slightest hint of readiness to ejaculate. (The squeeze technique can also be used by the man during masturbation to teach himself to delay his ejaculation.)

Other techniques are sometimes used in treating premature ejaculation but are generally not effective. These include the use of several condoms (one man used six), ointments such as Detane that anesthetize the head of the penis, and distraction (counting, playing tennis in one's head). Half of the 65,000 plus men referred to earlier who reported premature ejaculation said they deal with the problem by stimulating their partner another way (Petersen et al., 1983a). One-fourth said they simply wait and start again.

Ejaculatory Incompetence

In contrast to the man who experiences rapid ejaculation, the man who experiences ejaculatory incompetence cannot ejaculate at all, even after prolonged intercourse. Also referred to as retarded ejaculation, absence of ejaculation, and inhibited ejaculation, ejaculatory incompetence may be primary or secondary. Primary ejaculatory incompetence describes the man who has never ejaculated inside a woman's vagina. Secondary ejaculatory incompetence, the more common form, refers to the current inability to ejaculate inside the woman. It is not unusual for ejaculatory incompetence to be situational—it may occur with one partner but not another or the same partner on one occasion but not on another.

CONSIDERATION • Most causes of ejaculatory incompetence are psychological. For example, one husband reported that for 33 years his wife would not let him ejaculate inside of her because she did not want to get pregnant. As a result, he learned to prolong his orgasm and to take his penis out of her vagina before ejaculating. After his wife's menopause, she wanted him to ejaculate inside of her but he could not.

Lack of sexual excitement and feeling that the vagina is a disgusting place to ejaculate are other psychological causes of ejaculatory incompetence.

In treating this condition, the therapist discusses the psychological issues and recommends sensate focus exercises. Following these exercises the woman manually stimulates the man to ejaculate. After they are confident that he can be brought to orgasm manually, she stimulates him to a high level of sexual excitement and, at the moment of orgasm, inserts his penis into her vagina so that he ejaculates inside her. After several sessions of first hand, then vaginal stimulation, the woman gradually reduces the amount of time she manually manipulates her partner and increases the amount of time she stimulates him with her vagina.

• SEXUAL FULFILLMENT IN MIDDLE AGE •

The assumed focus of our discussion on sexual fulfillment has been on the sexuality of youthful partners. Although the same information is relevant to those in their middle years, some people seem reluctant to think about sex among older people. Perhaps this is a result of not viewing one's parents as sexual partners. "Only perverts think of their parents having sex," said one person.

Since it may be perverse *not* to explore sexuality beyond youth, this section will focus on the sexuality of women and men during the middle years. These are the years your parents are now experiencing, and these are the times through which you will also pass (or are already passing through).

When does a person become middle-aged? The U.S. Census Bureau regards you as middle-aged when you reach 45. Family life specialists define middle age as that time when the last child leaves home and continues until retirement or either spouse dies. Humorist Laurence Peter (1982) has provided a couple of additional definitions: "Middle age is when you can do just as much as you could ever do—but would rather not" and "Middle age is when work is a lot less fun and fun is a lot more work" (pp. Oct. 9 and May 4).

Regardless of how middle age is defined, it is a time of transition. Let us examine what happens to women, men, and their sexuality during this period.

Women in Middle Age

Women in middle age undergo a number of physical and psychological changes.

PHYSICAL CHANGES

Menopause is the primary physical event during this period. Defined as the permanent cessation of menstruation, menopause is caused by the gradual decline of estrogen produced by the ovaries. It occurs around age 50 for most women but may begin earlier or later. Signs that the woman may be nearing menopause include decreased menstrual flow and a less predictable cycle. After 12 months with no period, the woman is said to be through menopause.

The term *climacteric* is often used synonymously with menopause. But menopause refers only to the time when the menstrual flow permanently stops, while climacteric refers to the whole process of hormonal change induced by the ovaries, pituitary gland, and hypothalmus.

A typical reaction to such hormonal changes is the "hot flash."

DATA • *About 70 percent of menopausal women report experiencing hot flashes.* (Budoff, 1983)

The experience is "a sudden rush of fiery heat from the waist up, increased reddening of the skin surface, and a drenching perspiration. Following the hot flash there may be a very cold chill, whitening of the skin surface, and sudden shivers" (Smallwood & VanDyck, 1979, p. 73). Other symptoms experienced, though less often, include heart palpitations, dizziness, irritability, headaches, weight gain, and backache.

Most women do not have these experiences during menopause, but many women report physiological and behavioral changes as a result of the aging process and of decreasing levels of estrogen: (a) a delay in the reaction of the clitoris to direct stimulation, (b) less lubrication during sexual excitement, (c) a less intense orgasm, (d) a smaller vaginal opening, and (e) perhaps increased sexual interest.

To minimize the effects of decreasing levels of estrogen, some physicians recommend estrogen replacement therapy or ERT, particularly to control hot flashes during the climacteric. But because the long-range results of ERT are not known and there is some evidence that it contributes to cancer of the uterus, many physicians are cautious about the use of such therapy. The combined use of estrogen and progesterone is thought to minimize this risk.

PSYCHOLOGICAL CHANGES

The psychological reaction to menopause is mixed. Some women are elated that they do not have to worry about contraception or contend with the monthly blood flow. "I wish I had gone through menopause 10 years ago," reflected one woman. "My sex life has never been better."

But other women are saddened because they view menopause as the end of their childbearing capacity. At the extreme, some women view it not as the change of life but as the end of life. Their negative feelings about the menopausal years are related partly to the value our society places on the youthful appearance of women. To improve their self-esteem, some menopausal women seek a relationship with a younger man to affirm that they are still sexually desirable.

CONSIDERATION • A cross-cultural look at menopause suggests that a woman's reaction to this phase of her life may be related to the society in which she lives. For example, among Chinese women, fewer menopausal symptoms have been observed. Researchers have suggested this may be owing to the fact that older women in China are highly respected, as are older people generally. It is possible that the magnitude of the symptoms associated with menopause is correlated with the few roles available to the older woman (Griffin, 1977).

Men in Middle Age

While middle-aged women are adjusting to the consequences of menopause, men too are having problems in middle age.

PSYCHOLOGICAL CHANGES

Middle age requires that men adjust to change—or lack of change—in their jobs. Most men reach the top level of their earning power during middle age, and some find themselves well short of the peak they had hoped to reach. "A man of 40 may be looking anxiously over his shoulder at the wolf pack yapping and slobbering at his heels as he slips along over competitive ice. At 40, the status of many a man, whether in business or on the assembly line, is frozen, so he feels stuck and fearful" (Henry, 1974, p. 440). One researcher suggested that a principal task for men in the midlife transition is deillusionment—realistically asking if the goals they have set for themselves are reasonable and attainable (Levinson, 1977).

For many there is the feeling of having reached a dead end. "Had I known this firm was never going to promote me," one man said, "I would have left 15 years ago. But now it's too late. Who wants to hire a 50-year-old when 30-year-olds are a dime a dozen?" Still others reach the top only to find that "success" is meaningless for them. "I've been with the government since I left school and now I'm the head of my division. But so what? I move papers around my desk and have conferences that are supposed to mean something but don't. I've always wanted to be a psychologist so I could work with people about something that matters, but now it's too late."

Whether they feel they have failed in the right career or succeeded in a meaningless one, some middle-aged men respond to their disappointments and anxi-

This middle-life thing has become a phobia; people think it's *got* to be a big problem, when it's simply not.

JACK NICHOLSON

eties by having an affair. Love and sex with a young woman is often regarded as the last chance to experience youth.

> For the man who does not find satisfaction in his work, who has done what he had to do, rather than what he wanted to do, or whose life work has turned out to be not quite what he thought it was . . . the cure to his lifelong disorder may seem to be the young and beautiful woman . . . She gives him a feeling that he is not lost after all, he is not as weak as he thinks. She will, he feels, give him new creative power, because her sex interest proves that he is not dead wood. (Henry, 1974, 440–441)

PHYSIOLOGICAL CHANGES

Physiological changes also accompany middle age in men. The production of testosterone usually begins to decline around age 40 and continues to decrease gradually until age 60 when it levels off. (The decline is not inevitable but is related to general health status.)

The consequences of lowered testosterone include (a) more difficulty in getting and maintaining a firm erection, (b) greater ejaculatory control with the possibility of more prolonged erections, (c) less consistency in achieving orgasm, (d) fewer genital spasms during orgasm, (e) a qualitative change from an intense, genitally focused sensation to a more diffused and generalized feeling of pleasure and (f) an increase in the length of the refractory period, during which time the man is unable to ejaculate or have another erection.

These physiological changes in the middle-aged man, along with psychological changes, have sometimes been referred to as male menopause. During this period the man may experience nervousness, hot flashes, insomnia, and no interest in sex. But these changes most often occur over a long period of time, and the anxiety and depression some men experience seem to be as much related to their career perceptions as to hormonal alterations.

> At midlife, men suddenly discover the value of intimacy, relationships, and care, the importance of which women have known from the beginning.
>
> CAROL GILLIGAN

> CONSIDERATION • A middle-aged man who is not successful in his career is often forced to recognize that he will never achieve what he had hoped but carry his unfulfilled dreams to the grave. This knowledge may be coupled with his awareness of diminishing sexual vigor. For the man who has been taught that masculinity is measured by career success and sexual prowess, middle age may be particularly traumatic.
>
> But middle age may also be the best of times. A character in the novel *Anthony Adverse* says, "Grow up as soon as you can. It pays. The only time you really live fully is from 30 to 60 . . . The young are slaves to dreams; the old, servants of regrets. Only the middle-aged have all their five senses in the keeping of their wits."

• SEXUAL FULFILLMENT IN THE LATER YEARS •

DATA • *About one in 10 Americans (25 million) is over the age of 65. By the year 2030 they will represent about 20 percent of our population.* (U.S. Bureau of the Census, 1983)

The way a society views the elderly influences the expression of their sexuality. Although our society tends to expect people to reduce their sexual activities as they age, this expectation is not characteristic of all societies. In one study (Winn & Newton, 1982), 70 percent of one group of societies had expectations of continued sexual activity for their aging males. Among the Tiv in Africa many older men "remain active and 'hot' for many years after they become gray-haired" (p. 288); and among the Taoist sects of China, there are records of men retaining their sexual desires past 100 years of age. Similar reports of continued sexual activity and interest among aging women were found in 84 percent of societies for which data on this age group were available. The researchers concluded "that cultural as well as biological factors may be key determinants in sexual behavior in the later part of life" (p. 283).

Sexuality of the Elderly: Some Facts

Growing old need not mean an end to a person's sex life. To the contrary, there may be an improvement. In a study of 800 elderly Americans (Starr & Weiner, 1982), three-fourths of those who were sexually active reported that their love-making had improved with the years. But let us take a more detailed look at sex among the elderly by reviewing some of the facts.

DATA ARE LACKING

Since no nationwide random sample of the elderly has been interviewed or completed a questionnaire about their sexual behavior, we have only scattered information based on what some of the elderly have told us in various small-scale studies.

SEXUAL BEHAVIOR AMONG THE ELDERLY IS VARIABLE

As is true of the sexual behavior of other age groups, there are great differences in sexual behavior among the elderly. Whereas some report frequent intercourse, masturbation, and oral sex experiences, others are disgusted with the implication that they would be interested in such activities. One elderly woman said to another, "I think that sex at my age is a waste of time." Her friend replied, "Speak for yourself."

FREQUENCY OF INTERCOURSE DECLINES WITH AGE

One study noted that beginning at age 46, the frequency of intercourse reported by males decreases every year (Pfeiffer, Verwoerdt, & David, 1974). Reasons for this decline include societal expectations, physical problems, and satiation. The elderly are sometimes forced into mandatory retirement from sexual activity, particularly in retirement facilities and nursing homes where husbands and wives are segregated.

Physical problems also take their toll. In men, diabetes, malfunctions of the thyroid and pituitary glands, and alcoholism may impair the man's ability to get and keep an erection.

DATA • *About half of men 75 and over are impotent. For the elderly man who is not impotent, it is not unusual for him to require 30 to 40 minutes of stimulation before he gets an erection.* (Rossman, 1978)

Although, as we noted, physical changes in women are owing to the decrease in estrogen, the primary factor affecting the declining frequency of intercourse in women is the waning interest of her partner or the absence of one. The presence of a culturally approved sexual partner (husband) is often regarded as a prerequisite for heterosexual expression among elderly women.

DATA • *Half of all women over the age of 65 are widowed compared with only 12 percent of elderly men.*   (U.S. Bureau of the Census, 1983)

MASTURBATION DECLINES WITH AGE

In a study of 1,000 males aged 51 to 95 (Hegeler & Mortensen, 1977), there was a steady decline of reported masturbation with increasing age. Whereas half of those in their early fifties reported they masturbated, less than a fourth did so in their early nineties. Masturbation rates also decline with age among females. However, there is a upswing in the rates following separation, divorce, and widowhood.

LOVEMAKING MAY IMPROVE WITH AGE

One definition of improvement is what two researchers call the "second language of sex." The first language is "involved largely with physical pleasure . . . but the second language of sex is emotional and communicative as well as physical" (Butler & Lewis, 1976, p. 140). One husband confided:

At sixty-five I am having the best sex life I have ever had. My wife and I have few inhibitions and try anything we like. I'm usually the aggressor, but she likes to pull me into the bedroom and I don't struggle. We wander around our apartment naked, bathe together, and love each other's body and mind. Our love has been a developing one. First it was more sexual. Now it is that plus many other things. (Hite, 1981, p. 860)

CONSIDERATION • Lack of anxiety about pregnancy and more time and opportunity make it easier for people to experience the second language of sex. "When the kids aren't running about the house and you're both home all day, you've got time to do a lot of things including sex," said a 76-year-old man.

ORGASM REMAINS AN IMPORTANT EXPERIENCE

Lest we think that sex for the elderly is confined to holding each other, orgasm was viewed by three-fourths of the 800 respondents in the Starr and Weiner (1982) study as important to a good sexual experience. Many feel like Woody Allen who said, "I've never had a bad orgasm."

SEX, IN GENERAL, REMAINS AN IMPORTANT EXPERIENCE

More important than orgasm is the whole idea of sex. More than 95 percent of the respondents in the previously cited study said they liked sex. This finding contradicts the myth that the elderly never think of sex and certainly do not do anything about it. Indeed, for those who have had an active sex life throughout their youth, there is no time they just stop being interested in sex any more than there is a time they stop being interested in food or music or anything else they have enjoyed.

Sexual Fulfillment among the Elderly

There are several things people can do to achieve sexual fulfillment in the later years: doing what they want to do sexually (including nothing), relabeling their "losses" as "transitions," and adapting as necessary. It is important that the elderly not view the publicity about sex in the later years as an obligation to enjoy an active sex life. Since sexual fulfillment is individually defined, each elderly person, like others, should decide what behaviors and frequencies she or he feels comfortable with. There are no right or wrong, normal or abnormal, definitions.

CONSIDERATION • Rather than viewing partial erection, impotence, lack of vaginal lubrication, or pain during intercourse as sexual losses, the elderly might see these as inevitable transitions. We expect change in all other areas of life and should not be dismayed to discover that our bodies change too. Adaptation to change is likely to be a more satisfying response.

The golden years are supposed to be golden in other ways [than sexually].

B. F. SKINNER AND M. E. VAUGHAN

Adaptation does not necessarily mean resignation. It may mean finding substitute techniques for sexual expression. For example, for a partial erection or impotence, some couples use the "stuffing technique," manually pushing the penis into the vagina. This often stimulates the penis to erection, which can be followed by intercourse. Another problem that can be helped is pain during intercourse, which was reported by slightly more than 10 percent of the women in the Starr and Weiner study (1982). Pain may be caused by decreased vaginal lubrication, a smaller vaginal opening, and friction against the thinner walls of the vagina. A liberal use of K-Y jelly, a sterile lubricant, is helpful in minimizing the pain. Applied to both the penis and vagina, it helps the penis slide in and out with less friction.

• TRENDS •

Trends in sexual fulfillment include greater access to information about sexual fulfillment, a widening of the range of expression of sexual fulfillment, and increased exploration of these alternatives. Magazines like *Cosmopolitan*, *Redbook*, *Ladies Home Journal*, *McCall's*, and *Family Circle* regularly feature articles on sexual aspects of the woman-man relationship. Masters and Johnson's research is available to every person who stands in line to pay for groceries. Such visibility of sexual topics is not limited to magazines but includes movies, television, and radio. The openness with which the media treat sex will continue.

One consequence of this visibility is an awareness of the widening range of sexual behaviors expressed by different people. "Donahue" once featured discussions on "safe" topics only, but later programs included such topics as polyg-

Many elderly
people are
interested in sex
and are sexually
active.

amy, bisexual marriage, celibacy, and transsexuality. Exposure to media-mediated sex alerts us to the tremendous variations in sexual experience. Finally, although people do not always try what they see, they are more likely to include new behaviors in their own repertoire than if they were not aware of what others are doing.

These trends will affect both young and old. In time, today's younger generation, socialized exclusively in our sex-conscious society, will become the older generation, and they will carry their socialization with them. Their awareness of alternative ways of sexual fulfillment, including abstinence, will allow them to select from among those behaviors and frequencies the kind of sex life they want.

In the meantime our society will become more encouraging of the elderly to express their sexuality. Physicians will lead this trend by initiating dialogue about sex with elderly patients. The goal is not to exert pressure on older people to engage in sexual activity but to encourage them to feel that such activity is appropriate.

Sexual fulfillment means different things to different people, and these meanings may vary over time. But there seem to be certain prerequisites for its existence, including self-knowledge, a good relationship, open communication, realistic expectations, and demonstration of sexual interest in the partner.

Sexual fulfillment also requires an awareness of basic facts about human sexuality. These include an awareness that sexual attitudes and behaviors are primarily learned, that sex is a natural function, that sexual communication takes effort, and that spectatoring interferes with sexual functioning. Also interfering with sexual fulfillment are such myths as the belief that simultaneous orgasm is the ultimate experience, that intercourse during menstruation is harmful, and that sexual boredom is inevitable.

Sexual dysfunctions are a concern in many relationships. Lack of sexual responsiveness, inability to achieve orgasm, pain during intercourse (dyspareunia), and involuntary constrictions of the vagina (vaginismus) are the main female sexual dysfunctions. Men may be troubled by sexual apathy, an inability to get and maintain an erection (erectile dysfunction), inability to delay ejaculation (premature ejaculation), or inability to ejaculate at all (ejaculatory incompetence).

Menopause and the woman's reaction to it are the primary physical and psychological concerns of the woman during middle age. Men during this period are adapting to changes in career goals and lower testosterone levels.

Growing old need not lead to the end of a person's sex life. Although frequency of intercourse declines with age, orgasm and sex in general remain important. There are several things people can do to achieve sexual fulfillment in the later years: doing want they want to do sexually (including nothing), relabeling their losses as transitions, and adapting as necessary.

Trends in sexual fulfillment include greater access to sexual information, an expanded awareness of the various avenues to sexual fulfillment, and an increased exploration of these alternatives.

Questions for Reflection

1. How do you define sexual fulfillment?
2. What physical changes, if any, are you experiencing which suggest to you that you are aging?
3. How willing would you be to consult a sex therapist for a sexual problem?

·CHOICES·

Some couples who are unable to resolve the sexual problems in their relationship become involved in sex therapy. Once the decision is made to consult a sex therapist, several choices must be made: whether one or both partners should attend sex therapy, whether to have private or group therapy, and whether one or two therapists (as a team) should be sought.

ALONE OR WITH PARTNER?

Should just the person experiencing the sexual problem or the person and her or his sexual partner become involved in sex therapy? It depends. Some people prefer to go alone (Zilbergeld, 1980). One woman said, "If I ask him to go to therapy with me, he'll think I'm more emotionally involved than I am. And since I don't want to encourage him I'll just work out my problems without him." Other reasons why a person might see a sex therapist alone are if no partner is available, if the partner won't come, or if the person feels more comfortable in discussing sex in the partner's absence.

But there are several reasons why a person might want her or his partner to become involved in sex therapy—to work on the problem *with* someone, to share the experience, and to prevent one partner from being identified as the "one with the problem."

Although there are exceptions, a greater proportion of sexual problems can be more effectively treated by engaging in sex therapy with a partner.

PRIVATELY OR IN A GROUP SETTING?

Once the decision to pursue therapy (with or without a partner) is made, another choice is whether to be seen in private or in groups with other people who are experiencing a similar problem. There are advantages and disadvantages of each treatment pattern.

Although being seen privately helps to ensure that therapy will be tailored to fit the specific needs of the client, the cost is considerably higher than if the client is treated in a group setting. Private therapy may cost $75 an hour but only $15 for the same amount of time in a group of five.

Another advantage of group therapy is that being surrounded by others who have a similar problem helps to reduce the feeling that "I'm the only one." One woman who had difficulty achieving orgasm said, "When I heard the other women discuss their difficulty with climaxing, I knew I wasn't abnormal." The empathy of a group of peers can be extremely effective in helping a person feel less isolated.

A group setting also furnishes the opportunity to try new behaviors. For example, some sexual problems may be part of a larger problem, such as the lack of social skills to attract and maintain a partner. Fear of rejection can perpetuate being alone. But group members, with the help of their therapist, can practice making requests of each other and getting turned down. Such an exercise helps to develop the social skill of approaching others while learning to deal with rejection. Practicing with other group members is safe and gives a person the necessary confidence to approach someone outside the group.

There are at least two disadvantages of group therapy. First is the possibility of not having enough time spent on one's own problem. Second is the risk to the relationship with the partner who may not be involved in the group. In one study of women in group therapy for lack of orgasm (Barbach & Flaherty, 1980), one in four reported a negative effect on their partner.

Before drawing conclusions about the comparative effectiveness of private versus group therapy, we now examine the types of groups available.

(continued)

Groups of Individuals

The preceding study is an example of group therapy for individuals with a common sexual problem. In one such group, five to seven women who lacked the ability to achieve an orgasm in a particular fashion met for 10 one-and-a-half-hour weekly sessions. During this time they shared their early sexual learning experiences, their current sexual problems, and their feelings about sexuality. But most of the time they discussed the weekly homework assignments they were to have completed between sessions. These included masturbating, having their partners stimulate them manually or orally to orgasm while not attempting intercourse, and having their partners stimulate them manually during intercourse.

Group therapy is not limited to women with sexual problems. Erectile dysfunction has been treated in all-male groups (Lobitz & Baker, 1979). Through a series of homework assignments, the men learned to minimize the anxiety that caused their inability to create and maintain an erection. These assignments included masturbating to full erection, letting the erection subside, relaxing, and restimulating to full erection. By gaining, deliberately losing, and regaining their erections in private, each man became less fearful of not being able to control loss of erection.

Groups of Couples

As an alternative to group therapy for individuals with specific sexual dysfunctions, you and your partner might choose to be seen in group therapy with other couples. Premature ejaculation and orgasmic dysfunction have been treated in group settings of three to four couples (Golden et al., 1978). The format included the discussion of between-session homework assignments. Such assignments included sensate focus for the first several weeks, followed by instructions about the squeeze technique for couples in which the man was a premature ejaculator. Another set of instructions was given to couples working on the woman's orgasmic capacity. These included the woman masturbating to orgasm and teaching her partner how to bring her to orgasm.

Comparative Effectiveness

What is the comparative effectiveness of couples being treated in a group or in private therapy? In the Golden et al. (1978) study, when group couple therapy for premature ejaculation and orgasmic dysfunction was compared with therapy for the same problems treated in private, there were no differences in outcome. Both treatment patterns were effective—men reported satisfaction with their ability to prolong intercourse and women reported satisfaction with their orgasmic ability. Other researchers have found similar results—couples in groups are as successful in achieving their goals as couples in private therapy (Duddle & Ingram, 1980).

This suggests that *couples* can be treated effectively in either a private or a group setting. It is therefore a matter of preference. But group therapy for *individuals* may not be as effective as therapy with a partner in private or in a couples group. However, most individuals in group sex therapy without a partner do benefit from the experience.

ONE OR TWO THERAPISTS?

Is it best to see one therapist or a male-female sex therapy team? Masters and Johnson recommend the latter for couple therapy, suggesting that the man can better relate to the man and the woman to the woman. A dual sex team also provides a model for appropriate male-female interaction.

Although other sex therapists also have adopted the dual sex team approach, there is no evidence that such a team is more effective than individual male or female therapists (Clement & Schmidt, 1983; Mehlman et al., 1983). Rather than how many therapists of what gender are in the therapy setting, the quality of the therapy seems to be the important variable.

· Part Four ·

FAMILIES

One hundred years ago, technology had little impact on the family. Automobiles and television were nonexistent and medical technology relatively primitive. Family members spent most of

their time working on the farm. Travel was by horse-drawn buggy and information sources were limited to word of mouth and the printed page.

Today automobiles of every color, style, and option are available to take courtship partners away from the watchful eyes of parents and families on extended cross-country vacations. Television news provides instant exposure to the happenings of the day throughout the United States and the world. Situation comedies comment on a variety of life-styles, values, and behaviors.

Medical advances such as artificial insemination, test-tube fertilization, ovum transfer, amniocentesis, and chorion biopsy offer infertile couples a way to increase the probability of

pregnancy and help ensure a healthy fetus and infant. In addition, new contraceptives (subdermal implants for women, a "pill" for men) are being developed to provide increased control over family size.

· Chapter 14 ·

PLANNING CHILDREN

CONTENTS

Do You Want to Have Children?
The Child-Free Alternative
Self-Assessment: **The Attitudes
  Toward Children Scale**
**How Many Children
  Do You Want?**
Timing Your Children
Timing Subsequent Births
Choices

*Love is a fourteen letter word—
family planning.*

PLANNED
PARENTHOOD
POSTER

Parenthood should begin with planning. As a student, before each academic term you decide how many courses you want to take and when you want to take them. You probably try to avoid an overload and feel pleased when you get the sequence of courses you want. Successful family planning means having the number of children you want and when you want to have them. Although this seems a sensible and practical way to approach parenthood, many couples leave the number and spacing of their children to chance.

Family planning has benefits for the mother and child. Since having several children at short intervals increases the chances of premature birth, infectious disease, and death for the mother or baby, parents can minimize such risks by planning fewer children at longer intervals.

DATA · *At the start of the nineteenth century, white women bore an average of about seven children.*   (Thornton & Freedman, 1983)

Fathers may also benefit from family planning by pacing the financial demands of parenthood. "We spaced our three children every four years," said one father, "so we would have only one child in college at a time."

Conscientious family planning may also reduce the number of children born to parents who do not want them. A child born to rejecting parents is a tragic situation—but a preventable one.

Family planning also benefits society by enabling people to avoid having children they cannot feed and clothe adequately—children whose rearing may have to be subsidized by the taxpayer. Finally, family planning is essential to halting the continuing expansion of the world population and the consequent drain on limited environmental resources.

DATA • *There are currently more than 4.5 billion people on this planet and the population is increasing at a rate of between 80 and 90 million per year.* (CBS News, 1984)

In this chapter you are encouraged to consider three basic questions: Do you want to be a parent? If so, how many children do you want? When is the best time to begin your family?

Well over 90 percent of all human births are the by-product of a moment of passion rather than of family planning per se.

ROY CREEP

• DO YOU WANT TO HAVE CHILDREN? •

Most young adults say they want to have children "some day." In this section we examine the positive and negative consequences of having children, the social influences on the decision to have children, and the reasons people give for wanting children.

Positive Aspects of Parenthood

In their book *Parents in Contemporary America*, researchers LeMasters and DeFrain (1983) write that "rearing children is probably the hardest, and most thankless, job in the world" (p.22). Yet more than 90 percent of Americans express a desire to have this experience. Some of the presumed benefits from having children include the following.

PLAY

Children give you an excuse to express the child in yourself that society assumes you have outgrown. One parent said, "I like to ride an inner tube down a river with my kids in the summer and swing off a rope into the water as I did when I was a kid. I can't ask my friends to play like that; they'd think I was nuts. With your own kids, you've got the chance to play, really play, again." It is also fun to observe and join in the spontaneity that children bring to their activities. Children have no internal schedule that tells them what they should do next. Being tickled, playing hide and seek, and flying a kite always have the potential of leading to another, perhaps surprising, adventure.

HONESTY

Children are honest. Unburdened by years of social programming, children express exactly what they feel. "When your 5-year-old wraps her or his arms around you and says 'I love you,' you know the feelings are real," one parent said; and every family therapist knows that a way to find out how mother and daddy get along is to ask the kids. "She's always yelling at him because he drinks too much," said one 7-year-old.

COMPANIONSHIP

A mother of three children remarked, "After you finish school, all your friends scatter. The only relationships that really last are family relationships. Having children gives you the chance to be intimately involved in a family over a long period of time."

PARENTAL PRIDE

"I can't describe the pleasure it gave me to see my daughter ride a horse for the first time," said a rancher. Pride in one's own children is a major reward of parenthood, and it is not dependent on the child's potential for becoming president. Parents feel pride when their children first roll over, walk, talk, ride a bike, and swim.

SPOUSE-CHILD RELATIONSHIP

An additional delight for parents is to observe the interaction between their child and their spouse. A young father said, "Amy asks when she awakens from her nap, 'When's Mama coming home?' And when 'Mama' gets home, she lifts Amy in the air and they begin laughing with each other. As a result of watching them play together, I've developed a special love for my wife."

Parents often delight in the relationship they share with their children.

Negative Aspects of Parenthood

These positive aspects of parenthood have a flip side. The spontaneity children exhibit may erupt at the wrong time—when the parents are making love, reading, watching the evening news, or talking on the telephone or to each other. The honesty of children may also include telling a neighbor that mommy said daddy was a "pompous ass" or telling grandma that the oil painting she gave the family is only hauled out on the occasion of her annual visit. Parent-child companionship may also leave one spouse feeling excluded. Finally, parental pride can become parental grief when the child fails a grade, shoplifts, gets pregnant at 15, or takes drugs.

One woman who does not want children said, "They take the best years of your life and turn them into the best years of their life." Some of the negative aspects of parenthood include the following.

INCREASED EXPENSES

Since the wife may drop out of the work force when she becomes a mother (about 50 percent of mothers with preschool children are at home with them), having a baby may mean that the couple's income is cut drastically. But whether or not she stops working, expenses will climb.

DATA • *Costs for the first year (prenatal, delivery, and postnatal care) are around $3,000. It is estimated that the direct out-of pocket cost to a middle-class family rearing a son from conception through four years of college is $215,000, or 23 percent of the family's total income. The cost of a daughter is an average of $900 more per year.* (Olson, 1983)

RESTRICTED SOCIAL LIFE

In a study of 102 first-time fathers (Gilman & Knox, 1976), the respondents were asked how often they went out with their wives to eat, see a movie, or take a drive before and after the baby was born. Half of the fathers said they spent less time sharing these events with their wives after the baby came. "Before you have a baby," said one father, "you assume that you can always get a baby-sitter when you want and that your social life won't change. The reality is that when you spontaneously decide to go out, it's too late to find a sitter. You have to plan every social event at least three days ahead. The result—you go less often."

Another father who had been married 10 years before his child arrived expressed bitter resentment about the baby's interference with the sailing weekends he and his wife had enjoyed from April through late fall. "You can't take a baby on a sailboat, and being with Carol was part of the fun. We fought it for three months but finally sold the boat. If we had known that a baby equals a blackout on our sailing together, we would have reconsidered having a child."

NEW ROUTINES

Children influence the total life-style of the couple, who must adjust to new routines. These include more frequent visits by and to parents and in-laws, less sleep (sometimes chronic exhaustion), family-focused entertainment (G-rated movies), and less lovemaking.

> CONSIDERATION • Parents experience these aspects of parenthood to a different extent at different times throughout the family life cycle. Parenthood is neither positive nor negative all the time but is a mixture of these experiences over the years.

Social Influences on Deciding to Have Children

We live in a pronatalistic, or prochild, society. Unless the members of a society have children, the society will cease to exist. We earlier mentioned the Shakers, also called United Society of Believers, as an example of the consequences of a social deemphasis on procreation. Founded in New York in 1787, the Shakers were a religious community that grew to more than 5000 members by winning others to their faith. Their doctrine included an emphasis on celibacy, which resulted in no marriage, no sexual intercourse, and no children. The effect of prohibiting reproduction was to ensure that the Shaker community would eventually cease to exist. Today there are only a few members remaining who were recruited into the community.

Aware of the importance of reproduction for its continued existence, our society tends to encourage childbearing, an attitude known as pronatalism. Our family, friends, religion, government, and schools help to develop positive attitudes toward parenthood. Cultural observances also function to reinforce these attitudes.

FAMILY

The fact that we are reared in families encourages us to have families of our own. Our parents are our models. They married, we marry; they had children, we have children. Some parents exert a much more active influence. "I'm 73 and don't have much time. Will I ever see a grandchild?" asked the mother of an only child. Other remarks parents have made include "If you don't hurry up, your younger sister is going to have a baby before you do," "We're setting up a trust fund for your brother's child, and we'll do the same for yours," "Did you know that Nash and Marilyn (the child's contemporaries) just had a daughter?" "I think you'll regret not having children when you're old," and "Don't you want a son to carry on your name?" Some parents view such tactics as necessary since they may value parenthood more positively than their own children do (Callan & Gallois, 1983).

FRIENDS

Our friends who have children influence us to do likewise. After sharing an enjoyable weekend with friends who had a little girl, one husband wrote to the host and hostess, "Lucy and I are always affected by Karen—she is such a good child to have around. We haven't made up our minds yet, but our desire to have a child of our own always increases after we leave your home." This couple became parents 16 months later.

> So I've realized there are other things grown-ups should be and need to be concerned with—such as kids.
>
> DAVID LETTERMAN

RELIGION

Religion may be a powerful influence on the decision to have children. Catholics are taught that having children is the basic purpose of marriage and gives meaning to the union. Although many Catholics use contraception and reject their church's emphasis on procreation, some internalize the church's message. One Catholic woman said, "My body was made by God and I should use it to produce children for Him. Other people may not understand it, but that's how I feel." Judaism also has a strong family orientation. Couples who choose to be child-free are less likely than couples with children to adhere to any set of religious beliefs.

GOVERNMENT

The tax structure imposed by our federal and state governments support parenthood. Married couples without children pay higher taxes than couples with children, although the reduction in taxes is not large enough to be a primary inducement to have children.

Governments in other countries have encouraged or discouraged childbearing in different ways. As a mark of status for women contributing to the so-called Aryan race, Adolf Hitler in the 1930s bestowed the German Mother's Cross on Nazi Germany's most fertile mothers—a gold cross to mothers of eight or more children, a silver cross for six or seven, and a bronze cross for four or five.

Today China has a set of incentives to encourage families to have a maximum of one child. Couples who have only one child are given a "one-child glory certificate," which entitles them to special priority housing, better salaries, a 5 percent supplementary pension, free medical care for the child, and an assured place for the child in school. If the couple has more than one child, they may lose their jobs, be assigned to less desirable housing, and be required to pay the government back for the benefits they have received.

EDUCATION

The content of many educational programs is pronatalistic. One-third of 29 high school family studies texts reflects a positive bias toward children (Patterson & DeFrain, 1981). Grade school books, such as the Dick and Jane series, also emphasize the family context.

SPECIAL OBSERVANCES

Our society reaffirms its approval of parents every year by allocating special days for mom and dad. Each year on Mother's Day and Father's Day, parenthood is celebrated across the nation with gifts and embraces. Notice that there is no counterpart such as a Child-free Day.

CONSIDERATION • Many of these pronatalism influences operate without our conscious awareness. For example, while growing up in a family, rarely are we told by our parents that children are a benefit and we should have them when we grow up. Rather, the experience of growing up in a family encourages us to duplicate the behavior of our adult models.

Personal Reasons for Having Children

The impact of pronatalism influences is reflected in the reasons people give for having children. Some of these reasons follow.

SOCIAL EXPECTATIONS

A sociologist and father of two daughters said, "Having children was never a deliberate decision. It was more of a feeling that one ought to have a family." A mother of two expressed a similar feeling: "All my friends were having babies, and I never questioned whether I would too." Our society expects its members to conform to certain conventions, not the least important of which is having children. Conforming to society's expectations assures a degree of acceptance from peers and places us in the mainstream of American life.

PERSONAL FULFILLMENT

Some parents encourage their daughters to anticipate having children of their own. Giving them dolls and a dollhouse as playthings reinforces this. In some cases the socialization is so strong that womanhood is equated with motherhood. "I suppose I felt I had to get pregnant to verify that I was a real woman," a young mother said.

Men also derive personal fulfillment from children. Paternalism—pride in supplying the needs of their offspring and affection for them—is a strong motive for some men. Men may also affirm their masculinity by proving that they can conceive children.

PERSONAL IDENTITY

Related to the quest for personal fulfillment is the feeling that a baby gives the parent an identity. As one women explained, "Before my son, Benny, I had nothing. I was bored, I hated my job, and I didn't have any goals or focus to my life. Now I know who I am—a mother—and I feel that I am needed." Some fathers express the same feeling. "Having my child is the meaning of life," remarked the father of a newborn. "I am a lousy employee, but I'm a great father. For the first time in my life, I really feel like somebody."

> You can learn many things from children. How much patience you have, for instance.
>
> FRANKLIN P. JONES

INFLUENCE OF SPOUSE

Some spouses have children primarily to please their mates. "I wasn't wild about the idea of having children but decided to go along with it because my husband wanted one. As it turns out, I'm glad we did," one mother said. When husband and wife feel differently about having children, the disagreement is not always resolved in favor of having them. However, since the woman bears the child, her preferences are usually given more weight.

ACCIDENT

A good many couples have children without intending to. "I was out of pills and we didn't have any condoms," recalled a young wife, "but we wanted to have intercourse and decided to take a chance. An 8-pound baby was the result." Such accidents are not unusual. They sometimes also occur before marriage.

DATA • *One-fourth of married women in a national study became pregnant before the wedding.* (Rogers and O'Connell, 1984)

IMMORTALITY

Some people try to achieve immortality through their offspring or their works. I prefer to achieve immortality by not dying.

WOODY ALLEN

Some people have children to ensure a kind of immortality. They view parenthood as a way of making a lasting mark on the world. "If you have kids, and they have kids, there will always be a part of you around," said one parent. In one study (Englund, 1983), men were more concerned about the biological and lineage aspects of parenthood than women. Having a son to continue the family line is an important issue for some men. After his fourth daughter was born, one father said, "I always wanted a son to carry on the family name, but it looks like I'll fill up the back yard with girls before I get one."

CLOSE PARENT-CHILD RELATIONSHIP

The most frequent reason given by 700 adolescent boys and girls for wanting children was the opportunity of experiencing a close affiliative relationship (Townes et al., 1979). "You're closest to your own people," said one 15-year-old. "And I want a close relationship with kids that are mine."

Whatever the reasons parents give for having children, the rewards of parenthood are basically intangible. Parents often speak of the delight of seeing children discover their world for the first time, the joy of holding a baby in their arms and realizing it is a part of them and their partner, and the pleasure of following their children's development through the years and of relating to them as adults. A clinical psychologist and mother of three said, "The real problem with children is not their coming but their going. My first daughter will soon be married and move six states away. I used to feel that babies were not worth the trouble, but now I know the joy of an adult relationship with them. I'm not only losing a daughter but my best friend."

For a variety of reasons, some couples choose not to have children.

• THE CHILD-FREE ALTERNATIVE •

For all the happiness they may give, children also cause problems. They tend to interfere with the marriage relationship, disrupt careers (particularly the mother's), cost money, and make noise. In addition, parenthood is a demanding role that not all people feel qualified to assume. For these and other reasons, some couples choose to remain child-free, particularly the college educated.

DATA • *In a national study of American women, 20 percent of those with five or more years of college/postgraduate education expected to remain child-free in contrast to 10 percent of those who did not go beyond high school.* (U.S. Bureau of the Census, 1983)

What are the reasons couples actually give for remaining child-free? When 55 couples who chose not to have children were asked about their reasons, the wives gave as the most important reasons their desire for more personal freedom, greater time and intimacy with their spouses, and career demands (Cooper et al., 1978). The most important reasons for husbands included the desire not to take on increased responsibilities. Less frequently, the couples mentioned financial reasons, concern with overpopulation, and dislike of children.

Other couples do not initially decide to be child-free. They put off having children—"we'll wait till we're out of school . . . until we get a house . . . until our careers get established . . . until we have more money"—become satisfied with the child-free life-style, and decide to continue it. But those who never have children voluntarily are a minority.

DATA • *Of a representative nationwide sample of 17,000 married women (ages 15–44), about 2 percent chose to be child-free.* (Mosher & Bachrach, 1982)

> Being a housewife and a mother is the biggest job in the world, but if it doesn't interest you, don't do it. It didn't interest me, so I didn't do it. Anyway, I would have made a terrible parent. The first time my child didn't do what I wanted, I'd kill him.
>
> KATHARINE HEPBURN

THE ATTITUDES TOWARD CHILDREN SCALE

This scale is designed to measure the way you feel about having and rearing children. There are no right or wrong answers. After reading each sentence carefully, circle the number that best represents your feelings.

1 Strongly disagree
2 Mildly disagree
3 Undecided
4 Mildly agree
5 Strongly agree

	SD	D	U	A	SA
1. I will be more fulfilled as a person if I have children.	1	2	3	4	5
2. I will be happier as a parent than just as a spouse.	1	2	3	4	5
3. Holding a baby is a very enjoyable experience.	1	2	3	4	5
4. Whatever children cost, they are worth it.	1	2	3	4	5
5. Children provide a type of satisfaction you get nowhere else in life.	1	2	3	4	5
6. Children may require more adjustments for a married couple, but those adjustments are worth the experience of having children.	1	2	3	4	5
7. Child-free couples are really missing a worthwhile experience.	1	2	3	4	5
8. Most child-free couples will regret not having children when they are old.	1	2	3	4	5
9. Children may tie you down more but they are worth it.	1	2	3	4	5
10. Children are worth sacrificing whatever career goals are necessary to have them and rear them properly.	1	2	3	4	5

		SD	D	U	A	SA
11.	Parenthood is more of an enriching experience than a burden.	1	2	3	4	5
12.	Spending time with your spouse and children would be more enjoyable than spending time alone with your spouse.	1	2	3	4	5
13.	I wouldn't mind doing the work taking care of a baby requires—feeding, changing diapers, giving them a bath, reading stories at bedtime.	1	2	3	4	5
14.	Children make a lot of noise and tear up the house but these are minor concerns in deciding to have children.	1	2	3	4	5
15.	The happiest couples are those who have children.	1	2	3	4	5
16.	When I see a baby in a department store I want to hold her or him.	1	2	3	4	5
17.	I enjoy the experience of taking care of a helpless infant.	1	2	3	4	5
18.	Rearing children through the teen years would be a challenging experience rather than an experience to avoid.	1	2	3	4	5
19.	Children usually appreciate what you do for them when they get older.	1	2	3	4	5
20.	I can't imagine not having children.	1	2	3	4	5

Scoring: Add the numbers you circled. Since 1 (strongly disagree) is the most negative feeling you could have and 5 (strongly agree) is the most positive feeling you could have, the lower your total score (20 is the lowest possible score), the more pessimistic you feel about parenthood, and the higher your score (100 is the highest possible score), the more optimistic you feel about parenthood. A score of 60 places you at the midpoint between wanting and not wanting to become a parent.

Table 14.1 **Ideal Family Size**

NUMBER OF CHILDREN WANTED	PERCENT
None	3
One	3
Two	54
Three	21
Four	11
Five	1
Six or more	2
No opinion	5

Source: The Gallup Report, Report No. 210, Princeton, N.J., 1983, p. 11.

• HOW MANY CHILDREN DO YOU WANT? •

If you decide to have children, how many children do you want? Table 14.1, based on a Gallup report, indicates the number of children Americans say they want. Two children continues to be the ideal number for most Americans.

An Only Child

Many people who are hesitant about having an only child make statements like "It's not fair to the child," "Only children are lonely," "Only children are spoiled," and "One child doesn't make a real family."

Are these beliefs justified? Is the one-child family bad for the child and the parents? To find out, Hawke and Knox (1977) asked 105 only children and 168 parents of only children to describe the advantages and disadvantages of the one-child family pattern (see Table 14.2).

When the parents of only children were asked how many children they would have if they were starting over, 23 percent said they would wish to have an only child, 40 percent would like to have two, and another 21 percent would like to have more than two. Although only children have often been maligned, they are reported to be brighter, more career oriented, and have higher self-esteem than children with siblings (Pines, 1981).

Two Children

The most preferred family size in the United States is the two-child family (Thornton & Freedman, 1983). How does having two children differ from having one? One hundred and forty-four mothers who had two children and whose second child was less than 5 years old revealed their motivations for having a second and the consequences of doing so (Knox & Wilson, 1978). About half of the mothers said they enjoyed their first child and wanted to repeat the experience. More than one-quarter stated they wanted a companion for the first child. Other reasons included the husband wanting another child, personal fulfillment, and wanting a child of the opposite gender.

One mother was asked the difference between having one and two children. She said that when her first child swallowed a quarter, they took him to the hospital to have his stomach pumped out. When the second child swallowed a coin, he was told, "It will come out of your allowance."

ANONYMOUS

Only fifty percent of parents who want one boy and one girl will achieve their desired sex combination with two births. (Bongaarts, 1984)

These mothers also commented on the consequences of having a second child. Almost half (49 percent) said the first child made a greater personal impact than the second child. Specific comments included "I lost my freedom to truly enjoy life and do what I wanted with the first child. Once I began forgetting myself, my second child had little effect"; "Childbirth and responsibility for a baby were new experiences with the first child. I felt more confident with the second child"; and "I got used to never being alone after my first child was born" (p. 24).

Although the second child had less personal impact than the first, the mothers reported that their marriages were more affected by their second child than by their first. One mother remarked, "The main difference I noticed with the second child was that I was more exhausted with the second child since I had to relate emotionally to two children throughout the day." Another woman said, "After I had listened to incessant pleading such as 'I need a fork,' 'Can I have some more apple juice?' and 'I don't like oatmeal,' there was little left of me for my husband. And when the children were finally in bed, I needed to use the rest of the evening to catch up on the housework I was unable to do during the day because of the constant interruptions" (p. 15).

Table 14.2   Advantages and Disadvantages of a One-Child Family as Reported by Only Children and Their Parents

ONLY CHILDREN (N = 105)		PARENTS OF ONLY CHILDREN (N = 168)	
Advantages	*Percent*	*Advantages*	*Percent*
More possessions, opportunities	34	Financial	35
More parental attention	30	Child gets more attention, experience, time	28
Better for personal development	16	Less demanding for parents	13
No sibling problems	20	Closer parent-child relationship	8
		Freedom of career for mother	5
		Other (no estate problems, no sibling comparisons, parents have more time for each other)	11
Disadvantages	*Percent*	*Disadvantages*	*Percent*
Lack of companionship	58	Too much attention, protection, focus, etc.	28
Parents overfocus, -protect, -expect, etc.	27	Child lonely	24
Personal development retarded	10	Child misses sibling experience	22
Other (no motherhood preparation, holidays lonely, no excitement, etc.)	5	Parents have to entertain child	5
		Other (parent criticized for having one child, parent feels child is deprived, etc.)	21

Source: From *One Child by Choice* by Sharryl Hawke and David Knox, pp. 188–189 and 198–199. © 1977 by Prentice-Hall, Inc. Published by Prentice-Hall, Inc., Englewood Cliffs, N.J. 07632.

Three Children

Some couples want three children, and wanting to have a third child is related to the perceived consequences of doing so. For example, 59 married women with two children were asked whether they intended to have another (Werner et al., 1975). Those who wanted a third child felt that the child would further their self-development, help fulfill them as wives and mothers, and strengthen the relationship with their husbands. Those not desiring another child felt that the opposite consequences would occur.

Having a third child creates a "middle child." This child may be neglected since parents of three children may focus on "the baby" and the firstborn and only rarely on the one in between.

But some middle children see their position in the family in positive terms.

> I feel that being a middle child has turned out to be a great advantage for me. I received the love, but not the overattention, that was given my older brother and younger sister. Although I have at times been envious of my siblings, I am very close to them (even though they cannot get along with each other). I feel that I am capable of being responsive and caring for others when they need someone. All things considered, it's great to be a middle child!

> I have one older brother and one younger sister and they are loved very much along with myself. However I am the one to be spoiled out of the three of us. I get whatever I want, not only from my parents, but also from my grandparents (my grandparents gave me a new Ford Mustang for graduation). At Christmas I get very unhappy because I can see that my brother and sister resent me very much, and I have been told by their best friends that they resent me. But what can I do?

Four or More Children

The percentage of Americans desiring four or more children has decreased in the last three decades.

DATA • *In 1983, 14 percent of Americans said that they wanted four or more children in contrast to 41 percent of Americans in 1953.* (Gallup Report, 1983)

Of children in all she bore twenty-four Thank the Lord there will be no more.

EPITAPH

Larger families have complex interactional patterns and different values. The addition of each subsequent child dramatically increases the possible relationships in the family. For example, in the one-child family, four interpersonal relationships are possible—mother-father, mother-child, father-child, and father-mother-child. In a family of four, 11 relationships are possible; in a family of five, 26; and in a family of six, 57 (Henry & Warson, 1951).

In addition to relationships, values change as families get larger. Whereas members of a small family tend to value independence and personal development, large-family members necessarily value cooperation, harmony, and sharing. A parent of nine children said, "Meals around our house are a cooperative

Parents don't always get the number of children they plan.

endeavor. One child prepares the drinks, another the bread, and still another sets the table. You have to develop cooperation or nobody gets fed."

Married women preferring smaller families tend to be from a small family and a higher social class, be currently employed, enjoy a high-status career, earn a good income, and perceive themselves as an equal partner with their husbands. Those preferring larger families tend to have the opposite characteristics.

Recent Demographics

In 1982 American women gave birth to about 3.7 million babies. This represented an increase of about 2 percent over 1981. According to projections of the U.S. Bureau of the Census, between 1982 and 1985 there will be only small increases in the annual number of births (Thornton & Freedman, 1983).

The birthrate (number of live births per 1,000 population) in 1982 was 16; 15.6 for 1983. The fertility rate (number of live births per 1,000 women aged 15–44) for 1982 was 67.8, which was slightly above the rate for 1981 (67.6) (National Center for Health Statistics, 1983). The birthrate for the 12 months ending with April 1984 was 15.5. The fertility rate for this period was 65.5 (National Center for Health Statistics, 1984).

The percentage of births to unmarried women has escalated sharply in recent years.

DATA • *Between 1940 and 1960, the proportion of babies born to unmarried mothers fluctuated between 4 and 5 percent. In 1980, 18 percent of all babies were born to women who were not married.* (Thornton & Freedman, 1983)

Since federal collection of national adoption statistics was discontinued in 1975, the number of adoptions per year is unknown. However, information from the National Survey of Family Growth revealed that those women most likely to adopt are married, between the ages of 30 and 44, child-free, and sterile (Bachrach, 1983).

Some couples want to select the gender of their baby. Exhibit 14.1 describes several controversial procedures.

• TIMING YOUR CHILDREN •

People who say they sleep like a baby usually don't have one.
LEO J. BURKE

Having decided how many children you want to have, when is the best time to begin having them? There are at least three issues to consider in planning the first pregnancy.

Mother's Age

Babies most likely to be carried to term and to be healthy are born to women in the prime of their reproductive life—between ages 18 and 30. Risk to the mother during childbirth is minimal. Although the chance of dying in childbirth is extremely low, the risks increase with age.

DATA • *Nine deaths occur per 100,000 births in the United States.* (National Center for Health Statistics, 1984)

· Exhibit 14.1 ·

GENDER SELECTION

In addition to wanting a specific number of children, some couples are concerned about the gender of their children. In his desire to have a male heir, King Henry VIII discarded several wives because they delivered only female children. The hapless Anne Boleyn was beheaded. But only the third of his six wives gave him a son, who died in childhood. Although few American men and women feel the same desperation to have a son, most express a slight preference for a male child.

Enter gametrics—the application of biological-mathematical theory to gamete separation. The biological part is the knowledge that Y chromosomes determine a male child and X chromosomes a female child. The mathematical part is increasing the probability of a male child by isolating the sperm carrying Y chromosomes, putting them together, and artificially inseminating the woman.

The Y sperm are isolated by putting all the sperm from an ejaculation on top of a thick substance in a test tube. Since Y sperm are stronger and swim faster, those sperm going through the substance and swimming to the bottom first are more often male sperm. These are collected from several ejaculations and are used for the artificial insemination procedure. The probability of conceiving a male child using the procedure is 75 percent. If left to chance, the probability is 50 percent. A list of Centers for Gender Selection in your area can be obtained from Gametrics Limited, 475 Gate Five Road, Sausalito, CA 94965 (phone: 415–332–3141).

An alternative to the gametrics method has been developed by Dr. Landrum Shettles (1984) who claims that the timing of intercourse (at ovulation for a boy; three days before ovulation for a girl) can affect the chances of having the desired gender.

The method of amniocentesis and abortion may also be used in gender selection. Fluid from the uterus in which the fetus floats contains fetal cells. These cells can be analyzed by withdrawing a sample of fluid with a needle inserted into the pregnant woman's abdomen to see if the cells carry XX (female) or XY (male) chromosomes. (The procedure is commonly used to test for certain genetic defects such as Down's syndrome and sickle-cell anemia.) If the fetus is the gender desired by the parents, it is allowed to develop. Otherwise, it may be aborted. Examples of the use of amniocentesis in baby gender selection include a couple who wanted a male child to satisfy the condition of a relative's will that they must have a male child to inherit a million dollars. In another case, amniocentesis was used to preclude the possibility of a male birth since a lethal inherited disease was characteristic of male babies in that family.

Although amniocentesis has been used for the purpose of having a baby of the desired gender, it is unlikely to become routine. Not only are there moral objections to this procedure (some regard abortion as murder and others see selecting males as sexist and biologically maladaptive), but there are also risks to the mother and baby.

Risks to the baby's life also increase with the mother's age. The chance of a chromosomal abnormality is 1 percent if the woman is in her early twenties, 2 percent at ages 35–39, 3 percent at 40, and 10 percent at 45 (Seashore, 1980). A higher proportion of babies born to older mothers die or have Down's syndrome (sometimes improperly called mongolism), a genetic defect caused by an extra chromosome. A Down's syndrome baby is physically deformed, mentally retarded, and has a shorter life span.

Having a Down's syndrome baby is a particular concern of women who become pregnant after age 40. Many physicians recommend amniocentesis, described earlier, for these women to determine the presence of this and other chromosomal abnormalities.

Amniocentesis is not without risks. In rare cases (about 2 percent of the time), the fetus may be damaged by the needle even though an ultrasound scan (sound waves beamed at the fetus which produce a detailed image) has been used to identify its position. Congenital orthopedic defects, such as clubfoot, and premature birth have been associated with amniocentesis. Also, if no abnormality is detected, this does not guarantee that the baby will be normal and healthy (Powledge, 1983).

An alternative to amniocentesis is chorion biopsy. Also risky, the procedure involves placing a tube through the vagina into the uterus. Chorionic tissue, which surrounds the developing embryo, is removed and analyzed in the laboratory to assess the presence of genetic defects. The procedure can be performed in a physician's office as early as the eighth week of pregnancy, and results are

I assumed that women got pregnant without thinking about it, because if they ever once considered what it really meant, they would surely be overwhelmed with doubt.

ERICA JONG

Proper medical attention is especially important in pregnancy when the mother is under 17 or over 35.

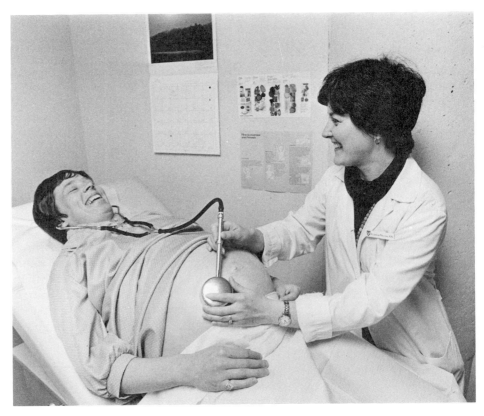

available within 24 hours. (Amniocentesis is not performed until the sixteenth week and results are not known for four weeks.)

There are also risks if the mother is too young. Studies have shown that mothers 17 or younger are more likely to give birth to babies who are premature, have birth defects, and die before they are a year old. Teenage mothers are also likely to be less psychologically competent than older ones. A nationwide study of 5,000 women aged 14 to 24 (McLaughlin & Micklin, 1983) noted that women who have their first child before age 19 seem to have reduced personal efficacy; that is, they are more likely to feel they are not in control of their environment.

Most women have their first child in their early to mid-twenties with more educated women waiting until later (Rindfuss & John, 1983). These ages have positive consequences for the mother and child and permit ample time for subsequent births. A woman who wants to become established in a career and waits until she is in her mid-thirties to become pregnant will have less time to work out fertility problems if they develop.

CONSIDERATION • As we noted earlier, increasing numbers of women are choosing to wait until their thirties to have children, and for these women the risks taken by delaying conception may be insignificant compared with the joy derived from motherhood (Bongaarts, 1982). "I'm 38 and just had my first baby," said one professional woman. "I am absolutely thrilled with being a mother and it frightens me that I might have thought it was too late to have a baby and missed this whole new terrific experience."

Father's Age

The father's age is also a consideration in deciding when to have the first child. Down's syndrome is associated with increased paternal as well as maternal age. Other abnormalities that may be related to the age of the father include achondroplasia (a type of dwarfism), Marfan syndrome (height, vision, and heart abnormalities), Apert syndrome (facial and limb deformities), and fibrodysplasia ossificans progressiva (bony growths).

DATA • *Approximately 2 percent of newborns have congenital defects that either result in an early death or are clinically significant because they require intensive or prolonged medical treatment.* (Bongaarts, 1984)

To help reduce birth defects of genetic origin, older couples and those whose family histories show evidence of hereditary defect or disease should consider genetic counseling. Such counseling helps the potential parents to be aware of the chance of having a defective child.

Number of Years Married

Although most spouses are confident in their decision to have children when in their twenties or early thirties, they are somewhat ambivalent about how long it is best to be married before having a baby.

DATA • *In one study 54 couples waited an average of 39 months between their marriage and the birth of their first child.* (Steffensmeier, 1982)

One viewpoint suggests that newlyweds need time to adjust to each other as spouses before becoming parents. If the marriage is dissolved, at least there will not be problems of child custody, child-support payments, and the single-parent status.

But if couples wait several years to have a baby, they may become so content with their child-free life-style that parenthood is an unwelcome change. "We were married for seven wonderful years before Helen was born," recalled one mother. "The adjustment hasn't been easy. We resented her intrusion into our relationship."

Another parent said, "We wanted to begin our family shortly after we were married because we wanted to be young enough to be able to do things with our children. Both of our children were born by the time we were 23 and we have had a terrific time as a family."

In one study (Marini, 1980), more than 5,000 parents were interviewed on the effect of delaying children versus having them soon after the marriage. Results indicated that marital satisfaction after children was about the same regardless of the length of time before having children.

CONSIDERATION • Whether a couple conceives their first child a long or a short time after the wedding does not seem to positively or negatively affect their marriage, but being pregnant before the wedding and having the first child within a few months after the marriage does have a significant negative effect (Marini, 1980).

• TIMING SUBSEQUENT BIRTHS •

Assuming you decide to have more than one child, what is the best interval between children? Most couples space their children within three years of each other. This interval allows parents to avoid being overwhelmed with the care of two infants, yet is short enough so that children can be companions. In addition, subsequent children conceived between four and 11 months of the last birth have a much higher mortality than children conceived at greater intervals (Winikoff, 1983). In general, the smaller the family, the longer the interval between the children and vice versa (National Center for Health Statistics, 1982).

A family's economic situation may influence the spacing of children, and also the economic situation of the family may be influenced by child spacing. In one study (Reimer & Maiolo, 1977), the slower the rate of family growth, the better the financial position of the family and the greater the probability of home ownership.

Your degree of commitment to your career is also an issue to consider in timing your first child. Although couples have different agreements about child care, most couples prefer that the wife be primarily responsible for child care. Such allocation of responsibility will be a major barrier to the woman who wants to pursue a full-time career with its demands of training, commitment, mobility, and continuity. Career-oriented women often decide to get their career going before beginning their family or to have their children first and then launch a career. Unless the partners opt to truly coparent, having a child while pursuing a career will be difficult. An alternative is the wife having a job rather than a career.

• TRENDS •

The future of family planning will include increased tolerance for the child-free alternative. Couples who decide not to have children will be viewed less often as selfish and immature. "You're no longer a sickie if you don't have kids," said one woman.

DATA • *Fifty-four percent of over 5000 students in four universities said that they believed that children were not necessary in marriage.* (Martin and Martin, 1984)

The one-child family will also become more prevalent as current concerns about inflation, personal freedom and growth, and the woman's career influence young couples to limit family size. In addition, as more parents become aware that only children tend to be bright, career oriented, and to have high self-esteem, fewer will have a second child out of obligation to the first.

More single people will want to have babies without the entanglements of marriage. Three in four Americans now consider it morally acceptable to be single and have children (Yankelovich, 1981). This issue is discussed in the Choices section.

A greater number of women will delay childbearing until their thirties because of later age at marriage and a desire to pursue their careers. As the risks to the baby increase with the mother's age, amniocentesis and chorion biopsy will be used more often to diagnose genetic abnormalities.

Finally, researchers in the field of immunology will develop ways to accurately isolate and selectively destroy Y or X sperm cells to produce the child of the desired gender.

• SUMMARY •

The decision whether to become a parent is one of the most important you will ever make. Unlike marriage, parenthood is a role from which there is no easy withdrawal. Individuals may try out marriage by living together, but there is no such trial run for would-be parents.

Spouses, children, and society all benefit from family planning. These benefits include less health risk to mother and child, fewer unwanted children, decreased economic burden for the parents and society, and population control.

Parenthood has both positive and negative aspects. The positive aspects include, the opportunity to engage in spontaneous play, developing a close relationship with your own daughter or son, feeling pride in your child's accomplishments, and delighting in a close spouse-child relationship. Negative aspects include expense, restricted social life, and the necessity to adjust to a series of new routines.

The decision to become a parent is encouraged (sometimes unconsciously) by family, peers, religion, government, education, and cultural observances. The reasons people give for having children include social expectations, influence of spouse, accident, the desire for immortality, personal fulfillment, and the desire for a close affiliative relationship.

Some couples opt for the child-free life-style. Reasons wives give for wanting to be child-free are more personal freedom, greater time and intimacy with their spouses, and career demands. Husbands also are motivated by the desire for more personal freedom. They mention disinterest in being a parent and the desire to avoid the responsibilities of parenthood as reasons for choosing a child-free life-style.

The most preferred family size in the United States is the two-child family. Some of the factors in a couple's decision to have more than one child are the desire to repeat a good experience, the feeling that two children provide companionship for each other, and the desire to have a child of each gender.

The timing of birth of the first child and the intervals between children are important choices. Issues to consider in planning your first child include the ages of both spouses, the number of years you have been married, your career commitment, and your financial situation. The desire to have children far enough apart in age to ease the burden of infant care and expenses, but close enough together to ensure their companionship, and the ability of the family to handle the expenses usually influence the spacing of children. Typical American couples have their first child about three years after their marriage and subsequent children at three-year intervals. The greater the number of children, the shorter the interval.

Trends in family planning include increased tolerance for the child-free alternative, more one-child families, and more people choosing single parenthood.

Questions for Reflection

1. Under what conditions do you regard the use of amniocentesis and chorion biopsy in gender selection appropriate?
2. What impact have your experiences in the family in which you were reared had on your desire for children? If you want children, how does the number of siblings you have influence the number of children you want?
3. To what degree do the only children you know fit the stereotype of being lonely and spoiled?

In 1980 out-of-wedlock births made up nearly half (48 percent) of total births to nonwhite women (of whom more than 90 percent are black), whereas the comparable figures for white women was 11 percent (Thornton & Freedman, 1983). Although most of these children were unplanned and born to women between the ages of 18 and 24, an increasing number are being conceived by women aged 30 and over. Many of these women are single or divorced. They want the experience of motherhood, yet feel they cannot delay having a baby indefinitely.

I was brought up on Cinderella and Snow White. I always was a dreamer. I thought you went to college, met somebody and then you have kids . . . I kept looking for that person, just waiting every year. I kept thinking I'd meet somebody. The years kept going by or things just didn't work out. Through your thirties you can be nostalgic and say: I should have done this or that. Then you get to 40, where if it is ever going to happen to you it is now. (Moore, 1983, p. 18)

Rather than wait until they meet someone they would like to marry, they choose to adopt or get pregnant without being married. Artificial insemination is one alternative. Other women seek impregnation from a man on the understanding that he will have no obligation, financial or otherwise, for the child.

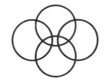

·CHOICES·

Some single and divorced men also want to be fathers but, like their women counterparts, are not in a socially legitimate sexual relationship—heterosexual marriage. Some advertise for a woman who is willing to become impregnated and to give up the child at birth. We discuss the issues of artificial insemination and surrogate motherhood in Chapter 15.

HAVING A CHILD WITHOUT A SPOUSE?

About seven million parents are rearing their children alone. More than six million are mothers; less than a million are fathers (Divorce statistics, 1983). Most of these mothers and fathers became single parents when their marriages ended in divorce. Since single parenthood is the role some unmarried people are seeking, let us examine what it is like for those already in the role of single parent.

Single parents are often stigmatized. Their families are often described as "broken," "disorganized," or "disin-tegrated" and the terms *motherless* and *fatherless* clearly imply that something is missing. But many single parents choose to ignore these labels. "My child and I have a tremendous relationship," said one single mother. "I can't imagine how a man around the house could improve our family life."

Nevertheless, there are certain problems with which single-parent families must cope. These include the following.

1. *Satisfaction of emotional needs of children.* Perhaps the greatest challenge for single parents is to satisfy the emotional needs of their children—alone. Children need love, which a parent may express in a hundred ways—from hugs and kisses to help with homework. But the single parent who is tired from working all day and has no one with whom to share parenting at night may be unable to express fully her or his love.

2. *Satisfaction of adult emotional needs.* Single parents have emotional needs of their own that children are often incapable of satisfying. The unmet need to share an emotional relationship with an adult can weigh heavily on the single parent. Most single parents seek such a relationship. All 71 of the divorced single

(continued)

parents in one study were extremely interested in dating and 80 percent were doing so (DeFrain & Eirick, 1981).

3. *Satisfaction of adult sexual needs.* Most single parents regard their role as interfering with their sexual relationships. They may be concerned that their children will find out if they have a sexual encounter at home and frustrated if they have to go away from home to enjoy a sexual relationship. They may have to deal with questions like "Do I wait until my children are asleep and then ask my lover to leave before morning?" "Do I openly acknowledge my lover's presence in my life to my children and ask them not to tell anybody?" and "Suppose my kids get attached to my lover who may not be a permanent part of our lives?" (Most single parents hide their sexual relationships from their children and make them aware of another person in their life only if the other person is of significant emotional importance to the single parent.)

4. *Child care and supervision.* Since the single parent is likely to be employed, adequate child-care arrangements must be made. Using a relative or a hired sitter are the most frequent arrangements for the preschool child. There are also commercial day-care centers. But when child-care services must be paid for, it may take a large slice out of the single parent's usually modest income.

5. *Money.* Lack of money is one of the most difficult aspects of single parenthood. The problem may be particularly acute when the single parent is a woman. The mean income for female-headed single-parent families is less than half the mean income for two-parent families. Male-headed single-parent families are less economically stressed because men typically make more money than women.

None of these concerns imply that the single-parent family is inferior or abnormal. Also, not all single-parent families have the problems just described. Even when the problems are present, there may be compensating factors. One single mother with two children said of her situation:

Sure, it's tough being a single parent. But when I need a kiss, when I need a hug, I've got it. There are people that are dying to be touched.

I think it's important for people to realize I'm happy. I don't have a big cross to bear. Lots of people are dealing with a lot tougher things than I am.

How can you not be happy with those two great kids of mine? We are a team. (Kuhn, 1983, p. 21)

Deciding to have a child without a spouse is probably the most difficult of all parenthood decisions. Some questions you might consider in making such a decision include the following. Do you have the financial resources to pay for the cost of rearing a child? Who will take care of the child while you are working? Do you have family and friends on whom you can call to help you in times of crisis? Do you want to allocate a major part of your life to rearing a child alone? Faye Dunaway and Jessica Lange are celebrity women who have chosen to have a child without a spouse.

Although most women will be married when they have their children, an increasing number will exercise their right to have a child without also choosing the role of spouse. Social acceptability of this lifestyle is increasing. Seventy-three percent of 1,000 women aged 18 to 65 found it acceptable for a woman who has never been married to have and rear children by herself (Women's Views Study, 1984).

Women contemplating single parenthood might want to contact the organization Single Mothers by Choice (501 Twelfth St., Brooklyn, NY 11215 (phone: 212–965–2148).

· Chapter 15 ·

FERTILIZATION AND BIRTH CONTROL

CONTENTS

Fertilization
Contraception
Self-Assessment: **The Contraceptive Use Scale**
Avoiding STDs and Pregnancy
Sterilization
Abortion
Choices

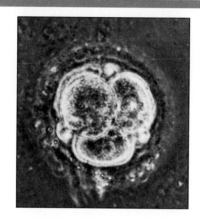

We have both the technology to increase or decrease the probability of fertilization. But whether we use it or not is up to us.

A UNIVERSITY
HEALTH SERVICE
PHYSICIAN

When a couple or individual decides to have a baby, getting pregnant becomes a goal. Recently, the natural way of pregnancy through sexual intercourse has been supplemented by the methods of artificial insemination, test-tube fertilization, and ovum transfer. For those who decide to remain child-free or to delay having children, use of effective birth control procedures is important. In this chapter we review the methods of fertilization and birth control. The latter include contraception, sterilization, and abortion. We conclude by examining the issues to consider when making choices about birth control.

· FERTILIZATION ·

Fertilization takes place when the female's egg, or ovum, unites with the male's sperm. This may occur through sexual intercourse or artificial insemination, or most recently, through the methods of test-tube fertilization and ovum transfer.

Sexual Intercourse

At orgasm the man ejaculates a thick white substance called semen.

DATA • *Each ejaculation contains from 300 to 500 million sperm cells.* (Mahoney, 1983)

Once the semen is deposited in or near the vagina, the sperm begin to travel up the vagina, through the opening of the cervix, up the uterus, and into the Fallopian tubes. If the woman has ovulated (released a mature egg from an ovary into a Fallopian tube) within eight hours, or if she ovulates during the two or three days the sperm may remain alive, a sperm may penetrate and fertilize the egg. About 30 percent of fertilized eggs die. Conception refers to a fertilized egg that survives through implantation on the uterine wall.

If the goal is to get pregnant, it is important to be aware of the probability of fertilization, keep anxiety about getting pregnant at a minimum, time intercourse to coincide with ovulation, and use the most efficient position during intercourse. Table 15.1 shows the chances of a fertile woman getting pregnant. Notice that the younger the woman, the greater her chance of getting pregnant in a fewer number of months. But regardless of age, it takes most women several months to conceive. Hence there should be no cause for alarm if pregnancy does not occur as soon as desired.

CONSIDERATION • A woman who gives herself time to get pregnant will be less anxious about doing so. This is important since anxiety may affect ovulation. Social workers in adoption agencies have noted that women, frustrated and despairing over their attempts to get pregnant and seeking to adopt a child, frequently become pregnant soon after they obtain a child and their anxiety disappears. "It was only after we had completed all the red tape and finally had our adopted daughter in the bassinet that I became pregnant," recalled one mother. Stress may affect male fertility too. Testicle biopsies performed on men who were awaiting execution revealed that they had a lower sperm count than men not under such stress.

When is the best time to have intercourse to maximize the chance of pregnancy? Since a woman is fertile for only about 48 hours each month, the timing of sexual intercourse is important. In general, 24 hours before ovulation is the best time. There are several ways to predict ovulation. Many women have breast tenderness and some experience a "pinging" sensation at the time of ovulation. Also, a woman may record her basal body temperature and examine her cervical mucus. These latter two methods are discussed in detail later in this chapter, but we briefly describe the cervical mucus timing method here. After menstruation, the vagina of most women is without noticeable discharge because the mucus is thick. As the time of ovulation nears, the mucus thins to the consistency of egg white, which may be experienced by the woman as increased vaginal discharge. Intercourse should occur during this time.

During intercourse the woman should be on her back and a pillow placed under her buttocks after receiving the sperm so a pool of semen will collect near her cervix. She should remain in this position for about 30 minutes to allow the

Table 15.1   Likelihood of Pregnancy in Fertile Women

AGE	PROBABILITY OF CONCEPTION PER MONTH	AVERAGE TIME TO CONCEPTION (MONTHS)	PROBABILITY OF CONCEPTION WITHIN A YEAR
Late 30s	8.3–10%	12–10	65–72%
Early 30s	10–15%	10–6.7	72–86%
Late 20s	15–20%	6.7–5	86–93%
Early 20s	20–25%	5–4	93–97%

Source: Sherman J. Silber, Table from *How to Get Pregnant.* Copyright © 1980 by Sherman J. Silber. Reprinted by permission of Charles Scribner's Sons.

sperm to reach the Fallopian tubes. "She may get tired of lying there," said one woman, "but if she wants to get pregnant, it's the thing to do."

DATA • *About 15 percent of the couples who have regular intercourse for a year or more and who do not use contraception are infertile.* (Shepard, 1980a) *Forty percent of the time the male is infertile; 40 percent of the time the female is infertile; 10 percent of the time both partners are infertile; and 10 percent of the time neither partner is determined to be infertile but the woman still cannot get pregnant.* (Crooks & Bauer, 1984)

Some of the more common causes of infertility in men include low sperm production, poor sperm motility, effects of sexually transmitted diseases such as gonorrhea and syphilis, and interference with the passage of sperm through the genital ducts owing to an enlarged prostate. The causes of infertility in women include blocked Fallopian tubes, endocrine imbalances that prevent ovulation, dysfunctional ovaries, chemically hostile cervical mucus that may kill sperm, and the effects of sexually transmitted diseases. About half of all infertility problems can be successfully treated so that a pregnancy will result. Couples not successful in becoming pregnant after trying to correct infertility sometimes opt for artificial insemination, test-tube fertilization, or ovum transfer.

DATA • *Three and one-half million couples in the United States currently experience a fertility problem.* (Porter & Christopher, 1984)

Artificial Insemination of Wife

When the sperm of the husband is low in number or motility, it sometimes helps to pool the sperm from several ejaculations and artificially inseminate the wife (known as AIH—artificial insemination by husband). In other cases, sperm from an unknown donor (AID—artificial insemination by donor) is used. Sometimes the donor's and husband's sperm are mixed so that the couple have the psychological benefit of knowing that the husband may be the biological father. "Our physician mixed my husband's sperm with a donor's sperm so that we could always feel that maybe it was my husband's sperm that fertilized the egg," said one wife. One situation in which the husband's sperm is not mixed with the donor's sperm is when the husband is the carrier of a genetic disease, such as Tay-Sachs disease.

I never thought getting pregnant would be so difficult.

DIANA BARGER

DATA • *The first documented artificial insemination occurred in London in the 1770s.* (Beck, 1984)

Some couples have sought sperm from the Repository for Germinal Choice. This controversial sperm bank in Escondido, California, specializes in providing sperm from men of known intellectual achievement. Among their donors have been three Nobel prize winners in science.

In the procedure of artificial insemination, a physician or the husband who has been trained by the physician deposits the sperm through a syringe in the wife's cervix and places a cervical cap over her cervix, which remains in place for 24 hours. On the average, it takes about three such inseminations before fertilization occurs.

One couple's experience with artificial insemination by donor follows.

Because of my need to get pregnant, my husband and I decided after long, hard thinking and sleepless nights to try artificial insemination. But I wasn't sure if that was what I wanted. I was very afraid that after the baby was born my husband would resent the child because it would be from another man's sperm. He tried to assure me that he would not feel that way. He wanted a baby almost as much as I did. So we began the procedures.

The first thing we had to do was to turn in my basal body temperature chart so the physicians could determine the exact time I ovulated. Then we had to give them a picture of my husband and his personal and biological traits (they also categorize donors according to these characteristics). Then they tried to find a donor with the characteristics that matched those of my husband.

The injections of the donor semen cost $25 and were done the day before and morning of ovulation. The actual procedure was very humiliating. I had to lay on the examination table after I received the injection with my feet up in the air at a 90-degree angle for 30 minutes.

I became pregnant after the first set of injections. It was really hard to believe that we were finally going to have a child. My husband was as excited as I was.

I carried the child full term and had no complications. It was hard to believe that after all those years of failing, some other man's sperm got me pregnant. Actually, I don't think about that now. We have a beautiful boy named Mark who is the joy of our lives. He is named after my husband, is very healthy, and we feel lucky to have him. As long as both parents agree, I feel that artificial insemination is the best answer to the problem of sterility. At least he is a part of one of us in flesh and bone! Our marriage is closer than ever now.

CONSIDERATION • Like this couple, most of the 62 AID couples who participated in a follow-up study reported having a positive experience (Czba & Chevret, 1979). Although couples recalled feeling severe emotional pain when they learned of the husband's inability to impregnate the wife, they decided on AID because, as the wife in the narrative noted, it would allow at least one-half of them as a couple to be biologically related to the prospective child. This fact was usually kept a secret and neither their friends nor the child was told.

DATA • *About 20,000 babies are born as a result of AID every year.* (Fleming, 1980)

Before AID is carried out, the parents-to-be agree that any child produced by this procedure will be their own and their legitimate heir.

The potential legal problems with AID have not been worked out. Only 18 states have laws pertaining to artificial insemination. One researcher observed, "A doctor could be charged with criminal conspiracy for producing an illegitimate child, and in the event the child were to be born with a severe defect, the parents or child could take legal action against the physician on grounds of negligence" (Zimmerman, 1982, p. 236).

Artificial Insemination of Surrogate Mother

Sometimes artificial insemination does not help a woman to get pregnant (for example, her Fallopian tubes may be blocked or her cervical mucus may be hostile to sperm). The couple who still want a child and who have decided against adoption may consider parenthood through a surrogate mother—a woman who is impregnated with the husband's sperm and carries the child to term. As with AIH, the motivation of the prospective parents is to have a child that is genetically related to at least one of them. For the surrogate mother, the apparent motivation is to help involuntary childless couples achieve their aspirations of parenthood.

The concept of surrogate pregnancy is not new. The Bible reports that Abraham and his wife Sarah could not conceive a child. Their solution was for Abraham to have intercourse with Sarah's Egyptian maid, Hagar, who bore a child for them.

In 1980 Elizabeth Kane (a fictitious name) gave birth to a healthy baby boy for a couple in which the wife could not get pregnant. Elizabeth Kane was artificially inseminated with the husband's sperm through Surrogate Parenting Associates, Inc., of Louisville, Kentucky (see Resources and Organizations in Part VI for address), and gave up her legal right to the baby. Mrs. Kane, the 38-year-old mother of three, indicated it was a fulfilling, sharing experience. In a study of 125 women who had applied for surrogate motherhood (Parker, 1983), more than 100 had already had children and described their pregnancies in glowing terms, saying that they felt "more complete" or "more feminine and attractive." Although nine in 10 said they would require a fee for their service, in no case was money the primary motivating factor.

> I had very easy pregnancies and I didn't think it would be a problem for me to carry another child. I figured maybe I could help someone.
>
> VALERIE, A SURROGATE MOTHER

CONSIDERATION • Legally, there are few guidelines to protect involuntary childless couples who engage a surrogate mother for procreative services. She could change her mind and decide to keep the child, leaving the childless couple little recourse with or without a contract (Zimmerman, 1982). Some states require that the social parents adopt the baby whose birth they have arranged.

DATA • *Engaging a surrogate mother is expensive. Total costs at Surrogates Parenting Associates in 1983 (excluding the cost for travel and board) began at approximately $25,000.* (Surrogates Parenting Associates, 1983) *Results are not assured and lawsuits have been filed against SPA by couples seeking to get their money back.*

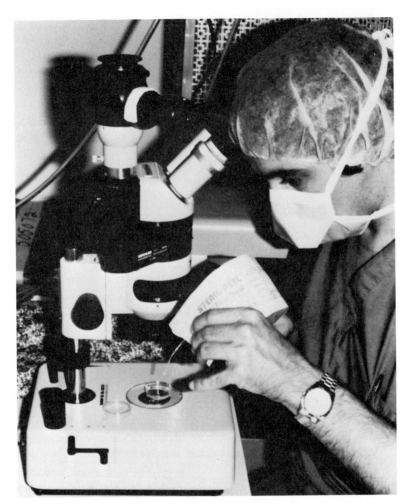

Test tube fertilization offers an additional option to many couples who once were not able to bear children.

Test Tube Fertilization

About two million couples cannot have a baby because the woman's Fallopian tubes are blocked or damaged, preventing the passage of the eggs to the uterus. Test-tube, or in-vitro, fertilization is an additional option to parenthood for infertile couples. Using a laparoscope (a narrow telescopelike instrument inserted through an incision just below the woman's navel to view the tubes and ovaries), the physician is able to see a mature egg as it is released from the woman's ovary. The time of release can be predicted accurately to within two hours. When the egg emerges, the physician uses an aspirator to remove the egg, placing it in a small tube containing a stabilizing fluid. The egg is taken to the laboratory, put in a culture dish, kept at a certain temperature-acidity level, and surrounded by sperm from the husband. After one of these sperm fertilizes the egg, it divides and is implanted by the physician in the wall of the wife's uterus (Edwards & Steptoe, 1980). Usually, several fertilized eggs are implanted in the hope that one will survive.

Louise Brown of Oldham, England, was the first baby to be born by in-vitro fertilization. After her birth in 1978, the first test-tube clinic in the United States opened at the Eastern Virginia Medical School in Norfolk, Virginia. Only women less than 35 years of age whose reproductive functions are normal (except for malfunctioning Fallopian tubes) are accepted. The procedure costs from $3,000 to $5,000, excluding hospitalization.

Other U.S. in-vitro fertilization clinics include those at the University of Texas, Duke University, and the University of North Carolina at Chapel Hill. As of this writing, eight "test-tube babies" have been born in the United States.

CONSIDERATION • Public opinion on the appropriateness of test-tube conception is divided. The readers of *Good Housekeeping* split 50-50 on the issue (GH Poll, 1980). Those approving felt that every couple should have the opportunity to have a child and viewed test-tube conception as offering that opportunity. Those who disapproved did so for religious reasons ("It's against God's plan") or for fear that a baby so conceived would be deformed.

Ovum Transfer

An alternative to test-tube fertilization for the infertile couple in which the woman's Fallopian tubes are blocked or damaged is ovum transfer. The man allows his sperm to be artificially inseminated in a surrogate woman. After about five days her uterus is flushed out (endometrial lavage) and the contents analyzed under a microscope to identify the presence of a fertilized ovum, which is inserted into the uterus of the otherwise infertile partner.

Infertile couples opt for ovum transfer, also called embryo transplant, because the baby will be half theirs (the man is the biological father) and the partner will have the experience of pregnancy and childbirth. The surrogate woman participates out of her desire to help an infertile couple.

Ovum transfers are being conducted at Harbor-UCLA Medical Center, 1000 W. Carson St., Torrance, CA 90509. Information about this and other fertility procedures may be obtained from calling the Infertility Hotline, 800-248-8877.

• CONTRACEPTION •

Most women have no problem getting pregnant. But many get pregnant when they do not want to. "I was a freshman and unmarried. The last thing I wanted at that time in my life was a baby," recalled one woman. Contraception, the prevention of pregnancy by one of several methods, is an alternative to pregnancy.

All contraceptive practices have a common purpose—to prevent the male sperm from fertilizing the female egg or to keep the fertilized egg from implanting in the uterus. In performing these functions, contraception permits couples to make love without making babies.

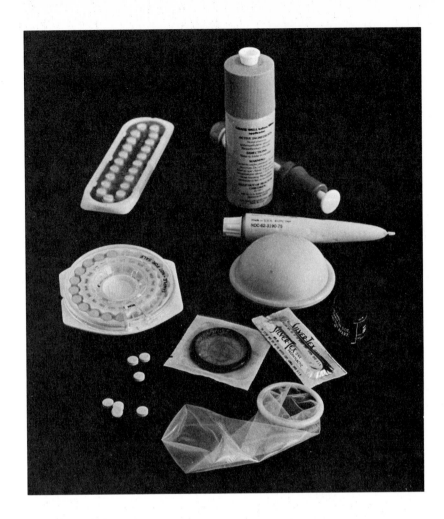

DATA • *If no method of contraception is used, the chance that a sexually active woman will get pregnant is 85 percent by the end of the second year. With contraception, the risk of becoming pregnant can be reduced to practically zero depending on the method and how systematically it is used.* (Shepard, 1980a)

Unmarried individuals most likely to use contraception consistently have positive feelings about their sexuality, are involved in serious heterosexual relationships, are not guilty about having intercourse, and have partners who encourage contraceptive use (Fisher, 1983; Herold & McNamee, 1982); but resistance to contraception use may be strong. Only 31 percent of 335 sexually active women and their partners used a birth control device every time they had intercourse (Herold & Goodwin, 1981). Reasons typically given for not using contraception include "I didn't want it to look like I was planning to have intercourse," "I thought I would be lucky and not get pregnant," "Sex should be spontaneous," and "It's against my religion to use birth control." You might want to assess the probability of your using birth control in your current relationship by taking the Contraceptive Use Scale.

THE CONTRACEPTIVE USE SCALE

This scale is designed to measure the probability of your using birth control in a current relationship. After reading each sentence carefully, circle the number that best represents your feelings.

1 Strongly disagree
2 Mildly disagree
3 Undecided
4 Mildly agree
5 Strongly agree

	SD	D	U	A	SA
1. I feel comfortable with my body and my sexuality.	1	2	3	4	5
2. I am seriously involved with my partner.	1	2	3	4	5
3. I do not feel guilty about my sexual experiences.	1	2	3	4	5
4. It is easy for me to talk about sex with my partner.	1	2	3	4	5
5. I feel that I am responsible to see that I or my partner use some form of birth control if we decide to have intercourse.	1	2	3	4	5
6. I am aware of several methods of birth control.	1	2	3	4	5
7. I feel it is important that a couple use a contraceptive each time they have intercourse.	1	2	3	4	5
8. I have discussed contraceptives with my partner.	1	2	3	4	5
9. My partner feels positively about her or his sexuality.	1	2	3	4	5
10. I care about my partner and our relationship.	1	2	3	4	5

Scoring: Add the numbers you circled. Since 1 (strongly disagree) reflects the lowest probability of your using a contraceptive and 5 (strongly agree) reflects the highest probability of contraceptive use, the lower your total score (10 is the lowest possible score), the less likely you are to use contraceptives, and the higher your score (50 is the highest possible score), the greater the likelihood that you would use contraceptives. A score of 30 places you at the midpoint between not using and using contraceptives.

When students in a marriage and family class were asked to describe their feelings when they had intercourse without using contraception, "worry," "anxiety," and "fear" were the most common descriptions. Specific comments follow:

Each time I have done it [had intercourse without protection], I always feel extremely guilty and every day I pray I get my period. It's not a very secure feeling at all since you know you can get pregnant.

.

I feel stupid and I talk to myself all month about how stupid I am. I always say, 'This is the last time I'll ever have sex without contraceptives.' I've been lucky so far but it's not worth it—the entire month after having sex I worry and work myself into a frenzy. The tension is on.

.

We had talked about sex for some time and had even talked about what type of contraceptive we would use if the need should arise. What happened, though, was we both got drunk, and without thinking about the consequences, one thing led to another. The next day she got scared and then I got scared. That is when I started to think, "It couldn't happen to us, it was our first time, she was a virgin." But it did happen to us. She got pregnant.

Students were also asked to describe their feelings when they did use contraceptives while having intercourse. "Self-confident," "secure," and "safe" were common feelings.

I feel good about myself knowing I'm on the pill. I tell myself that I'm not going to get pregnant. My boyfriend and I can enjoy sex so much better. It's a relief not having to sweat out the month wondering whether I'm pregnant.

.

I have congratulated myself on gathering the courage to go to the infirmary and get the pill. I believe that if you are mature enough to have intercourse, you are mature enough to prevent mistakes. I find that now I feel more self-confident and that I don't worry during sex. It's having pleasure without the tension of worry.

.

I told myself when I had intercourse and used contraception that she would not get pregnant and we would not have to worry about having a baby. We were both more relaxed.

Married couples are the most likely to consistently use some form of contraception. Table 15.2 shows the percentage of wives between the ages of 15 and 44 using various contraceptives. Each of these contraceptives is discussed in the following pages.

Oral Contraceptives

Birth control pills are the contraceptive preferred by most women—married and unmarried. Although there are more than 40 brands available in North America, there are basically two types of pills—the combination pill and the minipill.

The combination pill contains the hormones estrogen and progesterone (also known as progestin), which act to prevent ovulation and implantation. The estrogen inhibits release of the follicle-stimulating hormone (FSH) from the pitu-

Table 15.2 Percentage of U.S. Wives Using Various Nonsurgical Contraceptives

TYPE OF CONTRACEPTIVE	PERCENT
Pill	46
Condom	15
IUD	13
Rhythm	7
Diaphragm	6
Foam	6
Withdrawal	4
Douche	1
Other	2

Source: National Center for Health Statistics, 1981.

itary gland so that no follicle will develop. In effect, an egg will not mature. In other words, A (estrogen) blocks B (FSH), which would have produced C (egg).

The progesterone inhibits release of luteinizing hormone (LH) from the pituitary, which during a normal cycle would cause the mature ovum to move to the periphery of the follicle and the follicle to rupture (ovulation). Hence, there is no ovulation. In this case, A (progestin) blocks B (LH), which would have caused C (ovulation).

The progesterone serves as a secondary protection by causing a change in the composition of the cervical mucus. It becomes both thick and acidic, creating a hostile environment for the sperm. So even if an egg were to mature and ovulation were to occur, the progesterone would ward off or destroy sperm. Another function of progesterone is to make the lining of the uterus unsuitable for implantation.

The combination pill is taken for 21 days, beginning on the fifth day after the start of the menstrual flow. Three or four days after the last pill is taken, menstruation occurs and the 28-day cycle begins again. To eliminate the problem of remembering when to begin taking the pill every month, some physicians prescribe a low-dose combination pill for the first 21 days and a placebo (sugar pill) or iron pill for the next seven days. In this way, the woman takes a pill every day.

The second type of oral contraceptive is the minipill, which contains the same progesterone found in the combination pill but at much lower doses. The minipill contains no estrogen. As in the combination pill, progesterone provides a hostile environment for sperm and inhibits implantation of a fertilized egg in the uterus.

Either the combination or minipill should be taken only when prescribed by a physician who has detailed information about the woman's previous medical history. Contraindications, or reasons for not prescribing birth control pills, include hypertension, impaired liver function, known or suspected tumors that are estrogen dependent, undiagnosed abnormal genital bleeding, pregnancy at the time of the examination, and a history of poor blood circulation. The major complications associated with taking oral contraceptives are blood clots and high blood pressure. Also, the risk of heart attack is increased in women over age 30, particularly those who smoke or have other risk factors. Women over 40 should generally use other forms of contraception as side effects of contracep-

A pill a day keeps the doctor away.

ANONYMOUS

tive pills increase with the age of the user. Infertility problems have also been noted in women who have used the combination pill for several years without the breaks in pill use recommended by most physicians.

Although the long-term negative consequences of taking birth control pills are still the subject of research, short-term negative effects are experienced by 25 percent of women. These mild side effects include increased susceptibility to vaginal infections, nausea, slight weight gain, vaginal bleeding between periods, breast tenderness, mild headaches, and mood changes (some women become depressed and experience a loss of sexual desire).

CONSIDERATION • In spite of these negative consequences associated with pill use, numerous studies involving hundreds of thousands of women show that the overall risk of pill use is less than that of full-term pregnancy and giving birth (Ory, Rosenfeld, & Landman, 1980).

There are also immediate health benefits for taking birth control pills. Oral contraceptives tend to protect the woman against breast tumors, ovarian cysts, rheumatoid arthritis, and pelvic inflammatory disease. They also regularize her menstrual cycle, reduce premenstrual tension, and may reduce menstrual cramps and blood loss during menstruation. Finally, oral contraceptives are convenient, do not interfere with intercourse, and most important, provide highly effective protection against pregnancy.

Whether to use birth control pills remains a controversial issue. Some women feel that it harms their body to take birth control pills; others feel it harms their body not to take them. Whatever a woman's choice, it should be made in conjunction with her physician who knows her medical history.

Condom

Also referred to as a "rubber," "safe," or "prophylactic," the condom is currently the only form of male contraception. The condom is a thin sheath, usually made of synthetic material or lamb intestine, which is rolled over and down the shaft of the erect penis before intercourse. When the man ejaculates, the sperm are caught inside the condom. When used in combination with a spermicidal, or sperm-killing, agent, which the woman inserts in her vagina, the condom is a highly effective contraceptive.

CONSIDERATION • The condom is also the only contraceptive that provides some protection against sexually transmitted diseases.

Although some men say they do not like to use a condom because it decreases sensation, others say that having the woman put the condom on their penis is an erotic experience and that the condom actually enhances pleasurable feelings during intercourse.

Like any contraceptive, the condom is effective only when properly used. A space should be left at the top of the condom (some condoms already have a recessed tip) when it is rolled onto the penis to leave room for the semen to collect. Otherwise the condom may break. In addition, the penis should be withdrawn from the vagina soon after ejaculation. If the penis is not withdrawn and the erection subsides, the semen will leak from the base of the condom into the vaginal lips. The sperm can then travel up the vagina into the uterus and fertilize the egg.

In addition to furnishing extra protection, spermicides also provide lubrication, which permits easy entrance of the condom-covered penis into the vagina. If no spermicide is used and the condom is not of the prelubricated variety, K-Y jelly, a sterile lubricant, may be needed. Vaseline or other kinds of petroleum jelly should not be used because they may increase the risk of vaginal infection.

Condoms can be purchased in drugstores and most convenience stores. Among the brand names are Trojan, Ramses, Sheik, Naturalamb, and Fourex. The latter two are made from lamb intestine and are considerably more expensive than those made from synthetic material.

Intrauterine Device (IUD)

The IUD, or intrauterine device, is a small object that is inserted by a physician into the woman's uterus through the vagina and cervix. Most IUDs have two plastic threads attached to them that hang down into the vagina so the woman can feel them and check regularly that the device is in place. The four most commonly used IUDs are the Lippes Loop, Saf-T-Coil, Copper-7, and Progestasert T. The latter contains a slow-releasing progesterone and must be replaced every year. The IUD stays inside the uterus until it is removed by the physician. Although used most frequently by women who have had a child, some women who have never been pregnant may also use the IUD.

> Whenever I hear people discussing birth control, I always remember that I was the fifth.
>
> CLARENCE DARROW

The IUD works by preventing implantation of the fertilized egg on the uterine wall. The exact chemistry is unknown, but one theory suggests that the IUD stimulates the entry of white blood cells into the uterus, which attack and destroy "invading" cells, in this case, the fertilized egg. Implantation may also be prevented by the IUD mechanically dislodging the egg from the uterine wall.

Side effects of the IUD include cramps, excessive menstrual bleeding, and irregular bleeding, or spotting, between menstrual periods. These effects may disappear after the first two months of use. Infection and perforation are more serious side effects. Users of the IUD have a higher incidence of pelvic inflammatory disease, which infects the uterus and Fallopian tubes and may lead to sterility. In addition, the IUD may cut or perforate the uterine walls or cervix, resulting in bleeding and pain.

CONSIDERATION • Because of these potential side effects, women who plan to have children should consider using another method of contraception.

Some women are unable to retain the IUD; it irritates the muscles of the uterus causing them to contract and expel the IUD.

DATA • *The discontinuation rate with the IUD is 43 percent at the end of two years. Increased menstrual bleeding, pain, expulsion soon after insertion and pelvic infection account for the high rate of discontinuation.* (Harper, 1983)

To make sure that the IUD remains in place, a woman should check it at least once a month just after her period.

The fact that the IUD does not prevent conception is both its greatest advantage and disadvantage. The advantage is that the IUD does not interfere with the body's normal hormonal and physiological responses. The disadvantage is that it permits conception and then destroys the fertilized egg, which is morally repugnant to some people. "It's the same as abortion," said one devout Catholic. Also, women who do get pregnant while using the IUD must make a decision about whether to leave it in or remove it. There is a 50 percent chance for miscarriage if the IUD is left in and a 25 percent chance for miscarriage if the IUD is taken out. In most cases, the IUD is removed. However, there are no reports of birth defects if the IUD is left in and the baby is carried to a term delivery.

Diaphragm

The diaphragm is a shallow rubber dome attached to a flexible, circular steel spring. Varying in diameter from 2 to 4 inches, the diaphragm covers the cervix and prevents sperm from moving beyond the vagina into the uterus. It should always be used with a spermicidal jelly or cream.

To obtain a diaphragm, the woman must have an internal pelvic examination by a physician or nurse practitioner who will select the appropriate size of diaphragm and instruct the woman how to insert it. She will be told to apply the spermicidal cream or jelly on the inside of the diaphragm and to insert it at least two hours before intercourse.

DATA • *The diaphragm must be left in place after intercourse for 6 to 8 hours to permit any lingering sperm to be killed by the spermicidal cream.* (Shepard, 1980b)

After the birth of a child, a miscarriage, abdominal surgery, or the gain or loss of 10 pounds, a woman who uses a diaphragm should consult her physician or health practitioner to ensure a continued good fit. In any case, the diaphragm should be checked every two years for fit.

A major advantage of the diaphragm is that it does not interfere with the woman's hormonal system and has few, if any, side effects. Also, for those couples who feel that menstruation diminishes their capacity to enjoy intercourse, the diaphragm may be used to catch the menstrual flow.

On the negative side, some women feel that use of the diaphragm with the spermicidal gel is messy and a nuisance. For some the use of the gel may produce an allergic reaction. Furthermore, some partners feel that the gel makes oral-genital contact less enjoyable. Finally, if the diaphragm does not fit properly, pregnancy can result.

Cervical Cap

Not to be confused with the diaphragm, the cervical cap is a small rubber or plastic cap that fits snugly over the cervix and is held in place by suction. It blocks sperm from entering the cervix but the newer models have a one-way valve that permits menstrual material and cervical secretions to flow outward. Unlike the diaphragm, the cervical cap can be left in place for a week.

Cervical caps are currently being tested in the United States for FDA approval. Of 550 women who requested the cap (Koch, 1982), about one-fourth could not be fitted with one of the four sizes available. Those who were able to obtain a proper fit were instructed to fill the cap completely with spermicide before inserting it, to leave it in place for no longer than seven days, and to avoid using it during menstruation. In a two-year follow up, 30 percent reported that the cap had become dislodged during intercourse and four in 10 said that the most objectionable feature of the cap was a noticeable odor during use.

Vaginal Spermicides

Spermicidal foam contains chemicals that kill sperm. The foam must be applied near the cervix (appropriate applicators are included when the product is purchased) no more than 20 minutes before intercourse; and each time intercourse is repeated, more foam must be applied. Spermicidal creams also kill sperm; each application comes individually packaged, and the packaging can be disposed of after use.

> CONSIDERATION • Foams such as Delfen and Emko should not be confused with vaginal deodorants such as Summer's Eve. The latter has no contraceptive value. Spermicidal foams should also not be confused with spermicidal gels that are used in conjunction with a diaphragm. These gels should never be used alone since they do not stick to the cervix as well as foam.

Foams are advantageous because they do not manipulate the woman's hormonal system and they have few side effects. These include allergic reactions in some men and women (their genitals may become irritated by the chemicals in the foam). The main disadvantage is that some regard its use as messy and its taste unpleasant if oral-genital contact is enjoyed.

Vaginal suppositories also contain spermicide and are inserted about 30 minutes before intercourse. Also known as pessaries, vaginal suppositories provide protection by killing sperm and weakening sperm motility.

Vaginal Sponge

One of the newest contraceptives to win approval by the FDA is the vaginal sponge. The sponge is 2 inches in diameter, 1¼ inches thick, and contains spermicide that is activated when the sponge is immersed in water before insertion into the vagina. A small loop allows for easy removal of the sponge. Like condoms and spermicidal foams, the sponge is available in drugstores without a prescription. The brand name for the sponge is Today. It prevents fertilization, not only by releasing spermicide to kill sperm but also by blocking the cervix to prevent the sperm entering and by absorbing sperm into the sponge.

A major advantage of the sponge is that it allows for spontaneity in lovemaking since it can be inserted early in the day, may be worn for up to 24 hours, and may be used for more than one act of intercourse without requiring additional applications of spermicide. According to FDA tests on 1,582 sponge users, the sponge is comparable to the diaphragm in effectiveness.

Rhythm Method

The rhythm method is based on the premise that fertilization cannot occur unless live sperm are present when the egg is in the Fallopian tubes.

DATA • *Sperm usually live two to three days, whereas an egg lives 24 hours.* (Nass et al., 1984)

Women who use the rhythm method must know their time of ovulation and avoid intercourse just before, during, and immediately after that time. There are three ways of predicting the presumed safe period: the calendar method, the basal body temperature method, and the cervical mucus method.

CALENDAR METHOD

When using the calendar method to predict when the egg is ready to be fertilized, the woman keeps a record of the length of her menstrual cycles for eight months. The menstrual cycle is counted from day one of the menstrual period through the last day before the onset of the next period. She then calculates her fertile period by subtracting 18 days from the shortest cycle and 11 days from the longest. The resulting figures indicate the range of her fertility period. It is during this time that she must avoid intercourse.

For example, suppose that during an eight-month period, a woman had cycle lengths of 26, 32, 27, 30, 28, 27, 28, and 29 days. Subtracting 18 from her shortest cycle (26) and 11 from her longest cycle (32), she knows the days the egg is likely to be in the Fallopian tubes. To avoid getting pregnant, she must avoid intercourse on days 8 through 21 of her cycle.

BASAL BODY TEMPERATURE (BBT) METHOD

This method is based upon temperature changes that occur in the woman's body shortly after ovulation. The basal body temperature is the temperature of the body at rest upon waking in the morning. To establish her BBT, the woman must take her temperature for three months at this time before she gets out of bed. Just before ovulation, her temperature will drop about 0.2 degrees F. Between 24 and 72 hours later, there will be a rise in temperature of about 0.6 to 0.8 degrees F above her normal BBT, signaling the time of ovulation. (See Exhibit 15.1, Basal Body Temperature By Computer, for an alternative method of computation.) Intercourse must be avoided from the time the woman's temperature drops until her temperature has remained elevated for three consecutive days. Beginning on the night of the third day after the temperature shift is observed, she may resume having intercourse.

CERVICAL MUCUS METHOD

The cervical mucus method is based on observations of changes in the mucus cycle from no perceptible mucus for several days after menstruation to sticky to very slippery during ovulation to a cloudy discharge after ovulation ends. The mucus becomes thin and slippery, very similar to raw egg white, during ovulation to create a favorable environment for sperm. The woman should abstain from intercourse as soon as mucus appears before ovulation and continue to do so for four complete days after the peak of cervical mucus. A woman can check her cervical mucus by wiping herself with toilet paper several times a day before she urinates and observing the changes. This method requires the woman to distinguish between mucus and semen, spermicidal agents, lubrication, and discharges by infection. Also, she must not douche since she will wash away what she is trying to observe.

Other labels for the cervical mucus method are natural family planning and the Billings method (named after Evelyn and John Billings). Associated with the Billings method is the woman's observation of the *Mittelschmerz*—the mid-cycle abdominal pain or "ping" sometimes associated with ovulation.

Postcoital Contraception

Some women who have engaged in unprotected intercourse in the middle of their cycle elect to take a morning-after pill, which contains high levels of estrogen to prevent implantation of the fertilized egg on the uterine wall. This is an emergency form of birth control, is potentially dangerous, and is available only by prescription from a physician.

Diethylstilbestrol (DES) is the most commonly used morning-after pill. The first of ten 25 milligram doses must be taken within 72 hours after intercourse and preferably within 12 to 24 hours. Normally, the pills are taken twice a day for five days. Of 5,593 women treated with DES, only 26 became pregnant (Hatcher et al., 1978).

CONSIDERATION • Side effects of nausea, vomiting, bleeding abnormalities, and blood clots make routine use of this drug undesirable. In addition, studies indicate that the offspring of women who took DES (not knowing they were pregnant) were more likely to have birth defects and have an increased risk of vaginal cancer and infertility. If the woman remains pregnant after taking DES, she might consider a therapeutic abortion.

Nonmethods

Some people erroneously regard withdrawal and douching as effective methods of contraception. They are not.

WITHDRAWAL

Withdrawal, also known as coitus interruptus, is the practice of the man taking his penis out of the vagina before he ejaculates. Not only does this technique interrupt sexual pleasure, but it is also an unreliable means of contraception. Even before ejaculation, the man may, without his awareness, emit a small amount of fluid from the Cowper's gland, which may contain sperm. In addition, the man may delay his withdrawal too long and inadvertently ejaculate some semen near the vaginal opening of his partner. Sperm deposited here can live in the moist vaginal lips and make their way up the vagina to the uterus.

DOUCHING

Douching refers to rinsing or cleansing of the vaginal canal. After intercourse the woman fills a syringe with water or a spermicidal agent and flushes (so she assumes) the sperm from her vagina. But in some cases, the fluid will actually force sperm up through the cervix. In other cases, a large number of sperm may already have passed through the cervix to the uterus so that the douche may do little good.

CONSIDERATION • In effect, a douche does little to deter conception and may encourage it. Also, most physicians question the advisability of douching since they feel that doing so may create chemical imbalances in the vagina that may lead to infection.

• AVOIDING STDs AND PREGNANCY •

As suggested earlier, a condom that is put on before the penis touches the other person's body will make it difficult for a sexually transmitted disease (including genital herpes) to pass from one person to another.

It isn't very romantic to talk about STDs with a partner you are about to have sex with. But to ignore STDs one minute is to risk contracting one the next. Contraception should also be discussed beforehand. Not to do so involves the risk of unwanted pregnancy.

What might a person say before having a sexual experience with a new partner about the issues of sexually transmitted diseases and protection from pregnancy? One marriage and family professor asked her students how they would handle the situation if they were on an isolated moonlit beach with a person they wanted to have sex with (Hayes, 1983). Some of their responses follow:

In a situation like this, you have to be open and discuss the consequences. If this "messes up the mood," maybe that's the best thing—better than ending up diseased or pregnant. You can't let your feelings and your hormones [urges] control this situation. (a female)

Even in the heat of passion, one still has to be concerned about herpes and pregnancy. I would first ask if he was going to share something with me that he knew I wouldn't want him to share. I would definitely clarify if necessary. I would also state that I am not ready to be a mother and that some sort of birth control is necessary to continue. (a female)

The discussion of protection against pregnancy could be entwined into the romance of the evening, perhaps even made part of verbiage in sexual play. The discussion would not probably be purely sensual, rather one where feelings of care and love are conveyed. The discussion of STD would not be nearly as simple. It would be next to impossible to keep this subject within the mood of the evening. One of the parties will probably be offended. Nonetheless, this topic is of vital importance to discuss, mind you lightly, but it must be done. Perhaps after putting it into perspective for "our future," not to hurt each other, the ground lost can be recovered later in the evening. (a female)

I would just have to come right out and question my partner point blank about the subjects. If she had no protection, I'd make a quick trip to the convenience store to buy a condom if possible or abstain if not. If she had an STD I would take her back to her place and ride off into the sunset as quickly as possible, never to return. (a male)

Bringing up a subject like herpes or contraception would seem to detract from the mood more than would abstinence. This fact, along with the guilt feelings I would have to deal with after the experience with or without protection, has been enough incentive in this situation in the past to get me to stop short of intercourse so that the beauty of the memory is as great as the beauty of the moment. I'll keep it that way. (a male)

Since this is a new experience for us, we would probably both be more comfortable if we completely leveled with each other about protection. This includes birth control as well as sexually transmitted disease. Is this agreeable with you? If the partner doesn't want to discuss it, I'd be wary of the partner. I'd also be aware that complete honesty is not always forthcoming in such situations. Open communication enhances any relationship—sexual or otherwise. (gender not specified)

DATA • *In a study of 856 college students, those having more egalitarian gender-role attitudes were more likely to take equal responsibility for contracep-*

tion, to talk about it before intercourse, and to use contraception effectively than those having traditional gender-role attitudes.   (MacCorquodale, 1984)

• STERILIZATION •

Unlike the temporary and reversible methods of contraception just discussed, sterilization is a surgical procedure that permanently prevents the capacity of either gender to reproduce. Sterilization is losing its stigma as an extreme and undesirable method of birth control. It may be a method of choice because the woman should not have more children for health reasons, because of a desire to have no more children, or because of a desire to remain child-free. Most couples complete their intended childbearing in their late twenties or early thirties. This leaves more than 15 years of continued risk of unwanted pregnancy. Because of the risk of pill use at older ages and the lower reliability of alternative methods, sterilization is being increasingly chosen as the primary method of fertility control.

DATA • *About 20 percent of married couples use sterilization as a means of contraception.*   (Lederer, 1983)   *Among married women, it is the most popular method of contraception.*   (Pratt & Bachrach, 1983)   *Only about 1 percent of women and men who have been sterilized change their mind and want a reversal.*   (Riggall, 1980)

Slightly more than half of all sterilizations are performed on women. Although male sterilization is easier and safer than female sterilization, women feel more certain they will not get pregnant if they are sterilized. "I'm the one that ends up being pregnant and having the baby," said one woman. "So I want to make sure that I never get pregnant again."

Female Sterilization

Although a woman may be sterilized by removal of her ovaries (oophorectomy) or uterus (hysterectomy), these operations are not normally undertaken for the sole purpose of sterilization because the ovaries produce important hormones as well as eggs and because both procedures carry the risks of major surgery. But sometimes there is another medical problem requiring hysterectomy.

The mother of the year should be a sterilized woman with two adopted children.

PAUL R. EHRLICH

The usual procedures of female sterilization are salpingectomy and a variant of it, laparoscopy. Salpingectomy, also known as "tubal ligation" or "tying the tubes," is often performed under a general anesthetic while the woman is in the hospital just after she has delivered a baby. An incision is made in the lower abdomen, just above the pubic line, and the Fallopian tubes are brought into view one at a time. A part of each tube is cut out, and the ends are tied, clamped, or cauterized (burned). The operation takes about 30 minutes. About 700,000 such procedures are performed annually.

A less expensive and quicker (about 15 minutes) form of salpingectomy, which is performed on an outpatient basis, is laparoscopy. Often using local anesthesia, the surgeon inserts a small, lighted viewing instrument (laparoscope) through the woman's abdominal wall just below the navel through which the uterus and the Fallopian tubes can be seen. The surgeon then makes another small incision in the lower abdomen and inserts a special pair of forceps that carry electricity to cauterize the tubes. The laparoscope and forceps are then withdrawn, the small wounds are closed with a single stitch, and small bandages are placed over the closed incisions (laparoscopy is also known as "the band-aid operation").

As an alternative to reaching the tubes through an opening below the navel, the surgeon may make a small incision in the back of the vaginal barrel (vaginal tubal ligation).

These procedures for female sterilization are highly effective. But sometimes there are complications. In rare cases, a blood vessel in the abdomen is torn open during the sterilization and bleeds into the abdominal cavity. When this happens, another operation is necessary to find the bleeding vessel and tie it closed. Occasionally, there is injury to the small or large intestine, which may cause nausea, vomiting, and loss of appetite. The fact that death may result, if only rarely, is a reminder that female sterilization is surgery and, like all surgery, involves some risks.

Male Sterilization

The most frequent form of male sterilization is vasectomy. About 750,000 are performed annually, usually in the physician's office under a local anesthetic. Vasectomy involves making two small incisions in the scrotum so that a small portion of each vas deferens (the sperm-carrying ducts) can be cut out and tied closed. Sperm are still produced in the testicles, but since there is no tube to the penis, they remain in the testicles and eventually dissolve. The operation takes about 15 minutes, costs about $300, and the man can leave the physician's office within a short time. Most vasectomies are performed Friday afternoon so that an employed man will not have to miss work.

Since sperm do not disappear from the ejaculate immediately after a vasectomy, another method of contraception should be used until the man has had about 20 ejaculations. He is then asked to bring a sample of his ejaculate to the physician's office so that it can be examined under a microscope for a sperm count. In about 1 percent of the cases, the vas deferens grows back and the man becomes fertile again. In other cases, the man may have more than two tubes, which the physician was not aware of.

A vasectomy does not affect the man's desire for sex, ability to have an erection, orgasm, or the amount of ejaculate (sperm comprise only a minute portion of the seminal fluid). In a follow-up study of 1,012 men who had vasectomies (Simon Population Trust, 1973), 98 percent reported their sex life had improved or was unchanged. Two percent said their sex life had become worse. In another study, husbands reported an increase in intercourse of 2.5 times per month following their vasectomies (Maschoff et al., 1976).

In contrast to mostly positive evaluations of vasectomy, there are some suspected long-term negative side effects. In some men, some of the sperm escape into the circulatory system with the result that the body produces antibodies to the sperm. Some physicians are concerned that this may lead to a breakdown in the body's immune system.

But these concerns are speculative. In a comparison of 4,385 vasectomized and 13,155 nonvasectomized men (matched by age and race), Petitti (1983) found no significant difference for a large number of symptoms and diseases, including those of the cardiovascular system. Her conclusion was that vasectomy does not lead to disease in humans. Another study compared more than 10,000 men who had had a vasectomy with a similar number matched for age, race, and marital status (National Institute of Child Health and Human Development Collaborative Study, 1983). The result—there is no evidence that vasectomy has any adverse health consequences.

• ABORTION •

What if an unwanted pregnancy occurs? One alternative is an abortion—the removal of the fetus from the woman's uterus early in pregnancy before it can survive on its own (90 percent of abortions are obtained within the first 12 weeks of gestation). Of the 1.5 million abortions performed annually in the United States, most are obtained by young (18–19-year-olds), white (70 percent of abortions), and unmarried (80 percent of abortions) women, including the never married, separated, divorced, and widowed (Henshaw & O'Reilly, 1983).

Reasons for getting an abortion are related to age (Lewis, 1980). Unmarried women 18 and over state, "I wasn't ready to take care of a child," "I couldn't stay home and take care of a baby," and "I didn't have the money to support a child" (p. 450). In contrast, those less than 18 often have an abortion because of social shame or parental pressure. "My folks told me I would have to get an abortion," said one 16-year-old.

DATA • *About 20 percent of U.S. women have had an abortion. If abortion rates continue, about 40 percent of women will have an abortion before they turn 45.* (Forrest & Henshaw, 1983)

The woman with an unwanted pregnancy may be beset by a number of strong feelings: fear ("What will I do now?"), self-anger ("How could I let this happen?"), guilt ("What would my parents think if they knew I was pregnant?"), ambivalence ("Will I be sorry if I have an abortion? Will I be sorry if I don't?"), and sometimes desperation ("Maybe suicide is a way out").

CONSIDERATION • One of the best decisions during this period of crisis is to talk with an abortion counselor or a counselor at a local mental health center. These professionals are trained to help women look at alternatives and to help them decide what is best. Perhaps most important, they can help the pregnant woman to make her decision with care and deliberation rather than under pressure.

Methods of Induced Abortion

An abortion may be spontaneous (by miscarriage) or induced. Methods of inducing an abortion include the following.

VACUUM CURETTAGE

In vacuum curettage a hollow plastic rod attached to a vacuum aspirator is inserted into the woman's uterus through the cervix, which has been dilated and anesthetized. The device draws the fetal tissue and surrounding matter out of the uterus. Vacuum curretage can be performed in a physician's office and takes about 10 minutes. If done within eight weeks of the last menstrual period, the dilation and anesthesia may not be necessary and the procedure is referred to as a menstrual extraction.

DILATION AND CURETTAGE (D AND C)

In place of the vacuum curettage, a sharp metal surgical instrument is used to scrape the fetal tissue and placenta from the walls of the uterus. A general anesthetic is usually administered. This more traditional procedure is regarded as inferior to the vacuum curettage method.

DILATION AND EVACUATION (D AND E)

Used in the second trimester, D and E is a combination of the vacuum curretage and D and C. But more dilation of the cervical opening is required.

DATA • *More than 95 percent of all abortions are done by vacuum curettage, D and C, or D and E.* (U.S. Department of Health and Human Services, 1983)

SALINE INJECTION

As pregnancy progresses, the fetus becomes too large to be removed safely by any of the preceding methods. Abortion by saline may be performed by inserting a long needle containing a concentrated salt solution through the abdominal and uterine walls into the amniotic cavity. This kills the fetus. From six to 48 hours later, the uterus contracts until the fetus is pushed out into the vagina.

CONSIDERATION • Because saline injection is a major surgical procedure, earlier termination of pregnancy is desirable.

A variation of the saline method of abortion is the use of prostaglandins— hormonelike substances that cause the uterus to contract. When introduced into the vagina as a suppository or injected into the amniotic sac, they induce labor and the fetus is aborted.

HYSTEROTOMY

Hysterotomy is abdominal surgery through a caesarean section in which the surgeon cuts through the uterine wall and takes out the fetus. Because it is major surgery and expensive, it is used when the pregnancy is between 16 and 24 weeks and when the mother's health precludes the use of induction methods.

DATA • *Less than 4 percent of abortions are of the saline, prostaglandin, or hysterotomy variety.* (U.S. Department of Health and Human Services, 1983)

Abortion is an experience that is different for each woman. Exhibit 15.2 describes three abortion experiences.

· Exhibit 15.2 ·

THREE ABORTION EXPERIENCES

Mary found out that she was pregnant a week after she and her partner had broken their engagement.

I had just begun the first quarter of my freshman year and did not know anyone on campus. At the time, I thought abortion was the only way out since none of my friends were close by. Little did I know I was about to go through what has been the most traumatic experience of my life.

I became fast friends with a campus minister, and approximately one month after I found out I was pregnant I had an appointment to have the abortion. The "day" came and my new friend drove me to the clinic. I went through the procedures of paying, talking with a therapist, and finally being taken to a small white room where all the equipment was. I lay on a table with nothing but a hospital "robe" for nearly a half hour during which I almost changed my mind. The doctor finally came in and the abortion was over in about 20 minutes—with some pain and the worst two needles I have ever received.

After "it" was over, I lay there for another 15 to 20 minutes feeling very scared and sick. I wanted to just burst out in tears but I was afraid if I did, I would never stop crying. I remember how I wished I had been strong enough to change my mind before. I then got dressed and went to rest in a small room where my friend was waiting. I was amazed at how calm and unfeeling I seemed to be— at least as far as the doctor and nurse saw.

But about a week later I found myself in bed one night crying . . . I just kept thinking what I had done. It took several months before I could go an entire day without thinking about it. I felt like I had a constant pain way down deep in my stomach—the loss of a part of me. I began to appreciate my life in a very different way—realizing that I had no right to take another person's life—my baby's. One thing is for sure, I would never have another abortion.

Pam had been involved in a four-year relationship with a man during which time she had two abortions.

The first pregnancy was an accident and happened when I was 18. It terrified me to know I was pregnant. Both of us were planning to go to college so we knew the pregnancy had to be terminated. Neither of us was ready for a child. He paid for the abortion and went with me to the clinic. The abortion was a frightening and painful experience, but I kept my head straight and only thought about the realistic view of the situation.

The second pregnancy was mostly my fault so we shared the expense of the abortion. As was true the first time, the abortion was painful but not as frightening because I knew what to expect. This time we gave the idea of keeping the baby more thought and it was through the process of pros and cons that we decided to terminate the pregnancy. I have no regrets about either abortion because I know it was the right thing for me and for the baby.

Joan was married and in her fifth month of pregnancy. Because of a genetic disorder that would prevent their baby from being born alive, the pregnancy had to be terminated.

The physician induced labor and I was in labor for 16 hours. The labor was followed by a very difficult breech birth. Each labor pain seemed to drive home the fact that the baby we had was lost. When the fetus was delivered, she was nearly the size of a newborn because of her genetic disorder. It was unreal to see them carry away our baby bundled in a blanket. There was no excitement or joy that went with the birth, only the realization that physically our ordeal was almost over. Emotionally, we would have a long way to go. One thing that stood out in our minds was the incredible feeling of death. One day I had been so enormously pregnant and the next day I wasn't—with no baby to show for it. All our hopes and expectations had been "terminated" with the pregnancy.

Abortion Legislation

In 1973 the U.S. Supreme Court ruled that during the first three months of pregnancy, a woman has the right to obtain an abortion from a licensed physician without interference by the state. From the fourth through the sixth month, the decision to have an abortion belongs to the woman and her physician, but because an abortion at this later stage of pregnancy is more dangerous, the state may require that the abortion be performed in a hospital. During the last three months of pregnancy, the state may prohibit abortion except in those cases where the life or health of the mother is in danger. Neither a woman's husband nor her parents may veto her decision. In effect, the Supreme Court ruled that the fetus is a *potential* life and not a "person." Since the Supreme Court ruling, the number of legal abortions has increased and the number of abortion-related deaths has vastly decreased (Binkin, 1982).

DATA • *Over the past decade, the replacement of unintended births and illegal abortions by legal abortions has averted perhaps 1,500 pregnancy-related deaths and several tens of thousands of life-threatening complications.* (Tietze, 1984)

In 1980 the Supreme Court ruled that federal funds could not be used to pay for abortions. This ruling upheld the Hyde Amendment (sponsored by Representative Henry Hyde), which restricted congressional spending of Medicaid funds for abortions where the mother's life was not in danger or in cases where she was not impregnated by rape or incest. Although the decision has had little effect on abortion among affluent women, women with limited income who have an unwanted pregnancy—about half a million women per year—are seriously affected. Many of these women carry their pregnancies to term rather than resort to nonmedical abortions that are likely to be unsafe.

In 1981 Senator Jesse Helms sponsored the Human Life Amendment to the Constitution, which would define life as beginning at conception. Passage of the amendment would mean that the developing embryo would have a right to life and those terminating a pregnancy by abortion could be prosecuted for murder.

On the issue of abortion, heated disagreement continues.

In 1983 another constitutional amendment was suggested that would give the states the power to ban abortion. This amendment sidestepped the issue of when life begins but would permit a mechanism to outlaw abortion.

But also in 1983, the Supreme Court reaffirmed its position on abortion and struck down several state and local regulations that had been designed to make obtaining an abortion more difficult. The court declared unconstitutional regulations requiring that (1) all abortions for women more than three months pregnant be performed in hospitals rather than clinics, (2) physicians tell women seeking abortions about possible birth-giving alternatives, abortion risks, and that the fetus is a human life, (3) there be at least a 24-hour waiting period between the time a woman signs a consent form and the abortion is performed, (4) and all pregnant, unwed girls under 15 must obtain a parent's consent or have a judge's approval before having an abortion.

• TRENDS •

Artificial insemination, in-vitro fertilization, and ovum transfer will be used by an increasing number of people who cannot conceive a child through sexual intercourse. Some new reproductive technology is already in place. The development of cryogen, a refrigerant, permits the storage of human embryos for later implantation in the womb so that couples may have children at the desired intervals (Zoe, a baby in Australia has already been born from a frozen embryo). Embryos will also be screened for desired gender and genetic and developmental defects. Also, before the twenty-first century, it may be possible to develop embryos in artificial wombs.

The legal issues raised by these developments will be numerous. Does a surrogate mother have a right to her baby if she changes her mind after delivery? If a deformed child results from an artificial insemination in a surrogate mother, do the parents who paid for the child have a right to reject it? What are the responsibilities of a sperm bank to provide sperm that is free of defects? Do frozen embryos have inheritance rights from the people who produced them?

Trends in contraception are continued difficulty in reaching sexually active adolescents, more people who choose sterilization, and new contraceptives. The latter include a subdermal implant of levonorgestrel (a synthetic progestin) under the skin of the woman's arm. The procedure takes about five minutes and furnishes protection against pregnancy for five years or more. A long-lasting (three months) injection of 150 milligrams of the progestin Depo Provera is also being tested for FDA approval.

For men, hormonal contraceptives such as MPA (medroxyprogesterone acetate) and TO (testosterone oenanthate) have been tested in Toronto, London, and Santiago, but have not received FDA approval for use in the United States. Gossypol, an extract of cottonseed oil, has also been tested in China as an oral contraceptive. U.S. research firms are now testing the long-term safety of gossypol. A male contraceptive in the form of a pill, nasal spray, or injection is expected to be on the market by 1990 (Lederer, 1983).

· SUMMARY ·

Fertilization is the result of the union of the egg and sperm. Pregnancy may occur through sexual intercourse, artificial insemination of the wife by husband (AIH) or donor (AID), artificial insemination of a surrogate mother by the husband, test tube fertilization, or ovum transfer. Artificial methods of contraception are being used increasingly by couples when one of the pair cannot or should not conceive. The primary methods of birth control are contraception, sterilization, and abortion. With contraception, the risk of becoming pregnant can be reduced to practically zero, depending on the method and how systematically it is used. Contraception includes birth control pills, which prevent ovulation; IUDs, which prevent implantation of the fertilized egg; condoms, diaphragms, and the cervical cap, which are barrier methods; vaginal spermicides and sponge, the rhythm method, withdrawal, and douching. These methods vary in effectiveness and safety.

Sterilization is a surgical procedure that prevents fertilization, usually by blocking the passage of eggs or sperm through the Fallopian tubes or vas deferens, respectively. The procedure for female sterilization is called salpingectomy, or tubal ligation. Laparoscopy is another method of tubal ligation. The most frequent form of male sterilization is vasectomy.

Abortion is one alternative if an unwanted pregnancy occurs. Methods of inducing abortion include vacuum curettage, dilation and curettage (D and C), and dilation and evacuation (D and E), all used in the earlier stages of pregnancy, and hysterotomy and saline and prostaglandin injection, used when the pregnancy is more advanced. In 1973 the U.S. Supreme Court ruled that the abortion decision rests with the woman and her physician. Although the right to abortion has come under increasing legislative attack, the Supreme Court in 1983 struck down a number of state and local regulations that were designed to restrict abortions.

The future of fertilization and contraception include the implantation of previously frozen human embryos, legal unraveling of the complex issues involved in surrogate motherhood, and new contraceptive procedures for both women and men.

Questions for Reflection

1. To what degree are artificial insemination, surrogate mothers, in-vitro fertilization, and ovum transfers options which you would consider if you and your partner had difficulty becoming pregnant?
2. How do you feel about becoming sterilized?
3. To what degree are you prochoice or prolife regarding abortion? (This question will become more relevant after you read the Choices section that follows.)

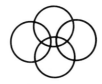

·CHOICES·

The availability of contraception, sterilization, and abortion involves a number of personal and couple choices.

CONTRACEPTION: WHICH METHOD?

Although age, marital status, partner preference, and whether you want a child later will affect your choice of a contraceptive, we discuss here the issues of personal values, health, reliability, sexual fulfillment, and psychological contentment. Do your personal values permit you to use one of the more reliable forms of contraception, that is, a mechanical or chemical method? "It's a sin to use anything but the rhythm method," one woman said. "I would feel immoral putting any of those devices in my body or contaminating my system with birth control pills." But others feel it is immoral *not* to use one of the more effective contraceptive procedures.

Another major concern is your health. Some women are at risk using the pill or IUD. If safety is the major concern, barrier methods such as the condom plus spermicide or diaphragm plus spermicide offer the greatest protection with the least risk to the wom-

an's health. Some women whose values permit abortion choose one of these methods for health reasons and consider abortion as a backup.

Reliability of the contraceptive chosen is another crucial concern. Abstinence is, of course, the ultimate contraceptive, but the various nonsurgical contraceptives have

varying rates of effectiveness. Table 15.3 indicates the failure rate of different contraceptive methods among one group of women. Other studies show that the pill and IUD are identical in effectiveness and that the condom with spermicidal agent and diaphragm with spermicidal agent approximate the effectiveness of birth control pills. The least effective method in all studies is the rhythm method.

Sexual fulfillment and psychological contentment are other issues. "It's important to me to have a good sex life," said one woman, "and fooling

(continued)

Table 15.3 Contraceptive Failure Experienced by U.S. Wives Who Wanted to Have Children in the Future

CONTRACEPTIVE METHOD	FAILURE PERCENTAGE
Pill	2.5
IUD	7.1
Condom	12.3
Diaphragm	17.2
Foam, cream, jelly, suppository	18.4
Other (withdrawal, douche, abstinence)	18.9
Rhythm	25.0

Source: Adapted with permission of the Population Council from William R. Grady, Marilyn B. Hirsch, Nelma Keen, & Barbara Vaughn's, "Contraceptive Failure and Continuation Among Married Women in the United States, 1970–1975." *Studies in Family Planning, 14,* 1 (January 1983), Table 1.

with a diaphragm every night is no fun. Yet I don't take the pill because I think it will harm my body." Her feelings emphasize that any decision about which contraceptive to use will involve some trade-offs.

In choosing a contraceptive, it should be kept in mind that any contraceptive method carries a lower death risk than childbirth itself. Summarizing his findings on this issue, Ory (1983) said:

Levels of mortality associated with all major methods of fertility control (tubal sterilization, the pill, IUD, condom, diaphragm, spermicides, rhythm and abortion) are low in comparison with the risk of death associated with childbirth and ectopic pregnancy when no fertility control method is used. The exceptions are the risks associated with pill use after the age of 40 for women who do not smoke, and with pill use after the age of 35 for smokers. The safest approach to fertility control is to use the condom and to back it up by abortion in case of method failure. (p. 62)

STERILIZATION: YES OR NO?

As we noted earlier, most couples complete their intended childbearing in their late twenties or early thirties. This leaves more than 15 years of continued risk of unwanted pregnancy. In conjunction with the risk of pill use at older ages and the lower reliability of alternative methods, sterilization is being increasingly chosen as a primary method of fertility control. It is the most frequently used method of birth control for those 30 and over.

Mumford (1983) studied 235 married and single men seeking a vasectomy and observed that there were seven basic stages in the decision-making process: becoming aware of vasectomy, discussing the procedure with a man who has had a vasectomy, deciding to have no children, beginning to seriously consider vasectomy, deciding that temporary contraceptive methods are no longer acceptable, deciding vasectomy is the best method, and having a scare (for example, the man's partner misses her period or has severe side effects from the pill).

Among the issues to be considered for sterilization in either the man or woman are the following:

1. *Permanence.* Sterilization should be considered permanent. Although microsurgery techniques do permit reversal of tubal ligations and vasectomies, the percentage of successful reversals that result in a baby is less than half.

2. *Self-image.* How do you predict you will feel about yourself following sterilization? As a woman, will you feel less feminine knowing that you are no longer capable of conceiving a child? As a man, will you feel less masculine because you can no longer father a child?

3. *Effect on Relationship.* How do you think sterilization will influence the relationship with your partner? Are you considering sterilization as a means of improving this relationship? In one follow-up study of vasectomy (Maschoff et al., 1976), both husbands and wives reported they received somewhat less affection from their spouses. But there were reported increases in the amount of communication and a marked decrease in the number of men who considered separation or divorce.

4. *The Future.* There are a number of questions you might ask yourself about the future. Are you certain you will never want another child under any conditions? If you are child-free, is it possible that you will change your mind and decide you want to have a

baby? If you have children, suppose they are killed by disease or accident? Would you then want to have another child? Suppose you were to get divorced (half of all married spouses do)? Might you want to have children with a new spouse? Suppose a new partner whom you love wouldn't marry you unless you could have a child?

There is also the possibility that your present spouse will die while you are still young enough to have children. One woman said, "I was 29 and had my tubes tied after my second child was born. Brock and I had the boy and girl we wanted and saw no reason for me to continue with birth control pills. But only a month after my laparoscopy, Brock had a heart attack and died. I'm now remarried and my new husband and I want a child of our own."

To keep their options open, some men who decide to get a vasectomy deposit some of their sperm in a sperm vault. The largest sperm banks are Xytex in Augusta, Georgia; the Infertility-Sperm Bank Service at the University of Oregon Medical School, Portland; and Idant Corporation in New York

City. Sperm storage the first year at Idant Corporation is $300. In subsequent years, the cost is $135. The probability of frozen sperm fertilizing an egg is somewhat less than that of fresh sperm.

In deciding about sterilization, it is important to balance considerations of its effect on you, your relationships, and the future against the costs and benefits associated with less permanent forms of contraception.

ABORTION: PROCHOICE OR PROLIFE?

When faced with an unwanted pregnancy, some couples decide on abortion. These prochoice advocates believe that legislation prohibiting abortion is governmental intrusion into a woman's personal, private decision. "Keep your laws and your morality off my body" reflects the anger as well as the message women want to convey to those who try to pass laws that would require women to continue with a pregnancy whether they choose to or not. The slogan "A woman's life is a human life" is a vivid reminder that Senator Jesse Helms's Human Life Amendment would inflict tragedy and suffering upon millions of women who would be forced to choose between

having babies they did not want or seeking an illegal abortion with the possibility of infection, permanent damage to the reproductive system, and even death. The prochoice proponents are a majority. Seventy percent of 1,000 women aged 18 to 65 said that abortion was their right (Women's Views Study, 1984).

Other couples faced with an unwanted pregnancy and who decide against abortion feel just as strongly that the unborn are defenseless human beings and that abortion is murder. "Choose life for your baby" and "Abortion is America's Holocaust" are two of the slogans on placards frequently carried by prolife advocates. They feel that legislation for the protection of the unborn is essential to prevent "helpless babies" being killed without caution. Prolife proponents are not without supporters. Twenty-six thousand demonstrated on the tenth anniversary of the 1973 Supreme Court decision legalizing abortion and vowed to restore protection for all innocent persons. About one-third of American women would favor a law that viewed abortion as a serious crime such as murder (Henshaw & Martire, 1982).

· Chapter 16 ·

HAVING CHILDREN

CONTENTS

Pregnancy
Labor
Childbirth Methods
**When a Woman
  Becomes a Mother**
**When a Man
  Becomes a Father**
**When a Couple
  Becomes a Family**
Self-Assessment:
  **Impact of Parenthood
  on Marriage Scale**
Choices

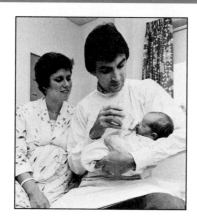

Before I got married I had six theories about bringing up children; now I have six children and no theories.

JOHN WILMOT, EARL
OF ROCHESTER
(1647–1680)

"We were both child development majors in college, had taken a preparation for parenthood class, and had been involved six weeks in a Lamaze course in anticipation of our baby. Although we thought we were prepared for the experience, we weren't. We're happy that we have Jennifer but we're still adjusting to her," said a new parent. This kind of reaction is not unique. Since the reality of parenthood is often different from the dreams and thoughts we have about it, parenthood remains a mystery until we experience it. In this chapter we look at parenthood from pregnancy through childbirth and how the new baby affects the woman, the man, and their marriage.

· PREGNANCY ·

Motherhood begins not with childbirth but with conception. Immediately after the egg is fertilized by the sperm in the Fallopian tube, it begins to divide and is pushed by hairlike cilia down the Fallopian tube into the uterus where it attaches itself to the inner wall of the uterus. Furnished with a rich supply of blood and nutrients, the developing organism is called an embryo for the first three months and a fetus thereafter.

Signs of Pregnancy

Although a missed period, morning sickness, enlarged and tender breasts, more frequent urination, and excessive fatigue are indications of pregnancy, the condition is best confirmed by laboratory tests and a physical examination.

There are several laboratory tests to assess pregnancy. All of them depend upon the presence of a hormone produced by the developing fetus, human chorionic gonadotropin (HCG), which appears in the pregnant woman's urine. One procedure, formally known as the lutex agglutination inhibition immunologic slide test, detects HCG in about 2 1/2 hours and can reveal if the woman is pregnant within 14 days after the first missed menstrual period.

> CONSIDERATION • Whereas all commercially available pregnancy tests (Early Pregnancy Test, Daisy 2, Answer, Fact) use the lutex agglutination principle, they are not as accurate as the slide tests conducted in the laboratory.

HCG also appears in the bloodstream of the pregnant woman. A radioimmunoassay test, a laboratory examination of the blood, can suggest if the woman is pregnant within eight days of conception. A new test, radioreceptorassay, also analyzes the blood and is 100 percent accurate on the first day after the first missed period.

If the laboratory test indicates pregnancy, the physician usually conducts a pelvic examination to find out if the woman's uterus has enlarged or changed color. These changes take place around the sixth week of pregnancy. Confirmation of the pregnancy is dependent on hearing and counting the fetal heart pulsations (to differentiate them from the mother's heartbeat). This occurs between the sixteenth and twentieth week.

On rare occasions women have a false pregnancy. All the usual signs of early pregnancy (morning sickness, cessation of menstrual period, and so on) are present but there is no developing fetus inside the woman's uterus. Such false pregnancies are usually the result of an intense desire to get pregnant. The mind induces what the body fails to provide. The woman is usually emotionally devastated when she learns that she is not pregnant. "We had wanted a baby so bad," said one woman, "that I knew that I was pregnant. I had already begun to look at bassinets. I was severely depressed after my doctor told me there was no baby."

The only time a woman wishes she were a year older is when she is expecting a baby.

MARY MARSH

Side Effects of Pregnancy

Pregnancy is divided into trimesters, or three-month periods, during which the woman may experience some minor discomforts owing to physical changes (Table 16.1).

Table 16.1 Some Discomforts During Pregnancy

	TRIMESTER		
	First: Week 0–14	*Second:* Week 15–26	*Third:* Week 27–40
Nausea	•		
Vomiting	•		
Frequent urination	•		•
Leg cramps	•		
Vaginal discharge	•	•	•
Fatigue	•	•	•
Constipation	•	•	•
Swelling		•	•
Varicose veins		•	•
Backache		•	•
Heartburn		•	
Shortness of breath		•	

One of the first discomforts the newly pregnant woman may experience is a feeling of nausea that may be accompanied by vomiting. The nauseous feeling occurs sometime after the first missed menstrual period and may be triggered by the odor of particular foods. Other women feel nauseated early in the morning or if they go too long without food. The specific cause of morning sickness is unknown, but hormonal and metabolic changes are the likely causes. Although the ultimate remedy is time (the nausea usually disappears by the fourth month), some women find that eating dry crackers or toast before getting out of bed each morning helps to prevent the onset of nausea. One woman said that "popcorn was the only thing I could eat without throwing up." Many physicians feel that medication to help control the nausea should be avoided because of possible negative effects on the developing embryo.

Frequent urination is also characteristic of the first trimester. The enlarging uterus presses against the bladder and causes the urgent feeling to urinate. When the uterus moves out of the pelvic area into the abdominal cavity, the urge to urinate lessens until the third trimester when the fetus presses against the bladder again. Although sometimes inconvenient, frequent urination is regarded as a normal part of pregnancy.

Vaginal discharge increases in the first trimester of pregnancy and continues until delivery. Known as leukorrhea, the discharge is a whitish mucus, and although not harmful, should be kept from accumulating by daily bathing.

CONSIDERATION • The pregnant woman should also wear cotton underpants as nylon retains heat and moisture, encouraging infection. If there are significant changes in the vaginal discharge, a physician should be consulted.

Leg cramps, particularly in the calf, may also be experienced during pregnancy. Such discomfort results from pressure on the nerves in the legs. Some physicians recommend calcium to reduce these cramps.

Other side effects are more likely to occur in the second and third trimesters. These include heartburn, constipation, backache, varicose veins, and ankle swelling. Each of these conditions tends to be temporary and the discomfort can be reduced. For example, aching varicose veins and ankle swelling can be lessened by lying on the floor and elevating the legs so that they rest on the seat of a sofa or chair. In this way, the blood can more easily flow from the legs. Heartburn can be reduced by avoiding greasy foods and eating smaller, more frequent meals. Constipation can be helped by drinking more water and eating more roughage like celery, apples, and lettuce. Backache can be eased by pelvic tilt exercises.

Nutrition During Pregnancy

Ensuring a healthy baby depends on adequate nutrition, controlled weight gain, and avoidance of substances such as alcohol and nicotine that are harmful to the fetus. A national Healthy Mothers, Healthy Babies Coalition has been established to improve maternal and infant health (Bratic, 1982).

DATA • *In one study one in five pregnant women ate more nutritional foods during their pregnancy.* (Gallup/Levi Poll, 1983)

Ideally, women should attend to their nutrition before becoming pregnant. Not only should they eat the proper type and quantity of foods, but also they should avoid foods high in sugar and fat. Table 16.2 details the foods by number of servings nonpregnant, pregnant, and lactating (breastfeeding) women need for the proper development of their infants.

CONSIDERATION • Underweight women should gain weight and overweight women should lose weight before becoming pregnant. If the woman begins her pregnancy at her ideal weight, she should gain about 20 to 24 pounds during pregnancy. Even if she is obese, she should still gain about 24 pounds to ensure adequate development of the fetus. If the mother does not gain enough weight, she may give birth to an underweight baby. A low-birthweight baby is defined as one weighing less than 5 1/2 pounds. Birthweight is the single most potent indicator of the infant's future health status. Low birthweight is associated with a higher incidence of disease and early mortality.

Pregnant women should also avoid alcohol. Fetal alcohol syndrome, refers to the negative consequences for the fetus and infant of the mother who drinks alcohol during pregnancy. These include increased risk of low birthweight, low birth length, smaller head circumference, distorted facial features, heart defects, and intellectual retardation. One of the most frightening aspects of fetal alcohol syndrome is that damage can occur as early as the third week after conception, well before most women even suspect they are pregnant. Likewise, smoking during pregnancy is associated with lower birthweight babies, premature babies, spontaneous abortions, and fetal deaths.

Table 16.2   Daily Food Guide for Pregnant Women

Food	NUMBER OF SERVINGS		
	Nonpregnant Woman	Pregnant Woman	Lactating Woman
Protein foods			
Animal (2 oz. serving)	2	2	2
Vegetable (at least one serving of legumes)	2	2	2
Milk and milk products	2	4	5
Enriched or whole-grain breads and cereals	4	4	4
Vitamin C-rich fruits and vegetables	1	1	1
Dark-green vegetables	1	1	1
Other fruits and vegetables	1	1	1

Source: Reprinted by permission from *Nutrition: Concepts and Controversies,* Second Edition, by Eva May Nunnelley Hamilton and Eleanor Noss Whitney, Copyright © 1978, 1982 by West Publishing Company. All rights reserved.

DATA • *One-third of the pregnant women in one study cut back or quit smoking during pregnancy, but one-third continued to smoke the same amount during pregnancy.*   (Gallup/Levi Poll, 1983)

Concerned about the health of their babies, some pregnant women avoid not only alcohol and cigarettes but also over-the-counter drugs such as aspirin and antihistamines, prescription drugs like amphetamines and tranquilizers, and illegal drugs like marijuana. Still others avoid caffeine since its use has been associated with birth defects. Finally, pregnant women should avoid exposure to photographic chemicals (Lappé, 1983).

Emotions During Pregnancy

Emotional reactions to pregnancy are varied. A woman may respond to her new state with excitement, viewing her morning sickness, frequent urination, and enlarging breasts as confirmation of her ability to create and sustain life. Her protruding abdomen announces to the world that her role in life is soon to change. Her husband, parents, and friends help to define her movement toward motherhood in positive terms.

But pregnancy may also trigger feelings of ambivalence. While the woman is developing an emotional attachment to her fetus, incompatible thoughts may flash through her mind. She may be excited about having a baby but apprehensive about its impact on her career and marriage. How can she balance career and family needs? Also, her husband may share her excitement about their baby, but will he still view her as sexually desirable during later pregnancy and after the baby is born?

Anxiety and fear also are not uncommon. One concern is that the baby will not be "perfect." "My closest friend was born with a birthmark that covered her right leg below the knee. I always avoid looking at her leg and hope it won't happen to my baby," remarked a woman in her seventh month. Other women are

> By far the most common craving of pregnant women is not to be pregnant.
>
> PHYLLIS DILLER

anxious about the gender of their baby. "Both of us want a boy," said one wife. "We tried the recommended procedure for having a boy and hope that it works. But my mother says you grow to love either sex child so I guess it doesn't really matter."

DATA • *Eighty percent of the pregnant women in one study had no desire to know the gender of their baby before the birth despite prenatal tests that allowed them to do so.* (Gallup/Levi Poll, 1983)

Near the end of pregnancy, a more serious concern may surface—fear of childbirth, or parturiphobia. Common fears are of pain during delivery, experiencing the unknown, and losing emotional control during delivery. Some women fear death. Various techniques of childbirth (Dick-Read, Lamaze, LeBoyer), discussed later in this chapter, are designed to help the woman work through her fears and to give her needed emotional support.

• LABOR •

Whatever emotions a woman experiences during pregnancy, they are likely to intensify as she nears the birth of her baby. Labor occurs in three stages and, although there are great variations, it lasts an average of 13 hours for the woman having her first baby (she is referred to as a primigravida) and about eight hours if the woman has given birth before (multigravida). It is not known what causes the onset of labor, which is marked by uterine contractions. But there are distinctions between the contractions of true and false labor. These include the following.

Contractions of true labor	*Contractions of false labor*
Occur at regular intervals	Occur at irregular intervals
Intervals gradually shorten	Intervals remain long
Intensity gradually increases	Intensity remains the same
Discomfort in back and abdomen	Discomfort chiefly in lower abdomen
Cervix dilates	Cervix does not dilate
Not affected by sedation	Usually relieved by sedation

First Stage of Labor

Figure 16.1 illustrates the stages of labor. Labor begins with regular uterine contractions at 15- to 20-minute intervals, which last from 10 to 30 seconds. The first stage of labor lasts for about nine hours if it is the first baby and about five hours in subsequent deliveries. During this time the woman often has cramps and backache. The membranes of the amniotic sac may rupture, spilling the amniotic fluid.

Throughout the first stage, the uterine contractions become stronger, lasting for 30 to 45 seconds, and more frequent (every three to five minutes). These contractions result in effacement and dilation of the cervix. With effacement the cervix flattens out and gets longer; with dilation the cervical opening through which the baby will pass gets larger. At the end of the first stage, the

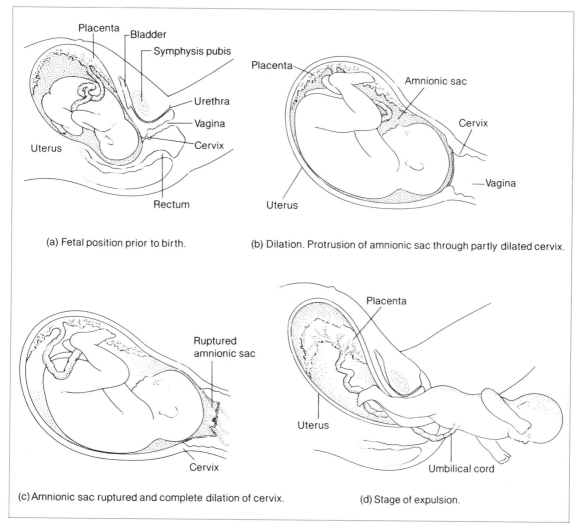

Figure 16.1 **The Birth Process**

cervix is dilated 3 1/2 to 4 inches; contractions occur every one to two minutes and last up to a minute.

During this stage the fetal heart rate is monitored continually by stethoscope or ultrasound and the woman's temperature and blood pressure are checked. She may experience leg cramps, nausea, irritability, or panic during this transitional phase of labor when the baby is getting into position to be born. Medication or anesthesia may be used at some point during this stage (see Exhibit 16.1).

Second Stage of Labor

Also known as the expulsive stage of labor, the second stage begins when the cervix is completely dilated and ends when the baby is born. It lasts about 50 minutes if it is a woman's first baby, 20 minutes if a later baby. Uterine contrac-

· Exhibit 16.1 ·

MEDICATION DURING CHILDBIRTH

Ninety-five percent of women take some type of medication to relieve the anxiety or pain of childbirth.

The four types of drugs used include the following:

1. Tranquilizers such as promethazine to reduce anxiety during labor.
2. Analgesics such as meperidine to relieve pain.
3. General anesthetics such as cyclopropane, which makes the woman unconscious during delivery.
4. Regional anesthetics, which block out pain in the vaginal area while the woman remains awake. An epidural is the most common form of regional anesthesia. Using a needle, the physician injects medication into the outer space around the spinal column, causing loss of sensation from the waist down.

There is professional disagreement on the possibility of harm to the baby from drugs. Some physicians feel that the risk is minimal and that judicious use of drugs helps to avoid a negative birth experience. Other physicians feel that the infant is at risk when drugs are introduced into the mother's body as they may depress the infant's breathing ability.

tions may last one and a half minutes and be one to two minutes apart. The contractions move the baby farther into the vaginal birth canal. The woman may help this process by pushing movements. The head of the baby emerges first followed by the shoulders and trunk. Although most babies are born head first, some are born breech. This means that the baby's feet or buttocks come out of the vagina first. Such deliveries are much more complicated. To ease the birth the physician may perform an episiotomy. This involves cutting the perineum, the area between the vagina and the anus, to make a larger opening for the baby and to prevent uncontrolled tearing.

Immediately after the baby is born, the nostrils are cleared of mucus using a small suction bulb. The umbilical cord is then clamped twice—about 1 and 2 inches from the infant's abdomen—and cut between the clamps. The baby is cleaned of placental matter and put in a temperature-controlled bassinet.

Third Stage of Labor

After the baby is born, the placenta, or afterbirth, is delivered. Usually within five minutes, the placenta separates itself from the uterine wall and is expelled from the vagina. If it does not disengage easily and by itself, the physician will remove it manually. After the placenta is delivered, if an episiotomy has been performed, the physician will repair the episiotomy by stitching up the incision.

The time from one to four hours after delivery is regarded by some physicians as a fourth stage of labor. During this time the mother's uterus relaxes and returns to a more normal state and bleeding of the cervix, resulting from the detachment of the placenta from the uterine wall, stops.

• CHILDBIRTH METHODS •

Among the alternatives to traditional childbirth preparation practices and hospital-managed deliveries are various childbirth methods, including Lamaze, Dick-Read, Bradley, and LeBoyer methods.

Lamaze Method of Childbirth

Preferred by an increasing number of couples, the Lamaze method of childbirth, often called natural childbirth, was developed by a French obstetrician, Dr. Fernand Lamaze. The method is essentially a preparation for childbirth, in which the woman and her partner take six one-and-a-half-hour classes during the last trimester of pregnancy, usually with several other couples. The goal of the sessions is to reduce the anxiety and pain of childbirth by viewing it as a natural process, by educating the couple about labor and delivery, and by giving them specific instructions to aid in the birth of their baby (see Special Topic 5 on page 615 on Resources and Organizations for the address of the American Society of Psychoprophylaxis in Obstetrics, which certifies Lamaze instructors).

There are several aspects of the Lamaze method.

1. *Education about childbirth.* The instructor explains the physiology of pregnancy, stages of labor, and delivery.
2. *Timed breathing exercises.* Specific breathing exercises are recommended for each stage of labor to help with the contractions by refocusing the laboring woman's attention and keeping the pressure of the diaphragm off the uterus. These exercises are practiced between sessions so that the couples will know when and how to use them when labor actually begins.
3. *Pain control exercises.* The woman is taught to selectively tense and relax various muscle groups of her body, for example, her arm muscles. She then learns how to tense these muscle groups while relaxing the rest of her body so that during labor she can relax the rest of her body while her uterus is contracting involuntarily.
4. *Husband's involvement.* A major advantage of the Lamaze method is the active involvement of the husband in the birthing event. His role (or that of a coach substitute if the father is not available) is to tell his wife when to start and stop the various breathing exercises, give her psychological support throughout labor, and in general, take care of her (get ice, keep her warm, and so on).

DATA • *In one study four out of five fathers were present in the delivery room at the births of their children.* (Gallup/Levi Poll, 1983)

Parenthood is the only profession that has been left exclusively to amateurs.

UNKNOWN

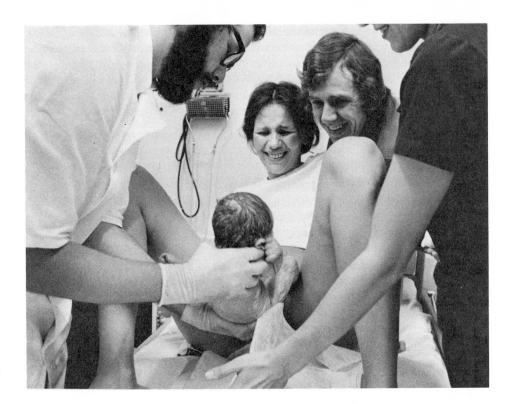

Many couples attend childbirth preparation classes and share in the births of their children.

Most husbands and wives report that the sharing of the labor and delivery is one of the most significant and memorable events of their lives. One woman described her Lamaze experience as follows:

> Just having him in the room was very comforting. He held my hand and he brought ice chips, which was very helpful. In the delivery room, he helped with the breathing and he told me to look when the baby was actually being born so I wouldn't miss it. He was very supportive. I think I would have panicked if he wasn't there. When I needed him, he was able to do whatever crazy thing I needed him to do. He understood my gestures to do this or not do that without my telling him. (Grossman et al., 1980, p. 75)

When the couple does not share the birth experience, the husband sits in the waiting room while his wife is in the labor room alone. One woman said, "The nurses were playing cards and between hands would come to check on me. I felt like a pig in the woods having her litter for all the help I got."

Dick-Read Method of Childbirth

Grantly Dick-Read introduced his concept of natural childbirth in the 1930s, about a decade before Lamaze. He believed it was a woman's fear of childbirth that produced the physical pain during delivery and that pain could be avoided by teaching the woman to relax. Similar to the Lamaze method, Dick-Read classes emphasize breathing and relaxation exercises, basic information about the birth event, and the husband's support. In addition, they focus on preparation for parenthood.

DATA • *A national poll of pregnant women and new mothers found that 60 percent of the husbands attended childbirth classes with their wives.* (Gallup/Levi Poll, 1983)

Bradley Method of Childbirth

Another method of childbirth less well known than the Lamaze method is one developed by a Denver obstetrician, Robert Bradley. Also known as "husband-coached childbirth," the Bradley method focuses on the couple—their marital communication, sexual relationship, and parental roles—as well as on relaxation exercises and proper nutrition during pregnancy. An important aspect of the Bradley method is the couple's relationship with their physician. They are encouraged to deal with issues such as the kind of delivery they want (hospital or home birth) and breast feeding well in advance. The Bradley method emphasizes a couple's freedom to choose the type of birth experience. If the physician is reluctant to cooperate, the couple is encouraged to seek another physician.

LeBoyer Method of Childbirth

The LeBoyer method of childbirth is named after its French founder, Frederick LeBoyer, who has delivered more than 10,000 babies in the way he has made famous. The goal of a LeBoyer birth experience is to make the infant's transition to the outer world as nontraumatic as possible. The delivery room into which the baby is born is quiet and dimly lit. After emerging from its mother, the baby is placed on the mother's abdomen where she gently strokes and rubs her child. The umbilical cord is cut only after it stops throbbing. This is thought to help the newborn's respiratory system adjust to its new environment.

After a few moments, the baby is immersed in water approximately the temperature of the amniotic sac in which she or he has been floating for the past nine months. The infant is allowed to relax and enjoy the bath. Then the baby is wrapped in layers of cotton and wool and placed on her or his side next to the mother. Placing the child on its back is avoided since it is felt that the spine should not be stressed this soon after birth.

To what degree is the LeBoyer method of childbirth beneficial to infants and mothers? A study comparing babies born LeBoyer style with babies born by conventional hospital procedures revealed no differences in responsiveness or irritability during the first three days of life (Nelson, 1979). Mothers delivering by the LeBoyer method did not see the experience any differently or make a different postnatal adjustment than those delivering by a conventional method.

Cesarean Births

Regardless of which method of childbirth a couple chooses, most anticipate that the baby will be born by passing through the vaginal canal. As a result they receive little information about cesarean births. In one study only 6 percent of the women who had had a cesarean birth reported receiving in-depth information from their physicians about such births (Erb et al., 1983). In cesarean sec-

> Health professionals must stimulate interest in prenatal education as a woman begins her pregnancy, not at the end.
>
> JOSEPH T. ANZALONE

tion an incision is made in the woman's abdomen and uterus and the baby is removed. The term does not derive from the Roman emperor Caesar being delivered in this way but from a law passed during Caesar's reign that made it mandatory for women dying in advanced pregnancy to have their babies removed by surgical means.

DATA • *About one in five babies are delivered by Cesarean section.* (Cohen and Estner, 1983)

Cesarean deliveries are most often performed when there would be risk to the mother or baby through normal delivery; for example, the fetus may be positioned abnormally, the head may be too large for the mother's pelvis, or the mother may have diabetes or develop toxemia during pregnancy. The woman is put to sleep with general anesthesia or given a spinal injection, enabling her to remain awake and aware of the delivery.

For most women, the knowledge that they will have a C-section is a surprise. In one study women reported they knew they were to deliver by cesarean less than two hours before the surgery was performed (Affonso & Stichler, 1980). Some women became anxious or upset at not being able to have a normal delivery; others were relieved since the cesarean meant the end to a long and agonizing labor. In one study mothers who gave birth vaginally or surgically did not differ in measured levels of anxiety, depression, or attitudes toward the baby in the hospital or at a one month follow-up (Bradley et al., 1983).

Although cesareans are major surgery, the risk of death to the mother is less than 2 percent. When death occurs it is usually the result of a preexisting condition such as severe toxemia or heart disease, not of the surgery itself. The cesarean section is regarded as one of the safest of all abdominal surgeries and has the record for the fewest postoperative problems (Stichler & Affonso, 1980).

CONSIDERATION • There has been considerable criticism of physicians who routinely perform cesarean surgery even when it is not medically indicated. As until recently a woman who had had a C-section had to have all subsequent births by C-section, these physicians were accused of creating a market for cesarean surgery. But owing to advances in surgical techniques, in 1982 the American College of Obstetricians and Gynecologists reversed its 75-year-old policy and said that some women who have a cesarean delivery for their first child could have subsequent vaginal deliveries. More than 28,000 such deliveries have taken place.

• WHEN A WOMAN BECOMES A MOTHER •

A mother is not a person to lean on, but a person to make leaning unnecessary.

DOROTHY
CANFIELD FISHER

There are about 3,650,000 babies born each year in the United States (National Center for Health Statistics, 1984). But this number does not reflect the individual experiences of the respective mothers. In general, motherhood results in a more profound change for the woman than fatherhood for the man (Harriman, 1983). What are the nature of these changes and how do women adjust to their new role of mother?

Reactions to Childbirth

Although childbirth and the labor preceding it are sometimes thought of as a painful ordeal, some women describe the birthing experience as "fantastic," "joyful," and "unsurpassed." One woman said, "I would rather give birth every day than any other thing I can think of. Having that baby come out of me was literally the grandest experience I have ever had."

Once her baby is born, the mother often feels an enormous sense of pride. This pride is heightened as parents and friends come to view the baby, give gifts, and assure the new mother that she has accomplished a miracle. A mother of three days explained, "I love to hear people tell me how beautiful my baby is. I immediately project into the future and count them lucky to have seen a baby who is destined for greatness."

The strong emotional bond between mother and baby develops early so that mother and infant resist separation. Some researchers feel that there is also a biological basis for the mother-infant bond (Marano, 1981). Studies of female rats suggest that oxytocin, a hormone of the pituitary gland released during the expulsive stage of labor, induces maternal behavior (Pederson & Prange, 1979).

But not all mothers feel immediate joy, and emotional bonding may be temporarily impeded by a mild depression characterized by irritability, crying, loss of appetite, and difficulty in sleeping.

DATA • *Well over half of all women experience what is known as postpartum depression (also referred to as postpartum blues or baby blues) after delivery.* (Calderone & Johnson, 1981).

The feeling is thought to be a result of the numerous physiological and psychological changes occurring during pregnancy, labor, and delivery. Although the woman may become depressed in the hospital, she more often experiences these feelings within the month after returning home with her baby. Most recover within a short time, and some (about 5 percent) seek therapy to speed their recovery.

CONSIDERATION • A study by Richard and Katherine Gordon at the Englewood Hospital in New Jersey (see Newton, 1976) revealed that adopting the following behavior patterns during pregnancy helped women avoid postpartum depression: (1) getting advice about parenthood, (2) making friends with couples who had young children, (3) continuing outside interests, (4) having the husband rearrange his schedule to be home more, and (5) having a relative or private nurse help with the baby soon after the arrival from the hospital.

Adjustments to Motherhood

"You can read about motherhood, watch your friends as they become mothers, and fantasize about having your own baby, but until you've done it, you can't really evaluate how you feel about motherhood," reflected a young mother. Whereas people can try out living together, they cannot try out being a parent.

Every woman goes into motherhood naively, and every woman has widely differing experiences in managing the role. For some women motherhood is the ultimate fulfillment; for others, the ultimate frustration. Most women report mixed emotions during their mothering experience. Whatever a woman's attitude before the birth of her baby, she is not likely to take her role lightly. From the time she knows she is pregnant (or about to become an adoptive mother), no woman's life is ever the same.

Motherhood brings with it changes in a woman's daily routine, an increased feeling of responsibility, worry, and often a need to balance the demands of job or career and family. For all of these she develops coping strategies. We now examine each of these adjustments.

ROUTINE WORK

The new mother finds herself with a new set of tasks. Feeding, diapering, and bathing the infant are added to the responsibilities she already has. "Extra work to care for the baby" and "loss of sleep" were the two most common problems mentioned by mothers of two-month-old infants (Kach & McGhee, 1982). In another study "having less time for yourself" and "feeling physically tired and fatigued" were the two most common changes reported by 132 first-time mothers (Harriman, 1983). These mothers also felt less interested in sex and less sexually responsive during intercourse.

RESPONSIBILITY

Most mothers contend that the actual day-to-day work of child care is not the factor that makes motherhood difficult, but it is rather the incessant and unrelenting responsibility. "The new mother starts out immediately on 24-hour duty, with responsibility for a fragile and mysterious infant totally dependent on her care. It is as if the woman shifted from a graduate student to a full professor with little intervening apprenticeship experience of slowly increasing responsibility" (Rossi, 1968, p. 35). Even in those relationships where the husband and wife say they share the responsibility for child care, the final responsibility more often falls on the wife.

The responsibility of motherhood is long term. A middle-class woman with two children observed:

> People tend to think of having children only in terms of the baby period. While it may seem like an eternity, the baby-toddler stage of a child is short compared with the 12 or 16 years of the school-age child. Parents may not be legally responsible for a child beyond 21, but morally and emotionally, once a parent, always a parent.

Tracy Ellis, age 4: Mother, I want you to be with me always. Diana Ross, mother of Tracy: I'll be with you always; and even when you don't want me to be with you.

WORRY

"You can make them go to their rooms but you can't get them out of your mind," said the mother of three daughters. Her observation reflects that children are an emotional as well as a physical drain. First, a child's safety is a major concern. "I look at the clock at three and know that my child will soon be crossing the street from school," one mother said, "and although there is a policewoman there, I don't relax until I see her when I get home from work." When mothers do not worry about busy streets, it is money (Will there be enough for them to complete college?) or peer persecution (Will they make fun of her because she has one crossed eye?) or health (Does a sore throat warrant a trip to the doctor?) or her own employment (Will my children suffer because I'm too involved in my career?). Confessions of a Supermom in Exhibit 16.2 illustrates the frustration of worrying too much about being the best possible mother.

THE EMPLOYED WOMAN AS MOTHER

DATA • *About 50 percent of mothers with preschool children are employed outside the home.* (Thornton and Freedman, 1983)

For the traditional housewife who stays at home, adding the role of mother may be relatively easy. She will have the time and resources (with her husband's economic support) to cope with her infant's demands. Indeed, being at home with her own baby is her dream come true.

But increasingly, more women are working outside the home and drop out of the labor force only long enough to have their children.

DATA • *In one study seventy percent of women employed during their pregnancy planned to return to work after their babies were born. Most of them (86 percent) expected to do so by the time their infants were 6 months old.* (Gallup/Levi Poll, 1983)

To the demanding roles of employee and wife, she must add that of mother. Even with her husband's support, the employed woman must find ways to fit the demands of motherhood into her busy schedule.

CONSIDERATION • Although most new mothers do return to the work force while their children are young, they are in conflict about doing so. In a study of 317 wives who had just had their first baby, most expressed a preference for staying home with their infants as opposed to taking outside employment. (Hock et al. 1984)

Priorities must be established. When forced to choose between her job and family responsibilities (the babysitter does not show up, the child is sick or hurt, or the like), the employed woman and mother generally responds to the latter role first. "Sarah, my 2-year-old, fell and cut her lip as I was about to leave for the office," remarked a young systems analyst. "Instead of dropping her at the day-care center, I took her to the doctor, who stitched her up. I didn't have to think about whether I was going to be late to work. My child is more important to me." Many employed women use their sick leave when their child is sick.

But other employed women have other priorities for a time of crisis. The managing editor for a local newspaper said, "My work comes first. I will see that my child is taken care of, but I'm not playing the role of resident nurse. Last week my son got sick, but I took him to the sitter anyway. Of course, there are occasions I will let my work go, but they are rare."

Some employed women give up their work completely. "No job is so fulfilling, no experience so rich as that of being with my baby," said one woman. "Your employed friends with children don't like it. They think you are a traitor. But many of them feel guilty about not being with their children."

My mother had a great deal of trouble with me but I think she enjoyed it.
SAMUEL CLEMENS

• Exhibit 16.2 •

CONFESSIONS OF A SUPERMOM*

I admit it. I did it. I broke the rules, the Supermom vows I held inviolate for so long. It all began when I started hiding my children's books. (The thought of reading aloud that same book, for the one hundredth time, made me breakout in a cold sweat.) I even drastically reduced trips to the library, down to a few token visits a year. I confess, I allowed sugar into my home, processed cheese singlets, and refined flour. (Imagine, buying bread instead of assuring my children received the proper ratio of B-vitamins found in homemade whole-wheat bread.) And, as a means of survival, I began serving hot dogs (nitrates included), frozen pizza, and raviolios. I permitted the "Smurfs" (one of the most violently-rated cartoons) to invade my living room on Saturday morning. Why? For the self-serving reason of affording myself the luxury of sleeping late. (Cardinal Rule #5: *NEVER* use the TV as a babysitter.)

For what it's worth, I did, and have held out against Count Chocula, Captain Crunch, and caffeine. This unfortunately, is countered by the fact that I confiscated the scissors from my first son at a time when the development of fine motor coordination was at its height. (I realize justifications aren't accepted, but he *had* cut his younger brother's hair. In fact, it was severe enough that my neighbors were convinced he had undergone brain surgery.)

Dare I confess to the times I relented and spanked my kids? I had done so well until then. I had maintained such control—the control only a Supermom could possess—even the time my second son tore my soft contact lens, the time he carved my living room sofa with the kitchen knife, or the time both boys, playing kamakazi pilots, dived through my sister-in-law's sliding glass door.

What kind of mother do you think I am? A reformed Supermom. A much more confident and self-assured mother. A mother who enjoys her children—in moderation—and actually laughs with them—occasionally. But it wasn't always this way. Two years ago I wouldn't have been able to admit to myself, much less to anyone else, that I had failed miserably at being a Supermom. Those were the days my self-worth was tied to my kids' performance. Those were the days that guilt pervaded my very being.

I did try. I embraced the ideal of the perfect mother with such zeal. I diligently prepared by faithfully attending childbirth classes and La Leche League meetings. I read every child care manual available. I was determined to succeed in every area my own parents had failed. I was, unknowingly, setting myself up for failure. For you see, the standards I was measuring my success by was perfection. I discovered too late that Supermom is a myth—a fairy tale mother who rarely exists except in our minds and on TV. She is the fantasy mother our society would have us believe was real. She is all-giving, all-loving, all of the time.

But, as so many other conscientious parents I believed it. I approached childrearing with high levels of caring, idealism, and enthusiasm. I was proud of my ability to do it all: to have a career and be a perfect mother too. I was driven by the delusion that I could equally "mother," cook, clean house, have sex, and pay bills (and not necessarily in that order). As the Enjoli commercial suggested, "I can bring home the bacon, fry it up in the pan, and never let him forget that he's a man."

The media, child care experts, and our own parents constantly bombard us with "good parent" criteria. And often, we unwittingly internalize their requirements which later resurface as compulsions to be the best mother, striving dutifully to produce the best/brightest kid on the block, in the classroom, and on stage. We push, push, push as if the child were a product whose worth was dependent solely upon performance. And the pressure is mounting. For now to be a *real* Supermom, one must produce a Superbaby. We are told we have but a few short years to determine our children's destinies. Intelligence and school performance can be determined by three years of age.

Alas, Supermom is on the move again. The prescription begins at conception: to create a Superbaby, and consequently a Superbeing, one must talk to the unborn child in utero. After birth, one must flash math and word cards before a baby's yet unfocused eyes. Then there's a rigorous gymnastics and swim program, and violin lessons by age two. And lest we forget, the world of commercials will remind us: Failure to present your daughter with a computer by her fourth birthday will ultimately make her a college reject.

The danger behind such expectations is that a mother's own sense of worth becomes dependent upon her child's achievements; her selfhood is as easily threatened as it is derived, in a large part, from the product she has so carefully and lovingly molded. The damage to the child can be equally disasterous. For when a child is made to feel that receiving his mother's love is contingent upon fulfilling certain rigid standards, his emotional development is jeopardized. For the young child, fear of losing a mother's love can be devastating.

Another danger to parent and child alike results when mother becomes disenchanted with her role and becomes a parent drop-out because she no longer has the physical and emotional energy to keep going, or giving. Dr. Joseph Procanccine of Loyola College in Baltimore terms this phenomenon, "Parent Burn-Out." He says, "Parents who burn-out have, in a sense, been 'on fire'. They have taken as a model for parenting a mythological ideal of the perfect parent." According to Dr. Procanccine, the greatest cause of parent burn-out is attempting to manage the anger—anger that results from "the guilt and frustration that occurs when these unrealistically high expectations for parenting (and for children's behavior) can't be met."

Preventing parent burn-out means re-evaluating your expectations for yourself and your child. It means taking care of yourself and exerting control over how and where you expend your energy. It means stressing to your children that you love them unconditionally, even if they don't get a part in the school play, even if they break your favorite coffee mug.

Yes, I admit it. I was a Supermom and I failed. I have, however, survived burn-out and by-passed a chronic state of disenchantment. And sure, it has been rough, but through it all I have gained a much greater understanding of myself. And it is comforting to hear my four-year-old daughter's words, as she assures me that my message to her has been clearly received: "Mommy, I love you *even* when you burp."

Suggested Reading:
The Growth and Development of Mothers
    by Angela Barron McBride
Parent Burn-Out
    by Dr. Joseph Procanccine
Parent Power, Child Power
    by Dr. Helen De Rosis

*Published in *Becoming . . .*
American Society for
Psychoprophylaxis in Obstetrics,
May/June 1984, Vol. 3, 4, p. 1 and 4.
© by Martha D. Ogburn. Used by
permission of author.

Some employed women arrange to see their babies during lunch.

Another woman who had been employed revealed what it was like to be at home all day with her 3-month-old baby (LaRossa & LaRossa, 1981).

> Well, it's different, but it's not what I had always thought it would be. I always thought it would be boring, and I always thought I would absolutely go stark raving mad the first three months. But it's really not like that, or at least it hasn't been so far, because she's really exciting and she's always doing something different. . . . you can see her do something today that she didn't do yesterday . . . (p. 106)

Nine months later, the same woman said:

> I'm getting to the place that I feel like I would enjoy being out a little more often. I'm not crawling the walls, but you get to a point you feel like you can leave the baby. She's not going to, you know, stop breathing if you're gone from the house for two minutes. . . . new mothers always have like a compulsion, nobody can take care of their baby better than themselves. (p. 115)

Like this woman, most women who were employed before their child's birth return to work.

COPING STRATEGIES

Before the birth of a woman's baby she spends her time in work, social life, marriage, and housekeeping. After the baby is born she still has these involvements, and in addition, she is a mother. Conflicts can result and coping strategies must be developed. Myers-Walls (1984), in a study of 42 women who had been mothers for two months, concluded that the use of four coping strategies was related to an easier transition to parenthood: "(1) holding a positive view of the situation, (2) establishing a salient role, (3) compartmentalizing roles, and (4) compromising standards" p. 270).

Holding a positive view of the situation is self-explanatory. Establishing a salient role means focusing on one role (like taking care of the baby) and managing the other roles in reference to it. Compartmentalizing means focusing on one role at a time and not thinking about other roles—for example, thinking only of her job while at work and only of her infant when at home. Compromising standards means letting the floor go unmopped and not trying to keep the house as orderly as before the baby was born.

• WHEN A MAN BECOMES A FATHER •

Whereas the woman may have dreamed of being a mother since early childhood and nourished the dream during pregnancy, her partner often has not fully considered the implications of fatherhood. In this section we examine how men view parenthood and their reactions to their new role.

How Men View Parenthood

Most fathers are guided by certain impressions they have of what a father is and does. They may variously view their role as provider, teacher, companion, and caretaker.

PROVIDER

Most fathers feel that one of their primary responsibilities is making money for their family. Earning money to support a family often means responsibility to an employer. A salesman must face his field manager periodically with a report on the number of items he has sold. If he has performed poorly, he loses his job. The employer is not interested in knowing if the employee goes camping with his children or eats lunch with them or picks them up after school. "How many did you sell?" is the only question.

But this need to be the main economic provider, which many men have been taught to see as part of their masculine role, may conflict with other needs. The conflict between family and career is particularly acute if the father chooses to climb the executive ladder in a large company. This requires taking work home at night, traveling extensively, and working more than the standard 40-hour week, all of which may interfere with spending time with children and relaxing as a family together. For the man whose family comes first, there will be fewer promotions, smaller raises, and generally less in the way of career rewards of all types.

Because men are rewarded for putting their career above their family, they often justify their minimal parenthood contribution in economic terms. One father said:

> I've given them everything they ever wanted. They want me to go on camping trips with them, but they also expect me to pay the country club dues so they

What does it feel like to be a father? I don't know yet; I've only been one for 15 minutes.

A NEW FATHER

can swim and to pay for their college educations. I'd really like to play, but somebody has to be responsible for the money.

But fathers are often criticized because making money is all they do. One 27-year-old graduate student said, "Yes, my dad put me through school and bought me a car, but he is a stranger to me. I'll never get over his not spending time with me when I was younger."

> CONSIDERATION • Because children are more likely to value being with their father than getting something from him, men might consider spending more time with their children than doing what employers reinforce, or reward, them for—staying away from home. (Some corporations approve of a man's divorce because it means he can throw himself into his work and not be encumbered by "external demands.") This change to a family orientation will not be easy for most men.

TEACHER

Few things are more rewarding emotionally than the delight a man gets from satisfactorily guiding his children from birth through their various stages of development until they are off on their own.

FITZHUGH DODSON

Some fathers believe it is their responsibility to make their child ready for life by teaching her or him to be independent, self-sufficient, and self-reliant. "I taught all my kids," said a father of three, "that there is always room at the top and the only way to get there is good morals and discipline."

COMPANION

"Regardless of how busy my dad was, he always spent some time with me in the evening and on weekends. We would talk about everything from football to what really matters in life. I've always felt my dad cared about me, and I've tried to be the same kind of father to my children," said the father of two youngsters.

Some fathers like to think of themselves as a friend and companion to their offspring, though the relationship varies with the age and gender of the children. For example, a father may relate quite differently to his son and daughter during their childhood and adolescence. "I've always been closer to my son, even when he was a kid," observed one father. "We just had more in common. When he was an adolescent, we worked on cars together and did some hunting. Now we're in business together. I love my daughter but have never had much in common with her."

But a father of two daughters said, "I can't imagine what it would be like to have a son because I've always related to my two children as people, not girls. I have enjoyed them since they were babies, and while we had our differences when they were teenagers, we are friends."

CARETAKER

The traditional father participated only minimally in the physical care of his children but his modern counterpart, especially one with a working wife, more often views child care as a shared responsibility. Putting them to bed, helping with homework, and playing with them are common behaviors of a father in two-income families (Kamerman, 1980). Some fathers do it all. "I enjoy taking care—feeding, bathing, singing to the baby—more than my wife," stated one husband. Beatle John Lennon provided all the child care for his infant son (Sean) and said he was proud of it.

Fathers and grandfathers enjoy the role of teacher.

Other fathers report that although they think taking care of their baby is important, they don't feel particularly good at it. One father remarked:

> I know that I simply have less tolerance and less patience for the, you know, well, not helping out, but the kinds of things, you know, with a crying child, who cries and cries and cries, and there's something wrong, and the mother's going to feel sympathy, or at least Sharon will very often feel sympathy, although she has her limits too, but her limits extend beyond mine. I can only take it for a short period of time. (LaRossa & LaRossa, 1981, p. 192)

Transition to Fatherhood

The fatherhood role begins with the woman's pregnancy and the husband relating to his wife as a mother-to-be. This means sharing her excitement about the pregnancy with parents and close friends. "It was like telling people that we were getting married," said one father. "We delighted in breaking the news to people who were as excited as we were."

Beyond this, husbands do very little to prepare for fatherhood. In a study of 102 first-time fathers (Knox & Gilman, 1974), only one-third attended parenthood classes offered by a local university, whereas one-fourth attended Lamaze classes. It would be inaccurate to assume that the fathers-to-be already knew what to expect from the fatherhood role. In fact, only 25 percent of them had discussed fatherhood with another male on several occasions and more than 40 percent had never fed a baby or changed a baby's diapers. In another study (Price-Bonham & Skeen, 1979), 160 fathers reported that "trial and error" was their first source of help with fatherhood.

When 30 husbands whose wives were in their last month of pregnancy were asked about their impending new role (Fein, 1976), most were concerned about what labor and delivery would be like and worried about how to actually take care of a baby. Others said their fathers had been emotionally distant with them when they were growing up and they did not want to repeat this pattern when they became fathers.

Participation in Child Care

After the mother and baby are home from the hospital, one of the discoveries of the new father is that a baby requires an enormous amount of physical care.

DATA • *In one study, virtually all fathers (96 percent) helped take care of their babies. Eighty percent changed diapers, 70 percent fed their babies, and 40 percent helped with bathing.* (Gallup/Levi Poll, 1983)

Those who advocate equal sharing in child-care responsibilities suggest that as men become increasingly involved in parenting, they will experience more of the emotional rewards of parenthood. Fathers may also bond with their newborns as mothers do.

CONSIDERATION • For fathers to participate more actively in child care, they need to be encouraged by their wives. However, some women who desire more egalitarian relationships with their husbands may still feel conflict about giving up control of the house and child care and about their husband becoming less competitive and more family oriented. Hence a role shift of the husband into greater child-care responsibility will require a concomitant shift of the wife's role and perceptions.

Reactions to Fatherhood

Since there is considerable social pressure to make only positive remarks about being a new parent, it is difficult to find out how fathers really feel about it. However, 25 percent of Knox and Gilman's (1974) sample agreed with the statement, "Sometimes I wish my wife and I could return to the time before my baby was born "(p. 33).

Men differ in the degree to which they are bothered by the irritations of early fatherhood. These differential reactions are related to the wife's feelings about motherhood, the effect of the baby on the marriage, and various characteristics of the father and the baby.

EFFECT OF WIFE'S ATTITUDE
A wife who responds favorably to her role as parent influences her husband to react in the same way. "To be honest, I could have gone either way," one father said. "After several nights of lost sleep, the sound of a crying baby during meals, and a drawer full of baby bills, I was ready to admit that we had made a big mistake. But Connie was excited about Pam and encouraged me to bathe her, feed her, and get involved. As a result, I began to enjoy the delight of fatherhood and

have developed an emotional bond with my daughter. Had it not been for Connie, my attitude would have been pretty negative."

EFFECT OF BABY ON MARRIAGE

Related to the wife's reaction is the way the husband perceives the effect of the baby on the marriage. In the Knox and Gilman (1974) study, if the marriage improved after the baby was born, the father reported a very favorable reaction to the baby. "Our baby gave us a common goal, a purpose," said the manager of a grocery store. "Since she was born, we have been much closer. She's the best thing that ever happened to our marriage."

In another study (Wente & Crockenberg, 1976), husbands who perceived the baby as having a disruptive effect on the relationship with their wives reported more difficulty in adjusting to fatherhood. "No baby is worth my marriage," said a computer programmer for IBM. "I wish the baby had never been born. My wife feels differently and it has cost us our relationship. We are getting together with our lawyers on Thursday to sign separation papers." Finally, in a study of 84 couples, the researchers (Grossman et al., 1984) concluded that the longer the men were married and the more children they had, the less satisfied they were with their marriages.

OTHER FACTORS

Fathers who are in their twenties are more likely to report a favorable reaction to parenthood than fathers who are in their thirties when their first child is born (Russell, 1974). In addition, fathers (and mothers) report a more favorable adjustment if the baby is quiet and healthy (Kirkland et al., 1983). Indeed, the birth of a chronically ill baby may induce severe strain in the marriage for both spouses (Patterson & McCubbin, 1983).

It is not clear whether taking classes in preparation for parenthood is effective in easing the transition to fatherhood. For example, results from two studies showed that fathers who attended parenthood classes reported more satisfaction with their infants than fathers who did not attend such classes (Beebe, 1978; Russell, 1974). But the researchers (Nicholson et al., 1983) in another study of 40 middle-class fathers who had taken preparation for parenthood classes observed:

> It is not possible to say that greater father involvement in pregnancy, and participation in labor and delivery, result in a more positive childbirth experience, attachment to the newborn, adaptation to fathering, and better marital adjustment, as some authors have claimed. (p. 9)

• WHEN A COUPLE BECOMES A FAMILY •

How does the prospect of having a child affect a couple's relationship, and what happens to their relationship after the baby is born?

The Couple During Pregnancy

As soon as the woman becomes aware that she is pregnant, the future infant begins to influence the couple's relationship. In anticipating the baby, the couple will deal with matters that are entirely new to them—talking to parents and friends about the pregnancy, allocating existing space for the baby (or getting a larger house or apartment), furnishing a nursery, choosing names for the child, and deciding whether to attend parenthood classes.

Pregnancy also affects the couple's sexual behavior. One husband said, "Sex has been a sticky subject lately. Linda's stomach has been so upset that just the thought of sex turns her off. The few times we have made love since we knew she was pregnant have been a little different for me too. Not negatively though. Something about a child growing inside makes me think about families, children, and reproduction rather than just love and pleasure" (Cass & Cass, 1980, pp. 62–63).

In a study of 43 women in their first pregnancies, 33 reported losing interest in lovemaking during the first three months (Masters & Johnson, 1966). Chronic fatigue, sleepiness, and contending with nausea were the primary reasons. Reduced interest also characterized the third but not the second trimester. During these middle three months, "sexual patterns generally reflected a marked increase in eroticism and effectiveness of performance" (p. 158). This finding should be viewed cautiously. At least six other studies failed to find evidence for an increase in sexual interest during the second trimester (Calhoun et al., 1981).

In another study of 260 pregnant women (98 percent were married), the average frequency of intercourse before getting pregnant was 17 times per month (Solberg et al., 1973). This frequency steadily decreased throughout pregnancy to less than three times per month during the ninth month. Reasons for decreased intercourse given by another group of wives included not feeling attractive and fear of hurting the baby (LaRossa, 1979).

CONSIDERATION • Does having intercourse during pregnancy involve a risk to the baby? Generally not. Women who have had a previous miscarriage or who are experiencing vaginal bleeding, ruptured membranes, or threatened premature labor should consult their physician about intercourse during pregnancy. In the absence of these complications, most couples can continue intercourse as late in pregnancy as they desire.

DATA • *Fifty percent of 328 women resumed having intercourse about five weeks after the birth of their baby. Forty percent reported some pain during their first intercourse after the birth.* (Grudzinskas & Atkinson, 1984)

The Baby's Impact on the Couple's Marriage

After the baby is born and brought home from the hospital, how does its presence affect the marital happiness of the spouses who are now mother and father? The answer is unclear. Some studies suggest that children increase marital happiness, whereas others suggest the opposite.

CHILDREN INCREASE MARITAL HAPPINESS

In several studies, parents reported that having a baby improved the relationship with their spouses. Sixty percent of the men and women in a national sam-

Nurturing the marriage relationship is important for total family well-being.

ple said their children had brought them closer together (Hoffman & Manis, 1978). In another study based on the responses of more than 200,000 readers of *Better Homes and Gardens* (1983), 40 percent said they felt closer to the spouse after they had children. Further, after an in-depth study of 84 married couples who had had a baby, the researchers concluded, "Overall, our couples seem to feel that, in general, the baby had enhanced their marital relationship even though it created more stresses on it" (Grossman et al., 1980, p. 201). Individually, spouses also report their babies have a very positive and surprising impact on them. "Feeling love and attachment" for the baby was the biggest surprise for mothers and among the biggest for fathers in a study of new parents (Kach & McGhee, 1982, p. 382). These spouses reported they were glad they had children, felt their marriages had improved since the baby, and looked forward to having more children.

CHILDREN DECREASE MARITAL HAPPINESS

But other parents seem to feel just the opposite. In a study of 72 couples, Belsky et al. (1983) observed that "the marriage becomes increasingly focused upon instrumental functions (making money, taking care of children) and decreasingly focused on emotional expression (being romantically together, making love) with the advent of parenthood . . ." (p. 576). The energy that spouses spend on each other is limited after a baby is born. Even mustering the energy to talk becomes a problem. One husband said:

> But three, two or three nights in a row, we sat down, both dead tired, turned on the TV, and I really wanted to talk, but I was so tired. I couldn't motivate myself to start the conversation, knowing that it would get involved and would take time . . . And every night, I'd say, "Well, tomorrow we're going, tomorrow night we'll do that." (LaRossa, 1983, p. 584)

Other researchers have found similar negative effects of children on the marriage relationship. In their study of 850 married couples, Feldman and Feldman (1977) compared the marriages of those who had an infant with those who had been married the same length of time but were child-free and found that lower marital satisfaction was characteristic of the couples with children. This remained true even in the middle and later years of marriage. Another researcher compared couples with and without children and concluded, "Those without children appear to be the most happily married" (Nock, 1979, p. 22).

Whereas all of these studies had relatively small samples, a more recent study included more than 9,000 respondents in six national surveys over a six-year period (Glenn & McLanahan, 1982). About the relationship between having children and marital happiness, the researchers said:

> [The data] indicate that the negative effects are quite pervasive, very likely outweighing positive effects among spouses in the United States of both sexes and of all races, major religious preferences, educational levels, and employment status . . . Children tend to interfere with marital companionship and to lessen the spontaneity of sexual relations, and their presence in the family creates the potential for jealousy and competition for affection, time, and attention. (p. 69)

Finally, one immediate effect of a baby on a couple's relationship is the recognition by both husbands and wives that the wife is less interested in and responsive to sex (Harriman, 1983).

CONSIDERATION • The answer to why children enhance satisfaction in some marriages but not in others may lie in the different way spouses cope with having a new baby. Fantasy (thinking back to prebaby times when things were less hectic) and going out together without the baby are two ways some couples try to adapt to the strains of parenthood. In a study focusing on how fathers coped with a new baby, the first coping mechanism didn't work; the second one did (Gilman & Knox, 1976). Staying at home thinking about how things used to be was not only unhelpful but also made things worse. But getting a baby-sitter and going out alone helped the couple to renew their relationship.

Couples also differ in their ability to reduce role strain. When the husband expects his wife, who is now a new mother, to give him the same time and attention that she did before the baby, he is likely to be disappointed. If the husband does not alter his expectations, the strain of managing the wife and mother roles may be particularly difficult for the woman.

You might want to complete the Impact of Parenthood on Marriage Scale, which may help to predict how a baby will affect your marriage.

IMPACT OF PARENTHOOD ON MARRIAGE SCALE

This inventory is designed to measure how a new baby will affect your marital happiness. After reading each sentence carefully, circle the number that best represents your feelings.

1 Strongly disagree   4 Mildly agree
2 Mildly disagree   5 Strongly agree
3 Undecided

	SD	D	U	A	SA
1. I am not a jealous person and will not be upset if my partner gives a lot of time and affection to the new baby.	1	2	3	4	5
2. My spouse is not a jealous person and will not be upset if I give a lot of time and affection to the new baby.	1	2	3	4	5
3. I want this baby to be born.	1	2	3	4	5
4. My spouse wants this baby to be born.	1	2	3	4	5
5. My spouse and I agree on which partner is to do how much of the child care—feeding, changing diapers, getting up at night when the baby cries.	1	2	3	4	5
6. I am not a selfish person.	1	2	3	4	5
7. My spouse is not a selfish person.	1	2	3	4	5
8. The baby will not be an undue financial burden.	1	2	3	4	5
9. My spouse and I plan to arrange for a baby-sitter to take care of our baby so that we can leave the house and be alone some of the time after the baby is born.	1	2	3	4	5
10. My spouse and I agree if and when the new mother will be employed after the baby is born.	1	2	3	4	5

Scoring: Add the numbers you circled. Since circling a 1 (strongly disagree) reflects the potentially most negative impact on the marriage and circling a 5 (strongly agree) reflects the potentially most positive impact on the marriage, the lower your total score (10 is the lowest possible score), the greater the chance of reduced marital happiness, and the higher your score (50 is the highest possible score), the greater the chance of increased marital happiness following the baby's birth. A score of 30 places you at the midpoint between decreased and increased marital happiness.

• TRENDS •

The future of parenthood will see a greater awareness of what the role involves, increased sharing by both spouses in the birth and rearing of their child, and a questioning of traditional delivery procedures. Although most couples will continue to opt for having children, they may enter parenthood with a greater understanding of the positive and negative aspects of that role. This awareness will result from the increased availability and use of preparation for parenthood classes and an active information search about the realities of parenthood. Higher marital satisfaction, parental satisfaction, and employment satisfaction were reported by 62 mothers who engaged in such a search (asking parents about parenthood, asking voluntarily child-free spouses about their decision not to have children, reading books, and the like) before they decided to have a child (Holahan, 1983).

The number of couples who want to share in the birth of their babies through some form of prepared, natural childbirth will also increase. In the past the mother was the only parent present at the birth of a couple's baby. Now the father may be part of the experience. This trend, coupled with more mothers working outside the home, will help the father assume a more active role in parenting.

Finally, traditional delivery procedures will be increasingly questioned. Physicians will be asked to justify to couples wanting natural childbirth the rationale for shaving pubic hair, enema, labor induction, episiotomy, forceps, delivery in the supine position, and anesthesia procedures. Although the physician will continue to be in control of the delivery process, the couple's wishes will be taken into account. In one case, a physician decided to have his partner deliver a baby rather than induce labor before his own vacation because the couple questioned—and protested—his original decision.

• SUMMARY •

The reality of parenthood is often different from the thoughts we have about it. Changes for the woman begin shortly after conception. During each trimester of pregnancy, the woman may experience some minor discomforts. Adequate nutrition to ensure a healthy baby is an important concern. The pregnant woman also has an array of emotional reactions to her pregnancy and impending delivery. Labor occurs in three stages and is sometimes thought of as a painful ordeal, but some women describe the experience as the most exciting and enjoyable experience of their lives.

Some expectant parents, dissatisfied with traditional, hospital-managed deliveries, are choosing alternative childbirth methods, including the Lamaze, Dick-Read, Bradley, and LeBoyer methods. When there is a risk to the mother or baby through vaginal delivery, a cesarean section may be performed.

A woman's reactions to childbirth may include temporary feelings of depression as well as a developing emotional bond with her infant. Motherhood brings with it changes in the woman's daily routine, an increased feeling of responsibility, worry, and often the need to balance the demands of job or career and family. For some women, motherhood is the ultimate fulfillment; for others, the ultimate frustration. Most women experience mixed emotions during their mothering experience.

The impact of becoming a parent is sometimes less profound for the man than for the woman since his daily routine doesn't change much after the baby is born. Most men are guided by certain impressions they have of the father's role. They tend to view the father as provider, teacher, companion, and caretaker. Although fathers participate less in child care than mothers, they are interested and capable and, if given opportunity and encouragement, do become involved. Their reactions to fatherhood are related to the wife's feelings about her role as parent, the effect of the baby on the marriage, and various characteristics of the father and the baby.

Having a baby affects the marriage relationship during pregnancy as well as after. During pregnancy the couple may have to adjust to a new division of labor and an altered sexual relationship. After the baby is born, the rosy expectations of parenthood give way to reality as the couple begin to adjust to the new family constellation.

The future of parenthood includes a greater understanding of the role, increased sharing of spouses in childbirth and childrearing, and a questioning of traditional childbirth procedures.

Questions for Reflection

1. How does a baby affect a woman's life more than a man's? Why?
2. As a woman, to what degree do you expect your husband to share the work of parenting if you have a baby?
3. As a man, to what degree do you want to share the work of parenting with your wife if you decide to have a baby?

·CHOICES·

Some couples want to have their baby at home. But should they? What issues need to be considered in deciding to have a child in the hospital or in the home? In addition, some fathers are making choices about the time they spend with their children. How should they allocate time to career and family?

HOME OR HOSPITAL BIRTH?

At the turn of the century, about 95 percent of babies were born at home (all 37 presidents before Jimmy Carter were born at home). Because there were few physicians and fewer hospitals, a midwife was usually summoned to assist the laboring mother-to-be with her delivery. Birthing was a family event with father, mother, and children competing to hold the new infant.

But because of infant mortality, the developing political strength of the medical profession, and the development of hospital facilities to handle difficult deliveries, home births became less common. Today more than 95 percent of all births take place in a hospital. When the woman experiences uterine contractions that are regular and intense, she checks in the hospital, is prepped (has her pubic hair shaved, an enema, and her vaginal area cleaned), and completes labor in a special room near the delivery room. Depending on whether the

couple has taken preparation for parenthood classes and also on hospital policy, her husband may or may not be allowed to remain with her during labor and delivery.

Some expectant parents are concerned that traditional childbirth procedures are too impersonal, costly, and potentially dangerous. Those who opt for home birth are primarily concerned about avoiding separation from the new infant, maintaining control over who can be present at the delivery, and avoiding "excessive obstetrical management" (Sacks and Donnenfeld, 1984, p. 471)

Safety is a primary concern in deciding to have a baby at home. Most physicians view home births as unsafe and do not support the movement toward home births (DeVries, 1983). However, some physicians feel that it is usually possible to predict a dangerous delivery since high-risk mothers (such as those with hypertension or diabetes) can be identified early in the pregnancy. Some proponents of the home birth movement feel that for the mother without prenatal complications, there is greater risk in having a baby in the hospital than at home.

The nurse-midwife is most often asked to assist in home births. Some are certified members of the American College of Nurse-Midwives and have successfully completed a master's degree in nurse-midwifery offered at various universities, including Georgetown, Emory, St. Louis, and Columbia.

Two organizations—ACAH (Association for Childbirth at Home) and HOME (Home Oriented Maternity Experience)—help couples prepare for home births. Couples may attend several classes during which the following issues are discussed.

1. *Advantages of home births.* These include the birthing of a child in a familiar environment with the women's spouse and children involved in the birthing process.
2. *Screening for home birth.* Home birth advocates recognize that some women should deliver their babies in the hospital. Such women with high-risk pregnancies are identified and encouraged not to have a home birth.
3. *Practical aspects of home birth.* Finding a midwife-nurse or obstetrician, proper nutrition, gathering necessary supplies, and developing a backup plan if the need for hospital assistance arises are among the practical concerns of a home birth.
4. *Psychological issues.* Attitudes of parents, friends,

and medical professionals toward home births, the emotional aspects of birthing, parenthood, and so on are discussed.

5. *Labor management.* This includes information about stages of labor, breathing exercises, and pain control.

What is the relative safety of home versus hospital births? A research study that attempts to answer this question must control for the screening of home birth choosers, who are for the most part women who are healthy and who have few risk factors. Also, since those choosing home birth have been educated in the techniques of prepared childbirth in some manner, home birthers must be compared with prepared hospital birthers.

A study that meets these criteria involved a sample of 1,146 pairs of home and hospital births matched on the basis of obstetrical history, general health, socioeconomic status, risk factors, and childbirth preparation (Mehl, 1976). Home birthers were all those who planned to birth at home, even if, for whatever reason, the actual birth took place in the hospital (88 percent of births begun at home were completed at home).

There were no differences in infant mortality rates between the home and hospital birth groups. However, infant and maternal morbidity (disease) rates were lower in the home birth group. Births injuries, maternal high blood pressure,

and episiotomies were also less frequent in the home births. Additional evidence comes from a review of studies of doctor and midwife-attended home births, in which it was noted that such births were as safe or safer than hospital births (Tew, 1978).

Table 16.3 summarizes the range of birthing alternatives and notes their suitability for different groups of women.

Underwater birth, in which the woman gives birth to her baby while her body is submerged in water, is the newest and most controversial alternative birth procedure. The assumed advantage of such a birth is that the baby is subjected to less stress, since there is no gravity in water and the baby may be totally relaxed. The baby receives oxygen through the umbilical cord and suffers no threat of drowning. Although this procedure has been used in the Soviet Union for the past 10 years, less than 50 babies have been born in the United States in this way. American physicians are divided on the acceptability of this procedure.

Sometimes preschool siblings observe the home births of their sisters and brothers. Some advocates of hospital births suggest that such observations have negative consequences for the children. But Lumley (1983) compared the short-term effects on preschool siblings who observed their brothers and sisters being born with preschool siblings who were not allowed such observations and found no significant differences.

FOR FATHERS: CAREER OR FAMILY?

Women have traditionally been socialized to give priority to their children over their careers, whereas men have been socialized to do the opposite. With the advent of preparation for parenthood classes, Lamaze births, and most wives working outside the home, men have the opportunity to rethink their socialization and make conscious choices. Some men still opt for their career. One man said:

I love my children but I really am not happy being around them for more than a weekend. By Monday I'm ready to go back to work and see them for a few minutes before bedtime during the week. I enjoy the competitive struggle of my work and making money is what I do best. I guess I'm lucky to be married to a woman who enjoys taking care of the kids.

But other men feel differently. One said:

I make about all the money I need, and I've learned that it is a dead-end trail. Here I am at middle age . . . my last child will be leaving for college in September and I hardly know him. I've spent more time with the mailman than I have with him and now he's leaving. I've got money but I don't have my boy. I think I've gotten my priorities mixed up.

Men might be aware that although they may be subject to enormous pressure for success, such success without taking time to "smell the roses" with their children may be less than fulfilling.

(continued)

Table 16.3 Birthing Alternatives

TYPE OF BIRTH	SUITABILITY	DESCRIPTION
Nonprofessionally supervised home birth	Questionably suitable	Includes do-it-yourself and unprepared or informally apprenticed lay midwifery care. Prenatal care may or may not be carried out, and a backup with the hospital system may or may not be available.
Professionally supervised home birth	Suitable for normal or low-risk births	Includes care supervised by a formally prepared practitioner duly licensed to provide maternity services, i.e., a physician (specialist or nonspecialist), nurse-midwife, or in some states lay-midwife. Prenatal care and postpartum follow-up are provided by the practitioner, and there are appropriate links to consultation and care within the hospital system.
Birth and childbearing centers	Suitable for normal or low-risk births	Includes independent and system-sponsored homelike settings away from, near, or within hospital, but with autonomous policies. Aspects of home birth are included, such as presence of family members, flexible routines, nonseparation of infant and parents, inclusion of family in decision making, and early discharge with follow-up. Care is provided by all levels of licensed practitioners with some technological supports available in the event of emergency. Effective linkage to the system and specialist consultation are available. Home visiting also included in follow-up. Consumer voice in policy making is an essential.
Humanized hospital birth	Suitable for "at-risk" or "complicated" births. May or may not be satisfactory for normal and uncomplicated births.	Includes birth rooms within labor-delivery suites, childbirth education, and rooming-in. Somewhat flexible care dominated by obstetrical practitioners with nurse support. May, but usually does not, include nurse-midwives or nonspecialist physicians. Priorities generally those of staff, based on institutional needs and student physician teaching requirements rather than consumers' requests. Technology in selective, rather than generalized, use.
Conventional hospital birth	Considered suitable for "at-risk" or "complicated" births. Low or no priority given to satisfaction.	Specialist-dominated birth with routine interventions such as amniotomy, use of ultrasound and electronic monitors, pitocin induction of labor, analgesia, regional and general anesthesia, lithotomy position for birth, separation of family members, deemphasis of childbirth education and breastfeeding. High value placed on "benefits" of caesarean section and emphasis on consumer "inability" and "lack of desire" to participate in decision making. Neonatal period also liable to be technologically conducted.

Source: Reprinted with permission of the publisher from "Alternative Maternity Care: Resistance and Change," by Ruth Watson Lubic, General Director, Maternity Center Association, in Shelly Romalis (Ed.), *Childbirth: Alternatives to Medical Control*, pp. 220–221. Copyright © 1981 by University of Texas Press, Austin, Texas.

· Chapter 17 ·

REARING CHILDREN

CONTENTS

Childrearing in Perspective
Folklore about Childrearing
Approaches to Childrearing
Childrearing Problems
Self-Assessment:
  Child Discipline Scale
Other Issues
  Concerning Parents
Choices

There are only two lasting bequests we can hope to give our children. One of these is roots; the other, wings.

HODDING CARTER

Most parents look forward to bringing up their children. They view childrearing as a process in which they will be teaching and instilling in their children values and behaviors that will make the children happy and themselves proud. In this chapter we examine childrearing in perspective, the folklore that surrounds childrearing, some childrearing theories, and examples of how these theories can be used in responding to behavior problems of children.

· CHILDREARING IN PERSPECTIVE ·

Although rearing children is a major undertaking, it is helpful to keep it in perspective. In this section we make some generalizations about the realities of parenthood.

Parenthood Is Only One Stage in Life

Children are a great comfort in your old age— and they help you reach it faster, too.

LIONEL KAUFFMAN

Parents of newly adult children often lament, "Before you know it, your children are grown and gone." Although parents of infants sometimes feel that the sleepless nights will never end, they do end. Unlike the marriage relationship, the parent-child relationship moves toward separation. Just as the couple were alone before their children came, they will be alone again after their children leave. Except for occasional visits with their children and possibly grandchildren, the couple will return to the child-free life-style.

Typical parents are in their early fifties when their last child leaves home. Since the average woman can expect to live until she is 78 and the man until he is 70, at a minimum the spouses in a continuous marriage will have about 20 years together after their children leave home. Hence parenthood might be perceived for what it is—one stage in marriage and in life.

DATA • *Assuming an individual marries at age 22, has 2 children at 3 year intervals, and dies at age 75, children will live with the individual about 30 percent of her or his lifetime and 50 percent of her or his marriage.*

One mother said:

> We had three kids and I loved taking care of all of them. I think the happiest time in my life was when my husband and I would wake up in the morning and they would all be there. But that's changed now. They are married and have moved several states away. I know they still love me and they call to stay in touch but I rarely see them anymore. I'm 55 and have at least 20 years left. I've gotten interested in Amway and am busy building my business. If I didn't have something to do, I would really be bored.

Parents Are Only One Influence in Their Children's Development

Although parents often take the credit and the blame for the way their children turn out, they are only one among many influences. Peers, siblings, teachers, relatives, and the mass media are also influential. Although parents are the first significant influence, peer influence becomes increasingly important and remains so into the college years. The values and behaviors of our friends and age-mates are likely to be mirrored in our own.

Siblings are not necessarily peers, but they too have an important and sometimes lasting effect on each other's development. For example, an older sibling who is required to take care of a younger sibling may resent such responsibility and be careless about fulfilling it. "I really didn't care if my younger sister fell down the steps or not," said one sibling. "She did and limps today because of it."

Siblings may also compete for the family's resources, particularly parental attention. One adolescent said:

> I can remember walking up to my mother (I was about 5) after my little baby brother was born. My mother was nursing him while she was sitting in the chair in the den. I wanted to sit in her lap but she said she couldn't hold both of us. I felt as though my mother had replaced me with my brother. It wasn't a good feeling.

Teachers and peers, as well as parents, are important influences on children.

Sibling influences may also be positive. "I've always been close to my sister," remarked one woman. "She's the best friend I have."

Relatives may also be significant childrearing agents, especially grandmothers and aunts. One graduate student remarked, "My grandmother is the one that reared me. She was a very polite person and although I resented her nagging me to be polite when I was a kid, I am very much the way she would have wanted me to turn out."

DATA • *In a study of new mothers, more than one-fourth said a relative, friend, or neighbor took care of their baby when they worked.* (Gallup/Levi Poll, 1983)

Teachers become influential once a child begins school, and they remain so as long as the child is exposed to the educational system. Since most teachers are middle class, they tend to stress the values of achievement and discipline. But teachers have another effect on their students. They may teach offspring things parents do not want them to know. One conservative parent told his son that he was more concerned about him getting a B.A. as a born-again Christian than a B.A. from the university he was attending. "You've got some liberal professors down there that are threatening your very soul," he said.

Children don't need to go to school to be exposed to influences their parents may not approve of. Television is a major means of exhibiting to children language, values, and life-styles that may be different from those of the parents.

> My mother loved children—she would have given anything if I had been one.
>
> GROUCHO MARX

One father had Home Box Office and Showtime disconnected because he did not want his children seeing the movies and specials on those channels. Another parent went through the TV guide each week and marked programs his children would not be allowed to watch. The TV guide was left on top of the television and they were to look at what programs had been approved before they turned it on.

Not all television viewing may have negative consequences.

DATA • *In a study of 116 households, the average amount of time spent viewing television together as a family unit was 2–3 hours daily, Monday through Friday, with an average of 4–6 hours on the weekend.* (Schroeder & Brocato, 1983)

These authors concluded that the more time a family spent watching television together, the greater their interaction, discussion of individual problems, and their feeling of having a "close, loving, and supportive family relationship" (p. 64).

In addition to being influenced by peers, siblings, relatives, teachers, and mass media, children are affected by different environmental situations. An only daughter adopted into an urban, Catholic, upper-class family will be exposed to a different environment than a girl born into a rural, Southern Baptist, working-class family with three male children. Some of the potentially important environmental variables include geographic location; family size; gender; how authoritarian or permissive the parents are; what the family's social class, religion, and racial or ethnic background is; and whether the children and parents are mentally and physically healthy.

CONSIDERATION • Because parents are only one of many influences on their children, they should be careful about taking the credit or the blame for the way they turn out. "It's not in the books," said a professor of psychology. "My wife and I have modeled a relatively conservative but ambitious life for our children and had hoped that they would want to become professionals. But they met a group in college and decided to drop out and join this commune. That was 10 years ago. It's not what we wanted for them but they're happy."

Parenthood Demands Change as Children Grow Up

The best way to keep children home is to make the home atmosphere pleasant—and let the air out of the tires.

DOROTHY PARKER

Parenthood is not the same in all of its innings. Enjoying children as infants and coping with the sleepless nights are characteristic of the first two years, but the issues change. The parent of a 10-year-old said, "It's getting my child to study, practice piano, and develop friends that keeps me frustrated." But the parent of a 17-year-old said, "Wait till it's your turn to have a teenager . . . you'll know why it's the stage most parents wish they could skip."

Each Child Is Different

Children differ in their tolerance for stress, in their capacity to learn, in their comfort in social situations, in their interests, and in innumerable other ways. Parents soon become aware of the specialness of each child—of her or his difference from every other child and from those they have read about. Parents of two or more children are often amazed at how children who have the same parents could be so different.

Most Parents Enjoy Their Role

Although parenthood is one of the most demanding roles a person may have, most parents feel good about the way their children turn out and would elect to have children again if they were to start over.

DATA • *Forty-eight percent of a national sample of parents said they were "very satisfied" with the way their children were turning out. Forty-four percent were "mostly satisfied." Only 6 percent said they would not have children if they had it to do over.* (Better Homes and Gardens, 1983)

Occasionally, parents get direct feedback from their children that they have done a good job. One parent said the following one-sentence letter was the first they received from their son after he left for college.

> You'll no doubt be pleased to know that I've come to the conclusion that you and Dad did a lot that was right—much more than I gave you credit for at the time.

Most Parents Choose Independence for Their Children

Parents are sometimes ambivalent about the kind of children they want. One alternative is to rear compliant and obedient children who will respond to parental wishes and do as they are told. Another goal is to rear courageous, independent, self-reliant children (Shea, 1984). Most parents opt for the latter. One parent said, "To the degree that you rear your children to be able to get along without you, you have been a successful parent."

Parenting Western Style Is Only One Way

Although parents in Western societies assume that parenting should be done by two parents per child, other societies, particularly the Polynesians, have a very different view. Polynesian children learn to view not only their mother and father but also their grandparents and all relatives of equivalent age and gender as parents. In practice, multiple parenting in Polynesia means there will be a number of people who will be involved in the life transition ceremonies, that the children will have a number of houses they regard as home, and that they will have an array of adults who nurture them, love them, and protect them (Ritchie & Ritchie, 1983).

To get adults to embark on the 20-year task of rearing children, certain folklore, whose purpose is to romanticize the job, has arisen. LeMasters and DeFrain (1983) identified some widely held beliefs about parenting that are not supported by facts.

Rearing Children Is Fun

Would-be parents see television commercials of young parents and children and are led to believe that drinking Pepsi in the park with their 4-year-old is what childrearing is all about. Parenthood is portrayed as being a lot of fun. The truth is somewhat different than the folklore.

> The idea of something being fun implies that you can take it or leave it, whereas parents do not have this choice. Fathers and mothers must stay with the child and keep trying, whether it is fun, or whether they are enjoying it or not. Any comparison to bowling, listening to jazz records, or sex is strictly coincidental . . . Rearing children is hard work; it is often nerve-racking work; it involves tremendous responsibility; it takes all the ability one has (and more); and once you have begun you cannot quit when you feel like it. (pp. 22, 23)

Good Parents Will Produce Good Kids

Children are unpredictable. You never know what inconsistency they're going to catch you in next.

FRANKLIN P. JONES

It is assumed that children who turn out wrong—who abuse drugs, steal, and the like—have parents who really did not do their job. We tend to blame parents when children fail. But there are good parents who have given both their emotional and material resources to their children and the children have not turned out well. One mother said:

> We live in one of the finer suburbs of our city, our children went to the best schools, and we spent a lot of time with them as a family (camping, going to the beach, skiing). But our son is now in prison. He held up a local grocery store one night and got shot in the leg. We've stopped asking ourselves what we did wrong. He was 23 and drifted into friendships with a group of guys who just decided they would pull a job one night.

Love Is the Essential Key to Effective Childrearing

Parents are taught that if they love their children enough, they will turn out okay. Love is seen as the primary ingredient, which if present in sufficient quantities, will ensure a successful child. But most parents love their children dearly and want only the best for them. Love is not enough and does not guarantee desirable behavior. One parent said:

> We planned our children in courtship, loved them before they got here, and have never stopped loving them. But they are rude, have despicable table manners, and hardly speak to us. We are frustrated beyond description. We've done

everything we know how to do in providing a loving home for them but it hasn't worked.

Childrearing Is Over When the Kids Leave Home

A joke is that two elderly parents got a divorce. A friend asked them why they waited to get a divorce until they were in their seventies. "We wanted to wait until our children were dead," replied the mother. Parents tend to think of childrearing as ending when the children grow up and leave home. The reality is that the role of parent may continue at some level as long as the child is alive.

Some offspring who have moved out of their parents' home need to move home again. They can't find a job and need a place to live until they have a steady source of income, or they are recently divorced, have children, and have difficulty surviving as a single parent. Still others miss the comforts of their own room and home and move back for the security.

DATA • *Twenty percent of more than 200,000 respondents said they would welcome their children returning home with no reservations, 56 percent said they would welcome them for a limited time, and 15 percent said they would refuse or agree reluctantly.* (Better Homes and Gardens, 1983)

One mother said:

> I told her it wasn't the happiest day of my life that she was returning home and I knew that it wasn't the happiest day of her life. But we decided that we would both live with it and make the best of it. And that's what we've done.

Feuerstein and Roberts (1981) conducted interviews with 250 families and 23 professionals before writing *The Not-So-Empty Nest*. They found only five families who reported feeling completely content with the parent-child relationship resumed under one roof. The children complained of lack of privacy, whereas the parents complained about the increased noise level and their children's slovenliness.

Children Appreciate What Parents Do for Them

Most people think of childrearing in terms of love, care, and nurturing and also of giving them things. They assume their children will appreciate their tender loving care and the material benefits, like stereos, computers, and cars. That assumption is wrong. Children think parents are supposed to love them and give them things. They view material benefits as their birthright.

CONSIDERATION • It is a mistake for would-be parents to embark on the adventure of having children with the expectation that they will be appreciated. For the most part, parenting involves a lot of selfless giving with no thought of a return. One parent said, "The best part about being a parent is loving your children. If they love you back or appreciate what you are doing, you get a bonus. But don't expect it."

We now explore five ways of viewing the childrearing process. Although socializing children may be viewed as teaching them the norms, roles, and values of society, there is no one or best way of accomplishing this goal. What works for one child may not work with another. It may not even work with the same child at two different times.

Developmental-Maturational Approach

Give me the children until they are seven and anyone may have them afterwards.

SAINT FRANCIS
XAVIER

For the past 60 years, Arnold Gesell and his colleagues at the Yale Clinic of Child Development have been known for their ages-and-stages approach to childrearing. Their developmental-maturational approach has been one of the most widely used in the United States. Let us examine the basic perspective of this approach, some considerations for childrearing, and some criticisms of the approach.

BASIC PERSPECTIVE

Gesell theorizes that what a child does, thinks, and feels is the result of her or his genetic inheritance. Although genes dictate the gradual unfolding of a unique person, every individual passes through the same basic pattern of growth. This pattern includes four aspects of development—motor behavior (sitting, crawling, walking), adaptive behavior (picking up objects, walking around objects), language behavior (words and gestures), and personal-social behavior (cooperativeness, helpfulness). Through observation of hundreds of normal infants and children, Gesell and his coworkers identified norms of development. Although there may be large variations, these norms suggest the ages at which an average child displays various behaviors.

DATA • *On the average, children begin to walk alone (although awkwardly) at age 13 months and use simple sentences between age 2 and 3.* (Mussen et al., 1984)

CONSIDERATIONS FOR CHILDREARING

Gesell suggests that if parents are aware of their children's developmental clock, they will avoid unreasonable expectations. For example, a child cannot walk or talk until the neurological structures necessary for those behaviors have matured. "Parents who provide special educational lessons for their babies are wasting their time," since the infants are not developmentally ready to profit from the exposure (Scarr, 1984, p. 60). Also, the hunger of a 4-week-old must be immediately appeased by food, but at 16 to 28 weeks, the child has some capacity to wait because the hunger pangs are less intense. In view of this and other developmental patterns, Gesell suggests that the infant's needs be cared for on a demand schedule that is, instead of having to submit to a schedule imposed by parents, infants are fed, changed, put to bed, and allowed to play when they want. Children are likely to be resistant to a hard and fast schedule because they may be developmentally unable to cope with it.

In addition, Gesell alerts parents to the importance of the first years of a child's life. In Gesell's view, these early years assume the greatest significance since this is when the child's first learning experiences occur.

CRITICISMS OF THE DEVELOPMENTAL-MATURATIONAL APPROACH

Gesell's work has been criticized because of (1) its overemphasis on the idea of a biological clock; (2) the deficiencies of the sample he used to develop maturational norms; and (3) his insistence on the merits of a demand schedule.

Most of the children studied to establish the developmental norms were from the upper-middle class. Children in other social classes are exposed to different environments, which influence their development. So norms established on upper-middle-class children may not adequately reflect those of children from other social classes.

Whereas parents may not be too concerned about the way developmental norms were established, they may be quite concerned about the suggestion that they do everything for the infant when the infant wants. Rearing an infant on the demand schedule can drastically interfere with the parents' personal and marital interests. As a result, most American parents feed their infants on a demand schedule but put them to bed to fit the parents' schedule (Shea, 1984).

Behavioral Approach

The behavioral approach to childrearing, also known as the social learning approach, is based on the work of B. F. Skinner. We now review the basic perspective, considerations, and criticisms of this approach to childrearing.

BASIC PERSPECTIVE

Behavior is learned through classical and operant conditioning. Classical conditioning involves presenting a stimulus with a reinforcer. For example, an infant comes to associate the faces of her or his parents with food, warmth, and comfort. Although initially only the food and feeling warm will satisfy the infant, later just the approach of the parent will soothe the infant. This may be observed when a father hands his infant to a stranger. The infant may cry because the stranger is not associated with pleasant events. But when the stranger hands the infant back to the parent, the crying may subside because the parent represents positive events and the stimulus of his or her face is associated with those pleasurable feelings.

Other behaviors are learned through operant conditioning, which focuses on the consequences of behavior. Two principles of learning are basic to the operant explanation of behavior—reward and punishment. The reward principle says that behaviors that are followed by a positive consequence will increase. If the goal is to teach the child to say "please," doing something the child likes after he or she says "please" will increase the use of "please" by the child. Rewards may be in the form of attention, praise, desired activities, or privileges. Whatever consequence increases the frequency of something happening is by definition a reward. If it doesn't change the behavior in the desired way, a different reinforcer needs to be tried.

In nature there are neither rewards nor punishments—there are consequences.

ROBERT GREEN INGERSOLL

The punishment principle is the opposite of the reward principle. A negative consequence following a behavior will decrease the frequency of that behavior, for example, isolating the child for five or ten minutes following an undesirable behavior. The most effective way to change behavior is to use the reward and punishment principles together to influence a specific behavior. British psychiatrist Michael Rutter (1984) commented:

> Not just stopping children from doing things—that doesn't seem to me to be the way, and in any case it doesn't work in the long run. You have to provide children with alternatives, to teach them what they should be doing, rather than what they should not be doing. (p. 64)

If a child is rewarded (gets to watch television) every time she or he makes the bed and punished (can't watch television for 24 hours) every time she or he doesn't, it is likely that the bed will get made most of the time. In addition, children of parents who use a behavioral approach to discipline perceive their parents as being congruent, that is, doing what they say they will do. This perception may result from parents following up rules with consequences (Haffey & Levant, 1984).

CONSIDERATIONS FOR CHILDREARING

Parents often ask, "Why does my child act this way and what can I do to change it?" The behavioral approach to childrearing suggests the answer to both questions—the child's behavior has been learned through his or her being rewarded for the behavior; the child's behavior can be changed by eliminating the reward for the undesirable behavior and rewarding the desirable behavior.

The child who cries when his or her parents are about to leave home for a movie is often reinforced for crying by the parents' staying home longer. To teach the child not to cry when the parents leave, the parents should reward the child for not crying when they are gone for progressively longer periods of time. For example, they might initially tell the child they are going outside to walk around the house and they will give the child a treat when they get back if he or she plays until they return. The parents might then walk around the house and reward the child for not crying. If the child cries, they should be out of sight for only a few seconds and gradually increase the amount of time they are away. The essential point is that children learn to cry or not depending on the consequences of crying. Since children learn what they are taught, parents might systematically structure learning experiences to achieve the behavioral goals they want.

CRITICISMS OF THE BEHAVIORAL APPROACH

Professionals and parents have attacked the behavioral approach to childrearing on the basis that it is deceptively simple, manipulative, and does not take into account cognitive issues. Although the behavioral approach is often presented as an easy-to-use set of procedures for child management, many parents do not have the background or skill to use the procedures effectively. What constitutes an effective reward or punishment, presented in what way, in what situation, with what child, to influence what behavior are decisions that need to be made before attempting to increase or decrease the frequency of a behavior. Parents often do not know the questions to ask or lack the training to make the appropriate decisions in the use of behavioral procedures. One parent locked her son in the closet for an hour to punish him for lying to her a week earlier—a gross misuse of learning principles.

Behavioral childrearing has also been charged with being manipulative and controlling, thereby devaluing human dignity and individuality.

Finally, the behavioral approach has been criticized because it ignores the influence of thought processes on behavior. Too much attention, say the critics, has been given to rewarding and punishing behavior and not enough to how the child perceives a situation. For example, parents might think they are rewarding a child by giving her or him a bicycle for good behavior. But the child may prefer to upset the parents by rejecting the bicycle and may be more rewarded by their anger than by the gift.

Parents who must cope with severe behavior problems may find practical help in Toughlove described in Exhibit 17.1.

Parent Effectiveness Training Approach

As B. F. Skinner is to behavior modification, so Thomas Gordon is to parent effectiveness training (P.E.T.).

BASIC PERSPECTIVE

Parent effectiveness training focuses on what the child is feeling and experiencing in the here and now—how she or he sees the world. The method of trying to understand what the child is experiencing is active listening in which the parent reflects the child's feelings. For example, the parent who is told by the child, "I want to quit taking piano lessons because I don't like the practicing" would reflect, "You're really bored by practicing piano and would rather have fun doing something else."

P.E.T. also focuses on the development of the child's positive self-concept. Such a self-concept is the result of other people reflecting positive images to the child—letting the child know he or she is liked, admired, and approved of.

> You can do anything with children if you only play with them.
>
> PRINCE OTTO VON BISMARCK

CONSIDERATIONS FOR CHILDREARING

To assist in the development of a positive self-concept and in the self-actualization of both children and parents, Gordon makes a number of recommendations. These include managing the environment rather than the child, engaging in active listening, using "I messages," and resolving conflicts through mutual negotiation. An example of environmental management is putting breakables out of reach of young children but towel racks and toy boxes within reach. It is sometimes easier and safer to manage the environment and not just the child.

The use of active listening becomes increasingly important as the child gets older. When Joanna is upset with her teacher, it is better for the parent to reflect the child's thoughts than to take sides with her. Saying "You're angry that Mrs. Jones made the whole class miss play period because Becky was chewing gum" rather than saying "Mrs. Jones was unfair and should not have made the whole class miss play period," shows empathy with the child without blaming the teacher.

Gordon also suggests using "I" rather than "you" messages. Parents are encouraged to say "I get upset when you're late and don't call," rather than "You're an insensitive, irresponsible kid for not calling me when you said you would."

· Exhibit 17.1 ·

TOUGHLOVE

Although not based on a specific childrearing theory, TOUGHLOVE is a self-help organization of parents (none of whom profess to have "professional qualifications" other than experience) who have difficulty controlling severe problem behaviors their teenage children engage in— drug abuse, physical abuse of parents, staying away from home without explanation, using obscene language to parents, and stealing from other family members. These parents feel overwhelmed with the magnitude of their child's unacceptable behavior and helpless to cope with it. They may have had "good kids" up until the teen years but are now experiencing something they never imagined.

TOUGHLOVE parents meet weekly with other parents in groups of about 10 to discuss their children and potential solutions to behavior problems. The typical format is for each parent to tell what problems she or he is experiencing. Other group members will comment on having had a similar problem, what they did, and how it worked. Although there is no pressure to talk about one's problems or to take action, once a parent decides to discuss a problem and becomes committed to a course of action, the group members will ask at the next meeting if the parent followed through and what the consequences were. TOUGHLOVE parents are very supportive of each other.

The group setting eliminates the parents' feeling that they are the only parents whose children have gotten out of control, that they are embarrassed at their inability to cope with the situation, and that they have something to be ashamed of. TOUGHLOVE parents take the position that they are people too and that they have a right to expect their children to behave appropriately. The TOUGH part becomes operative in the withdrawal of family resources when children consistently disregard parental requests. "The way you get cooperation from unruly young people is to withdraw the family resources that allow them to exploit their parents" (York et al., 1982, p. 114). For example, a child who says, "I am going to smoke dope whether you like it or not," may, as a last resort, be asked to find somewhere else to live, or the child who is arrested for drunk driving for the third time is left in jail for three days even though his parents could bail him out.

The larger community consisting of teachers, probation officers, social workers, therapists, and citizens may also be involved in helping parents in TOUGHLOVE. For example, a child who takes drugs and has a history of lying about doing so may be taken to school by the parents, watched carefully at school by the teacher, have weekly meetings with a caseworker, and be taken home by another member of the TOUGHLOVE group. The community pulls together to try to help the parents control their child's negative behavior. The emphasis is not on blaming anyone but on correcting the behavior problem. There are more than 500 chapters of TOUGHLOVE in the United States (York & York, 1982). Information about a chapter in your community can be obtained from the cofounders of TOUGHLOVE, David and Phyllis York, P.O. Box 70, Sellersville, PA 18960, phone: 215-257-0421.

The former avoids damaging the child's self-concept while still encouraging the desired behavior.

Gordon's fourth suggestion for parenting is the no-lose method of resolving conflicts. He rejects the use of power by parent or child. In the authoritarian home the parent dictates what the child is to do and the child is expected to obey. In this system the parent wins and the child loses. At the other extreme is the permissive home in which the child wins and the parent loses. The alternative, Gordon says, is for the parent and child to seek a solution acceptable to both and to keep trying until they find one. In this way neither parent nor child loses and both win.

CRITICISMS OF THE PARENT EFFECTIVENESS TRAINING APPROACH

Although much is commendable about P.E.T., parents may have problems with two of Gordon's suggestions. First, he recommends that because older children have a right to their own values, parents should not interfere with their dress, career plans, and sexual behavior. Some parents may feel they do have a right (and obligation) to "interfere."

Second, the no-lose method of resolving conflict is sometimes unrealistic. Suppose a 16-year-old wants to spend the weekend at the beach with her boyfriend and her parents do not want her to do so. Gordon says to negotiate until a decision is reached that is acceptable to both. But what if neither the parents nor the daughter can suggest a compromise or shift their position? To encourage parents to find a mutually agreeable solution is commendable, but the specifics of how to do so are not always clear.

Socioteleological Approach

Alfred Adler, a physician and former student of Sigmund Freud, saw a parallel between psychological and physical development. When a person loses her or his sight, the other senses (hearing, touch, taste) become more sensitive—they compensate for the loss. According to Adler, the same occurs in the psychological realm. When an individual feels inferior in one area, she or he will strive to compensate and become superior in another. Rudolph Dreikurs, a student of Adler, developed an approach to childrearing that alerts parents to how their children might be trying to compensate for feelings of inferiority. Dreikurs's suggestions are based on Adler's theory.

BASIC PERSPECTIVE

According to Adler, it is understandable that most children feel they are inferior and weak. From the child's point of view, the world is filled with strong giants who tower above him or her. Because children feel powerless in the face of adult superiority, they try to compensate by gaining attention (making noise, becoming disruptive), exerting power (becoming aggressive, hostile), seeking revenge (becoming violent, hurting others), and acting inadequate (giving up, not trying). Adler suggested that such misbehavior is evidence that the child is discouraged or feels insecure about her or his place in the family. The term socioteleological refers to social striving or seeking a social goal—in the child's case, the goal of a secure place within the family.

Mealtimes can be a good time to have family discussions.

CONSIDERATIONS FOR CHILDREARING

When parents observe misbehavior in their children, they should recognize it as an attempt to find security. According to Dreikurs, parents should not fall into playing the child's game by, say, responding to a child's disruptiveness with anger, but should encourage the child, hold regular family councils, and let natural consequences occur. To encourage the child, the parents should be willing to let the child make mistakes. If John wants to help Dad carry logs to the fireplace, rather than Dad's saying "You're too small to carry the logs," John should be allowed to try and encouraged to carry the size limb or stick that he can manage. Furthermore, Dad should praise John for his helpfulness.

> The best way to make children is to make them happy.
>
> OSCAR WILDE

Along with constant encouragement, the child should be included in a weekly family council (see Exhibit 17.2). During this meeting, family issues such as bedtimes, the appropriateness of between-meal snacks, assignment of chores, and family fun are discussed. Since the meeting is democratic, each family member has a vote. Such participation in family decision making is designed to enhance the self-concept of each child.

Finally, Dreikurs suggests that the parents let natural consequences occur for their child's behavior. If a daughter misses the school bus, she walks or is charged "taxi fare" out of her allowance. If she won't wear a coat and boots, she gets cold and wet. Of course, parents are to arrange suitable consequences where natural consequences either will not occur or would be dangerous. For example, a child who leaves the video games on the living room floor will have them taken away for a month. Love & McVoy (1981) noted, "If we are not exposed to the natural consequences of our behavior, we will never learn the hard-

· Exhibit 17.2 ·

FAMILY MEETINGS

The family meeting is a regularly scheduled meeting of all family members who want to attend. The purpose is to make plans for family chores and family fun, to express complaints and positive feelings, to resolve conflicts, and to make other decisions.

Guidelines for Family Meetings
1. Meet at a regularly scheduled time.

2. Treat all members as equals. Let everyone be heard.
3. Use reflective listening and I-messages to encourage members to express their feelings and beliefs clearly.
4. Pinpoint real issues. Avoid being sidetracked by other issues.

5. Encourage members by recognizing the good things happening in the family.
6. Remember to plan family fun and recreation.
7. Agree upon the length of the meeting and hold to the limits established.
8. Record plans and decisions made. Post the record as a reminder.

Pitfalls to Avoid
1. Meeting only to handle crises; skipping meetings; changing meeting times.
2. Dominating by members who believe they have more rights.
3. Failing to listen to and encourage each other.

4. Dealing with symptoms (such as bickering and quarreling) instead of the purposes of the behavior.
5. Focusing on complaints and criticisms.

6. Limiting the meetings to job distribution and discipline.
7. Ignoring established time limits.

8. Failing to put agreements into action.

Source: Systematic Training for Effective Parenting (STEP) © 1982 by Don Dinkmeyer and Gary D. McKay. Reproduced by permission of American Guidance Service, Inc., Publishers' Bldg., Circle Pines, MN 55014.

working, cooperative behaviors that lead to social, economic, or personal success . . . This is the kind of abuse that will cripple us throughout our lives" (p. 13).

CRITICISMS OF THE SOCIOTELEOLOGICAL APPROACH

This approach to childrearing has been criticized because of its lack of supporting empirical research and its occasional impracticality. Regarding research, "The approach has been used and 'tested' clinically, but such research does not impress the empirical-minded. Science tends to pass over theories which fail to demonstrate their usefulness in predicting specific outcomes which can be demonstrated in nature" (Mead, 1976, p. 63). It is fair to say that some of the other childrearing approaches already discussed also lack solid empirical support.

The impracticality of the socioteleological approach is sometimes illustrated in letting the child take natural consequences. This may be an effective child-rearing procedure for most behaviors, but it can backfire. Letting the child develop a sore throat with the hope that it will teach the importance of a raincoat is questionable.

Reality Therapy Approach

Based on the work of William Glasser and his parent involvement program (P.I.P.), the reality therapy approach to childrearing focuses on the developing child and teenager.

BASIC PERSPECTIVE

In bringing up children, spend on them half as much money and twice as much time.

LAURENCE PETER

Glasser suggests that the young child is irrationally narcissistic, emotionally precocious, and incapable of coping with frustration and stress. These qualities cause the behavioral problems children exhibit, from not cleaning their rooms to taking drugs. By irrational narcissism, Glasser means that the child is completely self-centered and views everything in terms of "what's in it for me." Emotional precociousness means that she or he is insensitive to the needs of others and seeks to manipulate others' emotions to her or his own ends. But Glasser sees the greatest character flaw as not being able to cope with stress and quitting rather than working through a problem. Children do not have the confidence in themselves to figure out what to do when something goes wrong or they do not have the perseverance to make it better.

Television is the villain behind these flaws. The hours children spend in front of this "mindless tube," according to Glasser, are destructive, not because the content of television is so awful, but because children aren't using this time to interact with others, to develop social skills, to learn about life by experiencing it. They are living vicariously.

CONSIDERATIONS FOR CHILDREARING

Glasser recommends that parents understand that nothing they can do for their children is more valuable than spending time with them. This communicates to children that they are loved and valued, which is a prerequisite for developing their confidence to persevere in spite of setbacks. Spending time with children also helps them to learn social skills, to learn another person's point of view, and to learn to share with others. Participation in family rituals such as Christmas, birthdays, vacations, Easter, and Sunday dinner also have the effect of bonding family members to each other (Schvaneveldt & Lee, 1983).

The reality therapy approach to childrearing also emphasizes the right of children to make their own choices. Parents are urged to give children responsibility for their choices and to let them take the consequences. This principle is similar to the Adlerian natural consequences principle. "My child has a right to fail in school," said one parent. This viewpoint acknowledges that only the child can decide what course of action to take (for example, whether to study or not) in life and that accepting the consequences for one's decisions is an effective way of learning how to make decisions.

According to Dr. William Glasser, spending time with your child is the most important thing you can do.

CRITICISMS OF THE REALITY THERAPY APPROACH

Like most childrearing approaches, the reality therapy approach looks good on paper. Spending time with children, giving children the right to make decisions, and letting natural consequences follow are suggestions with which parents might find it easy to agree. However, the basic premise of the reality therapy approach is that the love relationship between the parent and the child is the critical variable determining the way the child turns out. This premise is suspect. One parent said:

> I've spent half my life with my son, including regular fishing trips when he was a small boy and working with him in scouts when he was older. His teacher told me the reason he is doing poorly in school is because I haven't spent enough time with him to show my love for him. Baloney!

As noted earlier, children are subject to a wide variety of influences and parent behavior, regardless of how loving or stable, is only one aspect of the child's socialization.

In addition, as with the socioteleological approach, some parents may have a difficult time standing by waiting for their child to learn from her or his own decisions. For example, does a parent allow a 15-year-old to buy a motorcycle and learn through experience that turning curves too fast can cost a leg? Does a parent permit his or her child to be unconcerned about grades to the point of not being able to graduate? Does the parent let the child decide who his or her friends will be even if these friends are known for drug abuse?

Although you may not adhere to any one approach to childrearing, you do have a perspective on permissiveness or strictness of child discipline. The Child Discipline Scale is designed to help you identify this perspective.

• CHILDREARING PROBLEMS •

Having reviewed several of the major childrearing theories, we now identify major problems parents report having with their children and suggest how these might be resolved using some of these approaches. Having between-meal snacks, crying, asking parents to buy them advertised items, not doing chores, and staying out after curfew are among the problems parents report having.

Having Between-Meal Snacks

Children sneak into the kitchen and eat food between regularly scheduled meals. The problem for parents is that such snacking on cookies and candy at 4 o'clock reduces their hunger for a more nourishing meal at 6:30. Some potential solutions follow.

BEHAVIORAL APPROACH

> You know children are growing up when they start asking questions that have answers.
>
> JOHN J. PLOMP

Assuming that a 6-year-old child had lunch at noon, a behaviorist might suggest that he or she be allowed to eat half a banana or a comparable snack around 3 o'clock so the child will not become ravenous by dinnertime. A behaviorist would view the problem as a behavior (eating unlimited nonnutritious foods between regularly scheduled meals) and arrange consequences to decrease such behavior and increase the limited eating of nutritious foods as snacks. The parents would reward the child (e.g. an extra long piggy back ride) after she or he ate limited amounts of nutritious foods between meals and would punish the child (withdrawal of privileges) for eating candy as a snack.

PARENT EFFECTIVENESS TRAINING APPROACH

A parent who has had parent effectiveness training might say something like, "It upsets me when you eat cookies and candy in the late afternoon and don't eat a good dinner," and try to elicit the child's cooperation in limiting snacks and eating a good dinner. But even if the child continued to eat cookies at 4, the parent would not punish the child for doing so or try to force the child to eat a good dinner. If a real conflict arose, the parent would view the child as having a right to choose what to eat and when.

Crying

Crying and whining are particularly irritating problems with children age 3 and below.

CHILD DISCIPLINE SCALE

This inventory is designed to measure the degree to which you have a permissive or strict view of childrearing. There are no right or wrong answers. After reading each sentence carefully, circle the number that best represents your view.

1 Strongly disagree
2 Mildly disagree
3 Undecided
4 Mildly agree
5 Strongly agree

	SD	D	U	A	SA
1. When you spare the rod you spoil the child.	1	2	3	4	5
2. It is better for your children to view you as an authority than as a friend.	1	2	3	4	5
3. Parents let their children get away with too much.	1	2	3	4	5
4. One of the most important qualities a child can have is to be obedient.	1	2	3	4	5
5. Children should do as they are told without asking why.	1	2	3	4	5
6. If you aren't strict with a child, she or he won't respect you.	1	2	3	4	5
7. The only thing children really understand is a good spanking.	1	2	3	4	5
8. Parents who try to be buddy-buddy with their children lose their respect.	1	2	3	4	5
9. When children have done something bad, punishing them is more effective than talking with them about doing better the next time.	1	2	3	4	5
10. The Bible is a good guidebook for child discipline.	1	2	3	4	5

Scoring: Add the numbers you circled. Since 1 (strongly disagree) is the most permissive response you could make and 5 (strongly agree) is the most strict response you could make, the lower your total score (10 is the lowest possible score), the more permissive your childrearing view, and the higher your score (50 is the highest possible score), the more strict you are about discipline. A score of 30 places you at the midpoint between being permissive and strict.

There are many ways parents can satisfy a child's desire for snacks between meals.

DEVELOPMENTAL-MATURATIONAL APPROACH

A 3-year-old girl began to cry whenever her father put her to bed. From a developmental-maturational point of view, the father would assume that her crying indicates she is not sleepy and that she should be allowed to stay up until she gets sleepy. In effect, children should be allowed to set their own bedtime since it is counterproductive to put a child to bed who is not biologically ready for sleep.

SOCIOTELEOLOGICAL APPROACH

A mother operating from this point of view would assume the crying child was attempting to control her by resisting going to bed. The mother would put her daughter to bed and let natural consequences flow. In this case, the natural consequence of the daughter's continued crying would be exhaustion and sleep.

Asking for Advertised Items

Every parent who has been to the grocery store with a child knows that the child wants bubble gum (Hubba Bubba is a current favorite) or candy at the checkout counter. Other parents are plagued by requests from their children to buy them what they see advertised on Saturday-morning cartoons. Millions of dollars in advertising are spent between 8 and noon on programming kids to request that their parent buy them item X.

PARENT EFFECTIVENESS TRAINING APPROACH
The parents would be sympathetic to their child's request for certain items. "You would really like to have that remote control robot, wouldn't you?" If the child is insistent on getting it, the parent might negotiate a way for the child to get it." "Let's talk about a way for you to get the robot. What chores would you be willing to do in exchange?"

BEHAVIORAL APPROACH
From the behavioral point of view, the parents might view such incessant requests as an undesirable learned behavior and set up contingencies (rewards and punishments) to change that behavior. The parent might say to the child, "If you don't ask me to buy you something, you can watch TV. If you do ask me to buy you something, you can't watch TV." Although setting up such contingencies may seem like a lot of trouble, for the parent who is upset with the "buy me this" syndrome, the alternative may be to cope with the requests.

Not Doing Chores

As children get older they may be expected to perform some chores around the house—take out the trash, empty the dishwasher, and keep their rooms in order. But few children do their chores without being reminded and it becomes a source of frustration for some parents.

SOCIOTELEOLOGICAL APPROACH
At a family council meeting, the parents would discuss the necessity of certain chores being performed for the household to function smoothly. The children would then have an opportunity to select certain chores they would do to help other family members. If they did not wish to cooperate, the natural consequence might be that other family members would stop cooperating with them.

BEHAVIOR MODIFICATION APPROACH
Parents operating from the behavioral perspective would view doing chores as a learned behavior. Children don't do chores because doing them isn't fun. This upsets their parents (some children enjoy watching their parents get angry), and children who put up a big enough fuss sometimes eventually get out of doing the chore (the parent ends up doing the chore because it is easier to do it than to nag the child into doing it.)

> If you want to see what children can do, you must stop giving them things.
>
> NORMAN DOUGLAS

Learning to engage in a behavior may be as easy as learning not to engage in it. The parent operating from a behavioral perspective would make clear what specific chore (taking out the trash in the evening) was to be completed, when it was to be performed (by 10:00 P.M.) each evening, and what consequences would follow. For performing the chore, the child would continue to be able to watch television or go to the pool the following day. If the child neglected to take out the trash, television and going to the pool would be forfeited.

Staying Out after Curfew

Although the previous problems are characteristic of younger children and preadolescents, staying out after curfew is a problem that parents have to cope with in teenagers.

REALITY THERAPY APPROACH

Parents using the reality therapy approach would asume that the child has a right to make her or his own decision about when to come in at night. This approach may teach responsibility and self-discipline. One father said to his teenage son, "Be reasonable. That's the only curfew you have. And since I know that you have good judgment, I know you will be reasonable." In this case, the result was positive. From age 16 to 19, this adolescent was always home between 12:00 and 1:00 A.M.

PARENT EFFECTIVENESS TRAINING APPROACH

Parents operating from this perspective would negotiate a time with the adolescent. "When do you think you should be home?" asked one parent. "I don't want a curfew, Mom," replied the teenager. From these different points of view the mother and son would continue to talk until each felt comfortable with the compromise. The benefit of the P.E.T. approach is teaching the adolescent how to negotiate with others and making him a part of the solution. People are much more likely to comply with a rule if they help formulate it.

• OTHER ISSUES CONCERNING PARENTS •

Beyond specific childrearing problems, parents are also concerned about the effect of the society at large, day care, and public education on childrearing.

Society at Large

Although the issue is very complex, eighty percent of more than 200,000 respondents said they felt family life in the United States today was in trouble (*Better Homes and Gardens*, 1983). The absence of a religious or spiritual foundation, inattentive parents, divorce, moral decay, economic hardship, and both parents working were viewed as the primary threats to family life. One conservative parent said:

> When you look at the mess our society is in, it isn't a fit place to bring up a child any more. The television is filled with permissiveness, everybody is

cheating on his wife or her husband or getting divorced. And we've moved off of the land into the big city where there is plenty to get kids into trouble.

Day Care

In a national study of pregnant women, seven in 10 said they intended to return to work within six months after their baby was born, mostly because of economic necessity (Gallup/Levi Poll, 1983). Their biggest concern about returning to work was the quality of care their baby would receive in their absence. Although most parents leave their children with a hired baby-sitter or relative, an increasing number are turning to day care centers.

DATA • *About 20 percent of mothers who work full time take their child to a day care center.* (U.S. children and their families, 1983)

But how confident can parents be that day care centers will take good care of their children? Snow (1983) reviewed the literature on the effectiveness of day care for children and noted several implications for parents:

CONSIDERATION • First, although day care is not an optimal arrangement, parents may utilize good quality day care with some degree of assurance that the effects will be relatively benign at worst and slightly enriching at best. Parents should be prepared to accept an increased risk of their child's exposure to contagious diseases and the possibility of increased negative interaction of their child with peers. The risks associated with average to poor day care are unknown.

Second, center day care and family day care are both viable options for child care. A good day care center would be preferable to a poor day care home and vice versa. Given a choice between a good day care center and a good day care home, the day care home would most likely be preferable, especially for infants. Variations in the quality of both homes and centers make it especially important for parents to examine specific situations carefully before making child-care placement decisions.

Third, child-care arrangements should be consistent and stable within quality settings. Stability and continuity of caregivers is especially important for children from broken homes.

Fourth, in shopping for child-care arrangements, parents should look for (a) homes or centers that are licensed and supported by a sponsoring agency and have external resources such as training and consultants; (b) small centers (less than 60 children) and facilities that serve children in small groups with a favorable staff-child ratio and that have caregivers with education and training relevant to young children; and (c) facilities that welcome parent participation.

Finally, if possible, parents who need day care services should place their child in care between one and seven months of age or wait until after 15 to 18 months to avoid the peak age for separation anxiety.

Public Education

Parental concern continues when their children move beyond day care into public education.

Many parents enjoy sharing learning experiences with their children.

DATA • *In a study of more than 200,000 respondents, 78 percent of their children attend public school, 16 percent attend parochial or religious private school, and 6 percent attend a nonreligious private school.* (Better Homes and Gardens, 1983)

Considerable media attention has been given to the problems of public school education—graduates can't read, work simple math problems, or write an intelligible sentence. Parents feel frustrated when their children don't learn these basic skills. One parent said, "For all the money that is pumped into education, you would think more learning would take place."

• TRENDS •

New parents will continue to enter their childrearing role more or less naively. The person they are most likely to ask for information about children is their pediatrician or family physician (Mullis & Mullis, 1983). This suggests that most couples wait until they have a child to begin talking about their concerns about the childrearing role. Of course, no book, lecture, or course can adequately prepare a person for what it means to rear a child. Those who have had a great deal of responsibility for the care of younger siblings probably have a better idea than most.

For parents who find that the role is more than they anticipated, there are a number of resources including a newsletter, *Effective Parenting*, developed by the sponsors of STEP (systematic training for effective parenting). In addition to P.E.T. (parent effectiveness training), STEP offers workshops and materials on subjects from toddlers to teens. (Contact Effective Parenting, American Guidance Service, 2026 Publisher's Building, Circle Pines, MN 55014-1796. Their toll free number is 800-328-2560.)

Unless new parents learn effective disciplining procedures such as time out and withdrawal of privileges (see Choices section) they will tend to use corporal punishment, which as will be noted, has long-term negative consequences.

· SUMMARY ·

Rearing children is one of the most demanding tasks an individual ever undertakes, and it requires that parents keep their role in perspective. Parenthood is only one stage in the person's marriage and life. In addition, parents are only one influence in the lives of their children; the joys and problems of childrearing change as the children mature; each child is different; and the goals of childrearing may differ. Some parents want obedient children, whereas others want children who are independent and self-reliant. The latter goal is in the best interests of the child.

To get adults to commit themselves to the role of parent, extensive folklore has arisen to make the role more palatable. Would-be parents are led to believe that childrearing is fun, that good parents will produce good children, that love is enough for successful parenting, and that their children will appreciate the sacrifices they make for them. These beliefs are not supported by facts.

There are a number of childrearing approaches to help parents with the problems of parenting. The developmental-maturational approach focuses on what the child will be able to do when and suggests that parents not demand of children what they are developmentally unable to deliver. The behavioral approach assumes that behavior is learned and that parents can get their children to engage in the behavior they want by rewarding the desirable behavior and punishing the undesirable behavior. Parent effectiveness training focuses on the communication between parent and child and encourages the parents to negotiate with their children when conflict occurs. The socioteleological approach views the negative behavior of children as a result of feelings of inferiority and suggests regular family council meetings to give children a voice in what happens in the family. The reality therapy approach focuses on the necessity of letting children make their own choices and learning from them.

Beyond specific behavioral problems, parents are also concerned about the way the society at large, day care, and public education affect childrearing.

New parents will continue to enter the parenting role naively, but they may make use of a large number of resources in the form of workshops, organizations, and books for parents who seek such help.

Questions for Reflection

1. Which childrearing approach appeals to you? Why?
2. How do you feel about putting your child in day care?
3. How do you feel about "spare the rod and spoil the child?" (This question will become more relevant after reading the Choices section which follows.)

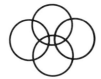

· CHOICES ·

Parents are faced with innumerable choices in rearing their children. These include which type of punishment to use, whether to reward positive behavior, how much freedom to give how soon, and whether to be a friend or an authority to their children.

WHICH TYPE OF PUNISHMENT IS BEST?

Infants are unsocialized persons. They know only one way—their own. Parents who adopt the behavioral approach to childrearing believe that to learn appropriate behavior, developing infants and children must be rewarded for certain behaviors and punished for others. Although parents may agree that praise and privileges are ways of rewarding children for positive behavior, they may choose different forms of punishment.

Some parents have the "spare the rod and spoil the child" philosophy and inflict physical pain on their children as punishment. Examples of such punishment include being beaten on the buttocks with a belt or leather strap, being whipped on the legs, buttocks, and back with a switch, and being slapped or knocked down. One parent said, "If you

don't give them a good beating now and then, they forget who's boss and they don't mind you. A good lickin' will snap a kid in line every time."

Other parents feel that corporal punishment is unnecessary or wrong and elect to put their children in time out or to withhold privileges for inappropriate behavior. "When my 6-year-old says 'Nah' rather than a polite 'No' or 'No ma'am,' I tell her to go to the bathroom. She knows that means she is being punished for being disrespectful," said one mother. "For her brother who didn't get home until 1:30 A.M. when he was supposed to be in at midnight, I took the car away from him for two weeks."

The decision to choose a corporal or noncorporal method of punishment should be based on the consequences of their respective use. In general, the use of time out (removing the child to a place of isolation) and withholding of privileges seem to be as effective in stopping a behavior as

corporal punishment. Young children who are consistently put in time out for inappropriate verbal behavior (saying "nah," talking back, having temper tantrums) decrease the frequency of those behaviors. Likewise, when meaningful privileges are withdrawn for inappropriate behavior (being late, not completing chores, drinking alcohol), the behaviors will decrease.

Beatings and whippings will also decrease the negative verbal and nonverbal behaviors. But there is a major side effect. The person who is physically beaten learns to fear and avoid the punisher. One student recalled, "My dad once beat me with his belt until I bled. I hated him for it and never wanted anything to do with him. And all I did was forget to bring his beer home." Parents who don't want their children to become fearful and avoid them should consider noncorporal forms of punishment.

TO REWARD OR NOT REWARD POSITIVE BEHAVIOR?

Most parents agree that some form of punishment is necessary to curb a child's inappropriate behavior, but there is disagreement over whether positive behavior (taking out the trash, cleaning up one's room, making good grades) should be rewarded by praise, extra privileges, or money. Some parents feel that a child should do the right things anyway and that to reward them is to bribe them. One parent said, "My kid is going to do what I say because I say so, not because I am going to give him something for doing it."

Other parents feel that both the child and parent benefit when the parents reward the child for good behavior. Since rewarding a child for a behavior will result in the child engaging in that behavior more often, the child develops a set of positive behaviors, feels good about herself or himself, and the parents, in turn, feel good about the child.

Rather than ask whether it is good or bad to reward children for positive behavior, parents might ask, "What behavior do I want my child to engage in?" Once that behavior is identified, it is necessary to ensure that positive things happen when the behavior occurs and negative things happen when it doesn't. Children who are rewarded by praise or privileges for being polite, completing their chores, and making good grades and punished by having privileges withdrawn for the opposite behaviors will soon learn to engage in the behavior their parents want them to engage in.

HOW MUCH
FREEDOM HOW SOON?

Becoming independent is one of the major tasks of adolescence. Successful parents may be defined as those who teach their children how to function as an independent adult in society, and they do this by learning to give less assistance to their offspring during adolescence. The parent giving too little or too much help and the adolescent taking too much or too little help will go through many adjustments before the adolescent becomes independent. One parent compared achieving a balance of freedom to flying a kite.

If a parent lets out too much string too quickly, the kite will fall to the ground. But letting out the string slowly as the kite finds the wind and braces against it seems to make the kite soar. And once the kite achieves flight, the parent must let out even more string. If the kite line is kept too tight it will snap and the kite will fall to the ground. So it is with the developing adolescent, letting out the line and waiting for the adolescent to adjust to that level of independence before letting out more line seems to work best for both parent and offspring.

PARENT AS
FRIEND OR AUTHORITY?

Parents are sometimes uncertain whether they want to be or should be a friend or authority to their children. Those who favor developing a friendship with their children sometimes feel their children take advantage of the friendship by trying to get extra privileges or get out of work. Those who favor being an authority sometimes feel like the police and miss an emotional bond with their children.

Another point of view suggests that being a friend does not cancel out being an authority and that both roles are necessary for the parent at different times. Children need a parent in whom they can confide and share the problems of growing up. But they also need an authority who will ensure that they learn the social skills and work habits necessary for their survival in society. Indeed, the New Right has suggested that parents have abandoned their proper role of authority and are responsible for undesirable social groups like the punk rockers and social effects like drug abuse and teenage pregnancy (Pogrebin, 1983).

Part Five

TRANSITIONS

Traditionally, the United States has had an adversary system of divorce in which one party was found innocent and the other guilty. Under the "fault doctrine," it was necessary to prove that one spouse had performed some specific act detrimental to the other spouse. For example, the wife might say (and prove), "He beat me"

(physical cruelty), or "He won't give me money for the children" (nonsupport). Likewise, the husband might accuse his wife of having an affair (adultery). Under any of these circumstances, the "innocent party" would be granted a divorce.

As an alternative to the adversary system of divorce, in 1970 California initiated the "no-fault divorce," allowing spouses to terminate their marriage if either spouse felt that there were "irreconcilable differences." Under the no-fault system, spouses who didn't want to live with each other because they were not happy, had grown apart, or didn't love each other could get a divorce with relative ease.

By 1985 almost all states had adopted similar no-fault provisions. Other labels for "irreconcilable differences" included "irretrievable

breakdown," "irremediable breakdown," and "no reasonable likelihood of preserving the marriage." Some states had adopted separation as a ground for divorce. Under this provision, the spouses need only live apart for six months to one year (depending on the state), this being evidence of "irreconcilable differences."

· Chapter 18 ·

DIVORCE, WIDOWHOOD, AND REMARRIAGE

CONTENTS

Divorce
Self-Assessment: **The Divorce Proneness Scale**
Widowhood
Preparation for Widowhood
Remarriage
Choices

Each American child learns, early and in terror, that his whole security depends on that single set of parents who, more often than not, are arguing in the next room over some detail in their lives. A desperate demand upon the permanence and all-satisfyingness of monogamous marriage is set up in the cradle. What will happen to me if anything goes wrong, if Mommy dies, if Daddy dies, if Daddy leaves Mommy, or Mommy leaves Daddy? are questions no American child can escape.

MARGARET MEAD

Divorce and death are the principal means by which marriages end (others are annulment and desertion). Such endings are accompanied by many emotions—frustration, disappointment, grief, relief, hope—and sometimes by growth. In this chapter we explore the process of, and adjustment to, marital dissolution by divorce and death. We also look at spouses who begin again through remarriage.

• DIVORCE •

DATA • *Every year there are more than one million divorces in the United States. The range is usually between 1,150,000 and 1,250,000.* (National Center for Health Statistics, 1984c)

Preceding these divorces, spouses typically express feelings like the following:

I'm tired of waiting for things to get better. I'm afraid that 20 years from now we'll be in the same stale relationship. Let's separate.

•

I feel trapped and want out.

•

It's not that I think bad things about you; it's just that I don't think about you at all anymore.

•

I am involved in a new relationship and want a divorce.

What began at a wedding ceremony usually with minister, parents, and friends ends in a courtroom with a judge, lawyers, and strangers. The reality of day-to-day living failed to meet the hopeful expectations the partners shared during courtship.

In this section we are concerned about marriage relationships that end in divorce. We all live under the illusion that divorce is something that happens to someone else. But the fact that one in two marriages ends in divorce, should shock us into the reality that it is a possibility for all of us. Before examining the societal and personal reasons for divorce, we look at divorce throughout history.

History of Divorce

For the ancient Greeks, Romans, and Hebrews, divorce (like marriage) was a private affair. Marital dissolutions were arranged by the spouses and their relatives. Particularly in the Mediterranean societies, from which our Judeo-Christian traditions spring, custom ruled that only the husband could initiate a divorce. The ancient Hebrew husband could say "I divorce thee" to his wife, and their marriage would immediately be terminated. Not until the days of the Roman Empire did wives acquire the right to divorce their husbands.

Under Christianity marriage was regarded as a sacrament, a religious act that only the church could validate and that could be dissolved only by death. But in time, the church fathers recognized that under conditions of extreme cruelty, married life might become intolerable. To deal with these unusual circumstances, ecclesiastical courts would sometimes issue a limited divorce that allowed the spouses to live separately, though neither could remarry.

After the Protestant reformation in the sixteenth century, marriage came to be viewed in other than sacramental terms. Some Christian denominations abandoned the concept of marriage as an insoluble bond, and with the growth of secular power, responsibility for the regulation of marriage was transferred from church to state. Non-Catholics began to recognize absolute divorce. In general, divorce was granted only for reasons of adultery, cruelty, and desertion, where one spouse had clearly "wronged" the other. But beginning in 1966 in the United States, divorces were granted for reasons not tied to misconduct, such as "irremedial breakdown."

DATA • *Divorces may now be granted in 48 states without regard to fault.* (Glass, 1984)

Frequency of Divorce

There are four ways of describing the frequency of divorce. The first is the crude divorce rate, which is the number of divorces for every 1000 members of the total population. In general, this description of divorce frequency is the least useful since not all members of our society are married.

The refined divorce rate is the number of divorces per 1,000 married women who are age 15 and over. Table 18.1 reflects the crude and refined divorce rate since 1965. Regardless of which index is used, they suggest divorce may be leveling off.

A third way of describing the frequency of divorce is by the ratio of marriages to divorces in a particular year. These statistics may be grossly misleading. For example, if 100 marriage licenses and 60 divorce decrees are granted in your county this year, one interpretation might be that 60 percent of the marriages in your county end in divorce. Such a conclusion is misleading because the 60 divorces granted this year represent not just marriages that began this year but also marriages that began long ago.

The only way to know what percentage of marriages actually end in divorce is to follow the marriages of those 100 couples until they are ended by divorce, death, desertion, or annulment (the fourth way of describing the frequency of divorce). This is difficult to do because a researcher would need to wait until all

Table 18.1   Crude and Refined Divorce Rates in the United States

YEAR	NUMBER OF DIVORCES	DIVORCES PER 1,000 TOTAL POPULATION (CRUDE DIVORCE RATE)	DIVORCES PER 1,000 MARRIED WOMEN 15 AND OVER (REFINED DIVORCE RATE)
1965	479,000	2.5	10.6
1970	708,000	3.5	14.9
1975	1,036,000	4.9	20.3
1978	1,130,000	5.1	21.9
1979	1,181,000	5.3	22.8
1980	1,189,000	5.2	22.6
1981	1,213,000	5.3	22.6
1982	1,183,000	5.1	
1983	1,179,000	5.0	
*1984	1,175,000	5.0	

*Estimate National Center for Health Statistics, 1984c.
Source: National Center for Health Statistics, 1984b.

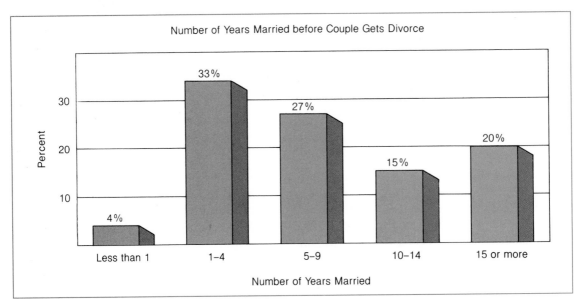

Figure 18.1   **Percent of Married Couples Divorcing by Duration of Marriage**

marriages were over before he or she could look at the reason each marriage ended. However, some estimates have been made.

DATA • *Almost 50 percent of persons ages 25 to 34 in 1980 had either ended their first marriage in divorce by 1980 or may be expected to do so before the age of 75.*   (Glick, 1984a)

Causes of Divorce

Finding the causes of divorce is not easy. The reasons are embedded in the individuals, their interaction, and the society in which they live. Let us look first at the larger social context.

SOCIETAL FACTORS

A number of factors have combined to make divorce increasingly common in America. They include the following.

Changing family functions   Many of the protective, religious, educational, and recreational functions of the family have largely been taken over by outside agencies. Family members may now look to the police, the church or synagogue, the school, and commercial recreational facilities rather than to each other for fulfilling these needs. The result is that although meeting emotional needs remains a primary function of the family, there is less reason to keep the family together.

Employed wives   In the past, the unemployed wife was dependent on her husband for food and shelter. No matter how unhappy her marriage, she could only think about divorce. Her husband literally represented her lifeline. Finding gainful employment outside the home made it possible for her to afford to leave her husband if she wanted to. Now that more than 60 percent of wives are employed (and this number is increasing), fewer and fewer wives are economically trapped in an unhappy marriage relationship.

DATA • *Career-oriented women who have attended graduate school have a greater likelihood of divorce than women who have less education.* (Glick, 1984a)

Fewer moral and religious sanctions The Catholic church no longer excommunicates divorced Catholics who remarry. Many priests and clergy recognize that divorce may be the only alternative in a particular marital relationship and attempt to minimize the guilt a member of their congregation may feel at the failure of his or her marriage. Increasingly, marriage is more often viewed in secular rather than in religious terms.

Divorce models As the number of divorced individuals in our society increases, the probability increases that a person's friends, parents, siblings, or children will be divorced. The more divorced people a person knows, the more normal divorce will seem to that person. The less deviant the person perceives divorce to be, the greater the probability that the person will divorce if his or her own marriage becomes strained.

Personal mate selection As noted in Chapter 6, American parents in the past had more control over whom their son or daughter married and factors such as family background, social class, and property were given priority. The result of such parentally controlled mate selection was that the partners had more in common than love feelings. But today love may be the primary consideration in the decision to marry, and feelings of love are sometimes not enough to weather 50 years together.

> Happiness is not a state to arrive at, but a manner of traveling.
>
> MARGARET LEE RUNBECK

Goal of happiness To achieve and maintain personal happiness is a major goal for most people who marry. Few are concerned about the functional and institutional aspects of marriage. When spouses become unhappy, the typical question they ask themselves is "Why should I stay married if I'm not happy?" Although the current answer of many Americans tends to be "You shouldn't," until the 1970s the answer of the great majority was "It's not unusual to be unhappy in marriage. Work it out. You've taken vows and owe it to yourselves, your children, and your parents to keep your marriage together."

Liberal divorce laws California has the highest annual number of divorces (more than 129,000) of all the states. It also has one of the most liberal divorce laws. A couple with no children, little personal property (less than $5,000), limited debts (less than $2,000), and married less than two years can fill out their own legal forms for dividing their property. After a waiting period of six months, either the husband or wife returns to the court and asks that the judge declare the divorce legal. In states that permit divorce with relative ease, there is a higher divorce rate than in those in which there are substantial legal barriers to divorce. Although a couple who want to get divorced will do so regardless of the laws, the legal system tends to make divorce convenient or not. Table 18.2 lists current grounds for divorce in the various states.

Table 18.2   Grounds for Divorce

STATE	BREAKDOWN OF MARRIAGE/ INCOMPATIBILITY	CRUELTY	DESERTION	NONSUPPORT	ALCOHOL AND/ OR DRUG ADDICTION	FELONY	IMPOTENCY	INSANITY	LIVING SEPARATE AND APART	OTHER GROUNDS	RESIDENCE TIME	TIME BETWEEN INTERLOCUTORY AND FINAL DECREES
Alabama	X	X	X	X	X	X	X	X	2 yrs.	A-B-E	6 mos.	none-M
Alaska	X	X	X	—	X	X	X	X		B-C-F	1 yr.	none
Arizona	X	—	—	—	—	—	—	—			90 days	none
Arkansas	—	X	X	X	X	X	X	X	3 yrs.	C-I	3 mos.	none
California[2]	X	—	—	—	—	—	—	X			6 mos.	6 mos.
Colorado[2]	X	—	—	—	—	—	—	—			90 days	none
Connecticut	X	X	X	X	X	X	—	X	18 mos.	B	1 yr.	none
Delaware	X[4]	—	—	—	—	—	—	—	6 mos.		6 mos.	none
Dist. of Columbia	—	—	—	—	—	—	—	—	6 mos.–1 yr.		6 mos.	none
Florida	X	—	—	—	—	—	—	X			6 mos.	none
Georgia	X	X	X	—	X	X	X	X	2 yrs.	A-B-F	6 mos.	L
Hawaii	X	—	—	—	—	—	—	X	5 yrs.	K	6 wks.	none
Idaho	X	X	X	X	X	X	X	—		H	90 days	none
Illinois	—	X	X	—	X	X	X	X		I-J	6 mos.	none
Indiana	X	—	—	—	—	X	—	—			6 mos.	none-N
Iowa	X	—	—	—	—	—	—	—			1 yr.	none-M
Kansas	X	—	—	—	—	—	—	—		H	60 days	none
Kentucky	X	X	—	X	X	X	—	—	1 yr.	C-J-K	180 days	none-N
Louisiana	—	X	X	X	X	X	X	X	1 yr.	H	12 mos.	none
Maine	X	X	X	—	X	X	X	X			6 mos.	none
Maryland	—	X	X	—	—	X	X	—	1–3 yrs.	D-I	1 yr.	none
Massachusetts	X[4]	X	X	X	X	X	X	—	6 mos.–1 yr.		1 yr.	6 mos.
Michigan	X	—	—	—	—	—	—	—			180 days	none
Minnesota	X	—	—	—	—	—	—	—		K	180 days	none-O
Mississippi	X[4]	X	X	—	X	X	X	X		A	6 mos.	none-P
Missouri	X[4]	—	—	—	—	—	—	—			90 days	none
Montana	X	—	—	—	—	—	—	—			90 days	none
Nebraska	X	—	—	—	—	—	—	—			1 yr.	6 mos.
Nevada	X	—	—	—	—	—	—	X	1 yr.	K	6 wks.	none
New Hampshire[3]	X	X	X	X	X	X	X	—	2 yrs.	K	1 yr.	none
New Jersey	—	X	X	—	X	X	—	X	18 mos.	E-K	1 yr.	none
New Mexico	X	X	X	—	—	—	—	—	6 mos.		6 mos.	none
New York	—	X	X	—	—	X	—	—	1 yr.	K	1 yr.	none

State												Sep.	Grounds	Res.	Res.
North Carolina	—	—	—	—	—	—	—	—	—	X	—	1 yr.	A-E	6 mos.	none
North Dakota	X	X	X	X	X	X	X	X	X	X	X		H-K	12 mos.	none
Ohio	X	X	X	X	X	X	X	X	X	—	X	2 yrs.	B-G-H-I	6 mos.	none
Oklahoma	X	X	X	X	X	X	X	X	X	X	X		A-B-G-H	6 mos.	none
Oregon²	X	—	—	—	—	—	—	—	—	—	—		B	6 mos.	30 days
Pennsylvania	X	X	X	X	X	X	X	X	X	X	X	3 yrs.	C-D-I	6 mos.	none
Rhode Island	X	X	X	X	X	X	X	X	X	—	X	3 yrs.		1 yr.	3 mos.
South Carolina	X	—	—	X	—	—	—	—	—	—	—	1 yr.		3 mos.	none
South Dakota	—	X	X	X	X	X	X	X	X	X	—			none	none
Tennessee	X	X	X	X	X	X	X	X	X	X	—		A-H-I-J-K	6 mos.	none
Texas	X	X	X	X	X	X	—	X	X	X	X	3 yrs.		6 mos.	none-O
Utah	X	X	X	X	X	X	X	X	X	—	—		K	3 mos.	3 mos.
Vermont	X	X	X	X	X	X	—	X	X	X	X	6 mos.		6 mos.	3 mos.
Virginia	X	X	X	X	X	X	—	X	X	—	—	6 mos.-1 yr.	E	6 mos.	none-P
Washington	X	—	—	X	—	—	—	—	—	—	—			none	none-R
West Virginia	X	X	X	X	X	X	X	X	X	X	X	1 yr.	U	1 yr.	none
Wisconsin	X	—	—	—	—	—	—	—	—	—	—	1 yr.	K	6 mos.	none-O
Wyoming	X	X	—	—	—	—	—	X	—	—	—	2 yrs.		60 days	none

Persons contemplating divorce should study latest decisions or secure legal advice before initiating proceedings since different interpretations or exceptions in each case can change the conclusion reached.

Adultery is either grounds for divorce or evidence of irreconcilable differences and breakdown of the marriage in all states. The plaintiff can invariably remarry in the same state where he or she procured a decree of divorce or annulment. Not so the defendant, who is barred in certain states for some offenses. After a period of time has elapsed even the offender can apply for permission.

(1) Generally 5 yrs. insanity but: permanent insanity in Ut.; incurable insanity in Col.; 1 yr. Wis.; 18 mos. Alas.; 2 yrs. Ga., Ha., Ind., Nev., N.J., Ore., Wash., Wy.; 3 yrs. Ark., Cal., Fla., Md., Minn., Miss., N.C., Tex., W. Va.; 6 yrs. Ida.; Kan: Incompability by reason of mental illness or incapacity. (2) Cal., Color, and Ore., have procedures whereby a couple can obtain a divorce without an attorney and without appearing in court provided certain requirements are met. (3) Other grounds existing only in N.H. are: Joining a religious order disbelieving in marriage, treatment which injures health or endangers reason, wife without the state for 10 years, and wife in state 2 yrs. husband never in state and intends to become a citizen of a foreign country. (4) Provable only by fault grounds, separation for some period, generally a year, proof of marital discord or commitment for mental illness. (A) Pregnancy at marriage. (B) Fraudulent contract.

(C) Indignities. (D) Consanguinity. (E) Crime against nature. (F) Mental incapacity at time of marriage. (G) Procurement of out-of-state divorce. (H) Gross neglect of duty. (I) Bigamy. (J) Attempted homicide. (K) Separation by decree in Conn.; after decree: one yr. in La., N.Y., Wis.; 18 mos. in N.H.; 2 yrs. in Ala., Ha., Minn., N.C. Tenn.; 3 yrs. in Ut.; 4 yrs. in N.J., N.D.; 5 yrs. in Md. (L) Determined by court order, La. 90 days to remarry. (M) 60 days to remarry. (N) One yr. to remarry except Ha. one yr. with minor child; La. 90 days (O) 6 mos. to remarry. (P) Adultery cases, remarriage in court's discretion. (Q) Plaintiff, 6 mos.; defendant 2 yrs. to remarry. (R) No remarriage if an appeal is pending. (S) Actual domicile in adultery cases. (U) Abuse and neglect of child; physical or mental injury to child. Enoch Arden Laws disappearance and unknown to be alive—Conn., S.C., Va., Vt., 7 yrs. absence, Ala., Ark., N.Y. 5 yrs. (called dissolution); N.H. 2 yrs.

N.B. Grounds not recognized for divorce may be recognized for separation or annulment. Local laws should be consulted.

Source: The World Almanac and Book of Facts 1984 edition. Grounds for Divorce. © Newspaper Enterprise Association, Inc., New York, NY 10166, 1984, p. 94. Compiled by William E. Mariana, Council on Marriage Relations, Inc., 110 E. 42d St., New York, NY 10017 (as of Aug. 24, 1982). Used by permission.

INDIVIDUAL FACTORS

Although various societal factors may make divorce a viable alternative to marital unhappiness, they are not sufficient to "cause" a divorce. One spouse must actually initiate divorce proceedings. Reasons why a spouse might seek a divorce include the following.

Negative behavior   People marry because they anticipate greater rewards from being married than from being single. During courtship each partner engages in a high frequency of positive verbal and nonverbal behavior (compliments, eye contact, physical affection) toward each other. The good feelings the partners share as a result of these high-frequency positive behaviors encourage them to get married to ensure that each will be able to share the same experiences tomorrow.

Just as love feelings are based on positive behavior from the partner, hostile feelings are created when the partner engages in a high frequency of negative behavior. In one study of spouses who got divorced (Kitson & Sussman, 1982), wives were irritated by their husband's being too domineering, drinking too much, and being unfaithful. Husbands complained that their wives were overcommitted to their work, were too involved with their relatives, and were unfaithful.

When a spouse's negative behavior continues to the point of creating more costs than rewards in the relationship, either partner may begin to seek a more reinforcing situation. Divorce (being single again) or remarriage may appear to be a more attractive alternative than being married to the present spouse.

DATA • *The median age for divorcing husbands is 33.1; for wives, 30.6.*   (National Center for Health Statistics, 1984)

> Without forgiveness life is governed by . . . an endless cycle of resentment and retaliation.
>
> ROBERTO ASSAGIOLI

Lack of conflict negotiation skills   Although getting a divorce is one way to handle negative behavior, negotiating the reduction of the negative and replacing it with more positive behavior is sometimes a more rewarding option. One wife said her husband never spent any time with her because he was always busy with his work. So she asked him what she could do to make him want to spend more time with her. He said she could stop criticizing him and approach him for lovemaking (he was always the initiator) twice a week. The exchange worked. He began to come home earlier and not go back to the office at night and she stopped the criticizing and initiated lovemaking. The result was a change in behavior by both partners with a subsequent change in their feelings toward each other. "I've got a husband who likes to spend time with me," said the wife. Her husband replied, "Yes, and I've got a wife who's fun to be with."

CONSIDERATION • On our wedding day we get three things: a wedding license, a wedding ring, and a little red wagon. As we pull our little red wagon down the marital road, inevitably stones (conflicts) flip into the wagon. If we don't get the stones out of the wagon as they collect—that is, if we don't have the negotiating skills to get the conflicts out of our marriage—the stones pile up and the wagon gets too heavy to pull. We give up and stop pulling the wagon—we get a divorce. Within a few years we have remarried and have gotten another little red wagon into which new stones flip. Unless we develop negotiation skills to reduce the conflicts in our relationships, we are likely to repeat the cycle.

Spouses who stop communicating begin the drift toward divorce.

Radical changes   "He's not the same man I married" is a not uncommon cry. People may undergo radical changes (philosophical or physical) after marriage. One minister married and decided seven years later that he did not like being a minister. He left the ministry, got a Ph.D. in psychology, and began to drink and have affairs. His wife, who had married him in the role of minister, now found herself married to a psychologist who spent his evenings at bars with other women. They divorced.

Spouses may also experience severe physical changes. One wife was in an automobile accident that broke her neck and put her in a wheelchair. "The car and my neck were not the only things that were wrecked," she said of the accident. "It changed our marriage. I was no longer the worker, companion, and lover I had been. We divorced."

Boredom   A 26 year-old woman who had been married for four years said, "It's not that my husband is terrible. I'm just tired of the same thing all the time. I dated a lot before I was married, and I miss the excitement of new people." "Satiated" best describes her feelings. As though she had been watching the third rerun of a TV movie, she is bored. She views divorce as a means of freeing herself from a stale relationship.

Extramarital relationship About half of all husbands and 30 to 40 percent of all wives have intercourse with someone other than their spouse during their marriages (Frank & Enos, 1983; Hassett, 1981, Petersen et. al., 1983a). Spouses who feel mistreated by their partners or bored and trapped sometimes consider the alternative of a relationship with someone who is good to them, exciting, new, and who offers an escape from the role of spouse to the role of lover.

DATA • *In one study of 51 divorced men, half were involved with another woman at the time they separated from their wives.* (Hayes, 1979)

> The vow of fidelity is an absurd commitment, but it is the heart of marriage.
>
> FATHER ROBERT CAPON

Extramarital involvements sometimes hurry a decaying marriage toward divorce because the partner begins to contrast the new lover with the spouse. Since the spouse is often associated with negatives (bills, screaming children, nagging) and the lover almost exclusively with positives (clandestine candlelight dinners), the choice is stacked in favor of the lover. Although most spouses do not leave their mate for a lover, the existence of the extramarital relationship may weaken the emotional tie between the spouses so that they are less inclined to stay married.

Movement toward Divorce

Relationships go through certain stages when they are winding down. Figure 18.2 illustrates the progressive movement toward divorce. These are stages you can see in a deteriorating relationship. First, the partners decrease the frequency of positive behavior and increase the frequency of negative behavior toward each other. This usually results in fewer compliments, less affection, and more criticism and hostility.

Then the partners often stop spending time together. A 32 year-old manager of a department store said, "Since my husband criticizes me every time I'm around him, I've started avoiding him. I go to bed after he's asleep and try to leave in the morning before he gets up. We rarely see each other any more." Failure to spend time together makes it impossible for spouses to recreate the positive feelings necessary to motivate them to stay married.

As feelings grow more distant, the deteriorating relationship is negatively labeled. One partner, more often the wife, eventually says, "I think we should get a divorce." This labeling is significant and seems to carry the couple to the lawyer. A husband and father of two children said, "After she told me she wanted a divorce, things haven't been the same. I feel dead inside."

Then comes a public demonstration that the marriage is ending. The spouses take off their rings, go alone (or with someone new) to events they would normally attend together, and tell those who call for the spouse, "I haven't seen him or her." Once the symbols of the marriage are withdrawn, one spouse often moves out. Once spouses separate, the chance that they will eventually get divorced dramatically increases. In a study of 300 couples who later dismissed their divorce suit and 300 couples who finalized the break, separation was strongly associated with the latter (Levinger, 1979).

Most divorces are accompanied by considerable hostility. A judge who presides over divorce cases remarked:

> You can have them! They're not pleasant. I'd opt for double murder-suicide; it's much easier! [laughs] A lot of arguing, that's all they are. (Glass, 1984, p. 60)

Figure 18.2 Stages in a Deteriorating Relationship

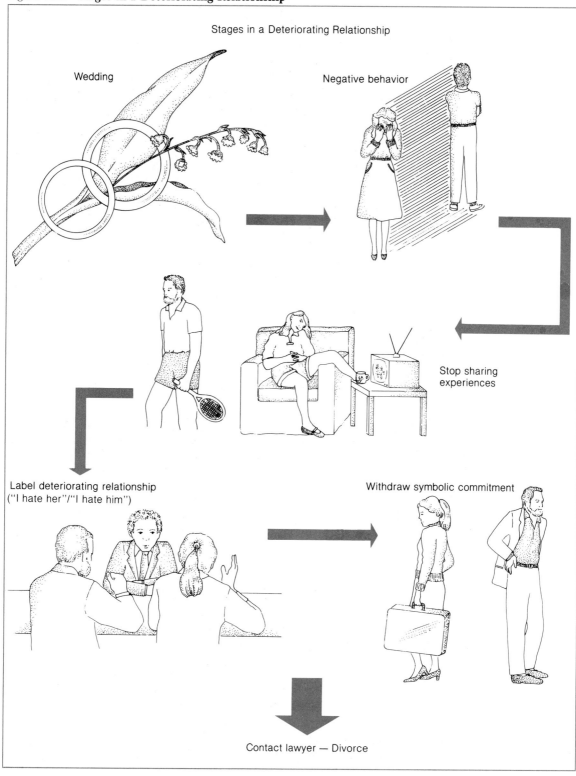

Stages in a Deteriorating Relationship

Wedding

Negative behavior

Stop sharing experiences

Label deteriorating relationship ("I hate her"/"I hate him")

Withdraw symbolic commitment

Contact lawyer — Divorce

Another judge said:

> I don't know where all the reasonable people go, but when they come in here they certainly aren't. Did I tell you about the case where the two of them argued about a plastic spice rack for two hours? (p. 62)

CONSIDERATION • The progression toward divorce can stop at any point, but the earlier the better. The best place to stop it is in the beginning when either partner becomes upset at the behavior of the other. Talking about what is upsetting and negotiating a change in the behavior will take the source of negative feelings out of the relationship. Otherwise, the negative feelings spin the spouses to the next stage and the difficulty of reversing the pattern increases.

For those committed to get a divorce, information about the legal road ahead may be valuable. One such source from a famous divorce lawyer is *Marvin Mitchelson: Everything You Wanted to Know about Divorce (But Couldn't Afford to Ask)* from Home Media Entertainment.

As noted earlier, grounds for divorce vary from state to state. Whereas some no-fault states require only a period of separation, others permit divorce for reasons of adultery, impotence at the time of the marriage, and pregnancy of the wife at the time of the marriage by someone other than the husband if he did not know of the pregnancy. A divorce becomes final when a judge issues a judgment that declares the marriage has ended under the laws of a particular state.

For many good people, divorce and the years that follow are angry, bitter times with two people who once held hands and said silly love things now lined up behind lawyers, ready to do battle.

DENNIS ROGERS

Characteristics of Divorced People

Spouses who don't reverse the movement toward divorce tend to have characteristics different from those who do. At least 12 characteristics are found among divorced people that are more likely to be absent among spouses who work out their differences and stay married (Palisi, 1984; Spanier and Glick, 1981; Yoder & Nichols, 1980). These include the following:

1. Marrying in teens
2. Premarital pregnancy
3. Having divorced parents
4. Limited income
5. Crowded home
6. No high school education
7. Not spending time together
8. Urban residence
9. Having no children
10. Having girl children only
11. Being black
12. Marital alternatives

The last item, marital alternatives, means that spouses who have good alternatives to the present partner are more likely to divorce than spouses who don't have alternatives (Udry, 1981).

This list should be viewed cautiously. Someone with all 12 characteristics could be happily married, just as someone with none of them could get divorced. Although each of us is a potential candidate for divorce, completing the

For people who are widowed or divorced, mealtimes alone may be hard to face.

Divorce Proneness Scale may help you to assess the probability of your getting a divorce.

Consequences of Divorce

For most people, divorce is one of the most devastating emotional experiences a person may encounter. Some reasons follow.

LOSS, DISRUPTIONS, AND NEGATIVE LABELING

A marriage and family counselor who divorced after 25 years of marriage said, "I knew all about divorce, except what it felt like." In spite of the prevalence of divorce and the suggestion that it is the path to greater self-actualization or fulfillment, most divorced people report some amount of personal disorganization, anxiety, unhappiness, and loneliness. "If I were miserable in a second marriage," said one spouse who was going through a divorce, "I'd stay married. I couldn't go through this again."

In a study of 500 male and female divorcées, almost one-fourth characterized their divorce experience as "traumatic, a nightmare" (Albrecht, 1980). Another 40 percent said it was "stressful, but bearable." The experience was much more difficult for the women than the men.

Feelings of depression and despair occur in response to three basic changes in the divorced person's life: termination of a major source of intimacy, disruption of the daily routine, and awareness of a new status—divorced person.

If you are married, you probably did so because you were in love and wanted to share your life with another. Like most people, you needed to experience feel-

Moving from marriage to divorce is like traveling to a foreign country. Few of us are eager for the journey; few can afford the fare; and few know how to cope en route or what to expect when we arrive.

ELEANOR
DIENSTAG

· Self-Assessment ·

THE DIVORCE PRONENESS SCALE

This scale is designed to indicate the degree to which you are prone to get a divorce. There are no right or wrong answers. After reading each sentence carefully, circle the number which best represents your feelings.

1 Strongly Agree
2 Mildly Agree
3 Undecided
4 Mildly Disagree
5 Strongly Disagree

	SA	A	U	D	SD
1. My parents have never been divorced.	1	2	3	4	5
2. My closest friends have never been divorced.	1	2	3	4	5
3. My partner and I can negotiate our differences.	1	2	3	4	5
4. This is my first marriage.	1	2	3	4	5
5. I am a religious person.	1	2	3	4	5
6. I married when I was over age 19.	1	2	3	4	5
7. I do not require a number of sexual relationships to be happy.	1	2	3	4	5
8. I married my partner after I had known her or him for more than 12 months.	1	2	3	4	5
9. My parents approved of the person I married.	1	2	3	4	5
10. My partner and I have an adequate source of income to meet all of our expenses and some money left to play with.	1	2	3	4	5

Scoring: Add the numbers you circled. Since 1 (strongly agree) is the least divorce prone response and 5 (strongly disagree) is the most divorce prone response, the lower your total score (10 is the lowest possible score) the lower your chance of getting a divorce, and the higher your score (50 is the highest possible score), the greater your chance of getting a divorce. A score of 30 places you at the midpoint between not getting and getting a divorce.

ings of intimacy in a world of secondary relationships. Others don't care about the intimate details of your life, nor do they have the background of a shared history to understand you. One reason divorce hurts is that you lose one of the few people who knew you and who, at least at one time, did care about you. Becoming aware that the marriage was not going to work out and thinking about divorce was the most difficult time in the divorce process for over half of the 500 divorced persons in the preceding study. "You feel like a personal failure and you miss the love you once had. When these feelings hit at the same time, it's awful," said one separated spouse.

Divorce also shatters your daily routine and emphasizes your aloneness. Eating alone, sleeping alone, driving alone to a friend's house for companionship are role adaptations made necessary by the destruction of your marital patterns. A divorced man said, "When you're married, things happen without your thinking about it. Eating, going out, visiting friends with your wife seem to occur with little effort. Once you're divorced, it's different. You feel like you have to make everything happen since there is just you. It reminds me that I depended more on her than I thought."

Compounding the loss of intimacy (which may have disappeared before the divorce) and disruption of daily habits is the acquisition of the negative label "divorced." Although divorce can be the wisest and most mature response to a failing marriage, our society still assigns some stigma to the divorced person. Even friends may regard the divorced person as having failed or at best with pity. Since an individual's self-concept is a result of how other people see him or her, maintaining a positive evaluation of one's self under these circumstances is difficult. One divorced woman said, "It's a pity that when you do what you think is right—get out of an emotionally dead relationship—people look down on you."

Telling others of the divorce isn't easy. In a study of 50 divorced members of Parents Without Partners,—the respondents said that mothers, fathers, and co-workers were the most difficult to tell (Ratcliff, 1982). Although most reacted supportively, some were unwilling to accept that the person was getting a divorce. One woman who had been married 23 years described what it was like to tell of her divorce:

> I think the hardest thing for me was breaking up the home and breaking down the image of the community that you had gone to church in, and had been on committees, etc. On the surface, everything looked fine. Everyone thought we were happy people. Most people would say, "You know you spent all those years together—you know you were happy—you're still happy." And I'd say, "Oh, yeah? Well look—how would you like to go live with him then?"

Of course, divorce is not necessarily a negative experience. About one in five spouses in one study characterized his or her divorce as "relatively painless" (Albrecht, 1980). A wife and mother of two children said of the divorce of her alcoholic husband, "It was, without a doubt, the happiest day of my life. I was finally free of him—I should have done it 20 years ago." For these people, the postdivorce period

> is one of exploration (at least for those who have the time, energy, and money to be adventuresome) of both one's inner world and changing outer environment. One may experiment with new activities, or resume hobbies that had been discarded. They may travel, return to school, or change jobs, and seek

I went through a terrible divorce . . . from the woman I loved very much . . . I was blown away as far as my views toward love and life were concerned.

ROBIN GIBB

out new social relationships. It can be a stimulating time of exciting, new challenges. (Kaslow, 1984, p. 36)

> CONSIDERATION • Several studies have been conducted to find out the conditions under which spouses seem to cope best with the divorce experience. Six of these conditions include:(a) terminating the marriage rather than having it terminated by the spouse (Ratcliff, 1982); (b) sharing the blame with the spouse for the marital failure rather than blaming it on the spouse (Newman & Langer, 1981); (c) not being emotionally attached to the ex-spouse and maintaining minimal contact with him or her after the divorce (Kitson, 1982a); (d) having a positive self-concept and high self-esteem (Kitson, 1982b); (e) maintaining social relationships with friends, relatives, and lovers (White & Bloom, 1981); and (f) not having a traditional family orientation (Bloom & Clement, 1984).

LOSS OF INCOME

The divorced person pays for the divorce in yet another way—financially. Two can only hope to live as cheaply as one if they live together. A divorced civil service worker said, "I went from a four-bedroom home and color television to a one-room studio apartment with a flickering black and white TV. It's all I can afford." One lawyer said, "Marriage counselors probably save some marriages, but when couples see the price tag of their divorce, they stop dreaming about the single and free life of the divorced. Most couples simply can't afford a divorce."

DATA • *When 293 divorced women were asked about the economic impact of their divorce, two-thirds said their incomes had significantly dropped.* (Albrecht, 1980) *Data from a national sample of middle-aged women revealed that their real income dropped 40 percent following divorce. The decline occurred in spite of the fact that these women were employed, receiving alimony, or other financial help.* (Corcoran, 1979) *Another study revealed that the drop in income persists across time.* (Weiss, 1984)

> Child support payments ought to be as well collected as car payments.
>
> JUDY GOLDSMITH, NATIONAL ORGANIZATION FOR WOMEN

Men seem less economically affected by divorce. Only 20 percent of 207 divorced males said their income dropped after their divorce. Twenty-five percent said that it increased (Albrecht, 1980). Men fair better economically following divorce because their incomes are higher than women's incomes, and in spite of the legal obligation to pay child support, half manage not to.

To increase support payments by parents who fail to make court-ordered child support payments after 30 days, Congress has passed legislation to withhold money from their paychecks and to take out back child support from tax refunds that are due.

DATA • *Although legally, willful neglect of refusal to pay child support is a criminal offense (for which the father can be imprisoned), only half of all divorced fathers pay child support.* (Jencks, 1982)

CHILDREN

More than half of all divorces involve children. "I'm caught between staying married for my children and living in an unhappy relationship. I don't want to

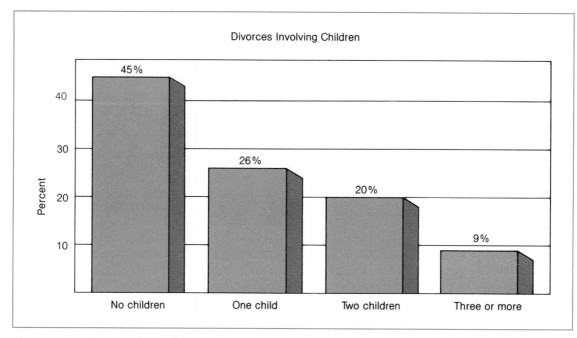

Figure 18.3 **Percent of Couples Getting Divorced Who Have Children**

take my children away from their other parent, but I'm too miserable to stay married either." The dilemma of this parent is not uncommon. Most resolve it in favor of divorce. However, as Figure 18.3 illustrates, the more children a couple has, the less likely they are to get a divorce.

DATA • *In one study 60 percent of more than 200,000 respondents said it was "right" for a couple with children to get divorced if they simply could not get along.* (Better Homes and Gardens, 1983)

But for the parent who does not get custody, actually being separated from one's children and not being able to remain an influence in their lives is a major negative consequence of divorce. "If I had realized that divorce means you don't get to see your kids at the dinner table or watch them play video games or be around them when you want to, I would probably still be married," said one father. "Divorce just isn't worth being separated from my kids."

Hal J. Daniel III, a divorced father, in his poem *Winding Down* (1984) expresses the unhappiness of being separated from his son.

Monday.
It's over.
Father's day is gone.
It never came
to my house.

My ten year old
no longer calls
me father.

My ten year old
no longer calls.

Although the parents will pay their own price for the divorce, what about the children? "How will divorce affect my children?" is the nagging concern of every unhappily married parent. The answer is unclear. In one study, when preschool children from divorced homes were compared with preschoolers from intact homes, relatively few significant differences were found (Hodges et al., 1979). But in another study preschool children who had experienced recent disruption showed more attention problems and more withdrawn behavior than children who had not experienced disruption (Kinard & Reinherz, 1984).

In still another study of 60 families five years after the divorce, 34 percent of the children were happy and thriving, 29 percent were doing reasonably well, and 37 percent were depressed (Wallerstein & Kelly, 1980). Perhaps the most crucial factor influencing a good readjustment was a stable, loving relationship with both parents, between whom friction had largely dissipated, leaving regular, dependable visiting patterns that the parent with custody encouraged. In contrast, children whose parents continued their hostility, resulting in infrequent or no contacts with the noncustodial parent, were still carrying feelings of abandonment and rejection.

Ideally, the conditions under which divorce is likely to have the least negative effect on children include the following:

1. The children understand that they are not personally responsible for the divorce. (Many children blame themselves for their parents' breakup—"My daddy left because he doesn't like me".)
2. Each parent continues to nurture a strong emotional tie with each child.
3. The divorce occurs when the children are very young (under 3 years) or grown up (18 or over). At these ages the children are either too young to feel the emotional impact of divorce or are old enough to perceive it as a not unusual phenomenon.
4. Each parent talks positively of the other. The most destructive effect divorce can have on children occurs when each parent downgrades the other. Fathers may be more likely to encourage their children to take sides with them against their ex-spouses. In one study comparing single-parent fathers and mothers, almost one-third of the fathers in contrast to only one mother had talked negatively about the other parent to the children (DeFrain & Eirick, 1981). One father told his son, "Your mother hates you and didn't want to live here." His son believed him.
5. Access to the other parent is not forbidden. The ex-spouses continue to encourage regular contact of their child or children with the noncustodial parent.

What are the long-term effects of divorce on children as they grow into adulthood? Research has shown conflicting results. In one study when adults who were reared in divorced homes were compared with adults who were reared in intact homes, those from divorced homes were more likely to be anxious, have lower self-esteem, experience marital problems, and be less happy (Rubenstein, 1980). Although this group still wanted to get married and have children, they were more likely to view divorce as an appropriate alternative to an unhappy marriage (Greenberg & Nay, 1982). Another study of more than 8,000 adults compared those who were living with both parents and those who were living with only one parent at age 16 (Nock, 1982). No significant differences were found between the groups. Few long-term effects were noted as being associated with family disruption of any sort. What effects were estimated as important were almost all positive, indicating that the individual may have been strengthened by the experience (p. 38).

CONSIDERATION • The differences in the findings of these studies may be related to the perception that an individual has of an event (divorce) and not the event itself. Divorce by itself doesn't do anything to children. It is how the parents teach them to regard the event and the relationship with the respective parents after the divorce that influences the eventual outcome.

Alternatives to Divorce

Divorce is not the only alternative to terminating a marriage. Others include annulment, separation (legal or informal), and desertion.

ANNULMENT

The concept of annulment has its origin in the Roman Catholic church, which takes the position that marriage is insoluble except by death. An annulment states that no valid marriage ever existed and returns both parties to their premarital status. Any property that has been exchanged as part of the marriage arrangement is returned to the original owner. Neither party has obligations to the other for economic support.

Common reasons for annulments are fraud, bigamy, under legal age, impotence, insanity, and lack of understanding. A university professor became involved in a relationship with one of his colleagues. During courtship he promised her that they would rear a "house full of babies." But after the marriage she discovered that he had had a vasectomy several years earlier and had no intention of having more children. The marriage was annulled on the basis of fraud—he misrepresented himself to her. Most annulments are for fraud.

Bigamy is another basis for annulment. In our society a person is allowed only one spouse at a time. If another marriage is contracted at the time a person is already married, the new spouse can have the marriage annulled. One hundred and four wives of confessed and convicted bigamist Giovanni Vigliotto were entitled to have their marriages to him annulled.

Most states have age requirements for marriage. When individuals are younger than the minimum age and marry without parental consent, the marriage may be annulled if either set of parents does not approve. However, if neither set of parents or guardians disapproves of the marriage and if the state recognizes common-law marriage, the marriage is not automatically annulled and may be regarded as legal.

Intercourse is a legal right of marriage. In some states if the male is impotent, his wife can have the marriage annulled. Likewise, if the wife refuses to have intercourse or is unable to do so for physical or psychological reasons, annulment is a possibility.

Insanity and lack of understanding of the marriage agreement are also reasons for annulment. Someone who is mentally deficient and incapable of understanding the meaning of a marriage ceremony can have such a marriage ceremony annuled. However, being drunk at the time of the wedding is insufficient grounds for annulment.

Although annulments are granted by our civil courts, a Catholic who divorces and wants to remarry in the church must have the first marriage annulled by the church. Grounds for church annulment vary widely; the result is that a Catholic seeking to annul his or her first marriage must find a reason the church will accept. In some cases, marriages have been annulled even though the couple had been married several years and had children.

DATA • *Annulments account for about one percent of all broken marriages.* (U.S. Cenus Bureau, 1981)

LEGAL SEPARATION

An equally small proportion of unhappy relationships end in separation. Separations, or limited divorces, are sought by couples who, for religious or personal reasons, do not want a divorce or do not want one yet and who do not have grounds for an annulment. They contact a lawyer and ask that he or she draw up separation papers.

Typical items in a separation agreement include the following: (1) The husband and wife live separately. (2) Their right to sexual intercourse with each other is ended. (3) The economic responsibilities of the spouses to each other is limited to the separation agreement. (4) Custody of the children is specified in the agreement with visitation privileges granted the other parent. The spouses may have relationships with others, but neither party has the right to remarry. Although some couples live under this agreement until the death of one spouse, others draw up a separation agreement as a prelude to divorce. In some states the fact that spouses have legally separated for one year is a ground for divorce.

INFORMAL SEPARATION

An informal separation is similar to a legal separation except that no lawyer is involved in the agreement. The husband and wife settle between themselves the issues of custody, visitation, alimony, and child support. Since no legal papers are drawn up, from the state's point of view, the couple is still married.

Attorneys advise against an informal separation (unless it is temporary) to avoid subsequent legal problems. For example, after three years of an informal separation, a mother decided that she wanted custody of her son. Although the father would have been willing earlier to sign a separation agreement that would have given her legal custody of her son, he was now unwilling to do so. Each spouse hired a lawyer and had a bitter and expensive court fight.

CONSIDERATION • If you decide that your marriage is not working out but you feel that divorce is premature, get a legal separation. This specifies the important elements (custody, alimony, child support, and so on) of your relationship and cannot be changed arbitrarily by either you or your partner. It is also important that you and your partner have different lawyers when entering into a separation agreement. Rarely can one lawyer serve the needs of two divorcing spouses.

DESERTION

Desertion differs from informal separation in that the deserter walks out and breaks off all contact. Although either spouse may desert, it is usually the husband who does so. A major reason for deserting is to escape the increasing financial responsibility of a family. One man with eight children said, "I'm in over my head; I've got to get away." A husband may also desert because he cannot afford the cost of a divorce.

The sudden withdrawal by desertion sometimes has more severe negative consequences for the wife than divorce. Unlike the divorced woman, the deserted woman is not free to remarry for several years. In addition, no child support or alimony payments are received and the children are deprived of a father.

Desertion is not unique to husbands. Although infrequent, wives and mothers also leave their husbands and children. Their primary reason for doing so is to escape from an intolerable marriage and feeling trapped by the role of mother. "I'm tired of having to think about my children and my husband all the time—I want a life for myself" said one woman who deserted her family. "I want to live too." But such desertion is not without its consequences. Most mothers who desert their children feel extremely guilty.

· WIDOWHOOD ·

A marriage relationship may also be ended by the death of one spouse. That spouse is usually the husband. The typical age at which the women, in one study, became widows was 65. The average length of time the women in the study had been in the role of widow was 18 years (Nuckols, 1983).

DATA • *There are 1,860,000 widowed men and 10,795,000 widowed women in the United States. As a group the widowed represent 2.4 percent of our population.* (*Statistical Abstract of the United States*, 1984)

The death of one's spouse requires as much or more social and personal readjustment than any other crisis. One widow described her husband's death as "the most difficult tragedy of my life which has caused a change in my lifestyle, friends, and finances . . . you never get over it completely. My husband has been dead 27 years and I still think about him and the life we shared every day."

The Bereavement Process

Although every individual will react somewhat differently, widows and widowers often go through several stages as they adjust to the death of their partner. For those whose spouses die suddenly, the initial reaction tends to be shock and disbelief. "I had just seen my wife earlier that morning," recalled a widower, "and I knew that she couldn't possibly be dead. I kept believing she was still alive until I reached into the casket and felt her cold stiff hand. Only then did I believe in her death." In the absence of a corpse, some spouses continue their disbelief. The wife of bandleader Glenn Miller kept his clothes in his closet awaiting his return for 20 years following his disappearance in a small plane over the English Channel during World War II.

After my husband died, I felt like one of those spiraled shells washed up on the beach. Poke a straw through the twisted tunnel, around and around, and there is nothing there. No flesh. No life. Whatever lived there is dried up and gone.

LYNN CAINE

Adjusting to the death of a spouse is one of the most difficult of life's experiences.

After accepting the reality of death, most widows and widowers go the next stage of bereavement—deep sorrow and grief. "I can't tell you how lonely I am," said one widow. "I feel like there is a heavy weight inside me. It takes a huge effort just to get up and go through the daily routines. You won't understand what it's like until it happens to you." Coupled with these feelings is a profound disorientation. "Everything is up in the air now. I don't know who I am anymore," said one widower.

During this period of sorrow, grief, and disorientation, widows and widowers often have fears of mental and physical breakdown and become inordinately dependent upon others. "I guess I wanted someone with me all the time during those first weeks after Philip died," recalled one widow. "I was afraid of what I might do because I had no reason to go on living without him."

While relatives, friends, and business associates are initially quite willing to assist the bereaved in every way possible, after a few weeks their support dwindles as they redirect their energies to their own families and job responsibilities. When such support is withdrawn, the bereaved often enter a new stage of grief as they are confronted with the reality of living without their mate and without continued help from others.

Adjustment for Widows

DATA • *About half of women over the age of 65 are widows*   (Fengler & Danigelis, 1982)

Although the bereavement process is experienced similarly by both widows and widowers, each person responds differently to particular aspects of the adjustment. Since many wives are married to husbands who make more money than they, the husband's death often means an end to the much-needed regular monthly check. "Aside from missing my husband terribly," recalled one widow, "it means I'll have to move out of this house because we didn't have insurance to pay off the house and my salary won't cover the house payment each month."

Other widows complain about difficulty in making decisions. "Paul and I always talked everything over and I depended on him to make the final decision. Now that he's gone I can hardly decide which salad dressing to buy." Decisions about selling property, moving into smaller living quarters, and buying health insurance may be particularly difficult for the woman who has always depended on her husband to make such decisions.

But for widows there are compensating factors. The widow is more likely than the widower to derive emotional satisfaction from her children and grandchildren and is more likely to be welcome in the home of the son or daughter because she can help with the household responsibilities. In one study of 1,400 widows, about 20 percent lived with their children (Fengler and Danigelis, 1982).

Widows also have more people with whom they share a similar role than do widowers. Large churches may have Sunday school classes for widows and community centers offer special programs for them. Between interactions with other widows and with children and grandchildren, the widow is likely to continue traditional domestic activities, which often give order and stability to her life. Although her husband is gone, what she does each day does not change that much.

Adjustment for Widowers

In the past it was thought that loss of a spouse was more difficult for men and that they were more likely to become victims of social isolation. But recent research has indicated that widowers are no more socially isolated than widows and are as likely as widows to have contact with neighbors, friends, relatives, and children (Ferraro & Barresi, 1982).

However, since the widower has probably not learned to perform regular domestic activities, he is less likely to take good care of himself, especially to eat properly. "If it weren't for the corner restaurant," said one widower, "I'd be dead. I really don't know how to cook."

• PREPARATION FOR WIDOWHOOD •

Planning ahead for eventual widowhood may be difficult because it forces us to confront our own and our spouse's mortality. But as one widow said, "It's not as hard as making the arrangements later." There are several key areas to consider in preparing for the death of either spouse. Such preparation includes giving careful early attention to wills, insurance, titles, and funeral expenses.

Wills

A will ensures that your money and property will go to those you want to have them. If you die intestate (without leaving a will), the state in which you lived will decide who gets what and how much. For example, suppose a married man with no children dies intestate. Although he may want his wife to have everything, she may get only half if the state law provides that his parents are entitled to half of his estate.

> CONSIDERATION • Before drawing up a will, consult a lawyer. He or she will be familiar with laws relating to the distribution of property and the guardianship of children in your state. If you move to another state, you might have a lawyer there check your will to make sure that it conforms to the laws in that state.

Under federal law an estate tax (also known as an inheritance or transfer tax) must be filed for every estate with gross assets of more than a certain amount, and any tax due must be paid at the time the return is filed. In 1985 the amount on which no tax is due is $400,000; in 1986, $500,000; in 1987, $600,000. Estates valued at less than these amounts in the respective years escape taxation. If you leave an estate valued at more than these amounts, the government looks to your survivors for its share of what you left. But by giving money or property to your children while you are alive—up to $10,000 annually per child—you can avoid their being taxed on the money at your death.

Also, by leaving a will you are permitted to give your surviving spouse everything you own, your entire estate, tax-free. This provision, allowed in every state by the Internal Revenue Service, is known as the "marital deduction." It applies to surviving spouses only and does not include live-in partners.

Insurance

Having made a will, check your life insurance poicy for amount, type of payment, and ownership of policy. Assuming that the insured feels that the face value of the policy is adequate, check to see if the payments are to be made monthly or in a lump sum. One widow was only allowed to receive monthly payments of $125 instead of receiving a lump sum that she needed to pay off her house.

Check your life insurance policy for ownership. If the husband owns the policy and names the beneficiary as his wife (which is the usual case), the face value of the policy will be included in his estate, and she may need to share the proceeds with the tax collector. If you are a man, you can keep money out of the tax collector's net by having your wife take out an insurance policy on your life. Because she is the owner of the policy, it is not included in your estate and hence is not taxable.

Titles

Just as life insurance benefits can be saved from estate taxes, so can your house, car, and checking accounts. If these are listed in the wife's name, they are considered her property and consequently not part of the husband's estate. Of course, if the wife dies first, the husband will face the inheritance tax problems she was to have avoided. So some balance of ownership is desirable. Retitling property to achieve a balance is only advisable, however, in a stable relationship. The transfer of ownership of large items followed by a divorce may create havoc.

Funeral Expenses

Currently, the cost of a funeral may range from $1,000 to $10,000, the average cost being around $5,000. This price includes embalming, casket, funeral service, use of the building for visitation, and cars for transportation to the cemetery.

The federal government now requires funeral homes to itemize the cost of their services and materials to individuals before the person agrees to any arrangements. In addition, funeral homes are required to give price information over the telephone to permit customers to shop around. Embalming is often not necessary since it is usually required only if the death was caused by a specific contagious disease such as polio, diphtheria or tuberculosis.

Alternative ways to avoid traditional funeral expenses are donating the body to medical research, cremation, and joining a memorial society. If you want to consider body donation, contact a medical school near you and ask them the procedure for donating your body for medical research and teaching. This usually involves completing an application specifying your wish that your body be donated to a certain medical school. At the time of your death, your spouse would then contact a local mortician and ask him or her to make the necessary arrangements with the medical school. Although you have donated your body to medicine, the traditional funeral service may still be held, with your body being transferred to the medical school rather than to a cemetery afterwards; or your body may be removed to the medical school immediately after death, and a memorial service can be held later. In either case, the medical school usually pays the embalming fee and cost of transporting your body up to 200 miles.

Cremation is another alternative. The cost is usually about $500. As with body donation, a memorial service may be held (cost is around $1,000).

• REMARRIAGE •

Marriage is like the army—everyone complains, but a surprising number reenlist.

LAURENCE PETER

Although ending a marriage through divorce or death is traumatic for most people, life goes on. For the divorced and widowed, remarrying is an alternative that may ease recovery from the termination of a previous marriage.

CONSIDERATION • Although remarriage is often viewed as the best method of adjusting to a divorce, a comparison of divorced persons who remarried and who remained single showed that there were no significant differences in the groups in terms of personal adjustment (Saul & Scherman, 1984).

Remarriage for the Divorced

DATA • *About 80 percent of divorced persons are likely to eventually remarry.* (Glick, 1984b) *Divorced women most likely to get remarried are white, were divorced before age 25, and have less than a high school education.* (U.S. Department of Health, Education, and Welfare, 1980)

The fact that a high percentage of divorced persons remarry emphasizes that spouses tire not of marriage but of the person they are married to. Going from one spouse to another does not occur haphazardly. Rather, there are identifiable stages through which a person passes on his or her way to a new partner (Goetting, 1982).

Emotional remarriage   The person begins to trust and love another person in a new relationship. Such feelings may come slowly as a result of negative experiences in the first marriage.

Psychic remarriage   The person gives up the freedom and autonomy of being single again and develops a mental set conducive to pairing. This transition may be particularly difficult for the person who sought a divorce as a means to personal growth and autonomy. The individual may fear that getting remarried will put unwanted constraints on her or him.

Community remarriage   This stage involves a change in focus from one's single friends to one's new mate and other couples with whom the new pair will interact. "Those bonds of friendship established during that period of time when one was divorced may be particularly valuable because they lent support at a time of personal crisis" (p. 219).

People who have been divorced tend to remarry within five years.

Parental remarriage Since most remarriages involve children, the nuances of living with someone else's children must be worked out. As will be noted in Chapter 19, the role of the stepparent is ambiguous. Society offers few guidelines for the sharing of rights and responsibilities with the natural parent. The result is sometimes confusion, frustration, and resentment.

Economic remarriage The second marriage may begin with economic responsibilities to the first marriage. Alimony and child support often threaten the harmony and sometimes even the economic survival of second marriages. One wife said that her paycheck was endorsed and mailed to her husband's first wife to cover his alimony and child support payments. "It irritates me beyond description to be working for a woman who lived with my husband for seven years," she added. In another case, a remarried woman receiving inadequate child support from her ex-spouse felt embarrassed to ask her new husband to pay for her son's braces.

Legal remarriage Partners in a second marriage have legal responsibilities to the former and current marriage. "Remarriage after divorce does not mean that a person exchanges one family for another; instead it means that the individual takes on an additional family. Since legal responsibilities associated with this action have not been clearly charted, individuals are left to base legal decisions on their own moral guidelines" (Goetting, 1982, p. 221). For example, if a spouse remarries and dies, does his estate go to the children of his first marriage, second marriage, or is it split, or none of these? Does the second wife inherit any or all of what the children of the first marriage might have inherited

> The first time you buy a house you see how pretty the paint is and buy it. The second time you look to see if the basement has termites. It's the same with men.
>
> LUPE VELEZ

had he not remarried? Deciding about these issues and having an appropriate will drawn up are necessary.

So most second marriages have to deal with former spouses (alimony, child support payments, and visitation), establishing relationships with stepchildren, and splitting income between two families. Spouses who remarry have a slightly higher chance for divorce than spouses in their first marriage.

DATA • *About 60 percent of second marriages will end in divorce. There is only a 5 percent chance that a person will have three divorces.* (Glick, 1984a)

Those who stay remarried are as likely to report that their marriages are happy as those who married only once (Glenn & Weaver, 1977; De Maris, 1984). "They feel particularly fortunate in their second marriages, as if they have been reborn out of the ashes and have managed to snatch victory out of defeat" (Hunt & Hunt, 1977, p. 258).

CONSIDERATION • An important factor which seems to contribute to the success of second marriages is a sufficient period of time (usually three to five years) between marriages. If remarriage occurs too soon, or the new relationship begins while the emerging partner-to-be is still with the first spouse, it is more likely that the old relationship will impede heavily on the new (Sager et al., 1983, p. 63).

Remarriage for the Widowed

Remarriage for the widowed is usually very different from remarriage for the divorced. The widowed are usually much older, their children are grown, and they are less likely to remarry.

DATA • *Thirteen percent of widowed women who were born around 1905 remarried; 30 percent of widowed men born around 1910 remarried.* (Espenshade & Braun, 1982)

A widow or widower may marry someone of similar age or someone who is radically older or younger. These marriages in which both spouses are elderly are typically referred to as December marriages. Those marriages in which only one spouse is considerably older than the other are referred to as May-December marriages. Since the latter were discussed in Chapter 9, we discuss only December marriages here.

In a study of 24 elderly couples, the need to escape loneliness or the need for companionship was the primary motivation for remarriage (Vinick, 1978). The men reported a greater need to remarry than the women. Most of the spouses met through a mutual friend or relative (75 percent) and married less than a year after their partner's death (63 percent).

The children of the couples had mixed reactions to their remarriage. Most of the children were happy that their parents were happy and felt relieved that the companionship needs of their elderly parent would now be met with someone on a more regular basis. But some children also disapproved of the marriage out

Most of the elderly who are widowed remarry within a year of the spouse's death.

of concern for their inheritance rights. "If that woman marries dad," said a woman with two children, "she'll get everything when he dies. I love him and hope he lives forever, but when he's gone, I want the farm."

More than 80 percent of the spouses described themselves as being either "very satisfied" or "satisfied" with their marriage. A typical response about how things were going was given by a woman who had been married two years: "We're like a couple of kids. We fool around—have fun. We go to dances and socialize a lot with our families. We enjoy life together. When you're with someone you're happy" (p. 362).

Most of the spouses had a live and let live attitude toward each other. "It doesn't pay to get angry," "It takes two to make an argument," and "A person should contain his feelings" were common statements of these elderly spouses.

• TRENDS •

The number of divorces in the United States will peak around 1990. Children of the baby-boom children will be in the 25 to 29 year age range—the years when most divorces take place (Glick, 1984b).

Divorce mediation will increase. In this process the spouses meet with a counselor and lawyer team for the purpose of reducing their hostility and reaching an out-of-court agreement on child support, custody, visitation rights, and property division issues. Such mediation avoids extended court fights and the buildup of extremely negative feelings against the ex-spouse.

Legal changes will include more granting of joint custody, custody to the husband, and assignment of child support responsibility to *both* parents. The legal precedent for the latter has already been established. In Silvia v. Silvia (1980), the Massachusetts court ruled that the incomes of both parents should be considered in assigning the economic responsibilities of the respective parents for the support of their children.

Finally, couples will find it even easier to get divorced through the use of do-it-yourself divorce kits. To avoid the $250 to $300 charged by an attorney for an uncontested divorce, a couple with no assets and no children will complete their own divorce documents. (For those divorces involving property, children, and/or alimony, a lawyer should be consulted.)

• SUMMARY •

The most frequent forms of marital dissolution are divorce and death. Divorce has not always been controlled by the state, nor has it always taken place under religious auspices. Throughout most of Western history, marriages and divorces have been arranged by the people involved and their kinship system.

Regardless of how the divorce rate is calculated (crude, refined, ratio of marriages to divorces, and percentage of marriages terminating in divorce), we have one of the highest divorce rates in the world. Societal factors contributing to such increases include the loss of family functions, more employed wives, and liberal divorce laws. Individual factors include negative behavior, lack of conflict negotiation skills, and extramarital relationships.

Certain categories of people have a higher probability than others of getting divorced. These include the premaritally pregnant, early married, black, and previously divorced.

For most, divorce represents a difficult transition. Loss of self-esteem, lack of money, and concern over children are among the potential consequences of divorce. But divorce may also represent a bridge from an unhappy relationship and personal confinement to new relationships and personal growth. For many, divorce is also the beginning of a new life.

Death terminates those marriages not ended by divorce, annulment, or desertion. Adjusting to the death of one's spouse is one of the most difficult life crises a person experiences. Although the trauma of widowhood cannot be avoided, it can be eased by anticipating one's own death and attending to various concerns such as wills, insurance, titles, and funeral arrangements. A great deal of money can often be saved by drawing up a will, making the wife the owner of the life insurance on her husband, putting property in the wife's name, and donating one's body to a medical school.

Many divorced and widowed people are in a stage of transition to another marriage. About one-third of all marriages are remarriages. Those who remarry and stay married report comparable marital happiness to those in their first marriages.

Trends regarding divorce include a peaking of the divorce rate by 1990, an increase in the frequencly of divorce mediation, and more couples opting for do-it-yourself divorces.

Questions for Reflection

1. To what degree do you share the characteristics of divorce-prone people? How do you feel these factors affect the probability that you might stay married or will eventually divorce?
2. Do you feel the people you know who have gotten divorced are glad they did so? Why do they feel this way? Do you think they are better off? How?
3. How comfortable would you be discussing funeral arrangements with your partner? Do you feel the potential money saved is worth the discomfort you may feel?

· CHOICES ·

Since 55 percent of divorces involve children, a basic decision to be made is who gets custody of the children? The options include mother, father, or joint custody. The latter decision also involves additional choices.

WHO GETS THE CHILDREN? CUSTODY CRITERIA OF PARENTS

Nine out of 10 custody decisions after divorce result in one parent (usually the mother) receiving custody of the children with the other parent (usually the father) receiving visitation rights. This arrangement is usually decided on by the divorcing couple. "That's good," said one attorney, "because if spouses don't make their own decisions, the courts will make their choices for them." Criteria parents use in deciding who will get custody include (1) the emotional quality of the parent-child relationship, (2) the parent's sense of responsibility to the child, (3) the parent's desire to have custody, (4) the parent's ability to maintain a good relationship with the other parent, (5) the parent's ability to provide continuity in the child's physical environment, (6) financial sufficiency, (7) the amount of time the parent has for the child, and (8) the par-

ent's reluctance to get into a legal dispute over custody (Lowery, 1982). Gender and age of the children are also important variables in parental custody decisions; boys and older children are more likely to go with the father.

CUSTODY TO ONE PARENT?

When the parents disagree over who should get custody of the children, a judge will decide. In the past, preference was given to mothers. In less than 5 percent of the cases has the father been given sole custody of his children (Spanier & Glick, 1981). Awarding custody to the mother, particularly of younger children, was based on the "tender years doctrine" which held that young children needed their mother and it was in their best interest to live with her. This doctrine was challenged by Ken Lewis, a divorced father of two daughters, who contended that the tender years doctrine was an insidious example of sex discrimination. He won custody of his children on the grounds that the word *mother* is a verb and

that he had demonstrated better mothering skills than the biological mother. (Fathers for Equal Rights of Michigan and Canada, P.O. Box 2272, Southfield, MI 48037 is an organization for fathers seeking divorce and custody reform.)

Although in most cases, fathers agree that their wives should have custody of their children, some fathers want custody and contest their wives' right to have them. In a study of contested child custody cases in Colorado, almost one in five fathers was awarded custody (Pearson et al., 1982). In such cases, the mother had been proven unfit (severe psychological problems, abandonment of child, history of child abuse) and the children expressed a preference to live with their father. In addition, the fathers had always been actively involved in his childrens' lives, felt responsible for them, and felt a deep emotional attachment.

JOINT CUSTODY?

An alternative to sole custody is joint custody. In one study joint custody was granted in 7 percent of the cases (Clingempeel & Reppucci, 1982).

Such an arrangement usually means that the parents will have equal access to the children and equal parenting rights. There are numerous choices in deciding on when the children are with each parent. Alternatives include the following:

1. Children rotate spending one week with each parent.
2. Children spend Monday through Thursday with mother, Friday, Saturday, and Sunday with father.
3. Children are separated with half living with each parent. Children spend weekends and holidays together with one parent on a rotated basis.
4. Children live with each parent for six months with regular visitation granted the other parent.
5. Children spend two weekdays with the mother, two weekdays with the father, and alternate weekends and holidays with each.

The alternative arrangements may seem complex, but not if they are "followed consistently so that the children are aware on any one day where they will be going" (Watson, 1981, p. 476).

Although the phrase "joint custody" sounds egalitarian, there are disadvantages to this arrangement. In some cases, the father uses the arrangement to avoid or reduce the amount of money he will be ordered by the court to pay in child support. Under a joint custody agreement, he will be ordered to pay less since it is assumed that he will be keeping the children with him some of the time. Other fathers may use the threat of joint custody to get their wives to ask for limited amounts of alimony and child support. The implicit threat is "If you ask for a lot of money, I will take the kids away from you as much as I can." Another disadvantage is that joint custody tends to put hostile ex-spouses in more frequent contact with each other so that the marital war continues. What the children might have escaped being exposed to in a sole custody decision, they are continually confronted with in a joint custody decision.

But joint custody has a positive side. Ex-spouses may fight less if they have joint custody because there is no problem about who gets the children and other inequities of the sole parent custody decision. Children will benefit from the resultant decrease in hostility between parents who have both "won" them.

Joint custody also allows both parents to continue to be involved in their children's lives. Unlike the sole parent custody outcome in which one parent, usually the mother, wins and the father is banished, the children under joint custody may continue to benefit from the love and attention of both parents.

Stahl (1983) observed the impact of joint physical custody on six families and concluded that the benefits far outweighed the drawbacks. All of the 10 children (ages 10–19) liked the arrangement. They were able to continue equal and easy access to each parent instead of having to choose between them. Although having to move between two homes was a problem, the benefit of being able to spend time with each parent made up for the disadvantage.

Eleven of the 12 parents were satisfied with joint custody. They felt they had divorced each other but not their children. The one parent who was dissatisfied felt that the ex-spouse was still too much in her life.

Depending on the level of hostility of the ex-partners, their motivations for seeking sole or joint custody, and the relationship with their children, any arrangement could have positive or negative consequences for the spouses and children. For those cases in which the spouses have minimal hostility toward each other and strong emotional relationships with their children as well as the desire to remain an active influence in their children's lives, joint custody may be the best of all possible choices.

· Chapter 19 ·

STEPFAMILIES

CONTENTS

Definition and Types of
Stepfamilies
Unique Aspects of Stepfamilies
Strengths of Stepfamilies
Weaknesses of Stepfamilies
Women in Stepfamilies
Men in Stepfamilies
Children in Stepfamilies
Developmental Tasks for
Stepfamilies
Self-Assessment:
Stepfamily Success Scale
Choices

*By 1990 there will be more
single parent and stepfamilies
combined than there will be
biological families.*

JOHN S. VISHER

With 50 percent of spouses getting divorced, 80 percent of the divorced remarrying, and 55 percent of those coming to the new marriage with children from a previous marriage, stepfamilies are not unusual. In this chapter we examine how stepfamilies differ from biological families, how they are experienced from the viewpoint of women, men, and children, and the developmental tasks that must be accomplished to make a successful stepfamily. We close the chapter with a look at the choices faced by those about to enter a stepfamily and suggest ways to make such decisions.

· DEFINITION AND TYPES OF STEPFAMILIES ·

Also referred to as a reconstituted, remarried, or binuclear family, a stepfamily is a married couple in which at least one of the spouses has had a child in a previous relationship. Stepfamilies are also known as blended families. The term *blended* is used because the new marriage relationship is blended with the children of at least one of their previous marriages.

DATA • *About one in six or about 17 percent of American families are stepfamilies. Every day 1,300 new stepfamilies are formed in the United States.* (Visher, 1984)

Types of stepfamilies include the following:

1. Families in which the children live with their remarried parent and stepparent. Such is the case of Roxie and Sherry who live with their mother who has recently remarried. Their stepfather is Mark.
2. Families in which the children from a previous marriage visit with their remarried parent and stepparent. Jack is the father of Roxie and Sherry. He has remarried and his children visit him and his new wife, Margaret, on weekends. When they visit, the four of them are a stepfamily.
3. An unmarried couple living together in which at least one of the partners has children from a previous relationship who live with them or visit. Susan and Bob are living together. Susan's daughter Michelle lives with them and Bob's son visits them on weekends.

• UNIQUE ASPECTS OF STEPFAMILIES •

Stepfamilies are unique when compared with couples who live with their own biological children. Some of these unique characteristics follow.

All Members Are Not Biologically Related

Unlike the biological family in which the children are genetically related to both parents, children in the stepfamily are related to only one parent. That parent is the mother in 97 percent of the cases.

DATA • *About 8.5 percent of all children live with either a stepfather or stepmother.* (Bachrach, 1983)

CONSIDERATION • The significance to the stepfamily of the biological tie between parent and child is the strong emotional bond that accompanies it. Although stepparents can develop love feelings for their stepchildren, they sometimes do not. The different levels of emotional bonds parents and stepparents have with their children and stepchildren create a context for negative feelings and conflict. "If you don't love my daughter, you don't love me," said a biological mother to the child's stepfather.

Stepfamilies Have Experienced a Crisis

Stepfamilies are born out of a crisis event. The children have been removed from one biological parent (whom they often desperately hope will reappear

Newly begun stepfamilies require adjustment from each family member.

and reunite with the parent) and the spouse has experienced emotional disengagement and physical separation from a once-loved partner because of divorce or death. Jane is divorced with two children. She said:

> It's been two years since I divorced Bill and it's been hard for all of us. The children miss their father a great deal and they still ask sometimes, "When are you and daddy getting back together?" It hurts me to know that they are separated from their father. But it would hurt even more for me to have to live with their father. Yet I miss being a family and look forward to getting remarried.

Members Have Different Beliefs and Values

Children in a biological family have been exposed to a relatively consistent set of beliefs, values, and behavior patterns. When entering a stepfamily, children get a new parent who brings into the unit a new way of living. One stepchild confided:

> As long as my mother was alive she cooked me plain ole meatloaf and potatoes for dinner. And her potatoes always were the real kind with lumps in them. My stepmother cooks all her meats in some fancy French wine sauce

The words "blended" and "reconstituted" remind you too much of the kitchen. It's as if you had to add water to make a new artificial family, something not quite as good as the real thing. We prefer the term *stepfamily*.

JOHN VISHER

and her potatoes are the instant variety. I don't like her cooking but didn't know how to tell her. And if I started to like her French cooking I might feel guilty because I would be betraying the memory of my mother.

Likewise, the new parent now lives with children who may have been reared differently from the way the stepparent would have reared them if he or she had been their parent all along. One stepfather explained:

It's been a difficult adjustment for me living with Molly's kids. I was reared to say "Yes sir" and "Yes ma'am" to adults and taught my own kids to do that. But Molly's kids just say yes and no. It rankles me to hear them say that but I know they mean no disrespect by it. I've talked to Molly about it and she says she doesn't see anything wrong with the yes and no as long as it is said politely and that it is just something that I am going to have to live with.

Parent-Child Relationship
Has Longer History Than the New Marriage

In the stepfamily the relationships between the biological parent and children have existed longer than those between the adults in the remarriage. Jane and her twin children have a nine-year relationship and are emotionally bonded to each other. But Jane has known her new partner only a year, and although her children like their new stepfather, they hardly know him.

CONSIDERATION • A parent's emotional bond with children (particularly if they are young and dependent) from a previous marriage may weaken a re-marriage from the start. As one parent says, "Nothing and nobody is going to come between me and my kids." However, new spouses may view such bonding differently. One spouse said that such concern for one's own children was a sign of a caring and nurturing person. "I wouldn't want to live with anyone who didn't care about his kids." But another said, "I feel left out and that she cares more about her kids than me. I don't like the feeling of being an outsider."

Children Have Two Homes

Unlike children in the biological family who have one home they regard as theirs, children in stepfamilies have two homes they regard as theirs. In cases of joint custody, some children spend half the week with one parent and half with the other parent; they have two sets of adult parents in two separate homes.

The respective adult couples may view the children being with the other couple as a negative influence on the children. One remarried mother whose children spend a week with their father in the summer said:

It takes them a week after they come home to settle down. He buys them everything, takes them to movies and pony shows, and shows them a terrific time. They come back here and it's rather drab. I dread their seeing their father because he interferes with the type of stable family life my new husband and I am trying to provide for them. (I won't go into the fact that my ex has a girlfriend who lives with him.)

Children in these relationships often feel torn. One child said:

> I love both my mom and my dad but feel like I'm not supposed to enjoy either of them when I'm with them. My mom makes me feel guilty if I act like I enjoy being with my father on Saturdays and my dad can't understand why I would rather live with my mom. It's a real bind.

Money from Ex-Spouse May Be Source of Conflict

In some stepfamilies the ex-spouse is expected to send child-support payments to the parent who has custody of the children. Although less than half of these fathers send any money, those who do may be irregular in their payments.

DATA • *The average amount of money received for child support each year is $1,799.* (Miller, 1983)

CONSIDERATION • The ex-husband sending money to the biological mother creates the illusion for the stepfather that the ex will take care of the expenses for the child. In reality, such payments will cover only a fraction of what is actually spent on the child, so that the new stepfather may feel burdened with more financial responsibility for his stepchildren than he bargained for. This may engender negative feelings toward the wife in the new marriage relationship.

Money to Ex-Spouse May Be Source of Conflict

The other side of child support is the remarried father paying money to his ex-wife who has custody of their children. One researcher studied 101 divorced men and observed that their remarriage was associated with an increase in voluntary support payments (Tropf, 1984).

One remarried father sent his ex-wife $500 each month in child support for their two children. But his new wife became upset that this money left their marriage every month and could not be spent to buy the things they wanted. She eventually told her husband that if he were going to send his money to a wife he hated for children he never saw, she was going to leave him. The husband stopped sending the money. His ex-wife did not take legal action because she wanted him out of her life and didn't value the money.

New Relationships Are in Flux

Each member of a new stepfamily has a great deal of adjustment to make. How the mate feels about the partner's children from a former marriage, how the children feel about the new stepparent, and how the never-before-married spouse feels about the spouse sending alimony and child-support payments to an ex-wife are issues that must be dealt with. Osborne (1983) reports that it takes at least two years for newly remarried spouses to feel comfortable together, to feel that they are a team as strong as the parent-child team. It takes four to

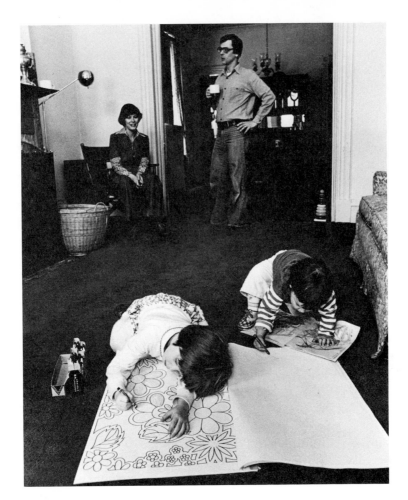

This newly remarried couple had no child-free period.

five years for the whole family to feel comfortable, to have a shared history and to feel inside rather than outside the family.

Stepfamilies Are Stigmatized

We all have a picture of a family. It is usually not a stepfamily.

JUDY OSBORNE

We are all familiar with the wicked stepmother in *Cinderella*. The fairy tale certainly gives us the impression that to be in a stepfamily with stepparents is a bad thing. Such a bad press has affected stepfamilies to the degree that remarried couples often hide the fact that their children are not biologically theirs. One remarried mother said:

> We moved to another state so no one would know that the children were from my former marriage. There is something better about my new husband saying "This is my son and daughter" rather than "This is my stepson and stepdaughter." The latter kind of assumes that there is something wrong with us (because we're divorced) and that something is wrong with the kids (they don't live in a "real family").

Table 19.1 Differences between Biological Families and Stepfamilies

BIOLOGICAL FAMILIES	STEPFAMILIES
1. Children are biologically related to both parents.	1. Children are biologically related to only one parent.
2. Both biological parents live with children.	2. One biological parent does not live with children because of divorce or death.
3. Beliefs and values of members tend to be similar.	3. Beliefs and values of members are more likely to be different because of different backgrounds.
4. Relationship between adults has existed longer than that between children.	4. Relationship between children and parents has existed longer than that between adults.
5. Children have one home they regard as theirs.	5. Children have two homes they regard as theirs.
6. The family's economic resources are from within.	6. Some economic resources come from ex-spouse.
7. All money generated stays in the family.	7. Some money generated may leave the family in form of alimony or child support.
8. Relationships are relatively stable.	8. Relationships are in flux: new adults adjusting to each other; children to stepparent; adults to stepchildren.
9. No stigma attached to biological family.	9. Stepfamilies are stigmatized.
10. Spouses had child-free period.	10. Spouses had no child-free period.

CONSIDERATION • Although stepfamilies are stigmatized, a study of 80 stepfamilies reported that the husbands and wives were aware of their problems, were able to suggest changes, and perceived themselves as strong and successful (Knaub et al., 1984). The researchers concluded that any suggestion that a stepfamily is inferior is inappropriate and is dysfunctional to that stepfamily's adjustment.

Stepparents Have No Child-free Period

Unlike the biological family in which the newly married couple have their first child about two and a half years after their wedding, the remarried couple begin their marriage with children in the house. "We've never been alone," said one wife. "We wouldn't know what it is like."

The differences between biological families and stepfamilies are summarized in Table 19.1.

• STRENGTHS OF STEPFAMILIES •

Stepfamilies have both strengths and weaknesses. Strengths include the early reality coping by children, their exposure to a variety of behavior patterns, and adaptation to sibling relationships inside the family unit.

Early Reality Coping

Children in stepfamilies learn early about life's realities. Whereas many children never have to cope with separation, divorce, and death, stepchildren have been around the track. They have had firsthand experience in losing someone close to them. More important, they have learned that life goes on no matter what happens and that transitions to new relationships can be for the better. One daughter said:

> Looking back on my parents' divorce, I wish they had done it long ago. While I miss my dad and am sorry that I don't see him more often, I was always upset listening to my parents argue. They would yell and scream and it would end with my mom crying. It was a lot more peaceful (and I know my mom was a lot more happy) after they got divorced. Besides, I like my stepdaddy. Although he isn't my real dad, I know he cares about me.

Exposure to Variety of Behavior Patterns

Children in stepfamilies also experience a variety of behaviors, values, and lifestyles. They have had the advantage of living on the inside of two families. One 12-year-old said:

> My real dad didn't like sports and rarely took me anywhere. My stepdad is different. He likes to take me fishing and roller skating. He recently bought me a knife and is showing me how to whittle a stake for our tent when we go camping this summer.

Adaptation to Stepsiblings

Children learning how to get along with other children in an intimate environment is another beneficial experience. Also, the child's world may be expanded by new playmates and companions. This is a particular benefit for an only child whose parent marries a person with one or more children.

• WEAKNESSES OF STEPFAMILIES •

Weaknesses of stepfamilies include unrealistic expectations and the necessity of continually dealing with an ex-spouse.

Unrealistic Expectations

Both spouses in the remarriage may expect that their present marriage will right all previous relationship disappointments—both parental and past marital failures. One spouse said:

> I was looking for a fresh start. I felt like a failure because I was divorced and separated from my kids. I wanted so desperately to be remarried and to be happy with my new wife and family. But it didn't work out that way. She had a problem with being faithful and her kids never looked on me as their dad.

Dealing with the Ex-Spouse

DATA • *In a study of 200 second wives, 26 percent reported that their husband's ex-wife was the primary problem in their relationship.* (Walker, 1984)

Another weakness of stepfamilies is dealing with the ex-spouse—the visible reminder of the first marriage who calls and comes by to pick up the children. Although new spouses may intellectually understand the necessity of such interaction between their spouse and the spouse's ex, emotionally they may feel jealous of the tie to the previous marriage.

> I can't stand it when his ex-wife calls and comes to visit the kids. I've asked my husband to go into another room to talk when she calls and I go to another room when she comes to pick up the kids. This thing gets me upset every time.

• WOMEN IN STEPFAMILIES •

Some of the concerns women in stepfamilies have include accepting the new partner's children, adjusting to alimony and child-support payments to an ex-wife, the new partner accepting her children and their accepting him, and having another child in the new marriage.

Accepting Partner's Children

"She better think a long time before she marries a guy with kids," said one 29-year-old woman who had done so.

DATA • *In a study of 200 second wives, 35 percent reported that children from the husband's first marriage was the top problem in their relationship.* (Walker, 1984)

This stepmother went on to explain:

> It's really difficult to love someone else's children. Particularly if the kid isn't very likable. A year after we were married, my husband's 9-year-old daughter visited us for a summer. It was a nightmare. She didn't like anything I cooked, was always dragging around making us late when we had to go somewhere, kept her room a mess, and acted like a gum-chewing smart aleck. I hated her

I don't have all the fond memories of you when you were a young child so don't expect me to enjoy these teen years without some good years to balance them.

STEPMOTHER TO STEPDAUGHTER

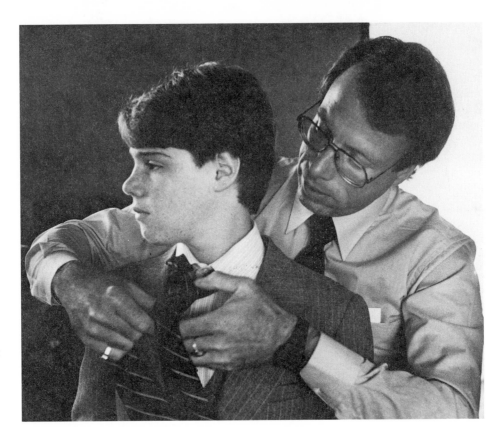

A woman who marries a divorced man who is a father must be aware of the strong bond he has with his children.

but felt guilty because I wanted to have feelings of love and tenderness. Instead, I was jealous of the relationship she had with her father and I wanted to get rid of her. I began counting how many days until she would be gone.

You can hide your dislike for awhile but eventually you must tell your partner how you feel. I was lucky. My husband also thought his daughter was horrible to live with and wasn't turned off by my feelings. He told her if she couldn't act more civil, she couldn't come back. The message to every woman about to marry a guy with kids is to be aware that your man is a package deal and that the kid is in the package.

Adjusting to Alimony and Child Support

DATA • *In a study of 200 second wives, 21 percent said that "financial problems" was the top problem in their relationship.* (Walker, 1984)

In addition to the potential problems of not liking the partner's children, there may be problems of alimony and child support. As noted earlier, it is not unusual for a wife to become upset when her husband mails a quarter or a third of his income to a woman he used to live with. This amount of money is often equal to the amount of money earned by the wife. Some wives see themselves as working for their husband's ex-wife, a perception that is very likely to create conflict.

New Partner Accepting Her Children and Their Accepting Him

In this situation a divorced woman has custody of her children and remarries a man without children. Her main concerns are how her new husband will accept her children and how the children will accept him. The ages of the children are important in these adjustments. If the children are young (age 3 or below), they are usually accepting of any new adult into the natural parent's life. On the other hand, if the children are in adolescence, not only are they struggling for independence from the natural parent, but they also do not want any new authority figures.

Whether the new spouse will accept the children is unpredictable. Some men enjoy children and relate to them easily, as did the man who built a new house "for my new family." Other men find it difficult to enjoy children, particularly those with whom they have no biological link. One man told his fiancée, "If those kids are going to live with us, I don't want to be married to you."

DATA • *Ninety-five percent of stepparents in one study said the husband and wife had equal duty to care for and bring up children from their present marriage; 59 percent said they had equal duty for children from the wife's prior marriage; and 52 percent said they had equal duty for children from the husband's prior marriage.* (Giles-Sims, 1984)

Having Another Child

Another important issue may be whether the new husband wants to have a child with the new wife. Some men delight in the prospect of a child with their new wife. But others feel that they have had enough children and do not want any more. One husband in a second marriage said, "I've got two kids of my own and I certainly don't want any more. But my new wife wants one so I guess we'll have one."

• MEN IN STEPFAMILIES •

Four combinations (among others) of men in stepfamilies are those with or without custody of their children who marry a woman with or without children.

Man without Custody Married to Woman without Children

A frequent stepfamily situation is the divorced man who is separated from his children and who is remarried to a woman without children. He is often concerned about the possibility that his new wife will resent his children visiting him or his visiting them.

DATA • *In a study of 101 divorced fathers, of those who were remarried, 47 percent saw their children at least once a month.* (Tropf, 1984)

Another concern is whether the new wife will accept the fact that he will be sending between a quarter and a third of his income in child-support payments to his ex-wife. In addition, since his wife is typically younger and childless, she may want children of her own. One divorced man said:

> I feel awful not being able to see my kids and I mope around the house a lot on weekends. When the time comes for them to visit, I get excited and really look forward to it. But my wife doesn't. She's tried to enjoy them but I know that she resents the relationship I have with them and their intrusion into our marriage. And the money has become a real problem. I send in child support the amount she makes each month. She told me that we could be living in a nice house for the money we are spending on "those kids." She's talking about "my kids."

Man with Custody Married to a Woman with Children

As more men are awarded custody of their children, an increasing number of stepfamilies will include two sets of children. Since the number of relationships to manage increases with each new person, such stepfamilies have most of the potential problems of stepfamilies: the adjustments of the spouses to their respective sets of stepchildren coupled with the stepchildrens' adjustment to their new stepparent and stepsiblings. The problems they avoid are those of child-support payments and lack of knowledge on the part of the adults as to what the parent-child bond is all about.

Man without Children Married to a Woman with Children

The adjustments of the never-married or divorced man who marries a woman with children are primarily about her children, their acceptance of him, and his awareness that his wife is emotionally bonded to her children. Unlike the child-free couple bonded only to each other, the husband entering a relationship with a woman who has children must accept her attachment with her children from the outset. One husband said:

> You better like children a lot if you marry a woman who already has children. I do love kids and it has worked out for us. But it hasn't been easy. I love for her to nurture her children and am not jealous of the time it takes to do so. Money is our problem. I'm always asked to pay for things the kids want even though they are her kids. Just this last week we found out that Marcy will need braces. That's $2,700, and since my wife's ex-husband doesn't pay a cent in child support, I end up with the bill.
>
> The good news is you have an instant family. You have kids you can do things with. And you're more like a friend to them than a parent. It's a different relationship.

CONSIDERATION • Here are some questions a man without children might ask a woman who has children:

1. How do you expect me to relate to your children? Am I supposed to be their friend, daddy, or what?

• CHILDREN IN STEPFAMILIES •

Stepchildren have viewpoints and adjustments of their own when their parents remarry. They have experienced the transition from a family in which their biological parents lived together to living alone with one parent (usually the mother) to a stepfamily with a new stepparent.

DATA • *Around 35 percent of all children in the United States will live with a stepparent during a part of their childhood.* (Glick, 1984)

Some adjustments revolve around feeling abandoned, divided loyalties, discipline, and stepsiblings.

Feeling Abandoned

Some stepchildren feel that they have been abandoned twice, once when their parents got divorced and again when the remaining parent turned his or her attention to a new adult partner in a remarriage. One adolescent explained:

> It hurt me when my parents got divorced and my dad moved out. I really missed him and felt he really didn't care about my feelings. But we adjusted with just my mom and when everything was going right again, she gets involved with this new guy and we've got baby-sitters all the time. I feel like I've lost both parents in two years.

CONSIDERATION • Coping with feelings of abandonment is not easy. It is best if the remaining parent assures the children that the divorce was not their fault and that they are loved a great deal. In addition, the remaining parent should be careful not to abandon the children to baby-sitters but to find a balance between time with the new partner and time with the children.

Divided Loyalties

Sometimes the children develop an attachment for a stepparent that is more positive than the relationship with the natural parent of the same gender. When these feelings develop, the children may feel they are in a bind. One adolescent boy explained:

> My real dad left my mother when I was six and my mom remarried. My stepdad has always been good to me and I really prefer to be with him. But when

Children in
stepfamilies
sometimes feel
abandoned by
both parents.

my dad comes to pick me up on weekends, I have to go. It's very uncomfortable for me but I don't know how to tell him I would just as soon he not come around.

DATA • *More than half of 103 adolescents living in stepfamilies reported they had experienced feeling divided loyalties.*   (Lutz, 1983)

For some adolescents, the more they care for the stepparent, the guiltier they feel, and they may try to hide their attachment. The stepparent may be aware of both positive and negative feelings coming from the child.

Stepchildren may also resent the new stepparent and feel that he or she is trying to rob them of their biological parent's love. One 14-year-old said:

My new stepdad made me feel guilty when I told him that I wanted to spend the summer with my dad. It was almost as though I was not supposed to have feelings for my real dad. I was in a bind. If I showed that I cared about my real dad, my stepdad would stop talking to me. If I didn't show the emotion I felt when my dad called to talk, I felt I was betraying myself and him. It can be a real bummer.

Discipline

"Adjusting to living with a new set of rules from your stepparent," "accepting discipline from a stepparent," and "dealing with the expectations of your step-parent" are situations 80 percent of more than 100 adolescents in stepfamilies said they had experienced (Lutz, 1983). Their main problem was accepting rules from an "outsider."

> I resented my stepdad telling me what to do. He wasn't my real dad and I didn't want my mom to marry him anyway. It's been a problem ever since he moved in. I liked it better when my mom was a single parent. It seems as though we were all happier then.

Stepsiblings

Stepchildren experience higher levels of stress in stepfamilies if they have step-siblings than if they do not (Lutz, 1983). The stress seems to be a result of more arguments among the adults when both sets of children are present and the per-ception that parents are more fair with their own children.

> I could bounce the ball in the den and my stepdad would jump all over me. But let my stepsister bounce it and he wouldn't say a word. All I want is to be treated fairly and that's not what's happening in this family.

• DEVELOPMENTAL TASKS FOR STEPFAMILIES •

A developmental task is a skill that if mastered will allow the family to grow as a cohesive unit. Tasks not mastered will move the family toward disintegra-tion.

Nurture New Marriage Relationship

Because the demands of family interaction can become intense—even exces-sive—it is important that the new wife and husband allocate time to be alone to nurture their relationship. They must take time to communicate, to share their lives, and to have fun. One remarried couple have a date each Saturday night for dinner and a movie—without the children. "If you don't spend time alone with your partner, you won't have one," said one stepparent.

Decide about Money

Money is an issue of potential conflict in stepfamilies because it is a scarce re-source and several people want to use it for their respective needs. The father wants a new computer; the mother wants a new car; the mother's children want bunk beds, a new stereo, and a satellite dish; the father's children want a larger room, clothes, and phone. How do the newly married couple and their children decide whose money is it and how it should be spent? There are two patterns of spending in stepfamilies (Fishman, 1983).

If two people who love each other let a single instant wedge itself between them, it grows—it be-comes a month, a year, a cen-tury; it becomes too late.

JEAN GIRAUDOUX

STEPFAMILY SUCCESS SCALE

This scale is designed to measure the degree to which you and your partner might expect to have a successful stepfamily. There are no right or wrong answers. After reading each sentence carefully, circle the number that best represents your feelings.

1 Strongly disagree
2 Mildly disagree
3 Undecided
4 Mildly agree
5 Strongly agree

	SD	D	U	A	SA
1. I am a flexible person.	1	2	3	4	5
2. I am not a jealous person.	1	2	3	4	5
3. I am a patient person.	1	2	3	4	5
4. My partner is a flexible person.	1	2	3	4	5
5. My partner is not a jealous person.	1	2	3	4	5
6. My partner is a patient person.	1	2	3	4	5
7. My partner values our relationship more than the relationship with his or her children.	1	2	3	4	5
8. My partner understands that it is not easy for me to love someone else's children.	1	2	3	4	5
9. I value the relationship with my partner more than the relationship with my children.	1	2	3	4	5

	SD	D	U	A	SA
10. I understand that it will be difficult for my partner to love my children as much as I do.	1	2	3	4	5
11. My partner and I will put our money in a common fund and use it for both of our children as necessary.	1	2	3	4	5
12. My children and those of my partner will live with the ex-spouse.	1	2	3	4	5
13. We will have plenty of money in our stepfamily.	1	2	3	4	5
14. I feel positively about my partner's children.	1	2	3	4	5
15. My partner feels positively about my children.	1	2	3	4	5
16. My children and those of my partner feel positively about each other.	1	2	3	4	5
17. My partner and I will begin our stepfamily in a place that neither of us has lived before.	1	2	3	4	5
18. My partner and I agree on how to discipline our children.	1	2	3	4	5
19. My children feel positively about my new partner.	1	2	3	4	5
20. My partner's children feel positively about me.	1	2	3	4	5

Scoring: Add the numbers you circled. Since 1 (strongly disagree) is the most negative response you could have made and 5 (strongly agree) is the most positive response you could have made, the lower your total score (20 is the lowest possible score), the greater the number of potential problems and the lower the chance of success in a stepfamily with this partner. The higher your score (100 is the highest possible score), the greater the chance of stepfamily success with this partner. A score of 60 places you at the midpoint between the extremes of having a difficult and easy stepfamily experience.

COMMON-MONEY-POT PATTERN

Under this arrangement, the marital partners put both their incomes from all sources (including alimony and child support) into a common pot and distribute money from it for themselves and the children without concern for who earned the money or whose child it will be spent on. Figure 19.1 shows how this family conceptualizes the distribution of their money.

One spouse commented:

> We see ourselves as one family, not as two families living under one roof. If any one of the children need something, we decide on a case-by-case basis whether or not we will purchase that item. We don't consider that it is "his" child or "my" child but what is the need of the child in reference to the whole family. And just because I make more money than my husband, I don't feel that I have a greater right to spend more of the money on "my children."

The common-pot pattern provides for a feeling of solidarity and family unity. Problems of two families lining up against each other are minimized. On the other hand, sacrifices and compromises must be made and this can occasion a lot of tension. In one case, the mother wanted to spend $800 to attend a professional conference. But this meant her husband's son wouldn't have the money to attend computer camp that summer. She decided not to attend the conference but felt as though her career was suffering because of her stepson.

TWO-MONEY-POT PATTERN

Under this arrangement, money is distributed primarily according to the biological identity of the children and only secondarily according to need. Figure 19.2 describes this pattern.

Figure 19.1 The Common-Money-Pot Pattern

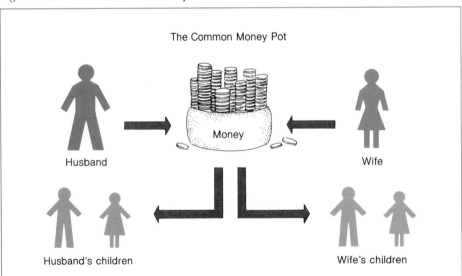

The Common Money Pot

Money

Husband

Wife

Husband's children

Wife's children

Source: Fishman, 1983.

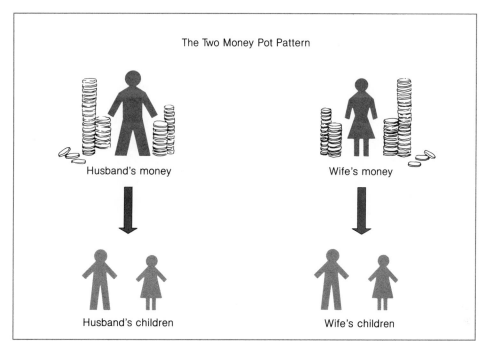

Figure 19.2　The Two-Money-Pot Pattern

Source: Fishman, 1983.

Fishman (1983) describes the money arrangement of Sheila and Harry, a re-married couple. She has three sons by a previous marriage, he has a daughter who does not live with them. Of their economic arrangement, Sheila said:

> When it comes to money, we take care of our own. Harry gives me $25 every week for his share of food and small expenses—dry-cleaning his clothes, things like that. I add the $200 a week I get from child support. Out of this to-tal, I run the house and pay for clothes for the boys and myself. Harry pays the fixed expenses—mortgage, gas and electric, and he supports his own children. (p. 364)

Harry's paycheck is deposited into his personal account, out of which he supports his child directly, giving her spending money and paying school tuition. He also gives his ex-wife a monthly stipend for Ginny's support. Sheila deposits her child-support check directly into her personal account. "They have no joint checking or savings account" (p. 364).

The advantage of the two-pot pattern is that the economic responsibilities are clear:

> Women who pay their own way do not have to account to a husband for the purchase of a personal item or a lunch out with friends. Men do not have to produce extra income to finance a stepchild. Couples do not argue over which partner is in control of money, as each partner is in control of his or her own. The very structure of their economy precludes this conflict. (p. 365.)

> The safest way to double your money is to fold it over once and put it in your pocket.
>
> FRANK McKINNEY HUBBARD

CONSIDERATION • Neither the one- nor the two-pot economic model is superi-or. They both have their advantages and limitations. What is important is that each family assess its situation and use the model that best fits its needs.

Decide Who May Discipline Whom

How much authority the stepparent will exercise over the children must be discussed by the adults before getting married. Some couples divide the authority, each spouse disciplining his or her own children. But children may test the stepparent in such an arrangement when the biological parent is not around. One stepmother said, "Jim's kids are wild when he isn't here because I'm not supposed to discipline them."

> CONSIDERATION • It is often helpful for the adults to tell their respective children that they must respect the wishes of the stepparent. Stepparents can't grab authority. They must become a partner with the natural parent who gives the authority to the new spouse. Unless children view each parent as an authority figure, they are likely to undermine the relationship between the adults.

Keep Communication Channels Open

Although open lines of communication are important in any relationship, they become critical in stepfamilies. As we have seen, because of the number of new relationships with varying histories and durations, the potential for problems is high. To prevent misunderstandings from festering, family members should agree that it is all right not to like something and to agree on a means to tell others how they are feeling. Some families do this through a family council meeting.

Support Child's Relationship with Absent Parent

Because a continued relationship with the absent biological parent is critical to the emotional well-being of the child, ex-spouses and stepparents should encourage that relationship. Regardless of the feelings the spouse and new partner may have about the ex, the children should be encouraged to talk with and see the biological parent.

> CONSIDERATION • In addition, stepparents need to communicate that they are not trying to take the place of the biological parent but want to be an additional person in the child's life who can, in time, become a friend. Suggesting that the child call the stepparent by a name the child feels comfortable with may help to encourage a friendly rather than an authoritarian relationship. Many stepparents recognize that it would be a mistake to force their stepchildren to call them mom or dad and ask the children to call them by their first name.

Support Child's Relationship with Natural Grandparents

A child's continued relationship with her or his natural grandparents is also in the best interest of that child. This is one of the more stable relationships in the stepchild's changing world of adult relationships. Regardless of how ex-spouses feel about their ex-in-laws, they should encourage such relationships. One mother said, "Although I am uncomfortable around my ex-in-laws, I know my children enjoy visiting them so I encourage their relationship."

• TRENDS •

Stepfamilies will become an increasingly visible phenomenon in American society. Schoolchildren play with other children in stepfamilies and adults have friends, relatives, and coworkers who are remarrying and beginning stepfamilies. As a result, stepfamilies will become more normative and lose the stigma they now carry.

Stepfamilies will continue to reach out for help. Members of stepfamilies have already established national organizations for support. These include the Stepfamily Association of America (900 Welch Road, Suite 400, Palo Alto, CA 94304) and Stepfamily Foundation (333 West End Ave., New York, NY 10023). Stepfamily Associates (353 Walnut St., Brookline, MA 02146) is a private organization that offers workshops and group meetings for stepfamily members to discuss their various concerns. Finally, for wives who do not have custody of their children or who are remarried to husbands who do not have custody of their children, Second Wife, First Class (2527 S. Randolph, Indianapolis, IN 46203) has been established.

• SUMMARY •

A stepfamily is a married couple in which at least one of the spouses has had a child in a previous relationship. These families include those in which the children live with their remarried parent and stepparent, those in which the children only visit their remarried parent and stepparent, and those in which the children of divorced parents either live with the remarried partners or visit.

There are a number of differences between biological families and stepfamilies. In stepfamilies the members are not all biologically related; they may have different values; they have experienced a crisis (divorce or death); and they are stigmatized as a stepfamily. In addition, the adults have known each other a shorter period of time than the parents have known their children and have never had a child-free period.

Stepfamilies have both strengths and weaknesses. The strengths include early reality testing, exposure to a variety of behavior patterns, and learning to mesh with stepsiblings in an intimate family environment. The weaknesses include the adults having unrealistic expectations and the occasional presence of the ex-spouse.

Women, men, and children sometimes experience stepfamily living differently. For women, learning to get along with the husband's children, not being resentful of his relationship with his children, and adapting to the fact that a quarter to a third of his income will be sent to his ex-wife as alimony or child support are skills she must develop. She may also want children with her new partner or may bring her own children into the remarriage. In the latter case, she is anxious that her new husband will accept her children.

Men in stepfamilies have similar concerns. Getting along with their wife's children, paying for many of the expenses of their stepchildren, having their new partner accept their own children, and dealing with the issue of having more children are among them.

Children must cope with feeling abandoned and problems of divided loyalties, discipline, and stepsiblings.

Developmental tasks of stepfamilies include nurturing the new marriage relationship, deciding whose money will be spent on whose children, deciding who will discipline the children and how, keeping communication channels open, and supporting the child's relationship with the absent parent and natural grandparents.

Trends include increased visibility of stepfamilies. By 1990 there will be more single-parent homes and stepfamilies than two-parent and biological homes. Such visibility will result in greater acceptance and less stigmatization. In addition, stepfamilies will continue to support each other through various organizations.

Questions for Reflection

1. How capable do you think you are of loving someone else's children?
2. How accepting would you be of a new spouse who could not accept your children?
3. As a woman, how easy would it be for you to encourage a positive relationship between your child and the child's natural father who divorced you without explanation?

·CHOICES·

Never-married and divorced individuals with children have choices to make about entering a stepfamily. The various issues for each of these individuals to consider follow.

SHOULD A NEVER-MARRIED MAN MARRY A DIVORCED WOMAN WITH CHILDREN?

The diagrams that follow, which were first presented in Chapter 4, emphasize the positive and negative consequences of a yes or no decision. They are helpful in making many kinds of decisions. First, we suggest how they may help the single man in deciding whether to marry a divorced woman with children.

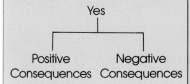

Yes
Positive Consequences   Negative Consequences

Yes
The positive consequences of marrying a divorced woman with children would include continuing the love relationship with the woman, having a ready-made family, and avoiding the pain of living without the beloved. Since the man making such a decision will be emotionally involved with the woman, a major factor in his decision will be emotional. One man said:

I love her and want to be with her whether she has kids or not. If you try to add and subtract everything about human relationships as though you are keeping a ledger, you are missing the point. My happiness depends on my being with her and marriage means that we will continue our lives together since we don't believe in living together.

In addition to being able to live with the loved person in a marriage relationship, another positive consequence of marrying a divorced person with children is having a ready-made family. "I've always wanted children, and I think her kids are great," said a prospective groom. "We've been camping together as a family, and it was nothing but fun. I don't see any problem down the road with these kids."

Another positive outcome is avoiding a negative one. "If I don't marry her, I'm forced to go back to bars and talk to people I'm not interested in. I love her and deciding not to marry her would mean loneliness and pain."

Since every decision has positive and negative consequences, what are the negative consequences of deciding to marry a divorced woman with children? The emotional bond between the woman and her children, the presence of an ex-husband who may be calling and coming by to get the kids, and the costs associated with rearing the children are potential problems. One man who married (and subsequently divorced) a woman with two children said:

It didn't work out for us. I was jealous of the time she gave to her own kids and knew that I was always second. I also didn't like her ex around even though it was for a brief time each week. Just to see the guy who had sex with my wife for 15 years unnerved me. And the money was a real problem. Her ex never paid enough child support to cover what the kids cost and I got tired of paying for kids who weren't really mine. Besides, they both needed braces and that got us deeply in debt. I'd say marrying a woman with kids isn't worth it no matter how much you love her.

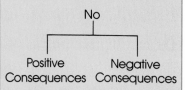

No
Positive Consequences   Negative Consequences

(continued)

No

Suppose a man decides not to marry the woman with two children. What are the positive and negative consequences of his decision? On the positive side, he has avoided the potential problems of feeling jealous of the bond between the woman and her children, of having to deal with an ex-spouse, and of feeling financially responsible for two children that are not biologically his. By making a single decision he has avoided a lot of potential headaches (and maybe a divorce since 60 percent of these marriages do not last). On the other hand, there are some losses associated with deciding not to marry her. The primary one is the emotional pain he would feel as a result of terminating the relationship with her. "In these situations," said one man, "I'm a real sucker for romance. I do what I feel every time. And living without this woman is something I can't do."

After listing the positive and negative consequences of a yes and no decision, a final decision can be made by examining how the consequences look on paper. Assign weights to the different consequences if necessary. For example, on a 10-point scale (10 = tops) how important is it to have a ready-made family, to continue the love relationship, or to avoid going in debt over children not biologically yours? Getting the issues on paper and looking at them sometimes makes it easy to make a decision.

How the decision feels is also important. Regardless of how it looks on paper, your feelings will play an important role in determining the final decision. "If the decision doesn't feel right in your heart, it isn't right," said one person.

SHOULD A NEVER-MARRIED WOMAN MARRY A DIVORCED MAN WITH CHILDREN?

It is not unusual for a single woman to become emotionally involved with a divorced man who has children. Al-though his wife frequently has custody of their children, they may visit and he probably pays child support. The process just described is helpful for examining the issues involved (see diagrams above).

Yes

Positive consequences for the single woman marrying a divorced man with children would be similar to those of the single man marrying a divorced woman with children: continuing the love relationship, benefiting from a ready-made family, and avoiding the pain of losing the partner.

The negative consequences of a yes decision may also include competing with the children for the husband's time. One woman said:

Since we both worked all week, I wanted the weekend to enjoy by ourselves. But he wanted his kids to visit us on weekends. I went along with it for awhile, but finally told him I didn't like it. He said, "My kids are coming to this house every Saturday as long as they want to. If you don't like it, leave." I tried to get along with them, but I just ended up cooking and doing the laundry for them. I felt like a maid for his kids who were interfering in our marriage.

No
The positive outcome of a decision not to marry is the avoiding problems of stepchildren visiting frequently, and taking money out of the marriage and giving it to the husband's ex-wife.

The negative consequence of deciding not to marry is the flood of bad feelings—loneliness, depression, and pain—that often follow a decision to walk away from an emotionally important relationship.

It is critical to keep in mind that no decision will have all good consequences and no negative ones. Every decision will involve trade-offs.

SHOULD A DIVORCED WOMAN WITH CHILDREN AND A DIVORCED MAN WITH CHILDREN MARRY?
Divorced people sometimes prefer each other because they know the person has an experiential understanding of the divorced state. "I won't date single people," said one divorced woman. "They have no appreciation for what it is like to be divorced and they certainly don't know anything about the parent-child bond." Marrying someone with children has its own problems. Refer again to the preceding diagrams.

Yes
Marrying someone who understands divorce and children is perhaps the greatest benefit of deciding to marry a divorced person with children. Because they know how intense the parent-child bond is, they are not as likely to feel jealous of this relationship. In addition, they have ex-spouses too and can empathize with the need and discomfort of interacting with one's ex.

Mother and father role models for each other's children are also a benefit for adults and children. "I need a mother for my kids and she needs a daddy for hers, so it's a good trade-off," said one father. "I wouldn't say I'm getting married for that reason, but it sure is a plus."

The negative consequences of a decision to blend two families together are problems of the wife's children accepting their stepfather, the husband's children accepting their stepmother, and the children accepting each other. These factors will influence the degree to which the new family "jells" and becomes a cohesive unit. To expect that such a fusion will occur quickly and smoothly is unrealistic.

No
The decision against blending two families will result in avoiding the potentially negative consequences just described. On the other hand, such a decision will terminate an emotional relationship with someone who knows what divorce, children, and single parenting is all about. "I'll take a chance," said one divorced male.

EPILOG

CONTENTS

Making Choices: Some Facts
Five Basic Choices
A Last Word

"Two roads diverged in a wood, and I—I took the one less traveled by, And that has made all the difference." *

ROBERT FROST

These words from Robert Frost's poem "The Road Not Taken" emphasize the importance of choices. In making choices in our own lives, we must be aware of our alternatives, alert to potential consequences, and choose with deliberation. Here, we review the nature of choices, then look again at some of the choices discussed in the previous chapters.

· MAKING CHOICES: SOME FACTS ·

In making choices, it is important to keep several ideas in mind.

Not to Decide Is to Decide

It is important to recognize that to not make a decision *is* a decision. The act of not deciding for something is to decide against something. For example, if you

* "The Road Not Taken" by Robert Frost. Garden City, New York: Garden City Publishing Co., Inc., 1942, p. 131.

are sexually active and do not use birth control, you have decided to increase the risk of pregnancy. Choosing—through action or inaction—means taking responsibility for the consequences of our decisions.

Choices Are Only Probabilities

The outcome of any choice is at best a probability since it is difficult, if not impossible, to know exactly what the best choice is for all time. We can only make decisions based on the information available to us at the time of the decision. Later we may become aware of new information which, had we known it initially, may have influenced us to have made a different decision. For example, one woman decided on the basis of a two-year courtship to marry a man with whom she was deeply in love. He was suave, attractive, and considerate. Not until their honeymoon did she discover that he was an alcoholic. "He literally passed out and his face hit the steak he was eating on our first dinner out after we were married," she said. "He had been hiding his alcoholism from me throughout our courtship." This is an extreme but true example.

Choices Are Continual

Making choices is a continual process. Life is not one or two BIG decisions. It is a series of some big decisions and a constant stream of smaller ones. For example, the bride just mentioned had to decide how to respond to her new (and drunken) husband. Should she leave the table, get in the car, and drive away? Should she help him back to their room? Should she divorce him? Should she stay with him, see if the behavior recurred, and reevaluate it later? She chose to stay with him through thirteen years of abusive alcoholism, which ended in his complete recovery through the help of Alcoholics Anonymous. They now have two small children and are happy as a couple and as a family—a situation that is not only the result of the woman's initial decision but also of innumerable ones over the years.

Choices Involve Trade-offs

Any choice we make will involve gains and losses. Rarely does a choice have all positive and no negative consequences. For example, if you decide to break up with a person because you feel that person doesn't meet your needs, you may avoid the continued frustration of living in an unsatisfactory relationship but you may experience a period of loneliness and pain as a result. Likewise, couples who decide to have a second child to be a companion for the first child soon become aware that two children cost more and that they may fight, bicker, and compete with one another. Or couples who decide that one spouse should quit work when the children are young must face the reality of lowered income. Every choice has its trade-offs.

Most Choices Are Revocable

Whether your choices involve a philosophy of life, a career, or selecting a mate, most are revocable. Although the price—emotional or financial—is higher for certain choices than others (for example, backing out of the role of spouse is somewhat less difficult than backing out of the role of parent), you can change your mind. Most choices can be modified or changed.

• FIVE BASIC CHOICES •

There are five basic choices for each of us about marriage and the family.

Singlehood or Marriage?

Although more than 90 percent of us eventually marry, it remains a choice. Some people are not suited for marriage and should not marry just because they feel society expects them to. One person said, "I can't stand living with other people. I need my own place with no one else there. Sure, I see other people and they come over to my place, but I don't want anyone living there but me. Marriage means that you are burdened with having to interact and consider another person in everything you do. I'm simply not cut out for that kind of life."

Children—Yes or No?

Just as most people marry, most express a desire for, and eventually have, children. But some people do not want children. Children take time and are a drain on financial and emotional resources. Individuals not anxious to share their lives with an infant, child, and teenager may decide not to have children.

One- or Two-Career Marriage?

The fact that more than 60 percent of married couples have two incomes illustrates their need for money to afford the life style they want. One partner, usually the wife, often has a job that permits easy entrance and exit from the labor force to accommodate the needs of the family. Couples who decide to pursue joint careers may enjoy economic advantages but may also have less time for each other, particularly if they have children. For the child-free couple, two careers are easier to manage.

Fidelity?

Most of us expect emotional and sexual fidelity from our partner, yet within marriage half of all husbands and as high as 40 percent of all wives have sexual relationships with someone other than their spouses. Although most couples continue the marriage after such involvements, each spouse must continually decide whether to be monogamous. "Someone is always available if you want to have an affair," said one spouse, "it's really up to you whether you do or not."

Positive or Negative View?

A final basic choice, perhaps the most important, is deciding how you wish to view something. Life has positive and negative aspects. Our choice of whether to focus on the positives or on the negatives is of critical importance to our personal happiness and the success of our personal relationships. When we look at our partners, we can focus on their loving eyes or the pimples on their noses. Similarly, we can focus on the times they did something we liked or the times they did something that offended or hurt us; we can focus on their preparing a meal rather than their forgetting to put salt on the table. In dissolving a relationship, we can view it as the end of life or the beginning of life. In other words, how we choose to view a situation will often have more to do with our happiness than the situation itself.

• A LAST WORD •

The story is told of a young boy who challenged a wise old person. The boy held a small bird tightly in his hand and asked the sage, "Is it alive or dead?" The sage looked thoughtfully at the boy, then answered, "As you choose." So it is, too, with you and your relationships.

· Part Six ·

SPECIAL TOPICS

Special Topic 1
Planning and Investing

Developing a Budget
Saving and Investing
Life Insurance

Special Topic 2
Credit

Types of Credit
Accounts

Three "C's" of Credit
Credit Snags to Avoid

Special Topic 3
Sexual Anatomy and
Physiology

Female External
Anatomy and
Physiology
Female Internal
Anatomy and
Physiology
Male External Anatomy
and Physiology
Male Internal Anatomy
and Physiology

Special Topic 4
Sexually Transmitted
Diseases

Gonorrhea
Syphilis
Genital Herpes

Acquired Immune
Deficiency Syndrome
(AIDS)
Getting Help
Prevention

Special Topic 5
Resources and
Organizations

PLANNING AND INVESTING

CONTENTS

Developing a Budget
Saving and Investing
Life Insurance

*Never ask of money spent
Where the spender thinks it
went;
Nobody was ever meant
To remember or invent
What he did with every cent.*

ROBERT FROST
*The Hardship of
Accounting*

One aspect of marriage is that it is an economic partnership in which the spouses conduct the business of getting and spending money. Problems may arise when this scarce resource is not managed properly. We now consider possible ways to prevent spending more than you and your partner are making and how to invest money for future needs.

· DEVELOPING A BUDGET ·

Developing a budget is a way of planning your spending. Since money spent on X cannot by spent on Y, budgeting requires conscious value choices about which bills should be paid, what items should be bought, and what expenditures should be delayed. Couples need to develop a budget if they are always out of money long before their next paycheck, if they cannot make partial payments or pay off existing bills yet keep incurring new debts, or if they cannot save money.

585

To develop a budget (see Table ST1.1), list and add up all your monthly take-home (after taxes) income from all sources. This figure should represent the amount of money your family will actually have to spend each month. Next, list and add up all of your fixed monthly expenses such as rent, utilities, telephone, and car payment. Other fixed expenses include items such as life, health, and car insurance. Since you may not receive a bill for these expenses every month, divide the yearly cost by 12 so that you can budget each item on a monthly basis. For example, if your annual life insurance premium is $240, you should budget $20 per month for that expense.

Set aside a minimum of 5 percent of your monthly income, and more if possible, for savings, and include this sum in your fixed expenses. By putting a fixed amount in a savings account each month, you will not only have money available for major purchases such as a car or major appliance but you will also have an emergency fund to cover unforeseen expenses like those caused by an extended illness or a long-distance move. The size of an emergency fund should be about twice your monthly income. Although you can personally set aside some of your monthly income for savings, an alternative is to instruct the bank to transfer a certain sum each month from your checking account to your savings account, or you can join a payroll savings plan. Under the latter arrangement, a

Table ST1.1 Monthly Budget for Two-Income Couple: Both Spouses Employed Full Time

Sources of Income	
Husband's take-home pay	$1,480
Wife's take-home pay	920
Interest earned on savings	17
TOTAL	$2,417
Fixed Expenses	
Rent	$ 350
Utilities	90
Telephone	50
Insurance	85
Car payments and expenses	290
Furniture payments	80
Savings	200
TOTAL	$1,145
DIFFERENCE	$1,272
(Amount available for day-to-day expenses)	
Day-to-Day and Discretionary Expenses	
Food	$ 250
Clothes	170
Personal care	90
Recreation	120
Miscellaneous	110
TOTAL	$ 740

This dual-income couple should have $532 extra at the end of each month. The reality is that many couples can't or don't live within their income and go into debt each month.

portion of your monthly salary is automatically deposited in your savings account without ever passing through your hands. "I always have the bank put money in a separate account," said one spouse. "If I don't, there won't be any savings. As soon as I get money, I spend it. I just can't keep money."

After adding together all your fixed monthly expenses, including savings, subtract this amount from your monthly take-home income. What remains can be used for such day-to-day expenses as food (groceries and restaurant meals), clothes (including laundry, dry cleaning, alterations, and new clothes), personal care (barber and hairdresser, toilet articles, cosmetics), and recreation (theater, movies, concerts, books, magazines).

> CONSIDERATION • If you come out even at the end of the month, you are living within your means. If you have money left over, you are living below your means. If you had to tap your savings or borrow money, you are living beyond your means. Knowing whether you are living within, below, or above your means depends on keeping accurate records.

• SAVING AND INVESTING •

As we noted, saving should be a part of every budget. By allocating a specific amount of your monthly income to savings, having your employer do so through the payroll savings plan, or putting your change every evening in a container on your dresser, you can accumulate money for both short-term goals (vacation, down payment on house) and long-term (college education for children, retirement income) goals.

Put not your trust in money, but put your money in trust.

O. W. HOLMES

> CONSIDERATION • Loose change in a container on your dresser is not earning you the money it could. By investing, you use money to make more money. All investments must be considered in terms of their risk and potential yield. In general, the higher the rate of return on an investment, the greater the risk. For example, putting your money in a bank or savings and loan institution is risk-free, since your deposit is insured by the federal government.

Another way to invest money for a fairly stable return is to buy a blue chip stock such as American Telephone and Telegraph or Eastman Kodak. The value of these stocks is likely to increase. Also, some stocks pay dividends as well as having the potential to appreciate. But although there is greater potential return from these investment stocks than from money in the bank, there is also more risk. For example, suppose Nikon Camera were to invent a new film that offered superior quality at a lower cost. Kodak stock might plummet and take your money with it.

There is an even greater risk with speculative stocks. These are stocks that might radically increase or decrease in value within a short time. Suppose you could afford to lose $500 and were willing to gamble on a high return. You could buy 100 shares of stock selling slightly below $5 per share. If the stock sold for $10 one year later, your original investment would have doubled in value—you would now have $1,000 for your initial investment of $500. But suppose the stock were selling for $1 per share one year later? You can lose money as fast as

Some people leave their investment decisions to professional brokers.

you can gain it. One spouse invested in a company specializing in bananas and looked forward to tripling her investment. But less than a week after she purchased the stock, a hurricane in Puerto Rico wiped out the banana crop, and the value of her stock dropped sharply.

CONSIDERATION • Don't invest in speculative stocks unless you can afford to lose the money.

Fortunately, investment opportunities are not limited to banks and stocks. Table ST1.2 illustrates several alternatives and furnishes information on other factors that should be considered in deciding on an investment. In addition to risk and return on investment, the liquidity, or the ease with which your investment can be converted into cash, is an important consideration. Stocks and bonds can be sold quickly to provide cash in hand. In contrast, if you have invested in a building or land, you must find a buyer willing to pay what you are asking before you can convert it to cash.

The amount of your time that is required to make your investment grow is also important. A real estate investment can give you a considerable return on your money, but it may also demand a lot of time perusing the newspaper, arranging for loans, placing ads, and showing houses, not to mention fixing leaky faucets, mowing grass, and painting rooms.

Also, consider the maturity date of your investment. For example, suppose you invest in a six-year certificate at a savings bank. Although the bank will pay you, say, 12 percent interest and guarantee your investment, you can't get your principle (the money you deposited) or the interest until the six years is up unless you are willing to pay a substantial penalty. Since regular savings accounts

Table ST1.2 Some Investment Alternatives

TYPE	RISK/YIELD	LIQUIDITY	MANAGEMENT	TAX ASPECTS
Savings account	Low/6%	Immediate	Self	Interest is taxed
Treasury bill	Low/8–9%	3 mths. to year	Self	Interest is taxed
Money market	Low/9–11%	Week	Broker	Interest is taxed
Annuity	Low/11%	Retirement	Company	Taxes deferred
Real estate	Depends/0–15%	months/years	Self or other	Good tax advant.
Mutual funds	Moderate/8–13%	Week	Agent	Lower tax if hold
Stocks	Depends/0–100%	Week	Broker	Depends on invest
Life ins	Low/6%	Years	Agent	Depends on invest
Bonds	Depends/8–14%	Week	Broker	Depends on invest
IRA	Low/9–12%	Retirement	Broker	Deferred
Certificates of Deposit	Low/9–12%	Variable	Self	Interest is taxed

have no maturity date, you can withdraw whatever amount you want whenever you want it, but you may earn only, say, 8 percent interest.

A final investment consideration is taxation. Investment decisions should be made on the basis of not how much money you can make but how much you can keep. Tax angles should be considered as carefully as risk and yield issues.

CONSIDERATION • Unless you are majoring in business or banking and have some expertise in money management, it may be wise to ask a broker in an investment firm like Merrill Lynch, Smith Barney or E. F. Hutton to advise you. He or she can tailor your investment program to accommodate your specific needs (high yield but low risk, go for broke, or whatever). Although there will be a commission if you decide to buy through the broker, there is usually no charge for the consultation.

Although savings, life insurance, real estate, and stock investments are probably familiar to you, the other types of investments listed in Table ST1.2 may need further clarification. (1) Annuities provide monthly income after age 65 (or earlier if desired) in exchange for your investing monthly premiums during your working years. For example, a 65-year-old man may receive $100 per month as long as he lives (or a lump sum) if he has paid the insurance company $238 annually since age 30. (2) Bonds are issued by corporations and federal, state, or local governments that need money. In exchange for your money, you get a piece of paper that entitles you to the return of the sum you lend at a specified date (up to 30 years) plus interest on that money. Although bonds are safer than stocks, you could lose all your money if the corporation you lend the money to goes bankrupt. United States Savings Bonds are safe but pay a comparatively low rate of interest. (3) Mutual funds offer a way of investing in a number of common stocks, corporate bonds, or government bonds at the same time. You invest your money in shares of the mutual fund, whose directors invest the fund's capital in various securities. If the securities they select increase in price, so does the value of your shares in the mutual fund, and vice versa. (4) Treasury

Anyone who thinks there's safety in numbers hasn't looked at the stock market pages.

IRENE PORTER

bills are issued by the Federal Reserve Bank. You pay a lower price for the bill than its cash value. For example, you may pay $900 for a T-bill that will be worth $1000 on maturity. Maturity of the bill occurs at three, six, nine, or 12 months. The longer the wait, the higher the interest. (5) Money market investments require a payment of $5,000 or more to a stockbroker who puts your money with that of others to buy high-interest-paying securities. Your money can be withdrawn in any amount at any time. As with all investments, you pay a fee to the broker or agent for investing your money. In the past several years, increasing numbers of people have put their money in money market funds. (6) Individual retirement accounts permit you to set aside up to $2,000 each year for your personal retirement fund. The money you put in your IRA will not be taxed until you withdraw it. Each spouse can open his or her own IRA. (7) Certificates of deposit are insured deposits given to the bank that earn interest at a rate from one day to several years. These have been extremely popular because of high yields and low risk. A minimum investment of $500 or more is usually required.

• LIFE INSURANCE •

In addition to saving and investing, it is important to be knowledgeable about life insurance. The major purpose of life insurance is to provide income for dependents when the primary wage earner dies. With dual-income couples, life insurance is often necessary to prevent having to give up one's home when one wage earner dies. Otherwise, the remaining wage earner may not be able to make the necessary payments.

When considering income protection for dependents, there are two basic types of life insurance policies: (1) term insurance and (2) insurance-plus-investment. As the name implies, term insurance offers protection for a specific time period, usually one, five, 10, or 20 years. At the end of the time period, the protection stops. Although a term insurance policy offers the greatest amount of protection for the least cost, it does not build up cash value (money the insured would get if he or she surrendered the policy for cash).

Insurance-plus-investment policies are sold under various names: (1) the first is straight life, ordinary life, or whole life, in which the individual pays a stated premium (based on age and health) as long as he or she lives. When the insured dies, the beneficiary is paid the face value of the policy, the amount of insurance that was bought. But during the life of the insured, the policy also builds up a cash value, which permits the insured to borrow money from the insurance company at a low rate of interest. (2) A second type is limited-payment policy, in which the premiums are paid up after a certain number of years (usually 20) or when the insured reaches a certain age (usually 60 or 65). As with straight, ordinary life, or whole life policies, limited-payment policies build up a cash value, and the face value of the policy is not paid until the insured dies. (3) The third type is endowment insurance, in which the premiums are paid up after a stated number of years and can be cashed in at a stated age.

Regardless of how they are sold, insurance-plus-investment policies divide the premium paid by the insured. Part pays for the actual life insurance, and part is invested for the insured, giving the policy a cash value. Unlike term insurance, insurance-plus-investment policies are not canceled at age 65.

Which type, term or insurance-plus-investment, should you buy? An insurance agent is likely to suggest the latter and point out the advantages of cash value, continued protection beyond age 65, and level premiums. But the agent has a personal incentive for your buying an insurance-plus-investment policy. The commission he or she gets on this type of policy is much higher than if you buy term insurance.

> When it is a question of money, everybody is of the same religion.
>
> VOLTAIRE

The annual premium for $50,000 worth of renewable term insurance at age 25 is about $175. The same coverage offered in an ordinary life policy, the most common of the insurance-plus-investment types, would cost $668 annually, so the difference is $493 per year. If you put this money in the bank at a minimum interest rate of 5 percent, at the end of five years you would have $2,860.32. In contrast, the cash value of an ordinary life policy after five years would be $2,350. But to get this money you would have to pay the insurance company interest to borrow it. If you didn't want to pay the interest, the company would give you this amount but cancel your policy. In effect, you would lose your insurance protection if you got the cash value of your policy. With term insurance, you have the $2,860.32 in the bank earning interest, and you can withdraw it any time without affecting your insurance program.

It should be clear that for term insurance to be cheaper, you must invest the money you would otherwise be paying for an ordinary life insurance policy. If you can't discipline yourself to save, buy an insurance-plus-investment policy, which will ensure savings.

Finally, what about the fact that term insurance stops when you are 65, just as you are moving closer to death and needing the protection more? Again, by investing the money that you would otherwise have spent on an insurance-plus-investment policy, you will have as much or more money for your beneficiary.

Whether you buy term or an insurance-plus-investment policy or both, there are three options to consider—guaranteed insurability, waiver of premiums, and double or triple indemnity. All are inexpensive and generally should be included.

Guaranteed insurability means that the company will sell you more insurance in the future regardless of your medical condition. For example, suppose you develop cancer after you have bought a policy for $10,000. If the guaranteed insurability provision is in your contract, you can buy additional insurance. If not, the company can refuse you more insurance.

Waiver of premiums provides that your premiums will be paid by the company if you become disabled for six months or longer and are unable to earn an income. Such an option ensures that your policy will stay in force because the premiums will be paid. Otherwise, the company would cancel your policy.

Double or triple indemnity means that if you die as the result of an accident, the company will pay your beneficiary twice or three times the face value of your policy.

An additional item you might consider adding to your life insurance policy is a disability income rider. If the wage earner becomes disabled and cannot work, the financial consequences for the family are the same as though he or she were dead. With disability insurance, the wage earner can continue to provide for the family up to a maximum of $3,500 per month or two-thirds of his or her salary, whichever is smaller. If the wage earner is disabled by accidental injury, payments are made for life. If illness is the cause, payments may be made only to age 65. A 27-year-old spouse and parent who was paralyzed in an automobile accident said, "It was the biggest mistake of my life to think I needed only life insurance to protect my family. Disability insurance turned out to be more important."

CONSIDERATION • In deciding to buy life insurance, it may be helpful to keep four issues in mind: (1) Compare prices. All policies and prices are not the same. In some cases, the higher premiums are for lower coverage. (2) Select your agent carefully. Only one in 10 life insurance agents stay in the business. The person you buy life insurance from today may be in the real estate business tomorrow. Choose an agent who has been selling life insurance for at least 10 years. (3) Seek group rates. Group life insurance is the least expensive coverage. See if your employer offers a group plan. (4) Proceed slowly. Don't rush into buying an insurance policy. Consult several agents, read *Consumer Reports* and talk with friends to find out what they are doing about their insurance needs.

· Special Topic 2 ·

CREDIT

CONTENTS

Types of Credit Accounts
Three C's of Credit
Credit Snags to Avoid

A creditor is worse than a master; for a master owns only your person, a creditor owns your dignity, and can belabor that.

VICTOR HUGO

You use credit when you take an item home today and pay for it later. The amount you pay later will depend on the arrangement you make with the seller.

· TYPES OF CREDIT ACCOUNTS ·

Suppose you want to buy a color television set that costs $600. Unless you pay cash, the seller will set up one of three types of credit accounts with you—installment, revolving charge, or open charge.

Under the installment plan, you make a down payment and sign a contract to pay the rest of the money in monthly installments. You and the seller negotiate the period of time over which payments will be spread and the amount you will pay each month. The seller adds a finance charge to the cash price of the television set and remains the legal owner until you have made your last payment. Most department stores and appliance and furniture stores, as well as automobile dealers, offer installment credit. The cost of buying the $600 color television set can be calculated as illustrated in Table ST2.1.

Table ST2.1 Calculating the Cost of Installment Credit

1. The amount to be financed

Cash price	$ 600.00
Minus down payment (if any)	– 50.00
Amount to be financed	$550.00

2. The amount that will be paid

Monthly payments	$ 35.00
Times number of payments	× 18
Total amount repaid	$630.00

3. The cost of the credit

Total amount repaid	$ 630.00
Minus amount financed	– 550.00
Cost of credit	$ 80.00

4. The total cost of the color TV

Total amount repaid	$ 630.00
Plus down payment (if any)	50.00
Total cost of TV	$ 680.00

Instead of buying your $600 television on the installment plan, you might want to buy it on the revolving charge plan. Most credit cards (MasterCard, Visa) represent revolving charge accounts that permit you to buy on credit up to a stated amount during each month. At the end of the month you may pay the total amount you owe or any amount over the stated "minimum payment due" amount. If you choose to pay less than the full amount, the cost of the credit on the unpaid amount would be 1.5 percent per month or 18 percent per year. For instance, if you paid $100 per month for six months, you would still owe $31.62 to be paid the next month for a total cost (television plus finance charges) of $631.62.

You can also purchase items on an open charge (30-day) account. Under this system you agree to pay in full within 30 days. Since there is no direct service charge or interest for this type of account, the television set would cost only the purchase price. Sears and J. C. Penney offer open charge (30-day) accounts. If you do not pay the full amount in 30 days, a finance charge is placed on the remaining balance. Both the use of revolving charge and open charge accounts are wise if you pay off the bill before finance charges begin. In deciding which type of credit account to use, remember that credit usually costs money, and the longer you take to pay for an item, the more the item will cost you. Exhibit ST2.1 describes the high cost of credit and one way parents of young married couples can help reduce the burden.

• THREE C'S OF CREDIT •

Whether you can get credit will depend on the rating you receive on the "three C's": character, capacity, and capital. *Character* refers to your honesty, sense of responsibility, soundness of judgment, and trustworthiness. *Capacity* refers to your ability to pay the bill when it is due. Such issues as the amount of money you earn and the length of time you have held a job will be considered in evaluating your capacity to pay. *Capital* refers to such assets as bank accounts, stocks, bonds, money market funds, real estate, and so on.

THE HIGH COST OF INTEREST OVER TIME

"What hurts young families so often is the high rate of interst they get saddled with over a 30-year-period when they buy a house," said one father of two children. "House payments in the early years are mostly interest, so it takes forever for the kids to pay off the principle." Jim Hicks, vice president of North Carolina National Bank, confirms this observation: *"The first payment on a $70,000 loan at 14 percent interest for 30 years is $829.50. Only $12.84 of this amount is allocated to the principle. The rest is for interest ($816.66)."* Taxes and fire insurance would be an additional $50 and $20, respectively, per month.

To shorten the total number of years during which a family must pay the bank $829.50 every month, spouses can make separate monthly payments that are applied specifically to the principle. The sooner the principle is paid off, the sooner all payments stop.

CONSIDERATION • It is particularly important that a married woman establish a credit rating in her own name in case she becomes widowed or divorced. Otherwise, her credit will depend on her husband, and when he goes, her credit does too. Although the law now furnishes some protection against financial discrimination by lenders, it remains the responsibility of the individual to establish his or her own credit rating.

• CREDIT SNAGS TO AVOID •

When you buy an item on the installment plan, you should be aware of several potential problems. One is the "add-on" clause, in which the seller keeps title to a whole list of items you are buying until all payments have been made on all items. For example, suppose you bought a stereo system from the same dealer who sold you the television set. If you fail to make any one payment, the seller may repossess both the stereo and the television set, even though you had paid all but a few dollars for both. The add-on clause permits the seller to add purchase after purchase to your original installment contract. In theory, a dealer who furnished your entire apartment under such an arrangement could collect all but 50 cents of the total amount you owed and then strip your apartment because you forgot the final payment.

CONSIDERATION • Don't sign a contract to buy something that has an add-on clause.

Credit purchases usually cost more, in the end.

Also, watch out for the "balloon" contract, which provides for a final payment considerably larger than the preceding monthly payments. For example, you might pay $50 down and $10 for 24 months for your television set and then face a final payment of $210. If you didn't have the $210, the seller could repossess the set before you could produce the money. Balloon contracts are illegal in some states.

An "acceleration" clause may also be a part of an installment contract. It not only permits the seller to repossess your television if you miss a payment but also requires you to make all remaining payments immediately if you lose your major source of income. If you lost your job after making payments on the television set for a couple of years, you would lose the set as well unless you could pay the balance due at once.

CONSIDERATION • If possible, try to buy items on a revolving or open charge account and avoid installment accounts. Sellers of major items on an installment plan often charge as high as 4 percent per month on the unpaid balance. This means a true annual interest rate of 48 percent. Hence the worst place to get credit for the purchase of expensive items is from the store or dealer that sells them. To get a lower interest rate, borrow the money from a commercial bank, savings and loan institution, or credit union and pay cash to the dealer.

SEXUAL ANATOMY AND PHYSIOLOGY

CONTENTS

Female External Anatomy and Physiology

Female Internal Anatomy and Physiology

Male External Anatomy and Physiology

Male Internal Anatomy and Physiology

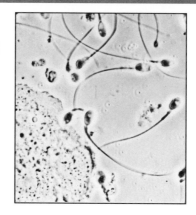

In the culture in which we live it is the custom to be least informed upon that subject concerning which every individual should know most, namely the structure and functions of his own body.

ASHLEY MONTAGUE

If we think of the human body as a special type of machine, *anatomy* refers to that machine's parts and *physiology* refers to how the parts work. In this topic we review the sexual anatomy and physiology of women and men and the reproductive process.

· FEMALE EXTERNAL ANATOMY AND PHYSIOLOGY ·

The external female genitalia are collectively known as the vulva (VUHL-vuh), a Latin term meaning "covering." The vulva consists of the mons veneris, the labia, the clitoris, and the vaginal and urethral openings (see Figure ST3.1). Like faces, the female genitalia differ in size, shape, and color, resulting in considerable variability in appearance.

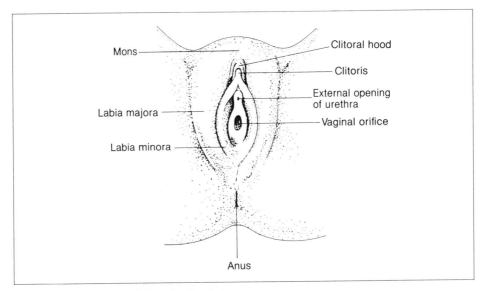

Figure ST3.1   **External Female Genitalia**

The Mons Veneris

The soft cushion of fatty tissue overlaying the pubic bone is called the mons veneris (mahns-vuh-NAIR-ihs), also known as mons pubis. This area becomes covered with hair at puberty and has numerous nerve endings. The purpose of the mons is to protect the pubic region during sexual intercourse.

The Labia

In the sexually unstimulated state, the urethral and vaginal openings are protected by the labia majora (LAY-bee-uh muh-JOR-uh) or "major lips," which are two elongated folds of fatty tissue that extend from the mons to the perineum, the area of skin between the opening of the vagina and the anus. Located between the labia majora are two additional hairless folds of skin called the labia minora (muh-NOR-uh), or "minor lips." They cover the urethral and vaginal openings and join at the top to form the hood of the clitoris. Both sets of labia, but particularly the inner labia minora, have a rich supply of nerve endings that are sensitive to sexual stimulation.

Clitoris

At the top of the inner lips is the clitoris (KLIHT-uh-ruhs), which also has a rich supply of nerve endings. The clitoris is the site of sexual excitement in the female and, like the penis, becomes erect during sexual excitation.

Vaginal Opening

The area between the labia minora is called the vestibule. This includes the urethral opening and the vaginal opening, or introitus (ihn-TROH-ih-tuhs), neither of which is visible unless the labia minora are parted. Like the anus, the vaginal opening is surrounded by a ring of sphincter muscles. Although the vaginal opening can expand to accommodate the passage of a baby at childbirth, under conditions of tension these muscles involuntarily contract, making it difficult to insert an object, including a tampon, into the vagina. The vaginal opening may be covered by a hymen, a thin membrane.

CONSIDERATION • Probably no other body part has caused as much grief to so many women as the hymen, which has been regarded throughout history as proof of virginity. A newly wed woman who was thought to be without a hymen was often returned to her parents, disgraced by exile, or even tortured and killed. It has been a common practice in many societies to parade a bloody bedsheet after the wedding night as proof of the bride's virginity. The anxieties caused by the absence of a hymen persist even today, and in Japan and other countries sexually experienced women may have a plastic surgeon reconstruct a hymen before marriage. Yet the hymen is really a poor indicator of virtue. Some women are born without a hymen or with incomplete hymens. In others the hymen is accidentally ruptured by vigorous physical activity or insertion of a tampon. In some women the hymen may not tear but only stretch during sexual intercourse. Even most doctors cannot easily determine whether a female is a virgin.

Urethral Opening

Just above the vaginal opening is the urethral opening where urine passes from the body. A short tube, the urethra, connects the bladder (where urine collects) with the urethral opening. Because of the shorter length of the female urethra and its close proximity to the anus, women are more susceptible than men to cystitis, a bladder inflammation.

• FEMALE INTERNAL ANATOMY AND PHYSIOLOGY •

The internal sex organs include the vagina, uterus, and the paired Fallopian tubes and ovaries (see Figure ST3.2).

Vagina

Leading from the vaginal opening into the woman's body is the vagina, a thin-walled elastic canal. In addition to receiving the penis during intercourse, the vagina functions as a passageway for menstrual flow and as the birth canal. The walls of the vagina are normally collapsed. Thus the vagina is actually a potential space.

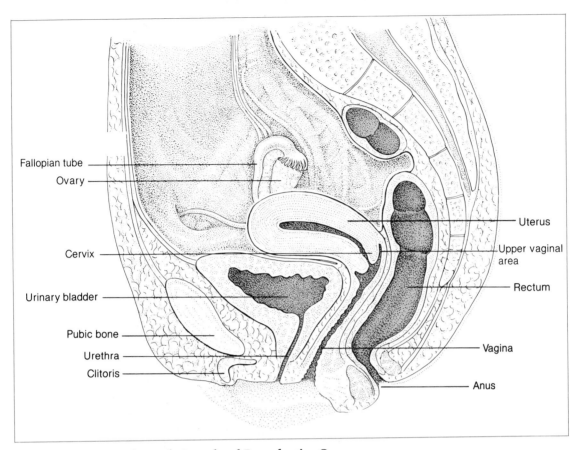

Figure ST3.2 **Internal Female Sexual and Reproductive Organs**

Fallopian tube
Ovary
Cervix
Urinary bladder
Pubic bone
Urethra
Clitoris
Uterus
Upper vaginal area
Rectum
Vagina
Anus

CONSIDERATION • The vagina is a self-cleansing organ. The bacteria that are found naturally in the vagina help to destroy other potentially harmful bacteria. In addition, secretions from the vaginal walls help maintain its normally acidic environment. The use of feminine hygiene sprays, as well as excessive douching, may cause irritation, allergic reactions, and in some cases, vaginal infection by altering the normal chemical balance of the vagina.

Some researchers believe that there is an extremely sensitive area in the front wall of the vagina about 1 to 2 inches into the opening. The spot swells during stimulation, and although a woman's initial response may be a need to urinate, continued stimulation generally leads to orgasm (Perry & Whipple, 1981). Other researchers disagree about the existence of the so-called Grafenberg spot, or G spot, named for gynecologist Ernest Grafenberg who discovered it. Hock (1983) said:

> The "G spot" does *not* exist as such, and the potential professional use of this term would be not only incorrect, but also misleading . . . The *entire* extent of the anterior wall of the vagina (rather than *one* specific spot), as well as the more deeply situated tissues, *including* the urinary bladder and urethral region, are extremely sensitive, being richly endowed with nerve endings. (p. 166)

In one study (Alzate & DipPsy, 1984), 48 women volunteered to allow one of several physicians to stimulate them digitally to assess the degree to which they felt erotic sensitivity in their vaginas. Forty-five reported erotic sensitivity located in most cases on the anterior wall and of those, 66.7 percent either reached orgasm or requested the physician to stop stimulation short of orgasm. The researchers concluded that the study supported the idea of erotic sensitivity in the vagina but that it did not support the idea of a particular location.

Uterus

The uterus (YOOT-uh-ruhs), or womb, resembles a small, inverted pear, which in women who have not given birth measures about 3 inches long and 3 inches wide at the top. A fertilized egg becomes implanted in the wall of the uterus and continues to grow and develop there until delivery. At the lower end of the uterus is the cervix, an opening that leads into the vagina.

Fallopian Tubes

Fallopian (fuh-LOH-pee-uhn) tubes (see Figure ST3.3) extend about 4 inches laterally from either side of the uterus to the ovaries. It is in the Fallopian tubes that fertilization normally occurs. The tubes transport the ovum, or egg, by means of cilia (hairlike structures) down the tube into the uterus.

Figure ST3.3 The Anatomical Relationships of the Vagina, Cervix, Uterus, Fallopian Tubes, and Ovaries
The ovaries are secured in the abdominal cavity by ligaments. The right ovary in the diagram has been opened to illustrate the progressive stages in the development of a follicle. A follicle has just ruptured, and the mature egg cell is swept into the funneled end of the Fallopian tube, the fimbria, by the action of cilia.

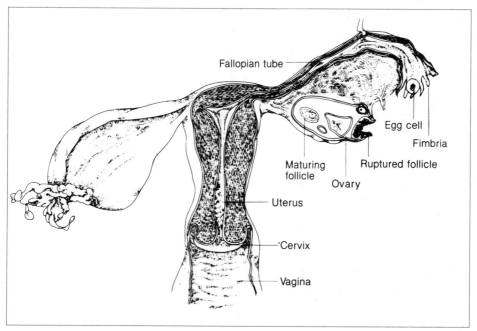

Ovaries

The ovaries (OH-vuhr-eez) are almond-shaped structures on both sides of the uterus. They produce eggs and the female hormones estrogen and progesterone. At birth the ovaries have about 400,000 immature ova, each contained in a thin capsule forming a follicle. Some of the follicles begin to mature at puberty, but only about 400 mature ova will be released in a woman's lifetime.

• MALE EXTERNAL ANATOMY AND PHYSIOLOGY •

Although they differ in appearance, many structures of the male (see Figure ST3.4) and female genitals develop from the same embryonic tissue (the penis and clitoris for example).

Figure ST3.4 **Internal and External Male Sexual Organs**

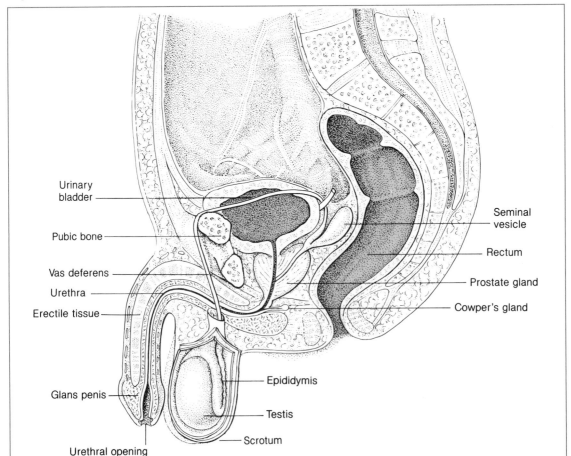

Penis

The penis (PEE-nihs) is the primary male sexual organ, which in the unaroused state is soft and hangs between the legs. When sexually stimulated, the penis enlarges and becomes erect, enabling penetration of the vagina. The penis functions not only to deposit sperm in the female's vagina but also as a passageway from the bladder to eliminate urine. In cross section the penis can be seen to consist of three parallel cylinders of tissue containing many cavities, two corpora cavernosa (cavernous bodies) and a corpus spongiosum (spongy body) through which the urethra passes. The penis has numerous blood vessels and when stimulated the arteries dilate and blood enters faster than it can leave. The cavities of the cavernous and spongy bodies fill with blood, and pressure against the fibrous membranes causes the penis to become erect. The head of the penis is called the glans, which at birth is covered by foreskin. The surgical procedure in which the foreskin is pulled forward and cut off is known as circumcision.

CONSIDERATION • Circumcision was performed by the Egyptians as early as 4000 B.C. and was an early religious rite for members of the Jewish and Moslem faiths. To Jewish people circumcision symbolizes the covenant with God made by Abraham. Today the primary reason for performing circumcision is to ensure proper hygiene. The smegma that can build up under the foreskin is a potential breeding ground for infection. But circumcision is a rather drastic procedure merely to ensure proper hygiene, which, as the Academy of Pediatrics suggests, can just as easily be accomplished by pulling back the foreskin and cleaning the glans during normal bathing. However, circumcision is indicated when the foreskin will not retract.

Scrotum

The scrotum (SCROH-tuhm) is the sac located below the penis, which contains the testes. Beneath the skin is a thin layer of muscle fibers that contract when it is cold, helping to draw the testes closer to the body to keep the temperature of the sperm constant. Sperm can only be produced at a temperature several degrees lower than normal body temperature and any prolonged variation can result in sterility.

CONSIDERATION • It is particularly hazardous for a male to contract a case of the mumps, a viral infection that often causes swelling of the testicles. The sheath in which the testes are enclosed does not readily expand and the resulting pressure can cause sterility.

• MALE INTERNAL ANATOMY AND PHYSIOLOGY •

The male internal organs, often referred to as the reproductive organs, include the testes where the sperm is produced, a duct system to transport the sperm out of the body, and some additional structures that produce the seminal fluid in which the sperm is mixed before ejaculation.

Testes

The paired testes, or testicles, are the male gonads and develop from the same embryonic tissue as the female gonads, the ovaries. The two oval-shaped testicles are suspended in the scrotum by the spermatic cord and enclosed within a fibrous sheath. The function of the testes is to produce spermatozoa and male hormones, primarily testosterone (see Figure ST3.5).

Duct System

The several hundred seminiferous tubules come together to form a tube in each testicle called the epididymus (ehp-uh-DIHD-uh-muhz), the first part of the duct system that transports sperm. If uncoiled, the tubes would measure 20 feet in length. Sperm spend from two to six weeks traveling through the epididy-

Figure ST3.5 Internal Structures of the Human Male Testes, Illustrating the Complex of Ducts Involved in Sperm Manufacture and Transport

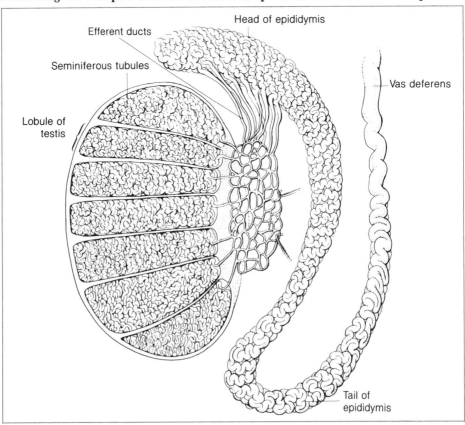

mus as they mature and are reabsorbed by the body if ejaculation does not occur. One ejaculation contains an average of 360 million sperm cells.

The sperm leave the scrotum through the second part of the duct system, the vas deferens (vas-DEF-uh-renz). These 14- to 16-inch paired ducts transport the sperm from the epididymus up and over the bladder to the prostate gland. Rhythmic contractions during ejaculation force the sperm into the paired ejaculatory ducts that run through the prostate gland. The entire length of this portion of the duct system is less than 1 inch. It is here that the sperm mix with seminal fluid to form semen before being propelled to the outside through the urethra.

Seminal Vesicles and Prostate Gland

The seminal vesicles resemble two small sacs about 2 inches in length located behind the bladder. They secrete their own fluids, which empty into the ejaculatory duct to mix with sperm and fluids from the prostate gland.

Most of the seminal fluid comes from the prostate gland, a chestnut-sized structure located below the bladder and in front of the rectum. The fluid is alkaline and serves to protect the sperm in the more acidic environments of the male urethra and female vagina.

A small amount of clear, sticky fluid is also secreted into the urethra before ejaculation by the two pea-sized Cowper's, or bulbourethral, glands located below the prostate.

CONSIDERATION • This fluid can often be noticed on the tip of the penis during sexual arousal. It may contain stray sperm, so that withdrawal of the penis from the vagina before ejaculation is a risky method of birth control.

· Special Topic 4 ·

SEXUALLY TRANSMITTED DISEASES

CONTENTS

Gonorrhea

Syphilis

Genital Herpes

Acquired Immune Deficiency
  Syndrome (AIDS)

Getting Help

Prevention

Evidence suggests that herpes is 400 million years old; it may be the oldest virus affecting humans.

LANE LENARD

Sexually transmitted diseases (STDs) are also known as venereal diseases. Venus was the Roman goddess of love, and since some diseases are transmitted through various acts of love—kissing, cunnilingus, fellatio, intercourse—the term venereal (from Venus) has been used to describe such diseases. These diseases are also referred to as social diseases because they are contracted primarily through sociosexual contact. In effect, any person who has a physical or sexual contact with someone who has a sexually transmitted disease may get that disease. The exposure may be through heterosexual or homosexual contacts. Table ST4.1 lists some of the myths and facts about STDs. We review some of the more common STDs in the following sections.

Table ST4.1 Myths and Facts about Sexually Transmitted Diseases (STDs)

MYTH	FACT
STDs in the genitals cannot be transmitted to the mouth and vice versa.	Transmission of STD infections from mouth to genitals and vice versa does occur.
If you have syphilis or gonorrhea, you will know it.	Some infected people show no signs of having syphilis or gonorrhea until many years later.
You can avoid having to see a physician by treating your suspected STD infection at home.	Only a physician can recommend a treatment plan for STDs.
You cannot have more than one STD at a time.	More than half of women who visited one STD clinic had two or more STDs.
Birth control pills protect you from STDs.	Birth control pills may increase a woman's chance of contracting various STDs when exposed.
Once you have been cured of an STD, you cannot get it again.	You can get an STD infection any time you come into contact with it whether you have had it or not.
Syphilis and gonorrhea can be contracted by contact with a toilet seat.	The germs of these diseases cannot live in the open air.

• GONORRHEA •

Also known as "the clap," "the whites," and "morning drop," gonorrhea is the number two communicable disease in the United States (number one is the cold). *Communicable* means that, like the common cold, the disease is easily "caught" from someone who has it.

DATA • *About one million cases of gonorrhea are reported every year. The highest percentage of these cases occur in those who are in their teens or early twenties.* (Zaidi et al., 1983)

Individuals most often contract gonorrhea through having genital contact with someone who is carrying the gonococcus (gahn-uh-KAH-us) bacteria. These bacteria live in the urethra and around the cervix of the female and in the urinary tract of the male. During intercourse some of the bacteria are transferred from the mucous membranes inside the urethra of one gender to the other. The bacteria may also enter the throat during oral-genital contact or the rectum during anal intercourse.

Although some infected men show no signs, 80 percent do so between three and eight days after exposure. They begin to discharge a thick, white pus from the penis (thus "the whites" and "morning drop") and feel pain or discomfort during urination. They may also have swollen lymph glands in the groin. Women are more likely to show no signs of the infection, but when they do, they are sometimes in the form of a discharge from the vagina along with a burning sensation. More often a woman becomes aware of gonorrhea only after she feels extreme discomfort, which is a result of the untreated infection traveling up into her uterus and Fallopian tubes. Pelvic inflammatory disease (PID) is the term used to describe the inflammation in these areas caused by the gonococci or other bacteria.

• SYPHILIS •

Although syphilis is less prevalent than gonorrhea, the effects of syphilis are more devastating, including mental illness, blindness, heart disease—even death. The spirochete (SPY-roh-keet) bacteria—the villain germs—enter the body through mucous membranes that line various body openings. With your tongue, feel the inside of your cheek. This is a layer of mucous membrane—the substance in which spirochetes thrive. Similar membranes are in the vagina and urethra of the penis. If you kiss or have genital contact with someone harboring these bacteria, they can be absorbed into your mucous membranes causing syphilitic infection. Your syphilis will then progress through at least three or four stages.

In stage one (primary-stage syphilis), between 10 and 90 days after exposure a small sore will appear at the site of the infection. The chancre (SHANK-er), as it is called, shows on the tip of the man's penis, in the labia or cervix of the woman, or in either partner's mouth or rectum. The chancre neither hurts nor itches, and if left untreated, will disappear in three to five weeks. This disappearance is one of the tricky aspects of syphilis since the person believes that she or he is cured. In reality, the disease is still present and doing great harm even though there are no visible signs.

During the second stage (secondary-stage syphilis), beginning from two to 12 weeks after the chancre has disappeared, other signs of syphilis appear. These may include a rash all over the body or just on the hands or feet. Welts and sores may also occur as well as fever, headaches, sore throat, and hair loss. Syphilis has been called "the great imitator" because it mimics so many other diseases (for example, infectious mononucleosis, cancer, and psoriasis). Whatever the symptoms, they too will disappear without treatment. The person may be tricked again into believing that nothing is wrong.

For about two-thirds of those with late untreated syphilis (latent-stage syphilis), the disease seems to have gone away with no subsequent effects. However, the spirochetes are still in the body and can attack any organ at any time. For the other third, serious harm results. Tertiary syphilis—the fourth stage—may disable or kill. In addition to heart disease and blindness, mentioned earlier, brain damage, loss of bowel and bladder control, difficulty in walking, and impotence may result.

Aside from avoiding contact with a person infected with syphilis, early detection and treatment is essential. Blood tests and examination of material from the infected site can help verify the existence of syphilis. But such tests are not always accurate. Blood tests reveal the presence of antibodies, not spirochetes, and it sometimes takes three months before the body produces detectable antibodies. Sometimes there is no chancre anywhere on the person's body.

Treatment for syphilis is similar to that for gonorrhea. Penicillin or other antibiotics (for those allergic to penicillin) is effective. Infected persons treated in the early stages can be completely cured with no ill effects. If the syphilis has progressed into the later stages, any damage that has been done cannot be repaired.

> CONSIDERATION • Another problem with syphilis is the effect it has on the newborn of an infected woman. If the pregnant woman does not receive treatment, her baby is likely to be born with congenital syphilis. If she is treated by the eighteenth week of pregnancy, the fetus will not be affected.

• GENITAL HERPES •

Herpes refers to more than 50 viruses related by size, shape, internal composition, and structure. One such herpes is genital herpes. Whereas the disease has been known for at least 2,000 years, the media attention to genital herpes (called "today's scarlett letter," "the VD of the Ivy League," and "Jerry Falwell's revenge") is relatively new. Also known as herpes simplex virus type 2 (HSV-2), genital herpes is a viral infection that is usually transmitted during sexual contact. Symptoms occur in the form of a cluster of small, painful blisters or sores on the penis or around the anus in men. In women the blisters usually appear around the vagina but may also develop inside the vagina, on the cervix, and sometimes on the anus.

DATA • *HSV-1 (lip herpes) causes 10 percent to 20 percent of the cases of type HSV-2 (genital herpes).* (Oriel, 1983)

Another type of herpes is labial or lip herpes, which originates in the mouth. Herpes simplex virus type 1 (HSV-1) is a biologically different herpes virus with which people are more familiar as cold sores on the lips. These sores can be transferred to the genitals by the fingers or oral-genital contact. In the past, genital and lip herpes had site specificity; that is, HSV-1 was always found on the lips or in the mouth and HSV-2 was always found in the genitals. But because of the increase in fellatio and cunnilingus, HSV-1 herpes may be found in the genitals and HSV-2 in the lips.

The first symptoms of genital herpes appear a couple of days to three weeks after exposure. At first these symptoms may include itching or a burning sensation during urination followed by headache, fever, aches, and swollen glands, and in women, vaginal discharge. The symptoms worsen over about 10 days, during which there is a skin eruption, followed by the appearance of painful sores, which soon break open and become very painful during genital contact or when touched. The acute illness may last from three to six weeks. "I've got herpes," said one sufferer, "and it's a very uneven discomfort. Somedays I'm okay, but other days I'm miserable."

As with syphilis, the symptoms of genital herpes subside (the sores dry up, scab over, and disappear) and the person feels good again. But the virus settles in the nerve cells in the spinal column and may cause repeated outbreaks of the symptoms in about a third of those infected.

Stress, menstruation, sunburn, fatigue, and the presence of other infections seem to be related to the reappearance of the virus. Although such recurrences are usually milder and of shorter duration than the initial outbreak, the resurfacing of the virus may occur throughout the person's life. "It's not knowing when the thing is going to come back that's the bad part about herpes," said one woman.

CONSIDERATION • The herpes virus is usually contagious during the time that a person has visible sores but not when the skin is healed. However, the person may have a mild recurrence yet be unaware that she or he is contagious. Aside from visible sores, itching, burning, or tingling sensations at the sore site also suggest that the person is contagious.

At the time of this writing, there is no cure for herpes. Because it is a virus, it does not respond to antibiotics as do syphilis and gonorrhea. There are a few procedures to help relieve the symptoms and promote healing of the sores. These include seeing a physician to look for and treat any other genital infections near the herpes sores, keeping the sores clean and dry, taking hot sitz-baths three times a day, and wearing loose-fitting cotton underwear to enhance air circulation. Acyclovir, marketed as Zovirax, is an ointment applied on the sores that helps to relieve pain, speed healing, and reduce the amount of time that live viruses are present in the sores. A more effective tablet form of acyclovir is also available which significantly reduces the rate of recurring episodes of genital herpes. Once acyclovir is stopped the herpetic recurrences resume (Straus, et al., 1984). While acyclovir seems to help manage the symptoms of first-episode genital herpes, it is less effective with subsequent outbreaks. Proper nutrition, adequate sleep and exercise, and avoiding physical or mental stress helps people to cope better with recurrences.

CONSIDERATION • A person with genital herpes can prevent infecting someone else by avoiding genital contact until the sores have healed. It is also recommended that the male use a condom and the female use a diaphragm for two weeks after the sores have healed. But using the condom or diaphragm is not completely effective since the herpes virus may pass through these synthetic membranes.

Coping with the psychological and emotional aspects of having genital herpes is often more difficult than coping with the physical aspects of the disease. Herpes victims typically go through a predictable pattern of shock, anger, bitterness, and depression. The latter may result in social withdrawal, not only from sexual encounters, but also from friends who are not sexual partners. Getting accurate information about the disease, dealing with a negative self-image, and learning how to tell someone they are sexually interested in that they have herpes are among the problems facing herpes sufferers (Greenwood & Bernstein, 1982).

· ACQUIRED IMMUNE DEFICIENCY SYNDROME (AIDS) ·

Acquired immune deficiency syndrome (AIDS) represents the appearance in previously healthy individuals of various aggressive infections and malignancies. AIDS was first seen among homosexual and bisexual males with multiple sex partners, intravenous drug users, hemophiliacs, and Haitian immigrants to the United States.

DATA · *More than 70 percent of AIDS victims have been homosexual and bisexual men who have had multiple sexual partners.* (Facts about AIDS, 1984)

The syndrome attacks the immune system of the body and makes it vulnerable to infection. The incubation period for AIDS ranges from a few months to about two years. Symptoms of AIDS include swollen glands, persistent fever, persistent dry cough, bruiselike markings on the skin, weight loss, night sweats, and persistent diarrhea.

Kaposi's sarcoma (KS), a type of cancer, and Pneumocystis carinii pneumonia (PCP) have been associated with AIDS. Patients often die since their bodies become incapable of combating other diseases and infection. Eighty percent of those who contract AIDS are dead within three years. A virus, HTLV–III, (Human T-Cell Leukemia/Lymphoma Virus) has been identified as the probable cause of AIDS and a vaccine to be available in 1986 or '87 is being developed to prevent it. Research is also being conducted to identify AIDS-contaminated blood to prevent transmitting it through blood transfusions.

CONSIDERATION · AIDS may be transmitted through anal intercourse, through penile-vaginal intercourse, through contact with infected urine and semen, through blood transfusions, and through the use of unsterilized needles. AIDS cannot be contracted by casual contact with someone who has AIDS. Family members other than sex partners of AIDS victims have not developed AIDS.

· GETTING HELP ·

If you suspect that you have had contact with someone who has a sexually transmitted disease or if you have any symptoms of the STDs mentioned, call the toll-free national VD hotline at 800-227-8922. For special information about AIDS, call 800-342-2437. In Washington, D.C. call 646-8182. You will not be asked to identify yourself but you can get information about your symptoms and local STD clinics that offer confidential, free treatment.

A newsletter, *The Helper*, is published quarterly to provide the latest information for herpes sufferers. The newsletter can be obtained by writing to HELP (Herpetics Engaged in Living Productively), 260 Sheridan Ave., Palo Alto, CA 94306. Herpes information is also available at 415-328-7710. Duke University in Durham, North Carolina, has opened an AIDS clinic to treat AIDS victims (phone 919-684-2660).

• PREVENTION •

The best way to avoid getting a sexually transmitted disease is to avoid sexual contact or to have contact only with those who are not infected. This means restricting your sexual contacts to those who limit their relationships to one person. The person most likely to get a sexually transmitted disease has sexual relations with a number of partners or with a partner who has a variety of partners.

In addition to restricting sexual contacts, a condom put on before the penis touches the other person's body will make it difficult for the sexually transmitted disease, including genital herpes, to pass from one person to the other. After genital contact, it is also a good idea for the partners to urinate and to wash their genitals with soap and hot water.

DATA • *Using a laboratory plunger model, researchers demonstrated that both natural and latex condoms were effective in blocking high concentrations of the genital herpes virus.* (Conant, et al., 1984)

· Special Topic 5 ·

RESOURCES AND ORGANIZATIONS

Abortion

Pro Choice
National Abortion Rights Action
League
1424 K St., NW
Washington, D.C. 20005

Pro Life
National Right to Life Committee
419 7th St., NW
Washington, D.C. 20045

Birth Alternatives

American Society for
Psychoprophylaxis in Obstetrics
1523 L St., NW
Washington, D.C. 20005

Nurse-Midwives
American College of Nurse-
Midwives
1522 K St., NW, Suite 1120
Washington, D.C. 20005

Breastfeeding

LaLeche International, Inc.
9616 Minneapolis Ave.
Franklin Park, IL 60123

Child Abuse

National Committee for Prevention
of Child Abuse
332 S. Michigan Ave., Suite 1250
Chicago, IL 60604–4357

Parents Anonymous
22330 Hawthorne Blvd., Suite 208
Torrance, CA 90505

National Child Abuse Hotline
800–421–0353

Divorced Fathers

Men's Rights Inc.
P.O. Box 163180
Sacramento, CA 95816

Family Planning

Planned Parenthood
1220 19th St., NW
Washington, D.C. 20036

Fertility

American Fertility Foundation
1608 13th Ave., S.
Suite 101
Birmingham, AL 35205

Resolve, Inc.
P.O. Box 2038
Washington, D.C. 20013

Gender Equality

National Organization for Women
425 13th St., NW
Washington, D.C. 20004

Gender Selection

Gametrics Limited
180 Harbor Dr.
Sausalito, CA 94965

Genetic Counseling

National Genetics Foundation
555 W. 57th St.
New York, NY 10019

Healthy Baby

Healthy Mothers–Healthy Babies
Coalition
Department of Public Affairs
600 Maryland Ave., SW
Washington, D.C. 20024

Homosexual Lifestyle

National Gay Task Force
80 Fifth Ave., Suite 1601
New York, NY 10011

Parents and Friends of Gays and
Lesbians
P.O. Box 24565
Los Angeles, CA 90025

or

5715 16th St., NW
Washington, D.C. 20011

Incest Prevention

Committee for Children
P.O. Box 15190
Seattle, WA 98115

Interracial Parenting

Council on Interracial Books for
Children
1841 Broadway
New York, NY 10023

Marriage Therapy

American Association for Marriage
and Family Therapy
1717 K St., NW
Suite 407
Washington, D.C. 20006

Moral Majority

Moral Majority, Inc.
Jerry Falwell
Thomas Road Baptist Church
305 6th St.
Lynchburg, VA 24502

Ovum Transfer

Harbor-UCLA Medical Center
1000 W. Carson St.
Torrance, CA 90509

Rape

National Rape Information Clearing
House
National Center for Prevention and
Control of Rape
5600 Fishers Lane
Rockville, MD 20857

Sex Education

Sex Information and Education
Council of the United States
(SIECUS)
80 Fifth Ave.
New York, NY 10011

Sexual Therapy

American Association of Sex
Educators, Counselors, and
Therapists (AASECT)
2000 N St., NW, Suite 110
Washington, D.C. 20036

Center For Marital and Sexual
Studies
5199 E. Pacific Coast Hy.
Long Beach, CA 90804

Masters and Johnson Institute
4910 Forest Park Blvd.
St. Louis, MO 63108

Loyola Sexual Dysfunction Clinic
Loyola University Hospital
2160 S. 1st Ave.
Maywood, IL 60153

Sexually Transmitted Diseases

American Social Health Association
260 Sheridan Rd.
Palo Alto, CA 94306

Center for Disease Control
Technical Information Services
Bureau of State Services
Atlanta, GA 30333

Herpes Resource Information
Box 100
Palo Alto, CA 94302

National VD Hotline
800-227-8922
(in California 800-982-5883)

National AIDS Hotline
800-342-2437

Single Parenthood

Parents Without Partners
7910 Woodmont Ave.
Washington, D.C. 20014

Single Mothers by Choice
501 12th St.
Brooklyn, NY 11215

Stepfamilies

Stepfamily Association of America,
Inc.
28 Allegheny Ave., Suite 1307
Baltimore, MD 21204

Sterilization

Association for Voluntary
Sterilization, Inc.
708 Third Ave.
New York, NY 10164

Test-tube Fertilization

Eastern Virginia Medical School
Norfolk General Hospital
Howard and Georgeanna Jones
Institute for Reproductive
Medicine
304 Medical Tower
Norfolk, VA 23507

· REFERENCES ·

CHAPTER 1

ABC (American Broadcasting Company) Television. Polygamy. "20/20." March 1, 1984.

Axelson, L. Department of Family and Child Development, Virginia Polytechnic Institute and State University, Blacksburg, Virginia. Personal communication, 1984. Used with permission.

Bader, E., Microys, G., Sinclair, C., Willett, E., & Conway, B. Do marriage preparation programs really work? A Canadian experiment. *Journal of Marital and Family Therapy*, 1980, *6*(2), 171–179.

Better Homes and Gardens. A report on American families. Des Moines, Iowa: Meredith Corporation, 1983.

Bobys, R. S. Research fraud factors and effects. *Free Inquiry in Creative Sociology,* 1983, *11,* 44–48.

Filsinger, E. E., & Lamke, L. K. The lineage transmission of interpersonal competence. *Journal of Marriage and the Family,* 1983, *45,* 75–80.

Freeman, D. *Margaret Mead and Samoa: The making and unmaking of an anthropological myth.* Cambridge, Mass.: Harvard University Press, 1983.

Glick, P. C. How American families are changing. *American Demographics,* 1984, *6*(1), 20–25.

King, C. E., & Christensen, A. The relationship events scale: A Guttman scaling of progress in courtship. *Journal of Marriage and the Family,* 1983, *44,* 671–678. © 1983 by the National Council on Family Relations, 1910 W. County Road B, Suite 147, St. Paul, Mn. 55113. Reprinted by permission.

Mead, M. *Coming of age in Samoa.* New York: Morrow, 1928.

National Center for Health Statistics. Births, marriages, divorces, and deaths for November 1983. *Monthly Vital Statistics Report, 32,* (11). DHHS Pub. No. (PHS) 84–1120. Hyattsville, Md.: U.S. Public Health Service, February 17, 1984.

Norton, A. J. Family life cycle: 1980. *Journal of Marriage and the Family,* 1983, *45,* 267–275.

Ridley, C. A., Lamke, L. K., Avery, A. W., & Harrell, J. E. The effects of interpersonal skills training on sex-role identity of premarital dating partners. *Journal of Research in Personality,* 1982, *16,* 335–342.

Rossi, A. S. Gender and parenthood. *American Sociological Review,* 1984, *49,* 1–19.

Rubenstein, C. Psychology's fruit flies. *Psychology Today,* July 1982, p. 83.

Stayton, W. R. Lifestyle spectrum 1984. *SIECUS Report,* 1984, *12,* 1–5.

CHAPTER 2

Alperson, B. L., & Friedman, W. J. Some aspects of the interpersonal phenomenology of heterosexual dyads with respect to sex-role stereotypes. *Sex Roles,* 1983, *9,* 453–474.

Balswick, J. Explaining inexpressive males: A reply to L'Abate. *Family Relations,* 1980, *29,* 231–233.

Bouchard, T. J., Eckert, E., Resnick, S., & Keys, M., The Minnesota study of twins reared apart: Project description and sample results. *Intelligence,* 1980. Reprinted by permission.

Bouchard, T. J., Jr. Do environmental similarities explain the similarity in intelligence of identical twins reared apart? *Intelligence,* 1983, *7,* 175–184.

Bradbard, M. R., & Endsley, R. C. The effects of sex-typed labeling on preschool children's information-seeking and retention. *Sex Roles,* 1983, *9,* 247–260.

Burchardt, C. J., & Serbin, L. A. Psychological androgyny and personality adjustment in college and psychiatric populations. *Sex Roles*, 1982, *8*, 835–851.

Bussey, K., & Perry, D. G. Same-sex imitation: The avoidance of cross-sex models or the acceptance of same-sex models? *Sex Roles*, 1982, *8*, 773–784.

Cahill, S. E. Reexamining the acquisition of sex roles: A social interactionist approach. *Sex Roles*, 1983, *9*, 1–16.

Chafetz, J. S., & Dworkin, A. G. Work pressure similarity for homemakers, managers & professionals. *Free Inquiry in Creative Sociology*, 1984, *12*, 47–50.

Culp, R. E., Cook, A. S., & Housley, P. A comparison of observed and reported adult-infant interactions: Effects of perceived sex. *Sex Roles*, 1983, *9*, 475–479.

Daniel, H. J. The brains of war and peace: A sexual dimorphism hypothesis. *Proceedings of the Ninth Annual Phi Kappa Phi Symposium*, East Carolina University, Greenville, N.C., 1984. Used by permission of H. J. Daniel.

Diamond, M. Sexual identity, monozygotic twins reared in discordant sex roles and BBC follow-up. *Archives of Sexual Behavior*, 1982, *11*, 181–185.

Erkut, S. Exploring sex differences in expectancy, attribution, and academic achievement. *Sex Roles*, 1983, *9*, 217–231.

Feldstein, J. H., & Feldstein, S. Sex differences on televised toy commercials. *Sex Roles*, 1982, *8*, 581–587.

Frankel, F., & Rathvon, S. *Whatever happened to Cinderella?* New York: St. Martin's Press, 1980.

Freud, S. *New introductory lectures in psychoanalysis.* (J. Strachey, Ed. and trans.). New York: W. W. Norton, 1965. Originally published, 1933.

_____. Some psychological consequences of an anatomical distinction between the sexes (1925). In J. Strouse (Ed.), *Women and analysis.* New York: Grossman, 1974.

Freudiger, P. Life satisfaction among three categories of married women. *Journal of Marriage and the Family*, 1983, *45*, 213–219.

Gerdes, E. P., & Garber, D. M. Sex bias in hiring: Effects of job demands and applicant competence. *Sex Roles*, 1983, *9*, 307–319.

Glick, P. C. How American families are changing. *American Demographics*, 1984, 6(1), 20–25.

Haber, S. Cognitive support for the career choices of college women. *Sex Roles*, 1980, *6*, 129–138.

Harvey, P. H. Macho and his mate. *Free Inquiry in Creative Sociology*, 1983, *11*, 167–170.

Herzog, A. R., Bachman, J. G., & Johnston, L. D. Paid work, child care, and housework: A national survey of high school seniors' preferences for sharing responsibilities between husband and wife. *Sex Roles*, 1983, *9*, 109–135.

Hoelter, J. W. Factorial invariance and self-esteem: Reassessing race and sex differences. *Social Forces*, 1983, *61*, 834–846.

Imperato-McGinley, J., Guerrero, L., Gautier, T., & Perterson, R. Steroid 5 and reductase deficiency in men: An inherited form of male pseudo hermaphroditism. *Science*, 1974, *186*, 1213–1215.

Isherwood, J. T. The male role: Limitations and interventions. *Free Inquiry in Creative Sociology*, 1983, *11*, 227–230.

Keating, K. What's happening to American families? Part II. *Better Homes and Gardens*, July 1983, p. 15 et passim.

Kenkel, W. F., & Gage, B. A. The restricted and gender-typed occupational aspirations of young women: Can they be modified? *Family Relations*, 1983, *32*, 129–138.

Knaub, P. K., Eversoll, D. B., & Voss, J. H. Is parenthood a desirable adult role? An assessment of attitudes held by contemporary women. *Sex Roles*, 1983, *9*, 355–362.

Kohlberg, L. A cognitive-developmental analysis of children's sex-role concepts and attitudes. In E. E. Macoby (Ed.). *The development of sex differences.* Stanford, Calif.: Stanford University Press, 1966.

_____. State and sequence: The cognitive-developmental approach to socialization. In D. A. Goslin (Ed.), *Handbook of socialization theory and research.* Chicago: Rand McNally, 1969. Pp. 347–480.

Kramarae, C. *Women and men speaking.* New York: Newbury House, 1981.

Lombardo, W. K., Cretser, G. A., Lombardo, B., & Mathis, S. L. Fer cryin' out loud—There is a sex difference. *Sex Roles*, 1983, *9*, 987–995.

Lull, J., Mulac, A., & Rosen, S. L. Feminism as a predictor of mass media use. *Sex Roles*, 1983, *9*, 165–177.

Lykken, D. T. Research with twins: The concept of emergenesis. *Psychophysiology*, 1982, *19*, 361–373.

McGhee, P. E., & Frueh, T. Television viewing and the learning of sex-role stereotypes. *Sex Roles*, 1980, *6*, 179–188.

McMahan, I. D. Expectancy of success on sex-linked tasks. *Sex Roles*, 1982, *8*, 949–958.

McVicar, P., & Herman, A. Assertiveness, self-actualization, and locus of control in women. *Sex Roles*, 1983, *9*, 555–562.

Mugford, S. & Lally, J. Sex, reported happiness, and the well-being of married individuals: A test of Bernard's hypothesis in an Australian sample. *Journal of Marriage and the Family*, 1981, *43*, 969–975.

O'Kelly, C. Sex-role imagery in modern art: Am empirical examination. *Sex Roles*, 1980, *6*, 99–111.

Paludi, M. A., & Bauer, W. D. Goldberg revisited: What's in an author's name. *Sex Roles*, 1983, *9*, 387–396.

Patterson, J. M., & McCubbin, H. I. Gender roles and coping. *Journal of Marriage and the Family*, 1984, *46*, 95–104.

Petersen, D. M., & Dressel, P. L. Equal time for women: Social notes on the male strip show. *Urban Life*, 1982, *11*, 185–208.

Pleck, J. H. Prisoners of manliness. *Psychology Today*, September 1981, pp. 69–83.

Rettig, K. D., & Bubolz, M. M. Interpersonal resource exchanges as indicators of quality of marriage. *Journal of Marriage and the Family*, 1983, *45*, 497–510.

Rhodes, A. L. Effects of religious denomination on sex differences in occupational expectations. *Sex Roles*, 1983, *9*, 93–108.

Ridley, C. A., Lamke, L. K., Avery, A. W., & Harrell, J. E. The effects of interpersonal skills training on sex-role identity of premarital dating partners. *Journal of Research and Personality*, 1982, *16*, 335–342.

Riemer, J. W., & Bridwell, L. M. How women survive in nontraditional occupations. *Free Inquiry in Creative Sociology*, 1982, *10*, 153–158.

Rombough, S., and Ventimiglia, J. C. Sexism: A tri-dimensional phenomenon. *Sex Roles*, 1981, *7*, 747–755.

Romer, N., & Cherry, D. Ethnic and social class differences in children's sex-role concepts. *Sex Roles*, 1980, *6*, 245–263.

Ross, L., Anderson, D. R., & Wisocki, P. A. Television viewing and adult sex-role attitudes. *Sex Roles*, 1982, *8*, 589–592.

Rossi, A. S. Gender and parenthood. *American Sociological Review*, 1984, *49*, 1–19.

Rotheram, M. J., & Weiner, N. Androgyny, stress, and satisfaction: Dual-career and traditional relationships. *Sex Roles*, 1983, *9*, 151–158.

Rubenstein, C. Wellness is all. *Psychology Today*, October 1982, pp. 27–37.

Stevens, G., & Boyd, M. The importance of mother: Labor force participation and intergenerational mobility of women. *Social Forces*, 1980, *59*, 186–199.

Stitt, C., Schmidt, S., Price, K., & Kipnis, D. Sex of leader, leader behavior, and subordinate satisfaction. *Sex Roles*, 1983, *9*, 31–42.

U.S. Bureau of the Census. Lifetime earnings for men and women in the United States: 1979. *Current Population Reports*, Series P-60, No. 139. Washington, D.C.: U.S. Government Printing Office, 1983.

Weisstein, N. Tired of arguing about biological inferiority? *Ms.*, May 1982, p. 42.

Wilson, K., & Knox, D. Sex role identity and dating appeal. Paper presented at the annual meeting of the National Council on Family Relations, Milwaukee 1981. Used with permission.

World Almanac & Book of Facts, 1984. New York: Newspaper Enterprise Association, 1984.

Zuckerman, D. M., & Sayre, D. H. Cultural sex-role expectations and children's sex-role concepts. *Sex Roles*, 1982, *8*, 853–862.

CHAPTER 3

Better Homes and Gardens. A report on American families. Des Moines, Iowa: Meredith Corporation, 1983.

Buehler, C. J., & Wells, B. Counseling the romantic. *Family Relations*, 1981, *30*, 452–458.

Buunk, B. Strategies of jealousy: Styles of coping with extramarital involvement of the spouse. *Family Relations*, 1982, *31*, 13–18.

Cook, K., Kretchmer, A., Hellis, B., Lever, J., & Hertz, R. The *Playboy* reader's sex survey: Part III. *Playboy*, May 1983, p. 126 et passim.

Corbett, S. L., & Morgan, K. D. The process of lesbian identification. *Free Inquiry in Creative Sociology*, 1983, *11*, 81–83.

Croake, J. Quoted in D. Knox, Married love. *Modern Bride*, August/September 1983, p. 166 et. passim.

Davidson, B., Balswick, J., & Halverson, C. Affective self- disclosure and marital adjustment: A test of equity theory. *Journal of Marriage and the Family,* 1983, *45,* 93–102.

Family Protection Act. H. R. 614, a Bill introduced into the 98th Congress, 1983 in the House of Representatives by Mr. Hansen of Idaho.

Folsom, J. K. Love and courtship. In R. Hill & H. Becker (Eds.), *Marriage and the Family,* Boston: D. C. Heath, 1948. Pp. 153–189.

Freedman, J. L. *Happy people.* New York: Harcourt Brace Jovanovich, 1978.

Freud, S. *Group psychotherapy and analysis of the ego.* J. Strachey, Trans. New York: Bantam Books, 1960.

Green, R. Sexual identity of 37 children raised by homosexual or transsexual parents. *American Journal of Psychiatry,* 1978, *135,* 692–697.

Hansen, G. L. Marital satisfaction and jealousy among men. *Psychological Reports,* 1983, 52, 363–366.

Harry, J., & Lovely, R. Gay marriages and communities of sexual orientation. *Alternative Lifestyles,* 1979, *2,* 177–200.

Hatkoff, T. S., & Lasswell, T. Male–female similarities and differences in conceptualizing love. In M. Cook & G. Wilson (Eds.), *Love and attraction.* Oxford: Pergamon Press, 1979. Pp. 221–227.

Hendrick, C., & Hendrick, S. *Liking, loving & relating.* Monterey, Calif.: Brooks/Cole, 1983.

Hirschberg, L. Cher wants to be taken seriously. *Rolling Stone,* March 29, 1984.

Huber, J., Gagnon, J., Keller, S., Lawson, R., Miller, P., & Simon, W. Report of the American Sociological Association's Task Group on Homosexuality. *American Sociologist,* 1982, *17,* 164–180.

Jay, K., & Young, A. *The gay report.* New York: Summit Books, 1979.

Jorgensen, S. R., & Gaudy, J. C. Self- disclosure and satisfaction in marriage: The relation examined. *Family Relations,* 1980, *29,* 281–288.

Kemper, T. D., & Bologh, R. W. What do you get when you fall in love? Some health status effects. *Sociology of Health and Illness,* 1981, *3,* 72–88.

Kinsey, A. C., Pomeroy, W. B., Martin, C. E., & Gebhard, P. H. *Sexual behavior in the human female.* Philadelphia: W. B. Saunders, 1953. Reprinted by permission of the Kinsey Institute for Research in Sex, Gender, and Reproduction, Inc. (Book reprinted in 1970 by Pocket Books).

Knox, D. Conceptions of love at three developmental levels. *Family Life Coordinator,* 1970, *19,* 151–157.

———. *What kind of love is yours?* Unpublished study, Department of Sociology, Anthropology, and Economics, East Carolina University, 1982.

———, & Sporakowski, M. J. Attitudes of college students toward love. *Journal of Marriage and the Family,* 1968, *30,* 638–642.

Lee, J. A. The styles of loving. *Psychology Today,* October 1974, 44–50. Reprinted from *Psychology Today* Magazine. Copyright © 1974 American Psychological Association.

Lewis, R. A., Kosac, E. B., Milardo, R. M., & Grosnick, W. A. Commitment in same-sex love relationships. *Alternative Lifestyles,* 1981, *4,* 22–42.

Liebowitz, M. *The chemistry of love.* Boston, Mass.: Little, Brown, 1983.

Lockhart, B. D. The "other" intimacy. *Family Perspective,* 1983, *17,* 35–39.

Lynch, J. J. *The broken heart: The medical consequences of loneliness in America.* New York: Basic Books, 1977.

Marmor, J. Overview: The multiple roots of homosexual behavior. In J. Marmor (Ed.), *Homosexual behavior: A modern reappraisal.* New York: Basic Books, 1980. Pp. 3–22.

Masters, W. H., & Johnson, V. E. *Human sexual response.* Boston: Little, Brown, 1966.

Meredith, N. The gay dilemma. *Psychology Today,* January 1984, pp. 56–62.

Money, J. *Love and sickness.* Baltimore: Johns Hopkins University Press, 1980.

Peele, S., & Brodsky, A. *Love and addiction.* New York: New American Library, 1976.

Peplau, L. A. What homosexuals want in relationships. *Psychology Today,* March 1981, pp. 28–38.

Petersen, J. R., Kretchmer, A., Hellis, B., Lever, J., & Hertz, B. The *Playboy* reader's sex survey, Part I. *Playboy,* January 1983a, p. 108 et passim.

Pines, A., & Aronson, E. Antecedents, correlates, and consequences of sexual jealousy. *Journal of Personality,* 1983, *51,* 108–109.

Raphael, S. M., & Robinson, M. K. The older lesbian: Love relationships and friendship patterns. *Alternative Lifestyles,* 1980, *3,* 207–229.

Reik, T. *Of love and lust.* New York: Farrar, Straus, & Cudahy, 1949.

Rettig, K. D., & Bubolz, M. M. Interpersonal resource exchanges as indicators of quality of marriage. *Journal of Marriage and the Family,* 1983, *45,* 3, 497–509.

Ridley, C. Quoted in D. Knox, Married love. *Modern Bride*, August/September 1983, p. 166 et passim.

Rubenstein, C. The modern art of courtly love. *Psychology Today*, July 1983, pp. 40–49.

Rubin, Z., Hill, C. T., Peplau, L. A., & Dunkel-Schetter, C. Self- disclosure in dating couples: Sex roles and the ethic of openness. *Journal of Marriage and the Family*, 1980, *42*, 305–318.

_____, Peplau, L. A., & Hill, C. T. Loving and leaving: Sex differences in romantic attachments. *Sex Roles*, 1981, *7*, 821–835.

Safilios-Rothschild, C. *Love, sex, and sex roles*. Englewood Cliffs, N.J.: Prentice-Hall, 1977.

Schacter, S. The interaction of cognitive and physiological determinants of emotional state. In Berkowitz L. (Ed.), *Advances in experimental social psychology*. New York: Academic Press, 1964. Pp. 49–80.

Suttie, I. D. *The origins of love and hate*. New York: Julian Press, 1952.

Tennov, D. *Love and limerence*. New York: Stein and Day, 1979.

Tillich, P. *Love, power, and justice*. New York: Oxford University Press, 1960.

Vannoy, R. *Sex without love: A philosophical exploration*. Buffalo, N.Y.: Prometheus Books, 1980.

Walster, E., & Walster, G. W. *A new look at love*. Reading, Mass: Addison-Wesley, 1978.

Women's Views Study. Sex, money, politics, family—where are women now? *Glamour*, January 1984, p. 144.

CHAPTER 4

Atwater, L. *The extramarital connection: Sex, intimacy, identity*. New York: Irvington Publishers, 1982.

Bell, R. R., and Coughey, K. Premarital sexual experience among college females, 1958, 1968, and 1978. *Family Relations*, 1980, *29*, 353–357.

Bermant, G. Sexual behavior: Hard times with the Coolidge Effect. In M. H. Siegel & H. P. Zeigler (Eds.), *Psychological research. The inside story*. New York: Harper & Row, 1976.

Blumstein, P., & Schwartz, P. *American couples*. New York: William Morrow, 1983.

Booth, A., Brinkerhoff, D. B., & White, L. K. The impact of parental divorce on courtship. *Journal of Marriage and the Family*, 1984, *46*, 85–94.

Boston Globe Newspaper Company, Washington Post Writer's Group, 1983.

Britton, T. Lenoir Community College, Kinston, N.C. *Personal communication*, 1984.

Connecticut Mutual Life report on American values in the '80s: The impact of belief. Hartford, Conn.: Connecticut Mutual Life Insurance Company, 1981.

Cook, K., Kretchmer, A., Nellis, B., Petersen, J. R., Lever, J., & Hertz, R. The *Playboy* reader's sex survey, Part 5. *Playboy*, October 1983, p. 92.

Davidson, Sr. J. and Darling, C. A. The stereotype of single women revisited: Sexual behavior and sexual satisfaction among professional women. Paper presented at the annual meeting of the Mid-South Sociological Association, Birmingham, 1983. Used with permission.

_____. Female sexual satisfaction: The effect of sexual experience. Paper presented at the Southern Sociological Society, Knoxville, Tennessee, 1984. Used by permission.

Diederen, I., & Rorer, L. Do attitudes and background influence college students' sexual behavior? Paper presented at the annual meeting of the American Psychological Association, Washington D.C., 1982. Used by permission.

Earle, J. R., & Perricone, P. J. *Correlates of permarital intercourse at a small southern university: Survey data for 1970, 1975, and 1981*. Unpublished manuscript, 1982. Used by permission.

Falwell, J. Falwell addresses nation live on moral and spiritual state of the union. *Moral Majority Report*, 1984, *5*(3),s-1.

Frank, E., & Enos, S. F. The lovelife of the American wife. *Ladies Home Journal*, February, 1983, p. 71.

Gallup Report-Mixed feelings expressed on Falwell group. Report No. 185, February 1981, pp. 38–39.

Graham, S. *Lecture to young men, on chastity, intended also for the serious consideration of parents and guardians*, 10th ed. Boston: C. H. Pierce, 1848.

Greenblat, C. S. The salience of sexuality in the early years of marriage. *Journal of Marriage and the Family*, 1983, *45*, 289–299.

Gregersen, E. *Sexual practices: The story of human sexuality*. New York: Franklin Watts, 1983.

Hassett, J. But that would be wrong. *Psychology Today*, December 1981, pp. 34–53.

Herold, E. S., & Way, L. Oral-genital sexual behavior in a sample of university females. *Journal of Sex Research*, 1983, *19*, 327–338.

Hill, C. T., Rubin, Z., & Peplau, L. A. Breakups before marriage: The end of 103 affairs. *Journal of Social Issues*, 1976, *32*, 147–168.

Hite, S. *The Hite report: A nationwide study of female sexuality.* New York: Dell, 1977.

Hudson, W. W., Murphy, G. J., & Nurius, P. S. A short-form scale to measure liberal vs. conservative orientations toward human sexual expression. *Journal of Sex Research*, 1983, *19*, 258–272.

Humphrey, F. G., & Strong, L. D. *A comparison of the effects of husband's versus wife's extramarital relationships upon the process and outcome of marital therapy.* Unpublished manuscript, University of Connecticut, 1978. Used with permission.

Kallen, D. J., Stephenson, J. J., & Doughty, A. The need to know: Recalled adolescent sources of sexual and contraceptive information and sexual behavior. *Journal of Sex Research*, 1983, *19*, 137–159.

Knox, D., & Wilson, K. Dating behaviors of university students. *Family Relations*, 1981, *30*, 83–86.

_____, & _____. Dating problems of university students. *College Student Journal*, 1983, *17*, 225–228.

Koblinsky, S. A., & Palmeter, J. G. Sex-role orientation, mother's expression of affection toward spouse, and college women's attitudes toward sexual behaviors. *Journal of Sex Research*, 1984, *20*, 32–43.

Levitt, E. E. Estimating the duration of sexual behavior: A laboratory analog study. *Archives of Sexual Behavior*, 1983, *12*, 329–335.

Moral Majority Report: What does Moral Majority believe about equal rights?, Censorship? Gays? March 1984, *5*(3), 21.

Negri, M. Moral majority versus humanism. *Humanist*, 1981, 41(2), 4–5.

Nurius, P. S., & Hudson, W. W. A sexual profile of social groups. *Journal of Sex Education and Therapy*, 1982, *8*(2), 15–30.

Notzer, N., Levran, D., Mashiach, S., & Soffer, S. Effect of reliogiosity on sex attitudes, experience and contraception among university students. *Journal of Sex and Marital Therapy*, 1984, *10*, 57–62.

Petersen, J. R., Kretchmer, A., Nellis, B., Lever, J., & Hertz, R. The *Playboy* readers' sex survey, Part 1. *Playboy*, January 1983a, p. 108.

_____, _____, _____, _____, _____. The *Playboy* reader's sex survey, Part 2. *Playboy*, March 1983b, p. 90.

Ratcliff, B., & Knox, D. University students' motivations for intercourse. Paper presented at the annual meeting of the Southern Sociological Society, Memphis, Tenn., 1982. Used with permission.

Reading, A. E., & Wiest, W. M. An analysis of self-reported sexual behavior in a sample of normal males. *Archives of Sexual Behavior*, 1984, *13*, 69–91.

Sack, A. R., Keller, J. F., & Hinkle, D. E. Premarital sexual intercourse: A test of the effects of peer group, religiosity, and sexual guilt. *Journal of Sex Research*, 1984, *20*, 168–185.

Schaefer, L. Women and extramarital affairs. *Sexuality Today*, 1981 *4*(13), 3.

Schmidt, G. Sex and society in the eighties. *Archives of Sexual Behavior*, 1982, *11*, 91–97.

Spanier, G. B., & Margolis, R. L. Marital separation and extramarital sexual behavior. *Journal of Sex Research*, 1983, 19, 23–48.

Symons, D. *The evolution of human sexuality.* New York: Oxford University Press, 1979.

Starr, B. D., & Weiner, M. B. *The Starr-Weiner report on sex and sexuality in the mature years.* New York: McGraw-Hill, 1982.

Tavris, C., & Sadd, S. *The Redbook report on female sexuality.* New York: Delacorte, 1977.

Thompson, A. P. Extramarital sex: A review of the research literature. *Journal of Sex Research*, 1983, *19*, 1–22.

_____. Emotional and sexual components of extramarital relations. *Journal of Marriage and the Family*, 1984, *46*, 35–42.

Tissot, S. A. (1766). *Onania, or a treatise upon the disorders produced by masturbation* (A. Hume, Trans.). London: J. Pridden. (Original work published in 1758).

Vaughn J. & Vaughn, P. *Beyond affairs.* Hilton Head, S.C.: Dialog Press, 1980.

Weiss, D. L. Affective reactions of women to their initial experience of coitus. *Journal of Sex Research*, 1983, *19*, 209–237.

Wheeler, J., & Kilmann, P. R. Comarital sexual behavior: Individual and relationship variables. *Archives of Sexual Behavior*, 1983, *12*, 295–306.

Women's Views Study. Sex, money, politics, family—Where are women now? *Glamour*, January 1984, p. 144.

Yablonsky, L. *The extra-sex factor: Why over half of America's married men play around.* New York: Times Books, 1979.

Yankelovich. D. The public mind/stepchildren of the moral majority. *Psychology Today,* November 1981, pp. 5–10.

Zelnik, M., & Kantner, J. F. Sexual and contraceptive experience of young unmarried women in the United States, 1976 and 1971. *Family Planning Perspectives,* 1977, *9,* 55–71.

_____, & _____. Sexual activity, contraceptive use and pregnancy among metropolitan-area teenagers: 1971–1979. *Family Planning Perspectives,* 1980, *12,* 230–237.

_____, & Shah, F. K. First intercourse among young Americans. *Family Planning Perspectives,* 1983, *15,* 64–70.

_____, Koenig, M. A., & Kim, Y. J. Sources of prescription contraceptives and subsequent pregnancy among young women. *Family Planning Perspectives,* 1984, *16,* 6–13.

CHAPTER 5

Cargan, L. Singles: An examination of two stereotypes. *Family Relations,* 1981, *30*(3), 377–385.

Connecticut Mutual Life Report on American Values in the 80's: The impact of belief. Hartford, Conn.: Connecticut Mutual Life Insurance Company, 1981.

Etaugh, C., & Malstrom, J. The effect of marital status on person perception. *Journal of Marriage and the Family,* 1981, *43*(4), 801–805.

Gardner, H. *The children of prosperity: Thirteen modern American communes.* New York: St. Martin's Press, 1978.

Glick, P. C. How American families are changing. *American Demographics,* 1984, *6*(1), 20–25.

Jansen, H. A. M. Communes. *Alternative Lifestyles,* 1980, *3*(3), 255–277.

Kephart, W. M. *Extraordinary groups* (2nd ed). New York: St. Martin's Press, 1982.

Levine, S. V. Radical departures. *Psychology Today,* August 1984, 20–27.

Mueller, C. W., & Campbell, B. G. Female occupational achievement and marital status: A research note. *Journal of Marriage and the Family.,* 1977, *39*(3), 587–593.

Pearlin, L. I., & Johnson, J. S. Marital status, life-strains, and depression. *American Sociological Review* 1977, *42,* 704–715.

Shaver, P. & Rubenstein, C. Healthy loners. *Psychology Today,* January 1980, pp. 27, 95.

Somers, A. R. Marital status, health, and use of health services: An old relationship revisited. *Journal of the American Medical Association,* 1979, *241*(17), 1818–1822.

Stein, P. J. *Single.* Englewood Cliffs, New Jersey: Prentice-Hall, 1976.

_____. Understanding single adulthood. In P. J. Stein (Ed.), *Single life: Unmarried adults in social context.* New York: St. Martin's Press, 1981.

Stewart, W. A look down the road. *Communities: Journal of Cooperation,* 1984, (61), Winter, 41–43.

Stolk, Y., & Brotherton, P. Attitudes towards single women. *Sex Roles,* 1981, *7*(1), 73–78.

Statistical Abstract of the United States: 1984 (104th ed.). Washington, D.C.: U.S. Bureau of the Census, 1983.

U.S. Bureau of the Census. Lifetime earnings for men and women in the United States: 1979. *Current Population Reports,* Series P-60, No. 139. Washington, D.C.: U.S. Government Printing Office, 1983.

Van Deusen, E. L. *Contract cohabitation.* New York: Grove Press, 1974.

_____. Personal communication, 1984. Material used by permission.

Ward, R. A. *The aging experience.* New York: Harper and Row, 1984.

CHAPTER 6

Booth, A., Brinkerhoff, D. B., & White, L. K. The impact of parental divorce on courtship. *Journal of Marriage and the Family,* 1984, *46,* 85–94.

Bytheway, W. R. The variation with age of age differences in marriage. *Journal of Marriage and the Family,* 1981, *43*(4), 923–927.

Daniel, H. J. The brains of war and peace: A sexual dimorphism hypothesis. *Proceedings of the Ninth Annual Phi Kappa Phi Symposium,* East Carolina University, Greenville, N.C., 1984. Used by permission of H. J. Daniel.

Harriman, L. C. Application of mate-selection theories in the classroom. *Family Perspective,* 1982, *16*(2), 91–92.

Janda, L. H., O'Gray, K. E., and Barnhart, S. A. Effects of sexual attitudes and physical attractiveness on person perception of men and women. *Sex Roles*, 1981, 7(2) 189–199.

Jedlicka, D. Formal mate selection networks in the United States. *Family Relations*, 1980, 29(2), 199–203.

_____. Indirect parental influence on mate choice: A test of the psychoanalytic theory. *Journal of Marriage and the Family*, 1984, 46, 65–70.

Kellogg, M. A. Could it be love at first cassette? *TV Guide*, July 2, 1982, pp. 33–36.

Knox, D., & Wilson, K. Dating behaviors of university students. *Family Relations*, 1981, 30, 255–258.

_____, & _____. Dating problems of university students. *College Student Journal*, 1983, 17, 225–228.

Kurian, G. (Ed.). *Cross-cultural perspectives of mate selection and marriage.* Westport, Conn.: Greenwood Press, 1979.

Lee, G., & Stone, L. H. Mate-selection systems and criteria: Variation according to family structure. *Journal of Marriage and the Family*, 1980, 42, 319–326.

Liddy, G. G. *Will.* New York: St. Martin's Press, 1980.

Lloyd, S. A., Cate, R. M., & Henton, J. M. Predicting premarital relationship stability: A methodological refinement. *Journal of Marriage and the Family*, 1984, 46, 71–76.

Meyer, J. P., & Pepper, S. Need compatibility and marital adjustment in young married couples. *Journal of Personality and Social Psychology*, 1977, 35(5), 331–342.

National Center for Health Statistics. Advance report of final marriage statistics, 1981. *Monthly Vital Statistics Report*, 32(11), Supp. DHHS Pub. No. (PHS) 84–1120. Hyattsville, Md.: U.S. Public Health Service, February 29, 1984.

Nye, F. I. Family mini theories as special instances of choice and exchange theory. *Journal of Marriage and the Family*, 1980, 42(3), 479–489.

Stephens, W. N. *The family in cross-cultural perspective.* Washington, D.C.: University Press of America, 1982.

Waller, W., & Hill, R. *The family: A dynamic interpretation.* New York: Holt, Rinehart and Winston, 1951.

Warner, L. A. Sociobiology and mate selection among humans. Paper presented at the Seventh Annual Alpha Kappa Delta Sociological Research Symposium, Richmond, Va., 1982.

Winch, R. F. The theory of complementary needs in mate selection: Final results on the test of the general hypothesis. *American Sociological Review*, 1955, 20, 552–555.

Woodfin, M. H., & Tinling, J. (Eds.). *Another secret diary of William Bryd of Westover, 1739–1741.* Richmond, Va.: 1942.

CHAPTER 7

Booth, A., Brinkerhoff, D. B., & White, L. K. The impact of parental divorce on courtship. *Journal of Marriage and the Family*, 1984, 46, 85–94.

DeMaris, A., & Leslie, G. R. Cohabitation with the future spouse: Its influence upon marital satisfaction and communication. *Journal of Marriage and the Family*, 1984, 46, 77–84.

Glick, P. C. How American families are changing. *American Demographics*, 1984, 6(1), 20–25.

Jacques, J.M., & Chason, K. J. Cohabitation: Its impact on marital success. *Family Relations*, 1979, 28(1), 35–39.

Mace, D. What is marriage beyond living together? Some Quaker reactions to cohabitation. *Family Relations*, 1981, 30(1), 17–20.

Macklin, E. D. Nontraditional family forms: A decade of research. *Journal of Marriage and the Family*, 1980, 42(4), 905–922.

_____. Education for choice: Implications of alternatives for family life education. *Family Relations*, 1981, 30(4), 567–577.

Markowski, E. M., & Johnston, M. J. Behavior, temperament, perceived temperament and idealization of cohabitating couples who married. *International Journal of Sociology*, 1980, 10, 115–125.

Martin, D., & Martin, M. Selected attitudes toward marriage and family life among college students. *Family Relations*, 1984, 33, 293–300.

Myricks, N. Palimony: The impact of Marvin V. Marvin. *Family Relations*, 1980, 29(2), 210–215.

Ratcliff, B. University students' motivations for intercourse. D. Knox (Ed.), In *Courtship, marriage, and the family.* Greenville, N.C.: Accucopy, (1983) pp. 24–28.

Ridley, C. A., Peterman, D. J. & Avery, A. W. Cohabitation: Does it make for a better marriage? *Family Coordinator*, 1978, 27, 129–136.

Risman, B. J., Hill, C. T., Rubin, Z. & Peplau, L. A. Living together in college: Implications for court-ship. *Journal of Marriage and the Family*, 1981, *43*(1), 77–83.

Spanier, G. B. Married and unmarried cohabitation in the United States: 1980. *Journal of Marriage and the Family*, 1983, *45*, 277–288.

Statistical Abstract of the United States:1984, 104th ed. Washington, D.C.: U.S. Bureau of the Census, 1983.

Toffler, A. *Future shock*. New York: Random House, 1979.

———. *The third wave*. New York: William Morrow, 1980.

Turner, L. *Lana*. New York: E. P. Dutton, 1982.

Watson, R. E. L. Premarital cohabitation vs. traditional courtship: Their effects on subsequent marital adjustment. *Family Relations*, 1983, *32*, 139–147.

Weitzman, L. J. *The marriage contract: Spouses, lovers, and the law*. New York: Free Press, 1981.

CHAPTER 8

Adams, B. N., & Cromwell, R. E. Morning and night people in the family: A preliminary statement. *The Family Coordinator* 1978, *27*(1), 5–13.

Bahr, S. J., Chappell, C. B., & Leigh, G. K. Age at marriage, role enactment, role consensus, and marital satisfaction. *Journal of Marriage and the Family*, 1983, *45*, (4), 795–803.

Carlson, E., & Stinson, K. Motherhood, marriage timing, and marital stability: A research note. *Social Forces*, 1982, *61*(1), 258–267.

Darnley, F. Periodicity in the family. *Family Relations*, 1981, *30*(1), 31–37.

Glick, P. C. How American families are changing. *American Demographics*, 1984, *6*(1), 20–27.

Hill, C. T., Rubin, Z., & Peplau, L. A. Breakups before marriage: The end of 103 affairs. *Journal of Social Issues*, 1976, *32*(1), 147–168.

Kraus, J. Shotgun weddings: Trends in the sociopathology of marriage. *Australian and New Zealand Journal of Psychiatry*, 1977, *11*, 259–264.

Landers, A. If you had it to do all over again, would you marry the same person? *Family Circle*, July 26, 1977.

Lasswell, M. E. Is there a best age to marry? An interpretation. *Family Coordinator*, 1974, *23*, 237–242.

Leigh, G. K., Holman, T. B., & Burr, W. R. An empirical test of sequence in Murstein's SVR theory of mate selection. *Family Relations*, 1984, *33*, 225–231.

Martin, D. & Martin, M. Selected attitudes toward marriage and family life among college students. *Family Relations*, 1984, *33*, 293–300.

Marriage and Divorce Today. For effective pre-marital programs use married couples. April 16, 1984, pp. 1, 3.

Mitchell, M. *Gone with the wind*. New York: Macmillan, 1977.

Rosenblatt, P. C., & Keller, L. O. Economic vulnerability and economic stress in farm couples. *Family Relations*, 1983, *32*, 567–573.

Rubin, Z., Peplau, L. A., & Hill C. T. Loving and leaving: Sex differences in romantic attachments. *Sex Roles*, 1981, *7*, 821–835.

Sammons, R. A., Jr. Personal communication. Charlottesville, VA, 1984.

Schumm, W. R., & Denton, W. Trends in premarital counseling. *Journal of Marital and Family Therapy*, 1979, *5*(4), 23–32.

Surra, C. A., & Wareham, J. V. Turning points in the decision to marry. Poster session at the National Council on Family Relations, Milwaukee, October 1981.

U.S. Bureau of the Census. Lifetime earnings estimates for men and women in the United States: 1979. *Current Population Reports*, Series P-60, No. 139. Washington, D.C.: U.S. Government Printing Office, 1983.

Vander Mey, B. J., & Rosher, J. H. Marriage contracting: Sex role liberation? Paper presented to the Southern Sociological Society, April 1981.

Walster, E., Walster, G. W. & Traupmann, J., Equity and premarital sex. *Journal of Personality and Social Psychology*, 1978, *36*(1), 82–92.

White, G. L. Inequality of emotional involvement, power, and jealousy in romantic couples. Paper presented to the American Psychological Association, 1977.

Wright, Jack W., Jr., Attorney at law. Personal communication. Monroe, L., 1984.

Zelnik, M., & Kantner, J. F. Sexual activity, contraceptive use and pregnancy among metropolitan-area teenagers: 1971–1979. *Family Planning Perspectives*, 1980, *12*, 230–237.

Adams, J. R., & Rubin, A. M. *Outcomes of sexually open marriages: A five year follow-up.* Unpublished study, 1984. Used by permission of Dr. Arline M. Rubin, Brooklyn College, New York.

Alder, C. The timing of marriage and educational attainment. Paper presented to the American Sociological Association, San Francisco, 1982.

Ammons, P., & Stinnett, N. The vital marriage: A closer look. *Family Relations,* 1980, *29*(1), 37–42.

Aschenbrenner, J., & Carr, C. H. Conjugal relationships in the context of the black extended family. *Alternative Lifestyles,* 1980, *3*(4), 463–484.

Ball, R. Marital quality in black families. Paper presented to the National Council on Family Relations, Washington, D.C., 1982.

_____, & Robbins, L. Marital status family/household structure and life satisfaction of black women. *Social Problems.* 1983.

Berardo, F. M., Vera, H. & Berardo, D. H. Age-discrepant marriages. *Medical Aspects of Human Sexuality.* In press.

Berkove, G. F. Perceptions of husband support by returning women students. *Family Relations,* 1979, *28*(4), 451–457.

Bumpass, L. L., & Sweet, J. A. Differentials in marital instability: 1970. *American Sociological Review,* 1972, 37, 754–766.

Buunk, B. Jealousy in sexually open marriages. *Alternative Lifestyles,* 1981, *4*(3), 357–372.

Cargan, L. Singles: An examination of two stereotypes. *Family Relations,* 1981, *30*(3), 377–385.

Cuber, J. F., & Harroff, P. B. *Sex and the significant Americans.* Baltimore, Md.: Penguin Books, 1965.

Darling, J. Late-marrying bachelors. In Peter J. Stein (Ed.), *Single Life.* New York: St. Martin's Press, 1981. Pp. 34–40.

Egelman, W., & Berlage, G. Catholic college students' attitudes toward interfaith marriage: An exploratory study. Paper presented to the Southern Sociological Society, Memphis, 1982.

Gary, L., & Leashore, B. Dyadic relationships as perceived by black men. Paper presented to the National Council on Family Relations, Washington, D.C., 1982.

Glick, P. C., & Spanier, G. B. Married and unmarried cohibitation in the United States. *Journal of Marriage and the Family,* 1980, *42*(1), 19–30.

Glenn, N. D. Interreligious marriage in the United States: Patterns and recent trends. *Journal of Marriage and the Family,* 1982, *44*(3), 555–566.

Gray-Little, B. G. Marital quality and power processes among black couples. *Journal of Marriage and the Family,* 1982, *44*(3), 633–646.

Harrington, W. What color are our children? *Washington Post Magazine,* October 17, 1982, p. 10 et passim.

Johnson, M. P., & Leslie, L. Couple involvement and network structure: A test of dyadic withdrawal hypothesis. *Social Psychology Quarterly,* 1982, *45*(1), 34–43.

Kelly, S. Returning to college. *Family Relations,* 1982, *31*(2), 287–294.

Knapp, J. J. An exploratory study of seventeen sexually open marriages. *Journal of Sex Research,* 1976, *12*, 206–219.

_____, & Whitehurst, R. N. Sexually open marriage relationships: Issues and prospects. In B. I. Murstein (Ed.), *Exploring intimate lifestyles.* New York: Springer, 1978, Pp. 35–52.

L'Abate, L., & L'Abate, B. L. Marriage: The dream and the reality. *Family Relations,* 1981, *30*(1), 131–136.

Landry, B., & Jendrek, M. P. The employment of wives in middle-class black families. *Journal of Marriage and the Family,* 1978, *40*(4), 787–797.

LaPatra, J. *The age factor: Love, sex and friendship in age-different relationships.* New York: M. Evans, 1980.

Ma, Li. Family ties as related to academic performance of college students. *College Student Journal,* 1983, *17*, 308–316.

Martin, D., & Martin, M. Selected attitudes toward marriage and family life among college students. *Family Relations,* 1984, *33*, 293–300.

McAdoo, H. P. Stress absorbing systems in black families. *Family Relations,* 1982, *31*(4), 478–488.

McRoy, S. and Fisher, V. Marital adjustment of graduate student couples. *Family Relations,* 1982, *31*(1), 37–41.

National Center for Health Statistics. Births, marriages, divorces, and deaths for November 1983. *Monthly Vital Statistics Report, 32*(11): DHHS Pub. No. (Phs) 84-1120. Hyattsville, Md.: U.S. Public Health Service, February 17, 1984.

O'Neill, N., & O'Neill, G. *Open marriage: A new life style for couples.* New York: Avon Books, 1972.

Peabody, S. A. Alternative lifestyles to monogamous marriage: Variants of normal behavior in psychotherapy clients. *Family Relations,* 1982, *31*(3), 425–434.

Porterfield, E. Black-American intermarriage in the United States. *Marriage & Family Review,* 1982, *5,* 17–34.

Price-Bonham, S., & Balswick, J. O. The noninstitutions: Divorce, desertion, and remarriage. *Journal of Marriage and the Family,* 1980, *42*(4), 959–972.

Quinn, N. "Commitment" in American marriage: A cultural analysis. *American Ethnologist,* 1982, *9,* 775–798.

Risman, B. J., Hill, C. T., Rubin, Z. & Peplau, L. A., Living together in college: Implications for courtship. *Journal of Marriage and the Family,* 1981, *43*(1), 77–83.

Rubin, A. M. Sexually open versus sexually exclusive marriage: A comparison of dyadic adjustment, *Alternative Lifestyles,* Winter, 1982, *5,* 101–108. (Dr. Arline M. Rubin, Professor, Brooklyn College, Bedford Ave. & Ave. H, Brooklyn, N.Y. 11210.

Spanier, G. B., & Glick, P. C. Mate selection differentials between whites and blacks in the United States. *Social Forces,* 1980, *58*(3), 707–725.

Staples, R. Race and marital status: An overview. In H. P. McAdoo's (ed.) *Black families.* Beverly Hills, California: Sage Publications, 1981, 173–175.

Statistical Abstract of the United States: 1984, 104th ed. Washington, D.C.: U.S. Bureau of the Census, 1983.

Stinnett, N., Sanders, G., DeFrain, J. & Parkhurst, A. A nationwide study of families who perceive themselves as strong. *Family Perspective,* 1982, *16*(1), 15–22.

_____. Interracial married couples, 1970 to 1980. *Statistical abstract of the United States,* 1981, 102d ed., p. 41.

U.S. Bureau of the Census. School enrollment—Social and economic characteristics of students: 1979. *Current Population Reports,* Series P-20, No. 360. Washington, D.C.: U.S. Government Printing Office, 1981.

Van Meter, M. J. S., & Agronow, S. J. The stress of multiple roles: The case for role strain among married college women. *Family Relations,* 1982, *31*(1), 131–138.

Ward, R. A. The never married in later life. *Journal of Gerontology,* 1979, *34,* 861–869.

CHAPTER 10

Aldous, J. From dual-earner to dual-career families and back again. *Journal of Family Issues,* 1981, *2*(2), 115–125.

American Council of Life Insurance. *The Economic Value of a Housewife.* Washington, D.C., 1983.

Atkinson, M. P. and Boles, J. WASP (Wives as Senior Partners) *Journal of Marriage and the Family,* in press.

Bacall, L. *By myself.* New York: Alfred A. Knopf, 1979. P. 172.

Bahr, S. J., & Day, R. D. Sex role attitudes, female employment, and marital satisfaction. *Journal of Comparative Family Studies,* 1978, *9*(1), 53–67.

Beer, W. R. *Househusbands.* South Hadley, Mass.: Bergin & Garvey, 1984.

Berardo, D. H. Dual-career families: A comparison with dual-occupation and traditional families. Paper presented at the National Council on Family Relations, Washington, D.C., 1982.

Bird, C. *The two paycheck marriage.* New York: Rawson, Wade, 1979.

Bird, G. W., Gird, G. A., & Scruggs, M. Determinants of family task sharing: A study of husbands and wives. *Journal of Marriage and the Family,* 1984, *46,* 345–355.

_____, & Ratcliff, B. Children's participation in family work: An analysis of parent data. Manuscript under review, 1984.

Blumstein, P., & Schwartz, P. *American couples.* New York: William Morrow, 1983.

Chafe, W. H. Looking backward in order to look forward: Women, work, and social values in America. In J. M. Kreps (Ed.), *Women and the American economy: A look to the 1980's.* Englewood Cliffs, N.J.: Prentice-Hall, 1976. Pp. 6–30.

Condran, J. G., & Bode, J. G. Rashomon, working wives, and family division of labor: Middleton, 1980. *Journal of Marriage and the Family,* 1982, *44*(2), 421–426.

Elman, M. R., & Gilbert, L. A. Coping strategies for role conflict in married professional women with children. *Family Relations,* 1984, *33,* 317–327.

Ferber, M. A. Labor market participation of young married women: Causes and effects. *Journal of Marriage and the Family,* 1982, *44*(2), 457–468.

Garbarino, J. "Latchkey" children: How much of a problem? *Education Digest*, February 1981, pp. 14–16.

Gerber, L. A. *Married to their careers.* New York: Tavistock Publications, 1983.

Gilbert, L. A., Holahan, C. K., & Manning, L. Coping with conflict between professional and maternal roles. *Family Relations*, 1981, 30(3), 419–426.

Gross, H. E. Dual- career couples who live apart: Two types. *Journal of Marriage and the Family*, 1980, 42(3), 567–576.

Houseknecht, S. K., & Macke, A. S. Combining marriage and career: The marital adjustment of professional women. *Journal of Marriage and the Family*, 1981, 43(3), 651–661.

Locksley, A. On the effects of wives' employment on marital adjustment and companionship. *Journal of Marriage and the Family*, 1980, 42(2), 337–346.

Long, L., & Long, T. *The handbook for latchkey children and their parents.* New York: Arbor House, 1983.

Maiolo, J. Department of Sociology, Anthropology, and Economics, East Carolina University. Personal communication, 1982.

Markham, W. T., Macken, P. O., Bonjean, C. M. & Corder, J. A. A note on sex, geographic mobility, and career advancement. *Social Forces*, 1983, 61, 1138–1146.

Mathis, J. L. Physician-physician marriages. *Medical Aspects of Human Sexuality*, January 1984, pp. 185–196.

Newsweek. The superwoman squeeze. May 19, 1980, pp. 72–79.

Nichols, S. Y., & Metzen, E. J. Impact of wife's employment upon husband's housework. *Journal of Family Issues*, 1982, 3(2), 199–216.

Piotrkowski, C. S., & Crits-Christoph, P. Women's jobs and family adjustment. *Journal of Family Issues*, 1981, 2(2), 126–147.

Poloma, M. M., Pendleton, B. F., & Garland, T. N. Reconsidering the dual-career marriage: A longitudinal approach. *Journal of Family Issues*, 1981, 2(2), 205–224.

Psychology Today. Dial-a friend. June 1983, pp. 76–77.

Presser, H. B., & Cain, V. S. Shift work among dual-earner couples with children. *Science*, 1983, 219, 876–979.

Rank, M. R. Determinants of conjugal influence in wives' employment decision making. *Journal of Marriage and the Family*, 1982, 44(3), 591–604.

Riemer, J. W., & Bridwell, L. M. How women survive in non-traditional occupations. *Free Inquiry in Creative Sociology*, 1982, 10(2), 153–158.

Robey, B., & Russell, C. A portrait of the American worker. *American Demographics*, 1984, 6(3), 17–21.

Rosenthal, D., & Hansen, J. The impact of maternal employment of children's perceptions of parents and personal development. *Sex Roles.*, 1981, (6), 593–598.

Rubenstein, C. Real men don't earn less than their wives. *Psychology Today*, November 1982, pp. 36–41.

Rubin, Z. Are working wives hazardous to their husband's mental health? *Psychology Today*, May 1983, pp. 70–72.

Sharda, B. D., & Nangle, B. Marital effects on occupational attainment. *Journal of Family Issues*, 1981, 2(1), 148–163.

Simpson, I. H., & England, P. Conjugal work roles and marital solidarity. *Journal of Family Issues*, 1981, 2(2), 180–204.

Smith, L. The relationship of interpersonal needs, role-of-work definitions, and occupational prestige to marital structure in dual-earner couples. Paper presented at the National Council on Family Relations, Washington, D.C., 1982.

Thornton, A., & Freedman, D. The changing American family. *Population Bulletin*, 1983, 38, 4.

Tittle, C. K. *Careers and family: Sex roles and adolescent life plans.* Beverly Hills, Calif.: Sage, 1981.

Trimberger, R., & MacLean, M. J. Maternal employment: The child's perspective. *Journal of Marriage and the Family*, 1982, 44(2), 457–468.

Tutchings, T. R. *Coping with the credit crisis.* Austin: Hogg Foundation for Mental Health, University of Texas, 1980.

U.S. Bureau of the Census. Wives who earn more than their husbands. *Special Demographic Analyses*, CDS-80-9. Washington, D.C.: U.S. Government Printing Office, 1983a.

_____. Lifetime earnings estimates for men and women in the United States: 1979, *Current Population Reports*, P-60, No. 139. Washington, D.C.: U.S. Government Printing Office, 1983b.

Yogev, S. Do professional women have egalitarian marital relationships? *Journal of Marriage and the Family*, 1981, 43(4), 865–872.

Alford, R. D. Intimacy and disputing styles within kin and nonkin relationships. *Journal of Family Issues*, 1982, *3*, 361–374.

Balswick, J. Explaining inexpressive males: A relpy to L'Abate. *Family Relations*, 1980, *29*, 231–233.

Bateson, G. *Steps to an ecology of mind.* New York: Ballantine, 1972.

Bavelas, J. B., & Segal, L. Family systems theory: Background and implications. *Journal of Communication*, 1982, *32*(3), 99–107.

Becnel, H., & Levy, L. Marriage encounter program effect on marital relations. *Inquiry in Creative Sociology*, 1983, *11*(1), 19–22.

Bell, D. C., Chafetz, J. S., & Horn, L. H. Marital conflict resolution: A study of strategies and outcomes. *Journal of Family Issues*, 1982, *3*, 111–132.

Bienvenu, M. J., Sr. Measurement of marital communication. *Family Coordinator*, 1970, *19*, 26–48.

Brandt, A. Avoiding couple karate: Lessons in the marital arts. *Psychology Today*, October 1982, pp. 38–43.

Cole, C. L., Cole, A. L., & Dean, D. G., Emotional maturity and marital adjustment: A decade replication. *Journal of Marriage and the Family*, 1980, *42*, 533–539.

Davis, E. C., Hovestadt, A. J., Piercy, F. P. & Cochran, S. W., Effects of weekend and weekly marriage enrichment program formats. *Family Relations*, 1982, *31*, 85–90.

Feldman, H. A comparison of intentional parents and intentionally childless couples. *Journal of Marriage and the Family*, 1981, *43*, 593–600.

Ford, J. D., Bashford, M. B., & DeWitt, K. N. Three approaches to marital enrichment: Toward optimal matching of participants and interventions. *Journal of Sex & Marital Therapy*, 1984, *10*, 41–48.

Galvin, K. M., & Brommel, B. J. *Family communication: Cohesion and change.* Glenview, Ill.: Scott, Foresman, 1982.

Garland, D. R. Training married couples in listening skills: Effects on behavior, perceptual accuracy and marital adjustment. *Family Relations*, 1981, *30*, 297–306.

Glenn, N. D., & McLanahan, S. Children and marital happiness: A further specification of the relationship. *Journal of Marriage and the Family*, 1982, *44*, 63–72.

Gottman, J. M. Emotional responsiveness in marital conversations. *Journal of Communication*, 1982, *32*(3), 108–120.

_____, Notarius, C., Gorso, J., and Markman, H. *A couple's guide to communication.* Champaign, Ill.: Research Press, 1976.

_____, & Porterfield, A. L. Communicative competence in the nonverbal behavior of married couples. *Journal of Marriage and the Family.* 1981, *43*, 817–824.

Hansen, G. L. Marital adjustment and conventionalization: A reexamination. *Journal of Marriage and the Family*, 1981, *43*, 855–863.

Hayes, M. P., Stinnett, N., & DeFrain, J. Learning about marriage from the divorced. *Journal of Divorce*, 1981, *4*, 23–29.

Hennon, C. B. Conflict management within cohabitation relationships. *Alternative Lifestyles*, 1981, *4*, 467–486.

Hof, L., & Miller, W. R. *Marriage enrichment.* Bowie, Md.: Robert J. Brady, 1981.

Honeycutt, J. M., Wilson, C., & Parker, C. Effects of sex and degrees of happiness on perceived styles of communication in and out of the marital relationship. *Journal of Marriage and the Family*, 1982, *44*, 395–406.

Joanning, H. The long term effects of the couple communication program. *Journal of Marital and Family Therapy*, 1983, *8*, 463–468.

Knox, D., & Wilson, K. Dating problems of university students. *College Student Journal*, 1983, *17*, 225–228.

Kramarae, C. *Women and men speaking.* New York: Newbury House, 1981.

Krueger, D. L., & Smith, P. Decision-making patterns of couples: A sequential analysis. *Journal of Communication*, 1982, *32*(3), 121–134.

Lederer, W. J., & Jackson, D. D. *The mirages of marriage.* New York: W. W. Norton, 1968.

Lester, M. E., & Doherty, W. J. Couple's long-term evaluations of their marriage encounter experience. *Journal of Marriage and the Family*, 1983, *9*, 183–188.

Locksley, A. Social class and martial attitudes and behavior. *Journal of Marriage and the Family*, 1982, *44*, 427–440.

Mace, D., & Mace, V. We open up our marriage. *Wellness Perspectives*, 1984, *1*(2), 21–29.

Markowski, E. M., and Cain, H. I. Live marital and family therapy supervision: A model for community mental health centers. *Clinical Supervisor*, 1983, *1*(3), 37–46.

Martin, D., & Martin, M. Selected attitudes toward marriage and family life among college students. *Family Relations*, 1984, *33*, 293–300.

Menaghan, E. G. Coping with marital problems: Assessing effectiveness. Paper presented at the annual meeting of the American Sociological Association, 1982. Used with permission.

Notarius, C. I., & Johnson, J. S. Emotional expression in husbands and wives. *Journal of Marriage and the Family*, 1982, *44*, 483–489.

Olson, D. H., McGuffin, H. I., and associates. *Families: What Makes Them Work*. Beverly Hills: Sage, 1983. Used with permission of D. H. Olson.

Powell, G. S., & Wampler, K. S. Marriage enrichment participants: Levels of marital satisfaction. *Family Relations*, 1982, *31*, 389–393.

Psychology Today, Embarrassing fact. December 1982, p. 84.

Rhyne, D. Bases of martial satisfaction among men and women. *Journal of Marriage and the Family*, 1981, *43*, 941–955.

Scoresby, A. L. *The marriage dialogue*. Reading, Mass.: Addison-Wesley, 1977.

Sherman, M. A., & Haas, A. Man to man, woman to woman. *Psychology Today*, June 1984, pp. 72–73.

Spanier, G. B. Measuring dyadic adjustment: New scales for assessing the quality of marriage and similar dyads. *Journal of Marriage and the Family*, 1976, *38*, 15–28.

Stedman, J. M. Marriage encounter: An "insiders" consideration of recent critiques. *Family Relations*, 1982, *31*, 123–130.

Stuart, R. B. *Helping couples change*. New York: Guilford Press, 1980.

Tiggle, R. B., Peters, M. D., Kelley, H. H., and Vincent, J. Correlational and discrepancey indices of understanding and their relation to marital satisfaction. *Journal of Marriage and the Family*, 1982, *44*, 209–216.

Warmbrod, M. T. Alternative generation in marital problem solving. *Family Relations*, 1982, *31*, 503–511.

Watzlawick, P., Beavin, J., & Jackson, D. *Pragmatics of human communication*. New York: Norton, 1967.

Wolcott, I. Marriage counseling services: Priorities and policy. *Policy Background Paper, No. 3*. Institute of Family Studies, March, 1984.

Zilbergeld, B. *The shrinking of America, Myths of psychological change*. Boston: Little, Brown, 1983.

CHAPTER 12

Barth, R. P., Blythe, B. J., Schinke, S. P., & Schilling, R. F., II. Self- control training with maltreating parents. *Child Welfare*, 1983, *72*, 313–324.

Bernard, M. L., & Bernard, J. L. Violent intimacy: The family as a model for love relationships. *Family Relations*, 1983, *32*, 283–286.

Brodbelt, S. College dating and aggression. *College Student Journal*, 1983, *17*, 273–277.

Burgess, R. L., & Garbarino, J. Doing what comes naturally? An evolutionary perspective on child abuse? In D. Finkelhor, R. J. Gelles, G. T. Hotaling, & M. A. Straus (Eds.), *The dark side of families: Current family violence research*. Beverly Hills, Calif.: Sage, 1983. Pp. 88–101.

Cate, R. M., Henton, J. M., Koval, J., Christopher, F. S., & Lloyd, S. Premarital abuse: A social psychological perspective. *Journal of Family Issues*, 1982, *3*(1), 79–90.

Dobash, R. E., & Dobash, R. *Violence against wives: A case against patriarchy*. New York: Free Press, 1979.

Downing, L. C. Substantiated reports of child abuse and neglect. *Free Inquiry in Creative Sociology*, 1982, *10*, 197–201.

Eastman, P. Elders under siege. *Psychology Today*, January 1984, p. 30.

Engfer, A., & Schneewind, K. A. Causes and consequences of harsh parental punishment. *Child Abuse & Neglect: The International Journal*, 1982, *6*, 129–140.

Finkelhor, D. Sex among siblings: A survey on prevalence, variety and effects. *Archives of Sexual Behavior*, 1980, *9*, 171–194.

———. Removing the child—Prosecuting the offender in cases of child abuse: Evidence from the national reporting system for child abuse and neglect. *Child Abuse & Neglect: The International Journal*, 1983, *7*, 195–206.

———, & Yllo, K. Forced sex in marriage: A preliminary research report. *Crime and Delinquency*, July 1982, Pp. 459–478.

_____, & _____. Rape in marriage: A sociological view. In D. Finkelhor, R. J. Gelles, G. T. Hotaling, & M. A. Straus (Eds.), *The dark side of families: Current family violence research*. Beverly Hills, Calif.: Sage, 1983. Pp. 119–130.

Garbarino, J., & Ebata, A. The significance of ethnic and cultural differences in child maltreatment. *Journal of Marriage and the Family*, 1983, *45*, 773–783.

Giarretto, H. A comprehensive child sexual abuse treatment program. *Child Abuse & Neglect: The International Journal*, 1982, *6*, 263–278.

Gordon, L., & O'Keefe, P. Incest as a form of family violence: Evidence from historical case records. *Journal of Marriage and the Family*, 1984, *46*, 27–34.

Helfer, R. E. A review of the literature on the prevention of child abuse and neglect. *Child Abuse & Neglect: The International Journal*, 1982, *6*, 251–262.

Henton, J., Cate, R., Koval, J., Lloyd, S., & Christopher, S. Romance and violence in dating relationships. *Journal of Family Issues*, 1983, *4*, 467–482.

Herrenkohl, E. C., Herrenkohl, R. C., & Toedter, L. J. Perspectives on the intergenerational transmission of abuse. In D. Finkelhor, R. J. Gelles, G. T. Hotaling, & M. A. Straus (Eds.), *The dark side of families: Current family violence research*. Beverly Hills, Calif.: Sage, 1983. Pp. 305–316.

Jeffords, C. R., & Dull, R. T. Demographic variations in attitudes towards marital rape immunity. *Journal of Marriage and the Family*, 1982, *44*, 755–762.

Kaduskin, A., & Martin, J. A. *Child abuse: An interactional event*. New York: Columbia University Press, 1981.

Kalmuss, D. The intergenerational transmission of marital aggression. *Journal of Marriage and the Family*, 1984, *46*, 11–19.

Knox, D., & Wilson, L. Dating problems of university students. *College Student Journal*, 1983, *17*, 225–228.

Makepeace, J. Courtship violence among college students. *Family Relations*, 1981, *30*, 97–102.

_____. Life events, stess and courtship violence. *Family Relations*, 1983, *32*, 101–109.

Miller, D. T., & Porter, C. A. Self-blame in victims of violence. *Journal of Social Issues*, 1983, *39*, 139–151.

Oates, R. K., Davis, A. A., & Ryan, M. G. Predictive factors for child abuse. In R. J. Gelles & C. P. Cornell (Eds.), *International perspectives on family violence*, 1983. Pp. 97–106.

O'Toole, R., Turbett, J. P., Linz, M., & Mehta, S. S. Defining parent abuse and neglect. *Free Inquiry in Creative Sociology*, 1983, *11*, 156–158.

Pagelow, M. D. *Woman-battering: Victims and their experiences*. Beverly Hils, Calif.: Sage, 1981.

Rapaport, K., & Burkhart, B. R. *Personality and attitudinal characteristics of sexually aggressive college males*. Paper submitted for publication.

Russell, D. *Rape in marriage*. New York: Macmillan, 1982.

Sarrel, P., & Masters, W. Sexual molestation of men by women. *Archives of Sexual Behavior*, 1982, *11*, 117–131.

Schumm, W. R., Martin, M. J., Bollman, S. R., & Jurich, A. P. Classifying family violence. *Journal of Family Issues*, 1982, *3*, 319–340.

Sherman, L. W. & Berk, R. A. *Police Foundation Report 1:* The Minneapolis domestic violence experiment, 1984. Used by permission of L. W. Sherman.

Smith, S. M., & Hansen, R. 134 battered children: A medical and psychological study. In R. J. Gelles & C. P. Cornell (Eds.), *International perspectives on family violence*, 1983. Pp. 83–96.

Stark, E. The unspeakable family secret. *Psychology Today*, May 1984, pp. 38–46.

Straus, M., Gelles, R., & Steinmetz, S. *Behind closed doors: Violence in the American family*. Garden City, N.Y.: Anchor Press/Doubleday, 1980.

Strube, M. J., & Barbour, L. S. The decision to leave an abusive relationship: Economic dependence and psychological commitment. *Journal of Marriage and the Family*, 1983, *45*, 785–793.

Szinovacz, M. E. Using couple data as a methodological tool: The case of marital violence. *Journal of Marriage and the Family*, 1983, *45*, 633–644.

Time Magazine. Wife beating: The silent crime. September 5, 1983, pp. 23–26.

Washburne, C. K. A feminist analysis of child abuse and neglect. In D. Finkelhor, R.J. Gelles, G. T. Hotaling, & M. A. Straus (Eds.), *The dark side of families: Current family violence research*. Beverly Hill, Calif.: Sage, 1983. Pp. 289–292.

Wilson, K., & Faison, R. *Victims of sexual assualt during courtship*. Unpublished paper, Department of Sociology, Anthropology, and Economics, East Carolina University, 1983.

_____, _____, & Britton, G. M. Cultural aspects of male sex aggression. *Deviant Behavior*, 1983, *4*, 241–255.

Yates, A., Hull, J. W., & Huebner, R. B. Predicting the abusive parent's response to intervention. *Child Abuse & Neglect: The International Journal*, 1983, *7*, 37–44.

Yllo, K., & Straus, M. A. Interpersonal violence among married and cohabiting couples. *Family Relations*, 1981, *30*, 339–346.

Ziegert, K. A. The Swedish prohibition of corporal punishment: A preliminary report. *Journal of Marriage and the Family*, 1983, *45*, 917–926.

Zimring, F. E., Mukherjee, S. K., & Winkle, B. V. Intimate violence: A study of intersexual homicide in Chicago. *University of Chicago Law Review*, 1983, *50*, 910–930.

CHAPTER 13

Barbach, L. G. *For each other: Sharing sexual intimacy.* New York: Doubleday, 1982.

_____, & Flaherty, M. Group treatment of situationally orgasmic women. *Journal of Sex and Marital Therapy*, 1980, *6*, 19–29.

Brewer, J. S. Duration of intromission and female orgasm rates. *Medical Aspects of Human Sexuality*, 1981, *15*(4), 70–71.

Butler, R. N., & Lewis, M. I. *Sex after sixty.* New York: Harper & Row, 1976.

Budoff, P. W. *No more hot flashes and other good news.* New York: G. P. Putnam, 1983.

Clement, U., & Schmidt, G. The outcome of couple therapy for sexual dyfunctions using three different formats. *Journal of Sex and Marital Therapy*, 1983, *9*, 67–78.

Clifford, R. E. Development of masturbation in college women. *Archives of Sexual Behavior*, 1978, *7*, 559–573.

Coleman, E. M., Hoon, P. W., & Hoon, E. F. Arousability and sexual satisfaction in lesbian and heterosexual women. *Journal of Sex Research*, 1983, *19*(1), 58–73.

Connecticut Mutual Life Report on American Values in the '80s: The Impact of Belief. Copyright © 1981, Connecticut Mutual Life Insurance Company, Hartford, Conn. Used by permission.

Dalton, K. *The premenstrual syndrome and progesterone therapy.* Chicago: Year Book Medical Publishers, 1977.

Duddle, C. M., & Ingram, A. Treating sexual dysfunction in couple's groups. In R. Forleo & W. Pasini (Eds.), *Medical sexology.* Littleton, Mass.: PSG Publishing, 1980. Pp. 598–605.

Frauman, D. C. The relationship between physical exercise, sexual activity, and the desire for sexual activity. *Journal of Sex Research*, 1982, *18*, 41–46.

Golden, J. S., Price, S., Heinrich, A. G., & Lobitz, W. C. Group vs. couple treatment of sexual dysfunctions. *Archives of Sexual Behavior*, 1978, *7*, 593–602.

Greenblatt, C. S. The salience of sexuality in the early years of marriage. *Journal of Marriage and the Family*, 1983, *45*, 289–299.

Greenblatt, R. B. Hormones to increase libido in women. *Medical Aspects of Human Sexuality*, 1980, *14*(11), 107.

Griffin, J. A. Cross-cultural investigation of behavioral changes at menopause. *Social Science Journal*, 1977, *14*, 49–55.

Grosskopf, D. *Sex and the married woman.* New York: Wallaby Books, 1983.

Harrison, M. *Self-help for premenstrual syndrome.* New York: St. Martin's Press, 1982.

Hatfield, E., Greenberger, D., Traupmann, J., & Lambert, P. Equity and sexual satisfaction in recently married couples. *Journal of Sex Research*, 1982, *18*, 18–32.

Hegeler, S., & Mortensen, M. Sexual behavior in elderly Danish males. In R. Gemme and C. Wheeler (Eds.), *Progress in sexology.* New York: Plenum Press, 1977. Pp. 285–292.

Heiman, J., LoPiccolo, L., & LoPiccolo, J. *Becoming orgasmic: A sexual growth program for women.* Englewood Cliffs, N.J.: Prentice-Hall, 1976.

Henry, J. Forty-year-old jitters in married urban women. In C. Perrucci and D. Tary (Eds.), *Marriage and the family.* New York: David McKay, 1974. Pp. 440–448.

Hite, S. *The Hite report on male sexuality.* New York: Alfred A. Knopf, 1981.

Hong, L. K. Survival of the fastest: On the origin of premature ejaculation. *Journal of Sex Research*, 1984, *20*, 109–122.

Johnson, F. A., Kaplan, E. A., & Tusel, D. J. Sexual dysfunction in the "two-career" family. *Medical Aspects of Human Sexuality*, 1979, *13*(1), 7–17.

Kaplan, H. The classification of the female sexual dysfunctions. *Journal of Sex and Marital Therapy*, 1974, *1*(2), 124–138.

Kilmann, P. R., Mills, K. H., Caid, C., Bella, B., Davidson, E., & Wanlass, R. The sexual interaction of women with secondary orgasmic dysfunction and their partners. *Archives of Sexual Behavior*, 1984, *13*, 41–49.

Kolodny, R. C., Masters, W. H., & Johnson, V. E. *Textbook of sexual medicine.* Boston, Mass.: Little, Brown, 1979.

Levinson, D. J. The mid-life transition: A period in adult psychosocial development. *Psychiatry,* 1977, *40,* 99–112.

Lobitz, W. C., & Baker, E. L. Group treatment of single males with erectile dysfunction. *Archives of Sexual Behavior,* 1979, *8,* 127–138.

Masters, W. H., and Johnson, V. E. *Human sexual inadequacy.* Boston: Little, Brown, 1970.

Mathew, R. J., & Weinman, M. L. Sexual dysfunctions in depression. *Archives in Sexual Behavior,* 1982, *11,* 323–328.

McCarthy, B. W. Sexual dysfunctions and dissatisfactions among middle-years couples. *Journal of Sex Education and Therapy,* 1982, *8*(2), 9–12.

McCary, J. L. Sexual myths and fallacies. In J. L. McCary and D. Copeland (Eds.), *Modern views of human sexual behavior.* Palo Alto, Calif.: Science Research Associates, 1976. Pp. 286–312.

Mehlman, S. K., Baucom, D. H., & Anderson, D. Effectiveness of cotherapists versus single therapists and immediate versus delayed treatment in behavioral marital therapy. *Journal of Consulting and Clinical Psychology,* 1983, *51,* 258–266.

Morgenstern, M. *How to make love to a woman.* New York: Crown, 1982.

Paige, K. E. The declining taboo against menstrual sex. *Psychology Today,* July 1978, pp. 50–51.

Penney, A. *How to make love to a man.* New York: Clarkson Potter, 1981.

Peter, L. *Peter's almanac.* New York: William Morrow, 1982.

Petersen, J. R., Kretchmer, A., Nellis, B., Lever, J., & Hertz, R. The *Playboy* reader's sex survey, Part 1. *Playboy,* January 1983a, p. 108 et passim.

———, ———, ———, ———, & ———. The *Playboy* readers' sex survey, Part 2. *Playboy,* March 1983b, p. 90 et passim.

Pfeiffer, E., Verwoerdt, A., & David, G. Sexual behavior in middle life. In E. Palmore (Ed.), *Normal aging II.* Durham, N.C.: Duke University Press, 1974. Pp. 243–251.

Rossman, I. Sexuality and aging: An internist's perspective. In R. L. Solnick (Ed.), *Sexuality and aging.* Los Angeles: Ethel Percy Andus Gerontology Center at the University of Southern California, 1978. Pp. 66–77.

Rubin, L. B. The marriage bed. *Psychology Today,* August 1976, p. 44 et passim.

Sarrel, P., & Sarrel, L. The *Redbook* report on sexual relationships. *Redbook,* October 1980, pp. 73–80.

Sholty, M. J., Ephross, P. H., Plant, S. M., Fischman, S. H. Charnas, J. F., & Cody, C. A. Female orgasmic experience: A subjective study. *Archives of Sexual Behavior,* 1984, *13,* 155–164.

Smallwood, K. B., & VanDyck, D. G. Menopause counseling: Coping with realities. *Journal of Sex Education and Therapy,* 1979, *1*(6) 72–76.

Starr, B. D., & Weiner, M. B. *The Starr-Weiner report on sex and sexuality in the mature years.* New York: McGraw-Hill, 1982.

U.S. Bureau of the Census. America in transition: An aging society. *Current population reports,* Series P-23, no. 128. Washington, D.C.: U.S. Government Printing Office, 1983.

Winn, R. L., & Newton, N. Sexuality in aging: A study of 106 cultures. *Archives of Sexual Behavior,* 1982, *11,* 283–298.

Zilbergeld, B. Alternative to couples counseling for sex problems: Group and individual therapy. *Journal of Sex and Marital Therapy,* 1980, *6,* 3–18.

CHAPTER 14

Bachrach, C. A. Adoption as a means of family formation: Data from the national growth survey of family growth. *Journal of Marriage and the Family,* 1983, *45,* 859–865.

Bongaarts, J. Infertility after age 30: A false alarm. *Family Planning Perspectives,* 1982, *14*(2), 75–78.

———. Building a family: Unplanned events. *Studies in Family Planning,* 1984, *15,* 14–19.

Callan, V. J., & Gallois, C. Perceptions about having children: Are daughters different from their mothers? *Journal of Marriage and the Family,* 1983, *45,* 607–612.

CBS News, June 12, 1984.

Cooper, P. E., Cumber, B., & Hartner, R. Decision-making patterns and post-decision adjustment of childfree husbands and wives. *Alternative Lifestyles,* 1978, *1,* 71–94.

DeFrain, J., & Eirick, R. Coping as divorced single parents: A comparative study of fathers and mothers. *Family Relations,* 1981, *30,* 265–274.

Divorce statistics. *Marriage and Divorce Today,* 1983, *8*(38), 4.

Durant, W. *The story of philosophy.* New York: Simon and Schuster, 1926. Reprinted as a Time Reading Program Special Edition, 1962. P. 292.

Elvenstar, D. *A child: To have or have not?* San Francisco: Harbor, 1982.

Englund, C. L. Parenting and parentage: Distinct aspects of children's importance. *Family Relations,* 1983, *32,* 21–28.

Gallup Report. *Ideal number of children.* Report No. 210, March 1983, p. 11.

Gilman, R. C., & Knox, D. Coping with fatherhood: The first year. *Child Psychiatry and Human Development,* 1976, *6,* 134–148.

Hawke, S., & Knox, D. *One child by choice.* Englewood Cliffs, N.J.: Prentice-Hall, 1977.

Henry, J., & Warson, S. Family structure and psychic development. *American Journal of Orthopsychiatry,* 1951, *21,* 59–73.

Knox, D., & Wilson, K. The differences between having one and two children. *Family Coordinator,* 1978, *27,* 23–25.

Kuhn, M. A. Mother load. *Washington Post Magazine,* November 27, 1983, pp. 13, 20, 21.

LeMasters, E. E., & DeFrain, J. *Parents in contemporary America.* Homewood, Ill.: Dorsey Press, 1983.

Marini, M. M. Effects of the number and spacing of children on marital and parental satisfaction. *Demography,* 1980, *17,* 225–242.

McLaughlin, S. D., & Micklin, M. The timing of the first birth and changes in personal efficacy. *Journal of Marriage and the Family,* 1983, *45,* 47–55.

Moore, C. Bye-bye, Ms. American pie. *Washington Post Magazine,* November 27, 1983, pp. 10, 11, 16–19.

Mosher, W. D., & Bachrach, C. A. Childlessness in the United States. *Journal of Family Issues,* 1982, *3,* 517–543.

National Center for Health Statistics. Advance report of final natality statistics, 1980. *Monthly Vital Statistics Report,* 31(8), Supp. DHHS Pub. No. (PHS) 83-1120. Hyattsville, Md.: U.S. Public Health Service, November 1982.

_____. Annual summary of births, deaths, marriages, and divorces: United States, 1982. *Monthly Vital Statistics Report,* 31(13). DHHS Pub. No. (PHS) 83-1120. Hyattsville, Md.: U.S. Public Health Service, October 1983.

Olson, L. *Costs of children.* Lexington, Mass: Lexington Books, 1983.

Patterson, L. A., & DeFrain, J. Pronatalism in high school family studies texts. *Family Relations,* 1981, *30,* 211–217.

Pines, M. Only isn't lonely (or spoiled or selfish). *Psychology today,* March 1981, pp. 15–19.

Powledge, T. M. Windows of the womb. *Psychology Today,* March 1983, pp. 37–42.

Reimer, R. J., & Maiolo, J. *Family growth and socioeconomic status among poor blacks.* Unpublished manuscript, East Carolina University, 1977. Used with permission of John Maiolo.

Rindfuss, R. R., & John, C. S. Social determinants of age at first birth. *Journal of Marriage and the Family,* 1983, *45,* 553–565.

Rogers, C. C. & O'Connell, M. Child-spacing among birth cohorts of American women (1905–1959). U.S. Bureau of the Census, Series P-20, No. 385. U.S. Government Printing Office, Washington, D.C. 1984.

Seashore, M. R. Counseling prospective parents about possible genetic disorders in offspring. *Medical Aspects of Human Sexuality,* 1980, *14*(11), 97–98.

Shettles, L. *How to choose the sex of your baby.* New York: Doubleday, 1984.

Steffensmeier, R. H. A role model of the transition to parenthood. *Journal of Marriage and the Family,* 1982, *44,* 319–334.

Thornton, A., & Freedman, D. The changing American family. *Population Bulletin,* 38(4), 1983.

Townes, B. D., Wood, R. J., Beach, L. R., & Campbell, F. L. Adolescent values for childbearing. *Journal of Sex Research,* 1979, 15, 21–26.

U.S. Bureau of the Census. Fertility of American women: June 1982 (advance report). *Current Population Reports,* Series P-20, No. 379. Washington, D.C.: U.S. Government Printing Office, 1983.

U.S. Department of Health, Education, and Welfare. Wanted and unwanted births reported by mothers 15–44 years of age: United States, 1976. *Vital & Health Statistics,* No. 56, 1980.

Veevers, J.E. Researching voluntary childlessness: A critical assessment of current strategies and findings. In E. Macklin & R. Rubin (Eds.), *Contemporary families and alternative lifestyles.* Beverly Hills, Calif.: Sage, 1983. Pp. 75–96.

Werner, P. D., Midlestadt-Carter, S. E., & Crawford, T. J. Having a third child: Predicting behavioral intentions. *Journal of Marriage and the Family,* 1975, 37, 348–358.

Winikoff, B. The effects of birth spacing on child and maternal health. *Studies in family planning,* 1983, *14,* 231–245.

Women's Views Study. Sex, money, politics, family—Where are women now? *Glamour,* January 1984, p. 144.

Yankelovich, D. *New Rules: Search for self-fulfillment in a world turned upside down.* New York: Random House, 1981.

CHAPTER 15

Beck, W. W., Jr. Two hundred years of artificial insemination. *Fertility and Sterility,* 1984, *41,* 193–195.

Binkin, N., Gold, J., & Cates, W., Jr. Illegal-abortion deaths in the United States: Why are they still occurring? *Family Planning Perspectives,* 1982, *14*(3), 163–167.

Czba, J. C., & Chevret, M. Psychological reactions of couples to artificial insemination with donor sperm. *International Journal of Fertility,* 1979, *24,* 240–245.

De Maris, A. A comparison of remarriages with first marriages on satisfaction in marriage and its relationship to prior cohabitation. *Family Relations* 1984, *33,* 443–449.

Edwards, R., & Steptoe, P. *A matter of life.* New York: William Morrow, 1980.

Fisher, C., Cohen, H. D., Schiavi, R. C., Davis, D., Furman, B., Ward, K., Edwards, A., & Cunningham, J. Patterns of female sexual arousal during sleep and waking: Vaginal thermo-conductance studies. *Archives of Sexual Behavior,* 1983, *12,* 97–122.

Fleming, A. T. New frontiers in conception. *New York Times Magazine* July 20, 1980, pp. 14–20.

Forrest, J. D., & Henshaw, S. K. What U.S. women think and do about contraception. *Family Planning Perspectives,* 1983, *15,* 157–166.

Good Housekeeping Poll. Test tube babies. *Good Housekeeping,* November 1980, pp. 58–60.

Harper, M. J. K. *Birth control technologies.* Austin, Texas: University of Texas Press, 1983.

Hatcher, R. A., Stewart, G. F., Stewart, F., Guest, F., Stratton, P., & Wright, A. H. *Contraceptive technology,* 9th rev. ed. New York: Irvington, 1978.

Hayes, M. School of Human Development, University of Oklahoma. Personal communication, 1983. Used by permission.

Henshaw, S. K., & Martire, G. Abortion and the public opinion polls: Morality and legality. *Family Planning Perspectives,* 1982, *14,* 53–60.

_____, & O'Reilly, K. Characteristics of abortion patients in the United States, 1970 and 1980. *Family Planning Perspectives,* 1983, *15,* 5–16.

Herold, E. S., & Goodwin, M. S. Premarital sexual guilt and contraceptive attitudes and behavior. *Family Relations,* 1981, *30,* 247–253.

_____, & McNamee, J. E. An explanatory model of contraceptive use among young single women. *Journal of Sex Research,* 1982, *18,* 289–304.

Kafka, D., & Gold, R. B. Food and drug administration approves vaginal sponge. *Family Planning Perspectives,* 1983, *15,* 146–148.

Koch, J. P. The Prentif contraceptive cervical cap: A contemporary study of its clinical safety and effectiveness. *Contraception,* 1982, *25,* 135.

Lederer, J. Birth-control decisions. *Psychology Today,* June 1983, pp. 32–38.

Lewis, C. C. Abortion decisions of adult and minor women. *American Journal of Orthopsychiatry,* 1980, *50,* 446–453.

MacCorquodale, P. L. Gender roles and premarital contraception. *Journal of Marriage and the Family,* 1984, *46,* 57–64.

Mahoney, E. R. *Human Sexuality.* New York: McGraw-Hill, 1983.

Maschoff, T., Fashier, H., & Hansen, D. Vasectomy: Effect upon marital stability. *Journal of Sex Research,* 1976, *12,* 295–314.

Mumford, S. D. The vasectomy decision-making process. *Studies in Family Planning,* 1983, *14,* 83–88.

Nass, G. D., Libby, R. W., & Fisher, M. P. *Sexual choices.* Monterey, Calif.: Brooks-Cole, 1984.

National Center for Health Statistics. Contraceptive utilization: United States 1976, Publication No. 81-1983. Hyattsville, Md.: U.S. Public Health Service, March 1981, p. 6.

National Institute of Child Health and Human Development Collaborative Study. The health status of American men. Paper presented at the annual meeting of the American Public Health Association, Dallas, 1983.

Ory, H. W. Mortality associated with fertility and fertility control: 1983. *Family Planning Perspectives*, 1983, *15*, 57–63.

_____, Rosenfeld, A., & Landman, L. C. The pill at 20: An assessment. *Family Planning Perspectives*, 1980, *12*, 278–283.

Parker, P. J. Motivation of surrogate mothers: Initial findings. *American Journal of Psychiatry*, 1983, *140*, 117–118.

Petitti, D. *Longitudinal study on safety of vasectomy*. Unpublished study, Kaiser-Permanente Medical Care Program, Oakland, California, 1983. Used with permission.

Porter, N. L., & Christopher, F. S. Infertility: Towards an awareness of a need among family life practitioners. *Family Relations*, 1984, *33*, 309–315.

Pratt, I. W. F., & Bachrach, C. A. Preliminary estimates of the population "At Risk" of pregnancy and of those using contraception: Finding from Cycle III of the National Survey of Family Growth. Paper presented at the annual meeting of the American Public Health Association, Dallas, 1983.

Riggall, F. C. Reversing female sterilization. *Medical Aspects of Human Sexuality*, 1980, *14*(7), p. 107.

Shepard, M. K. Infertility. In R. N. Shain and C. J. Pauerstein (Eds.), *Fertility control*. New York: Harper and Row, 1980a. Pp. 57–70.

_____. Nonsurgical methods of contraception. In R. N. Shain and C. J. Pauerstein (Eds.), *Fertility control*. New York: Harper and Row, 1980b. Pp. 71–84.

Silber, S. J. *How to get pregnant*. New York: Scribner's, 1980.

Simon Population Trust. Vasectomy: Follow-up of a thousand cases. In L. Lader (Ed.), *Foolproof birth control: Male and female sterilization*. Boston: Beacon Press, 1973. Pp. 131–140.

Tietze, C. The public health effects of legal abortion in the United States. *Family Planning Perspectives*, 1984, *16*, 26–28.

U.S. Department of Health and Human Services. *Morbidity and Mortality Weekly Report*, 32(5). Atlanta: Center for Disease Control, February 11, 1983.

Women's Views Study. Sex, money, politics, and family—Where are women now? *Glamour*, January 1984, p. 144.

Zimmerman, S. L. Alternatives in human reproduction for involuntary childless couples. *Family Relations*, 1982, *31*, 233–242.

CHAPTER 16

Affonso, D. D., & Stichler, J. F. Caesarean birth: Women's reactions. *American Journal of Nursing*, 1980, *80*, 468–470.

Beebe, E. R. Expectant parent classes: A case study. *Family Coordinator*, 1978, *27*,, 55–58.

Belsky, J., Spanier, G. B., & Rovine, M. Stability and change in marriage across the transition to parenthood. *Journal of Marriage and the Family*, 1983, *45*, 567–577.

Better Homes and Gardens. A report on American families. Des Moines, Iowa: Meredith Corporation, 1983.

Bradley, C. F., Ross, S. E., & Warnyca, J. A prospective study of mothers' attitudes and feelings following Cesarean and vaginal births. *Birth*, 1983, *10*(2), 79–84.

Bradley, R. A. *Husband-coached childbirth*. New York: Harper and Row, 1981.

Bratic, E. B. Healthy Mothers, Healthy Babies Coalition. *Prevention*, 1982, *97*, 503–509.

Calderone, M. S., & Johnson, E. W. *The Family Book About Sexuality*. New York: Harper and Row, 1981.

Calhoun, L. G., Selby, J. W., & King, H. E. The influence of pregnancy on sexuality: A review of current evidence. *Journal of Sex Research*, 1981, *17*, 139–151.

Cass, L., & Cass, R. Pregnancy diary: The first months. *Parents Magazine*, May 1980, pp. 59–65.

Cohen, N. W., & Estner, L. J. *Silent Knife*. South Hadley, Mass.: Bergin and Garvey, 1983.

Crooks, R. & Baur, K. *Our Sexuality*. Menlo Park, California: The Benjamin/Cummings Publishing Co., 1984.

DeVries, R. B. Image and reality: An evaluation of hospital alternative birth centers. *Journal of Nurse-Midwifery*, 1983, *28*(3), 3–9.

Erb, L., Hill, G., & Houston, D. A survey of parents' attitudes toward their Cesarean births in Manitoba hospitals. *Birth Issues in Perinatal Care and Education*, 1983, *10*, 85–92.

Fein, R. A. Men's entrance into parenthood. *Family Coordinator*, 1976, *25*, 341–348.

Feldman, H., & Feldman, M. *Effect of parenthood at three points in marriage*. Unpublished manuscript, Cornell University, 1977. Used with permission.

Gallup/Levi Maternity Wear National Poll of Pregnant Women and New Mothers. San Francisco, Calif.: Levi Strauss & Co., 1983.

Gilman, R. C., & Knox, D. Coping with fatherhood: The first year. *Child Psychiatry and Human Development*, 1976, 6, 134–148.

Glenn, N. D., & McLanahan, S. Children and marital happiness: A further specification of the relationship. *Journal of Marriage and the Family*, 1982, 44, 63–72.

Grossman, F. K., Eichler, L. S., & Winickoff, S. A. *Pregnancy, birth, and parenthood*. San Francisco, Calif.: Jossey-Bass, 1980.

Grudzinskas, J. G., & Atkinson, L. Sexual function during the puerperium. *Archives of Sexual Behavior*, 1984, 13, 85–91.

Harriman, L. C. Personal and marital changes accompanying parenthood. *Family Relations*, 1983, 32, 387–394.

Hock, E., Gnezda, M. T., & McBride, S. L. Mothers of infants: Attitudes toward employment and motherhood following birth of the first child. *Journal of Marriage and the Family*, 1984, 46, 425–432.

Hoffman, L. W., & Manis, J. D. Influences of children on marital interaction and parental satisfactions and dissatisfactions. In R. M. Lerner & G. B. Spanier (Eds.). *Child influences on marital and family interaction*. New York: Academic Press, 1978. Pp. 165–213.

Holahan, C. K. The relationship between information search in the childbearing decision and life satisfaction for parents and nonparents. *Family Relations*, 1983, 32, 527–535.

Kach, J. A., & McGhee, P. E. Adjustment of early parenthood: The role of accuracy of preparenthood expectations. *Journal of Family Issues*, 1982, 3, 375–388.

Kamerman, S. B. *Parenting in an unresponsive society*. New York: Free Press, 1980.

Kirkland, J., Deal, F., & Brennan, M. About CrySOS, a clinic for people with crying babies. *Family Relations*, 1983, 32, 537–543.

Knox, D., & Gilman, R. C. The first year of fatherhood. *Family Perspective*, 1974, 9, 31–34.

Lappé, M. Risks from maternal exposure to photographic chemicals in pregnancy. *Birth Issues in Perinatal Care and Education*. 1983, 10, 173–177.

LaRossa, R. Sex during pregnancy: A symbolic interactionist analysis. *Journal of Sex Research*, 1979, 15, 119–128.

_____. The transition to parenthood and the social reality of time. *Journal of Marriage and the Family*, 1983, 45, 579–589.

_____, & LaRossa, M. M. *Transition to parenthood: How infants change families*. Beverly Hills, Calif.: Sage, 1981.

Lubic, R. W. Alternative maternity care: Resistance and change. In Shelly Romalis (Ed.), *Childbirth: Alternatives to Medical Control*. Austin, Texas: University of Texas Press, 1981.

Lumley, J. Preschool siblings at birth: Short-term effects. *Birth Issues in Perinatal Care and Education*, 1983, 10, 11–16.

Marano, H. E. Biology is one key to the bonding of mothers and babies. *Smithsonian*, December 1981, pp. 60–69.

Masters, W. H., & Johnson, V. E. *Human sexual response*. Boston: Little, Brown, 1966.

Mehl, L. Statistical outcomes of home births in the United States: Current status. In D. Stewart & L. Stewart (Eds.), *Safe Alternatives in Childbirth*, 2nd ed. Chapel Hill, N.C.: NASPSAC, 1976. Pp. 73–100.

Myers-Walls, J. A. Balancing multiple role responsibilities during the transition to parenthood. *Family Relations*, 1984, 33, 267–272.

National Center for Health Statistics. Births, marriages, divorces, and deaths for November 1983. *Monthly Vital Statistics Report*, 32(1): DHHS Pub. No. (Phs) 84-1120. Hyattsville, Md.: U.S. Public Health Service, February 17, 1984.

Nelson, N. M. A randomized controlled trial of the LeBoyer approach to childbirth. Paper presented at the *Birth and Family Journal* Conference on Technological Approaches to Obstetrics, 1979.

Newton, M. New baby! Why so sad? *Family Health*, 1976, 8(5), 17.

Nicholson, J., Gist, N. F., Klein, R. P., & Standley, K. Outcomes of father involvement in pregnancy and birth. *Birth Issues in Perinatal Care and Education*, 1983, 10, 5–9.

Nock, S. L. The family life cycle: Empirical or conceptual tool. *Journal of Marriage and the Family*, 1979, 41, 15–26.

Patterson, J. M., & McCubbin, H. The impact of family life events and changes on the health of a chronically ill child. *Family Relations*, 1983, 32, 255–264.

Pedersen, C. A., & Prange, A. J., Jr. Induction of maternal behavior in virgin rats after intracerebroventricular administration of oxytocin. *Neurobiology*, 1979, 76, 6661–6665.

Price-Bonham, S., & Skeen, P. A comparison of black and white fathers with implications for parent education. *Family Coordinator*, 1979, *28*, 53–59.

Russell, C. S. Transition to parenthood: Problems and gratifications. *Journal of Marriage and the Family*, 1974, *36*, 294–303.

Rossi, A. S. Transition to parenthood. *Journal of Marriage and the Family*, 1968, *30*, 26–39.

Sacks, S. R., & Donnenfeld, P. B. Parental choice of alternative birth environments and attitudes toward childrearing philosophy. *Journal of Marriage and the Family*, 1984, *46*, 469–475.

Solberg, D. A., Butler, J., & Wagner, N. W. Sexual behavior during pregnancy. *New England Journal of Medicine*, 1973, *288*, 1098–1103.

Stichler, J. F., & Affonso, D. D. Caesarean birth. *American Journal of Nursing*, 1980, *80*, 466–468.

Tew, M. The case against hospital deliveries: The statistical evidence. In S. Kitzinger & J.A. Davis (Eds.), *The place of birth*. London and New York: Oxford University Press, 1978. Pp. 55–65.

Thornton, A., & Freedman, D. The changing American family. *Population Bulletin*, *38*(4), 1983.

Wente, A. S., & Crockenberg, S. B. Transition to fatherhood: Lamaze preparation, adjustment difficulty and the husband-wife relationship. *Family Coordinator*, 1976, *25*, 351–357.

CHAPTER 17

Better Homes and Gardens. A report on American families. Des Moines, Iowa: Meredith Corporation, 1983.

Dreikurs, R., & Grey, L. *A parent's guide to child discipline*. New York: Duell, Sloan, and Pearce, 1958.

Feuerstein, P., & Roberts, C. *The not-so-empty nest*. Piscataway, N.J. New Century, 1981.

Ford, E. E., & Englund, S. *For the love of children: A reality therapy approach to raising your child*. New York: Anchor Press, 1978.

Gallup/Levi Maternity Wear National Poll of Pregnant Women and New Mothers. Opinions About Motherhood. San Francisco: Levi Strauss & Co., 1983.

Gesell, A. *The child from five to ten*. New York: Harper, 1946.

_____, & Ilg, F. L. *Infant and child in the culture of today*. New York: Harper, 1943.

Gordon, T. *P.E.T. in action*. New York: Bantam Books, 1976.

Haffey, N. A., & Levant, R. F. The differential effectiveness of two models of skills training for working class parents. *Family Relations*, 1984, *33*, 209–216.

LeMasters, E. E., & DeFrain, J. *Parents in contemporary America: A sympathetic view*. Homewood, Ill.: Dorsey Press, 1983.

Love, N. W., Jr., & McVoy, J. H. Child abuse by the unaware. *Marriage and Family Living*, 1981, *65*(11), 12–29.

Mead, D. E. *Six approaches to child rearing*. Provo, Utah: Brigham Young University Press, 1976.

Mullis, A. K., & Mullis, R. L. Making parent education relevant. *Family Perspective*, 1983, *17*, 167–173.

Mussen, T. H., Gonger, J. J., Kagan, J., & Huston, A. C. *Child Development and Personality*. New York: Harper and Row, 1984.

Pogrebin, L. C. *Family politics*. New York: McGraw-Hill, 1983.

Ritchie, J., & Ritchie, J. Polynesian child rearing: An alternative model. *Alternative Lifestyles*, 1983, *5*, 126–141.

Rutter, M. Resilient children. *Psychology Today*, March 1984, pp. 57–65.

Scarr, S. What's a parent to do? *Psychology Today*, May 1984, pp. 58–63.

Schroeder, A. B., & Brocato, B. R. Television and family interaction. *Free Inquiry in Creative Sociology*, 1983, *11*, 61–64.

Schvaneveldt, J. D., & Lee, T. R. The emergence and practices of ritual in the American family. *Family Perspective*, 1983, *17*, 137–143.

Shea, J. Department of Child Development and Family Relations, East Carolina University, Greenville, N.C. Personal communication, 1984. Used by permission.

Skinner, B. F. *About behaviorism*. New York: Alfred A. Knopf, 1974.

Snow, C. W. As the twig is bent: A review of research on the consequences of day care with implications for caregiving. Paper presented at the National Association for the Education of Young Children, Atlanta, 1983. Used by permission.

U.S. children and their families: Current conditions and recent trends. A report together with additional views of the Select Committee on Children, Youth, and Families, Ninety-eighth Congress,

1st Sess. Washington, D.C.: U.S. Government Printing Office, 1983. Figure cited in text is for 1985 projection.

York, P., York, D., & Wachtel, T. *Toughlove*, New York: Bantam Books, 1982.

_____, & _____. D. Toughlove. *Family Therapy Networker*, September-October 1982, pp. 32–37.

CHAPTER 18

Albrecht, S. l. Reactions and adjustments to divorce: Differences in the experiences of males and females. *Family Relations*, 1980, *29*, 59–68.

Bloom, B. L., & Clement, C. Marital sex role orientation and adjustment to separation and divorce. *Journal of Divorce*, 1984, *7*(3), 87–98.

The Connecticut Mutual Life Report on American Values in the '80s: The Impact of Belief. Hartford, Conn.: Connecticut Mutual Life Insurance Company, 1981.

Clingempeel, W. G., & Reppucci, N. D. Joint custody after divorce: Major issues and goals for research. *Psychological Bulletin*, 1982, *91*(1), 101–127.

Corcoran, M. The economic consequences of marital dissolution for women in the middle years. *Sex Roles*, 1979, *5*(3), 343–353.

Daniel, H. J., III. *As long as you're not cold.* Greenville, N.C., 1984.

DeFrain, J., & Eirick, R. Coping as divorced single parents: A comparative study of fathers and mothers. *Family Relations*, 1981, *30*, *(2)*, 265–273.

Espenshade, T. J., & Braun, R. E. Life course analysis and multistate demography: An application to marriage, divorce, and remarriage. *Journal of Marriage and the Family*, 1982, *44*, 1025–1036.

Fengler, A. P., & Danigelis, N. Residence, the elderly widow, and life satisfaction. *Research on Aging*, 1982, *4*, 113–135.

Ferraro, K. F., & Barresi, C. M. The impact of widowhood on the social relations of older persons. *Research on Aging*, 1982, *4*, 227–247.

Frank, E., & Enos, S. F. The lovelife of the American wife. *Ladies Home Journal*, February 1983, p. 71 et passim.

Glass, B. L. No-fault divorce law: Impact on judge and client. *Journal of Family Issues*, 1984, *5*, 47–69.

Glenn, N. D., & Weaver, C. N. The marital happiness of remarried divorced persons. *Journal of Marriage and the Family*, 1977, *39*(2), 331–337.

Glick, P. How American families are changing. *American Demographics*, 1984a, *6*(1), 20–27.

_____. Marriage, divorce, and living arrangements. *Journal of Family Issues*, 1984b, *5*, 7–26.

Goetting, A. The six stations of remarriage: Developmental tasks of remarriage after divorce. *Family Coordinator*, 1982, *31*, 213–222.

Greenberg, E. F., & Nay, W. R. The intergenerational transmission of marital instability reconsidered. *Journal of Marriage and the Family*, 1982, *44*, 335–347.

Hassett, J. But that would be wrong. *Psychology Today*, November 1981, pp. 34–53.

Hayes, M. P. Strengthening marriage in the middle years. *Family Perspective*, 1979, *13*, 1–19.

Hodges, W. F., Wechsler, R., & Ballantine, C. Divorce and the preschool child: Cumulative stress. *Journal of Divorce*, 1979, *3*, 33–69.

Hunt, M., & Hunt, B. *The divorce experience.* New York: McGraw-Hill, 1977.

Jencks, C. Divorced mothers, Unite! *Psychology Today*, November 1982, pp. 73–75.

Kaslow, F. W. Divorce: An evolutionary process of change in the family system. *Journal of Divorce*, 1984, *7*(3) 23–39.

Kinard, E. M., & Reinherz, H. Marital disruption: Effects on behavioral and emotional functioning in children. *Journal of Family Issues*, 1984, *5*, 90–115.

Kitson, G. C. Attachment to the spouse in divorce: A scale and its application. *Journal of Marriage and the Family*, 1982a, *44*, 379–393.

_____. Predictors of post-divorce adjustment: Eighteen months after separation. Paper presented at the American Sociological Association, San Francisco, 1982b.

_____, & Sussman, M. B. Marital complaints, demographic characteristics, and symptoms of mental distress in divorce. *Journal of Marriage and the Family*, 1982, *44*, 87–101.

Knaub, P. K., Hanna, S. L., & Stinnett, N. Strengths of remarried families. *Journal of Divorce*, 1984, *7*(3), 41–55.

Levinger, G. Marital cohesiveness at the brink: The fate of applications for divorce. In G. Levinger and O. Moles (Eds.), *Divorce and separation.* New York: Basic Books, 1979. Pp. 137–150.

Lowery, C. R. Child custody in divorce: How parents decide. Paper presented at the American Psychological Association, 1982.

Mead, M. Anomalies in American postdivorce relationships. In P. Bohannon (Ed.), *Divorce and after: An analysis of the emotional and social problems of divorce.* New York: Doubleday, 1970. Pp. 107–125.

National Center for Health Statistics. Advance report of final divorce statistics, 1981. *Monthly Vital Statistics Report, 32*(9), Supp. 2: DHHS Pub. No. (PHS) 84-1120. Hyattsville, Md.: U.S. Public Health Service, January 1984a.

_____. Births, marriages, divorces, and deaths for November 1983. *Monthly Vital Statistics Report, 32*(11): DHHS Pub. No. (PHS) 84-1120. Hyattsville, Md.: U.S. Public Health Service, February 17, 1984b.

_____. Advance report of final divorce statistics, 1981. *Monthly Vital Statistics Report, 32*(9), Supp. 2: DHHS Pub. No. (PHS) 84-1120. Hyattsville, Md.: U.S. Public Health Service, January 17, 1984c.

_____. Births, marriages, divorces, and deaths for February 1984. *Monthly Vital Statistics Report, 33*(2) DHHS Pub. No. (PHS) 84-1120. Hyattsville, Md.: U.S. Public Health Service, May 23, 1984d.

Newman, H. M., & Langer, E. J. Post-divorce adaptation and the attribution of responsibility. *Sex Roles,* 1981, *7,* 223–232.

Nock, S. L. Enduring effect of marital disruption and subsequent living arrangements. *Journal of Family Issues,* 1982, *3,* 25–40.

Nuckols, R. C. Family systems and inheritance patterns. *Marriage and Family Review Series.* New York: Haworth Press, Winter 1983.

Palisi, B. J. Symptoms of readiness for divorce. *Journal of Family Issues,* 1984, *5,* 7–89.

Pearson, J., Munson, P., and Thoennes, N. Legal change and child custody awards. *Journal of Family Issues,* 1982, *3,* 5–24.

Petersen, J. R., Kretchmer, A., Nellis, B., Lever, J., & Hertz, R. The *Playboy* reader's sex survey, Part 1. *Playboy,* January 1983a, p. 108 et passim.

Ratcliff, B. B. *Patterns of divorce disclosure.* Unpublished thesis, Department of Sociology, Anthropology, and Economics, East Carolina University, Greenville, N.C., 1982.

Better Homes and Gardens, A report on American families. Des Moines, Iowa: Meredith Corporation, 1983.

Rofes, E., (Ed.). *The kids book of divorce.* Lexington, Mass.: Lewis, 1981.

Roll, S. Ties that bind. *Psychology Today,* September 1983, pp. 6–7.

Rubenstein, C. The children of divorce as adults. *Psychology Today,* August 1980, pp. 74–75.

Sager, C. J., Brown, H. S., Crohn, H., Engle, T., Rodstein, E., & Walker, L. *Treating the remarried family.* New York: Brunner/Mazel, 1983.

Saul, S. C., & Scherman, A. Divorce grief and personal adjustment in divorced persons who remarry or remain single. *Journal of Divorce,* 1984, *7*(3), 75–85.

Silvia v. Silvia, 400 N.E. 2nd 1330 (Mass. 1980).

Spanier, G. B., & Glick, P. C. Marital instability in the United States: Some correlates and recent changes. *Family Relations,* 1981, *30,* 329–338.

Stahl, P. M. Joint custody. Unpublished dissertation, University of Michigan, Ann Arbor, Michigan, 1983.

Statistical Abstract of the United States: 1984 (104th ed.). Washington, D.C.: U.S. Bureau of the Census, 1983.

Udry, J. R. Marital alternatives and marital disruption. *Journal of Marriage and the Family,* 1981, *43,* 889–897.

U.S. Bureau of the Census, America in transition: An aging society, *Current Population Reports,* Series p-23, No. 128. Washington, D. C.: U.S. Government Printing Office, 1983.

U.S. Department of Health, Education, and Welfare. Remarriages of women 15–44 years of age whose first marriage ended in divorce: United States, 1976. U.S. Public Health Service, Office of Health Research, Statistics, and Technology, no. 58, February 14, 1980.

Vinick, B. Remarriage in old age. *The Family Coordinator,* 1978, *27,* 359–363.

Wallerstein, J. S., & Kelly, J. B. *Surviving the break-up: How children actually cope with divorce.* New York: Basic Books, 1980.

Watson, M. A. Custody alternatives: Defining the best interests of the children. *Family Relations,* 1981, *30,* 474–479.

Weiss, R. S. The impact of marital dissolution on income and consumption in single-parent households. *Journal of Marriage and the Family,* 1984, *46,* 115–127.

White, S. W., & Bloom, B. Factors related to the adjustment of divorcing men. *Family Relations,* 1981, *30,* 349–360.

Yoder, J. D., & Nichols, R. C. A life perspective comparison of married and divorced persons. *Journal of Marriage and the Family,* 1980, *42*, 413–419.

CHAPTER 19

Bachrach, C. A. Children in families: Characteristics of biological, step- and adopted children. *Journal of Marriage and the Family,* 1983, *45*, 171–179.

Fishman, B. The economic behavior of stepfamilies. *Family Relations,* 1983, *32*, 359–366. © National Council on Family Relations, Fairview Community School Center, 1910 W. County Rd. B, Suite 147, St. Paul, MN. 55113.

Giles-Sims, J. The stepparent role: Expectations, behavior, and sanctions. *Journal of Family Issues,* 1984, *5*, 116–130.

Glick, P. C. How American families are changing. *American Demographics,* 1984, *6(1)*, 20–25.

Knaub, P. K., Hanna, S. L., & Stinnett, N. Strengths of remarried families. *Journal of Divorce,* 1984, *7*(3), 41–55.

Lutz, P. The stepfamily: An adolescent perspective. *Family Relations,* 1983, *32*, 367–375.

Miller, G. Select Committee on Children, Youth and Families. Committee Report: U.S. children and their families: Current conditions and recent trends. Washington, D.C.: Room H2-385 House Office Building Annex 2, 1983.

Osborne, J. How to provide effective help for remarried couples. *Marriage and Divorce Today,* 1983, 8 (52), p. 2–3.

Tropf, W. D. An exploratory examination of the effect of remarriage on child support and personal contacts. *Journal of Divorce,* 7(3), 57–73.

Visher, J. S. Seven myths about stepfamilies. *Medical Aspects of Human Sexuality,* January 1984, pp. 52–76.

Walker, G. *Second Wife, second best?* New York: Doubleday, 1984.

EPILOG

Frost, R. "The Road Not Taken." from Lathem, E. C. (ed.), *The Poetry of Robert Frost.* Copyright 1916, © 1969 by Holt, Rinehart and Winston. Copyright 1944 by Robert Frost. Reprinted by permission of Holt, Rinehart and Winston, Publishers.

SPECIAL TOPICS

Alzate, H., & Dippsy, M. L. L. Vaginal erotic sensitivity. *Journal of Sex and Marital Therapy,* 1984, *10*(1), 49–56.

Conant, M. A., Spicer, D. W., & Smith, C. D. Herpes simplex virus transmission: Condom studies. *Sexually Transmitted Diseases,* 1984, *11*, 94–95.

Facts about AIDS. Washington, D.C.: U.S. Public Health Service, June 1984.

Greenwood, V. B., & Bernstein, R. *Coping with herpes: The emotional problems.* Washington, DC: WCCT, 1982. (Pamphlet available from Washington Center for Cognitive Therapy, P.O. Box 39119, Washington, D.C. 20013)

Hock, Z. The G spot. *Journal of Sex and Marital Therapy,* 1983, *9*, 166–167.

Oriel, J.D. Genital lesions. McCormack (Ed.), *Sexually Transmitted Diseases.* Boston, Mass.: John Wright, 1983. Pp. 95–115.

Perry, J. D., & Whipple, B. Pelvic muscle strength of female ejaculation: Evidence in support of a new theory of orgasm. *Journal of Sex Research,* 1981, *17*, 22–39.

Straus, S. E., Takiff, H. E., Seidlin, M., Bachrach, S., Lininger, L., DiGiovanna, J. J., Western, K. A., Smith, H. A., Lehrman, S. N., Creagh-Kirk, T., & Alling, D. W. Suppression of frequently recurring genital herpes. *New England Journal of Medicine,* 1984, *310*, 1546–1550.

Zaidi, A. A., Aral, S. O., Reynolds, G. H., Blount, J. H., Jones, O. G., & Fichtner, R. R. Gonorrhea in the United States: 1967–1979. *Sexually Transmitted Diseases,* 1983, *10*(2), 72–76.

· INDEX ·

Abortion, 446–450, 455, 615
Abuse. *See also* Violence
  of children, 344–350, 615. *See*
    also Incest
  of parents, 354–355
  sexual. *See* Incest; Sexual
    violence
Acceleration clauses, 596
Acquaintance rape, 335–336
Acquired immune deficiency
  syndrome (AIDS), 79, 80, 612
Add-on clauses in credit, 595
Adler, Alfred, 323, 501
Adlerian therapy for marital
  problems, 323
Adolescence:
  curfew violation in, 510
  independence in, 515
Advertised items as childrearing
  problem, 509
Affairs, sexual, 116. *See also*
  Extramarital intercourse
Agapic love, 77
Age:
  at marriage, 221–222, 256–257,
    259–261
  and masturbation rates, 393
  in mate selection, 173–174, 259–
    261
  at pregnancy, 416, 418–419
  and sexual intercourse, 199, 392–
    393
Age-discrepant marriages, 259–261
Aggression in child abuse, 347, 349.
    See also Violence
AID (artificial insemination by
  donor), 427–429
AIDS (acquired immune deficiency
  syndrome), 79, 80, 612
AIH (artificial insemination by
  husband), 427
Alcohol. *See also* Drugs
  marital problems with, 321
  during pregnancy, 460, 461
  in sexual dysfunctions, 383, 386

Alimony as stepfamily problem,
  562. *See also* Child support
  payments; Palimony
Amniocentesis, 417–419
Anatomy and physiology, 33–34
  sexual. *See* Sexual anatomy and
    physiology
Androgyny and living together, 190
Annulment of marriages, 537–538
Anorgasmia in women, 381–384
Arranged marriages, 171–172
Artificial insemination, 427–429,
  450, 451
Asceticism, 91
Assets and Liabilities Inventory, 178
Attitudes. *See specific entries, for
  example*: Love Attitudes
  Scale; Singles, attitudes
  toward
Attitudes toward Children Scale,
  410–411

Balloon contracts, 596
Basal body temperature (BBT)
  method of contraception,
  440–441
Battered women, shelters for, 343–
  344. *See also* Violence, in
  relationships
Battering rape, 341. *See also* Rape
BBT (basal body temperature)
  method of contraception,
  440–441
Behavior:
  altering, communication in, 305
  as divorce factor, 526
  in marriage conflicts, 309–310
  sexual. *See* Sexual behavior
Behavioral approach to childrearing,
  497–500, 506, 509–510, 514–
  515
Behavioral origin of love, 62
Behavioral theory of gender roles,
  35–36

Behavior contracts, 321, 322
Behavior therapy for marriage
  problems, 321–322
Bereavement process in
  widowhood, 539–541
Between-meal snacks as
  childrearing problem, 506
Bias in research, 23
Billings method of contraception,
  441
Biological families, 13–14, 554–559.
  See also Families;
  Stepfamilies
Biological inheritance, 30–34, *See
  also* Genetic counseling;
  Genetic defects
  versus environment, in gender
    roles, 40–43
Birth control. *See* Abortion;
  Contraception; Sterilization
Birth control pills, 434–436, 441–
  442
Blacks. *See* Race
Body clock compatibility in
  marriage, 212–213
Boredom:
  as divorce factor, 527
  sexual, avoiding, 377
Bradley method of childbirth, 467
Breastfeeding, 615
Breast stimulation in petting, 106
Brief sexual encounters, 116. *See
  also* Extramarital intercourse
Brother-sister incest, 352–353
Budgeting, 585–587
Burt, Cyril, 24

Calendar method of contraception,
  440
Careers. *See also* Employment
  criteria for, 278–279 in marriage:
    compatibility of, 209, 214
    dual versus single, 580. *See also*
    Dual-career marriages

645

versus families, for fathers, 475–476, 487
and marriage timing, 223
and relationship balancing, 234
for women. *See* Dual-career marriages; Employment, of married women; of women
Caretaker role of fathers, 476–477
Cervical caps in contraception, 438–439
Cervical mucus method of contraception, 441
Cesarean section childbirth, 467–468
Child abuse, 344–350, 615. *See also* Incest
Child abusers, 346, 348–350
Childbirth, *See also* Pregnancy
  drugs during, 464
  fear of (parturiphobia), 462
  home versus hospital, 486–488, 615
  labor in, stages of, 462–465
  methods of, 465–468, 484
  reactions of mothers to, 469
Child care. *See also* Childrearing
  fathers in, 478
  in single-parent families, 424
Child custody, 535, 548. *See also* Child support payments
  choices in, 550–551
  joint, 548, 550–551, 556
  in living-together relationships, 200–202
  in stepfamilies, 564
Child Discipline Scale, 507
Child-free life-style, 409, 580
Childrearing, 489–513
  approaches to, 496–510
    behavioral, 497–500, 506, 509–510, 514–515
    developmental-maturational, 496–497, 508
    parent effectiveness training (P.E.T.), 499, 501, 506, 509, 510
    reality therapy, 504–506, 510
    restrictive, in lack of sexual desire, 378
    socioteleological, 501–504, 508, 509
  choices in, 514–515
  effects on, types of, 510–512
  ending of, 495
  folklore about, 494–495
  perspectives on, 489–493
  problems of, 506, 508–510
  procedures for, child abusers taught, 349–350
  in stepfamilies, 567, 572
  trends in, 512–513

Children. *See also* Families; Pregnancy
  abuse of, 344–350, 615. *See also* Incest
  attitudes toward, scale of, 410–411
  benefiting, methods of, 9
  differences among, 493
  divorce affecting, 534–537, *See also* Child custody; Child support payments
  emotional needs of, 423
  expenses of, 404
  genders of, selecting, 417
  honesty of, 402–403
  independence of, 493, 515
  influences on, 490–492
  irrational narcissism of, 504
  "latchkey," 291–292
  in marriages. *See also* divorce affecting, *above*
    age-discrepant, 260
    as legitimate, 11
    marital happiness affected by, 480–483
    marriage relationship affected by, 479–483
    myths about, 299
    problems with, in marriage therapy, 320
  and mothers, emotional bond between, 469. *See also* Mothers
  numbers of, choosing, 412–416
  parental social life restricted by, 404
  and parents, relationships of, 403, 408, 469. *See also* Parenthood; Parenting; Parents
    effects on, 250, 273–274
    in stepfamilies, 556–557, 561, 572
  parents abused by, 354–355
  planning for. *See* Family planning
  playing with, 402
  responsibility for, 279–280
  returning home as adults, 495
  self-concept of, 290, 499, 501
  in single-parent families, 423
  in stepfamilies, 556–557, 560–563, 565–567, 572–573, 575–577
Child support payments, 534, 548, 557, 562
Choices:
  in abortion, 455
  basic, 580–581
  in childbirth, home versus hospital, 486–488, 615

in child custody, 550–551
in childrearing, 514–515
as continual, 582
in contraception, 453–454
in dating, 183–184
in gender roles, 56–57
of life-styles, 139–142, 151, 153–155
in living-together relationships, 204–205
in love relationships, 87–88
making, facts about, 581–582
in marriage:
  in careers. *See* Careers, in marriage
  in communication and conflict, 329–330
  about employment of married women, 294–295
  and family, 15–17, 26–27
  in sexual monogamy, 580–581
  versus singlehood, 580
of marriage partners, 207–216
in marriage relationships, 268–269
of parenthood:
  versus child-free life-style, 580
  single, 423–424
of positive versus negative view of life, 581
as probabilities, 581–582
revocability of, 580
in sex therapy, 397–398
about sexual intercourse, 124–127
in stepfamilies, 575–577
in sterilization, 454–455
trade-offs in, 579
in violent relationship termination, 358–359
Chores as childrearing problem, 509–510
Chorion biopsy, 418–419
Chromosomes:
  in biological inheritance, 30–31
  in gender determination, 417
  in genetic defects, 418–419
Circumcision, 603
Class. *See entries beginning with* Social class
Classical conditioning, 497
Climacteric, 389–391
Clitoris, 598
Coed dorms in living-together relationships, 188
Cognitive conditions of love, 67–68
Cognitive-developmental theory of gender-role learning, 36–37
Cohabitation, contract, 143–145, 150, 155. *See also* Living-together relationships

Coitus. *See* Sexual intercourse
Coitus interruptus as contraceptive method, 442
College marriages, 253–257
Commitment in marriage, 242–243, 264
Common-money-pot pattern, 570
Communes as life-style, 16, 145–150
Communication. *See also* Conflict
  with dating partners, 168, 169
  in marriage, 297, 301, 304–308
    choices in, 329–330
    and compatibility, 212, 214–216
    intensity of, 306–307
    nonproductive, 312–316
    problems of, in marriage therapy, 320
    productive, 312–318
    trends in, 326–327
  patterns of, gender differences in, 307–308
  sexual, in sexual fulfillment, 366–367, 369–370
  in stepfamilies, 572
Community property in living-together relationships, 200, 201
Community remarriage, 544
Commuter marriages, 285
Companion role of fathers, 476
Companionship:
  of children, 403
  as dating motivation, 161
  in marriage, 134
Compatibility in marriage, types of, 208–216
Complementary conflict style, 311
Complementary needs in mate selection, 175–177
Computers as dating partner source, 164–165
Conditioning. *See also entries beginning with* Behavioral
  classical, 497
  operant, 497–498, 514–515
Conditioning origin of love, 61
Condoms, 436–437, 442
Conflict. *See also* Communication
  in communes, 149
  in marriage, 268, 298–299, 308–312, 314–316, 329–330
    sources of, 274–275, 309–310, 320
    styles of, 311–312
    trends in, 326–327
    and violence, 340
Conflict-habituated marriage relationships, 268

Conflict negotiation skills, 5, 501, 526
Conjugal love, 69–74, 87–88
Conservative view of sexual values, 96–99
Constricted vaginas, 384
Contraception, 431–444. *See also* Abortion; Sterilization
  methods of:
    choices of, 453–454
    for men, 436–437, 451
    for women, 434–442, 451
    and premarital intercourse, 125, 187
    trends in, 451
Contraceptive Use Scale, 433
Contract cohabitation, 143–145, 150, 155
Contracts:
  balloon, 596
  behavior, 321, 322
  marriage (prenuptial), 229–233, 237–238
Control groups in research, 22
Coolidge Effect, 117
Coping strategies of mothers, 474–475
Credit, acquiring, 594–596
Credit accounts, types of, 593–594
Crisis events, 20, 554–555
Crude divorce rate, 521
Cruising, 80
Crying as childrearing problem, 506, 508
C-section childbirth, 467–468
Cultural aspects of mate selection, 170–173
Cunnilingus in petting, 106–107
Curfews as childrearing problem, 510
Custody of children. *See* Child custody

D and C (dilation and curettage), 447
D and E (dilation and evacuation), 447
Date rape, 335–336
Dating, 157–181
  choices in, 183–184
  history of, 158–160
  men in, 56–57, 169–170
  motivations for and function of, 160–162
  parental influence on, 159–160
  realities of, 162–167
  trends in, 180–181
  women in, 56–57, 167–169
Dating activities, 166–167

Dating partners:
  communication with, 168, 169
  desired, characteristics of, 165–166
  honesty and openness of, 169, 170
  sexual pressure by, 167–168
  shyness of, 169
  sources of, 162–165
  violence of, 332–336
    sexual, 334–336
    and termination of dating relationship, 358–359
Dating service organizations, 164
Daughters, incest with, 351–352
Day care in childrearing, 511
Deception
  before marriage, 230, 234
  in research, 23–24
Dependency love, 77
DES (diethylstilbestrol), 442
Desertion by marriage partners, 539
Developmental-maturational approach to childrearing, 496–497, 508
Devitalized marriage relationships, 268
Diaphragms in contraception, 438
Dick-Read method of childbirth, 466
Diethylstilbestrol (DES), 442
Differential involvement in mate rejection, 217
Dilation and curettage (D and C), 447
Dilation and evacuation (D and E), 447
Discrimination:
  economic, black marriages affected by, 261
  in employment of women, 47, 48
Displacement:
  in child abuse, 347
  in marital conflicts, 315
  in marital violence, 340
Division of labor:
  in communes, 149
  in living-together relationships, 192
Divorce, 520–539, 550–551
  alternatives to, 537–539
  causes of:
    individual, 359, 524–528
    societal, 522–523
  effects of, 531, 533–537
    on children, 534–537. *See also* Child custody; Child support payments
    on premarital intercourse, 113
  and extramarital intercourse, 117
  frequency of, 521–522

grounds for, 524–525, 530
history of, 520–521
legislation about, 523–525, 530
and religion, 520, 523
stages preceding, 528–530
trends in, 547–548
Divorced people:
characteristics of, 530–532
money problems of, 534
organization for, 615
remarriage of, 544–546, 575–577.
   See also Stepfamilies
sexual intercourse among, 119–121
as singles, 136
Divorce models as divorce factor, 523
Divorce Proneness Scale, 532
Donors, artificial insemination by (AID), 427–429
Double standard, sexual, 96, 187
Douching as contraceptive method, 442
Down's syndrome, 417, 418
Dreikurs, Rudolph, 501–502
Drugs, *See also* Alcohol
during childbirth, 464
on dates, 166–167
in living-together relationships, 189–190
marriage problems with, 321
during pregnancy, 461
Dual-career marriages, 282–287. *See also* Employment, of married women
choices about, 294–295, 580
jobs versus careers in, 278–282
obstacles to, 279–282
and sexual fulfillment, 364–365
Dual-income marriages. *See* Employment, of married women
Duct system in men, 604–605
Dyadic Adjustment Scale, 302–303
Dyspareunia (pain during intercourse), 384, 394

Economic discrimination affecting black marriages, 261
Economic life-styles in marriage, compatibility of, 211, 214, 215
Economic maintenance of communes, 149
Economic remarriage, 545
Economic self-sufficiency and singlehood, 154–155
Education. *See also* College marriages; Teachers

effects of:
   on childrearing, 511–512
   on parenthood, 406
in marriage timing, 222–223
in mate selection, 173–174
and premarital intercourse, 112
public, 511–512
sex, 616
and singlehood, 155
of women, 46
Egos:
enhancement of, sexual intercourse in, 109
in happy marriages, 264–265
Ejaculation, 605
premature (rapid), 387–388
retarded (ejaculatory incompetence), 388
Elderly, sexual fulfillment among, 391–394
Electra complex, 38
Ellis, Albert, 322
Emancipation relationships, 197
Emotional bond of mother and child, 469
Emotional insulation in marital conflicts, 316
Emotional intimacy in sexual intercourse, 108
Emotional needs in single-parent families, 423–424
Emotional relationship of marriage, 10
Emotional remarriage, 544
Emotional stereotypes for men, 51
Emotions. *See also* Feelings
love affecting, 64
of mothers, 470–473
during pregnancy, 461–462
Empathy in happy marriages, 264
Employment. *See also* Careers; Job requirements for men
gender-role flexibility in, 57
of married women, 46–49
choices about, 294–295
consequences of, 285, 287–292, 295, 471, 474, 522–523
currently, 277
historically, 276–277
jobs versus careers in, 278–282
   See also Dual-career marriages
motivations for, 277–278
trends in, 292–293
of women, 46–49
discrimination in, 47, 48
married. *See* of married women, *above*
Endogamous pressures on mate selection, 172–173
Engagements, 223–229

Environment:
in gender roles, 34. *See also* Socialization
versus heredity, 40–43
stressors of, in child abuse, 347
Erectile dysfunction (impotence), 386–387, 394
Erotic love, 75. *See also* Romantic love
ERT (estrogen replacement therapy), 389
Escapism:
from marital conflicts, 314
marriage for, 228
Estate taxes, 542
Estrogen replacement therapy (ERT), 389
Ethics, 90–92. *See also* Sexual values
Exchange theory in mate selection, 176, 178, 179
Exogamous pressures on mate selection, 172, 173
Expectations:
realistic:
   in marriage, developing, 5
   in sexual fulfillment, 367–368
social, influencing parenthood, 407
unrealistic:
   in orgasmic dysfunction, 383
   of stepfamilies, 560–561
Ex-spouses:
as conflict source in stepfamilies, 557
dealing with, 561
parent-child relationships of, 556–557, 561, 572
Extended families, 14
Extramarital intercourse, 115–119, 122, 125–127, 528

Fallopian tubes, 601
False labor, 462
False pregnancy, 458
Families:
versus careers, for fathers, 475–476, 487
defined, 13
functions of, changing, 522
influences of:
   on marital violence, 338, 340
   on parenthood, 405
and marriage, *See* Marriage, and family
types of, 13–15
   extended, 14
   nuclear, 14
   of orientation (biological), 13, 554–559
   of procreation, 13–14

single-parent, 423–424, 617
step-. *See* Stepfamilies
Family goal compatibility in
    marriage, 209, 214
Family life cycle view of marriage
    and family, 17–19
Family meetings, 502, 503
Family network systems, 16
Family planning, 401–421, 615. *See
    also* Pregnancy
    choices in, 423–424
    family size determination in,
        412–416
    parenthood timing in, 416, 418–
        421. *See also* Parenthood
    trends in, 421
Farm, the (commune), 148
Father-daughter incest, 351–352
Fatherhood, implications of, 475–
    479. *See also* Motherhood;
    Parenthood
Fathers:
    age of, at pregnancy of mothers,
        419
    careers versus family of, 475–476,
        487
    in child care, 478
    divorced, 615
    roles of, 475–477
Father's Day, 406
Feelings, *See also* Emotions; *entries
    beginning with* Emotional
    altering, communication in, 305
    about marriage, in living-together
        relationships, 191–192
    in marriage enrichment
        programs, 325
    of marriage partners,
        determining, 215
    negative, about partners, 382–383
    about parents, 215
Fellatio in petting, 107
Fertilization, 425–431, 450–451,
    617
Fetal alcohol syndrome, 460
Folsom, Joseph, 61
Freedom:
    loss of, in living-together
        relationships, 193–194
    money affecting, 273
Freud, Sigmund, 37–38, 60
Friends:
    as dating partner sources, 163–
        165
    extramarital intercourse with,
        118
    and marriage, 250, 321
    parenthood influences of, 405
    parents as, 515
Friendship love, 76
Fun. *See also* Recreation

childrearing as, myth of, 494
    as sexual intercourse motive, 95,
        109
Function-structure perspective of
    marriage and family, 17
Funeral expenses, 543–544

Gametrics, 417
Gays. *See* Homosexuality;
    Homosexual love
    relationships
Gender identity, 30
Gender roles:
    choices in, 56–57
    defined, 30
    environment in, 34
        versus heredity, controversy
            about, 40–43
    flexibility of, and employment
        choices, 57
    learning, theories of, 34–38
    in marriage, sharing, 57
    of men, 49–53
    and socialization, 34–40
    trends in, 53–54
    of women, 43–49, 53
Genders. *See also* Men; Women
    biological inheritance of, 30–32
    defined, 30
    equality of, organization for, 615
    selection of, 417, 616
Genetic counseling, 616
Genetic defects, 418–419
Genetics. *See* Biological inheritance
Genital herpes, 609–610
Genitals, stimulation of, 106–107.
    See also Sexual anatomy and
    physiology
Gesell, Arnold, 496–497
Glasser, William, 504
Gonorrhea, 608–609
Gordon, Thomas, 499, 501
Grafenberg spot (G spot), 600–601
Grandparent-child relationships,
    572–573
Group marriages, 16
Groups, control, in research, 22
Group sex (swinging), 16, 116, 137–
    138
Group therapy for sexual problems,
    397–398
G spot (Grafenberg spot), 600–601

Happiness:
    as goal, in divorce, 523
    love affecting, 64
    in marriage:
        chances for, improving, 8
        influences on, 263–265, 480–
            483

lack of, as extramarital
    intercourse motive, 118
and marital adjustment, 300–
    303
myths about, 298, 299
predicting, 230, 234–235
scale of, 266
perception of, 300–301
HCG (human chorionic
    gonadotropin), 458
Health:
    love affecting, 64
    sexual functioning affected by,
        371–372, 374–375
Hedonism, 91
Helms, Jesse, 449
Heredity. *See* Biological inheritance;
    Genetic counseling; Genetic
    defects
Herpes, 609
    genital, 609–610
Heterosexual love relationships, 79
Homogamy in mate selection, 173–
    175
Homosexuality, 78–79, 616
Homosexual love relationships, 78–
    81
Honesty:
    of children, 402–403
    of dating partners, 169, 170
Honeymoons, 247–248
Hormones in biological inheritance,
    31–32
Hostility in living-together
    relationships, 197
Human chorionic gonadotropin
    (HCG), 458
Human Life Amendment to
    Constitution, 449
Human sexuality. *See* Sexuality
Husbands. *See* Married men
Hyde Amendment, 449
Hysterotomy as abortion method,
    447

Identical twins, studies of, 41
Identification theory of gender-role
    learning, 37–38
Identity-equals-job syndrome of
    men, 50–51. *See also* Gender
    identity; Personal identity
Immortality as parenthood
    influence, 408
Impact of Parenthood on Marriage
    Scale, 484
Impotence (erectile dysfunction),
    386–387, 394
Incest, 350–354, 616
Income. *See* Employment, of
    married women; Money

Inconsistent rules as marital conflict source, 310–311

Induced abortion, methods of, 446–447. *See also* Abortion

Industrial Revolution and dating, 158–159

Infertility, 427, 615

Informal separations in marriage, 538

Inheritance:
biological. *See* Biological inheritance
legal, 200, 201, 542–543, 545–546

Inheritance taxes, 542

Insurance, life, 542–543, 590–592

Insurance-plus-investment policies, 591, 592

Intense dependency love, 77

Intercourse. *See* Sexual intercourse

Interracial marriages, 258–259

Interracial parenting, 616

Interreligious marriages, 257–258

Intimacy:
emotional, in sexual intercourse, 108
in living-together relationships, 192

Intrauterine devices (IUDs), 437–438

Investment alternatives, 589–590

Investments and saving, 587–590

In vitro fertilization, 430–431, 450, 617

Irrational narcissism of children, 504

IUDs (intrauterine devices), 437–438

Jealousy, 83–85, 193

Job requirements for men, 49–50, *See also* Careers; Employment; Identity-equals-job syndrome of men

Johnson, Virginia E., 381, 387

Joint custody of children, 548, 550–551, 556

Kinship ties of black marriage partners, 262

Kissing in petting, 105

Labia majora, 598

Labia minora, 598

Labor:
in childbirth, stages of, 462–465. *See also* Childbirth
in work, division of. *See* Division of labor

Lamaze method of childbirth, 465–466

Laparoscopy, 444–445

"Latchkey" children, 291–292

Leadership ambiguity in marital conflict, 311

LeBoyer method of childbirth, 467

Legal aspects:
of living-together relationships, 198, 200–202
of marriage, 11, 243–245, 251. *See also* Marriage contracts

Legalistic view of sexual ethics, 90

Legal remarriage, 545–546

Legal separations in marriage, 538

Legislation:
abortion, 449–450
divorce, 523–525, 530
obscenity, 96

Legitimacy:
of children, 11
social, of marital intercourse, 113

Lesbians, 78, 81. *See also* Homosexuality; Homosexual love relationships

Levirate system of marriage, 171

Libido, low, 378, 381, 385

Life, positive versus negative view of, 581

Life cycles of families, 17–19

Life insurance, 542–543, 590–592

Life-style Preference Inventory, 151

Life-styles, 131–151
choices of, 139–142, 151, 153–155
in marriage, compatibility of, 211, 214, 215
menu of, 16
of parents, changes in, 404–405. *See also* Parenthood
racial changes in, as divorce factor, 527
trends in, 150
types of. *See specific entries, for example*: Child-free life-style; Living-together relationships

Limerance, 69. *See also* Romantic love

"Linus blanket" relationships, 197

Living together, defined, 186

Living-Together Consequences Scale, 199

Living-together partners:
characteristics of, 189–190
violence by, 336

Living-together relationships, 185–202. *See also* Contact cohabitation; Premarital intercourse
advantages of, 195–196, 199
and androgyny, 190
child custody in, 200–202

choices in, 204–205
court cases on, 201
day-to-day issues in, 190–194
disadvantages of, 196–199
division of labor in, 192
drugs in, 189–190
hostility in, 197
increases in, reasons for, 186–189
intimacy in, 192
jealousy in, 193
legal implications of, 198, 200–202
as life-style, 16
loss of freedom in, 193–194
marriage feelings in, 191–192
as marriage preparation, 194–195
and parents, 189, 193
as permanent alternative, 198, 200–202
and previous marriages, 190
race in, 190
religion in, 189
trends in, 202
types of, 186
to avoid, 197–198
urban-rural differences in, 190

Logical-sensible love, 77–78

Loneliness and singlehood, 138, 154

Lonely loser stereotype of singles, 138

Love:
in childrearing, 494–495
conditions of, 64–68
definitions of, 62–63
dilemmas of, 63
importance of, 63–64
in marriage, 213
and money, 274
origins of, 60–62
and sex, 81–83, 88
types of, 69–78, 87–88

Love Attitudes Scale, 69–71, 73

Love relationships:
choices in, 87–88
heterosexual, 79
homosexual, 78–81. *See also* Homosexuality
jealousy in, 83–85
and premarital intercourse, 112
trends in, 85

Lover role, elements of, 68–69

Loving, styles of, 75–78

Loyalties of stepchildren, 565–566

Ludic love, 75–76

Magazines as dating partner source, 163–164

Males. *See* Men

Manic love, 77

Manual genital stimulation, 106

Marital status:
  and masturbation, 105, 377
  previous, in mate selection, 175
Marriage. *See also* Engagements;
    Remarriage
  adjustment to, 300–303
  age at, 221–222, 256–257, 259–
    261. *See also* Age, in mate
    selection
  careers in. *See* Careers, in
    marriage
  changes in:
    legal, 251
    personal, 249–250
    sexual, 251–252
    social, 250–251
  children in. *See* Children, in
    marriages
  in college, 253–257
  commitment in, 242–243, 264
  communication in. *See*
    Communication, in marriage
  companionship in, 134
  compatibility in, types of, 208–
    216
  confinement of, 234
  conflict in. *See* Conflict, in
    marriage
  dating as leading to, 162
  deception before, 230, 234
  defined, 10–12
  disadvantages of, 139, 141–142
  egos in, 264–265
  as emotional relationship, 10
  empathy in, 264
  employment of married women
    affecting, 289–290. *See also*
    Employment, of married
    women
  for escape, 228
  and family:
    choices involving, 26–27
    as commitment, 242–243
    conceptual frameworks for, 15–20
    differences between, 15
    research on, cautions about,
      21–24
    studying, 4–9, 26–27
    trends in, 24
  feelings about, in living-together
    relationships, 191–192
  flexibility in, 212
  and friends, 250, 321
  happiness in. *See* Happiness, in
    marriage
  insight into, 8
  legal aspects of, 11, 243–245, 251.
    See also Marriage contracts
  length of, 117, 419–420
  as life-style, 132–135, 150, 153–
    154

living together before, 194–195.
    See also Living-together
    relationships
  love in, 213
  masturbation in, 377
  money in. *See* Money, in marriage
  myths about, 298–300
  negative reasons for, 227–229
  and parenthood, 135, 483. *See
    also* Children; Parenthood;
    Parenting; Parents
  and parents, 215, 227, 250, 269
  and parents-in-law, 226, 250, 320
  personal fulfillment in, 134
  for pity, 228–229
  previous, and living-together
    relationships, 190
  problems in, brought to marriage
    therapy, 320–321
  public ceremony of, 11–12. *See
    also* rites of passage
    associated with, *below*
  race in, 258–259, 261–263
  rape in, 340–343
  realistic expectations about,
    developing, 5
  religion in, 175, 210–211, 214–
    215, 257–258, 320–321
    and annulment, 537, 538
  rites of passage associated with,
    11–12, 243–248
    honeymoons, 247–248
    weddings, 243–247
  roles in, 57, 210, 255, 262–263.
    See also Fathers, roles of;
    Gender roles
  security in, 135
  self-actualization in, 211–212,
    215
  sexual intercourse in. *See* Sexual
    intercourse, in marriage
  versus singlehood, 4, 580
  and society, 132–133
  termination of. *See* Annulment of
    marriages; Desertion by
    marriage partners; Divorce;
    Separation, from marriage
    partners; Widowhood
  timing of, 195, 221–223, 226–229
  trends in, 235, 265
  types of:
    age-discrepant, 259–261. *See
      also* ages at, *above*
    arranged, 171–172
    commuter, 285
    dual-career. *See* Dual-career
      marriages
    dual-income. *See* Employment,
      of married women
    group, 16
    interracial, 258–259

  interreligious, 257–258
    mixed, 257–261
    modern, 132
    monogamous, 12. *See also*
      Sexual monogamy
    polyandrous, 13
    polygamous, 12–13
    polygynous, 12–13
    rebound, 227–228
    sexually open, 16, 252–253
    synergamous, 16
    traditional, 132
  unsatisfactory relationships
    before, 195
  values in, 210–212, 310
  women in. *See* Married women
Marriage contracts, 229–233, 237–
    238
Marriage enrichment, 9, 323–326
Marriage Happiness Scale, 266
Marriage licenses, 11
Marriage partners:
  absence from, 119
  apathetic or uncooperative, 118
  black, 262–263
  compatible, identifying, 4
  death of. *See* Widowed people;
    Widowhood
  desertion of, 539
  ex-. *See* Ex-spouses
  feelings of, determining, 215
  female. *See* Married women
  male. *See* Married men
  and parenthood, 403, 407. *See
    also* Parenthood; Parenting;
    Parents
  rejection of, 213, 217–221
  selection of, 170–180
    criteria in, 207–216
    cultural aspects of, 170–173
    personal, as divorce factor, 523
    psychological aspects of, 175–
      179
    sociobiological aspects of, 179–
      180
    sociological aspects of, 173–
      175, 259–261
  separations from, legal and
    informal, 538
  trust between, 268
  vacations of, 269
  violence by, 337–338, 340–344,
    359
Marriage relationships, 241–266
  demands of, balanced with career
    demands, 234
  effects on:
    of children, 479–480
    of money, 273–275. *See also*
      Employment, of married
      women

during pregnancy, 479–480
in stepfamilies, 567
types of, 268–269
Marriage therapy, 9, 318–323, 329–
330, 344, 616. *See also* Sex
therapy
Married men. *See also* Fathers
artificial insemination by (AIH),
427. *See also* Artificial
insemination
attitudes of, as career obstacle for
married women, 281–282
in dual-income marriages,
consequences for, 287, 289
Married women. *See also* Mothers
achievement barriers of, 46–47
artificial insemination of, 427–
429
careers of. *See* Dual-career
marriages
credit for, 595
in dual-income marriages, 285,
287
education of, 46
employment of. *See* Dual-career
marriages; Employment, of
married women
problems of, 44
Mass media:
children influenced by, 491–492
as dating partner source, 163–164
socialization by, 39–40
Masters, William H., 381, 387
Masturbation, 99, 102–105, 121
and age, 393
and marital status, 105, 377
by men, 103–104, 377
and religion, 99, 102, 104
by women, 103–104, 377, 381,
383–384
Mates. *See* Marriage partners
Mating gradient, 173–174
Mead, Margaret, 23
Media. *See* Mass media
Medical community on
masturbation, 102
Medications, *See* Drugs
Men:
anatomy and physiology of,
33–34
sexual. *See* sexual anatomy and
physiology of, *below*
in changing relationships, 51–52
communication patterns of, 307–
308
contraceptives for, 436–437, 451
in dating, 56–57, 169–170
emotional stereotypes for, 51
fatherhood views of, 475–477
gender roles of, 49–53

homosexual, love relationships
of, 79–80. *See also*
Homosexuality
ideal, characteristics of, 52–53
identity-equals-job syndrome of,
50–51
infertility in, 427
job requirements for, 49–50. *See
also* Careers; Employment
married. *See* Married men
masturbation by, 103–104, 377.
See also Masturbation
menopause of, 391
in middle age, 390–391
as parents. *See* Fatherhood,
implications of; Fathers;
Parenthood; Parenting;
Parents
sexual anatomy and physiology
of:
external, 602–603
internal, 603–605
sexual apathy of, 385
sexual dysfunctions of, 385–388,
394
sexual intercourse of. *See also*
Sexual intercourse
extramarital, 117
premarital, 112
sexual response cycles of, 370–
372
sterilization of, 445–446
widowed, 541–542. *See also*
Widowed people;
Widowhood
Menopause, 389–391
Menstruation, sexual intercourse
during, 375–376. *See also*
Premenstrual syndrome
(PMS); Toxic shock syndrome
Mental. *See entries beginning with*
Psychological
Middle age:
of men, 390–391
of women, 389–390
physiological changes in, 389–391
psychological changes in, 390–
391
sexual fulfillment in, 388–391
Midwifery, 486–488
Minimal involvement in mate
rejection, 213, 217
Miscarriages, 446. *See also* Abortion
Mixed marriages, 257–261
Modeling:
in child abuse, 347
in gender-role learning, 35–36
Money:
effects of, 272–275
and love, 274

in marriage, 214. *See also* Dual-
career marriages;
Employment, of married
women
during college, 255
as conflict source, 274–275,
320. *See also* problems with,
below
dual income, 295
effects of, 273–275
management of, 269
in marriage delays, 227
meanings of, 271–275
problems with. *See also* in
marriage, as conflict source,
above
in college marriages, 255
of divorced people, 534
in single-parent families, 424
in stepfamilies, 557
in stepfamilies, 557, 567, 570–571
Monogamy, sexual, 11, 12, 16, 580–
581
Mons veneris (mons pubis), 598
Moral Majority, 97–99, 616
Moral sanctions and divorce, 523
Morning-after pill for contraception,
441–442
Motherhood. *See also* Fatherhood,
implications of; Parenthood
achievement barriers of, 46–47
adjustments to, 469–475
brevity of, 44, 46
and education, 46
and employment, 46–49
implications of, 468–475
Mothers:
age of, at pregnancy, 416, 418–419
childbirth reactions of, 469
and children, emotional bonds
between, 469
coping strategies of, 474–475
employment of, 288–292, 471, 474
responsibility of, 470
super- (Supermoms), 472–473
surrogate, 429, 451
worries of, 470–473
Mother's Day, 406
Mother-son incest, 352
Multiple parenting, 493

Narcissism of children, 504
Nature versus nurture controversy
about gender roles, 40–43
Need-for-partner compatibility in
marriage, 208
Needs:
complementary, in mate
selection, 175–177

emotional, in single-parent families, 423–424
Needs Assessment Inventory, 177
Negative behavior as divorce factor, 526
Negative feelings about partners, 382–383
Negative view of life, 581
Never-married singles, 135–136
Newspapers as dating partner source, 163–164
No-lose method of conflict resolution, 501
Nonbattering rape, 341–342. *See also* Rape
Nonproductive communication in marriage, 312–316
Nuclear families, 14
Nurse-midwives, 486–488
Nutrition during pregnancy, 460–461

Obscenity laws, 96
Obsessive rape, 342. *See also* Rape
Oedipal complex, 37–38
Off-campus apartments in living-together relationships, 188
One-sided convenience relationships, 198
Open marriages, 16, 252–253
Openness. *See also* Communication of dating partners, 169, 170
sexual, 95
Operant conditioning, 497–498, 514–515. *See also entries beginning with* Behavioral
Oral contraceptives, 434–436, 441–442
Organizations and resources, 615–617
Orgasm:
in elderly, 393
myth about, 376–377
simultaneous, 373, 375
Orgasmic dysfunction, 381–384
Ovaries, 602
Ovum transfers, 431, 450, 616

Pain during sexual intercourse, 384, 394
Palimony, 200, 201
Parallel conflict style, 311
Parent abuse, 354–355
Parent effectiveness training (P.E.T.), 499, 501, 506, 509, 510
Parenthood. *See also* Children; Fatherhood, implications of; Motherhood; Pregnancy

accidental, 407–408
versus child-free life-style, 580
demands of, 492
enjoyment of, 493
influences on:
personal, 407–409
social, 405–407
and marriage, 135, 483
negative aspects of, 404–405
planning for. *See* Family planning
positive aspects of, 402–403, 493
single, 423–424, 617
as stage in life, 490
timing of, 416, 418–421
trends in, 484
Parenting. *See also* Children
effective, systematic training for (STEP), 513
interracial, 616
preparing for, 7
styles of, 493
Parent involvement program (P.I.P.), 504
Parents:
of blacks, and kinship ties, 262
child abuse by, 344–350, 615. *See also* incest committed by, *below*
and children, relationships of. *See* Children, and parents, relationships of
dating influence of, 159–160
desires of, 493
divorced, and premarital intercourse, 113. *See also* Stepfamilies
as friends versus authorities, 515
images of, in mate selection, 179
incest committed by, 350–354, 616
life-style changes of, 404–405
and living-together relationships, 189, 193
and marriage, 215, 227, 250, 269
remarriage of, 545. *See also* Stepfamilies
single, emotional needs of, 423–424
socialization by, 38–39
social life of, restricted by children, 404
Parents-in-law, 226, 250, 320
Partner Abuse Scale, 339
Partners. *See specific entries, for example:* Dating partners; Marriage partners
Parturiphobia (fear of childbirth), 462
Passive-cogenial marriage relationships, 268

Peers:
influence of:
on children, 490
on extramarital intercourse, 117
on living-together relationships, 188–189
on love, 65
on premarital intercourse, 112
on sexual intercourse, 109
on socialization, 39
relationships with, money affecting, 274
Pelvic inflammatory disease, 437
Penile implants, 386
Penis, 603
Personal changes in marriage, 249–250
Personal fulfillment:
in marriage, 134
parenthood influenced by, 407
Personal identity. *See also* Self-concept
in parenthood, 407
in singlehood, 155
Personal reasons for parenthood, 407–409
Personal Sex History Inventory, 379–380
Personal sexual values, clarifying, 93–94
P.E.T. (parent effectiveness training), 499, 501, 506, 509, 510
Petting, 105–107
Philosophical origin of love, 61
Physical appearance in mate selection, 174
Physical factors in low libido, 378
Physical health in sexual functioning, 371–372, 374–375
Physiological changes in middle age, 389–391
Physiological conditions of love, 67–68
Physiology and anatomy, 33–34
sexual. *See* Sexual anatomy and physiology
P.I.P. (parent involvement program), 504
PMS (premenstrual syndrome), 372, 374–375
Politics in marriage, compatibility of, 211
Polyandry, 13
Polygamy, 12–13
Polygyny, 12–13
Positive reinforcement in childrearing, 349–350

Positive self-concept and love, 66
Positive view of life, 581
Postcoital contraception, 441–442
Postmarital intercourse, 119–121
Postpartum depression, 469
Power, sense of, money affecting, 272
Pragmatic love, 77–78
Pregnancy, 457–462. *See also* Abortion; Childbirth; Contraception; Sterilization
  age at, 416, 418–419
  alcohol during, 460, 461
  amniocentesis in, 417–419
  chorion biopsy in, 418–419
  drugs during, 461
  emotions during, 461–462
  false, 458
  fertilization in, 425–431, 450–451, 617
  marriage delayed by, 227
  marriage length at, 419–420
  marriage relationship during, 479–480
  nutrition during, 460–461
  sexual intercourse during, 426–427, 480
  side effects of, 458–460
  signs of, 458
  smoking during, 460–461
Premarital counseling, 226
Premarital intercourse, 110–113, 117, 122, 124–125, 187. *See also* Living-together relationships
Premarital pregnancy in marriage delays, 227
Premature ejaculation, 387–388
Premenstrual syndrome (PMS), 372, 374–375
Prenuptial contracts, 229–233, 237–238
Primary ejaculatory incompetence, 388
Primary impotence, 386
Primary orgasmic dysfunction, 381
Primary-stage syphilis, 609
Primary vaginismus, 384
Productive communication in marriage, 312–318. *See also* Communication
Projection in marital conflicts, 314–315
Propinquity in mate selection, 175
Prostate gland, 605
Provider role of fathers, 475–476
Psychic origin of love, 61
Psychic remarriage, 544
Psychological aspects of mate selection, 175–179

Psychological changes in middle age, 390–391
Psychological conditions of love, 65–67
Psychological factors in low libido, 378
Psychological health in sexual functioning, 371–372, 374–375
Psychopathology of parents in child abuse, 346–347
Psychotherapy on masturbation, 102
Public ceremony of marriage, 11–12. *See also* Rites of passage associated with marriage
Public education and childrearing, 511–512. *See also* Education; Teachers
Punishment principle, 498, 514

Race:
  in living-together relationships, 190
  in marriage, 258–259, 261–263
  and parenting, 616
  in premarital intercourse, 112
Racism context of black marriages, 261
Radical life-style changes as divorce factor, 527
Rape. *See also* Sexual violence
  acquaintance (date), 335–336
  battering, 341
  in marriage, 340–343
  nonbattering, 341–342
  obsessive, 342
  organization to contact about, 616
Rapid ejaculation, 387–388
Rational-emotive therapy for marital problems, 322
Rationalism as sexual value system, 91–92
Rationalization of marital conflicts, 314
Realistic expectations:
  in marriage, developing, 5
  in sexual fulfillment, 367–368
Realistic love, 69–74, 87–88
Reality therapy approach to childrearing, 504–506, 510
Rebound marriages, 227–228
Recreation. *See also* Fun
  as dating motivation, 160–161
  marital problems with, 320
Recreational compatibility in marriage, 208
Recreational sex, 95, 109

Referees, lack of, in marital violence, 340
Refined divorce rate, 521
Reik, Theodore, 61
Reinforcement:
  positive, in childrearing, 349–350
  of violence, in marital violence, 340
Relationship Assessment Inventory, 214–216
Relationship Events Scale, 6
Relationships:
  changes in, 9, 51–52
  improvement of, sexual intercourse in, 110
  quality of, and sexual fulfillment, 364–366
  types of. *See specific entries, for example*: Emancipation relationships; Marriage relationships
  violence and abuse in, 355–356. *See also* Violence
Relatives as influencing children, 491
Religion:
  conservatism in, 97–99, 616
  in living-together relationships, 189
  in marriage, 175, 210–211, 214–215, 257–258, 320–321
  and annulment, 537, 538
  and divorce, 520, 523
  and masturbation, 99, 102, 104
  in parenthood, 405, 406
  and premarital intercourse, 112
Remarriage:
  of divorced people, 544–546, 575–577. *See also* Stepfamilies
  of widowed people, 546–547
Research, cautions about, 21–24
Researcher bias, 23
Research terminology, 22–23
Resources and organizations, 615–617
Responsibility of mothers, 470
Retarded ejaculation, 388
Reward principle, 497, 514–515
Rhythm method of contraception, 440–441
Rites of passage associated with marriage, 11–12, 243–248
  honeymoons, 247–248
  weddings, 243–247
Roles:
  of fathers, 476–477
  gender. *See* Gender roles
  lover, 68–69
  in marriage, 57, 210, 255, 262–263
  sexual, passive, in low libido, 378

Romantic love, 69–74, 87–88
Rules, inconsistency of, in marital
 conflict, 310–311
Rural-urban differences in living-
 together relationships, 190

Saline injection method of abortion,
 447
Salpingectomy (tubal ligation), 444–
 445
Sampling in research, 21–22
Satiation, 114
Saving:
 in budgets, 586–587
 and investing, 587–590
Scrotum, 603
Secondary ejaculatory
 incompetence, 388
Secondary impotence, 386
Secondary orgasmic dysfunction,
 381
Secondary-stage syphilis, 609
Secondary vaginismus, 384
Second language of sex, 393
Security:
 in marriage, 135
 money affecting, 272–273
Self, social, confirmation of, 160
Self-actualization in marriage, 211–
 212, 215
Self-assessments:
 Assets and Liabilities Inventory,
  178
 Attitudes toward Children Scale,
  410–411
 Child Discipline Scale, 507
 Contraceptive Use Scale, 433
 Divorce Proneness Scale, 532
 Dyadic Adjustment Scale, 302–
  303
 Employment of Mothers with
  Small Children, Financial
  Costs of, 288–289
 Impact of Parenthood on Marriage
  Scale, 483
 Life-style Preference Inventory,
  151
 Living-Together Consequences
  Scale, 199
 Love Attitudes Scale, 69–71, 73
 Marriage Happiness Scale, 266
 Needs Assessment Inventory,
  177
 Partner Abuse Scale, 339
 Personal Sex History Inventory,
  379–380
 Relationship Assessment
  Inventory, 214–216
 Relationship Events Scale, 6

Sexist Attitudes Scale, 45
Sexual Attitude Scale, 100–101
Stepfamily Success Scale, 568–
 569
 value of, 5
Self-centered love, 75–76
Self-concept:
 of children, 290, 499, 501
 effects on, 18, 66, 272
 of women, 43–45
Self-control, training in, 349, 350
Self-disclosure and love, 66–67
Self-fulfilling prophecies, 19
Self-knowledge:
 lack of, in orgasmic dysfunction,
  383
 and sexual fulfillment, 364
Self-sufficiency, economic, and
 singlehood, 154–155
Seminal vesicles, 605
Sensate focus exercises, 381, 382,
 387, 388
Sensible-logical love, 77–78
Separated singles, 136
Separation:
 from marriage partners, 538
 in mate rejection, 217
Serial monogamy, 16
Sex. See also Sexual behavior;
 Sexual intercourse
 attitudes toward, and sexual
  fulfillment, 368
 for elderly, 393–394
 group (swinging), 16, 116, 137–
  138
 and love, 81–83, 88
 myth of, 376–377
 as natural function, 368–369
 as recreation, 95, 109
 second language of, 393
Sex education, 616
Sex History Inventory, 379–380
Sexist Attitudes Scale, 45
Sex norms (double standard), 96,
 187
Sex roles. See Gender roles; Sexual
 roles, passive, in low libido
Sex therapy, 381, 397–398. See also
 Marriage therapy
Sexual abuse of children, 350–354,
 616
Sexual anatomy and physiology. See
 also Genitals, stimulation of
 of men:
  external, 602–603
  internal, 603–605
 of women:
  external, 597–599
  internal, 599–602
Sexual Attitude Scale, 100–101

Sexual behavior:
 attitudes about, 100–101
 as learned, 368
 pressure for, in dating, 167–168
 and sexual values, 89–122, 124–
  127
 trends in, 121–122
Sexual boredom, avoiding, 377
Sexual changes in marriage, 251–
 252
Sexual communication in sexual
 fulfillment, 366–367, 369–
 370
Sexual compatibility in marriage,
 209, 215
Sexual desire, lack of (low libido),
 378, 381, 385
Sexual double standard, 96, 187
Sexual dysfunctions. See also
 Sexual functioning, effects on
 alcohol in, 383, 386
 of men, 385–388, 394
 organizations concerned with, 616
 of women, 377–378, 381–384, 394
Sexual encounters, brief, 116. See
 also Extramarital intercourse
Sexual fulfillment, 361–395. See
 also Sexual dysfunctions
 among elderly, 391–394
 meanings of, 362–364
 in middle age, 388–391
 myths about, 372–373, 375–377
 prerequisites for, 364–370
 sex therapy in, 381, 397–398. See
  also Marriage therapy
 and sexual intercourse, 362–363.
  See also Sexual intercourse
 sexuality awareness in, 368–372
 over time, 363–364
 trends in, 396–397
Sexual functioning, effects on, 370–
 372, 374–375. See also Sexual
 dysfunctions
Sexual intercourse, 107–121. See
 also Contraception; Sex;
 Sexual behavior
 and age, 199, 392–393
 choices about, 124–127
 among divorced people, 119–121
 first experience of, 110–113
 frequency of, 113–114, 392–393
 in marriage, 113–115, 260, 264,
  320. See also postmarital;
  premarital, below
 extramarital, 115–119, 122,
  125–127, 528
 of men:
  extramarital, 117
  premarital, 112
 monogamous, 11, 580–581. See

also Sexual monogamy
motivations for, 95, 108–110
myth of, 376–377
of parents and children or siblings
(incest), 350–354, 616
postmarital, 119–121
premarital, 110–113, 117, 122,
124–125, 187. *See also*
Living-together relationships
and sexual fulfillment, 362–363.
See also Sexual fulfillment
among widowed people, 121
of women:
extramarital, 117
and fertilization, 426–427
forced. *See* Rape
during menstruation, 375–376
pain during, 384, 394
during pregnancy, 426–427, 480
premarital 112
Sexuality:
awareness of, in sexual
fulfillment, 368–372
of elderly, 392–394
studying, 5
Sexual life-styles in marriage,
compatibility of, 211, 214,
215
Sexually open marriages, 16, 252–
253
Sexually transmitted diseases
(STDs), 607–613
acquired immune deficiency
syndrome (AIDS), 79, 80, 612
avoiding, 125, 442–444, 613
genital herpes, 609–610
gonorrhea, 608–609
help for, obtaining, 612–613, 616–
617
myths and facts about, 608
syphilis, 609–610
Sexual monogamy, 11, 12, 16, 580–
581
Sexual needs of single parents, 424
Sexual openness, 95
Sexual origin of love, 60
Sexual partners. *See also* Dating
partners; Living-together
partners; Marriage partners
numbers of, 113
pressure from, 109
Sexual response cycles, 370–372
Sexual roles, passive, in low libido,
378. *See also* Gender roles
Sexual values:
personal, clarifying, 93–94
and sexual behavior, 89–122, 124–
127
of society, 94–99
systems of, 90–92

Sexual variety as extramarital
intercourse motive, 117–118
Sexual violence:
by dating partners, 334–336
by marriage partners, 340–343
organization to contact about,
616
Shelters for battered women, 343–
344
Shettles, Dr. Landrum, 417
Shyness of dating partners, 169
Siblings:
children influenced by, 490–491
incest by, 352–353
step-, 560, 567
Simultaneous orgasm, 373, 375
Singlehood:
benefits of, 139–141
and economic self-sufficiency,
154–155
and education, 155
as life-style, 16, 135–143, 154–155
and loneliness, 138, 154
versus marriage, 4, 580
personal identity in, 155
as stage, 143
Single-parent families, 423–424, 617
Singles:
attitudes toward, 137
categories of, 135–137
stereotypes of, 137–138
Sister-brother incest, 352–353
Situational impotence, 386
Situation ethics, 90–92
Skinner, B. F., 497
Smoking during pregnancy, 460–461
Social changes in marriage, 250–251
Social class in mate selection, 173–
174
Social-class view of marriage and
family, 19–20
Social conditions of love, 65
Social expectations in parenthood,
407
Social influences on parenthood,
405–407
Social interaction theory of gender-
role learning, 37
Socialization:
as dating function, 161–162
and gender roles, 34–40
sources of, 38–40
Social learning theory of gender
roles, 35–36. *See also entries
beginning with* Behavioral
Social legitimacy of sexual
intercourse in marriage, 113
Social life of parents, children
restricting, 404
Social origin of love, 60–61

Social-psychological view of
marriage and family, 18–19
Social relationships, money
affecting, 273–274
Social self, confirmation of, in
dating, 160
Social-value differences in marital
conflict, 310
Society:
as divorce factor, 522–523
childrearing effects of, 510–511
and marriage, 132–133, 340
sexual values of, 94–99
violence in, 340
Sociobiological aspects of mate
selection, 179–180
Sociological aspects of mate
selection, 173–175, 259–261
Socioteleological approach to
childrearing, 501–504, 508,
509
Sons, incest with, 352
Sororate system of marriage, 171
Spectatoring as obstacle to sexual
functioning, 370
Sperm, 604–605
Sperm banks, 428, 451
Spermicides, vaginal, 436, 437, 439
Spontaneous abortion (miscarriage),
446. *See also* Abortion
Spouses. *See* Marriage partners;
Married men; Married
women
Squeeze technique for treating
premature ejaculation, 387
STDs. *See* Sexually transmitted
diseases (STDs)
STEP (systematic training for
effective parenting), 513
Stepfamilies. *See also* Families;
Remarriage
adjustments in, 557
alimony problems of, 562
and biological families,
differences between, 554–559
childrearing in, 567, 572
children in, 556–557, 560–563,
565–567, 572–573, 575–577
choices in, 575–577
communication in, 572
defined, 553
developmental tasks for, 567–573
men in, 563–565
money in, 557, 567, 570–571
organization to contact about,
617
stigmatization of, 558–559
strengths of, 559–560
trends in, 573
types of, 554

uniqueness of, 554–559
unrealistic expectations of, 560–561
weaknesses of, 560–561
women in, 561–563
Stepfamily Success Scale, 568–569
Stepsiblings, 560, 567
Stereotypes:
  emotional, for men, 51
  of singles, 137–138
Sterilization, 444–446, 454–455, 617
Stimulation:
  lack of, in orgasmic dysfunction, 383
  in petting, 106–107
Storgic love, 76
Stratification, 19–20
Structure-function perspective of marriage and family, 17
Stuffing technique, 394
Supermoms, 472–473
Surrogate mothers, 429, 451
Suttie, Dr. Ian, 60–61
Swinging (group sex), 16, 116, 137–138
Symmetrical conflict style, 311
Synergamous marriages, 16
Syphilis, 609–610
Systematic training for effective parenting (STEP), 513
Systems therapy for marital problems, 321

TA (transactional analysis), 323
Taxes, 406, 542
Teacher role of fathers, 476
Teachers:
  children influenced by, 491
  socialization by, 39
Television. See Mass media
Tension, displacement of, in marital violence, 340
Term insurance, 591–592
Testes, 604
Test tube fertilization, 430–431, 450, 617
Thou-centered love, 77
Tillich, Paul, 61
Time lags in research, 23
Time out technique in childrearing, 349–350
Timing:
  of marriage, 195, 221–223, 226–229
  of parenthood, 416, 418–421
Titles in widowhood preparation, 543
Total marriage relationships, 268

TOUGHLOVE self-help organization, 500
Toxic shock syndrome, 440
Traditional monogamy, 16
Transactional analysis (TA), 323
Transfer taxes, 542
Transitions, preparing for, 5, 7
Trends:
  in childrearing, 512–513
  in contraception, 451
  in dating, 180–181
  in divorce, 547–548
  in employment of married women, 292–293
  in family planning, 421
  in fertilization, 450–451
  in gender roles, 53–54
  in life-styles, 150
  in living-together relationships, 202
  in love relationships, 85
  in marriage, 235, 265
    and family, 24
    in communication and conflict, 326–327
  in parenthood, 484
  in sexual behavior, 121–122
  in sexual fulfillment, 396–397
  in stepfamilies, 573
  in violence and abuse handling, 355–356
True labor, 462
Trust between marriage partners, 268
Tubal ligation (salpingectomy), 444–445
Twin studies, 41
Two-money-pot pattern, 570–571

Unrealistic expectations of stepfamilies, 560–561
Urban-rural differences in living-together relationships, 190
Urethral opening in women, 599
Uterus, 601

Vacations of marriage partners, 269
Vacuum curettage abortion method, 446–447
Vaginal opening, 599
Vaginal spermicides, 436, 437, 439
Vaginal sponges in contraception, 439–440
Vaginal tubal ligation, 445
Vaginas, 599–601
  constricted, 384
Vaginismus (constricted vagina), 384

Values:
  in marriage, 210–212, 310
  sexual. See Sexual values
Van Deusen, Edmund, 143–145
Vasectomies, 445–446
Venereal diseases. See Sexually transmitted diseases (STDs)
Video cassettes as dating partner source, 165
Violence:
  to children, 344–350, 615. See also Incest
  in relationships:
    countering, 343–344, 355–356
    dating. See Dating partners, violence by
    marriage, 337–338, 340–344, 359
    sexual, 334–336, 340–343. See also Incest
Virginity, 95–96, 599
Vital marriage relationships, 268
Vulva, 597

Weddings, 243–247
Whining as childrearing problem, 506, 508
Widowed people:
  remarriage of, 546–547
  sexual intercourse among, 121
  as singles, 136–137
Widowhood, 539–544
  adjustment to, 541–542
  bereavement process in, 539–541
  early, in age-discrepant marriages, 260–261
  preparation for, 542–544
Wills, need for, 542, 546
Withdrawal as contraceptive method, 442
Women:
  abortion of, 446–450, 455, 615
  achievement by, barriers to, 46–49
  anatomy and physiology of, 33–34. See also sexual anatomy and physiology of below
  battered, shelters for, 343–344. See also Violence, in relationships; sexual
  communication patterns of, 307–308
  contraceptives for, 434–442, 451
  in dating, 56–57, 167–169
  education of, 46. See also Education
  employment of. See Dual-career marriages; Employment, of married women; of women

gender roles of, 43–49, 53
homosexual, 78, 81. *See also*
    Homosexuality; Homosexual
    love relationships
ideal, characteristics of, 53
married. *See* Married women
masturbation by, 103–104, 377,
    381, 383–384
as mothers. *See* Motherhood;
    Mothers
pregnant. *See* Childbirth;
    Pregnancy

self-concepts of, 43–45
sexual anatomy and physiology
    of:
    external, 597–599
    internal, 599–602
sexual dysfunctions of, 377–378,
    381–384, 394
sexual intercourse of. *See* Sexual
    intercourse, of women
sexual response cycles of, 370–
    371

sexual violence against. *See*
    Sexual violence
in stepfamilies, 561–563
sterilization of, 444–445
violence against. *See* Violence, in
    relationships, sexual
widowed, adjustment of, 541. *See*
    also Widowed people;
    Widowhood
Worries of mothers, 470–473